# Lecture Notes in Computer Science 8430

*Commenced Publication in 1973*
Founding and Former Series Editors:
Gerhard Goos, Juris Hartmanis, and Jan van Leeuwen

Julia M. Badger   Kristin Yvonne Rozier (Eds.)

# NASA
# Formal Methods

6th International Symposium, NFM 2014
Houston, TX, USA, April 29 – May 1, 2014
Proceedings

 Springer

Volume Editors

Julia M. Badger
NASA-Johnson Space Center
2101 NASA Parkway, M/C ER4
Houston, TX 77058, USA
E-mail: julia.m.badger@nasa.gov

Kristin Yvonne Rozier
NASA Ames Research Center
Intelligent Systems Division
Moffett Field, CA 94035, USA
E-mail: kristin.y.rozier@nasa.gov

ISSN 0302-9743          e-ISSN 1611-3349
ISBN 978-3-319-06199-3      e-ISBN 978-3-319-06200-6
DOI 10.1007/978-3-319-06200-6
Springer Cham Heidelberg New York Dordrecht London

Library of Congress Control Number: 2014935174

LNCS Sublibrary: SL 2 – Programming and Software Engineering

*Typesetting:* Camera-ready by author, data conversion by Scientific Publishing Services, Chennai, India

Printed on acid-free paper

Springer is part of Springer Science+Business Media (www.springer.com)

# Preface

This publication contains the proceedings of the Sixth NASA Formal Methods Symposium (NFM 2014), which was held April 29 - May 1, 2014 at NASA Johnson Space Center (JSC) in Houston, Texas, USA.

The widespread use and increasing complexity of mission- and safety-critical systems require advanced techniques that address their specification, verification, validation, and certification requirements.

The NASA Formal Methods Symposium is a forum for theoreticians and practitioners from academia, industry, and government, with the goals of identifying challenges and providing solutions to achieving assurance in mission- and safety-critical systems. Within NASA such systems include autonomous robots, separation assurance algorithms for aircraft, Next Generation Air Transportation (NextGen), and autonomous rendezvous and docking for spacecraft. Moreover, emerging paradigms such as property-based design, code generation, and safety cases are bringing with them new challenges and opportunities. The focus of the symposium was on formal techniques, their theory, current capabilities, and limitations, as well as their application to aerospace, robotics, and other safety-critical systems in all design life-cycle stages. We encouraged work on cross-cutting approaches marrying formal verification techniques with advances in safety-critical system development, such as requirements generation, analysis of aerospace operational concepts, and formal methods integrated in early design stages carrying throughout system development.

The NASA Formal Methods Symposium is an annual event that was created to highlight the state of the art in formal methods, both in theory and in practice. The series is a spinoff of the original Langley Formal Methods Workshop (LFM). LFM was held six times in 1990, 1992, 1995, 1997, 2000, and 2008 near NASA Langley in Virginia, USA. In 2009 the first NASA Formal Methods Symposium was organized by NASA Ames Research Center in Moffett Field, CA. In 2010, the Symposium was organized by NASA Langley Research Center and NASA Goddard Space Flight Center, and held at NASA Headquarters in Washington, D.C. The third NFM symposium was organized by the Laboratory for Reliable Software at the NASA Jet Propulsion Laboratory/California Institute of Technology, and held in Pasadena, CA in 2011. NFM returned to NASA Langley Research Center in 2012; the Symposium was organized by the NASA Langley Formal Methods Group in nearby Norfolk, Virginia. NASA Ames Research Center organized and hosted NFM 2013, the fifth Symposium in the series. This year's Symposium was organized via a collaboration between NASA Goddard Space Flight Center, NASA Johnson Space Center, and NASA Ames Research Center.

The topics covered by NFM 2014 include but are not limited to: model checking; theorem proving; static analysis; model-based development; runtime monitoring; formal approaches to fault tolerance; applications of formal methods to aerospace systems; formal analysis of cyber-physical systems, including hybrid and embedded systems; formal methods in systems engineering, modeling, requirements, and specifications; requirements generation, specification debugging, formal validation of specifications; use of formal methods in safety cases; use of formal methods in human-machine interaction analysis; formal methods for parallel hardware implementations; use of formal methods in automated software engineering and testing; correct-by-design, design for verification, and property-based design techniques; techniques and algorithms for scaling formal methods, e.g., abstraction and symbolic methods, compositional techniques, parallel and distributed techniques; application of formal methods to emerging technologies.

Two types of papers were considered: regular papers describing fully developed work and complete results, and short papers describing tools, experience reports, or descriptions of work in progress with preliminary results. The Symposium received 107 abstract submissions, 83 of which resulted in full papers: 50 regular papers, and 33 short papers in total. Out of these, 20 regular papers and 9 short papers were accepted, giving an overall acceptance rate of 35% (a 40% rate for regular papers and a 27% rate for short papers). All submissions went through a rigorous reviewing process, where each paper was read by at least three reviewers.

In addition to the refereed papers, the symposium featured three invited talks and a panel feature. NASA provided a special guest talk on "NASA Future Challenges in Formal Methods," delivered by Bill McAllister, Chief, Safety and Mission Assurance, International Space Station Safety Panels, Avionics and Software Branch, NASA Johnson Space Center. Professor Lawrence C. Paulson from the University of Cambridge gave a keynote talk on "Theorem Proving and the Real Numbers: Overview and Challenges." Professor Moshe Y. Vardi from Rice University gave a keynote talk on "Compositional Temporal Synthesis."

The NFM 2014 panel feature, titled "Future Directions of Specifications for Formal Methods," featured panelists Matt Dwyer of the University of Nebraska, Hadas Kress-Gazit of Cornell University, and Moshe Y. Vardi of Rice University. Specifications are required for all applications of formal methods yet extracting specifications for real-life safety critical systems often proves to be a huge bottleneck or even an insurmountable hurdle to the application of formal methods in practice. This is the state for safety-critical systems today and as these systems grow more complex, more pervasive, and more powerful in the future, there is not a clear path even for maintaining the bleak status quo. Therefore, NFM2014 highlighted this issue in the home of an important critical system, the Mission Control Center of NASA's most famous critical systems, and asked our panelists where we can go from here.

The organizers are grateful to the authors for submitting their work to NFM 2014 and to the invited speakers and panelists for sharing their insights. NFM 2014 would not have been possible without the collaboration of the Steering

Committee, Program Committee, external reviewers, and the support of the NASA Formal Methods community. We are also grateful to our collaborators at the LERO the Irish Software Engineering Research Centre. The NFM 2014 website can be found at http://www.NASAFormalMethods.org.

February 2014                                                Julia M. Badger
                                                    Kristin Yvonne Rozier

# Organization

## Program Committee

| | |
|---|---|
| Domagoj Babic | Google Research, USA |
| Calin Belta | Boston University, USA |
| Armin Biere | Johannes Kepler University, Austria |
| Nikolaj Bjorner | Microsoft Research, USA |
| Jonathan P. Bowen | Museophile Limited, UK |
| Guillaume Brat | CMU/NASA Ames Research Center, USA |
| Gianfranco Ciardo | Iowa State University, USA |
| Frederic Dadeau | FEMTO-ST/Inria, France |
| Ewen Denney | SGT/NASA Ames Research Center, USA |
| Ben Di Vito | NASA Langley Research Center, USA |
| James Disbrow | NASA Dryden Flight Research Center, USA |
| Steven Drager | Air Force Research Laboratory, USA |
| Alexandre Duret-Lutz | LRDE/EPITA, France |
| Cindy Eisner | IBM Research - Haifa, Israel |
| Éric Féron | Georgia Institute of Technology, USA |
| Shalini Ghosh | SRI, USA |
| Alwyn Goodloe | NASA Langley Research Center, USA |
| Arie Gurfinkel | Software Engineering Institute, Carnegie Mellon University, USA |
| John Harrison | Intel Corporation, USA |
| Klaus Havelund | NASA/Jet Propulsion Laboratory, California Institute of Technology, USA |
| Connie Heitmeyer | Naval Research Laboratory, USA |
| Gerard Holzmann | NASA/Jet Propulsion Laboratory, California Institute of Technology, USA |
| Hadas Kress-Gazit | Cornell University, USA |
| Joe Leslie-Hurd | Intel Corporation, USA |
| David Lester | Manchester University, UK |
| Kenneth McMillan | Microsoft Research, USA |
| Sheena Miller | Barrios Technology/NASA Johnson Space Center, USA |
| Steven Miller | Rockwell Collins, USA |
| Cesar Munoz | NASA Langley Research Center, USA |
| Suzette Person | NASA Langley Research Center, USA |
| Lee Pike | Galois, Inc., USA |
| André Platzer | Carnegie Mellon University, USA |
| Neha Rungta | SGT/NASA Ames Research Center, USA |

Johann Schumann                SGT/NASA Ames Research Center, USA
Cristina Seceleanu             Mälardalen University, Sweden
Sandeep Shukla                 Virginia Tech, USA
Radu Siminiceanu               Amazon, USA
Oksana Tkachuk                 SGT/NASA Ames Research Center, USA
Stefano Tonetta                FBK-irst, Italy
Helmut Veith                   Vienna University of Technology, Austria
Arnaud Venet                   CMU/NASA Ames Research Center, USA
Mike Whalen                    University of Minnesota Software Engineering
                               Center, USA
Nok Wongpiromsarn              Singapore-MIT Alliance for Research and
                               Technology, Singapore
Karen Yorav                    IBM Research - Haifa, Israel

## Steering Committee

Ewen Denney                    SGT/NASA Ames Research Center, USA
Ben Di Vito                    NASA Langley Research Center, USA
Klaus Havelund                 NASA/Jet Propulsion Laboratory, California
                               Institute of Technology, USA
Gerard Holzmann                NASA/Jet Propulsion Laboratory, California
                               Institute of Technology, USA
Cesar Munoz                    NASA Langley Research Center, USA
Corina Pasareanu               CMU/NASA Ames Research Center, USA
Suzette Person                 NASA Langley Research Center, USA
Kristin Yvonne Rozier          NASA Ames Research Center, USA

## Additional Reviewers

Anderson, Matthew                          Fischer, Bernd
Archer, Myla                               Fulton, Nathan
Aydin Gol, Ebru                            Gario, Marco
Bak, Stan                                  Gascón, Adrià
Bartocci, Ezio                             Guralnik, Elena
Breuer, Peter                              Hatvani, Leo
Bushnell, David                            Hendrix, Joe
Dagit, Jason                               Jobredeaux, Romain
Deng, Yi                                   Jovanović, Dejan
Diatchki, Iavor                            Julliand, Jacques
Donzé, Alexandre                           Kong, Zhaodan
Duggirala, Parasara Sridhar                Koyfman, Anatoly
Elenius, Daniel                            Li, Wenchao
Faber, Johannes                            Mallet, Frederic

Marinescu, Raluca
Mitsch, Stefan
Moran, Shiri
Mover, Sergio
Müller, Andreas
Nanjundappa, Mahesh
Orni, Avigail
Owre, Sam
Pai, Ganesh
Pan, Guoqiang
Pham, Hung
Pidan, Dmitry
Renault, Etienne

Rodriguez-Navas, Guillermo
Rozier, Eric
Saeedloi, Neda
Seidl, Martina
Swei, Sean
Thompson, Sarah
Tiwari, Ashish
Veksler, Tatyana
Völp, Marcus
Wang, Timothy
Whiteside, Iain
Zawadzki, Erik

# Keynotes/Panel

# NASA Future Challenges in Formal Methods

R. William McAllister

NASA Johnson Space Center,
Houston, TX 77058, USA

The introduction of formal methods into a legacy software development process like the International Space Station Programs presents many of the same challenges impeding the wide acceptance of formal methods by industry. Not the least of these being budget and schedule targets and process inertia. While prior work shows that even the highly regarded Shuttle flight software development process could have benefited from the use of formal methods, the approach was never integrated into the baseline process.

Further, NASA software safety and quality assurance engineers face significant challenges of oversight and insight where NASA, rather than acquiring a software product in support of a program, contracts for a program service that happens to require software. For example, the ISS program levies no more than thirty computer based control system (software safety) and ten software quality assurance requirements on the Commercial Resupply Services and the Commercial Crew providers. While the providers compliance data is reviewed and approved by NASA, there is only the slightest opportunity to influence the software development methods employed.

Regardless, any mature development process includes corrective actions to eliminate the recurrence of escapes. Because single corrective actions routinely identify multiple escapes in the development cycle, these investigations provide an opportunity to examine the utility of formal methods.

# Theorem Proving and the Real Numbers: Overview and Challenges

Lawrence C. Paulson

Computer Laboratory, University of Cambridge, England
lp15@cl.cam.ac.uk

One of the first achievements in automated theorem proving was Jutting's construction of the real numbers using AUTOMATH [14]. But for years afterwards, formal proofs focused on problems from functional programming and elementary number theory. In the early 90s, John Harrison revived work on the reals by formalising their construction using HOL [8] and by undertaking an extensive programme of research into verifying floating point arithmetic, including the exponential and trigonometric functions [9–11].

MetiTarski represents a different approach to theorem proving about the reals. Reducing everything to first principles is rigorous, but makes proofs of the simplest statements extremely time-consuming. Many other automatic theorem provers are confined to linear arithmetic, or at best, polynomial comparisons. MetiTarski can prove complicated assertions involving transcendental functions. It takes many of their properties as axioms, and reasons from these properties using sophisticated decision procedures. MetiTarski has recently been integrated with other powerful reasoning tools, including KeYmaera [19] and PVS [17]. With this power, proofs involving such things as aircraft manoeuvres and the stability of hybrid systems can be undertaken, even when the dynamics are described by complicated formulas involving many special functions. Examples of this research can be found in these proceedings, for example, Denman's work on qualitative abstraction of hybrid systems [6].

This very success raises the question of how to recover the rigour of LCF-style theorem proving without losing the power of MetiTarski. The standard answer to this question (used by Isabelle's Sledgehammer for example [18]) is for the external prover to generate some sort of certificate that can be checked rigorously. The point is that the expensive proof search does not need to be checked, but only the proof that was actually found.

Checking a certificate using a separate theorem prover, such as Isabelle, requires machine formalisations of all the underlying mathematics. Since Harrison's work mentioned above, researchers worldwide have formalised substantial chunks of real analysis, including measure theory and probability theory [12, 16]. Independently, from the 1960s onwards, computer algebra systems enjoyed rapid development, as did decision procedures for real arithmetic. Much recent work has focused on formalising computer algebra algorithms within theorem provers, especially Coq [2, 15]. Investigations into special function inequalities have been conducted using PVS [5].

Nevertheless, the mathematics needed to certify the sort of proofs found by MetiTarski does not appear to have been formalised as yet. MetiTarski relies on an external decision procedure for *real-closed fields* (RCF) [7] to test the satisfiability of first-order formulas involving polynomials. The underlying algorithm is called CAD (Cylindrical Algebraic Decomposition) and QEPCAD [3] is a well-known implementation, although it has also been implemented in Mathematica and Z3 [13]. Each of these implementations is very complicated, and there is no obvious way to verify their results.

The underlying mathematics is real algebraic geometry [1]. MetiTarski also relies upon upper and lower bounds for the fractions it reasons about, given in the form of truncated power series or rational functions derived from continued fractions [4]. The necessary mathematics here belongs to approximation theory, and unusually, we are not concerned with the closeness of the approximations; the soundness of MetiTarski relies only upon the property that they are indeed upper or lower bounds. Proving these properties formally appears to require a substantial effort. And although we are only concerned with the real numbers, the necessary theory is most easily reached via complex analysis. That branch of mathematics remains largely unformalised at the moment, so we have much to do.

**Acknowledgements.** The Edinburgh members of the project team are Paul Jackson, Grant Passmore and Andrew Sogokon. The Cambridge team includes James Bridge, William Denman and Zongyan Huang. We are grateful to our outside collaborators such as César Muñoz, Eva Navarro-López, André Platzer, and others not listed here.

The research was supported by the Engineering and Physical Sciences Research Council [grant numbers EP/I011005/1, EP/I010335/1].

# References

1. Basu, S., Pollack, R., Roy, M.-F.: Algorithms in Real Algebraic Geometry, 2nd edn. Springer, Heidelberg (2006)
2. Bertot, Y., Guilhot, F., Mahboubi, A.: A formal study of Bernstein coefficients and polynomials. Mathematical Structures in Computer Science 21(04), 731–761 (2011), http://hal.inria.fr/inria-00503017
3. Brown, C.W.: QEPCAD B: a program for computing with semi-algebraic sets using CADs. SIGSAM Bulletin 37(4), 97–108 (2003), http://doi.acm.org/10.1145/968708.968710, doi:10.1145/968708.968710
4. Cuyt, A., Petersen, V., Verdonk, B., Waadeland, H., Jones, W.B.: Handbook of Continued Fractions for Special Functions. Springer, Heidelberg (2008), http://www.springer.com/math/analysis/book/978-1-4020-6948-2
5. Daumas, M., Muñoz, C., Lester, D.: Verified real number calculations: A library for integer arithmetic. IEEE Trans. Computers 58(2), 226–237 (2009), http://dx.doi.org/10.1109/TC.2008.213

6. Denman, W.: Verifying nonpolynomial hybrid systems by qualitative abstraction and automated theorem proving. In: 6th International Symposium on NASA Formal Methods, NFM 2014 (2014) (these proceedings)
7. Dolzmann, A., Sturm, T., Weispfenning, V.: Real quantifier elimination in practice. In: Matzat, B.H., Greuel, G.-M., Hiss, G. (eds.) Algorithmic Algebra and Number Theory, pp. 221–247. Springer, Heidelberg (1999), http://dx.doi.org/10.1007/978-3-642-59932-3_11
8. Harrison, J.: Constructing the real numbers in HOL. Formal Methods in System Design 5, 35–59 (1994)
9. Harrison, J.: Floating point verification in HOL Light: the exponential function. Formal Methods in System Design 16, 271–305 (2000)
10. Harrison, J.V.: Formal verification of floating point trigonometric functions. In: Johnson, S.D., Hunt Jr., W.A. (eds.) FMCAD 2000. LNCS, vol. 1954, pp. 217–233. Springer, Heidelberg (2000)
11. Harrison, J.: Formal verification of IA-64 division algorithms. In: Aagaard, M.D., Harrison, J. (eds.) TPHOLs 2000. LNCS, vol. 1869, pp. 233–251. Springer, Heidelberg (2000)
12. Hurd, J.: Verification of the Miller-Rabin probabilistic primality test. Journal of Logic and Algebraic Programming 56, 3–21 (2002)
13. Jovanović, D., de Moura, L.: Solving non-linear arithmetic. In: Gramlich, B., Miller, D., Sattler, U. (eds.) IJCAR 2012. LNCS, vol. 7364, pp. 339–354. Springer, Heidelberg (2012)
14. van Benthem Jutting, L.S.: Checking Landau's "Grundlagen" in the AUTOMATH System. PhD thesis, Eindhoven University of Technology (1977)
15. Mahboubi, A.: Implementing the CAD algorithm within the Coq system. Mathematical Structure in Computer Sciences 17 (2007)
16. Mhamdi, T., Hasan, O., Tahar, S.: Formalization of measure theory and Lebesgue integration for probabilistic analysis in HOL. ACM Trans. Embedded Comput. Syst. 12(1), 13 (2013)
17. Owre, S., Rajan, S., Rushby, J.M., Shankar, N., Srivas, M.K.: PVS: Combining specification, proof checking, and model checking. In: Alur, R., Henzinger, T.A. (eds.) CAV 1996. LNCS, vol. 1102, pp. 411–414. Springer, Heidelberg (1996)
18. Paulson, L.C., Susanto, K.W.: Source-level proof reconstruction for interactive theorem proving. In: Schneider, K., Brandt, J. (eds.) TPHOLs 2007. LNCS, vol. 4732, pp. 232–245. Springer, Heidelberg (2007)
19. Platzer, A., Quesel, J.-D.: KeYmaera: A hybrid theorem prover for hybrid systems. In: Armando, A., Baumgartner, P., Dowek, G. (eds.) IJCAR 2008. LNCS (LNAI), vol. 5195, pp. 171–178. Springer, Heidelberg (2008)

# Compositional Temporal Synthesis

Moshe Y. Vardi

Rice University, Houston, Texas, USA
vardi@cs.rice.edu

Synthesis is the automated construction of a system from its specification. In standard temporal-synthesis algorithms, it is assumed the system is constructed from scratch. This, of course, rarely happens in real life. In real life, almost every non-trivial system, either in hardware or in software, relies heavily on using libraries of reusable components. Furthermore, other contexts, such as web-service orchestration and choreography, can also be modeled as synthesis of a system from a library of components.

In this talk we describe and study the problem of compositional temporal synthesis, in which we synthesize systems from libraries of reusable components. We define two notions of composition: data-flow composition, which we show is undecidable, and control-flow composition, which we show is decidable. We then explore a variation of control-flow compositional synthesis, in which we construct reliable systems from libraries of unreliable components.

**Acknowledgements.** Joint work with Yoad Lustig and Sumit Nain.

# References

1. Lustig, Y., Nain, S., Vardi, M.Y.: Synthesis from probabilistic components. In: Bezem, M. (ed.) CSL. LIPIcs, vol. 12, pp. 412–427. Schloss Dagstuhl - Leibniz-Zentrum fuer Informatik, http://dblp.uni-trier.de/db/conf/csl/csl2011.html#LustigNV11
2. Lustig, Y., Vardi, M.Y.: Synthesis from component libraries. STTT 15(5-6), 603–618 (2013)
3. Nain, S., Vardi, M.Y.: Synthesizing Probabilistic Composers. In: Birkedal, L. (ed.) FOSSACS 2012. LNCS, vol. 7213, pp. 421–436. Springer, Heidelberg (2012)

# Panel: Future Directions of Specifications for Formal Methods

Julia M. Badger[1] and Kristin Yvonne Rozier[2],*

[1]NASA Johnson Space Center, Houston, Texas, USA
Julia.M.Badger@nasa.gov
[2]NASA Ames Research Center, Moffett Field, California, USA
Kristin.Y.Rozier@nasa.gov

Specifications are required for all applications of formal methods, yet extracting specifications for real-life safety critical systems often proves to be a huge bottleneck or even an insurmountable hurdle to the application of formal methods in practice. This is the state for safety-critical systems today and as these systems grow more complex, more pervasive, and more powerful in the future, there is not a clear path even for maintaining the bleak status quo. Therefore, we propose highlighting this issue in the home of an important critical system, the Mission Control Center of NASA's most famous critical systems, and asking our panelists where we can go from here.

## Panelists

- Matt Dwyer, University of Nebraska, USA
- Hadas Kress-Gazit, Cornell University, USA
- Moshe Y. Vardi, Rice University, USA

## Panel Questions

1. **Where are we now?** Please outline your background and answer the question "Where are we now?" with regards to specifications.
2. **Where will we get specifications from?** At NASA in particular, extracting specifications needed for any formal analysis is a huge challenge. Some critical systems are designed without ever having what this community would consider to be a formal set of requirements. Some design processes don't formally define requirements until the testing phase, far too late to use them for design or design-time analysis, or other key periods in the system development life-cycle where formal methods are applicable. Even for critical systems where specifications are defined early in the system development life-cycle, they often mix many different objectives, mixing many different levels of detail and describing things like how the system is defined, how the system should behave, legal-speak on why the system satisfies rules, and

---

* Panel Moderator

more – sometimes all in the same sentence! As safety-critical systems become increasingly complex and the budgetary and other constraints tighten, where can we look in the future to hope to extract the specifications we need for formal analysis?

3. **How should we measure specification quality?** How can we know when we're "done" extracting specifications or have some idea of how well we've done? As critical systems continue to grow in complexity, how will we measure the completeness, coverage, or general quality of a specification or a set of specifications?

4. **How do we best use specifications?** How should formal specifications (both those we are given and those we must extract) fit into the design life-cycle for different kinds of critical systems? How can we indoctrinate formal specifications into diverse teams of system designers without hitting barriers to adoption such as huge costs in terms of time and learning curves? What should our roadmap look like for a future full of well-specified (formally analyzable) critical systems?

5. **We are now open for questions from the audience.**

# Table of Contents

DO-333 Certification Case Studies .............................. 1
  *Darren Cofer and Steven Miller*

A Compositional Monitoring Framework for Hard Real-Time
Systems ...................................................... 16
  *André de Matos Pedro, David Pereira, Luís Miguel Pinho, and
  Jorge Sousa Pinto*

Leadership Election: An Industrial SoS Application of Compositional
Deadlock Verification ......................................... 31
  *Pedro R.G. Antonino, Marcel Medeiros Oliveira,
  Augusto C.A. Sampaio, Klaus E. Kristensen, and
  Jeremy W. Bryans*

Verification of Certifying Computations through AutoCorres and
Simpl ........................................................ 46
  *Lars Noschinski, Christine Rizkallah, and Kurt Mehlhorn*

Distinguishing Sequences for Partially Specified FSMs ................. 62
  *Robert M. Hierons and Uraz Cengiz Türker*

On Proving Recoverability of Smart Electrical Grids.................. 77
  *Seppo Horsmanheimo, Maryam Kamali, Mikko Kolehmainen,
  Mats Neovius, Luigia Petre, Mauno Rönkkö, and Petter Sandvik*

Providing Early Warnings of Specification Problems .................. 92
  *Dustin Hoffman, Aditi Tagore, Diego Zaccai, and Bruce W. Weide*

Mechanized, Compositional Verification of Low-Level Code ............ 98
  *Björn Bartels and Nils Jähnig*

Formally Verified Computation of Enclosures of Solutions of Ordinary
Differential Equations ........................................ 113
  *Fabian Immler*

On the Quantum Formalization of Coherent Light in HOL ............ 128
  *Mohamed Yousri Mahmoud and Sofiène Tahar*

Refinement Types for TLA$^+$ .................................. 143
  *Stephan Merz and Hernán Vanzetto*

Using Lightweight Theorem Proving in an Asynchronous Systems
Context . . . . . . . . . . . . . . . . . . . . . . . . . . . . . . . . . . . . . . . . . . . . . . . . . . . . . . . .    158
   *Matthew Danish and Hongwei Xi*

JKelloy: A Proof Assistant for Relational Specifications of Java
Programs . . . . . . . . . . . . . . . . . . . . . . . . . . . . . . . . . . . . . . . . . . . . . . . . . . . . . .    173
   *Aboubakr Achraf El Ghazi, Mattias Ulbrich, Christoph Gladisch,
Shmuel Tyszberowicz, and Mana Taghdiri*

Verifying Hybrid Systems Involving Transcendental Functions . . . . . . . . .    188
   *Paul Jackson, Andrew Sogokon, James Bridge, and
Lawrence Paulson*

Verifying Nonpolynomial Hybrid Systems by Qualitative Abstraction
and Automated Theorem Proving . . . . . . . . . . . . . . . . . . . . . . . . . . . . . . . . .    203
   *William Denman*

Combining PVSio with Stateflow . . . . . . . . . . . . . . . . . . . . . . . . . . . . . . . . . .    209
   *Paolo Masci, Yi Zhang, Paul Jones, Patrick Oladimeji,
Enrico D'Urso, Cinzia Bernardeschi, Paul Curzon, and
Harold Thimbleby*

Qed. Computing What Remains to Be Proved . . . . . . . . . . . . . . . . . . . . . . .    215
   *Loïc Correnson*

Warps and Atomics: Beyond Barrier Synchronization in the Verification
of GPU Kernels . . . . . . . . . . . . . . . . . . . . . . . . . . . . . . . . . . . . . . . . . . . . . . . . .    230
   *Ethel Bardsley and Alastair F. Donaldson*

Testing-Based Compiler Validation for Synchronous Languages . . . . . . . .    246
   *Pierre-Loïc Garoche, Falk Howar, Temesghen Kahsai, and
Xavier Thirioux*

Automated Testcase Generation for Numerical Support Functions in
Embedded Systems . . . . . . . . . . . . . . . . . . . . . . . . . . . . . . . . . . . . . . . . . . . . . .    252
   *Johann Schumann and Stefan-Alexander Schneider*

REFINER: Towards Formal Verification of Model Transformations . . . . .    258
   *Anton Wijs and Luc Engelen*

Designing a Deadlock-Free Train Scheduler: A Model Checking
Approach . . . . . . . . . . . . . . . . . . . . . . . . . . . . . . . . . . . . . . . . . . . . . . . . . . . . . . .    264
   *Franco Mazzanti, Giorgio Oronzo Spagnolo, and Alessio Ferrari*

A Synthesized Algorithm for Interactive Consistency . . . . . . . . . . . . . . . . .    270
   *Adrià Gascón and Ashish Tiwari*

Energy-Utility Quantiles . . . . . . . . . . . . . . . . . . . . . . . . . . . . . . . . . . . . . . . . .    285
   *Christel Baier, Marcus Daum, Clemens Dubslaff, Joachim Klein,
and Sascha Klüppelholz*

Incremental Verification of Compiler Optimizations.................... 300
  *Grigory Fedyukovich, Arie Gurfinkel, and Natasha Sharygina*

Memory Efficient Data Structures for Explicit Verification of Timed
Systems ......................................................... 307
  *Peter Gjøl Jensen, Kim Guldstrand Larsen, Jiří Srba,*
  *Mathias Grund Sørensen, and Jakob Haar Taankvist*

The Gradual Verifier ............................................. 313
  *Stephan Arlt, Cindy Rubio-González, Philipp Rümmer,*
  *Martin Schäf, and Natarajan Shankar*

Synthesizing Predicates from Abstract Domain Losses ............... 328
  *Bogdan Mihaila and Axel Simon*

Formal Verification of kLIBC with the WP Frama-C Plug-in .......... 343
  *Nuno Carvalho, Cristiano da Silva Sousa, Jorge Sousa Pinto, and*
  *Aaron Tomb*

Author Index...................................................... 359

# DO-333 Certification Case Studies

Darren Cofer and Steven Miller

Rockwell Collins Advanced Technology Center
{ddcofer,spmiller}@rockwellcollins.com

**Abstract.** RTCA DO-333, *Formal Methods Supplement to DO-178C and DO-278A*, provides guidance for software developers wishing to use formal methods in the certification of airborne systems and air traffic management systems. This paper presents three case studies describing the use of different classes of formal methods to satisfy DO-178C certification objectives. The case studies examine different aspects of a common avionics example, a dual-channel Flight Guidance System (FGS), which is representative of the issues encountered in actual developments. The three case studies illustrate the use of theorem proving, model checking, and abstract interpretation. Each of these techniques has strengths and weaknesses and each could be applied to different life cycle data items and different objectives than those described here. Our purpose is to illustrate a reasonable application of each of these techniques to produce the evidence needed to satisfy certification objectives in a realistic avionics application. We hope that these case studies will be useful to industry and government personnel in understanding formal methods and the benefits they can provide.

**Keywords:** Formal methods, certification, model checking, theorem proving, abstract interpretation.

## 1 Introduction

Certification can be defined as legal recognition by a government authority that a product, service, organization, or person complies with specified requirements. In the context of commercial aircraft, certification consists primarily of convincing the relevant certification authority (the FAA in the U.S. or EASA in Europe) that all required steps have been taken to ensure the safety, reliability, and integrity of the aircraft. Software itself is not certified in isolation, but only as part of an aircraft design. Certification differs from verification in that it focuses on evidence provided to a third party to demonstrate that the required activities were performed completely and correctly, rather on performance of the activities themselves.

For software in commercial aircraft, the relevant certification guidance is found in DO-178C, "Software Considerations in Airborne Systems and Equipment Certification" (known in Europe as ED-12C) [10]. Certification authorities in North American and Europe have agreed that an applicant (aircraft manufacturer) can use this guidance as a means of compliance with the regulations governing aircraft certification.

J.M. Badger and K.Y. Rozier (Eds.): NFM 2014, LNCS 8430, pp. 1–15, 2014.

Its predecessor, DO-178B, allowed for the use of formal methods to satisfy certification objectives, but did so only as an "Alternative Method." DO-178C now provides guidance specific to newer software technologies including formal methods, model-based development, and object-oriented software. This technology-specific guidance is contained in supplemental documents which may add, modify, or replace objectives in the core document. With the publication of DO-333, *Formal Methods Supplement to DO-178C and DO-278A* [12], the use of formal methods has become a recognized means of compliance (rather than an alternative method), streamlining the process for aircraft manufacturers to obtain certification credit through the use of formal verification techniques.

This paper presents three case studies describing the use of different classes of formal methods to satisfy DO-178C certification objectives using the guidance in DO-333. The three case studies illustrate the use of theorem proving, model checking, and abstract interpretation. Each of these techniques has strengths and weaknesses, and each could be applied to different life cycle data items and different objectives than those described here. The material presented is not intended to represent a complete certification effort. Rather, the purpose is to show how formal methods can be used in a realistic avionics software development, focusing on the evidence produced that could be used to satisfy the verification objectives found in DO-178C. The complete version of the case studies along with all the associated models, code, and verification artifacts will be available as a NASA contractor report in 2014.

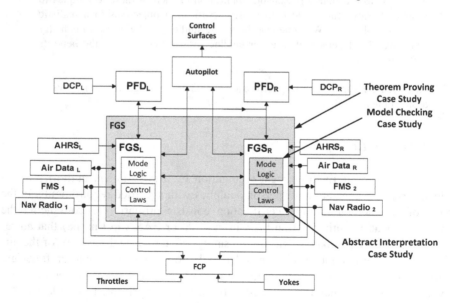

**Fig. 1.** Formal Methods applications in the Flight Guidance System example

The case studies examine different aspects of a common avionics system, a dual-channel Flight Guidance System (FGS), shown in Fig. 1. While not intended as a complete example, it is representative of the issues encountered in actual development projects and includes design artifacts specified using PVS, MATLAB Simulink/ Stateflow®, and C source code.

An FGS is a component of the overall Flight Control System (FCS). It compares the measured state of an aircraft (position, speed, and attitude) to the desired state and generates pitch and roll guidance commands to minimize the difference between the measured and desired state. The pilots interact with the FGS via the Flight Control Panel (FCP), Primary Flight Display (PFD), and the Display Control Panel (DCP).

The FGS subsystem accepts input about the aircraft's state from the Attitude Heading Reference System (AHRS), the Air Data System (ADS), the Flight Management System (FMS), and the Navigation Radios. Using this information, it computes pitch and roll guidance commands that are provided to the autopilot (AP). When engaged, the AP translates these commands into movement of the aircraft's control surfaces necessary to achieve the commanded changes about the lateral and vertical axes.

The FGS has two physical sides, or channels – one on the left side and one on the right side of the aircraft. These provide redundant implementations that communicate with each other over a cross-channel bus. Each channel of the FGS can be further broken down into the mode logic and the flight control laws. The flight control laws accept information about the aircraft's current and desired state, and compute the pitch and roll guidance commands. A flight control law is active if its guidance commands are being used to control the aircraft or to provide visual cues to the flight crew. A flight control law that is operational but that is not yet active is armed. The mode logic determines which lateral and vertical modes of operation are active (e.g. controlling the aircraft or providing visual guidance cues to the flight crew) and armed (e.g. operational but not yet active) at any given time. These in turn determine which flight control laws are active and armed.

## 2    Certification and DO-333

General guidance is provided in DO-333 that is applicable to the overall verification process when formal methods are used. This includes the following requirements:

- All formal notations used must have unambiguous, mathematically defined syntax and semantics.
- The soundness of each formal analysis method should be documented. A sound method never asserts that a property is true when it may not be true. Soundness here refers to the underlying analysis method, not soundness of the tool implementation. Tool soundness issues are addressed separately as part of the tool qualification process described in DO-330 [11].
- All assumptions related to the formal analysis should be described and justified (e.g. assumptions about execution semantics on the target computer, or assumptions about data range limits).

Beyond these general requirements, specific guidance is provided to describe how formal methods can be applied within each of the verification activities and objectives defined in DO-178C. This is illustrated in Fig. 2 for Level A software, the highest criticality level defined in DO-178C. These include compliance with requirements, accuracy and consistency of requirements, compatibility with the target computer, verifiability of requirements, conformance to standards, traceability between life cycle data items, and algorithmic correctness.

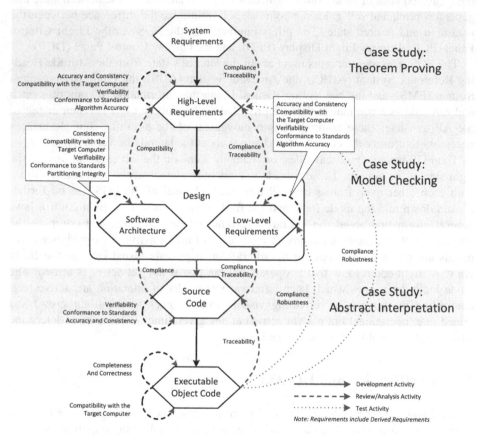

**Fig. 2.** Relationship of Case Studies to DO-178C Level A Objectives (adapted from DO-333)

Fig. 2 also shows the relationship between the three case studies and DO-178C objectives. Theorem proving was applied to the verification of the High-Level Requirements (HLR) for the Pilot Flying synchronization logic of the two channels of the FGS, focusing on the objectives of DO-333 Table FM.A-3. Theorem proving is generally considered the most powerful and versatile class of formal methods, but it is also the least automated, and usually requires the significant expertise and user training. This case study is described in Section 3.

Model checking has been applied to the verification of the Low-Level Requirements (LLR) for the mode logic of a single FGS channel, focusing on the objectives of DO-333 Table FM.A-4. Current model checking tools are very powerful and provide much more automation than theorem provers. In general, less user expertise is required, but the user must be able to specify requirements to be analyzed in a formal language. These tools are relatively mature and (in our opinion) the benefits of using formal methods are greatest at this level. This case study is described in Section 4.

Abstract interpretation has been applied to the Source Code implementing one of the control laws of the FGS, focusing on the objectives of DO-333 Table FM.A-5. Abstract interpretation is the most automated of the three techniques, at least as used in currently available commercial tools, and typically requires the least expertise from users. Part of this is due to the use of abstract interpretation to check non-functional requirements, eliminating the need to formally specify requirements. We should note, however, that more powerful versions of abstract interpretation tools exist which require much more expertise to specify and check user-defined abstract domains. This case study is described in Section 5.

Another issue we address in each case study is *tool qualification*. Tool qualification is the process necessary to obtain certification credit for the use of a software tool within the context of a specific airborne system. The purpose of qualification is to ensure that the tool provides confidence at least equivalent to that of any process which is eliminated, reduced, or automated. DO-178C specifies that tool qualification should be performed in accordance with *DO-330, Software Tool Qualification Considerations* [11].

Each case study includes:

- The objectives to be satisfied and the evidence produced
- A general description of the portion of the example system to be verified
- A description of the verification approach, including the life cycle data items produced and the tools used, corresponding to some of the information that should be included in a Software Verification Plan
- Tool qualification issues for the formal methods tools used
- A detailed description of the verification effort that was performed

There are some parts of DO-333 that are not covered in these case studies. In particular, we do not address the verification of Executable Object Code (DO-333 Table FM.A-6), nor do we address the replacement of coverage testing by formal analysis (DO-333 Table FM.A-7).

# 3 Theorem Proving Case Study

This case study illustrates the use of the PVS [9] and the HOL4 [7] theorem proving systems to verify the outputs of the software requirements process (DO-178C Section 5.1) focusing on the objectives of Table A-3 in DO-178C and Table FM.A-3 in DO-333. The purpose of these verification activities is to detect any errors that may have been introduced during the software requirements process. The DO-178C and DO-333 objectives satisfied through theorem proving are summarized in Table 1. The table indicates whether an objective was satisfied (fully or partially) in the case study for each software level, A through D. Some objectives do not need to be satisfied for the less critical Level C or Level D software and are indicated by shaded boxes in the corresponding columns of the table.

**Table 1.** Summary of Objectives Satisfied by Theorem Proving

| Obj | Description | A | B | C | D | Notes |
|---|---|---|---|---|---|---|
| A-3.1 | High-level requirements comply with system requirements. | ■ | ■ | ■ | ■ | Established by proof the system requirements are implemented by the high-level requirements and the system architecture. |
| A-3.2 | High-level requirements are accurate and consistent. | ■ | ■ | ■ | ■ | Accuracy is established by formalization of the high-level requirements. Consistency is established by proving the absence of logical conflicts. |
| A-3.3 | High-level requirements are compatible with target computer. | | | | | Not addressed |
| A-3.4 | High-level requirements are verifiable. | ■ | ■ | ■ | | Established by formalizing the requirements and completion of the proof. |
| A-3.5 | High-level requirements conform to standards. | □ | □ | □ | | Partially established by specifying the high-level requirements as formal properties. |
| A-3.6 | High-level requirements are traceable to system requirements. | ■ | ■ | ■ | ■ | Established by verification of the system requirements, and by demonstrating the necessity of each high-level requirement for satisfying some system requirement. |
| A-3.7 | Algorithms are accurate. | ■ | ■ | ■ | | Correctness of the pilot flying selection logic is established by proof. |
| FM.A-3.8 | Formal analysis cases and procedures are correct. | ■ | ■ | ■ | | Established by review. |
| FM.A-3.9 | Formal analysis results are correct and discrepancies explained. | ■ | ■ | ■ | | Established by review. |
| FM.A-3.10 | Requirements formalization is correct. | ■ | ■ | ■ | | Established by review. |
| FM.A-3.11 | Formal method is correctly defined, justified, and appropriate. | ■ | ■ | ■ | ■ | Established by review. |

■ *Full credit claimed*     □ *Partial credit claimed*     ▨ *Satisfaction of objective is at applicant's discretion*

Consider Objective A-3.1 in Table 1 (high-level requirements comply with system requirements). The system architecture is captured in the PVS theory *Pilot_Flying_System*. This theory describes how the system components interact in the overall system. The system requirements are stated formally as theorems in the PVS theory *Pilot_Flying_System_Requirements*. Machine checked proofs are developed in PVS to prove that these requirements are satisfied by the system architecture and the high-level requirements for the system components. The high-level software requirements are specified for each FGS side in the *Side_HLR* theory. This theory uses axioms and uninterpreted types, constants, and functions to eliminate design detail from the requirements. The axioms are proven consistent by demonstrating that at least one concrete implementation exists that satisfies the axioms. The objective is satisfied by proving with the PVS theorem prover that the system level requirements specified as theorems in theory *Pilot_Flying_System_Requirements* are implemented by the system architecture defined in theory *Pilot_Flying_System*, the high-level software requirements specified as axioms in theory *Side_HLR* and the high-level hardware requirements specified as axioms in theory *Bus_HLR*. A more detailed discussion of how each objective is satisfied is provided in the full contractor report available from NASA.

The specific example used in the theorem proving case study is the synchronization of the Pilot Flying side of the aircraft. The overall FGS system has two physical sides, or channels, one on the left side and one on the right side of the aircraft. These provide redundant implementations that communicate with each other over a cross-channel bus as shown in Fig. 3. Bidirectional communication between the left and right sides is modeled separately as LR_Bus and RL_Bus.

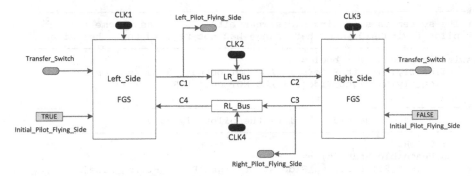

**Fig. 3.** Overview of the Dual FGS System

Most of the time, the FGS operates in *dependent* mode where only one FGS channel is *active* and provides guidance to the AP. In this mode, the flight crew can choose whether the left or the right FGS is the active, or *pilot flying*, side by pressing the Transfer Switch. The other side serves as a hot spare and sets its modes to agree with those of the active side. In this example, there are five system-level requirements related to the synchronization of the pilot flying side. Stated informally, these are:

R1. At least one side shall be the pilot flying side.

R2. At most one side shall be the pilot flying side.

R3. Pressing the Transfer Switch shall always change the pilot flying side.

R4. The system shall start with the Primary Side as the pilot flying side.

R5. The system shall not change the pilot flying side unless the Transfer Switch is pressed.

The case study formalizes these system-level requirements in PVS and HOL4, develops high-level software and hardware requirements for each side and the cross-channel bus, and proves that that the system architecture, the high-level software requirements, and the high-level hardware requirements comply with the system requirements. This is done in both PVS and HOL4 for a synchronous design in which all components are driven from single master clock. The example was repeated in PVS for an asynchronous design in which the components are driven by separate clocks.

For example, the PVS specification of the requirements R1 and R2 for the synchronous design is shown in Fig. 4. Note that formalizing these requirements required a precise statement of what it means for the system to be switching sides.

The case study then develops a set of high-level requirements for each subcomponent, i.e., the FGS sides and the buses of Fig. 3, that are completely free of design detail by using uninterpreted PVS types and axioms specifying the relationship of their outputs to their inputs. These high-level requirements are then proven to be consistent (i.e. to not contradict each other) by creating a concrete implementation using interpreted PVS types and functions and showing that the concrete implementation is a PVS theory interpretation of the high-level component requirements. Finally, we prove that the system architecture and the high-level requirements of the components comply with the system requirements by proving that the system requirements are satisfied by the synchronous design instantiated with any components that satisfy the high-level component requirements

```
%-------------------------------------------------------------
% The system is switching sides when either side has become the
% pilot flying side and that change has not reached the other side
%-------------------------------------------------------------
switching_sides(s) : bool =
    pilot_flying(Left_Side(s))  AND NOT output(LR_Bus(s)) OR
    pilot_flying(Right_Side(s)) AND NOT output(RL_Bus(s))

%-------------------------------------------------------------
% R1. At least one side shall be the pilot flying side.
%-------------------------------------------------------------
  R1: THEOREM
      Reachable_State(s) =>
          Left_Pilot_Flying_Side(s) or Right_Pilot_Flying_Side(s)
%-------------------------------------------------------------
% R2. At most one side shall be the pilot flying side
%     except while the system is switching sides.
%-------------------------------------------------------------
  R2: THEOREM
      Reachable_State(s) AND NOT switching_sides(s) =>
          Left_Pilot_Flying_Side(s) /= Right_Pilot_Flying_Side(s)
```

**Fig. 4.** Example of FGS System Requirements in PVS

The verification was then repeated for an asynchronous design in which each side and each bus is driven by its own independent clock (CLK1-4 in Fig. 3). We followed the same process for the asynchronous case. However, the sides and the buses needed to be modified to allow an acknowledgement signal to be exchanged between the two sides to implement a hand-shaking protocol to synchronize on the pilot flying side. Aside from changing the definition of what it meant to be switching sides, the system level requirements did not need to be modified.

The synchronous Dual FGS example was also verified using HOL4. HOL4 proofs were developed using both the next-state approach used with PVS and a stream approach similar to that used in synchronous data flow languages such as Lustre [4]. In the next-state approach, the evolution of each component and the overall system was specified by defining a next-state function that returns the next state given its current state and inputs as arguments. In the stream-based approach, each system variable is specified as a mapping from a natural number representing the system step to the variable's value on that step. The evolution of each component and the overall system is then specified by defining the value of each system variable for each step.

Qualification of a theorem prover may be a difficult task. The largest part of a normal qualification effort is focused on defining operational requirements for the tool (what the tool claims to do – the processes eliminated, reduced, or automated), and then developing a comprehensive test suite to show that those requirements are satisfied over an appropriate range of tool inputs. An alternative approach is to avoid the need to qualify the theorem prover itself by providing an independent check of the proof it produces. This may be feasible depending on the nature of the proof artifacts generated by a particular theorem prover.

PVS is based on a classical strongly-typed higher-order logic and the theorem prover itself is a based on a sequent calculus for this logic. PVS does not normally emit a proof that could be checked by a separate (qualified) proof checking tool, though this option is available. Depending upon the nature of the proof rules used, this expansion could in principle be independently checked by a separate tool. However, we are not aware of this having been done in practice and development of an appropriate independent checker for PVS is still a research topic.

**Table 2.** Summary of Objectives Satisfied by Model Checking

| Objective | Description | A | B | C | D | Notes |
|---|---|---|---|---|---|---|
| A-4.1 | Low-level requirements comply with high-level requirements. | ■ | ■ | ■ | | Established by proof that the high-level requirements are implemented by the low-level requirements and the software architecture. |
| A-4.2 | Low-level requirements are accurate and consistent. | ■ | ■ | ■ | | Established by modeling using an executable language and translation to a formal specification language. |
| A-4.3 | Low-level requirements are compatible with target computer. | | | | | Not addressed |
| A-4.4 | Low-level requirements are verifiable. | ■ | ■ | | | Established by modeling using an executable language and translation to a formal specification language. |
| A-4.5 | Low-level requirements conform to standards. | □ | □ | □ | | Established by use of Simulink/Stateflow design language. |
| A-4.6 | Low-level requirements are traceable to high-level requirements. | □ | □ | □ | | Established by verification of the high-level requirements. |
| A-4.7 | Algorithms are accurate. | ■ | ■ | ■ | | The accuracy of the mode logic is established by model checking. |
| A-4.8 | Software architecture is compatible with high-level requirements. | ■ | ■ | ■ | | Established by proof that the high-level requirements are implemented by the low-level requirements and the software architecture. |
| A-4.9 | Software architecture is consistent | ■ | ■ | ■ | | Established by modeling using an executable language and translation to a formal specification language. |
| A-4.10 | Software architecture is compatible with target computer. | | | | | Not addressed |
| A-4.11 | Software architecture is verifiable. | ■ | ■ | | | Established by modeling using an executable language and translation to a formal specification language. |
| A-4.12 | Software architecture conforms to standards. | □ | □ | □ | | Partially established by use of Simulink/Stateflow. |
| A-4.13 | Software partitioning integrity is confirmed. | | | | | Partitioning integrity has been established using formal methods for several commercial operating systems. This is not addressed in the current case study. |
| FM.A-4.14 | Formal analysis cases and procedures are correct. | ■ | ■ | ■ | | Established by review |
| FM.A-4.15 | Formal analysis results are correct and discrepancies explained. | ■ | ■ | ■ | | Established by review |
| FM.A-4.16 | Requirements formalization is correct. | ■ | ■ | ■ | | Established by review |
| FM.A-4.17 | Formal method is correctly defined, justified, and appropriate. | ■ | ■ | ■ | ■ | Established by review |

■ *Full credit claimed*　　□ *Partial credit claimed*　　■ *Satisfaction of objective is at applicant's discretion*

The HOL4 implementation is based on a small trusted kernel, which encapsulates just the primitive inference rules, axioms, and definition mechanisms of the logic. The logic kernel is an abstract data type, having the property that the only way a theorem can be obtained is ultimately by making primitive inference steps, which are very close in granularity to those in the mathematical definition of the logic. As a consequence, it is straightforward to instrument HOL kernels so that they emit formal proofs. This has been done in a variety of research projects [8] [5]. Programs that check the correctness of such proofs are small and relatively easy to verify.

# 4    Model Checking Case Study

This case study illustrates the use of the Kind [3] and MathWork's Design Verifier model checkers to perform verification activities associated with the outputs of the software design process, focusing on the objectives of Table A-4 in DO-178C and Table FM.A-4 in DO-333. The purpose of these verification activities is to detect any errors that may have been introduced during the software design process (DO-178C Section 5.2). The DO-178C and DO-333 objectives satisfied through model checking are summarized in Table 2.

The specific example used in the model checking case study is the verification of the mode logic of one side of the FGS. Specifically as it relates to the FGS, FAA Advisory Circular AC/ACJ 25.1329 defines a mode as *a system configuration that corresponds to a single (or set of) FGS behavior(s)* [2]. In the FGS, the modes are actually abstractions of their associated flight control law and reflect the current state of the flight control law. The FGS modes are organized into the lateral modes, which control the behavior of the aircraft about the roll and yaw axes of the aircraft and the vertical modes, which control the behavior of the aircraft about the pitch axis of the aircraft. The lateral modes in the example include *Roll Hold, Lateral Navigation, Lateral Approach,* and *Lateral Go Around.* The vertical modes include *Pitch Hold, Vertical Speed, Flight Level Change, Altitude Hold, Altitude Select, Vertical Approach,* and *Vertical Go Around.*

In the case study, the mode logic is viewed as the software low-level requirements and is specified using MATLAB Simulink and Stateflow. For example, the Stateflow diagram for the Lateral Navigation (NAV) mode is shown in Fig. 5. Details of the transition guards are specified as Stateflow truth tables.

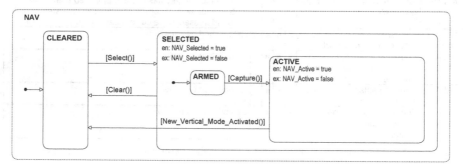

**Fig. 5.** Lateral Navigation (NAV) Mode Low-Level Requirements in Stateflow

The mode logic of the FGS specifies these individual modes and the rules for transitioning between them. To provide proper guidance of the aircraft, these modes are tightly synchronized so that only a small portion of their total state space is actually reachable. For example, since at least one lateral and one vertical mode must be active and providing guidance whenever the AP is engaged, one mode is designated as the *basic* mode for each axis. The basic mode is automatically activated if no other mode is active for that axis. In this example, the basic modes are *Roll Hold* and *Pitch Hold*. In similar fashion, only one lateral mode and one vertical mode can provide guidance to the AP at the same time, so the mode logic must ensure that at most one lateral and one vertical mode are ever active at the same time.

Other constraints enforce relationships between the modes that are dictated by the characteristics of the aircraft and the airspace. For example, *Vertical Approach* mode is not allowed to become active until *Lateral Approach* mode has become active to ensure that the aircraft is horizontally centered on the localizer before tracking the glideslope. These constraints constitute the high-level software requirements for the mode logic and are captured as 118 high-level properties written in the Lustre specification language. For example, the requirement that at least one lateral mode is always active is specified in Lustre as

```
At_Least_One_Lateral_Mode_Active =
    ROLL_Active or HDG_Active or NAV_Active or
    LAPPR_Active or LGA_Active;
```

To verify that the Simulink and Stateflow low-level requirements for the mode logic satisfy these high-level requirements, the Simlink/Stateflow model of the mode logic is translated into Lustre, the input language of the Kind model checker, using the Rockwell Collins formal translation framework [6] and merged with the high-level requirements written in Lustre. This file can then be analyzed by the Kind model checker. Sixteen errors were discovered in the mode logic using the Kind model checker and three errors are discussed in detail in the full report.

Once these error were corrected, the model checker showed that the Simulink/Stateflow model (the software LLR) complies with the Lustre specifications (the software HLR). This corresponds to Objective A-4.1 in Table 2.

The mode logic was also verified using MATLAB Design Verifier. Properties can be specified either textually as MATLAB function blocks or graphically as Simulink/Stateflow models. For example, the requirement that at least one vertical mode is active is specified textually as a MATLAB function block.

```
function At_Least_One_Vertical_Mode_Active(PITCH_Active, VS_Active,
    FLC_Active, ALT_Active, ALTSEL_Active, VAPPR_Active, VGA_Active)
    % At least one vertical mode shall be active.
    P = ( PITCH_Active    || FLC_Active    || ALT_Active    ||
        ALTSEL_Active || VAPPR_Active || VGA_Active);
sldv.prove(P);
```

The command *sldv.prove(P)* instructs Design Verifier to attempt to prove that P is true for all combinations of inputs and outputs.

Model checkers do not (in general) produce independently checkable output. This means that a model checker must be qualified if its outputs are to be used for certification credit. In addition to the development artifacts that must be provided, tool qualification requires that Tool Operational Requirements (TOR) be defined. The TORs describe what the tool claims to do relative to the certification objectives. Then a comprehensive test suite must be developed to show that those requirements are satisfied over an appropriate range of tool inputs. For a model checker, this would mean producing a collection of models and properties that span the full range of constructs found in the model and property specification language(s) of the tool. These example models would need to contain property errors which the model checker would have to be shown to identify correctly. We are not aware of any existing efforts to qualify an academic open source model checker like Kind. For commercial tools like Simulink Design Verifier, some support from the tool vendor may be needed to achieve qualification.

**Table 3.** Summary of Objectives Satisfied by Abstract Interpretation

| Objective | Description | A | B | C | D | Notes |
|-----------|-------------|---|---|---|---|-------|
| A-5.1 | Source Code complies with low level requirements. | | | | | Not addressed |
| A-5.2 | Source Code complies with software architecture. | | | | | Not addressed |
| A-5.3 | Source Code is verifiable. | □ | □ | | | This may be partially satisfied by demonstrating that the code conforms to input restrictions for the tool. |
| A-5.4 | Source Code conforms to standards | □ | □ | □ | | This may be partially or fully satisfied by different analysis tools, depending upon the coding standards and tool qualification |
| A-5.5 | Source Code is traceable to low-level requirements. | | | | | Not addressed |
| A-5.6 | Source Code is accurate and consistent. | □ | □ | □ | | The absence of some classes of run-time errors is established through analysis with abstract interpretation tools. |
| A-5.7 | Output of software integration process is complete and correct. | | | | | Not addressed |
| A-5.8 | Parametric Data Item File is correct and complete. | | | | | Not addressed |
| A-5.9 | Verification of Parametric Data Item File is achieved. | | | | | Not addressed |
| FM.A-5.10 | Formal analysis cases and procedures are correct. | ■ | ■ | ■ | | Established by review |
| FM.A-5.11 | Formal analysis results are correct and discrepancies explained. | ■ | ■ | ■ | | Established by review |
| FM.A-5.12 | Requirements formalization is correct. | ■ | ■ | ■ | | Established by review |
| FM.A-5.13 | Formal method is correctly defined, justified, and appropriate. | ■ | ■ | ■ | ■ | Established by review |

■ *Full credit claimed*     □ *Partial credit claimed*          ▨ *Satisfaction of objective is at applicant's discretion*

## 5      Abstract Interpretation Case Study

This case study illustrates the use of two commercial static analysis tools (AbsInt's Astrée and MathWorks' Polyspace) to perform verification activities associated with the outputs of the software coding process, focusing on the objectives of Table A-5 in DO-178C and Table FM.A-5 in DO-333. The purpose of these verification activities is to detect any errors that may have been introduced during the software coding process (DO-178C Section 5.3). The DO-178C and DO-333 objectives satisfied through abstract interpretation are summarized in Table 3.

The Heading Control Law (Fig. 6) is one of the flight modes in the FGS that is selected by the mode logic. It computes aileron, elevator, rudder, and throttle commands based on sensor inputs and commanded aircraft heading, altitude, and speed. For this case study, we are using a publicly available model provided by researchers at the University of Minnesota (UMN) [1]. The complete flight software implemented by UMN consists of a sensor data acquisition module, a navigation module, a guidance law, a main control law, and a number of other modules associated with sensor faults and system identification. The heading control law that we are using is one mode available in the main control law. It is comparable in many ways to flight control laws that would be found in commercial aircraft. The other functions of the UMN flight test platform would be carried out by other parts of our FGS example system.

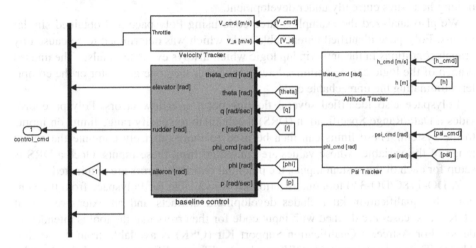

**Fig. 6.** Heading Control Law Model

In this case study, we have used abstract interpretation to verify the outputs of the software coding and integration process. In the example, this corresponds to verification that the source code implementing the Heading Control Law is correct. Current abstract interpretation tools are best suited to detecting run-time errors in the code rather than satisfaction of behavioral requirements. Verification was performed on C source code generated from the Simulink control law model. Our primary objective was to check the code for accuracy and consistency (DO-333 Section 6.3.4.f and Objective A-5.6 in Table 3). We can also check for unreachable code. We assume that the code will be tested against high and low level requirements–based test cases as part of a traditional test-based verification process.

Astrée can be used to prove that no floating-point overflow errors can occur during the execution of the control code, but this is only possible if the user does some fine-tuning in order to eliminate false alarms. This fine-tuning is done by indicating to Astrée that at certain points in the program, different cases need to be distinguished, which is called *partitioning* in the terminology of Astrée. In order to find the places in the code where partitioning needs to be done, and to determine the conditions which distinguish the different cases in the partitioning, the user needs to have some understanding of the implemented system.

Astrée initially reported four potential issues in the source code, corresponding to C statements which might cause floating-point overflow errors. The code of the control law implements four integrators, which are protected from overflow by *anti-windup* mechanisms. However, the abstraction made by Astrée keeps the tool from detecting the effectiveness of the overflow prevention. To enable Astrée to prove that these mechanisms are effective, the analysis needs to be guided by some partitioning information provided by the user.

Astrée is, in general, not able to provide direct user feedback to show where the case partitions must be done. However, an experienced user can find the necessary fine-tuning relatively easily. Also, there is some hope that future versions of Astrée will be able to treat this kind of program completely automatically using new partitioning heuristics currently under development.

We also analyzed the example source code using Polyspace and obtained similar results. Polyspace identified unreachable code which was determined to be caused by branch conditions in the anti-windup logic which always evaluate to false. The unused branch of the logic can be optimized away by either the code generator or the compiler, eliminating the unreachable code.

Polyspace also identified several floating-point overflow errors. Polyspace provides a Data Range Specification (DRS) mechanism to specify range limits on inputs to the system. These limits can then be used to more precisely compute the actual range of the variables whose values are computed from these inputs. Once a DRS is setup for each of the system inputs, the potential overflow errors are eliminated.

A DO-178C/DO-330 tool qualification kit is available for Polyspace from the vendor. The qualification kit includes development artifacts and an extensive list of TORs. Test cases are defined with input code for the errors that the tool is intended to detect. For Astrée, a Qualification Support Kit (QSK) is available from its vendor, AbsInt. The currently available QSK can be used for qualification up to level A under DO-178B.

## 6   Conclusion

We have provided an overview of three case studies illustrating the use of different formal methods tools to satisfy the certification objectives defined in DO-178C and its accompanying formal methods supplement, DO-333. These case studies provide a practical demonstration of theorem proving, model checking, and abstract interpretation applied to a Flight Guidance System design that is representative of systems deployed in commercial aircraft. The case studies show how the evidence produced by these three techniques might be used in an actual certification effort. Each technique has strengths and weaknesses and each could be applied to different life cycle data items and different objectives from those described here.

Formal methods and tools have already been used to a limited extent in several actual aircraft certification efforts. However, due to the proprietary nature of the models, code, and other artifacts, it has not been possible to make these results public. We hope that by providing a collection of publicly available examples, our case studies will be useful to industry and government personnel in understanding both the new certification guidance in DO-333 and the benefits that can be realized through the use of formal methods.

The complete version of the case studies along with all the associated models, code, and verification artifacts will be available as a NASA contractor report.

**Acknowledgements.** This work was sponsored by NASA under contract NNL12AB85T, under subcontract from The Boeing Company. The authors thank Hugh Taylor at Boeing, and Konrad Slind, Jennifer Davis, Siddhartha Bhattacharrya, and Michael Dierkes at Rockwell Collins for their contributions to the case studies.

# References

[1] Dorobantu, A., Johnson, W., Lie, F.A.P., Murch, A., Paw, Y.C., Gebre-Egziabher, D., Balas, G.J.: An Airborne Experimental Test Platform: From Theory to Flight. In: Proceedings of the 2013 American Control Conference, Washington DC (June 2013)

[2] Federal Aviation Administration, Joint Advisory Circular: Flight Guidance System Appraisal, AC/ACJ 25.1329 (2001)

[3] Hagen, G., Tinelli, C.: Scaling up the formal verification of Lustre programs with SMT-based techniques. In: Proceedings of the 8th International Conference on Formal Methods in Computer-Aided Design (FMCAD 2008), Portland, Oregon. IEEE (2008)

[4] Halbwachs, N., Caspi, P., Raymond, P., Pilaud, D.: The Synchronous Dataflow Programming Language LUSTRE. In: Proceedings of the IEEE (1991)

[5] Hurd, J.: Composable packages for higher order logic theories. In: Aderhold, M., Autexier, S., Mantel, H. (eds.) Proceedings of the 6th International Verification Workshop, VERIFY 2010 (July 2010), http://gilith.com/research/papers

[6] Miller, S.P., Whalen, M.W., Cofer, D.D.: Software Model Checking Takes Off. Communications of the ACM 33(2) (February 2010)

[7] Norrish, M., Slind, K.: HOL-4 Manual (1998-2013), http://hol.sourceforge.net/.

[8] Obua, S., Skalberg, S.: Importing HOL into isabelle/HOL. In: Furbach, U., Shankar, N. (eds.) IJCAR 2006. LNCS (LNAI), vol. 4130, pp. 298–302. Springer, Heidelberg (2006)

[9] Owre, S., Shankar, N.: The Formal Semantics of PVS, NASA Technical Report CS-1999-209321 (May 1999)

[10] RTCA DO-178C, Software Considerations in Airborne Software (December 2011)

[11] RTCA DO-330, Software Tool Qualification Considerations (December 2011)

[12] RTCA DO-333, Formal Methods Supplement to DO-178C and DO-278A (December 2011)

# A Compositional Monitoring Framework for Hard Real-Time Systems

André de Matos Pedro[1], David Pereira[1],
Luís Miguel Pinho[1], and Jorge Sousa Pinto[2]

[1] CISTER/INESC TEC, ISEP, Polytechnic Institute of Porto, Portugal
{anmap,dmrpe,lmp}@isep.ipp.pt
[2] HASLab/INESC TEC & Universidade do Minho, Portugal
jsp@di.uminho.pt

**Abstract.** Runtime Monitoring of hard real-time embedded systems is a promising technique for ensuring that a running system respects timing constraints, possibly combined with faults originated by the software and/or hardware. This is particularly important when we have real-time embedded systems made of several components that must combine different levels of criticality, and different levels of correctness requirements. This paper introduces a compositional monitoring framework coupled with guarantees that include time isolation and the response time of a monitor for a predicted violation. The kind of monitors that we propose are automatically generated by synthesizing logic formulas of a timed temporal logic, and their correctness is ensured by construction.

## 1 Introduction

*Real-time systems* (RTSs) range from simple, isolated components to large, highly complex and inherently concurrent systems. They act upon a variety of environments which are frequently very dynamic and hard to capture during design time. Therefore, developing an RTS can easily become a very difficult task to complete. However, even in the presence of potentially complex requirements, the design and development processes for RTSs limit themselves to model-driven techniques and intensive testing and fault-injection, which are known to allow the existence of human introduced errors. At later stages of the development cycle such errors can become highly expensive and very hard to tackle, even with the number of static analysis tools available. A notable example is in the area of scheduling analysis, where schedules for task sets are obtained by a rigorously defined scheduling algorithm. In hard RTSs the scheduling guarantees for task sets are obtained prior to the execution of the system. It is also often the case that schedulability analysis has to be performed in a compositional framework, such as the one presented in [9,22], in order to determine a valid schedule for the system (*e.g.*, when the system is made of a set components, each of which with its own set of tasks and local scheduling policy).

On the more rigorous side of RTS development, formal methods have been introduced progressively in the development cycle, most of which are based on

J.M. Badger and K.Y. Rozier (Eds.): NFM 2014, LNCS 8430, pp. 16–30, 2014.

temporal logic. While standard temporal logics yield a natural and abstract framework for the analysis of safety and liveness properties [21], these logics fail to capture the specific timing properties of RTSs [13]. This limitation is tackled by a set of timed temporal logics [1], and many of these logics have already been used to develop model checking tools [5]. However, model checking has its own pitfalls, namely when the size of the state space of the model that captures the RTS under consideration is too large to be mechanically analyzed by a tool implementing a model checking algorithm. Moreover, it might be the case that the properties to be checked cannot be captured rigorously at the abstract level of the model of the system.

In order to address the cases where static analyses of an RTS fail, researchers have introduced the concept of *runtime verification* (RV). RV is a major complement to static methods because it can be used to check errors for which it is possible to conclude some property of interest based exclusively in knowledge that can be gathered only at execution time. Contrary to *ad hoc* instrumentation of runtime behavior, RV based approaches use formal specifications and synthesize them into *monitors*, that is, pieces of code that take partial traces of execution of the system and match them against the referred specifications and make a verdict. Moreover, monitors can be used both to verify and enforce the properties which are provided by components, even when the components assume the form of a black-box, as long as each component is coupled with a formal specification. A simple example of the power of RV is the case when the response to a property violation detection consists in shutting down a complex component and give control to a simpler, yet formally verified component. RV has been progressively adopted by the industry of real-time operating systems as described in [6].

In this paper we introduce a *compositional monitoring framework* (CMF) that allows us to make assumptions about the time isolation between components as well as the response times of the monitors. We apply this notion to components with different criticality assurances, and whose specific requirements shall be ensured statically and dynamically through schedulability analysis and runtime monitoring, respectively. To guarantee these frameworks' assumptions we use a fragment of the *metric temporal logic with durations* (MTL-$\int$) [14] to analyze the schedulability of the CMF, and to statically check the maximum response times of each of the generated monitors. To the best of our knowledge, this is the first approach that combines MTL-$\int$ with the generation of *monitors* with explicit durations, for RV of hard RTSs. The timing enforcers of the CMF are synthesized from MTL-$\int$ formulas.

The paper is organized as follows: in Section 2 we describe work that is related to the subject of this paper; in Section 3, we describe the model and architecture of the CMF; in Section 4 we introduce a version of MTL-$\int$, with a restricted syntax and augmented axiomatic system to handle the properties of our CMF; in Section 5 we describe the process that synthesizes MTL-$\int$ formulae into monitors; in Section 6 a set of guarantees provided by the CMF is introduced, including the response time bound guarantee of each monitor; in Section 7 it is exemplified how to use monitors and a practical applicability of the proposed schedulability analysis is given; finally, Section 8 draws some conclusions and directions for further work.

## 2    Related Work

RV is being progressively introduced in RTS development in those corner cases for which static approaches are not strong enough. In the following we review theories and tools that are related to the ideas we are proposing in this paper, namely, monitor synthesis approaches based on timed temporal logics and their tools, as well as alternative techniques for schedulability analysis.

### 2.1    Monitor Based Approaches

Auguston and Takhtenbrot [3] describe a model-driven approach which dynamically enforces properties specified from statechart-based models via runtime monitoring. Monitors are automatically generated from formulas that specify the system's behavior, in a proposed assertion language, and their expressiveness always depends on the assertion language. Bauer *et al.* [4] propose an algorithm to efficiently generate monitors from TLTL formulae. Such monitors are able to specify real-time constraints from which verdicts can be made at any point of the execution. The three-valued notion of *timed linear-time temporal logic* (TLTL)$_3$ is specially suitable for runtime monitoring since a complete set of traces is not available at runtime, and the monitors' specifications are increasingly evaluated. Nickovic *et al.* [16] describe a translation of MTL into deterministic timed automata. The full MTL language is considered, and no bounds are imposed in the future temporal connectives. The process first converts *metric temporal logic* (MTL) into non-deterministic timed automata, and then determinizes them. Another close research effort is the *runtime enforcement* of timed properties. In Pinisetty *et al.* [20], monitors are introduced to enforce properties with explicit time. This approach is useful to delay events (or messages) that arrive before the allowed time (e.g., when a buffer becomes full due to a premature arrival of an event).

Tool support for the monitorization of RTSs is scarce. Temporal Rover [8] is appropriate for monitoring of hard real-time systems due to the temporal constraints being specified by the MTL. However, the monitoring software is proprietary and many specifications are hidden from common users. Alves *et al.* [2] present the results of a formal computer-aided validation and verification of critical time-constrained requirements of the Brazilian Satellite Launcher flight software based on Temporal Rover. Pike *et al.* [17] introduce the Copilot tool which is able to monitor hard real-time systems. The tool is a compiler that supports a pre-defined streaming language in which properties shall be specified. The tool also generates a scheduler that guarantees the timing constraints of the system, and outcomes a constant-execution time and constant-space C program. However, no time specifications are allowed by the tool since they are statically ensured by a scheduler that is automatically generated. The correctness of the timed properties depends of this step. New features have later been added into the tool for distributed systems. A case study of a Byzantine fault-tolerant airspeed sensor system is described in [18]. More prominent experiments have been carried out recently as described by the report [19], where two case-studies using Copilot monitors are tested in a true avionic system. The authors also show the capability of their approach to cover such realistic settings.

## 2.2 Schedulability Analysis and Predictable Monitoring

Fersman et al. [11,12] introduces an interesting research effort that discards the classic schedulability analysis for uni-processor systems. The authors use *timed automata extended with real-time tasks* to specify the system behavior together with the scheduler behavior. Regarding these, the schedulability test remains a reachability analysis problem, which is normally solved by model checkers such as UPPAAL [5]. Recently, Fersman et al. [10] have showed that the schedulability for multi-processor systems is possible for non-preemptive and preemptive schedulers with constant execution time.

Work that addresses a predictable monitoring framework of temporal properties is proposed by Zhu et al. [24]. The authors take inspiration from classical schedulability analysis to find a response time bound for monitors using sporadic servers. However, no composability or duration of real time tasks were considered for runtime monitoring.

## 3 Proposed Framework

In this section we introduce our CMF, an abstract component-based framework that includes runtime monitors, thus supporting external observations at runtime. We begin by introducing the definitions of real-time task-sets and periodic resource models; event sequences; and lastly the framework.

We will assume *tasks sets* $\Gamma = \{\tau_1, \tau_2, ..., \tau_n\}$, such that $n \in \mathbb{N}^+$ is the number of tasks $\tau_i = (p_i, e_i)$ where $p_i$ and $e_i$ are, respectively, the period and the worst-case execution time of $\tau_i$. Each task $\tau_i \in \tau$ is periodic. A *periodic resource model* $\omega$ is a tuple $(\tau, \pi, \theta, rm)$, where $\tau \subseteq \Gamma$, $\pi$ is the *replenishment period*, $\theta$ is the *server budget*, and $rm$ is the *rate monotonic* (RM) scheduling algorithm. The set of periodic resource models is denoted by $\Omega$. The outputs of a resource model $\omega$ are *sequences of events*. Considering a pair $(\omega, \tau_i)$ with $\omega \in \Omega$ and $\tau_i \in \tau$, each event can be of one of the following types: a *release-event* erelease$(\omega, \tau_i)$; a *start-event* estart$(\omega, \tau_i)$; a *sleep-event* esleep$(\omega, \tau_i)$; a *resume-event* eresume$(\omega, \tau_i)$; or a *stop-event* estop$(\omega, \tau_i)$. In addition, we assume a parameterized event $\varepsilon(\omega_j, \tau_i, id)$ that denotes the critical events of a task, where $id$ is the event identifier, and erenewal$(\omega)$ denotes the budget release of a resource model. We denote sets of events by $\mathcal{E}$.

*Event sequences* are a formalism that allows us to describe the scheduler behavior, creating a generic event language that a system can produce. If a system produces unexpected event words, we shall consider it a faulty system. This abstraction also establishes an interface for temporal logic observations [14]. A sequence of events, also known as *execution trace*, is an infinite sequence

$$\rho = (e_1, t_1)(e_2, t_2) \cdots$$

of time-stamped events $(e_i, t_i)$ with $e_i \in \mathcal{E}$ and $t_i \in \mathbb{R}^+$. The sequence satisfies monotonicity and progresses, *i.e.*, $t_i \leq t_{i+1}$ for all $i \in \mathbb{N}^+$, and for all $t \in \mathbb{R}^+$ there is some $i > 0$ such that $t_i > t$, respectively.

### 3.1    CMF Model and Architecture

The CMF model is composed of a set of elements of one of the following types:

- (Component) A *simple component* $C = (\Gamma, \omega, \vartheta, \phi)$ is a component, where $\omega$ is a resource model, $\vartheta$ is a scheduler, and $\phi$ is a set of properties to be verified at runtime. The scheduler $\vartheta$ behaves accordingly to a scheduling policy, such as a fixed-priority scheduler. The variable $\phi$ is a set of properties defined in a *program logic* to monitor the behavior of the task set $\Gamma$.
- (Hypervisor) A supervisor component manages several components allowing us to coordinate component executions with lower interference among them. Let $H = (\Omega, \eta_p, \eta_m, \phi_h)$ denote a hypervisor, where $\Omega$ is a set of periodic resource models, $\eta_p$ is a set of notational processors (these is for future work) that may be assigned to the required components, $\eta_m$ is a set of notational memory blocks that each component is able to use, and $\phi_h$ is a set of properties that the hypervisor H shall employ.

The CMF architecture accommodates the previously defined components as depicted in Fig. 1. The monitor for each component is synthesized automatically by the set of monitor properties $\phi$ assigned to each component. $\phi$ is a logic formula corresponding to a specification, which can be seen as an assume/guarantee condition of a component. Our architecture manages the monitors by three levels of criticality, and joins similar monitors in similar resource models: $M^h$, $M^m$, and $M^l$, respectively. This management can be composed by n-levels. A monitor resource model is viewed as a resource model of a component. However, each component or hypervisor has a set of quasi omniscient monitors (resp. hypervisor monitor) that draws a verdict about the assumptions of the architecture that may be violated.

## 4    Metric Temporal Logic with Durations

In this section we introduce a fragment of the formal logic MTL-$\int$ [14], whose evaluation is carried out with respect to sequences of events produced by resource models. MTL-$\int$ enables the automatic generation of monitors and, at the same time, it allows us to statically ensure properties about our architecture (resp. the response time bound of monitors). Such monitors are able to observe and

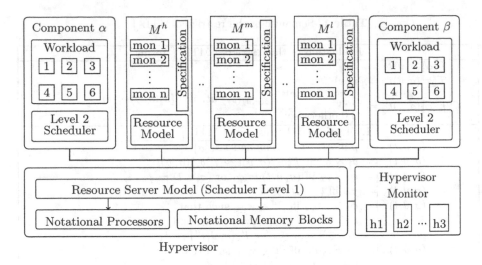

**Fig. 1.** Component-based Monitoring Architecture (CMA)

check timed constraints, as well as the *worst case execution time* (WCET) of the tasks of a given resource model. Nevertheless, computing the value of MTL-$\int$ formulae may not always be possible. In order to cope with this limitation, we consider a fragment of MTL-$\int$ that uses only the $\leq$, $<$, and $=$ relations over terms, and and we exclude occurrences of functions in terms. We also consider a strong form of the existential quantifier operator, which we denote by $\exists'$.

**Definition 1 (MTL-$\int$).** *Let $\mathcal{P}$ be a set of propositions and $\mathcal{V}$ a set of logical variables. Logical variables in $\mathcal{V}$ are mapped to $\mathbb{R}$. The syntax of MTL-$\int$ is defined inductively, as follows:*

$$\delta ::= \alpha \mid x \mid \textstyle\int^\delta \varphi$$

$$\varphi ::= p \mid \delta_1 \sim \delta_2 \mid \varphi_1 \lor \varphi_2 \mid \neg\varphi \mid \varphi_1\, U_{\sim\gamma}\, \varphi_2 \mid \varphi_1\, S_{\sim\gamma}\, \varphi_2 \mid \exists x\, \varphi \mid \exists' x\, \varphi$$

*where $\delta$ are terms, $\int^\delta \varphi$ is the duration of the subformula $\varphi$ in the interval $[0, \delta]$, $x$ is a continuous variable in $\mathcal{V}$, $p \in \mathcal{P}$ is an atomic proposition, $\gamma \in \mathbb{R}_{\geq 0}$, $\sim\, \in \{<, \leq, =\}$, and $\alpha \in \mathbb{R}$.*

We are now able to define the semantic of the MTL-$\int$. The semantic of MTL-$\int$ is separated in two parts: *terms* and *formulas*. The semantic of terms is defined using the notation $\mathcal{T}[\![\tau]\!](\sigma, \vartheta)t$ in Table 1. All terms represent numerical values in $\mathbb{R}_0^+$. The term $\int^\delta \varphi$ is the integral over the Boolean function $B_{\phi(\sigma, \vartheta)}(t)$ (whose return value is 1 if $(\sigma, \vartheta, t) \models \phi$, and 0 otherwise). Since $B_{\phi(\sigma, \vartheta)}(t)$ behaves as a step function, it is always Riemann integrable. The same is not true in the full MTL-$\int$ logic. The semantic of the MTL-$\int$ formula is defined inductively in Table 1, where the satisfability of a formula $\phi$ in a model $(\sigma, \vartheta)$ at time $t$ is defined by $(\sigma, \vartheta, t) \models \phi$. $\sigma$ and $\vartheta$ are an observation function and a logic environment

**Table 1.** Semantic of the restricted MTL-$\int$

| Evaluation of the restricted MTL-$\int$ terms |
|---|
| $\mathcal{T}[\![\alpha]\!](\sigma,\vartheta)t \;=\; \alpha$ |
| $\mathcal{T}[\![x]\!](\sigma,\vartheta)t \;=\; \vartheta(x)$ |
| $\mathcal{T}[\![\int^{\delta}\phi]\!](\sigma,\vartheta)t \;=\; \begin{cases} \int_{t}^{t+\mathcal{T}[\![\delta]\!](\sigma,\vartheta)t} B_{\phi(\sigma,\vartheta)}(t_*)\,dt_* & \text{if } \mathcal{T}[\![\delta]\!](\sigma,\vartheta)t \geq 0 \\ 0 & \text{otherwise} \end{cases}$ |
| **Evaluation of the restricted MTL-$\int$ formulas** |
| $(\sigma,\vartheta,t) \models p$ iff $\sigma(p)(t) = true$ and $t < |\sigma|$ |
| $(\sigma,\vartheta,t) \models \delta_1 \sim \delta_2$ iff $\mathcal{T}[\![\delta_1]\!](\sigma,\vartheta)t \sim \mathcal{T}[\![\delta_2]\!](\sigma,\vartheta)t$ |
| $(\sigma,\vartheta,t) \models \phi_1 \vee \phi_2$ iff $(\sigma,\vartheta,t) \models \phi_1$ or $(\sigma,\vartheta,t) \models \phi_2$ |
| $(\sigma,\vartheta,t) \models \neg\phi$ iff $(\sigma,\vartheta,t) \not\models \phi$ |
| $(\sigma,\vartheta,t) \models \phi_1 \, U_{\sim\gamma} \, \phi_2$ iff $\exists t' \in \mathbb{R}_{\geq 0}$ such that $t \leq t' \sim t + \gamma \wedge (\sigma,\vartheta,t') \models \phi_2$, and $\forall t'' \in \mathbb{R}_{\geq 0},\, t \leq t'' < t',\, (\sigma,\vartheta,t'') \models \phi_1$ |
| $(\sigma,\vartheta,t) \models \phi_1 \, S_{\sim\gamma} \, \phi_2$ iff $\exists t' \in \mathbb{R}_{\geq 0}$ such that $t - \gamma \sim t' \leq t \wedge (\sigma,\vartheta,t') \models \phi_2$, and $\forall t'' \in \mathbb{R}_{\geq 0},\, t' < t'' \leq t,\, (\sigma,\vartheta,t'') \models \phi_1$ |
| $(\sigma,\vartheta,t) \models \exists x\,\varphi$ iff there exists a value $v \in \mathbb{R}$ such that $(\sigma,\vartheta_x^v,t) \models \phi$ |
| $(\sigma,\vartheta,t) \models \exists' x\,\varphi$ iff there exists a value $v \in \nu$ such that $(\sigma,\vartheta_x^v,t) \models \phi$ |

**Table 2.** Syntactic abbreviations for our MTL-$\int$ fragment

| Operator | Abbreviation | Equivalent Formula |
|---|---|---|
| Eventually | $\Diamond_{\sim\gamma}\phi$ | $true\; U_{\sim\gamma}\,\phi$ |
| Always | $\square_{\sim\gamma}\phi$ | $\neg(\Diamond_{\sim\gamma}\neg\phi)$ |
| Next | $\bigcirc_{\phi_1}\phi_2$ | $\phi_1\, U_{\sim\infty}\,\phi_2$ |
| Implies Next | $\phi_1 \overset{\bigcirc}{\Longrightarrow} \phi_2$ | $\neg\phi_1 \vee \bigcirc_{\phi_1}\phi_2$ |

defined as usual [14]. The set $\nu$ contains the time stamps for the differential between the observed truth values given by the $\sigma$ function (allowing us to formulate some axioms to turn our logic evaluation in a computable function). We will use the abbreviations *eventually* ($\Diamond$) and *always* ($\square$) as usual.

In the remaining of the paper we will frequently refer to the abbreviations presented in Table 2 in order to ease the presentation of properties that describes the monitor behavior. For illustrative purposes, we now introduce a practical example of the expressive power of MTL-$\int$'s language.

*Example 1.* To ensure that a monitor task responds in a bounded response time, the formula $\psi_1 \implies \Diamond_{\leq\gamma}\psi_2$ is sufficient. The proposition $\psi_1$ describes a set of events that may violate the system, the proposition $\psi_2$ describes the task invocation, and $\gamma$ is the maximum expected response time bound. Informally, the formula means that if a fault event occurs, then the task executes within $\gamma$ time units.

## 4.1  MTL-$\int$ Axiomatization

Having restricted the original MTL-$\int$ described in [14], we are able to fix new axioms for durations. Most interesting is that such axioms will allow us to turn our MTL-$\int$ fragment computable. As the meaning of the duration term $\int^r \phi$ is defined as an integral, and the relation $\leq$ as a term operator, we have axioms that capture properties of integrals over the $\leq$ operator. They are, as follows:

A1. $\exists x\ \alpha \leq \int^\alpha \phi \equiv \alpha \leq \int^\alpha \phi$;

A1$'$. $\exists x\ \int^\alpha \phi \leq \alpha \equiv \int^\alpha \phi \leq \alpha$;

A2. $\exists x\ x \leq \int^\alpha \phi \equiv \min(x) \leq \int^\alpha \phi$;

A2$'$. $\exists x\ \int^\alpha \phi \leq x \equiv \int^\alpha \phi \leq \max(x)$;

A3. $\exists x\ \alpha \leq \int^x \phi \equiv \alpha \leq \int^{\max x} \phi$;

A3$'$. $\exists x\ \int^x \phi \leq \alpha \equiv \int^{\min x} \phi \leq \alpha$;

A4. $\exists x\ \alpha \leq \int^{\int^{\int^x \phi_n} \phi_1} \phi \equiv \alpha \leq \int^{\int^{\int^{\max x} \phi_n} \phi_1} \phi$;

A4$'$. $\exists x\ \int^{\int^{\int^x \phi_n} \phi_1} \phi \leq \alpha \equiv \int^{\int^{\int^{\min x} \phi_n} \phi_1} \phi \leq \alpha$;

A5. $\exists x\ \exists y\ \int^x \phi_1 \leq \int^y \phi_2 \equiv \int^{\min(x)} \phi_1 \leq \int^{\max(y)} \phi_2$;

A6. $\exists x\ \int^x \phi_1 \leq \int^x \phi_2 \equiv \exists' p\ \int^p \phi_1 \leq \int^p \phi_2$.

Axioms A1 and A1$'$ remove the existential operator in the evaluation of a constant inequality over a constant interval. Axioms A2 and A2$'$ substitute the existential quantification with a minimum and maximum that a variable $x$ can take according to the constraints applied to $x$. If $x$ is unbounded the minimum is zero, and the maximum is infinity. Axioms A3 and A3$'$ reduce the existential operator over a duration into a minimum and maximum inequality. Axioms A4 and A4$'$ deal with nested durations. For the remaining axioms we have variables and duration primitives of MTL-$\int$ in both sides of the operator $\leq$. Once we have an infinite observation over a path composed by finite pieces we have a procedure to compute the truth value of this type of formula. Axiom A5 establishes that the order relation between two durations specified by different variables is the same as if their minimum and maximum allowed values are considered. This can be seen as a desynchronization of durations axiom. Axiom A6 means that the existential quantification of duration terms over the $\leq$ operator can be reduced by substituting the existential quantification in points along the path where observation of MTL-$\int$ formulas is made. This can be seen as a synchronization of durations axiom.

*Example 2.* Consider an application of Axiom A6 with the two MTL- formulas $\phi_1 = \int^{|\rho|}(\epsilon_\beta \wedge \epsilon_\alpha) \leq 10$ and $\phi_2 = \int^{|\rho|}(\epsilon_\beta) \leq 10$. To easily understand their use we will show two figures. Figure 2a depicts the sequence of events $\rho$, their respective activation times as well as the evaluation of three formulas $\epsilon_\beta\ U\ \epsilon_\alpha$, $\phi_1$, and $\phi_2$ over the duration of the sequence $\rho$. Figure 2b depict an evaluation of the formula $\exists x\ \int^x(\epsilon_\beta) \leq \int^x(\epsilon_\beta \wedge \epsilon_\alpha)$, where the undefined values are shown in gray. Note that the duration of any MTL-$\int$ formula cannot be greater than the duration of a *true* formula as depicted by the figure. In practice, we shall conclude that the points to compare are the time stamps of events of each path $\rho$ since these points form a set of monotonic increasing piecewise linear segments.

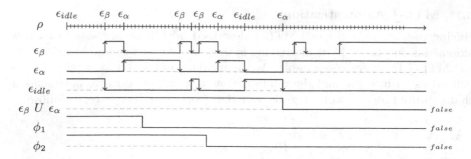

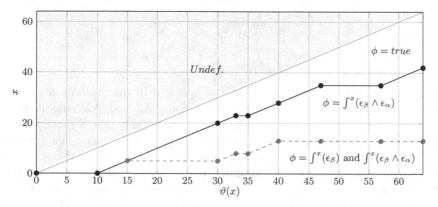

(a) A diagram containing: a path $\rho$; three event releases $\epsilon_\beta$, $\epsilon_\alpha$, and $\epsilon_{idle}$; and the respective truth value of the logic formulas $\epsilon_\beta \; U \; \epsilon_\alpha$, $\phi_1$, and $\phi_2$.

(b) The graph depicts the formula $\int^x(\epsilon_\beta)$ and $\int^x(\epsilon_\beta \wedge \epsilon_\alpha)$ which allows us to visually check the formula $\forall x \; \int^x(\epsilon_\beta) \leq \int^x(\epsilon_\beta \wedge \epsilon_\alpha)$ in the finite interval $[0, 64)$.

**Fig. 2.** Diagram of a path (a) and respective duration computation (b)

## 5   Evaluation of MTL-$\int$ Formulas

In order to synthesize monitors for our CMF we have defined a fragment of MTL-$\int$ that is able to describe durations for RTS, an algorithm to evaluate logic and their WCET estimation, and the time complexity analysis of the algorithm. We have implemented the semantics of our MTL-$\int$ fragment and implemented it in OCaml language [23].

### 5.1   The Evaluation Algorithm

The semantics of MTL-$\int$ introduced in [14] may not be fully computable due to the real numbered existential and universal quantifications. In addition, the axioms established previously allow us to compute the non negative real number existential and universal quantifications, and to enable the WCET estimation.

However, the validity of the argument is also shown by the evaluation function of Algorithm 1 where the MTL-$\int$ semantics is codified exclusively using functions applied to lists. This algorithm evaluates MTL-$\int$ formulas and produces Boolean verdicts.

Some notations need to be introduced before the description of the algorithm, obs is a function that corresponds to an observation, env is a logical environment, and mt is a term function which evaluates terms such as $\alpha$, $x$, and $\int^\alpha \phi$. These functions are defined according to the semantics of [14]. Note that these terms are always computable, *i.e.*, terms are non negative real valued numbers.

The functions $\Phi_\int$, $\Phi_x$, and $\Phi$ are special functions that rewrite formulas by applying the axioms described previously to compute new values. Next, we present an example to clarify the role of these functions.

*Example 3.* Suppose that we have an existential quantification of $x$ over the formula $\alpha \leq \int^{\Phi(\sigma, \vartheta) tr_1} \phi$. This formula will be rewritten to $\alpha \leq \int^{\max(mt\,(\sigma, \vartheta)\,t\,r_1)} \phi$ which means that the maximum allowed value is enough to know if there exists an $x$ sufficiently large to validate the inequality condition. The other functions follow the same principle, but considering $x \leq \int$, $\int \leq x$, and $\int \leq \int$.

## 5.2   The Time Complexity of Our Evaluation Algorithm

In order to provide an analysis of the CMF, the WCET of monitors should be supplied. We address a pessimistic bound for our evaluation function EVAL based on time complexity, $T(m, n) = n \times m$, where $n$ is the length of the formula and $m$ the length of the trace to be consumed by the monitor. This means that in the worst case we have $n \times m$ comparisons between list elements, and the WCET can be computed by multiplying the constant cost that each list element takes. Note that our algorithm is based on functions applied to lists, *forall*, *exists*, and *fold_left*, and a more accurate estimation of the WCET defining a recursive cost function could easily be employed.

## 5.3   Runtime Monitoring as the Evaluation of an MTL-$\int$ Formula

After establishing a computable logic, a monitor may be seen as a procedure to evaluate a formula. Thus, we introduce the notion of monitor generated from an MTL-$\int$ formula.

**Definition 2.** *A monitor is a process that evaluates one specific bounded formula in the MTL-$\int$ fragment.*

Monitors belong to resources models (or components), and are represented by tasks (one formula produces one task). Our algorithm is adequate to estimate the WCET of a monitor even with a pessimistic bound, and also to be employed in practice (as will be seen later). Note that WCET parameters of monitors are required in order to make a prior schedulability analysis which ensures a certain responsiveness for the monitor components. Note also that this process is an alternative to the synthesis approaches using automata theory [16].

---

**in** : An execution trace $\rho$ of length $|\rho|$, and a logic formula $\phi$.
**out**: A Boolean evaluation of the logic formula $\phi$ over the trace $\rho$.

1    **let** EVAL $\rho$ t $\phi$ = **let** $\sigma$ = obs $\rho$ **in let** $\vartheta$ = **env in** MODELS $(\sigma, \vartheta, t)$ $\phi$

2

3    **let** MODELS $(\sigma, \vartheta, t)$ $\phi$ = **match** $\phi$ **with**

4      | p $\rightarrow$ $\sigma$.evaluate p t **and** $\sigma$.interval t

5      | $\neg$ $(\phi_1)$ $\rightarrow$ not (MODELS $(\sigma, \vartheta, t)$ $\phi_1$)

6      | $\vee$ $(\phi_1, \phi_2)$ $\rightarrow$ MODELS $(\sigma, \vartheta, t)$ $\phi_1$ **or** MODELS $(\sigma, \vartheta, t)$ $\phi_2$

7      | $U_{<\gamma}$ $(\phi_1, \phi_2)$ $\rightarrow$ **let** (b,t') = exists (**fun** a $\rightarrow$ MODELS $(\sigma, \vartheta, a)$ $\phi_2$) $(\sigma$.intrv t $(t + \gamma - \epsilon))$ **in** b **and** forall (**fun** $t''$ $\rightarrow$ MODELS $(\sigma, \vartheta, t'')$ $\phi_1$) $(\sigma$.intrv t $(t' - \epsilon))$

8      | $U_{=\gamma}(\phi_1, \phi_2)$ $\rightarrow$ MODELS $(\sigma, \vartheta, \gamma)$ $\phi_2$ **and** forall (**fun** $t''$ $\rightarrow$ MODELS $(\sigma, \vartheta, t'')$ $\phi_1$) $(\sigma$.intrv t $(t' - \epsilon))$

9      | $\exists$ $(var, \phi_1)$ $\rightarrow$ exists (**fun** n $\rightarrow$ **let** () = $\vartheta$.add $var$ n **in** MODELS $(\sigma, \vartheta, t)$ $\phi_1$) $(\sigma$.intrv t $(\vartheta$.bound var))

10    | $\sim$ $(\int^{r_1} \phi_1, \alpha)$ $\rightarrow$ MT $(\sigma, \vartheta)$ t $(\int^{\Phi(\sigma, \vartheta) \, t \, r_1} \phi_1)$ $\sim$ MT $(\sigma, \vartheta)$ t $\alpha$

11    | $\sim$ $(\alpha, \int^{r_1} \phi_1)$ $\rightarrow$ MT $(\sigma, \vartheta)$ t $\alpha$ $\sim$ MT $(\sigma, \vartheta)$ t $(\int^{\Phi(\sigma, \vartheta) \, t \, r_1} \phi_1)$

12    | $\sim$ $(\int^{r_1} \phi_1, x)$ $\rightarrow$ MT $(\sigma, \vartheta)$ t $(\int^{\Phi_x(\sigma, \vartheta) \, t \, r_1} \phi_1)$ $\sim$ MT $(\sigma, \vartheta)$ t $x$

13    | $\sim$ $(x, \int^{r_1} \phi_1)$ $\rightarrow$ MT $(\sigma, \vartheta)$ t $x$ $\sim$ MT $(\sigma, \vartheta)$ t $(\int^{\Phi_x(\sigma, \vartheta) \, t \, r_1} \phi_1)$

14    | $\sim$ $(\int^{r_1} \phi_1, \int^{r_2} \phi_2)$ $\rightarrow$ MT $(\sigma, \vartheta)$ t $(\int^{\Phi_{\int}(\sigma, \vartheta) \, t \, r_1} \phi_1)$ $\sim$ MT $(\sigma, \vartheta)$ t $(\int^{\Phi_{\int}(\sigma, \vartheta) \, t \, r_1} \phi_1)$

15

16 **let** MT $(\sigma, \vartheta)$ t $r$ = **match** $r$ **with**

17    | $\alpha \rightarrow \alpha$

18    | $x \rightarrow \vartheta(x)$

19    | $\int^r \phi \rightarrow$ **if** MT $(\sigma, \vartheta)$ t $r \geq 0$ **and** $(\sigma$.intrv t $(t + \text{MT}(\sigma, \vartheta) \, t \, r)) \geq 2$ **then** INT t $(t + \text{MT}(\sigma, \vartheta) \, t \, r)$ (ONE $\phi$ $(\sigma, \vartheta)$ $t_1$) **else** 0

20

21 **let** ONE $\phi$ $(\sigma, \vartheta)$ $t_1$ = **if** MODELS $(\sigma, \vartheta, t_1)$ $\phi$ **then** 1 **else** 0

22

23 **let** INT $t_b$ $t_e$ $f$ = **let** v,_ = fold_left (**fun** $(a, t_l), t \rightarrow (a + f(t) \cdot (t - t_l), t))$ (0, hd $\sigma$.intrv $t_b$ $t_e$) (tl $\sigma$.intrv $t_b$ $t_e$) **in** v

---

**Algorithm 1.** MTL-$\int$ Evaluation Algorithm, with $\sim \in \{<, \leq, =\}$

Our approach is particularly suited to handle the reorganization of monitors that belong to different resource models. Once the monitor synthesis process provides one task per logical formula, the performance is affected. This is due to the increasing number of tasks that may reduce substantially the systems' utilization (a known problem of the fixed-priorities schedulers). To relax this problem, a clustering of monitor tasks based on the execution time, deadline, and response time bound is a possible solution.

After generating series of monitors the clusters are classified within n-level components, *i.e.*, each cluster is assigned to one resource model independently of the system under monitoring. This guarantees non-interference of time between monitors and the system's schedulability.

# 6    Guaranteeing Real-Time Constraints Using MTL-∫ for CMF

Constraints for our CMF shall be statically ensured using our logic fragment as basis [7]. WCET violations of one or more tasks may interfere with other non monitoring tasks resulting in an undesirable environment. This can be tackled by using higher priority tasks for monitor processes or by assigning monitors to independent resource models. However, to guarantee non interference between resource models, we shall ensure the correct behavior of such models by specifying their allowed budgets and periods. Other formulas are required to establish a complete formalization as described in [7].

Assuming a correct release of events, namely the $\mathsf{erenewal}(\omega)$, the budget supply is specified by the formula $\phi(\omega)$ equivalent to

$$\Box_{\leq\infty} \left( \mathsf{erenewal}(\omega) \overset{\bigcirc}{\Longrightarrow} (\Diamond_{=\pi} \mathsf{erenewal}(\omega)) \wedge \int^{\pi} \bigvee_{\tau_i \in \tau} evs^+(\omega, \tau_i) \leq \theta \right),$$

where $\omega$ is one resource model; $\pi$ and $\theta$ their renewal period and budget, respectively; $\mathsf{erenewal}(\omega)$ is the budget renewal event, and $evs^+(\omega_j, \tau_i) \overset{def}{=} \mathsf{estart}(\omega_j, \tau_i) \vee \mathsf{eresume}(\omega_j, \tau_i) \vee \mathsf{erenewal}(\omega) \vee \mathsf{estop}(\omega_j, \tau_i) \vee \varepsilon(\omega_j, \tau_i, \cdot) \vee \mathsf{erelease}(\omega_j, \tau_i)$. This formula states that for each occurrence of the event $\mathsf{erenewal}(\omega)$ in the resource model $\omega$, the duration of the other events until $\pi$ time units does not overpasses the budget $\theta$ per period $\pi$. In this formula we assume the correct specification of the periodic event releases ($\mathsf{erenewal}(\omega, \tau_i)$), and the schedulability of the workload according to a fixed priority policy. Note that this assumption can be discarded using schedulability analysis based on task automata or following the instruction provided in [7].

In addition, the predictability of our framework with respect to event sequences can be established by identifying the relevant or critical events, and preserving the partial order of events arrival for monitor processes. We denote the critical events by the subset $\mathcal{E}_{cr}^{\phi} \subseteq \mathcal{E}$, and the prefix-tree which preserves the partial order of events for all possible executions by $pt$. Given these predictable traces $pt$ we are able to ensure the response time of the monitor $\mathsf{mon\_id}$ for each trace $\rho \in pt$ by the formula

$$\bigwedge_{e \in \mathcal{E}_{cr}^{\phi}} e \Longrightarrow \Diamond_{\leq \gamma} \mathsf{estop}(\omega, \tau_1), \tag{1}$$

where $\mathsf{estop}(\omega, \tau_1)$ is the triggered event that monitors generate at the end of their complete execution, and $\mathcal{E}_{cr}^{\phi}$ is a set of the events used by formula $\phi$.

*Example 4.* Assuming two resource models RS-A($\pi = 10$, $\theta = 8$) and RS-C($\pi = 5$, $\theta = 1$) described in Figure 3 containing three tasks (ts1 with period of 14 and WCET of 3; ts2 with period of 20 and WCET of 5; and ts3 with period of 27 and WCET of 7), and one task (ts1 with period of 33 and WCET of 4), respectively. We could see that to guarantee the maximum detection delay of the monitor task ts1 in RS-C, the trace depicted in the Figure 3 need to be generated. This trace assumes the critical instant theorem [15] (to find the worst execution trace) as

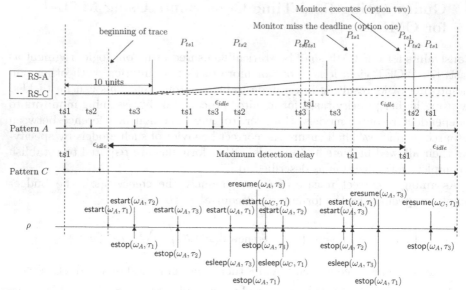

**Fig. 3.** Example of patterns and the global trace generated by the composition of resource models defined in the Example 4

well as the hyper-period of the resource model (to define the length of the trace). Replacing the event estop($\omega, \tau_1$) with estop($RS - C, ts1$) in Equation 1 we are able to obtain the maximum detection delay of our trace, which corresponds to value $\gamma$ equal to 34 time units. We also known that the deadline of 27 time units for monitor period is not enough for the established resource models settings, RS-A and RS-C, respectively. However, if we increase the period of the monitor task to a value greater than 39 time units we obtain a schedulable taskset.

## 7    Performance Evaluation of our MTL-∫ Approach

To estimate the performance of our evaluation algorithm we define some classical properties in MTL-∫ and monitor them using our evaluation algorithm, such as: $true$ $U_{\leq t}$ $\phi$ (eventually); $\phi \to \Box_{\leq t} \psi$ (bounded-invariance); $\phi \to \Diamond_{\leq t} \psi$ (bounded-response); $\Box_{\leq t} \int^t \phi \leq \beta$ (limited-duration); and $\phi \to \int^t \psi \leq \beta$ (bounded-duration). Results of the performance analysis are depicted in Table 3. The values are presented in milliseconds. Average values are computed over multiple runs provided by a stochastic model. The length of the input trace is denoted by $|\rho|$. The entry $t_{average}$ is the execution time that a set of monitors takes, on average, to the evaluation algorithm. The throughput shows how many events can be processed by the monitor as the trace increases, i.e., $\frac{|\rho|}{t_{monitor}}$.

The experiments were performed on an Intel Core i3-3110M at 2.40GHz CPU, and 8 GB RAM running on Fedora 18 X64. Note that all the monitors are time bounded in $t$, indicating that only one trace that has this duration should assign a truth value for the formula (a verdict). Our algorithm executes in polynomial time as the experiments also show.

**Table 3.** Performance analysis of enforcement monitors (milliseconds)

| Monitors | $|\rho|$ | | | | throughput |
|---|---|---|---|---|---|
| | 10 | 100 | 1000 | 10000 | |
| $true\ U_{\leq t}\ \phi$ | 0.051 | 1.717 | 171.376 | 26366.48 | 196.1, 0.379 |
| $\phi \to \Box_{\leq t}\ \psi$ | 0.065 | 1.834 | 172.683 | 26159.36 | 153.8, 0.382 |
| $\phi \to \Diamond_{\leq t}\ \psi$ | 0.055 | 1.765 | 174.594 | 26944.16 | 181.8, 0.371 |
| $\Box_{\leq t} \int^t \phi \leq \beta$ | 0.309 | 65.950 | 76682.652 | > 10min | indef |
| $\phi \to \int^t \psi \leq \beta$ | 0.011 | 0.195 | 14.033 | 1993.12 | 909.1, 5.01 |
| $t_{average}$ | 0.098 | 14.192 | 15443.068 | indef | no value |

# 8   Conclusion and Further Work

In this paper we have introduced a novel approach to runtime monitoring. Compared with currently available methods our approach extends runtime monitoring for component-based approaches; introduces the monitor synthesis for duration formulas; establishes guarantees such as time interference of monitors, predictability, and avoidance of catastrophic scenarios due to WCET violations for our compositional framework; and supplies a platform for design of hard real-time embedded system where knowledge provided at execution time is required. In terms of current and future research goals, we are presently working on formally establishing the correctness of the algorithm as well as several properties of our MTL-$\int$ fragment. Our preliminary empirical findings strongly suggest that our fragment is well suited in terms of expressiveness for schedulability analysis of uni-processor and multi-processor systems.

**Acknowledgments.** The authors would like to thank the anonymous reviewers for their detailed and helpful comments. This work was partially supported by National Funds through FCT (Portuguese Foundation for Science and Technology) and by ERDF (European Regional Development Fund) through COMPETE (Operational Programme 'Thematic Factors of Competitiveness'), within projects Ref. FCOMP-01-0124-FEDER-022701 (CISTER), FCOMP-01-0124-FEDER-015006 (VIPCORE) and FCOMP-01-0124-FEDER-020486 (AVIACC).

# References

1. Alur, R., Henzinger, T.A.: Logics and Models of Real Time: A Survey. In: Real-Time: Theory in Practice, REX Workshop, pp. 74–106 (1992)
2. Alves, M.C.B., Drusinsky, D., Michael, J.B., Shing, M.: Formal validation and verification of space flight software using statechart-assertions and runtime execution monitoring. In: SOSE 2011, pp. 155–160 (2011)
3. Auguston, M., Trakhtenbrot, M.: Synthesis of Monitors for Real-Time Analysis of Reactive Systems. In: Avron, A., Dershowitz, N., Rabinovich, A. (eds.) Pillars of Computer Science. LNCS, vol. 4800, pp. 72–86. Springer, Heidelberg (2008)
4. Bauer, A., Leucker, M., Schallhart, C.: Runtime Verification for LTL and TLTL. ACM Trans. Softw. Eng. Methodol. 20(4), 14:1–14:64 (2011)

5. Behrmann, G., David, A., Larsen, K.G., Hakansson, J., Petterson, P., Yi, W., Hendriks, M.: UPPAAL 4.0. In: QEST 2006, pp. 125–126 (2006)
6. Cotard, S., Faucou, S., Bechennec, J., Queudet, A., Trinquet, Y.: A Data Flow Monitoring Service Based on Runtime Verification for AUTOSAR. In: HPCC 2012, pp. 1508–1515 (2012)
7. Pedro, A.M., Pereira, D., Pinho, L.M., Pinto, J.S.: Logic-based Schedulability Analysis for Compositional Hard Real-Time Embedded Systems. In: Proceedings of the 6th International Workshop on Compositional Theory and Technology for Real-Time Embedded Systems, CRTS 2013 (2013)
8. Drusinsky, D.: The Temporal Rover and the ATG Rover. In: Havelund, K., Penix, J., Visser, W. (eds.) SPIN 2000. LNCS, vol. 1885, pp. 323–330. Springer, Heidelberg (2000)
9. Easwaran, A., Lee, I., Sokolsky, O., Vestal, S.: A Compositional Scheduling Framework for Digital Avionics Systems. In: RTCSA 2009, pp. 371–380 (2009)
10. Fersman, E., Krcal, P., Pettersson, P., Yi, W.: Task automata: Schedulability, decidability and undecidability. Inf. Comput. 205(8), 1149–1172 (2007)
11. Fersman, E., Mokrushin, L., Pettersson, P., Yi, W.: Schedulability analysis of fixed-priority systems using timed automata. Theor. Comput. Sci. 354(2), 301–317 (2006)
12. Fersman, E., Pettersson, P., Yi, W.: Timed Automata with Asynchronous Processes: Schedulability and Decidability. In: Katoen, J.-P., Stevens, P. (eds.) TACAS 2002. LNCS, vol. 2280, pp. 67–82. Springer, Heidelberg (2002)
13. Koymans, R.: Specifying real-time properties with metric temporal logic. Real-Time Systems 2(4), 255–299 (1990)
14. Lakhneche, Y., Hooman, J.: Metric temporal logic with durations. Theor. Comput. Sci. 138(1), 169–199 (1995)
15. Liu, C.L., Layland, J.W.: Scheduling algorithms for multiprogramming in a hard-real-time environment. J. ACM 20(1), 46–61 (1973)
16. Ničković, D., Piterman, N.: From MTL to deterministic timed automata. In: Chatterjee, K., Henzinger, T.A. (eds.) FORMATS 2010. LNCS, vol. 6246, pp. 152–167. Springer, Heidelberg (2010)
17. Pike, L., Goodloe, A., Morisset, R., Niller, S.: Copilot: A hard real-time runtime monitor. In: Barringer, H., Falcone, Y., Finkbeiner, B., Havelund, K., Lee, I., Pace, G., Roşu, G., Sokolsky, O., Tillmann, N. (eds.) RV 2010. LNCS, vol. 6418, pp. 345–359. Springer, Heidelberg (2010)
18. Pike, L., Niller, S., Wegmann, N.: Runtime verification for ultra-critical systems. In: Khurshid, S., Sen, K. (eds.) RV 2011. LNCS, vol. 7186, pp. 310–324. Springer, Heidelberg (2012)
19. Pike, L., Wegmann, N., Niller, S., Goodloe, A.: Copilot: Monitoring Embedded Systems. Innovations in Systems and Software Engineering, 1–21 (2013)
20. Pinisetty, S., Falcone, Y., Jéron, T., Marchand, H., Rollet, A., Nguena Timo, O.L.: Runtime enforcement of timed properties. In: Qadeer, S., Tasiran, S. (eds.) RV 2012. LNCS, vol. 7687, pp. 229–244. Springer, Heidelberg (2013)
21. Pnueli, A.: The temporal logic of programs. In: SFCS 1977, pp. 46–57 (1977)
22. Shin, I., Lee, I.: Compositional real-time scheduling framework with periodic model. ACM Trans. Embed. Comput. Syst. 7(30), 30:1–30:39 (2008)
23. The OCaml Development Team. Ocaml programming language (2013)
24. Zhu, H., Dwyer, M.B., Goddard, S.: Predictable Runtime Monitoring. In: ECRTS 2009, pp. 173–183 (2009)

# Leadership Election: An Industrial SoS Application of Compositional Deadlock Verification

Pedro R.G. Antonino[1,*], Marcel Medeiros Oliveira[2], Augusto C.A. Sampaio[1], Klaus E. Kristensen[3], and Jeremy W. Bryans[4]

[1] Centro de Informática, Universidade Federal de Pernambuco, Brazil
prga2@cin.ufpe.br
[2] Departamento de Informática e Matemática Aplicada,
Universidade Federal do Rio Grande do Norte, Brazil
[3] Bang & Olufsen, Denmark
[4] School of Computing Science, University of Newcastle upon Tyne, UK

**Abstract.** In distributed computing, the leadership election has been used to distributively designate a node as the central controller (leader) of a network of nodes. The complexity of the algorithm arises due to the unawareness of every node of who the current leader is. After running the algorithm, however, a unique node in the network must be elected as the leader and recognized as so by the remaining nodes. In this paper, using CSP, we formalise the leadership election algorithm used by our industrial partner. Its verification is feasible only due to the use of a pattern based strategy that allows the verification to be carried out in a fully local manner. The pattern used here is novel and a further contribution of the paper. A refinement relation together with predicate abstraction is used to describe pattern conformance. The mechanisation of the behavioural conformance is carried out using FDR.

**Keywords:** Leadership Election, Local Analysis, Deadlock Freedom.

## 1 Introduction

The complexity inherent to most distributed algorithms (and systems) can turn their development into a very laborious and error-prone task. The use of formal methods like CSP [12] considerably simplifies this task and provides a better understanding and means for verification of phenomena that are exclusive to the concurrent world, like deadlock and livelock. For CSP, the model checker FDR [6] provides an automatic check of finite state specifications for correctness and properties like deadlock and divergence freedom.

Component-based or Systems of Systems (SoS) development are only feasible in an industrial context of high-quality critical systems if trustworthy architectures are obtained by carefully designing and systematically verifying the constituents integration in a scalable fashion. A naive practice has been to verify and

---

* Corresponding Author.

J.M. Badger and K.Y. Rozier (Eds.): NFM 2014, LNCS 8430, pp. 31–45, 2014.
© Springer International Publishing Switzerland 2014

validate them after they have been built [8,9,4]. The major issue is the high cost to fix a problem that is found in a late stage of development. Instead of verifying the entire system, more promising approaches focus on iteratively identifying problems in compositions. However, in most approaches the cost of subsequent compositions is not alleviated by the results of the previous ones [1,3,5]. Every composition is taken as a monolithic system for verification, and properties of its constituting parts are not considered. Hence, these methods are not compositional and have scalability problems by not considering local analysis.

In [11,10], we proposed an approach to build trustworthy component-based systems underpinned by CSP [12]. In this approach, constituents may only be composed using composition rules that impose the necessary constraints for a safe interaction among components. Together, the composition rules systematise the approach preserving deadlock-freedom by construction. Although systematic, this approach is not local for cyclic communicating systems, potentially presenting a state explosion in the verification of such systems. This drawback can make our approach inapplicable to complex cyclic systems.

In this paper, we formalise and analyse the version of the leadership election algorithm used at B&O[1], which is an example of a class of cyclic networks. This algorithm is used in B&O's networks of Audio and Video (AV) systems with up to 32 systems. There are other solutions to this problem [7,15], whose details are discussed in the conclusions. They make different assumptions on the networks topology and faults. Like [15], we use CSP as our modelling language as it is a well-established notation with industrial strength tools for verification of communicating systems.

The use of standard approaches in the formal verification of our model presented scalability issues. This motivated the use of a local analysis strategy based on architectural patterns. However, none of the existing architectural patterns in the literature (including those in [15]) match directly the structure of our case study. As a further contribution, we formalise a new pattern that allows local deadlock analysis of our example. We use CSP to specify the pattern's behaviour and its stable failures refinement to formalise a conformance relation. We compare the application of our local analysis with a standard global analysis using FDR.

In Section 2, we introduce the CSP notation. Section 3 presents the underpinning model and theory used to analyse systems for deadlocks. In Section 4 we formalise a verification approach that allows local analysis of systems that obey a communication pattern suitable for our case study. The leadership algorithm, its practical use at B&O, and its formalisation in CSP is presented in Section 5. In Section 6, we apply the verification approach of Section 4 to our example. We also present an empirical analysis of the approach and contrast its verification effort against the standard approach based on a global analysis. Finally, in Section 7, we present our concluding remarks and future work.

---

[1] http://www.bang-olufsen.com/

## 2   CSP

CSP is a process algebra that can be used to describe systems as interacting components, which are independent self-contained processes with interfaces that are used to interact with the environment [12]. Most of the CSP tools, like FDR2 and ProBE, accept a machine-processable CSP, called $CSP_M$, used in this paper.

The two basic CSP processes are STOP and SKIP; the former deadlocks, and the latter does nothing and terminates. The prefixing a -> P is initially able to perform only the event a; afterwards it behaves like process P. A boolean guard may be associated with a process: g & P behaves like P if the predicate g is true; it deadlocks otherwise. The alternation if b then P else Q is available and has a standard behaviour. The operator P1;P2 combines P1 and P2 in sequence. The external choice P1[]P2 initially offers events of both processes; the occurrence of the first event or termination resolves the choice in favour of the process that performs either of them. The environment has no control over the internal choice P1|~|P2, in which the choice is resolved internally. The synchronised parallel composition P1[|cs|]P2 synchronises P1 and P2 on the events in the set cs; events that are not listed occur independently. Processes composed in interleaving P1|||P2 run independently. The event hiding P\cs encapsulates the events that are in cs. The renamed process P[[a<-b]] behaves like P except that all occurrences of a in P are replaced by b. The interrupt operator allows a process Q to take over from another process P: P /\ Q specifies that, while behaving as P, this process always offers the choice of P and Q, once Q is chosen, then it behaves as Q.

CSP also provides replicated versions for most of its compositional operators. For instance, ||| x : S @ P(x) stands for the interleaving of all P(x), for $x \in$ S. Local processes are defined using the let Id = P within Q construct, which behaves as Q and restricts the scope of process Id to Q.

There are three major semantic models for CSP: *traces*, *stable failures*, and the *failures-divergences* model. In this work we only use the *stable failures* one. In this model processes are described by their traces, a set of finite sequences of events it can perform given by $traces(P)$, and by its set of stable failures, given by the function $failures(P)$. The stable failures set contains all pairs $(s, X)$ where $s$ is a finite trace of $P$ and $X$ is a set of events that $P$ can refuse after performing $s$. All states in which $P$ may perform an internal action are considered unstable: they are not taken into account. Finally, the function $refusals(P, s)$ gives the set of events the process $P$ can refuse after the trace $s$. This model also possesses a refinement relation ([F=) on processes. The relation P [F= Q holds if and only if $traces(P) \supseteq traces(Q) \wedge failures(P) \supseteq failures(Q)$ holds.

## 3   Networks of Processes

The concepts presented in this section are essentially drawn from [13,14], which present an approach to deadlock analysis of systems described as a network of CSP processes. The most fundamental concept is the one of *atomic tuples*, which represents the most fundamental components of a system. These are triples that contain an identifier for the component, the process describing the behaviour of this component and an alphabet that represents the set of events that this component can perform. A *network* is a finite set of atomic tuples.

**Definition 1 (Network).** *Let $CSP\_Processes$ be the set of all possible CSP processes, $\Sigma$ the set of CSP events and $IdType$ the set for identifiers of atomic tuples. A network is a finite set $V$, such that:*

$$V \subset Atomics$$

*where: $Atomics \mathrel{\widehat{=}} IdType \times CSP\_Processes \times \mathbf{P}\,\Sigma$.*

The behaviour of a network is given as the alphabetised parallel composition of the behaviour of each component, where processes and alphabets are extracted from atomic tuples. We use an indexed version of the alphabetised parallel operator, which generalises the binary one with processes interacting in the alphabet intersection. The functions $A(id, V)$ and $B(id, V)$ extract the alphabet, and the behaviour of an atomic process $id$ from the network $V$, respectively.

**Definition 2 (Behaviour of a network).** *Let $V$ be a network.*
$B(V) =$ || id : dom V @ [A(id,V)] B(id,V)

By way of illustration, let $V = \{(id_1, B1, A1), (id_2, B2, A2), (id_3, B3, A3)\}$. The behaviour of this network is given by $B(V) =$ B1 [A1||A2] B2 [A2||A3] B3.

A *live* network is a structure that satisfies three assumptions. The first one is *busyness*. A busy network is a network whose atomic components are deadlock free. The second assumption is *atomic non-termination*, i.e. no atomic component can terminate. The last assumption concerns interactions. A network is *triple-disjoint* if at most two processes share an event, i.e. if for any three different atomic tuples their alphabet intersection is the empty set.

In a *live* network, a deadlock state can only arise from an improper interaction between processes, since no process can individually deadlock. This particular misinteraction is captured by the concept of *ungranted requests*. The states $\sigma$ of a network are pairs $(s, R)$, such that $s$ is a trace of the network and $R$ is a vector of refusal sets. The function $R(id)$ returns the refusal set of the process $id$ after $s \upharpoonright A(id)$. The projection $t \upharpoonright s$ takes a trace $t$ and a set of events $s$ as arguments and yields the trace $t$ restricted to $s$. An ungranted request arises in a state $\sigma$ when an atom, say $id_1$, is offering an event to communicate with another atom, say $id_2$, but $id_2$ cannot offer any of the events expected by $id_1$. In addition, both processes must not be able to perform internal actions.

A proper cycle of ungranted requests is an important element of deadlock analysis. It is represented as a sequence of different process identifiers, $C$, where each element at the position $i$, $C(i)$, has an ungranted request to the element at the position $i \oplus 1$, $C(i \oplus 1)$, where $\oplus$ is addition modulo length of the sequence. A *conflict* is a proper cycle of ungranted requests with length 2, and a *long cycle* is one with length greater than 2. After these definitions two fundamental theorems extracted from [13] are introduced.

**Theorem 1.** *Let V be a live network. Any deadlocked state has a cycle of un-granted requests. If V is conflict-free then a deadlock state has a long cycle.*

The next theorem requires the introduction of three important concepts. A *communication graph* is a representation of the topology of the network where vertexes represent atomic components of the network and edges represent the alphabet intersection between components. A *disconnecting edge* is an edge that, if removed, increases the number of connected components of the graph, i.e., an edge that is not part of a cycle in the communication graph. The components left after the removal of every disconnecting edge are called *essential components*.

**Theorem 2.** *Let V be a live network with essential components $V_1, \ldots, V_k$ where the pair of processes joined by each disconnecting edge are conflict-free. Then if each $V_i$ of the network is deadlock free, then so is V.*

Theorem 1 allows one to reduce the problem of avoiding deadlock by pre-venting cycles of ungranted requests. Theorem 2 allows the decomposition of a network in subnetworks called essential components that can be independently verified for deadlock freedom.

With these two results it is already possible to fully verify a tree topology network in a local way, by checking only pairs of processes, due to the fact that only proper cycles of length two can arise in tree networks. Nevertheless, cyclic networks cannot be locally verified by these methods. Moreover, if one tries to verify the freedom of long cycles of ungranted requests, based on Theorem 1, this might be as complex as exploring the whole state space. Therefore, for networks with cycles in their topology a complete and local method for checking deadlock freedom is not generally available.

## 4    Pattern Based Approach to Cyclic Network Verification

As a complementary approach to the decomposition strategy presented in the previous section, we consider the adoption of communication patterns in order to support local analysis of cyclic networks. Our approach is based on the design rules described in [12], which proposes resource sharing and client/server design rules, among others. As a novel contribution, we propose a pattern so as to prevent deadlocks by avoiding the emerging of cycles of ungranted requests. The pattern proposed in this section can be used to design and analyse networks that are asynchronous and dynamic (in the sense that nodes might turn on and off) and whose transport layer possesses a mechanism allowing to detect whether a node is on or off.

The pattern can be applied to networks with two different types of nodes: the participants and the transport layer. The participants of the network do not interact directly with each other, but exchange messages via the transport layer. The participants recursively send messages to all its peer participants and receives messages from them. Both sending and receiving must follow an order. Furthermore, participants can turn on and off at any time. The transport layer, composed of a set of transport entities, provides communication point-to-point between participants of the network. It has also the ability to identify whether participants are on or off.

The proposed pattern imposes behavioural and structural restrictions on a network as a means to guarantee deadlock freedom. Our approach uses CSP processes, which are parametrised, to capture pattern specifications and the stable failures refinement relation to capture a notion of pattern conformance. Structural restrictions are captured as predicates over the network structure and conformance through a predicate satisfaction relation.

A transport entity connects two participants: a sender and a receiver. It is entitled to receive data from its sender participant and to pass this data on to its receiver participant. This communication is unidirectional from the sender to the receiver. It also detects whether its sender is switched on or off.

**Definition 3 (Transport entity specification).** *Let id be an identifier of a transport entity, source(id) and target(id) the identifiers of the sender and receiver participants associated to the transport entity id, and offCh, sendCh, receiveCh, onCh, timeoutCh functions that, given the identifiers of source and target participants, yield the channels used for detecting that the sender is off, receiving data, sending data, detecting that the sender is on, and signalling a timeout, respectively. The transport entity CSP specification is:*

```
TransportSpec(id) =
let
    idS = source(id)
    idT = target(id)
    On = offCh(idS,idT) -> Off [] sendCh(idS,idT)?data -> OnF(data)
    OnF(d) = offCh(idS,idT) -> Off
        [] sendCh(idS,idT)?data -> OnF(data)
        [] receiveCh(idS,idT)!d -> On
    Off = onCh(idS,idT) -> On [] timeoutCh(idS,idT) -> Off
within Off
```

The processes On, OnF and Off specify the expected behaviour of a transport entity in a sender detected as on and no data available state, in a sender detected as off and data available state, and in a sender detected as off state, respectively. The transport entity initially behaves as Off, in which case it offers two events to its participants: a *timeout* that informs the receiver that the sender is switched off, and a *turn on* that detects when the sender turns on, in which case it behaves as the process On. In this state the transport entity is on and empty: it can receive data from the sender participant or detect a switching off event from it. In the case of the latter, the entity behaves as Off again. However, if it receives data, the transport entity stores this data and starts behaving as OnF. In the OnF state, the transport entity can receive new data from its sender participant, in which case the new data overwrites the data previously stored. However, it can also transmit the data stored to its receiver participant, in which case the transport entity behaves as On again. Finally, it can also detect whether its sender participant has turned off, in which case it behaves as the process Off.

The participants specify the domain related behaviour (business logic) of the network. They have a dynamic behavioural feature that allows them to turn on and off and a functional behaviour that involves data exchange and any business related function. The behavioural specification of a participant is given as follows.

**Definition 4 (Participant specification).** *Let id be the identifier of the participant and sequence(id) a function that yields a sequence of ids representing the order in which this participant interacts with its neighbours. The participant CSP specification is:*

```
ParticipantSpec(id) =
   let s = sequence(id)
       SendReceive(id,s) = Send(id,s);Receive(id,s);SendReceive(id,s)
   within OnDetect(id,s); (SendReceive(id,s) /\ (SKIP |~| STOP));
          OffDetect(id,s); ParticipantSpec(id,s)
```

A participant first behaves as the process `OnDetect`, which sends a signal to inform that it is on to each transport entity to which it acts as a sender. This mechanism abstracts the ability of the transport layer to detect participant status. The **s** parameter gives the order in which the participant interacts with its transport entities. After turning on, it acts recursively, first behaving as a sender (**Send**) and then as a receiver (**Receive**). When behaving as a sender, it sends messages to all transport entities that have this participant as sender, following the order recorded in **s**. When acting as a receiver, in the same way, it interacts with the transport entities that have it as a receiver, also following the order stated in **s**: it accepts both the incoming data and a timeout signal that indicates the sender associated with the transport entity is off. The process (`SKIP |~| STOP`) is used as a mechanism to abstract the fact that the sending and receiving behaviours might be interrupted due to a failure of a node. When `SKIP` is chosen, the participant might fail; conversely, when `STOP` is chosen, the participant cannot fail.

In order to check whether a concrete model of either a transport entity or a participant conforms to the corresponding abstract behaviour, we use a refinement relation in the stable failures model of CSP. We restrict the behaviour of the processes being tested for conformance to the events that are related interactions, as these are the only events of interest for deadlock analysis. This restriction is given by the **Abs** function. Hence, transport entity and participant conformance is given by the following definition.

**Definition 5 (Transport entity and Participant conformance).** *Let Spec stand for the specification of either a transport entity or of a participant (as in Definitions 3 and 4). Let id be the identifier of the candidate concrete model. Then id conforms to Spec if, and only if, the following refinement holds:*

```
Spec [F= Abs(id,V)
```

   *where:*

   - `Abs(id,V) = B(id,V) \ diff(A(id,V),AVoc(id,V))`, `diff` *standing for set difference.*
   - `AVoc(id,V) = Union({inter(A(id,V),A_(a)) | a <- V, ID_(a) != id})`
   - `a <- V` *states that* `a` *is an atomic tuple from* `V`
   - `A_(a)` *and* `ID_(a)` *give the alphabet and identifier of* `a`, *respectively.*

In addition to the behavioural restrictions, the pattern also imposes structural restrictions. The first one restricts the alphabet of any two participants or transport entities to be disjoint. This restriction is encoded in the *disjointAlpha* predicate. This ensures that two participants or two transport entities may interact directly. The *controlledAlpha* predicate is satisfied if the alphabet of the interaction between constituents is the set composed of the send, receive, on, off and timeout events. This ensures that the behaviour related to the interaction between constituents of the network is restricted to the controlled behaviour. The sequence of ids used to guide the order of interaction for the participant's behavioural restriction must have only one occurrence of each neighbour of this participant. This restriction is guaranteed by the *validOrder* predicate. Hence, the conformance of a network to this pattern is given by the following predicate, which is a conjunction of the restrictions presented.

**Definition 6 (Async Dynamic network).** *Let $V$ be a network, participants a set of participants and transport_entities a set of transport entities.*

$AsyncDynamic(V, participants, transport\_entities) \triangleq$

   $disjointAlpha(participants) \wedge disjointAlpha(transport\_entities) \wedge$

   $partition(V, participants, transport\_entities) \wedge$

   $\forall id : participants \bullet ParticipantBehaviouralRestriction(id) \wedge$

   $\forall id : transport\_entities \bullet TransportBehaviouralRestriction(id) \wedge$

   $\forall id : participants \bullet validOrder(id) \wedge$

   $\forall id_1 : participants, id_2 : transport\_entities \bullet controlledAlpha(id_1, id_2)$

*where:*

- $disjointAlpha(set) \triangleq \forall id_1, id_2 : set \bullet A(id_1) \cap A(id_2) = \emptyset$
- $partition(v, s_1, s_2) \triangleq s_1 \cap s_2 = \emptyset \wedge s_1 \cup s_2 = dom\, v$
- $ParticipantBehaviouralRestriction(id, V) \triangleq \texttt{ParticipantSpec(id,V)}$ [F= Abs(id,V)
- $TransportBehaviouralRestriction(id, V) \triangleq \texttt{TransportSpec(id,V)}$ [F= Abs(id,V)
- $validOrder(id) \triangleq$

     $neighbours(id) = ran\, sequence(id) \wedge functional(sequence(id))$
- $controlledAlpha(id_1, id_2) \triangleq$

     $A(id_1) \cap A(id_2) = \{|sendCh(source(id_2), target(id_2)),$

     $receiveCh(source(id_2), target(id_2)), onCh(source(id_2), target(id_2)),$

     $offCh(source(id_2), target(id_2)), timeoutCh(source(id_2), target(id_2))|\}$

The following theorem ensures the ability of our pattern to prevent deadlock. A proof sketch can be found in [2].

**Theorem 3.** *Let $V$ be a network, and participants and transport_entities two partitions of the domain of this network, then:*

   $AsyncDynamic(V, participants, transport\_entities) \Rightarrow V\ is\ deadlock\ free$

# 5    Industrial Case Study: The Leadership Election at B&O

A critical concept in B&O product networks is that of the *dynamic global system configuration*, which describes the current combined configuration of all the products in the network. For example, the currently active user experiences (such as current song, planned playlist, volume) are stored in the system configuration, enabling the B&O system to allow the experiences to be reproduced as the user moves around the home, thus giving the impression that the experiences follow the user.

The requirements for availability and consistency of the system configuration must be realised by the communications architecture, which is based on a publisher-subscriber pattern. To enable this communication pattern the underlying network must always be able to identify a leader (the publisher). Conceptually the architecture of a B&O product network contains two global states:

- The publisher-subscriber state: a single publisher (the leader) is present and the product network can guarantee availability and consistency of user experience. All other connected products are subscribers (followers), and newly joined products are undecided, until they learn the identity of the leader.
- The election state: no publisher is present and the user experiences are inconsistent or unavailable. In this state all connected products are undecided.

In the election state a leadership protocol is executed by the products in the network. During this state each product reacts to a set of local transition rules that will guarantee the desired emergent property. A B&O network is inherently asynchronous, and therefore the algorithm must tolerate the following cases:

- Products may join or leave the network at any point during or after an election. Products may enter a power-saving state, restart because of defects, or be turned on or off by their users. As a consequence, the algorithm must handle the disappearance of leaders and the appearance of new contenders for leadership.
- Communication is asynchronous, with some latency in the network. There is, therefore, no coordination of when an election is started, and so any product can initiate an election independently. The likelihood of simultaneously initiated elections is increased by network latency.

One of the risks that such a fluid environment increases is that the protocol might reach a deadlocked state. To mitigate this, we develop a formal model of the B&O leadership election protocol and show that it is deadlock-free. B&O invests in a formal analysis of this kind because of its desire to develop and analyse models in the early design stages, before expensive implementation commitments are made.

Our leadership election model is composed of distributed nodes that store internal data in a set of memory cells; this data storage is managed by a memory controller. A node communicates with another node through a bus cell, which provides a point-to-point unidirectional communication. To illustrate these connections, a 2-node configuration architecture is given in Figure 1(a).

The nodes are distinguished by their `id` parameter, which is drawn from the set {0..N}. The processes prefixed with `BroadCast` specify the order in which messages are sent and received by nodes: the process `BroadCastData(id,data)` is used by node `id` to broadcast `data` to all other processes, while the process `BroadCastControl(id,..)` distributes status messages throughout the network.

A node that is off is modelled by the process `OffNode`:

```
OffNode(id, priority) = switchOn.id ->
        BroadCastControl(id,onSource,OnNode(id, max(LOWER_LIMIT_PET,priority-1)))
```

When a node is turned on it broadcasts that fact, then behaves as a switched on node. The priority is decremented as a heuristic strategy to elect a stable leader, *i.e.* the one that has the least occurrences of leaving the network. Following an initialisation, the process `Node` repeatedly checks for updates in the network configuration. Using the CSP interruption (/\), we specify that this behaviour can be interrupted at any time via a `switchOff` event. When switched off, the node first informs all other nodes that it has been turned off (by broadcasting the message `offSource`). This behaviour, of broadcasting messages after having been turned off, abstracts the behaviour of the B&O protocol, in which any node can always detect when another node is off.

```
OnNode(id, priority) = Node(id, <id..N>, priority, undecided)
    /\ ((switchOff.id -> BroadCastControl(id,offSource,OffNode(id, priority))) |~| STOP)
```

The main behaviour of a node, given by process `Node`, regulates the status exchange cycle between nodes, controlled by the list `<id..N>`, as well as the election process. The process `Node` either broadcasts its local state or receives status updates from other nodes. The list of nodes is re-initialised to `<id..N>` when it is empty. The local state is given by the *priority* of a node and its *claim*: its current state in the election process – `undecided`, `leader` or `follower`. After this initial broadcast it waits for the local state of each of its neighbours in turn. The node receives either the current state of the neighbour (through channel `cp_pack.in.a.id`) or a timeout event (through channel `timeout.in.a.id`) if the corresponding neighbour is turned off.

```
Node(id, <a>^list, mypriority, myclaim) =
    if a == id then BroadCastData(id, myclaim.mypriority);
        Node(id, list, mypriority, myclaim)
    else ((cp_pack.in.a.id?valC?valP -> setPack.id.a!valC!valP -> SKIP)
        []
        (commTimeout.in.id.a -> setPack.id.a!off!0 -> SKIP));
        Choice(id, <a>^list, mypriority, myclaim)
```

Each incoming message is stored, and the node reassesses its own local state in `Choice`.

```
Choice(id, <a>^list, mypriority, myclaim) =
    if myclaim == undecided then Undecided(id, <a>^list, mypriority)
    else if myclaim == leader then Leader(id, <a>^list, mypriority)
        else Follower(id, list, mypriority)
```

A **Leader** begins by retrieving the number of other nodes that are also claiming to be leaders. If this is not zero, the node becomes **undecided**; otherwise it remains a leader. The priority of a leader node is incremented (up to an upper limit) when it has completed a full cycle of status exchanges. This ensures that stable nodes are more likely to become leaders.

```
Leader(id, <a>^list, mypriority) =
    nleaders.id?valLeaders ->
        if valLeaders > 0 then Node(id, list, mypriority, undecided)
        else if id == next(a) then Node(id, list, min(UP_LMT,mypriority+1),
        leader) else Node(id, list, mypriority, leader)
```

A **Follower** remains so if there exists a leader; it becomes undecided, otherwise.

```
Follower(id, list, mypriority) =
    nleaders.id?valLeaders ->
        if valLeaders == 0 then Node(id, list, mypriority, undecided)
        else Node(id, list, mypriority, follower)
```

An **Undecided** node decides to lead or follow by first retrieving the number of competing leaders, the value of the highest priority among these, and the value of the largest identity among the highest priority nodes. The node follows a leader if it finds one. Otherwise, it remains undecided until the end of the status exchange cycle (`id = next(a)`). It then becomes a leader if its priority is higher than all other nodes. If multiple nodes have the same priority, the node becomes a leader if it has the highest `id`.

```
Undecided(id, <a>^list, mypriority) =
    nleaders.id?valLeaders -> hpetition.id?highest -> hpetitionid.id?highestid ->
    (let myclaim =
            if valLeaders > 0 then  follower
            else if id == next(a) then
                    if highest == mypriority and highestid < id
                        or highest < mypriority then leader
                    else follower
                else undecided
        within Node(id, list, mypriority, myclaim))
```

Communication between nodes takes place over a **Bus** that provides bidirectional communication between every pair of nodes. The **Bus** is composed of various **BusCells**, each of which provides an unidirectional channel between a source and a target node.

```
BusCell(idSource,idTarget) =
    let On(data) = cp_pack.out.idSource.idTarget?val -> On(val)
            [] data != -1 & cp_pack.in.idSource.idTarget!data -> On(-1)
            [] offSource.idSource.idTarget -> Idle
        Idle = timeout.idSource.idTarget -> Idle
            [] onSource.idSource.idTarget -> On(-1)
    within Idle
```

We create our fully connected model using the alphabetised parallel operator to connect bus cells and nodes.

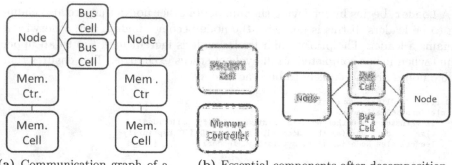

(a) Communication graph of a 2-node configuration.

(b) Essential components after decomposition.

**Fig. 1.** Views of the system

## 6  A Local Strategy for Deadlock Analysis of the Leadership Election and Experimental Results

Although, in principle, our CSP model can be fully analysed by tools like FDR, this approach to analyse the complete model for deadlock freedom is not local and incurs in an exponential growth in the number of states to be analysed, becoming infeasible at early stages. Our alternative to this problem is to use a strategy that combines the theory for deadlock analysis presented in Section 3 together with the pattern based approach that we proposed in Section 4.

The model presented for the leadership election can be decomposed based on Theorem 2. This decomposition gives the memory cells, the memory controllers, and the subnetwork as essential components. The latter is composed of interconnected nodes and bus cells as depicted in Figure 1(b).

This decomposition alone enables the local verification for deadlock freedom of both memory cells and memory controllers. Nevertheless, based on the results of [14,13] summarised in Section 3, the verification of the subnetwork of bus cells and nodes is still left to be verified as a single component, which also leads to an exponential analysis in the number of nodes, as shown later in this section. As a demonstration of the benefits brought by this pattern, we show that, using the pattern proposed in Section 4, we need to verify only local behavioural conditions for guaranteeing deadlock freedom. As an example of how the conformance notions are encoded as assertions that can be automatically verified by FDR, we present the following two assertions, which verify the conformance of atom BUS_CELL.0.1 to the transport entity specification and the conformance of atom NODE.0 to the participant specification, respectively.

```
assert TransportSpec(BUS_CELL.0.1,LENetwork) [F= Abs(BUS_CELL.0.1,LENetwork)
assert ParticipantSpec(NODE.0,LENetwork) [F= Abs(NODE.0,LENetwork)
```

As expected, by conducting a full local analysis using FDR, we verified that all the restrictions imposed by the pattern are satisfied. This guarantees that that our example is indeed deadlock free.

In order to demonstrate that our local analysis avoids combinatorial explosion, we conducted a comparative analysis of three verification approaches, all using FDR: (i) analysis of the complete model; (ii) local analysis based on the decomposition supported by [14,13], as presented in Section 3 and Figure 1b; (iii) the decomposition considered in (ii) in addition to the pattern based approach proposed in Section 4. For the analysis of our strategy (iii), we only evaluate state, transitions and time for behavioural restriction as this is the most complex task in checking pattern adherence, the predicate satisfaction time being insignificant in comparison to that time.

Our goal was to analyse a model with 32 nodes, which is the maximal number of nodes of a B&O network of devices. For this reason, we conducted the analysis for 2, 3, 4, 5, 10, 20 and 32 node instances of this model. The results are presented in Table 1, in which we provide the number of states analysed, the number of transitions, the number of processes in the network and the amount of time spent in the verification. The number of states and transitions are the ones of the Labelled Transitions System generated and analysed by FDR. The time is measured in seconds, and transitions and states in thousands. We used a dedicated server with an 8 core Intel(R) Xeon(R) 2.67GHz and 16 GB of RAM in an Ubuntu 4.4.3 system.

**Table 1.** Practical comparison

| Nodes | #Procs | (iii) Proposed strategy | | | (ii) Decomposed model | | | (i) Complete model | | |
|---|---|---|---|---|---|---|---|---|---|---|
| | | States | Trans | Time | States | Trans | Time | States | Trans | Time |
| 2 | 8 | 0.4 | 1.5 | 0.5 | 17.5 | 81.5 | 0.3 | 1,695 | 7,663 | 11.27 |
| 3 | 18 | 1.7 | 6.7 | 1.7 | 242,626 | 1,886,533 | 3,115 | * | * | * |
| 4 | 32 | 4.7 | 19.9 | 3.86 | * | * | * | * | * | * |
| 5 | 50 | 10 | 47 | 7 | * | * | * | * | * | * |
| 10 | 200 | 156 | 740 | 46 | * | * | * | * | * | * |
| 20 | 800 | 2,490 | 12,149 | 659 | * | * | * | * | * | * |
| 32 | 2,048 | 16,414 | 80,939 | 5,161 | * | * | * | * | * | * |

* FDR exceeds the machine's memory available

As expected, the exponential explosion quickly makes the leadership election model intractable by the strategy (i). The verification time for deadlock freedom for a 2-node configuration is 11 seconds, but the 3-node instance needs more than 16 GB of memory, which is beyond the configuration of the server used. Even if the decomposition strategy is applied, as described in (ii), FDR is not capable of analysing further than the 3-node configuration. Also, the state space explosion in this case is very clear as the number of states leaps from about 17,500 in the 2-node configuration to 242,626,600 in the 3-node configuration. Our strategy (iii) is by far the only viable option, being able to analyse the 2,048 processes of the 32-node configuration, in 1.43 hours. Note that, in addition to the state explosion, the processes being analysed also grow in complexity as the number of nodes in the configuration increases because every node needs to communicate with more nodes, making the analysis of this example even more expensive.

# 7    Conclusion and Related Work

In this paper, we proposed a pattern that prevents deadlocks and the formalisation of a notion of pattern conformance using first order logic and refinement expressions. We also presented a formal specification of the leadership election algorithm. This algorithm is used by one of our industrial partners, B&O, to define the *publisher* of their *publisher-subscriber* protocol, in which one of the products (the publisher) is the leader of the other products (the subscribers). We applied the proposed pattern to this industrial case study and compared the efficiency of our verification approach to a global approach.

As demonstrated by the analysis in Section 6, the verification of a complex algorithm using a global approach rapidly becomes infeasible. Our pattern based approach is a valid and promising alternative to verifying complex systems for deadlock freedom. By verifying adherence to a pattern that requires only local analysis, we were able to guarantee that a complex distributed algorithm used in industry is deadlock free. In the case of B&O, we were able to guarantee the deadlock freedom of their distributed algorithm with up to 32-nodes (the maximum number of nodes in a B&O network), involving 2,048 processes. Moreover, during the development and verification of this model several issues were identified and the real C++ implementation was modified as a result.

A CSP specification of the leadership election "Bully algorithm" of [7] is given in [15]. The assumptions on processes are similar to the ones we make: processes may fail and revive at any time, and contain some stable storage. Although both models assume that messages will not be duplicated or lost, their network assumptions differ. The Bully algorithm does not allow a failed communication between two live processes. We model this possibility using a `timeout`. Furthermore, in the Bully algorithm, messages may not overtake each other: they must be processed in the order in which they are sent. In our model, message may overtake each other. Finally, in the Bully algorithm communication is synchronous, whilst we model asynchronous communications.

In terms of algorithm design, a leadership competition in the Bully algorithm is resolved by the node with the highest identifier "bullying" the other nodes into accepting its claim. In the case of competing claims in the algorithm we present, the primary decision mechanism is the value of `priority`, although the node `id` may be used as a last resource.

In the future, we plan to increase the range of systems to which our approach is applicable through the development and verification of new architectural patterns. Furthermore, we also intend to extend the application of our approach to other properties such as livelock-freedom. Finally, we plan to apply the pattern-based strategy to a wide spectrum of real systems.

**Acknowledgments.** The EU Framework 7 Integrated Project COMPASS (Grant Agreement 287829) financed most of the work presented here. INES and CNPq supports the work of Marcel Oliveira: grants 573964/2008-4, 560014/2010-4 and 483329/2012-6.

# References

1. Allen, R., Douence, R., Garlan, D.: Specifying and analyzing dynamic software architectures. In: Astesiano, E. (ed.) ETAPS 1998 and FASE 1998. LNCS, vol. 1382, pp. 21–37. Springer, Heidelberg (1998)
2. Antonino, P.R.G., Oliveira, M.V.M., Sampaio, A.C.A., Kristensen, K.E., Bryans, J.W.: Leadership Election: An Industrial SoS Application of Compositional Deadlock Verification — Extended version. Technical report, UFPE (2013), http://www.cin.ufpe.br/~prga2/tech/techNFM2014.html
3. Bernardo, M., Ciancarini, P., Donatiello, L.: Architecting families of software systems with process algebras. ACM Transactions on Software Engineering and Methodology 11(4), 386–426 (2002)
4. Cheung, E., Chen, X., Hsieh, H., Davare, A., Sangiovanni-Vincentelli, A., Watanabe, Y.: Runtime deadlock analysis for system level design. Design Automation for Embedded Systems 13(4), 287–310 (2009)
5. Cheung, S., Kramer, J.: Context constraints for compositional reachability analysis. ACM Transactions on Software Engineering and Methodology 5(4), 334–377 (1996)
6. Formal Systems Ltd. FDR: User Manual and Tutorial, version 2.82 (2005)
7. Garcia-Molina, H.: Elections in a distributed computing system. IEEE Transactions on Computers C-31(1), 48–59 (1982)
8. He, J., Li, X., Liu, Z.: A theory of reactive components. Electronic Notes in Theoretical Computer Science 160, 173–195 (2006)
9. Plasil, F., Visnovsky, S.: Behavior protocols for software components. IEEE Transactions on Software Engineering 28(11), 1056–1076 (2002)
10. Ramos, R., Sampaio, A., Mota, A.: Systematic development of trustworthy component systems. In: Cavalcanti, A., Dams, D.R. (eds.) FM 2009. LNCS, vol. 5850, pp. 140–156. Springer, Heidelberg (2009)
11. Ramos, R.T., Sampaio, A.C.A., Mota, A.C.: Conformance notions for the coordination of interaction components. Science of Computer Programming 75(5), 350–373 (2010)
12. Roscoe, A.W.: The Theory and Practice of Concurrency. Prentice-Hall Series in Computer Science. Prentice-Hall (1998)
13. Roscoe, A.W., Brookes, S.D.: Deadlock analysis in networks of communicating processes. Distributed Computing (4), 209–230 (1991)
14. Roscoe, A.W., Dathi, N.: The pursuit of deadlock freedom. Information and Computation 75(3), 289–327 (1987)
15. Roscoe, A.W.: Understanding Concurrent Systems, 1st edn. Springer-Verlag New York, Inc., New York (2010)

# Verification of Certifying Computations through AutoCorres and Simpl

Lars Noschinski[1,*], Christine Rizkallah[2,*], and Kurt Mehlhorn[2,*]

[1] Institut für Informatik, Technische Universität München, Germany
[2] Max-Planck-Institut für Informatik, Saarbrücken, Germany

**Abstract.** Certifying algorithms compute not only an output, but also a witness that certifies the correctness of the output for a particular input. A checker program uses this certificate to ascertain the correctness of the output. Recent work used the verification tools VCC and Isabelle to verify checker implementations and their mathematical background theory. The checkers verified stem from the widely-used algorithms library LEDA and are written in C. The drawback of this approach is the use of two different tools. The advantage is that it could be carried out with reasonable effort in 2011. In this article, we evaluate the feasibility of performing the entire verification within Isabelle. For this purpose, we consider checkers written in the imperative languages C and Simpl. We re-verify the checker for connectedness of graphs and present a verification of the LEDA checker for non-planarity of graphs. For the checkers written in C, we translate from C to Isabelle using the AutoCorres tool set and then reason in Isabelle. For the checkers written in Simpl, Isabelle is the only tool needed. We compare the new approach with the previous approach and discuss advantages and disadvantages. We conclude that the new approach provides higher trust guarantees and it is particularly promising for checkers that require domain-specific reasoning.

## 1   Introduction

A user of a program has in general no easy means to know whether the result computed by the program is correct or has been compromised by a bug. While formal verification is one solution, for complex programs the cost is often prohibitive. We are interested in complex programs for combinatorial and geometric problems as, for example, discussed in [1,4,21]. For an input $x$, a *certifying algorithm* [7,26,19] produces an output $y$ and a *witness* $w$. The accompanying *checker* is a simpler and more efficient program that uses the witness $w$ to ascertain that $y$ is a correct output for input $x$. The checker is supposed to return *true* if and only if the witness $w$ indeed proves that $y$ is the correct output for $x$. A small example helps understanding the concept. The input for a planarity test is a graph. A certifying planarity test witnesses the output "is-planar" by a planar embedding and the output "is-not-planar" by a Kuratowski subgraph. Certifying algorithms are a key design principle of the algorithms library LEDA [21]. Checkers are an integral part of the library and are optionally invoked after every execution of a LEDA program. Adoption of the principle greatly improved the reliability of the library [20].

---

* The first two authors contributed equally to this work. The third author supervised the work.

J.M. Badger and K.Y. Rozier (Eds.): NFM 2014, LNCS 8430, pp. 46–61, 2014.

The (relative) simplicity of checkers makes them amenable to formal verification. Recent work [2] provides a framework for verifying certifying computations. The approach uses the interactive theorem prover Isabelle as a backend to the automatic code verifier VCC. Low level properties of the C code are proven using VCC. These are then translated to Isabelle and used to derive the desired mathematical properties, which are translated back to VCC. This framework (the *VCC approach*) is illustrated on several examples in the domain of graphs. Using two proof tools has the advantage of using the strength of each tool: verification of C code with VCC and mathematical reasoning with Isabelle/HOL.

In this work, we investigate the feasibility of carrying out the entire verification of the checkers within Isabelle/HOL. We implement the checkers both in Simpl and in C. Simpl [25] is a generic imperative programming language embedded into Isabelle/HOL that was designed as an intermediate language for program verification. The Simpl checkers are verified directly within Isabelle. To translate from C to Isabelle we use the C-to-Isabelle parser that was developed as part of the seL4 project [17] and was used to verify a full operating system kernel. We do not work on the output of the parser directly, but use the AutoCorres tool [15] that simplifies reasoning about C in Isabelle/HOL. This approach (the *AutoCorres approach*) avoids double formalizations in two systems and reduces the trusted code base: instead of trusting VCC, one now has to trust the C-to-Isabelle parser, a significantly simpler program. Since we are the first external users of AutoCorres, it was not clear at the beginning of our work, whether the AutoCorres approach is competitive. At least for our examples, it is competitive, if not superior.

Why do we verify implementations both in C and in Simpl? It allows us to separate the verification of the checker algorithm and of the checker implementation. Simpl has a very powerful expression language as all Isabelle expressions are Simpl expressions. Therefore, one can write pseudo-code like Simpl programs. Verifying both a C and a Simpl implementation allows us to estimate how much additional effort for the full verification is needed in addition to the pseudo-code verification. The hope was that after the Simpl verification is done the verification of the C-program would be only dealing with C-intricacies and hence be relatively straight-forward.

Section 3 introduces the implementations and verifications of the checkers both in Simpl and in C and discusses lessons learned. In Section 4 we suggest a refinement framework for using Autocorres. Then in Sections 5 and 6 we give an evaluation and talk about related work. The full implementation and all proofs are available on the companion website.[1]

## 2  Preliminaries

As in the VCC approach, we consider algorithms taking an input $x$ from a set $X$ and producing an output $y$ from a set $Y$ and a witness $w$ from a set $W$. Input $x$ is supposed to satisfy a precondition $\varphi(x)$, and $x$ and $y$ are supposed to satisfy a postcondition $\psi(x, y)$. A *witness predicate* for a specification with precondition $\varphi$ and postcondition $\psi$ is a predicate $\mathcal{W} \subseteq X \times Y \times W$ with the following *witness property*:

---

[1] http://www21.in.tum.de/~noschinl/Verifying_Certifying

$$\forall x, y, w. \; \varphi(x) \land \mathcal{W}(x, y, w) \longrightarrow \psi(x, y) \tag{1}$$

In contrast to algorithms, which work on abstract sets $X$, $Y$, and $W$, programs as their implementations operate on concrete representations of abstract objects. We use $\overline{X}$, $\overline{Y}$, and $\overline{W}$ for the set of representations of objects in $X$, $Y$, and $W$, respectively and assume mappings $i_X : \overline{X} \to X$, $i_Y : \overline{Y} \to Y$, and $i_W : \overline{W} \to W$. The checker program $C$ receives a triple $(\overline{x}, \overline{y}, \overline{w})$ and is supposed to check whether it fulfills the witness property. More precisely, let $x = i_X(\overline{x})$, $y = i_Y(\overline{y})$, and $w = i_W(\overline{w})$. If $\neg\varphi(x)$, $C$ may do anything (e.g., run forever or halt with an arbitrary output). If $\varphi(x)$, $C$ must halt and either accept or reject. A correct checker $C$ will accept if $\mathcal{W}(x, y, w)$ holds and reject otherwise. The following proof obligations arise:

**Witness Property:** A proof for the implication (1).
**Checker Correctness:** A proof that $C$ checks the witness predicate if the precondition
   $\varphi$ is satisfied. I.e., for an input $(\overline{x}, \overline{y}, \overline{w})$ with $x = i_X(\overline{x})$, $y = i_Y(\overline{y})$, $w = i_W(\overline{w})$:
   1. If $\varphi(x)$, $C$ halts.
   2. If $\varphi(x)$, $C$ accepts if and only if $\mathcal{W}(x, y, w)$.

*Tools.* Isabelle/HOL [23] is an interactive theorem prover for classical higher-order logic based on Church's simply-typed lambda calculus. The system is built on top of a kernel providing a small number of inference rules; complex deductions (especially by automatic proof methods) ultimately rely on these rules only. This strategy [14] guarantees correctness as long as the inference kernel is correct. Isabelle/HOL comes with a rich set of already formalized theories, e.g., natural numbers, integers, sets, finite sets, and as a recent addition graphs [24]. Proofs in Isabelle/HOL can be written in a style close to that of mathematical textbooks. The user structures the proof and the system fills in the gaps by its automatic proof methods.

   Simpl [25] is a generic imperative language designed to allow a deep embedding of real programming languages such as C into Isabelle/HOL for the purpose of program verification. The C-to-Isabelle parser converts a large subset of C99-code into low-level Simpl code. Simpl provides the usual imperative language constructs such as functions, variable assignments, sequential composition, conditional statements, while loops, and exceptions. There is no return statement for abrupt termination; it is emulated by exceptions. Simpl has no expression language of its own; rather, every Isabelle expression is also a Simpl expression. Programs may be annotated by invariants. Specifications for Simpl programs are given as Hoare triples, where pre- and post-condition are arbitrary Isabelle expressions. A verification condition generator (*VCG*) converts Hoare Triples to a set of higher-order formulas.

   The C-to-Isabelle parser makes no effort to abstract from details of the C-language. AutoCorres [15] builds upon this parser and, in a fully verified way, provides a simpler representation of the original program. Apart from simplifying the control flow, it transforms the deeply embedded Simpl code into a shallowly embedded monadic representation where local variables are modeled as bound Isabelle variables. There are multiple monads from which AutoCorres chooses depending on the C features used; the most common one is the nondeterministic state monad. In this monad, program statements are a function from a heap to a tuple consisting of a failure flag and the nondeterministic state, represented as a set of pairs of return value and heap. The monadic bind operation implements sequential composition. Again, specifications are given as Hoare triples and a VCG converts these to higher-order formulas [11].

VCC [12] is an assertional, automatic, deductive code verifier for full C code. Source code is annotated with specifications in the form of function contracts, data invariants, loop invariants, and further annotations to guide the verifier. Annotated code can still be compiled with a normal C compiler. From the annotated program, VCC generates verification conditions for partial or total correctness, which it then tries to discharge automatically.

## 3   Verification of Checkers within Isabelle/HOL

The VCC approach was used to verify several checkers in the field of graphs from the algorithmic library LEDA. For the sake of comparison, we rework the verification of the connectedness checker. Moreover, we verify the LEDA checker for testing graph non-planarity. In order to get a measure of the effort dedicated to the verification of the algorithm respectively that of dealing with C-intricacies, we use two methods to verify the checker in Isabelle/HOL: First, we verify an implementation in Simpl. Second, we use AutoCorres to verify a C implementation. We compare the approaches in Section 5.

**Connectedness of Graphs.** Given an undirected graph $G = (V, E)$, we consider an algorithm that decides whether $G$ is connected, i.e., whether there is a path between any pair of vertices [21, Section 7.4]. Non-connectedness is certified by a cut, i.e., a nonempty subset $S$ of the vertices with $S \neq V$, such that every edge of the graph has either both or no endpoint in $S$. Connectedness is certified by a spanning tree of $G$. On a high level, we instantiate the general framework as follows:

$$
\begin{aligned}
\text{input } x &= \text{ an undirected graph } G = (V, E) \\
\text{output } y &= \text{ either } \textit{True} \text{ or } \textit{False} \text{ indicating whether } G \text{ is connected} \\
\text{witness } w &= \text{ a cut or a spanning tree} \\
\varphi(x) &= G \text{ is well-formed, i.e., } E \subseteq V \times V, V \text{ and } E \text{ are finite sets} \\
\mathcal{W}(x, y, w) &= y \text{ is } \textit{True} \text{ and } w \text{ is a spanning tree or } y \text{ is } \textit{False} \text{ and } w \text{ is a cut} \\
\psi(x, y) &= \text{ if } y \text{ is } \textit{True}, G \text{ is connected and if } y \text{ is } \textit{False}, G \text{ is not connected.}
\end{aligned}
$$

As in previous work [2], we restrict ourselves to the positive case $y = \textit{True}$. For an example of a graph and its witnessing spanning tree see Fig. 3 in [2]. We represent spanning trees by functions *parent-edge* and *num* and a root vertex $r$ and view the edges of the tree oriented towards $r$: for each $v$, *parent-edge*$(v)$ is the first edge on the path from $v$ to $r$ (we set *parent-edge*$(r) = \textit{None}$), and *num*$(v)$ is the length of this path. Undirected graphs are represented as bidirected graphs, i.e., for every unordered edge $\{u, v\}$ of $G$, we have ordered pairs $(u, v)$ and $(v, u)$ in the representation of $G$.

*Witness Property.* The witness property states that if the conditions in Fig. 1 hold, the graph is connected. This was already proven in Isabelle/HOL by Alkassar et al. [2]. We extend the theorem to also state that the conditions imply that the *num*-value of each vertex is its depth in the spanning tree. This is important for the C-verification.

**locale** *connected-components-locale* = *pseudo-digraph* +
  **fixes** *num* : $\alpha \Rightarrow$ *nat* **and** *parent-edge* : $\alpha \Rightarrow \beta$ *option* **and** $r$ : $\alpha$
  **assumes** *r-assms*: $r \in$ *verts* $G \wedge$ *parent-edge* $r$ = *None* $\wedge$ *num* $r$ = 0
  **assumes** *parent-num-assms*: $\bigwedge v.\ v \in$ *verts* $G \wedge v \neq r \Longrightarrow$
    $\exists\, e \in$ arcs $G$. *parent-edge* $v$ = *Some* $e \wedge$ *head* $G\ e$ = $v \wedge$ *num* $v$ = *num* (*tail* $G\ e$) + 1

**Fig. 1.** Preconditions for the connectedness proof in Isabelle. $G$ is a well-formed graph with vertices of type $\alpha$ and edges of type $\beta$.

*Simpl Implementation and Verification.* We represent graphs as in previous work [2]. The type *IGraph* represents a graph $G$ by the numbers *ivertex-cnt* $G$ and *iedge-cnt* $G$ of its vertices and edges and a function *iedges* $G$, mapping $0 \leq i <$ *iedge-cnt* $G$ to the pair of endpoints of the $i$-th edge. A graph is *well-formed* if all endpoints are smaller than *ivertex-cnt* $G$.

Each of the conditions in Fig. 1 is checked by a procedure. For example, the procedure *parent-num-assms* in Fig. 2 checks *parent-num-assms* in the obvious way. The loop invariant *parent-num-assms-inv* states that *parent-num-assms* holds up to vertex $i$. **VAR MEASURE** introduces the measure function used for the termination proof and the command **ANNO** binds logical variables to be used in the invariant. Total correctness of each function is formulated as a Hoare triple; see Lemma *parent-num-assms-spec* in Fig. 2. Invoking the VCG and using the annotations (loop invariant and measure function) is sufficient for the correctness proof.

*C Implementation and Verification.* The C representation of graphs is similar to that in Simpl. In particular, numbers are now of bounded precision. This means we need to prove absence of overflows during verification. The number of vertices and edges are now **unsigned int**s. We represent spanning trees as explained above, but use arrays instead of functions. The function *parent-edge* is represented as an array of (signed) **int**, and *num* as an array of **unsigned int**. As in previous work [2], we require as a precondition that the input graph is well-formed.

The *check-connected* checker is a function that accepts exactly when the two functions *check-r* and *check-parent-num* accept. The first function checks that $r$ is indeed the root of the spanning tree. The second function checks for every vertex $v$ different from $r$ that the edge *parent-edge*[$v$] is incident to $v$ and that the other endpoint of the edge has a number one smaller than *num*[$v$].

The first step in the C verification is calling the C-to-Isabelle parser and invoking AutoCorres. As in Simpl, for each function in the code we prove a corresponding specification lemma, formulated as a Hoare triple and reasoned about using a VCG. The termination proof of the checkers is as trivial as in the Simpl case. For proving functional correctness, we introduce some helper functions that assist in relating the implementation types to Isabelle types. For example, the abstraction predicate array list, *arrlist*, takes as input the state of the heap $h$, a list $l$ and a pointer $p$ and checks whether $p$ points in $h$ to an array containing the values of $l$. We also introduce a set of lemmas to ease dealing with bounded numbers.

We prove that the checker function checks the conditions in Fig. 1. This proof happens under the assumption that the pointers to the graph, to its edges, to *num* and to *parent-edge* can be abstracted to Isabelle datatypes (using the *arrlist* predicate).

**definition** *parent-num-assms-inv* : $IGraph \Rightarrow IVert \Rightarrow IPEdge \Rightarrow INum \Rightarrow nat \Rightarrow bool$
**where** *parent-num-assms-inv* $G\ r\ p\ n\ k \equiv \forall\ k < i.\ i \neq r \rightarrow$ (**case** $p\ i$ of *None* $\Rightarrow$ *False*
  | *Some* $x \Rightarrow x <$ *iedge-cnt* $G \wedge snd$ (*iedges* $G\ x$) $= i \wedge n\ i = n$ (*fst* (*iedges* $G\ x$)) $+ 1$)

**procedures** *parent-num-assms*
  (G : *IGraph*, r : *IVert*, parent-edge : *IPEdge*, num : *INum* | R : *bool*)
**in ANNO** ($G, r, p, n$). {| G = $G$ ∧ r = $r$ ∧ parent-edge = $p$ ∧ num = $n$ |}
  **where** vertex : *IVert*, edge-id : *Edge-Id*
    R := *True* ; vertex := 0 ;
  **TRY**
    **WHILE** vertex < *ivertex-cnt* G
    **INV** {| R = *parent-num-assms-inv* G r parent-edge num vertex
      ∧ vertex ≤ *ivertex-cnt* G|} **VAR MEASURE** (*ivertex-cnt* G − vertex)
    **DO**
      **IF** (vertex ≠ r) **THEN**
        **IF** parent-edge vertex = *None* **THEN** R := *False* ; **THROW FI** ;
        edge-id := the (parent-edge vertex) ;
        **IF** edge-id ≥ *iedge-cnt* G ∨ *snd* (*iedges* G edge-id) ≠ vertex
          ∨ num vertex ≠ num (*fst* (*iedges* G edge-id)) + 1 **THEN** R := *False* ; **THROW FI**
      **FI** ;
      vertex := vertex + 1
    **OD**
  **CATCH SKIP END** {|R=*parent-num-assms-inv* G r parent-edge num (*ivertex-cnt* G)|}

**lemma** (**in** *parent-num-assms-impl*) *parent-num-assms-spec*:
  $\forall G\ r\ p\ n.\ \Gamma \vdash_t$ {|G = $G$ ∧ r = $r$ ∧ parent-edge = $p$ ∧ num = $n$|}
  R := **PROC** *parent-num-assms*(G, r, parent-edge, num)
  {| R = *parent-num-assms-inv* $G\ r\ p\ n$ (*ivertex-cnt* $G$)|}

**Fig. 2.** Excerpts from the Simpl implementation and verification of connectedness. The Lemma *parent-num-assms-spec*, formulated as a Hoare triple, states that the procedure *parent-num-assms* terminates (indicated by $\vdash_t$) and computes *parent-num-assms-inv*. Observe the distinction between logical and program variables; $x$ versus x for a variable with name x.

*Experiences and Lessons Learned.* The verification of this checker assures us that the AutoCorres approach is feasible. The effort for the verification of the C-version of the connectedness checker was about the same as in the VCC approach. VCC knows more about C and this made it easier to reason about the C-program. This advantage would show even more clearly in programs that use low-level features of C more intensively, e.g., bit operations on words. On the other hand, one is forced to formalize a small number of graph-theoretic concepts such as path in two logical systems, this complicates the VCC-approach. A small number sufficed because verifying that the C-checker correctly checks the assumptions from Fig. 1 needs no graph-theoretic knowledge and hence there is a clear separation of labor between VCC and Isabelle/HOL. The disadvantage of double formalization shows more clearly in programs that need complex mathematical reasoning in the checker correctness proof and hence would require formalizing more advanced concepts in VCC. The checker for non-planarity presented in the next section is an example to this effect. There the correctness proof of the program requires graph-theoretic reasoning. If we had tried to verify this example using the VCC-approach, we would have had to formalize a non-trivial theory twice.

The connectedness checker verified using the VCC approach [2] has an unintended weakness. Not every representable connected graph has a spanning tree that could be represented as input to the checker. This is because the vertices of the graph were represented as **unsigned int** and the array $num$ had type **unsigned short**; this holds true for the program actually verified, not for the program listed in the paper. Thus graphs having no spanning tree of depth bounded by the size of **unsigned short** had no representable witness. VCC had no difficulties in automatically verifying that the addition in the C equivalent of num (*fst (iedges* G edge-id*)*) + 1 (see Fig. 2) does not overflow, because types smaller than **int** are lifted to **int** for arithmetic operations in C. In the AutoCorres verification, we had to manually prove that $s + 1 \leq u$, where $s$ and $u$ are the maximum values of **unsigned short** and **int**, respectively. This led us to notice and modify the type of $num$ in the checker to **unsigned int**. Now the addition could potentially overflow and we need to show that it does not. This is proven by strengthening the loop invariant to infer that $num$-value cannot exceed the number of vertices and hence does not overflow in a correct witness. In order to prove that the checker accepts if and only if the assumptions in Listing 1 hold one needs the stronger witness property mentioned above. Even though in this case manually discharging guards was useful, it demonstrates that VCC saves effort when it comes to automatically discharging guards.

**Non-planarity of Graphs.** One of the motivating examples for the introduction of certified algorithms in the LEDA library is the planarity test [21]. The planarity check in LEDA takes as input a graph $x$ and returns $y = True$ and a combinatorial planar embedding $w$ of $x$ if $x$ is planar or $y = False$ and a Kuratowski subgraph $w$ of $x$ otherwise. On a high level, we instantiate the general framework as follows:

$$
\begin{aligned}
\text{input } x &= \text{an undirected graph } G = (V, E), \text{ possibly with loops} \\
\text{output } y &= \text{either } True \text{ or } False \\
\text{witness } w &= \text{combinatorial planar embedding or Kuratowski subgraph} \\
\varphi(x) &= G \text{ is well-formed, i.e., } E \subseteq V \times V \text{ where } V \text{ and } E \text{ are finite.} \\
\psi(x, y) &= \text{If } y \text{ is } True, x \text{ is planar, else } x \text{ is not planar.}
\end{aligned}
$$

In this paper, we restrict ourselves to the case $y = False$. Then $\mathcal{W}(x, False, w)$ holds iff $w$ is a Kuratowski subgraph of $x$. Let $K_5$ be the complete graph on five vertices and $K_{3,3}$ the complete bipartite graph on three and three vertices. We call $K_{3,3}$ and $K_5$ *Kuratowski graphs*. Kuratowki's theorem is the basis for our formalization of non-planarity (see Fig. 3).

**Theorem 1 (Kuratowski).** *A graph $K$ is a* Kuratowski subgraph *of $G$ if $K$ is a subgraph of $G$ and the subdivision of a Kuratowski graph. A graph $G$ is planar if and only if it has no Kuratowski subgraph.*

*Witness Predicate.* The key step of the checker is testing whether the certificate $K$ is a subdivision of a $K_{3,3}$ or $K_5$. One option is to repeatedly take a node of degree 2 and contract it. In an imperative implementation this requires the program to work on a

$$subdivide(K, (u, v), w) = (V(K) \cup \{w\}, (E(K) \setminus \{uv\}) \cup \{uw, vw\})$$

$$planar(G) = \neg(\exists K. \ K \leq G \land (\exists H. \ subdivision(H, K) \land (K_{3,3}(H) \lor K_5(H))))$$

**Fig. 3.** Characterization of planarity. $subdivision(H, K)$ is the minimal predicate satisfying the following rules: $H$ is a subdivision of itself and if $K$ is a subdivision of $H$, $e$ is an edge of $K$, and $w$ is a new vertex, then $subdivide(K, e, w)$ is a subdivision of $H$. By $\leq$, we denote the subgraph relation.

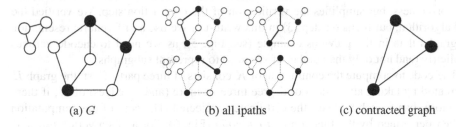

        (a) $G$                   (b) all ipaths           (c) contracted graph

**Fig. 4.** A graph $G$ and its ipaths and contracted graph ($V_3(G)$ in black). Neither the isolated circle nor the node of degree 1 are on any ipath (or in $V_3(G)$), so they do not contribute to the contracted graph.

copy of $K$ (or to modify the input). Instead, we follow the method used in LEDA [21] and compute the *contraction* of $K$ in single step and check whether the contraction is a Kuratowski graph. This requires only a constant amount of memory.

**Definition 1 (Contraction).** *Let $G$ be a graph and $V_3(G)$ be the set of all vertices of $G$ with degree at least three. Let $E'$ be such that $uv \in E'$ iff $u, v \in V_3(G)$ and there is a path in $G$ connecting $u$ and $v$ whose interior vertices are not in $V_3(G)$. Then $G' = (V_3(G), E')$ is the contraction of $G$. A path with end nodes in $V_3(G)$ and interior nodes in $V(G) \setminus V_3(G)$ is called an ipath. See Fig. 4 for an illustration.*

Note that in general $G$ is not a subdivision of its contraction. In particular, vertices of degree one or less and isolated cycles are discarded and cannot be reconstructed by subdivision. Nevertheless, contraction gives us a useful over-approximation of the Kuratowski subgraphs, as demonstrated by the following lemmas.

**Lemma 1.** *Let $K$ be a graph and $H$ the contracted graph of $K$. Then there exists a subgraph $K'$ of $K$ such that $K'$ is a subdivision of $H$. In particular, if $H$ is a $K_{3,3}$ or $K_5$ and $K$ a subgraph of a graph $G$, then $G$ is not planar.*

**Lemma 2.** *Let $H$ be a Kuratowski graph. If $K$ is a subdivision of $H$, then $H$ is the contracted graph of $K$. In particular, if $K$ is a Kuratowski subgraph of a graph $G$, then the contracted graph of $K$ is a Kuratowski graph.*

We prove both properties in Isabelle. To this end, we introduce the class of slim graphs. These correspond to those graphs on which contraction is an inverse to subdivision. The contraction of a non-slim graph $G$ is also the contraction of a slim subgraph of $G$ and the above lemmas derive from that. For details of the proof see [24].

Based on this, we give a new witness predicate $\mathcal{W}'$ as follows: $\mathcal{W}'(x, \textit{False}, w)$ holds if and only if $w$ is well-formed and a loop-free subgraph of $x$ such that the contracted graph of $w$ is a Kuratowski graph. Then Lemma 1 ensures the witness property. Lemma 2 ensures that $\mathcal{W} \subseteq \mathcal{W}'$, i.e., all certificates of non-planarity are accepted.

*Implementation and Verification.* The implementation of the checker is roughly divided into four steps: (1) Test whether $K$ is a subgraph of $G$. (2) Test whether $K$ is loop-free. (3) Compute $H$ by contracting $K$. (4) Test whether $H$ is a Kuratowski graph. The input is accepted if and only if all four tests succeed. The test for loop-freeness is not needed for correctness, but simplifies the verification of the contraction step. We verified the full algorithm, but focus on step (3) in this write-up. We use a different representation of graphs than in the previous example (see Fig. 5), as we need to encode vertices explicitly (and not only the number of vertices) to represent subgraphs.

The code to compute the contraction of $K$ consists of three parts: First, the graph $H$ is created by taking all vertices of degree three or more (and no edges) of $K$; if there are more than 6 such vertices, the certificate is rejected. The core of the computation is then performed by the function *find-endpoint* (Fig. 6): For a given vertex $v_{start} \in V(H)$ and an incident edge $e \in E(G)$ (given by its other endpoint $v_{next}$), it computes implicitly the ipath of $G$ starting with this edge end returns its last vertex (if it exists). The contracted edge described by this ipath is then added to $H$.

*Checker Correctness.* We assume that the input and certificate are well-formed graphs. Most of the termination arguments are pretty trivial (loops counting upwards to some constant), but termination of *find-endpoint* is not obvious: The procedure implicitly constructs an ipath, adding a vertex in every iteration. Termination follows as the length of an ipath is bounded by the number of vertices.

For partial correctness, the checker returns true if and only if $\mathcal{W}'(x, \textit{False}, y)$ holds. In the verification, most of the work is needed for step (3). To prove the specification of *find-endpoint* (Fig. 7) one needs to show that a maximal path where all interior nodes are of degree two is uniquely determined by its first edge. From this it follows relatively easily that calling *find-endpoint* for all nodes and their incident edges determines all edges of the contracted graph. Without referring to the mathematical background theory, both termination and partial correctness would be hard to prove.

*Verifying the C Implementation.* There are some differences between the Simpl and C implementations. In C, Graphs are not represented as a pair of lists, but as a struct with two pointers to arrays, and instead of natural numbers, we use bounded machine words. Finally, in Simpl, basic graph operations like "vertex contained" were stated as Isabelle expressions. In C, they need to be implemented and verified.

AutoCorres provides a natural translation of C code, so we hoped that for the verification of the C program, we could start with the the Simpl proof and fill in the gaps: i.e., abstract memory accesses and datatypes to the ones used in the Simpl proof and verify the functions not implemented before. The latter was indeed straight-forward. Similarly, abstracting the heap to the graph datatypes of Isabelle was tedious, but straight-forward, following established schemes [22]. Most of the additional effort was needed because of the bounded precision integers. This was somewhat surprising, because the only arithmetic operations occurring in the program are equality and increment against a fixed upper bound.

```
struct edge_t {              struct graph_t {              struct contr_t {
   unsigned start;              unsigned vert_cnt;             unsigned char vert_cnt;
   unsigned target; };          unsigned edge_cnt;            unsigned verts[6];
                                unsigned *verts;              unsigned char
                                struct edge_t *edges; };         edges[6][6]; };
```

**Fig. 5.** C datastructures for graphs. *graph_t* represents a graph by a list of vertices and a list of edges. *contr_t* represents the contracted graph as an adjacency matrix.

**procedures** *find-endpoint* (G : *IGraph'*,
  H : *IGraph'*, $v_{start}$ : *IVert*, $v_{next}$ : *IVert*
  | R : *IVert option*)
**where**
  found : *bool*, i : *nat*, len : *nat*, $v_0$ : *IVert*,
  $v_1$ : *IVert*, $v_t$ : *IVert* io-edges : *ig-edge list*,
**TRY**
  **IF** $v_{start}$ = $v_{next}$ **THEN RAISE** R := *None* **FI** ;
  $v_0$ := $v_{start}$ ; $v_1$ := $v_{next}$ ; len := *1* ;
  **WHILE** $v_1 \notin$ *set* (*ig-verts* H) **DO**
    io-edges := *ig-in-out-edges* G $v_1$ ;
    i := *0* ; found := *False* ;
    **WHILE** ¬found ∧ i < *length* io-edges **DO**
      $v_t$ := *ig-opposite* G (io-edges *!* i) $v_1$ ;
      **IF** $v_t \neq v_0$ **THEN**
        found := *True* ; $v_0$ := $v_1$ ; $v_1$ := $v_t$ **FI** ;
      i := i + *1*
    **OD** ;
    len := len + *1* ;
    **IF** ¬ found **THEN RAISE** R := *None* **FI**
  **OD** ;
  **IF** $v_1$ = $v_{start}$ **THEN RAISE** R := *None* **FI** ;
  R := *Some* $v_1$
**CATCH SKIP END**

```
unsigned find_endpoint(struct graph_t *g,
   struct contr_t *h, unsigned v_start,
   unsigned v_next) {
   unsigned v0 = v_start;
   unsigned v1 = v_next;

   while (tmp_get_index(h, v1) ≡ −1) {
      unsigned i;
      for (i=0; i < edge_cnt(g); i++) {
         unsigned vt = opposite(v1,
            edge(g,i));
         if (vt ≠ v0 ∧ vt ≠ −1) {
            v0 = v1;
            v1 = vt;
            break;
         }
      }
      if (i ≡ edge_cnt(g)) return −1;
   }
   if (v1 ≡ v_start) return −1;
   return v1;
}
```

**Fig. 6.** The function *find-endpoint* in Simpl and C. H (resp. *h*) is the preliminary contracted graph. The function implicitly constructs an ipath by adding vertices until a vertex of degree 3 (i.e., in H) is reached. The if-statement in the inner loop ensures that the algorithm does not go back the edge from the previous iteration. If the outer loop aborts abnormally, then no vertex in H is reachable from $v_{start}$ via ($v_{start}$, $v_{next}$). The Simpl implementation uses relatively high-level datastructures, like sets and list.

$\forall \sigma.\ \Gamma \vdash_t \{\!|\sigma.\ iverts$ H = $iverts_3$ G ∧ *loop-free* (*mk-graph* G) ∧ $v_{start} \in$ *set* (*iverts* H)
  ∧ *iadj* G $v_{start}$ $v_{next}$ ∧ *IGraph-inv* G$|\!\}$
  R := **PROC** *find-endpoint*(G, H, $v_{start}$, $v_{next}$)
$\{\!|$**case** R of *None* ⇒ ¬(∃p w. *ipath* (*mk-graph* $^\sigma$G) $^\sigma v_{start}$ ($^\sigma v_{start}\,^\sigma v_{next}$ # p) w)
  | *Some* w ⇒ (∃p. *ipath* (*mk-graph* $^\sigma$G) $^\sigma v_{start}$ ($^\sigma v_{start}\,^\sigma v_{next}$ # p) w) $|\!\}$

**Fig. 7.** Specification of *find-endpoint*: If H has all degree-3 nodes of G and G has no loops, then the procedure decides the existence of an ipath starting with the nodes $v_{start}$ and $v_{next}$. *mk-graph* abstracts a graph and $^\sigma$x refers to the value of x before the execution.

There are mainly two reasons for the problems we encountered with words: First, Isabelle has only weak support for proving properties involving words automatically. Second, such properties often occur not on their own, but as side-conditions in a larger proof. While Isabelle's automatic proof tools can often discharge such properties for natural numbers, they cannot do so for words and therefore fail, leaving the user to solve the goal mostly manually.

## 4   Abstraction

The issues with reasoning about functions using words motivated us to implement an abstraction framework for AutoCorres programs. The idea is to take the original function $f$ and give a modified implementation $f'$ that uses natural numbers instead of words. With the help of the abstraction framework, we prove $f$ and $f'$ to be equivalent and then perform verification on the abstracted function.

*Abstraction* or *refinement* is a well-known idea going back to Dijsktra [13] and Wirth [28] and put into a formal calculus by Back [3]. In particular, AutoCorres uses this technique to get from the Simpl program generated by the C parser to the simplified version presented to the user. We want to change two things in the abstraction process: Where appropriate, we want to replace words by natural numbers. For this, we also need to insert a guard before each operation on words that asserts that there will be no overflow (these guards then need to be discharged in the correctness proof of the abstract function). Moreover, we want to be able to insert ghost code (and ghost state), i.e., additional computations which have no influence on the outcome of the function. Such ghost code is often useful for stating loop invariants.

However, the abstraction framework used by AutoCorres [27] is unsuited for our purposes: It expects that each state in the concrete program corresponds to at most one state in the abstract program. This makes it difficult to insert ghost code. Moreover, although the given proof rules are syntax directed they must be applied in a guided manner, this makes them harder to use. Therefore, we give our own definition.

Recall that a computation in the nondeterministic state monad returns a failure flag and a set of states. For a relation *rel* on states, we define a relation *refines* on abstract. resp. concrete program statements $A$ and $C$:

$$refines\ rel\ A\ C = (\neg fail\ A \longrightarrow (\neg fail\ C \land \forall c \in st\ C.\ \exists a \in st\ A.\ (a, c) \in rel)$$

In particular, instead of proving correctness for the concrete program, we can prove correctness for the abstract program. We only give a simplified version here, which does not allow abstracting the heap. A state is a pair $(r, h)$, where $r$ is the return value of the previous command (often a tuple) and $h$ is the heap.

**Lemma 3.** *Let $P_A$ and $P_C$ be programs (i.e., functions from state to program state) and rel be a relation on states. The Hoare triple*

$$\{Q\}\ P_C\ \{R\ \}!$$

*states that $P_C$ is totally correct w.r.t. to the precondition $Q$ (a predicate on heaps) and the postcondition $R$ (a predicate on value/heap pairs). Assume that*

$$\forall h.\ Q\ h \longrightarrow refines\ rel\ (P_A\ h)\ (P_C\ h)$$

*i.e., for all heaps satisfying a precondition $Q$ the result of the abstract and concrete programs are related. In addition, assume that*

$$\{Q\}P_A\{\lambda r_A\, s_A.\ \forall r_C\, s_C.\ ((r_A, s_A), (r_C, s_C)) \in rel \longrightarrow R\, r_C\, s_C\}!$$

*i.e., for a heap $h$ satisfying $Q$, the result of $P_A\ h$ is related to a concrete program state satisfying $R$. Then the concrete program $P_C$ satisfies the specification above.*

To prove that two programs are related, we provide a syntax directed proof procedure which compares the two programs instruction by instruction. This requires the two programs to be very similar in structure. This is the case in our application. The central rule of the proof procedure is the rule for sequential composition.

**Lemma 4 (Refinement of Sequential Composition).** *Let $P_{A,1}$ be a program and $P_{A,2}$ a function mapping a return value of $P_{A,1}$ to a program (similarly for $P_{C,1}$, $P_{C,2}$).*

$$[refines\ rel\ (P_{A,1}\ h_A)\ (P_{C,1}\ h_C);$$
$$\forall((r_A, h_A), (r_C, h_C)) \in rel.\ refines\ rel'\ (P_{A,2}\ r_A\ h_A)\ (P_{C,2}\ r_C\ h_C)]$$
$$\implies refines\ rel'\ ((P_{A,1} \ggcurly P_{A,2})\ h_A)\ ((P_{C,1} \ggcurly P_{C,2})\ h_C)$$

*Here, $\ggcurly$ is the operator for sequential composition. $(P_1 \ggcurly P_2)\ h$ calls $P_1$ with heap $h$, and, for every pair $(r_2, h_2)$ in the result of $P_1\ h$, calls $P_2\ r_2\ h_2$. The union of the results is returned.*

Note that the relation $rel$ w.r.t. which $P_{A,1}$ and $P_{C,1}$ are refined is not fixed a priori. Our verification condition generator will synthesize it during the proof, using the following basic blocks:

– A refinement relation for words: $\{(n, w) \mid n = unat\ w\}$. Here, *unat* is the conversion from words to natural numbers.
– The identity relation.
– A ghost relation, allowing the introduction of an additional stack variable in the abstracted program: $\{(((g, r), h), (r', h')) \mid ((r, h), (r', h'))\}$

These are put together with the help of a pairing relation $\{((r, h), (r', h')) \mid (r, r') \in rrel \wedge (h, h') \in hrel\}$.

*Putting Abstraction to Use.* For the Kuratowski checker, our proof process is as follows: For each function $f$ containing word arithmetic, we make a copy $f'$ of this function, in which we replace words by natural numbers. For each arithmetic operation, we insert a guard stating that this operation would not overflow on words (see Fig. 8). Where necessary, we also add ghost code and annotate loops with invariants. One example of this is function *find-endpoint*, where we add an variable holding the computed ipath and use this in the invariant. Note that the ghost code can use arbitrary Isabelle expressions. Then we prove that $f'$ is an abstraction of $f$, using the verification condition generator sketched in the previous section. The proof is mostly automatic; we only need to prove simple properties about words and natural numbers.

return $((i : 32 \ word) + 1)$            $guard \ (\lambda\_. \ (i : nat) < unat \ (max\text{-}word : 32 \ word));$
                                          return $(i + 1)$

(a) concrete program                              (b) abstract program

**Fig. 8.** Abstraction of word arithmetic. The guard ensures that the operations on words and natural numbers behave the same. For the refinement proof, we write $ADD\_guard$ instead of $guard$ as a hint for our syntax directed VCG.

## 5   Evaluation

After abstraction, verification of the non-planarity checker follows closely the proof of the Simpl program. Overall, we conclude that the use of AutoCorres provides a viable alternative to the VCC approach for the verification of certifying computations. Moreover, we can profit from a previous verification of the algorithm. However, it is necessary to lift the C program to a similar level of abstraction as the pseudo code. This could not be achieved with the facilities provided by AutoCorres alone, but required us to implement our own refinement framework. The effort of developing this framework is required only once and can be reused for future verifications.

It is worth noting that there is parallel work adding automatic abstraction of words into AutoCorres [16]. However, when verifying a program, one is likely to encounter other datatypes that need a custom abstraction. In addition, our abstraction framework gives the option of adding ghost code, which is known to ease the formulation of invariants.

Both the Simpl and the C implementation of the Kuratowski checker consist of around 300 lines of code (the Simpl syntax is more verbose than C). The verification of the Simpl checker was done in 1300 lines. The verification of the C checker required 3200 lines and 1400 lines for the refinement framework. Of the 3200 lines, 900 deal with heap abstraction and access and the verification of basic graph operations not implemented in the Simpl code.

## 6   Related Work

Verifying code within interactive theorem provers is a an active field of research. The seL4 microkernel that is written in low-level C was verified within Isabelle/HOL using the C-to-Isabelle parser [17]. The underlying approach is refinement starting from an abstract specification via an intermediate implementation in Haskell to the final C code. Coq [5] was used both for programming the CompCert compiler and for proving its correctness [18]. CFML is a verification tool embedded in Coq that targets imperative Caml programs [10]. It was used to verify several imperative data structures.

Shortest path algorithms, especially imperative implementations thereof, are popular as case studies for demonstrating code verification [10,8]. They target full functional correctness as opposed to instance correctness. Verifying instance correctness is orthogonal to verifying the implementation of a particular algorithm and it is a tempting choice that also attracted much attention. In 1997, a checker for sorting algorithms has been developed and verified [9]. The DeCert project aims to design an architecture where either decision procedures are proven correct within Coq or produce witnesses allowing external checkers to verify the validity of their results, [6] provides an example. In recent work [2], a general framework to verify certifying computations is developed.

## 7 Conclusion

In this paper, we explored an alternative to the VCC approach, which provides higher trust guarantees, and verified checker for graph non-planarity. To our knowledge, no algorithm or checker for graph non-planarity was verified before.

The LEDA project [21] has shown that the concept of certifying computations eases the construction of libraries of reliable implementations of complex combinatorial and geometric algorithms. Reliability is increased because the output of every computation is checked for correctness by a checker program. Checker programs are relatively simple and hence easier to implement correctly than the corresponding solution algorithms. Certifying algorithms are available for a large number of algorithmic problems [19].

Our AutoCorres approach does not use VCC; the entire verification is done in Isabelle/HOL. We did so for three reasons: (1) The VCC approach, with its use of two different tools requires the formalization of certain concepts in two theories, a duplication of effort. (2) Furthermore, it requires trust in VCC, a fairly complex program. We have no reason not to trust the program. However, as a matter of principle, the trusted code base should be kept as small and simple as possible. (3) The recent tool AutoCorres [15] promised to greatly simplify reasoning about C in Isabelle.

Our experience with AutoCorres is positive. The AutoCorres approach presented in this paper yields a viable alternative to the VCC approach. It is particularly useful when the verification requires domain-specific reasoning (e.g., graph theory, as it was the case for the non-planarity checker).

The implementation of each of the advanced algorithms in LEDA took several man-months (recollection of the third author). In comparison, with either approach, it took less time to verify the checker. Note that the non-planarity checker is amongst the most complex checkers in LEDA. The verification time is likely to go down with increased experience and development of the tools (cf. [16]). In particular, we extended Auto-Corres with a reusable abstraction framework. We find that our work demonstrates that the development of libraries of certifying programs with formally verified checkers is feasible at reasonable cost.

**Acknowledgement.** We thank David Greenaway and Thomas Sewell for their advice on using AutoCorres and for their feedback on the paper. We also thank Jasmin Christian Blanchette for his feedback on the paper.

## References

1. Ahuja, R.K., Magnanti, T.L., Orlin, J.B.: Network Flows. Prentice-Hall (1993)
2. Alkassar, E., Böhme, S., Mehlhorn, K., Rizkallah, C.: A framework for the verification of certifying computations. JAR (2013), doi:10.1007/s10817-013-9289-2

3. Back, R.J.R.: Correctness preserving program refinements: Proof theory and applications. Mathematical Centre tracts. Mathematisch centrum (1980)
4. de Berg, M., Kreveld, M., Overmars, M., Schwarzkopf, O.: Computational Geometry: Algorithms and Applications. Springer (1997)
5. Bertot, Y., Castéran, P.: Interactive Theorem Proving and Program Development—Coq'Art: The Calculus of Inductive Constructions. Springer (2004)
6. Besson, F., Jensen, T., Pichardie, D., Turpin, T.: Certified result checking for polyhedral analysis of bytecode programs. In: Wirsing, M., Hofmann, M., Rauschmayer, A. (eds.) TGC 2010, LNCS, vol. 6084, pp. 253–267. Springer, Heidelberg (2010)
7. Blum, M., Kannan, S.: Designing programs that check their work. In: STOC, pp. 86–97 (1989)
8. Böhme, S., Leino, K.R.M., Wolff, B.: HOL-Boogie—An interactive prover for the Boogie program-verifier. In: Mohamed, O.A., Muñoz, C., Tahar, S. (eds.) TPHOLs 2008. LNCS, vol. 5170, pp. 150–166. Springer, Heidelberg (2008)
9. Bright, J.D., Sullivan, G.F., Masson, G.M.: A formally verified sorting certifier. IEEE Transactions on Computers 46(12), 1304–1312 (1997)
10. Charguéraud, A.: Characteristic formulae for the verification of imperative programs. In: ICFP, pp. 418–430 (2011)
11. Cock, D., Klein, G., Sewell, T.: Secure microkernels, state monads and scalable refinement. In: Mohamed, O.A., Muñoz, C., Tahar, S. (eds.) TPHOLs 2008. LNCS, vol. 5170, pp. 167–182. Springer, Heidelberg (2008)
12. Cohen, E., Dahlweid, M., Hillebrand, M., Leinenbach, D., Moskal, M., Santen, T., Schulte, W., Tobies, S.: VCC: A practical system for verifying concurrent C. In: Berghofer, S., Nipkow, T., Urban, C., Wenzel, M. (eds.) TPHOLs 2009. LNCS, vol. 5674, pp. 23–42. Springer, Heidelberg (2009)
13. Dijkstra, E.W.: Notes on structured programming. Technological University Eindhoven Netherlands (1970)
14. Gordon, M.J., Milner, A.J., Wadsworth, C.P.: Edinburgh LCF: A Mechanised Logic of Computation. LNCS, vol. 78. Springer, Heidelberg (1979)
15. Greenaway, D., Andronick, J., Klein, G.: Bridging the gap: Automatic verified abstraction of C. In: Beringer, L., Felty, A. (eds.) ITP 2012. LNCS, vol. 7406, pp. 99–115. Springer, Heidelberg (2012)
16. Greenaway, D., Lim, J., Andronick, J., Klein, G.: Don't sweat the small stuff: Formal verification of c code without the pain. In: PLDI (2014) (to appear)
17. Klein, G., Andronick, J., Elphinstone, K., Heiser, G., Cock, D., Derrin, P., Elkaduwe, D., Engelhardt, K., Kolanski, R., Norrish, M., Sewell, T., Tuch, H., Winwood, S.: seL4: Formal verification of an operating-system kernel. CACM 53(6), 107–115 (2010)
18. Leroy, X.: Formal verification of a realistic compiler. CACM 52(7), 107–115 (2009)
19. McConnell, R.M., Mehlhorn, K., Näher, S., Schweitzer, P.: Certifying algorithms. Computer Science Review 5(2), 119–161 (2011)
20. Mehlhorn, K., Näher, S.: From algorithms to working programs: On the use of program checking in LEDA. In: Brim, L., Gruska, J., Zlatuška, J. (eds.) MFCS 1998. LNCS, vol. 1450, pp. 84–93. Springer, Heidelberg (1998)
21. Mehlhorn, K., Näher, S.: The LEDA Platform for Combinatorial and Geometric Computing. Cambridge University Press (1999)
22. Mehta, F., Nipkow, T.: Proving pointer programs in higher-order logic. Information and Computation 199, 200–227 (2005)
23. Nipkow, T., Paulson, L.C., Wenzel, M.T.: Isabelle/HOL — A Proof Assistant for Higher-Order Logic. LNCS, vol. 2283. Springer, Heidelberg (2002)

24. Noschinski, L.: A graph library for Isabelle (2013),
    `http://www21.in.tum.de/~noschinl/documents/`
    `noschinski2013graphs.pdf` (submitted)
25. Schirmer, N.: Verification of sequential imperative programs in Isabelle/HOL. Ph.D. thesis,
    Technische Universität München (2006)
26. Sullivan, G.F., Masson, G.M.: Using certification trails to achieve software fault tolerance.
    In: FTCS, pp. 423–431 (1990)
27. Winwood, S., Klein, G., Sewell, T., Andronick, J., Cock, D., Norrish, M.: Mind the gap: A
    verification framework for low-level C. In: Berghofer, S., Nipkow, T., Urban, C., Wenzel, M.
    (eds.) TPHOLs 2009. LNCS, vol. 5674, pp. 500–515. Springer, Heidelberg (2009)
28. Wirth, N.: Program development by stepwise refinement. CACM 14(4), 221–227 (1971)

# Distinguishing Sequences for Partially Specified FSMs

Robert M. Hierons[1] and Uraz Cengiz Türker[2]

[1] School of Information Systems, Computing and Mathematics, Brunel University,
Uxbridge, Middlesex, UK
rob.hierons@brunel.ac.uk
[2] Sabancı Üniversitesi Orta Mahalle, Üniversite Caddesi No: 27, 34956
Tuzla-Istanbul, Turkey
urazc@sabanciuniv.edu

**Abstract.** Distinguishing Sequences (DSs) are used in many Finite State Machine (FSM) based test techniques. Although Partially Specified FSMs (PSFSMs) generalise FSMs, the computational complexity of constructing Adaptive and Preset DSs (ADSs/PDSs) for PSFSMs has not been addressed. This paper shows that it is possible to check the existence of an ADS in polynomial time but the corresponding problem for PDSs is PSPACE-complete. We also report on the results of experiments with benchmarks and over $8 * 10^6$ PSFSMs.

## 1 Introduction

Model Based Testing (MBT) techniques and tools use behavioural models and generally operate on either finite state machines (FSMs) or labelled transition systems (LTSs) that define the semantics of the underlying model. There has been significant interest in automating testing based on an FSM or LTS model in areas such as sequential circuits [1], lexical analysis [2], software design [3], communication protocols [3–12], object-oriented systems [13], and web services [14–17]. Such techniques have also been shown to be effective when used in significant industrial projects [18].

The literature contains many approaches that automatically generate test sequences from FSM models of systems [11, 19–26]. The reader may also refer to [8, 27, 28] for detailed surveys of such methods. These methods are based on *fault detection experiments* [29], a methodology in which an input sequence $\bar{x}$ is applied to the implementation under test (IUT) $N$ and the resultant output sequence is compared to that produced when $\bar{x}$ is applied to the specification $M$. The core principles of fault detection experiments were outlined by Moore [30], who introduced *Checking Experiments* and *Checking Sequences* (CEs, CSs). A CS is a single test case (input sequence) that is guaranteed to lead to a failure if the IUT is faulty, assuming that it has no more states than the specification. A CE is a set of test cases that has this guaranteed fault detection ability.

The literature contains many techniques that automatically generate checking sequences [3, 30–36]. Most approaches consist, in-principle, of three parts:

J.M. Badger and K.Y. Rozier (Eds.): NFM 2014, LNCS 8430, pp. 62–76, 2014.

*initialization*, *state identification*, and *transition verification*. The third part can be seen as identifying the starting and ending states of the transitions. Many techniques for constructing CSs use distinguishing sequences (DSs) to resolve the state identification problem. There are two reasons for the interest in DSs: there are polynomial time algorithms that generate CSs when there is a known DS and the length of the CS is relatively short when designed with a DS [31, 32, 37, 33, 34][1]. There are other approaches such as *Unique Input Output (UIO) sequences* or *Characterizing Sets (W-Set)* that can be used to identify the current state of the IUT. However, these lead to longer CSs [38]. A DS can be preset or adaptive: if the input sequence applied is fixed then the DS is a *Preset Distinguishing Sequence (PDS)* and otherwise, when the next input to be applied depends on the response to the previous input, it is an *Adaptive Distinguishing Sequence (ADS)*[2]. Throughout the paper we refer to PDS or ADS when we write DS.

## 1.1 Motivation and Problem Statement

It has been long known that in practice, FSM specifications are often partial meaning that some state-input combinations do not have corresponding transitions [40–43]. Such FSMs are called Partially Specified FSMs (PSFSMs). For PSFSMs the traditional state identification methodologies usually are not applicable [20, 44]. The FSM based testing literature usually applies the *Completeness Assumption* [45, 46], which states that the FSMs used are completely specified. This is justified by assuming that a PSFSM can be completed by, for example, adding transitions with null output.

Although it is sometimes possible to complete a PSFSM, as reported by Petrenko and Yevtushenko [44], this is far from being a solution to the general state identification problem for PSFSMs. For example, sometimes there being no transition from state $s$ with input $x$ corresponds to the situation in which $x$ should not be received in state $s$ and testing should respect such a restriction. This might be the case if the test cases are to be applied by a context that cannot supply the unspecified inputs [44]. It has been observed that it is possible to test the IUT via another FSM (tester FSM) such that the tester FSM may never execute the missing transitions, which partially bypasses the completeness assumption [47, 48]. Nevertheless, in the FSM based testing literature we know of only one paper [39] in which the CS generation problem is addressed for PSFSMs. Although the method proposed [39] introduces a polynomial time algorithm, the algorithm assumes that DSs are known in advance but does no report how one can derive DSs for the underlying PSFSM. As far as we are aware, no previous work has investigated the problem of generating a DS from a PSFSM.

These observations form the motivation for the work reported in this paper, which explores the complexity of deciding the existence of a DS for a given PSFSM. We examine the following problems.

---

[1] While the upper bound on PDS length is exponential, test generation takes polynomial time if there is a known PDS.

[2] ADSs are also called *Distinguishing Sets* [31, 39].

**Definition 1 (PDS-Existence Problem).** *Given a PSFSM M, is there a* PDS *for M?*

**Definition 2 (ADS-Existence Problem).** *Given a PSFSM M, is there an* ADS *for M?*

## 1.2 Practical Implications of Our Results and Future Directions

We show that it is possible to decide in polynomial time whether a PSFSM has an ADS. As a result of this, where a PSFSM has an ADS it is possible to generate a CS in polynomial time using a previously defined algorithm [39] and there is the potential to extend other technique for generating a CS from an FSM. This can all be achieved without making the Completeness Assumption, leading to test generation algorithms that can be applied where there being no transition from state $s$ with input $x$ corresponds to the situation in which $x$ should not be received in state $s$ and testing should respect such a restriction. This paper reports the results of initial experimental studies in which PSFSMs were randomly generated and it was found that relatively few of these PSFSMs had an ADS or a PDS. In contrast, we analysed a benchmark that has PSFSM specifications of digital circuits and found that where a PSFSM had a DS it was usually of a reasonable length.

The computational complexity results regarding PDSs are less positive. However, there may be scope to develop Greedy Algorithms for constructing PDSs for PSFSMs and we see this as an interesting research direction. While it might seem that ADSs are preferable to PDSs, there are benefits to using preset DSs. In particular, preset sequences can be applied using a simpler test infrastructure and sometimes there are timing constraints that make it difficult to apply adaptive tests since, for example, they can lead to the IUT timing out.

## 1.3 Summary of the Paper

Section 2 introduces terminology and notation that we use throughout the paper. Section 3 examines the computational complexity of checking the existence of PDSs and Section 4 considers the complexity of checking the existence of ADSs. Section 5 presents the results of experiments. Finally we conclude our discussion.

## 2 Preliminaries

A PSFSM $M$ is defined by tuple $(S, X, Y, \delta, \lambda, D)$ where $S = \{s_1, s_2 \ldots s_n\}$ is the finite set of states, $X = \{a, b, \ldots, p\}$ and $Y = \{1, 2, \ldots, q\}$ are finite sets of inputs and outputs, $D \subseteq S \times X$ is the domain, $\delta : D \to S$ is the transition function, and $\lambda : D \to Y$ is the output function. If $(s, x) \in D$ then $x$ is *defined* at $s$. Given input sequence $\bar{x} = x_1 x_2 \ldots x_k$ and $s \in S$, $\bar{x}$ *is defined at* $s$ if there exist $s_1, s_2, \ldots s_{k+1} \in S$ such that $s = s_1$ and for all $1 \leq i \leq k$, $x_i$ is defined at $s_i$ and $\delta(s_i, x_i) = s_{i+1}$. $M$ is *completely specified* if $D = S \times X$ and otherwise is *partially specified.* If $(s, x) \in D$ and $x$ is applied when $M$ is in state $s$, $M$ moves to state $s' = \delta(s, x)$ and produces output $y = \lambda(s, x)$. This defines *transition* $\tau = (s, x/y, s')$ and we say that $x/y$ is the *label* of $\tau$, $s$ is the *start state* of $\tau$, and $s'$ is the *end state* of $\tau$.

We use juxtaposition to denote concatenation. The transition and output functions can be extended to input sequences as follows in which $\epsilon$ is the empty sequence, $x \in X$, $\bar{x} \in X^*$, and $x\bar{x}$ is defined at $s$: $\delta(s, \epsilon) = s$ and $\delta(x\bar{x}) = \delta(\delta(s, x), \bar{x})$; $\lambda(s, \epsilon) = \epsilon$ and $\lambda(s, x\bar{x}) = \lambda(s, x)\lambda(\delta(s, x), \bar{x})$. If there exists $\bar{x} \in X^*$ defined in $s$ and $s'$ such that $\lambda(s, \bar{x}) \neq \lambda(s', \bar{x})$, then $\bar{x}$ *distinguishes* $s$ and $s'$. We now define *Preset DSs* and *Adaptive DSs*.

**Definition 3.** *Given PSFSM $M$, $\bar{x} \in X^*$ is a Preset Distinguishing Sequence for $M$ if all distinct states of $M$ are distinguished by $\bar{x}$.*

**Definition 4.** *Given PSFSM $M = (S, X, Y, \delta, \lambda, D)$, an Adaptive Distinguishing Sequence is a rooted tree $\mathcal{A}$ such that the following hold. Each node is labeled by a set of states and the root is labeled by $S$. Each leaf of $\mathcal{A}$ is labeled by a singleton set. Each edge is labeled by an input/output pair.*

*Let us suppose that node $v$ has state set $S'$. If $v$ has one or more outgoing edges then these edges are labeled by the same input $x$, $x$ is defined in all states in $S'$, and if there exists $s \in S'$ such that $\lambda(s, x) = y$ then there is a unique edge $(v, x/y, v')$ such that $v'$ is labeled with the set $S'' = \{s'' \in S | \exists s' \in S'.\lambda(s', x) = y \wedge \delta(s', x) = s''\}$ of states reached from $S'$ by a transition with label $x/y$.*

*If $v$ has state set $S' \subseteq S$ and has one or more outgoing edges then the input $x$ on these edges satisfies the following property: for all $s, s' \in S'$ with $s \neq s'$ we have that either $\lambda(s, x) \neq \lambda(s', x)$ or $\delta(s, x) \neq \delta(s', x)$.*

An ADS defines an experiment ending in a leaf. From the last condition, two states cannot be mapped to the same state unless they have already been distinguished. Applying $\mathcal{A}$ in $s \in S$ leads to the input/output sequence that labels both a path from the root of $\mathcal{A}$ to a leaf and a path of $M$ with start state $s$. From the definition, the input/output sequences for distinct states differ and so $\mathcal{A}$ distinguishes the states of $M$.

## 3  Preset Distinguishing Sequences

The following immediately follows from the PSPACE hardness of PDS existence problem for completely specified FSMs [34].

**Lemma 1.** *The problem of deciding whether a PSFSM has a PDS is PSPACE-hard.*

We now give an upper bound for the length of a minimal PDS to use in the proof that the PDS existence problem is in PSPACE, adapting the approach for FSMs [49]. Throughout the following $S$, $\bar{S}$ are sets of states. Sequence $\bar{x} \in X^*$ *splits* $\bar{S}$ if it distinguishes two or more states of $\bar{S}$ and for all distinct $s, s' \in \bar{S}$, $\delta(s, \bar{x}) = \delta(s', \bar{x}) \Rightarrow \lambda(s, \bar{x}) \neq \lambda(s', \bar{x})$. We let $n = |S|$, $m = |\bar{S}|$ and $\nu = |\bar{x}|$. We write $\bar{x}^i$ to denote the $i^{th}$ input of $\bar{x}$ and $pre_i(\bar{x})$ to denote the prefix of length $i$.

We also write $\delta(s, pre_i(\bar{x}))$ to denote the state reached when we apply $pre_i(\bar{x})$ at $s$ and by abusing notation we write $\delta(\bar{S}, pre_i(\bar{x})) =< \delta(s, pre_i(\bar{x}))|s \in \bar{S} >$ to denote a vector of states called a *state configuration*.

A minimal PDS $\bar{x}$ is of the form $\bar{x}_1\bar{x}_2 \ldots \bar{x}_p$ where the partition on $S$ induced by prefixes of $\bar{x}$ changes (becomes more refined) on the last inputs of the $\bar{x}_k$. In the worst case, prefix $\bar{x}_1\bar{x}_2 \ldots \bar{x}_k$ distinguishes $k$ states from all others and so at the end of this either the start state is known or we have a set $\bar{S}$ of $n - k$ states that are possible 'current states'. This is the worst case because it maximises the size of $\bar{S}$. Consider $\bar{x}_k$ and $\bar{S}$. When reasoning about the application of $\bar{x}_k$ from $\bar{S}$ we can can refer to the set of states reached from $\bar{S}$ by a prefix $\bar{x}_k^i$. This leads to a data structure, that we call an *input-state configuration*, that combines the prefix $\bar{x}_k^i$ with the state information and is represented by $< \bar{x}_k^i.\delta(\bar{S}, pre_i(\bar{x}_k)) >$. Then the application of $\bar{x}_k$ in $\bar{S}$ defines a sequence $< \bar{x}_k^1.\delta(\bar{S}, pre_1(\bar{x}_k)) > < \bar{x}_k^2.\delta(\bar{S}, pre_2(\bar{x}_k)) > \cdots < \bar{x}_k^\nu.\delta(\bar{S}, pre_\nu(\bar{x}_k)) >$ of configurations. If $< \bar{x}_k^j.\delta(\bar{S}, pre_j(\bar{x}_k)) >=< \bar{x}_k^i.\delta(\bar{S}, pre_i(\bar{x}_k)) >$ for $j < i$ then $\bar{x}_k' =< \bar{x}_k^1.\delta(\bar{S}, pre_1(\bar{x}_k)) > \cdots < \bar{x}_k^j.\delta(\bar{S}, pre_j(\bar{x}_k)) > < \bar{x}_k^{i+1}.\delta(\bar{S}, pre_{i+1}(\bar{x}_k)) > \cdots < \bar{x}_k^\nu.\delta(\bar{S}, pre_\nu(\bar{x}_k)) >$ can replace $\bar{x}_k$ in $\bar{x}$. Thus, if $\bar{x}$ is minimal then the configurations obtained by applying $\bar{x}_k$ to $\bar{S}$ have no repetitions. The maximum number of state configurations reached from $\bar{S}$ is $C\binom{n}{m}$. Thus, since $m = |\bar{S}|$ changes from 2 to $n$, the length of the minimal PDS is bounded above by $\ell = \sum_{i=2}^{i=n} C\binom{n}{i} < 2^n$.

**Lemma 2.** *One can check if PSFSM M has a PDS using polynomial space.*

*Proof.* We show that a non-deterministic Turing Machine (TM) $\mathcal{T}$ can solve the problem using polynomial space. $\mathcal{T}$ guesses one input at a time, maintaining a set $\pi$ of pairs of states such that $(s, s') \in \pi$ if and only if the current input sequence $\bar{x}$ takes $s \in S$ to $s'$. $\mathcal{T}$ also maintains equivalence relation $r$ such that $(s, s') \in r$ if and only if $s$ and $s'$ are not distinguished by $\bar{x}$. When $\mathcal{T}$ guesses an input it updates $\pi$ and $r$. The input sequence received defines a PDS if no two different states are related under $r$. Thus, $\mathcal{T}$ can generate a PDS from a PSFSM $M$ that has a PDS and requires polynomial space.

Now consider the case where there is no PDS for $M$ and we have to guarantee that $\mathcal{T}$ terminates with failure. In order to achieve this goal, $\mathcal{T}$ will use an extra $log_2(\ell) = n$ bits of space as a counter. It increments the counter each time it guesses an input and before each guess $\mathcal{T}$ checks this counter to see whether it has reached the upper bound. $\mathcal{T}$ terminates with failure if the states have not been distinguished (determined by examining $r$) and the counter reaches the upper bound value $\ell$. Thus the problem can be solved in polynomial space by a non-deterministic TM. The result follows from non-deterministic PSPACE being equal to PSPACE [50]. ∎

Using Lemmas 1 and 2 we have the following result.

**Theorem 1.** *The problem of deciding whether a PSFSM has a PDS is* PSPACE-complete.

## 4    Adaptive Distinguishing Sequences

Let us assume that we have been given a PSFSM $M$ and that we wish to decide whether it has an ADS and, if it does, generate such an ADS. We will show how given $M$ we can construct a completely specified FSM $\mathcal{M}(M)$ such that there is a suitable correspondence between ADSs for $M$ and $\mathcal{M}(M)$. Given $M = (S', X', Y', \delta, \lambda, D)$ we will define $\mathcal{M}(M) = (Q, X, Y, \delta_Q, \lambda_Q)$ as follows.

We take two copies $M_1 = (S^1, X', Y', \delta, \lambda, D^1)$, $M_2 = (S^2, X', Y', \delta, \lambda, D^2)$ of $M$, we give the states superscripts to distinguish between states of $M_1$ and $M_2$ and so if $s$ is a state of $M$ then the corresponding states of $M_1$ and $M_2$ are $s^1$ and $s^2$ respectively. The state set of $\mathcal{M}(M)$ is $S = S^1 \cup S^2$. We add a new input $d$ and new outputs $y, y_1, y_2$ and so the set of input symbols of $\mathcal{M}(M)$ is $X = X' \cup \{d\}$ and the set of output symbols is $Y = Y' \cup \{y, y_1, y_2\}$. We let $s_0$ denote some fixed state from $S^2$: the choice of state does not affect the proof. The transition function $\delta_Q$ of $\mathcal{M}(M)$ is defined as follows:

$$
\delta_Q(s, x) = \begin{cases} s_b^1, & s = s_a^1, x \text{ is specified at } s_a \wedge \delta(s_a, x) = s_b, \\ s_b^2, & s = s_a^2, x \text{ is specified at } s_a \wedge \delta(s_a, x) = s_b, \\ s_0, & x \text{ is not specified at } s, \\ s_0, & x = d \end{cases}
$$

The output function $\lambda_Q$ of $\mathcal{M}(M)$ is defined as follows in which $i \in \{1, 2\}$,

$$
\lambda_Q(s^i, x) = \begin{cases} \lambda(s, x), & \text{If } x \text{ is specified at } s, \\ y, & x \text{ is not specified at } s \text{ and } x \neq d, \\ y_1, & x \text{ is not specified at } s \wedge x = d \wedge i = 1, \\ y_2, & x \text{ is not specified at } s \wedge x = d \wedge i = 2, \end{cases}
$$

It is clear that $\mathcal{M}(M)$ is completely specified. The construction also ensures that we cannot distinguish states $s^1$ and $s^2$ without using input $d$. It also ensures that in forming an ADS we cannot apply $d$ in a node whose current set of states contains states $s_i^k$ and $s_j^k$ in which $i \neq j$: the application of $d$ would map these to state $s_0$ with common output $y_k$. Further, until $d$ has been applied, for every state $s$ we have that $s^1$ and $s^2$ are in the same block (have yet to be distinguished) and so an ADS cannot apply an input that is not specified in $s$; such an input takes $s^1$ and $s^2$ to the same state with common output $y$.

Recall that each node of an ADS has an associated set of states, which is the set of possible states given the observed input/output sequence that labels the path from the root of the ADS to this node. We will say that an ADS $\mathcal{A}$ is *non-redundant* if the only nodes of $\mathcal{A}$ that have singleton sets are the leaves of $\mathcal{A}$. If this property does not hold then the use of $\mathcal{A}$ in a state $s$ can lead to the application of input in the situations in which $s$ has already been distinguished from the other states of $M$ (the current state set is a singleton); such an ADS can be replaced by a non-redundant ADS. We will now prove that we have the required correspondence between non-redundant ADSs for $M$ and $\mathcal{M}(M)$. We demonstrate the construction in Figure 3.

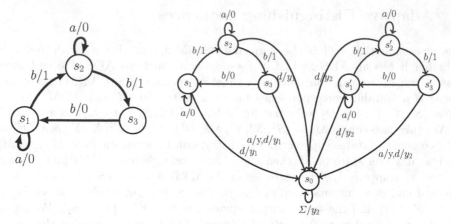

**Fig. 1.** PSFSM $M_1$

**Fig. 2.** Completely specified FSM $\mathcal{M}(M)$ constructed from PSFSM $M_1$ given in Figure 1

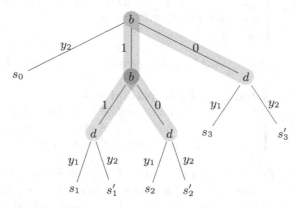

**Fig. 3.** ADS constructed for $\mathcal{M}(M)$ given in Figure 2. Highlighted tree is an ADS for PSFSM $M_1$ given in Figure 1

Let $\mathcal{A}d$ denote the ADS $\mathcal{A}'$ that applies input $d$ when a leaf of $\mathcal{A}$ has been reached. Then, clearly, if a given PSFSM $M$ has an ADS $\mathcal{A}$, then $\mathcal{A}d$ is an ADS for $\mathcal{M}(M)$. Formally;

**Lemma 3.** *If $\mathcal{A}$ is an ADS for the PSFSM $M$ then $\mathcal{A}d$ is an ADS for $\mathcal{M}(M)$.*

On the other hand if, there exist an ADS $\mathcal{A}$ for $\mathcal{M}(M)$ then the machine $M$ has an ADS.

**Lemma 4.** *Given PSFSM $M$, if $\mathcal{A}$ is a non-redundant ADS for $\mathcal{M}(M)$ then $\mathcal{A} = \mathcal{A}'d$ for some ADS $\mathcal{A}'$ for $M$.*

*Proof.* First observe that since $\mathcal{A}$ is an ADS for $\mathcal{M}(M)$, for each state $s$ of $M$ the application of $\mathcal{A}$ in $s^1$ and $s^2$ must lead to $d$ being applied; otherwise $\mathcal{A}$ does not distinguish $s^1$ and $s^2$. Further, $d$ maps all states to $s_0$ and so a non-redundant ADS does not apply any further input after $d$. Thus, there exists some $\mathcal{A}'$ such that $\mathcal{A} = \mathcal{A}'d$ and $\mathcal{A}'$ does not contain input $d$.

Let us suppose that the input of $\mathcal{A}'$ in state $s^k$ ($1 \leq k \leq 2$) leads to the sequence $(s_1^k, x_1/y_1, s_2^k) \ldots (s_m^k, x_m/y_m, s_{m+1}^k)$ of transitions. Then we must have $(s_1, x_1/y_1, s_2), \ldots, (s_m, x_m/y_m, s_{m+1})$ are transitions of $M$ since otherwise $\mathcal{A}$ would not distinguish between $s^1$ and $s^2$; some input $x_i$ would be applied in a state $s_i^k$ such that $x_i$ is not specified in $s_i$ and so $s^1$ and $s^2$ would be mapped to the same state before $d$ is applied. Thus, the application of $\mathcal{A}'$ in a state $s$ of $M$ leads to a sequence of inputs begin applied in states where they are specified. Now consider states $s_i$ and $s_j$ of $M$. Since $\mathcal{A}$ distinguishes between $s_i^1$ and $s_j^1$ we must have that $\mathcal{A}'$ distinguishes $s_i^1$ and $s_j^1$. Since the application of $\mathcal{A}'$ in a state $s$ of $M$ does not lead to an input begin applied in a state where it is not specified, we have that the output produced by applying $\mathcal{A}'$ in state $s$ of $M$ is the same as the output produced by applying $\mathcal{A}'$ in state $s^1$ of $\mathcal{M}(M)$. Thus, since $\mathcal{A}'$ distinguishes states $s_i^1$ and $s_j^1$ of $\mathcal{M}(M)$ we have that $\mathcal{A}'$ distinguishes states $s_i$ and $s_j$ of $M$. Since this holds for all $s_i, s_j \in S$ with $s_i \neq s_j$ we have that $\mathcal{A}'$ is an ADS for $M$ as required.

**Theorem 2.** *Given an incomplete FSM $M$ with $n$ states and $p$ inputs, it is possible to decide in time $O(pn \log n)$ whether $M$ has an ADS and, if it does, it is possible to construct such an ADS in $O(pn^2)$ time.*

*Proof.* By Lemmas 3 and 4 we know that $M$ has an ADS if and only if $\mathcal{M}(M)$ has an ADS. Thus, the first part of the result follows from it being possible to decide in $O(pn \log n)$ whether $\mathcal{M}(M)$ has an ADS [34]. The second part of the result follows from there being an $O(pn^2)$ algorithm that will generate an ADS for $\mathcal{M}(M)$ if it has such an ADS [34].

It is known that if a completely specified FSM $M$ has an ADS then it has one of length at most $\frac{\pi^2 n^2}{12}$. Thus, given a partially specified FSM $M$ with $n$ states we have that if $\mathcal{M}(M)$ has an ADS then it has an ADS of depth at most $\frac{\pi^2 n^2}{3}$ since $\mathcal{M}(M)$ has $2n$ states. Since the last input of a non-redundant ADS $\mu$ for $\mathcal{M}(M)$ is $d$, and this can be removed when constructing the ADS for $M$ from $\mu$, we can conclude that if $M$ has an ADS then it has an ADS of depth at most $\frac{\pi^2 n^2}{3} - 1$. However, whether this is a tight bound is an open problem.

# 5   Experimental Results

This section describes the results of experiments using $8 * 10^6$ randomly generated PSFSMs and PSFSMs of digital circuits from a benchmark. We found that PSFSM specifications usually have DSs of a reasonable length, when they exist.

## 5.1  PSFSM Generation

To construct a PSFSM with $n$ states, $p$ inputs and $q$ outputs, we first randomly generated a minimal, strongly connected, completely specified FSM using the tool utilised in [37, 51]. In this process we randomly assigned the values of $\delta(s, x)$ and $\lambda(s, x)$ for each state $s$ and input $x$. We then checked whether the machine $M$ was strongly connected, minimal, and had an ADS[3]. If the FSM failed one or more of these tests then we omitted this FSM and produced another.

Having constructed an FSM $M$, we randomly selected an integer $K$ between $n$ and $n * p$. Afterwards, we randomly selected $K$ state-input pairs. For each pair $(s, x)$ we erased the transition of $M$ whose start state is $s$ and input label is $x$. If deleting a transition disconnected the FSM then we did not delete this transition and guessed another state input pair.

By following this scheme we formed four classes of PSFSMs where each class had $2 * 10^6$ PSFSMs. The sizes of the input/output alphabets and the state sets were $(2/2, 9)$, $(2/2, 17)$, $(3/3, 9)$, and $(3/3, 17)$ respectively. To carry out these experiments we used an Intel Xeon E5-1650 @3.2-GHZ CPU with 16 GB RAM.

## 5.2  Results

In Table 1, we show how many PSFMSs had an ADS/PDS and the average time taken to compute an ADS/PDS for a given PSFSM. In the third column we see the number of PSFSMs that had an ADS and in the fourth column we see the number of PSFSMs that had a PDS.

Comparing the first and the third or the second and the fourth rows of the third column, we can see that the number of PSFSMs that have an ADS appears to increase with the size of the input and output alphabets. The results in the first and the second or the third and the fourth rows of the third column suggest that as the number of states increases the number of PSFSMs that have an ADS reduces. The number of PSFSMs that possess an ADS is larger than the

**Table 1.** Number of PSFSMs that have ADS/PDS. $|S|$, $|\Sigma|$, $|\mathcal{Q}|$, ADS, PDS, $T_{ADS}$ and $T_{PDS}$ are the number of states, the cardinality of the input/output alphabets, the number of PSFSMs, the number of PSFSMs that have an ADS, the number of PSFSMs that have a PDS, the average time to compute an ADS and the average time to compute a PDS respectively.

| | $|S|$ | $|\mathcal{Q}|$ | ADS | PDS | $T_{ADS}$ (msec) | $T_{PDS}$ (msec) |
|---|---|---|---|---|---|---|
| $|\Sigma| = 2$ | | | | | | |
| | 9 | $2 * 10^6$ | 120.575 (6.02%) | 16.365 (0.81%) | 0.006 | 0.097 |
| | 17 | $2 * 10^6$ | 40.368 (2.01%) | 26.784 (1.33%) | 0.012 | 0.106 |
| $|\Sigma| = 3$ | | | | | | |
| | 9 | $2 * 10^6$ | 415.101 (20.75%) | 23.561 (1.17%) | 0.008 | 0.113 |
| | 17 | $2 * 10^6$ | 113.023 (5.65%) | 33.590 (1.67%) | 0.017 | 0.121 |

---

[3] We used the LY-Algorithm from [34].

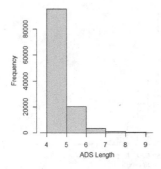

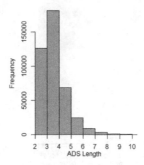

**Fig. 4.** ADS lengths and frequencies of 120575 PSFSMs where $|S| = 9, |\Sigma| = 2$

**Fig. 5.** ADS lengths and frequencies of 415101 PSFSMs where $|S| = 9, |\Sigma| = 3$

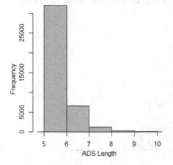

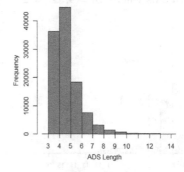

**Fig. 6.** ADS lengths and frequencies of 40368 PSFSMs where $|S| = 17, |\Sigma| = 2$

**Fig. 7.** ADS lengths and frequencies of 113023 PSFSMs where $|S| = 17, |\Sigma| = 3$

number with a PDS, which is to be expected since a PDS defines an ADS but the converse is not the case. These results are just as expected since it is well known that the ratio of the number of states to the number of outputs affects the distinguishablity of the states [29]. When we compare the timings we see that, on average, the PDS computation takes longer. But this is expected since for a given PSFSM a brute–force algorithm is used to find a PDS. Moreover, Figures 4, 5, 6, and 7 show that the average length of PDSs is longer than the average for ADSs.

Consider now the depths of the ADSs shown in Figures 4, 5, 6 and 7. Here we find that most ADSs have depth close to the lower bound formula $log_q|S|$, where $q$ is the size of the output alphabet. Moreover, comparing Figures 4 with 6 and 5 with 11, we see that the depths of the ADSs increases with the number of states. Figures 4-5 and 6-7 reveal that depths seem to decrease as the number of inputs and outputs increase.

The lengths of the PDSs are presented in Figures 8, 9, 10 and 11. Interestingly, although there is no polynomial upper bound on PDS length, these PSFSMs are relatively short. In fact, most of the lengths are lower than $|S|$ and the results are similar to those for ADSs. However, fewer PSFSMs had a PDS than had an ADS.

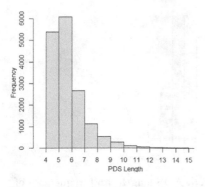

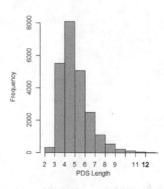

**Fig. 8.** PDS length distribution of 16365 PSFSMs where $|S| = 9$, $|\Sigma| = 2$

**Fig. 9.** PDS length distribution of 23561 PSFSMs where $|S| = 9$, $|\Sigma| = 3$

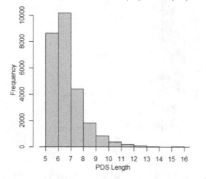

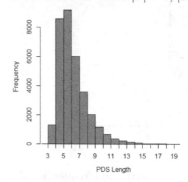

**Fig. 10.** PDS length distribution of 26784 PSFSMs where $|S| = 17$, $|\Sigma| = 2$

**Fig. 11.** PDS length distribution of 33590 PSFSMs where $|S| = 17$, $|\Sigma| = 3$

In the experiments only a relatively small percentage of PSFSMs had DSs. This can be explained by the high number of transitions left undefined; at least one per state on average and up to one per state/input pair. Observe that a PSFSM $M$ is guaranteed not to have a DS if for every input $x$ we have that $M$ has a state $s$ from which there is no transition with input $x$. The choices made in the experiments made it extremely likely that a randomly generated PSFSM $M$ had this property. It is unclear what proportion of transitions are typically unspecified in practice, a factor that is likely to significantly influence how many PSFSMs have DSs, and so we explored a set of benchmark PSFSMs.

## 5.3   Benchmark Dataset

We considered the ACM/SIGDA benchmarks. This benchmark has 59 FSM specifications, representing circuits, obtained from industry [52]. The FSM specifications are presented in kiss2 format where "don't care" inputs are specified as $-$. We converted the kiss2 format to our FSM specification format. The analysis revealed that 25.42% of the specifications have partial transitions and so we

determined how many of these PSFSMs had DSs. For each PSFSM we applied
the adapted LY algorithm and found that 20% of the PSFSMs had ADSs. We
also executed the brute–force algorithm presented in [29] to compute the PDSs of
the PSFSMs and found that all PSFSMs with ADSs also had PDSs. In Table 2
we present the size of the PSFSMs and the length of the ADSs/PDSs and the
time required to compute ADSs/PDSs. As with the randomly generated FSMs,
DS computation took very little time but took longer for PDSs than ADSs.
Scalability to larger FSMs is a topic for future work.

**Table 2.** Average lengths and computation times of ADSs and PDSs

| Name | ADS-PDS lengths | $|S|$ | $|X|$ | $T_{ADS}$ (msec) | $T_{PDS}$ (msec) |
|------|-----------------|-------|-------|------------------|------------------|
| ex1  | 3-4             | 20    | $2^9$ | 0.103            | 0.730            |
| ex4  | 3-7             | 14    | $2^6$ | 0.073            | 0.188            |
| ex6  | 4-6             | 8     | $2^5$ | 0.019            | 0.124            |
| opus | 3-7             | 10    | $2^5$ | 0.014            | 0.127            |

These results are important and justify our initial claims. Without applying a completeness assumption to the PSFSMs in the benchmark (if such an
assumption is applicable for these PSFSMs), one can compute ADSs and use
a checking sequence generation algorithm similar to that in [39] to construct
polynomial length checking sequences for the PSFSMs in the benchmark.

# 6    Conclusions

In this paper we addressed the state identification problem for partially specified
deterministic finite state machines (PSFSMs). Specifically, we considered adaptive and preset distinguishing sequences (ADS/PDS) motivated by the fact that
a checking experiment can be constructed in polynomial time if we have a PDS
or ADS. We determined the complexity of checking the existence of ADSs and
PDSs for PSFSMs: it is polynomial time solvable to test if a PSFSM possesses
an ADS and it is PSPACE-complete in the case of PDSs. The results of experiments suggest that ADSs and PDSs are relatively short where they exist. This
suggests that where DSs exist they can form the basis for generating checking
sequences of reasonable size.

We showed that the depth of an ADS is bounded above by $\frac{\pi^2 n^2}{3} - 1$ for
PSFSMs. As we do not know whether the bound on ADS depth is tight, it
would be interesting to find a tight bound on ADSs length. The PDS problem is
PSPACE-complete and so it would also be interesting to explore heuristics, such as
Greedy algorithms, for this problem. Finally, there is a need to run experiments
with more PSFSMs representing real specifications in order to further explore
how often there are DSs and how long these tend to be.

# References

1. Friedman, A.D., Menon, P.R.: Fault detection in digital circuits. Computer Applications in Electrical Engineering Series (1971)
2. Aho, A.V., Sethi, R., Ullman, J.D.: Compilers, principles, techniques, and tools. Addison-Wesley series in computer science
3. Chow, T.S.: Testing software design modelled by finite state machines. IEEE Transactions on Software Engineering 4, 178–187 (1978)
4. Holzmann, G.J.: Design and validation of computer protocols. Prentice-Hall software series
5. Brinksma, E.: A theory for the derivation of tests. In: Proceedings of Protocol Specification, Testing, and Verification VIII, pp. 63–74. North-Holland, Atlantic City (1988)
6. Dahbura, A.T., Sabnani, K.K., Uyar, M.U.: Formal methods for generating protocol conformance test sequences. Proceedings of the IEEE 78(8), 1317–1326 (August)
7. Lee, D., Sabnani, K.K., Kristol, D.M., Paul, S.: Conformance testing of protocols specified as communicating finite state machines-a guided random walk based approach. IEEE Transactions on Communications 44(5), 631–640 (May)
8. Lee, D., Yannakakis, M.: Principles and methods of testing finite-state machines - a survey. Proceedings of the IEEE 84(8), 1089–1123 (1996)
9. Low, S.H.: Probabilistic conformance testing of protocols with unobservable transitions. In: Proceedings of the 1993 International Conference on Network Protocols, pp. 368–375 (October 1993)
10. Mihail, M., Papadimitriou, C.H.: On the random walk method for protocol testing. In: Dill, D.L. (ed.) CAV 1994. LNCS, vol. 818, pp. 132–141. Springer, Heidelberg (1994)
11. Sabnani, K., Dahbura, A.: A protocol test generation procedure. Computer Networks 15(4), 285–297 (1988)
12. Sidhu, D.P., Leung, T.-K.: Formal methods for protocol testing: A detailed study. IEEE Transactions on Software Engineering 15(4), 413–426 (1989)
13. Binder, R.V.: Testing Object-Oriented Systems: Models, Patterns, and Tools. Addison-Wesley (1999)
14. Haydar, M., Petrenko, A., Sahraoui, H.A.: Formal verification of web applications modeled by communicating automata. In: de Frutos-Escrig, D., Núñez, M. (eds.) FORTE 2004. LNCS, vol. 3235, pp. 115–132. Springer, Heidelberg (2004)
15. Betin-Can, A., Bultan, T.: Verifiable concurrent programming using concurrency controllers. In: Proceedings of the 19th IEEE International Conference on Automated Software Engineering, pp. 248–257. IEEE Computer Society (2004)
16. Pomeranz, I., Reddy, S.M.: Test generation for multiple state-table faults in finite-state machines. IEEE Transactions on Computers 46(7), 783–794 (1997)
17. Utting, M., Pretschner, A., Legeard, B.: A taxonomy of model-based testing approaches. Software Testing, Verification and Reliability 22(5), 297–312 (2012)
18. Grieskamp, W., Kicillof, N., Stobie, K., Braberman, V.A.: Model-based quality assurance of protocol documentation: Tools and methodology. Software Testing, Verification and Reliability 21(1), 55–71 (2011)
19. Aho, A.V., Dahbura, A.T., Lee, D., Uyar, M.U.: An optimization technique for protocol conformance test generation based on UIO sequences and rural chinese postman tours. In: Protocol Specification, Testing, and Verification VIII, Atlantic City, pp. 75–86. Elsevier, North-Holland (1988)

20. Hennie, F.C.: Fault-detecting experiments for sequential circuits. In: Proceedings of Fifth Annual Symposium on Switching Circuit Theory and Logical Design, pp. 95–110. Princeton, New Jersey (November 1964)
21. Gonenc, G.: A method for the design of fault detection experiments. IEEE Transactions on Computers 19, 551–558 (1970)
22. Vasilevskii, M.P.: Failure diagnosis of automata. Cybernetics and Systems Analysis 9, 653–665
23. Vuong, S.T., Chan, W.W.L., Ito, M.R.: The UIOv-method for protocol test sequence generation. In: The 2nd International Workshop on Protocol Test Systems, Berlin (1989)
24. Fujiwara, S., von Bochmann, G., Khendek, F., Amalou, M., Ghedamsi, A.: Test selection based on finite state models. IEEE Transactions on Software Engineering 17(6), 591–603 (1991)
25. Ural, H., Zhu, K.: Optimal length test sequence generation using distinguishing sequences. IEEE/ACM Transactions on Networking 1(3), 358–371 (1993)
26. Petrenko, A., Yevtushenko, N.: Testing from partial deterministic FSM specifications. IEEE Transactions on Computers 54(9), 1154–1165 (2005)
27. von Bochmann, G., Petrenko, A.: Protocol testing: Review of methods and relevance for software testing. In: ACM International Symposium on Software Testing and Analysis, Seattle USA, pp. 109–123 (1994)
28. Lai, R.: A survey of communication protocol testing. Journal of Systems and Software 62(1), 21–46 (2002)
29. Kohavi, Z.: Switching and Finite State Automata Theory. McGraw-Hill, New York (1978)
30. Moore, E.P.: Gedanken-experiments. In: Shannon, C., McCarthy, J. (eds.) Automata Studies. Princeton University Press (1956)
31. Boute, R.T.: Distinguishing sets for optimal state identification in checking experiments. IEEE Trans. Comput. 23, 874–877 (1974)
32. Hierons, R.M., Ural, H.: Optimizing the length of checking sequences. IEEE Trans. Comput. 55, 618–629 (2006)
33. Jourdan, G.-V., Ural, H., Yenigun, H., Zhang, J.: Lower bounds on lengths of checking sequences. Formal Aspects of Computing 22(6), 667–679 (2010)
34. Lee, D., Yannakakis, M.: Testing finite-state machines: State identification and verification. IEEE Trans. on Computers 43(3), 306–320 (1994)
35. da Silva Simão, A., Petrenko, A.: Checking completeness of tests for finite state machines. IEEE Transactions on Computers 59(8), 1023–1032 (2010)
36. da Silva Simão, A., Petrenko, A., Yevtushenko, N.: On reducing test length for FSMs with extra states. Software Testing, Verification and Reliability 22(6), 435–454 (2012)
37. Hierons, R.M., Jourdan, G.-V., Ural, H., Yenigun, H.: Checking sequence construction using adaptive and preset distinguishing sequences. In: SEFM, pp. 157–166 (2009)
38. Ural, H.: Formal methods for test sequence generation. Computer Communications 15(5), 311–325 (1992)
39. da Silva Simão, A., Petrenko, A.: Generating checking sequences for partial reduced finite state machines. Testing of Software and Communicating Systems, 153–168 (2008)
40. Tsai, P.-C., Wang, S.-J., Chang, F.-M.: FSM-based programmable memory bist with macro command. In: 2005 IEEE International Workshop on Memory Technology, Design, and Testing, MTDT 2005, pp. 72–77 (August 2005)

41. Zarrineh, K., Upadhyaya, S.J.: Programmable memory bist and a new synthesis framework. In: Twenty-Ninth Annual International Symposium on Fault-Tolerant Computing. Digest of Papers, pp. 352–355 (June 1999)
42. Xie, L., Wei, J., Zhu, G.: An improved FSM-based method for BGP protocol conformance testing. In: International Conference on Communications, Circuits and Systems, pp. 557–561 (2008)
43. Drumea, A., Popescu, C.: Finite state machines and their applications in software for industrial control. In: 27th Int. Spring Seminar on Electronics Technology: Meeting the Challenges of Electronics Technology Progress, vol. 1, pp. 25–29 (2004)
44. Petrenko, A., Yevtushenko, N.: Testing from partial deterministic FSM specifications. IEEE Transactions on Computers 54(9), 1154–1165 (2005)
45. Yannakakis, M., Lee, D.: Testing finite state machines: Fault detection. Journal of Computer and System Sciences 50(2), 209–227 (1995)
46. Yevtushenko, N., Petrenko, A.: Synthesis of test experiments in some classes of automata. Automatic Control and Computer Sciences 4 (1990)
47. Gill, A.: Introduction to The Theory of Finite State Machines. McGraw-Hill, New York (1962)
48. Rho, J.-K., Hachtel, G., Somenzi, F.: Don't care sequences and the optimization of interacting finite state machines. In: IEEE International Conference on Computer-Aided Design, ICCAD 1991. Digest of Technical Papers, pp. 418–421 (November 1991)
49. Sokolovskii, M.N.: Diagnostic experiments with automata. Kibernetica (6), 44–49 (1971)
50. Savitch, W.J.: Relationships between nondeterministic and deterministic tape complexities. Journal of Computer and System Sciences 4(2), 177–192 (1970)
51. Güniçen, C., Türker, U.C., Ural, H., Yenigün, H.: Generating preset distinguishing sequences using sat. In: Computer and Information Sciences II, pp. 487–493. Springer (2012)
52. Brglez, F.: ACM/SIGMOD benchmark dataset, http://cbl.ncsu.edu:16080/benchmarks/Benchmarks-upto-1996.html

# On Proving Recoverability
# of Smart Electrical Grids

Seppo Horsmanheimo[1], Maryam Kamali[2], Mikko Kolehmainen[3],
Mats Neovius[2], Luigia Petre[2], Mauno Rönkkö[3], and Petter Sandvik[2,4]

[1] VTT Technical Research Centre of Finland
[2] Åbo Akademi University
[3] University of Eastern Finland
[4] TUCS – Turku Centre for Computer Science

**Abstract.** Smart electrical grids refer to networked systems for distributing and transporting electricity from producers to consumers, by
dynamically configuring the network through remotely controlled
(dis)connectors. The consumers of the grid have typically distinct priorities, e.g., a hospital and an airport have the highest priority and the street
lighting has a lower priority. This means that when electricity supply is
compromised, e.g., during a storm, then the highest priority consumers
should either not be affected or should be the first for whom electricity
provision is recovered. In this paper, we propose a general formal model
to study the provability of such a property. We have chosen Event-B as our
formal framework due to its abstraction and refinement capabilities that
support correct-by-construction stepwise development of models; also,
Event-B is tool supported. Being able to prove various properties for such
critical systems is fundamental nowadays, as our society is increasingly
powered by dynamic digital solutions to traditional problems.

# 1 Introduction

Our society and lifestyles are rapidly changing to being powered by digital technologies. One prominent example is provided by the electrical grids that are
increasingly digital. In grids, as well as in other control systems, action is determined by sensing, monitoring, and measuring. The control part of the paradigm
is nowadays implemented in software, which forms a critical infrastructure for
decision making in these *smart grids*. Hence, the high-quality of the controlling
software is of utmost importance.

This modus operandi of smart grids leads to a high degree of flexibility for
the grid configuration and functions. Smart grids are networked systems for
connecting electricity generators to consumers, by dynamically configuring the
network through remotely controlled (dis)connectors. The consumers of the grid
have typically distinct priorities, e.g., a hospital and an airport have the highest
priority and the street lighting has a lower priority. This means that when electricity supply is compromised, e.g., due to a storm or peak consumption, then
the order of (re-establishing) electricity provision is with respect to the priorities. Another example of functional flexibility of smart grids is the possibility of

J.M. Badger and K.Y. Rozier (Eds.): NFM 2014, LNCS 8430, pp. 77–91, 2014.

(regularly) changing priorities, e.g., in the evenings, factories and office buildings have a lower lighting priority than living areas. In this context, the *problem* that we address here is how can we trust that consumers with the highest priority have almost always a path in the grid from an electricity generator; and, if such a connection is lost, is finding an alternative one guaranteed?

The *solution* that we propose in this paper is based on formal methods. Some example of formal method usage in industry can be seen for instance with Siemens [8], Space Systems [12] and SAP [5]. The fundamental design techniques of formal methods that we employ here are *abstraction* and *refinement*. We start from a simple, abstract model of the smart grid, that is striped away of many details (including connections among grid nodes), so that it is easy to prove some desired properties for it. Among others, we prove that high-priority consumers can recover from failure. Then, we add details in a stepwise manner to our model, until we reach a level of abstraction that agrees to our purposes. In this paper, we prove that, when connections to high-priority consumers fail, the smart grid can find alternative connections for these consumers, whenever there are connections available. We also *prove* that the more detailed models correctly refine the less detailed models.

In our work we use the Event-B formal method [2] for system modelling and analysis, due to its abstraction and refinement capabilities. Event-B comes with an associated toolset, the Rodin Platform, a theorem prover-based environment where proofs about the models are generated automatically and discharged either automatically or interactively.

Our contribution is thus twofold:

1. We propose smart grid models at different levels of abstraction and prove that the more concrete models refine the more abstract ones.
2. We demonstrate the recoverability property for smart grids as an invariant for our models.

Importantly, as our proving is based on assumptions, we are able to reason on when we can prove the recoverability property for smart grids and discuss why. Also, our modelling is developed for reusability: depending on various criteria, our recovery methodology can produce different reconnected paths, thus our most detailed model can be reused for various purposes.

We proceed as follows. In Section 2 we describe the smart grids and our model restrictions, in Section 3 we outline Event-B, and in Section 4 we describe our Event-B model to the extent needed in this paper. In Section 5 we discuss some interesting proving aspects of our approach. Related work is reviewed in Section 6 and some conclusions are presented in Section 7.

## 2   Smart Grids

The term *grid* indicates a structured framework of interconnected elements. Within the domain of the electricity, the electrical grid refers to the interconnected network delivering electricity from power plants to consumers. The grid comprises electricity generators labelled $G_i$, substations labelled $S_j$, and consumers labelled

$C_k$, where i,j,k denote natural numbers. This is illustrated in Fig. 1a) where edges between $G_i$ and $S_j$ or in between $S_j$ denote the (high-voltage) transmission network and the edges between $S_j$ and $C_k$ denote the distribution network.

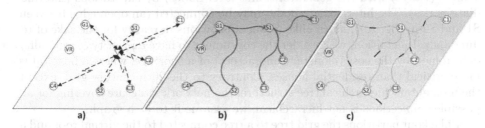

**Fig. 1.** Smart Grid's Layers of Operation: a) Information Flow; b) Power Flow Tree; c) Smart Grid (SG) graph

The term *Smart Grid* (SG) comprises an intelligent grid of this kind, typically considered an enhancement of the traditional 20th century grid. Some significant differences are presented in [11]. Gharavi and Ghafurian [13] define SG as a system that uses information and provides two-way, cyber-secure communication. This enables computational intelligence for a safe, secure, reliable, resilient, efficient and sustainable system. On the differences between the 20th century grid and SG, we note that the bidirectional communication is fundamental, implying several of the others. This connects SG with the information revolution era, where "smart" refers to using information regarding the grid for enabling pervasive self* properties. A categorisation on the physical realisation of the bidirectional communication [11] and a survey on SG [10] may be found elsewhere.

Research on SG has several points of focus. First, smart infrastructure systems are studied, in particular the communication infrastructure (the information flow layer in Fig. 1a)). This addresses the communication technology and protocols, the information subsystem concerned with information interoperability and the energy subsystem concerned with, among others, small scale energy production such as solar panels. Second, the management system is of interest, considering energy efficiency, operation costs reduction, demand and supply balance, emission control and utility maximization. Third, the smart protection system is very relevant, being concerned with user errors, equipment failures, natural disasters and deliberate cyber attacks [11]. Of these, in this paper we are concerned with the smart protection system and its feature of failure recovery, implemented in software. This is of outmost importance to increase the SG reliability and is strongly motivated by the annual costs of outage; for example, in 2002 these were estimated to 79 billion dollars in the US [19].

To study failure recovery, we assume reliable outage detection; reports on this by phasor measurement may be found elsewhere [23]. With respect to failure recovery, we formally outline the requirements of a fully and a partly connected grid (network) topology. We do recovery by switching (dis)connectors on the edges of this network, i.e. by operating the dis(connectors) depicted on the edges in Fig. 1c). Hence, we assume each element of the network to be remotely controllable. We assume the momentary topology to be of a tree structure with an added virtual root node, labelled VR in Fig. 1b). This tree connects all consumers (leaves) with the generators (first level nodes) by substations (intermediate nodes). The intermediate nodes may be connected (an open edge between S1 and S2 in Fig. 1c)), much alike power substations in reality for the sake of redundancy. In addition, we consider the consumers to have a priority of criticality determined by the cost (monetary, moral, etc) of a shortage, where a hospital is more critical than residential houses. Contrary to the 20th century grid, except the momentary hierarchical tree structure, the network structure covering for all possible connections is not hierarchical; we assume it to be a graph.

A blackout partitions the grid tree to a tree connected to the virtual root and a disconnected compromised subtree. Recovery effectively means reconnecting this compromised subtree's leaves to the virtual root node by finding an alternative route in the smart grid graph. As the recovery strategy implemented may vary depending on the setting, we implement a general strategy of circumventing the compromised subtree's root node; this general strategy can be adapted to many settings later. When recovery is not possible (there are no alternative paths to choose from), an operator could dispatch human resources for repairing the point of failure. The priorities of consumers set the recovery order when needed. An optimal condition with respect to our problem is thereby reached when the tree is fully connected, i.e. all leaves, independently of priority, have a path to the root.

## 3 Event-B

The Event-B [2] formalism is derived from the B-Method [1] and the Action Systems [3] framework, and was created for modelling and reasoning about parallel, distributed and reactive systems. The associated Rodin Platform [9] tool provides automated support for modelling and verification by theorem proving in Event-B.

In Event-B, a model of a system consists of a dynamic part, *machine*, and optionally also a static part, *context*. An Event-B context can specify constants, carrier sets, and axioms about these. A machine in Event-B optionally *sees* a context, and describes the model state by *variables*, updated by *events*. Events are atomic sets of (simultaneous) variable updates, and each event may contain *guards*, which are associated predicates, that must evaluate to true for the event to be enabled, i.e., be able to execute. If more than one event is enabled simultaneously, the choice between the events is non-deterministic. An Event-B machine should also include *invariants*, i.e., properties that must hold for any reachable state of the model. Thus, these properties must be established by a special initialisation event and hold before and after every occurrence of any other event. The proof manager in the Rodin Platform [9] tool automatically generates what needs to be proved in order for an invariant to hold.

Event-B provides a stepwise refinement-based approach to system development, preserving correctness by gradually detailing a model. In this paper, starting from an abstract model, refinement [2,4] refers to adding new variables, events and constants in addition to existing ones. Old events can also be modified, typically either updating the newly introduced variables or introducing more deterministic assignments on the old variables, while also strengthening the event guards.

# 4    Three Smart Grid Models: $M_0, M_1, M_2$

In this section we describe the high-level models $M_0$, $M_1$ and $M_2$ for SG; due to space restrictions, we only discuss here $M_0$ and $M_1$ and refer for more details in [16]. Our models are at three increasing levels of detail so that each model is a refinement of the previous one: $M_0 \sqsubseteq M_1 \sqsubseteq M_2$. In the initial model, we specify the set of consumers with different priorities, introduce random electricity outage and specify the behaviour of a recovery mechanism. We define the correctness properties of the recovery mechanism based on the priority of the consumers. We fold (hide) further detail of SG and magically recover from the outage problem. In the second model, we unfold (add) new data, refine events to model the tree structures in SG as well as link failures. We design the recovery mechanism in a way that guarantees that, after recovery, the structure of the momentary SG remains a tree and all consumers with higher priority are connected to a generator. In the third model, we detail our recovery mechanism by refining (splitting) events to distinguish between successful and unsuccessful recovery; in the latter case, we provide information on the failed subtree, for human-directed reconfiguration, that we assume to take place.

## 4.1    The Initial Model $M_0$

The initial model $M_0$ that we construct is very abstract: we do not consider the underlying SG connections but only the SG consumers; the SG connections are introduced in the subsequent refinement. $M_0$ thus allows us to specify our recovery goal very abstractly. The model $M_0$ is formed of the static part and the dynamic part, as follows.

**The Static Part.** The static part of our model is described below and contains the sets $NODE$, $MODE$, $STATE$ and the constants $consumer$, $generator$, $pr1$, $pr2$, $normal$, $recovery$, $on$ and $off$. The SG nodes are elements of the finite and non-empty $NODE$ set (**axm1**). Nodes can be either consumers or generators, so the $NODE$ set is partitioned into $consumer$ and $generator$ (**axm2**). Some consumers have higher priority, so we partition $consumer$ into $pr1$ and $pr2$ (**axm3**). SG can be in two different modes (**axm4**) and the state of consumers can be either $on$ or $off$ (**axm6**). In [16] we have also a third SG mode, called $optimal$.

```
CONSTANTS consumer  generator   pr1   pr2   normal   recovery   on   off
SETS  NODE MODE STATE
AXIOMS
   @axm1  finite(NODE) ∧ NODE ≠ ∅
   @axm2  partition(NODE, consumer, generator)
   @axm3  partition(consumer, pr1, pr2)
   @axm4  partition(MODE, {normal}, {recovery})
   @axm5  partition(STATE, {on}, {off})
```

**The Dynamic Part.** In the dynamic part of the model $M_0$, we define the state of consumers and the SG mode. We specify that whenever there is some power outage in higher priority consumers, there would be a mechanism to recover from the outage. We model a magical recovery mechanism which eventually recovers high-priority consumers from the outage. In [16] we also model a mechanism that provides the recovery of lower priority consumers as well, called optimising.

The outline of the dynamic part is shown below. The *cons_st* variable models the state of each consumer (**inv1**) and the *mode* variable models the current mode of SG (**inv2**). The *pr1* consumers have higher priority than the *pr2* consumers with respect to recovery, modelled by invariant **inv3**: when SG is in *normal* mode, all higher priority consumers are in *on* state. When SG is in *recovery* mode, there is power outage of at least one higher priority consumer (**inv4**).

```
VARIABLES    cons_st  mode
INVARIANTS
  @inv1 cons_st ∈ consumer → STATE
  @inv2 mode ∈ MODE
  @inv3 mode = normal ⇒ (∀c · c ∈ pr1 ⇒ cons_st(c) = on)
  @inv4 mode = recovery ⇒ (∃c · c ∈ pr1 ∧ cons_st(c) = off)
```

Our assumption is that initially all consumers are *on* and as a consequence, to satisfy the invariants, SG is in the *normal* state, as shown in the **INITIALISATION** event above. The **failure** event models a random power outage that happens to a subset $i$ of consumers, at least one of which is a high priority consumer. SG mode changes from *normal* to *recovery* and the state of the consumer subset $i$ with power outage updates from *on* to *off*.

```
INITIALISATION
BEGIN
  @act1  mode := normal
  @act2  cons_st := consumer × {on}
END
```

```
failure
ANY i WHERE
  @grd1  mode = normal
  @grd2  i ⊂ consumer
  @grd3  i ≠ ∅ ∧ i ∩ pr1 ≠ ∅
THEN
  @act1  mode := recovery
  @act2  cons_st := cons_st ⩤ (i × {off})
END
```

Two events **failure_recovery** and **recovery_complete** magically solve the outage, gradually reconnecting the compromised consumers, by switching their state to *on*. When the state of the last subset of consumers updates to *on* in **recovery_ complete**, the SG mode switches to *normal*. When SG is in *normal* mode, there might still be some lower priority consumers with power outage.

```
failure_recovery
ANY i WHERE
  @grd1  i ⊂ pr1
  @grd2  cons_st[i] = {off} ∧ i ≠ ∅
  @grd3  mode = recovery
  @grd4  ∃j·j ∉ i ∧ j ∈ pr1 ∧ cons_st(j) = off
THEN
  @act1  cons_st := cons_st ⩤ (i × {on})
END
```

```
recovery_complete
ANY i WHERE
  @grd1  i ⊂ pr1
  @grd2  cons_st[i] = {off} ∧ i ≠ ∅
  @grd3  mode = recovery
  @grd4  cons_st[(pr1\i)] = {on}
THEN
  @act1  cons_st := cons_st ⩤ (i × {on})
  @act2  mode := normal
END
```

## 4.2 The Second Model $M_1$

Recovery from the power outage that affects high priority consumers is achieved in the model $M_0$ simply by switching their state from $off$ to $on$. In this section, we refine the initial model $M_0$ to also specify links between nodes in SG. For this, we keep two structures. The SG *graph* denotes the entire grid, with all the available links and nodes. The momentary SG *tree* denotes the currently used links and nodes. This is illustrated in Fig. 2. The SG tree is, in fact, extracted from the SG graph. When the momentary SG tree suffers a failure, it needs to find an alternative path, in the SG graph, to make all the higher priority consumers connected to SG again.

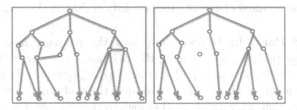

**Fig. 2.** An SG graph and an instance of one of its trees

**The Static Part.** In order to express and reason about the recovery property, we need to define a *closure* property for relations. In the context shown below, the constant $cl$ is defined as a total function from $netrel$ ($NODE \leftrightarrow NODE$, **axm6**) to $netrel$ (**axm7**). The characteristic properties of $cl(r)$ are: (i) The relation $r$ is included in $cl(r)$. (ii) The forward composition of $cl(r)$ with $r$ is included in $cl(r)$. (iii) The relation $cl(r)$ is the smallest relation dealing with (i) and (ii). These properties are modelled respectively by **axm8**, **axm9**, and **axm10**; the closure theorems are introduced in **thm1-3**.

---

**CONSTANTS** $netrel$   $cl$   $tree$   $root$   $net$   $initial\_net\_setting$
**AXIOMS**
@**axm6** $netrel = NODE \leftrightarrow NODE$
@**axm7** $cl \in netrel \rightarrow netrel$
@**axm8** $\forall r \cdot r \subseteq cl(r)$
@**axm9** $\forall r \cdot r ; cl(r) \subseteq cl(r)$
@**axm10** $\forall r, t \cdot (r \subseteq t \wedge r ; t \subseteq t \Rightarrow cl(r) \subseteq t)$
**theorem** @**thm1** $\forall r \cdot r \in netrel \Rightarrow cl(r) = r \cup (r ; cl(r))$
**theorem** @**thm2** $\forall t \cdot (\forall s \cdot s \subseteq t^{-1}[s] \Rightarrow s = \varnothing) \Rightarrow cl(t) \cap (NODE \lhd id) = \varnothing$
**theorem** @**thm3** $cl(\varnothing) = \varnothing$
@**axm11** $tree \in NODE \setminus \{root\} \rightarrow NODE \setminus consumer$
@**axm12** $\forall s \cdot s \subseteq tree^{-1}[s] \Rightarrow s = \varnothing$
**theorem** @**thm4** $\forall T \cdot root \in T \wedge tree^{-1}[T] \subseteq T \Rightarrow NODE \subseteq T$
**theorem** @**thm5** $cl(tree^{-1})[\{root\}] \cup \{root\} = NODE$
**theorem** @**thm6** $cl(tree)[consumer] \cup consumer = NODE$
**theorem** @**thm7** $\forall T \cdot consumer \subseteq T \wedge tree[T] \subseteq T \Rightarrow NODE \subseteq T$
**theorem** @**thm8** $\forall S \cdot S \subseteq tree[S] \Rightarrow S = \varnothing$
**theorem** @**thm9** $cl(tree) \cap (NODE \lhd id) = \varnothing$
@**axm13** $net \in NODE \setminus \{root\} \leftrightarrow\!\!\rightarrow generator$
@**axm14** $net \cap net^{-1} = \varnothing \wedge NODE \lhd id \cap net = \varnothing$
@**axm15** $initial\_net\_setting \in NODE \setminus \{root\} \rightarrow NODE \setminus consumer$
@**axm16** $cl(initial\_net\_setting^{-1})[root] \cup \{root\} = NODE$
@**axm17** $\forall S \cdot S \subseteq initial\_net\_setting[S] \Rightarrow S = \varnothing$
@**axm18** $initial\_net\_setting \subseteq net$

We also model a tree structure of the network, in the constant *tree*, with the following properties: (i) A tree is a total surjection function from $NODE \backslash \{root\}$ to $NODE \backslash consumer$ (**axm11**). (ii) The *consumer* set are leaves of tree and *root* is the top point in a tree (**axm11**). (iii) The tree is acyclic (**axm12**). The theorems (**thm4-9**) further describe tree properties.

Moreover, we define the *net* and *initial_net_setting* constants. The *net* constant is an asymmetric, irreflexive and total surjective function modelling the SG graph (**axm13**, **axm14**). The *initial_net_setting* constant is a tree (**axm15-17**), extracted from *net* (**axm18**).

The adapted theorems for closure allow us to prove the adapted theorems of the tree structure which will be used in the dynamic part of the second model to guarantee the correctness of the SG tree evolution during the recovery process.

**The Dynamic Part.** In $M_1$, we show how the recovery mechanism solves the power outage problem by changing the SG momentary tree. There are five variables in $M_1$: *node*, *dyn_net*, *failed_link*, *failed_path* and *failed_flag*. The *node* variable is a subset of $NODE$ and models the nodes of the SG momentary tree (**inv5**). In our model, *root* always belongs to the SG tree, hence $root \in node$ (**inv6**). In **inv7** we link *node* to the abstract variable *cons_st* from $M_0$: we model that there is no consumer with state *off* in set *node*, but all consumers that are in state *on* are members of *node*. The *dyn_net* models the SG tree with nodes and links between them: a total function from $node \backslash \{root\}$ to *node* (**inv8**) that is loop-free (**inv9**). We introduce **inv10** to restrict the range of *dyn_net* so that consumers can only be leaves in *dyn_net*.

```
VARIABLES  node  dyn_net  failed_link  failed_path  failed_flag
INVARIANTS
  @inv5  node ⊆ NODE
  @inv6  root ∈ node
  @inv7  cons_st⁻¹[{off}] ∩ node = ∅ ∧ cons_st⁻¹[{on}] ⊆ node
  @inv8  dyn_net ∈ node \ {root} → node
  @inv9  ∀s·(s ⊆ dyn_net⁻¹[s] ⇒ s = ∅)
  @inv10  (consumer ∩ node) ∩ ran(dyn_net) = ∅
  @inv11  failed_link ∈ NODE \ {root} ⤖ NODE \ {root}
  @inv12  failed_path ∈ failed_link ⤖ (NODE ↔ NODE)
  @inv13  ∀f·f ∈ dom(failed_path) ⇒ failed_path(f) ∈ NODE \ {root} ⤖ NODE \ {root}
  @inv14  ∀i,j·i ↦ j ∈ dom(failed_path) ⇒ (∀k·k ∈ ((dom(failed_path(i ↦ j))∪
            ran(failed_path(i ↦ j))) \ {j}) ∧ k ∈ (cl(failed_path(i ↦ j)))⁻¹[{j}])
  @inv15  ∀i,j·i ↦ j ∈ dom(failed_path) ⇒ consumer ∩ ran(failed_path(i ↦ j)) = ∅
  @inv16  failed_flag ∈ BOOL
  @inv17  mode = recovery ⇒ dom(failed_path) = failed_link
  @inv18  failed_link ≠ ∅ ∧ dyn_net ∩ failed_link = ∅ ⇒
            (∃r·r ∈ consumer ∧ r ∉ (cl(dyn_net))⁻¹[{root}])
  @inv19  failed_flag = FALSE ∧ mode ≠ recovery ⇒ failed_link = ∅ ∧ failed_path = ∅
  @inv20  ∀r·r ∈ consumer ∧ r ∉ (cl(dyn_net))⁻¹[{root}] ∧ failed_link ≠ ∅∧
            dyn_net ∩ failed_link = ∅ ⇒ cons_st(r) = off
  theorem @mthm1  ∀S·(root ∈ S ∧ dyn_net⁻¹[S] ⊆ S ⇒ node ⊆ S)
  theorem @mthm2  node \ {root} ⊆ (cl(dyn_net))⁻¹[{root}]
  theorem @mthm3  cl(dyn_net) ∩ (NODE ◁ id) = ∅
```

In the initial model, power outage hits a subset of consumers nondeterministically. In $M_1$, it happens due to some link failures in the SG tree. The partial function *failed_link* denotes the set of link failures in SG (**inv11**). We note that the root cannot fail, because the root is virtual and actually not belonging to SG. We use it for the sake of modelling. Each link failure leads to disconnectivity in a part of tree. We store the disconnected subtree for each link failure in $failed\_path$ function (**inv12**). In order to guarantee that a disconnected subtree of each link failure is a tree we introduce **inv13** and **inv14**. Invariant **inv13** denotes that each subtree is a partial function from $NODE \setminus \{root\}$ to $NODE \setminus \{root\}$. Invariant **inv14** denotes that all the nodes in a subtree of a failed link, say $i \mapsto j$, can be reached from both nodes $i$ and $j$. In other words, any node in the subtree is a child of node $i$ and $j$. In addition, we ensure that the built subtree of each $failed\_link$ satisfies **inv10**: consumers are leaves of the subtree (**inv15**).

To update the value of the $failed\_path$ variable after a link failure, we need to define a flag to allow us to do preprocessing before recovery. This is just for modelling purposes. The flag $failed\_flag$ is modelled by **inv16**. When $failed\_flag = TRUE$ the preprocessing should be initiated and the SG mode be updated to $recovery$. In other words, when the network is in $recovery$ mode, it means that $failed\_path$ contains all subtrees of all failures (**inv17**). The consequence of any failure is having at least one consumer which suffers from power outage due to the tree structure of SG (**inv18**). Finally, invariant **inv19** denotes that when the network is not in recovery mode, $failed\_link$ is empty. It is formulated as shown in **inv20**.

In order to ensure that every node in the $dyn\_net$ is reachable from the root node, we model the theorems **mthm1-3**, derived from existing invariants. Theorem **mthm2** denotes that all nodes in $node$ except $root$ are reachable from $root$. Theorem **mthm1** is used in the proof of **mthm2** and **mthm3** is introduced to satisfy the no-loop property.

To address the newly added structures we add three new events in $M_1$ as well as refine the abstract events. The newly introduced events define failure of links (**Link_fail** event), preprocessing to update function $failed\_path$ (**Failed_path_update** event) and distributing the knowledge about link failure to the grid (**Failed_tree_update** event). We explain these in more detail below.

| Link_fail | Failed_path_update |
|---|---|
| **ANY** l **WHERE** | **ANY** f des subtree l i **WHERE** |
| @**grd1** $l \subseteq dyn\_net \rhd \{root\}$ | @**grd1** $failed\_flag = TRUE$ |
| @**grd2** $failed\_flag = FALSE$ | @**grd2** $l \in failed\_link \wedge l = i \mapsto f$ |
| @**grd3** $l \neq \varnothing$ | @**grd3** $l \notin dom(failed\_path)$ |
| @**grd4** $mode = normal$ | @**grd4** $des = (cl(dyn\_net))^{-1}[\{f\}]$ |
| **THEN** | @**grd5** $subtree = des \lhd dyn\_net$ |
| @**act1** $failed\_flag := TRUE$ | **THEN** |
| @**act2** $failed\_link := l$ | @**act1** $failed\_path := failed\_path \cup$ |
| @**act3** $failed\_path := \varnothing$ | $(\{l\} \times \{subtree\})$ |
| **END** | **END** |

**Link_fail.** This event models the failure of a non-empty (**grd3**) subset of links in SG, except virtual links to root (**grd1**) when SG is in normal mode (**grd4**). The $failed\_flag$ variable which is initially $FALSE$ (**grd2**) is set to $TRUE$ (**act1**) in order to enable the preprocessing event. The $failed\_link$ set updates to the list of failed links(**act2**) and $failed\_path$ initiates to $\varnothing$ (**act3**). The only enabled event after the execution of the **Link_fail** event is **Failed_path_update** event, to ensure that preprocessing is performed before any further actions.

**Failed_path_update.** This event is enabled when $failed\_flag$ is $TRUE$ (**grd1**). It is enabled until all failed links (**grd2**) become members of $dom(failed\_path)$ (**grd3**). This event is aimed at storing a set of subtrees of the grid that are unreachable due to link failures. In order to compute the subtree for each individual failed link, we need to add two computational parameters $des$ and $subtree$. Parameter $des$ is the set of all descendants of nodes of a failed link (**grd3**). Parameter $subtree$ is the set of all links which form the subtree (**grd5**). Function $failed\_path$ is updated so that $failed\_link$ becomes a symbolic 'root' for $subtree$ (**act1**).

```
Failed_tree_update
ANY f des subtree l i r WHERE
  @grd1 failed_flag = TRUE
  @grd2 dom(failed_path) = failed_link
  @grd3 l ∈ failed_link
  @grd4 l ∈ dyn_net
  @grd5 l = i ↦ f
  @grd6 l ∉ dom(failed_path)
  @grd7 des = (cl(dyn_net))⁻¹[{f}]
  @grd8 subtree = des ◁ dyn_net
  @grd9 ∀k·k ∈ consumer ∧ k ∈ des ⇒ k ∈ r
THEN
  @act1 dyn_net := dyn_net\({l}∪subtree)
  @act2 node := node \ des
  @act3 cons_st := cons_st ⩤ (r × {off})
END
```

```
Failure refines failure
WHERE
  @grd1 mode = normal
  @grd2 failed_flag = TRUE
  @grd3 failed_link ≠ ∅
  @grd4 ∀f·f ∈ failed_link⇒
            f ∈ dom(failed_path)
  @grd5 ∀f·f ∈ failed_link ⇒ f ∉ dyn_net
THEN
  @act1 mode := recovery
  @act2 failed_flag := FALSE
END
```

**Failed_tree_update.** This event is enabled when preprocessing is complete: the subtree of all failed links are assigned (**grd2**). In order to update SG based on link failures, we remove a failed link, say $l$, with its subtree, stored in $failed\_path(l)$ from $dyn\_net$. The $node$ set, the set of reachable nodes from root, and the function $cons\_st$ update accordingly. Function $cons\_st$ updates in this event in order to guarantee that if a consumer is unreachable in the grid, the consumer is in $off$ state (**inv7** and **inv20**).

**Failure event:** This event is enabled when the preprocessing and the grid updating is completed. It simply resets the $failed\_flag$ and updates the grid mode.

```
Fail_rec extends failure_recovery
ANY i rec_set last res WHERE
  @grd5 ∀r·r ∈ failed_link ⇒ failed_path(r) ⊆ res
  @grd6 ∀k·k ∈ res ⇒ (∃i·i ∈ failed_link ∧ failed_path(i) ⊆ res)
  @grd7 rec_set ⊆ res ∪ (net \ failed_link)
  @grd8 dyn_net ∪ rec_set ∈ NODE \ {root} ⇸ NODE
  @grd7 dyn_net ∪ rec_set ∈
        (node ∪ dom(rec_set) ∪ ran(rec_set)) \ {root} → (node ∪ dom(rec_set) ∪ ran(rec_set))
  @grd9 ∀s·(s ⊆ (dyn_net ∪ recovery_set)⁻¹[s] ⇒ s = ∅)
  @grd10 ∀p·p ∈ pr1 \ last ⇒ p ∈ (cl(dyn_net ∪ recovery_set))⁻¹[{root}]
  @grd11 last ⊆ pr1
  @grd12 cons_st[last] = {off} ∧ (last ∩ cl(dyn_net ∪ rec_set)⁻¹[{root}] = ∅)
  @grd13 (cons_st⁻¹[{off}] ∩ pr1) \ last ⊆ dom(rec_set ∪ dyn_net)
  @grd14 (node ∪ dom(rec_set) ∪ ran(rec_set)) ⊆ {root} ∪ (cl(dyn_net ∪ rec_set))⁻¹[{root}]
  @grd15 i ⊆ dom(rec_set)
THEN
  @act2 dyn_net := dyn_net ∪ rec_set
  @act3 node := node ∪ dom(rec_set) ∪ ran(rec_set)
END
```

**Fail_rec event:** There are two approaches for power outage recovery: (i) to find an alternative path from the original graph, modelled as *net* in the static part of the second model and (ii) to repair failed links (human intervention). The **Fail_rec** event combines these two approaches which can be taken to solve the power outage problem for high priority consumers. The abstract event is extended by adding three computational parameters *res*, *rec_set* and *last*. Parameter *res* is a subset of all subtrees, extracted from *failed_path* function. Parameter *rec_set* is a subset of parameter *res* and all existing links in the original graph except those failed ones with the following conditions: (i) The union of *rec_set* and *dyn_net* does not introduce a loop and preserve the tree structure of the grid (ii) Consumers are either leaves or unreachable (iii) the set of consumers that belongs to *rec_set* are reachable (from *root*).

Parameter *last* is a subset of high priority consumers that are neither reachable in *dyn_net* nor reachable in $dyn\_net \cup dom(rec\_set)$. Parameter *last* is an evidence that the recovery is not completed yet. Parameter *rec_set* is a solution for power outage problem of a subset of high priority consumers, represented as $i$ in the event. The set of recovery links are added to the current grid (**act2**) and correspondingly the subset of *node* is updated (**act3**).

```
Recovery_complete extends Recovery_complete
ANY rec_set res WHERE
   @grd5 ∀r·r ∈ failed_link ⇒ failed_path(r) ⊆ res
   @grd6 ∀k·k ∈ res ⇒ (∃i·i ∈ failed_link ∧ failed_path(i) ⊆ res)
   @grd7 rec_set ⊆ res ∪ (net \ failed_link)
   @grd8 dyn_net ∪ rec_set ∈
       (node ∪ dom(rec_set) ∪ ran(rec_set)) \ {root} → (node ∪ dom(rec_set) ∪ ran(rec_set))
   @grd9 ∀s·(s ⊆ (dyn_net ∪ rec_set)⁻¹[s] ⇒ s = ∅)
   @grd10 ∀p·p ∈ pr1 ⇒ p ∈ (cl(dyn_net ∪ recovery_set))⁻¹[{root}]
   @grd11 (node ∪ dom(rec_set) ∪ ran(rec_set)) ⊆ {root} ∪ (cl(dyn_net ∪ rec_set))⁻¹[{root}]
THEN
   @act2 failed_link := ∅
   @act3 failed_path := ∅
   @act4 node := node ∪ dom(rec_set) ∪ ran(re_set)
   @act5 dyn_net := dyn_net ∪ rec_set
END
```

**Recovery_complete event:** This event is similar to **Fail_ rec** event, except it is the final stage of recovery and the grid mode changes to *normal* after the event execution. In order to show that it is the last recovery step, we need to add **grd10** that denotes all high priority consumers are reachable in $dyn\_net \cup recovery\_set$: there is no power outage problem that hits any high priority consumers. Therefore, the grid mode can switch to *normal* and *failed_link* and *failed_path* update to *emptyset*.

### 4.3   The Third Model $M_2$

In $M_1$, we have defined the tree structure of the grid and non-deterministically constructed a solution for power outage of high priority consumers regardless of its cost. For instance, a solution could be repairing some failed links while there would be other alternatives in the original network graph. In the second model $M_1$, we have not included any policy for selecting a solution from a set of possible solutions because we intended to construct a reusable correct source model. The generic source model supports further refinements following particular policies.

One basic policy for selecting a recovery solution can be first searching the original network graph for existing links. If there are links in the network graph, those alternatives are used first and then the rest of failures are recovered by repairing the failed links. In this refined model $M_2$, we specify this policy by restricting the non-determinism of the abstract model $M_1$ [16].

## 5  Verification of Models

Deciding from what kind of abstraction to start modelling and what details to add at each refinement step is problem-specific. Often, we take decisions that address modelling/proving complexity and enable reusability of models.

In order to prove that the models satisfy their correctness properties we have to check that they respect their invariants, in our case, the tree properties for SG and the gradual reconstruction of the tree due to node failures. To prove this, we have generated the proof obligations for all the models using the Rodin platform tool. The proof statistics for our models are shown in Table 1. These figures express the number of proof obligations generated by the Rodin platform as well as the number of obligations automatically discharged by the platform and those interactively proved.

**Table 1.** Proof Statistics

| Model | Number of Proof Obligations | Automatically Discharged | Interactively Discharged |
|---|---|---|---|
| Context | 19 | 11 | 8 |
| $M_0$ Model | 41 | 30 | 11 |
| $M_1$ Model | 112 | 83 | 29 |
| $M_2$ Model | 76 | 54 | 22 |
| Total | 248 | 178 | 70 |

One of the most essential requirements for proving the correctness of the recovery mechanism is to show that each step of the recovery reduces the number of disconnected high priority consumers. To prove this, we define the recovery events as *convergent* [2] and introduce a numeric variant. The Rodin platform generates a variant proof obligation ensuring that each convergent event decreases the proposed numeric variant. The other essential requirements are to construct a correct tree: each step of the recovery preserves the tree structure of *dyn_net*. For instance, to prove the preservation of the invariant **inv10**, stating that all consumers which are in set *node* are leaves, for the event **Fail_rec** of model $M_1$, we have distributed union and intersection throughout the generated proof obligation. The distribution allowed us to split the proof obligation into three simple ones:

$$(1)\ consumer\ \cap\ node\ \cap\ (ran(dyn\_net)\ \cup ran(rec\_set)) = \varnothing$$
$$(2)\ consumer\ \cap\ dom(rec\_set)\ \cap\ (ran(dyn\_net)\ \cup ran(rec\_set)) = \varnothing$$
$$(3)\ consumer\ \cap\ dom(rec\_set)\ \cap\ (ran(dyn\_net)\ \cup ran(rec\_set)) = \varnothing$$

To prove these proof obligations, we applied case distinction for the parameter *rec_set*. When links in *rec_set* were corresponding links in the range of *failed_path*, we could not prove the proof obligation. This was due to a missing invariant: denoting links in range of *failed_path* also follows the requirement that consumers are leaves. We added the invariant **inv15** and those discharged branches of proof obligation were proved.

Hence, our most important result in this paper can be formulated as follows. If an SG is constructed according to our modelling, then we can recover from link failures by providing alternative paths from generator to high-priority consumers, when there are paths available. There are two important issues to note here. First, if there are no available paths to choose from, then, obviously, we cannot provide any. However, in this case, we save (in $failed\_path$) the subtrees corresponding to the failed links and at least human resources could be dispatched to repair them. Second, our modelling is fundamentally based on the momentary SG having a tree structure. We can recover from failure because we have the consumers as leaves in this tree, i.e., they are not distributing electricity further. They might have this capability in smart grids, and the available SG graph may have them as substations. But in the momentary SG tree, they are leaves. This illustrates the strength of abstraction (and proof) in modelling.

## 6   Related Work

The area of failure identification, diagnosis and recovery in smart grids has been extensively studied. Clark and Pavlovski have presented their experiences as a case study in deploying a cellular wireless solution to support smart grid solutions [7]. In [15], a system-level simulation model including interdependencies between electricity distribution and mobile communication networks has been presented and evaluated with field trials. The formal aspects of electrical grids have also been studied before, for instance by Calderaro et al: they captured the details of modelling a protection system for the grid, using Petri Nets [6]. Probabilistic graphical models for modelling spatially correlated data from phasor measurement units, as well as using statistical hypothesis testing for fault diagnosis, was proposed by He and Zhang [14]. Apart from electrical grids, other types of distributed networks have also previously been formally modelled, for instance sensor-actor networks [18], peer-to-peer networks [22], and network recovery [17].

The general formal model proposed in this article addresses the safety and recoverability analysis of many of the advanced properties of smart grids as discussed for instance by Moslehi et al [21]. It can be extended to cover the main aspects of smart grids, as discussed by Fang et al [10], and it should be noted that the proposed model could be refined further to take into account various load profiles or personalised electricity use information, to provide further adaptation capabilities against failures and power outages. The proposed method is of high interest also to smart grid (communication) capacity planning, as discussed for instance by Luan et al [20]. The plan must take into account various modes of operation. Luan et al discussed two modes, or scenarios, which they called "Blue Sky Day" and "Storm Day". Such scenario based planning can be verified and proven correct with the proposed method.

## 7   Conclusions

In this paper we have illustrated the use of formal methods, notably the abstraction and refinement techniques, in modelling recovery in smart electrical grids.

This is useful from several points of view. First, there is no report of *proving* this kind of properties in related literature, hence our methodology proposes a novel view on addressing these problems. Second, our modelling is intended for reusability and can be extended in several directions. For instance, consumers could be divided into more than the two classes of priority that we have modelled. However, by abstracting away details we have captured the basic problem of addressing first the high-priority consumers and the rest of the consumers could now be modelled by partitioning $pr2$ consumers into other sets. Also, our link failures are non-deterministic; however, we might need to simulate particular failures to see what happens, if alternative paths are found. For instance, this is useful when a storm is forecasted and the SG operators need to ensure that their high-priority consumers are safe. To model this, we only need to refine the non-deterministic choice with a particular choice and our models continue to work. Moreover, when we have several recovery paths to choose from, some may be preferred with respect to various criteria; in that case, the nondeterministic choice in $M_2$ can be refined.

We have employed Event-B as our formal method due to its integrated support of abstraction and refinement; also, the tool support from the Rodin platform is very useful and can help for an easier acceptance of this methodology in industry. An interesting aspect of Event-B is that the context modelling the constants, sets and axioms on them needs, in principle, no proofs. However, for proving recovery as an invariant of our modelling, we needed to ensure the tree structure of the momentary SG, and so in $M_1$ we have part of the axioms proved, to ensure consistency of our context. This makes for a stronger model and it was largely facilitated due to the Event-B tool support.

In our model we have only considered a binary situation, i.e., there is a failure or not. In reality, this type of failure is called blackout; there is at least another type of failure, called brownout, referring to a situation where the power is not completely disconnected but the voltage drops below acceptable levels. Furthermore, brownouts can be intentional, whereby dropping the voltage overall can prevent a blackout in some part of the grid. As we have not modelled this situation in our work, it remains a future research topic.

**Acknowledgement.** This research is based on the cooperation between the Academy of Finland FResCo project (grant numbers 264060 and 263925, "FResCo: High-quality Measurement Infrastructure for Future Resilient Control Systems") and the Tekes/SHOK Smart Grids and Energy Markets (SGEM) programme.

# References

1. Abrial, J.R.: The B-Book: Assigning Programs to Meanings. Cambridge University Press (1996)
2. Abrial, J.R.: Modeling in Event-B: System and Software Engineering. Cambridge University Press (2010)
3. Back, R., Sere, K.: From Modular Systems to Action Systems. Software - Concepts and Tools 13, 26–39 (1996)
4. Back, R., Sere, K.: Superposition Refinement of Reactive Systems. Formal Asp. Comput. 8(3), 324–346 (1996)

5. Bryans, J.W., Wei, W.: Formal Analysis of BPMN Models Using Event-B. In: Kowalewski, S., Roveri, M. (eds.) FMICS 2010. LNCS, vol. 6371, pp. 33–49. Springer, Heidelberg (2010)
6. Calderaro, V., Hadjicostis, C.N., Piccolo, A., Siano, P.: Failure identification in smart grids based on Petri Net modeling. IEEE Transactions on Industrial Electronics 58(10), 4613–4623 (2011)
7. Clark, A., Pavlovski, C.: Wireless Networks for the Smart Energy Grid: Application Aware Networks. In: Proceedings of the International Multi Conference of Engineers and Computer Scientists, vol. 2 (2010)
8. Craigen, D., Gerhart, S., Ralson, T.: Case Study: Paris Metro Signaling System. In: Proceedings of IEEE Software, pp. 32–35. IEEE (1994)
9. Event-B and the Rodin Platform, http://www.event-b.org/ (accessed January 2014)
10. Fang, X., Misra, S., Xue, G., Yang, D.: Smart grid - the new and improved power grid: A survey. IEEE Communications Surveys and Tutorials 14(4), 944–980 (2012)
11. Farhangi, H.: The path of the smart grid. IEEE Power & Energy Mag. 8(1), 18–28 (2010)
12. Salehi Fathabadi, A., Rezazadeh, A., Butler, M.: Applying Atomicity and Model Decomposition to a Space Craft System in Event-B. In: Bobaru, M., Havelund, K., Holzmann, G.J., Joshi, R. (eds.) NFM 2011. LNCS, vol. 6617, pp. 328–342. Springer, Heidelberg (2011)
13. Gharavi, H., Ghafurian, R.: Smart grid: The electric energy system of the future. Proc. IEEE 99(6), 917–921 (2011)
14. He, M., Zhang, J.: Fault detection and localization in smart grid: A probabilistic dependence graph approach. In: IEEE SmartGridComm 2010, pp. 43–48 (2010)
15. Horsmanheimo, S., Maskey, N., Kokkoniemi-Tarkkanen, H., Savolainen, P., Tuomimäki, L.: Evaluation of Interdependencies between Mobile Communication and Electricity Distribution Networks in Fault Scenarios. In: IEEE ISGT Asia 2013 (2013)
16. Horsmanheimo, S., Kamali, M., Kolehmainen, M., Neovius, M., Petre, L., Rönkkö, M., Sandvik, P.: On Proving Recoverability of Smart Electrical Grids. Tech. Rep. 1096, TUCS – Turku Centre for Computer Science (2013)
17. Kamali, M., Laibinis, L., Petre, L., Sere, K.: A Distributed Design of a Network Recovery Algorithm. International Journal of Critical Computer-Based Systems 4(1), 45–68 (2013)
18. Kamali, M., Laibinis, L., Petre, L., Sere, K.: Formal development of wireless sensor-actor networks. Science of Computer Programming 80, 25–49 (2014)
19. LaCommare, K., Eto, J.: Cost of power interruptions to electricity consumers in the United States. Tech. rep., Ernest Orlando Lawrence Berkeley National Laboratory, lBNL-58164 (2006)
20. Luan, W., Sharp, D., Lancashire, S.: Smart grid communication network capacity planning for power utilities. In: Proceedings of Transmission and Distribution Conference and Exposition, pp. 1–4. IEEE (2010)
21. Moslehi, K., Kumar, R.: A Reliability Perspective of the Smart Grid. IEEE Transaction on Smart Grid 1(1), 57–64 (2010)
22. Petre, L., Sandvik, P., Sere, K.: Node Coordination in Peer-to-Peer Networks. In: Sirjani, M. (ed.) COORDINATION 2012. LNCS, vol. 7274, pp. 196–211. Springer, Heidelberg (2012)
23. Tate, J., Overbye, T.: Double line outage detection using phasor angle measurements. In: Power & Energy Society General Meeting, PES 2009, pp. 1–5. IEEE (2009)

# Providing Early Warnings
# of Specification Problems

Dustin Hoffman, Aditi Tagore, Diego Zaccai, and Bruce W. Weide

Department of Computer Science and Engineering
The Ohio State University
Columbus, Ohio 43210, USA
{hoffman.373,tagore.2,zaccai.1,weide.1}@osu.edu

**Abstract.** A formal software verification system relies upon a software engineer writing mathematically precise specifications of intended behavior. Humans often introduce defects into such specifications. Techniques and tools capable of warning about common defects can help them develop correct specifications by finding subtle issues that would permit unintended behavior. New specification-checking techniques and a tool that implements them, *SpecChec*, are described.

## 1 Introduction

A formal verification system normally tries to prove that implementations satisfy formal specifications, but it cannot show that those specifications properly capture informal requirements. Therefore, specifications that erroneously encode requirements, combined with verified implementations of those specifications, could lead to false confidence in a system. Deciding whether specifications match requirements is a problem that generally has been regarded as beyond the scope of formal methods because, essentially by definition, formal specifications are developed from *informal* requirements. However, some specification defects can be caught by performing internal consistency checks on specifications alone (see [1]). This paper expands upon previous work in automatic detection of specification errors by describing a new specification-checking technique along with the implementation of a tool, *SpecChec*, capable of detecting certain kinds of inadmissible specifications as described here and in previous work.

Our experience with writing formal specifications suggests that simply identifying which parameters might be modified by an operation is generally an easy part of the process of formalizing requirements. Writing a sensible post-condition is normally more prone to both logical errors and typos. So, if a parameter has been identified as one that might be (i.e., is intended to be) modified by the operation—but the post-condition as written admits a correct implementation that *never* changes it—the postcondition is probably wrong. We submit that such a specification should receive what we call a **trivial-update** warning.

For example, consider fire-control software for a torpedo. The launch system needs to increase the pressure in the tube to equalize with sea pressure.

J.M. Badger and K.Y. Rozier (Eds.): NFM 2014, LNCS 8430, pp. 92–97, 2014.

The design of this system might involve an operation IncreaseP. If its specification inadvertently allows a correct implementation to do *nothing* to the pressure (even though the pressure parameter is marked as modifiable), the torpedo might not be able to launch. Thus a verified system fails.

Our proposed technique identifies trivial-update defects when a specification is being created. Typically, errors are detected by a verification system (in our case, the RESOLVE tools [2]) when a verification condition (VC) cannot be discharged by a theorem-prover (in our case, Z3 [3] and/or SplitDecision [4]) and subsequently the VC is traced back to its origin in implementation code. The specification-checking approach used here also involves generating VCs and feeding them to a theorem-prover—but much earlier in the design process. Since the cost of detecting and fixing errors increases as software development reaches the later stages of its life-cycle, eliminating errors early is widely regarded as a best practice in software engineering [5].

We assume familiarity with formal design-by-contract specifications using pre- and post-conditions. However, except as noted here, no prior knowledge of the RESOLVE language [6] or tools [2] or any specific theorem-prover is necessary. The ideas apply to specification and verification more generally.

The primary contributions of this work are in codifying and automating certain checks on the quality of specification engineering:

- A technique to detect trivial-update defects: specification errors that admit unintended behavior, i.e., failure of the specification to capture requirements.
- A tool to warn the developer of this and other specification defects.

## 2   Specification Modes

Most formal specification languages have syntax to mark each formal parameter whose value might be changed by an operation, such as the modifies clause in Dafny [7], JML [8], and Spec# [9]; by default, a parameter's value is unchanged. RESOLVE uses a slightly different approach. Every formal parameter to an operation has a **specification mode** ("mode" for short) that concisely declares something about how its value is affected by the operation, and about the relevance of the incoming and/or outgoing value of that parameter to the operation's overall effect. There are multiple modes in RESOLVE, four of which are of particular interest for this paper: restores, updates, replaces, and clears. The latter three can be viewed as specializations of the all-encompassing modifies of other languages. The mode restores indicates that the outgoing value is the same as the incoming value. The mode updates indicates that the outgoing value might be different from the incoming value, and that both are relevant. The mode replaces indicates that the outgoing value is set by the operation, and that the incoming value is irrelevant. The mode clears indicates that that the outgoing value is an initial value for its type, and that the incoming value is relevant.

## 3   Trivial-Update Defects

### 3.1   Examples

The following two examples illustrate trivial-update defects. Both exemplify actual specification errors we have made ourselves or have observed others making. The first involves a trivial typo, the second a logical mistake.

```
procedure IncreaseP (                 procedure RemoveAny(
    updates  p: Integer,                  updates s: Set,
    restores max: Integer)                replaces x: Item)
  requires                              requires
    p < max                               s /= empty_set
  ensures                               ensures
    p >= #p                               x is in #s and
                                          #s = s union {x}
```

Fig. 1. Specifications of IncreaseP and RemoveAny

The error in IncreaseP is that the post-condition should read p > #p (i.e., the outgoing value of p exceeds its incoming value). [1] Other than performing some kind of natural-language processing on the name of the operation, how can this defect be detected?

RemoveAny is intended to remove an arbitrary element from a non-empty set. What is the defect here, and how can it be detected?

### 3.2   Identifying Trivial-Update Defects

The updates mode is unique in that it introduces some redundancy: it summarizes the specifier's intent for the parameter at a coarse level, while the pre-condition and post-condition pin down the details. It is this redundancy that allows a trivial-update defect to be identified.

```
procedure Foo(restores r: T1, updates u: T2,
              replaces s: T3, clears c: T4)
  requires
    pre ⟨r, u, c⟩
  ensures
    post⟨r, #u, u, s, #c, c⟩
```

Listing 1.1. A general operation specification schema

Consider the general schema for an operation shown in Listing 1.1 (in which the types of the parameters are unimportant). The modes determine which parameters' incoming and outgoing values may be mentioned in the pre-condition and post-condition. Indeed, conformance to this schema is one of the purely syntactic specification admissibility checks discussed in [1].

---

[1] A formal parameter appearing with a # prefix in an ensures clause denotes the parameter's value before the call. This is omitted in a requires clause, where all parameters necessarily denote their values before the call.

The process of identifying trivial-update defects begins by building sentence (1) claiming that there *exist* incoming values of the parameters that satisfy the pre-condition—because if not, the specification is inadmissible [1] since *any* implementation of it is correct:

$$\exists r, u, c \ (pre\langle r, u, c\rangle) \tag{1}$$

Assuming this first admissibility check is passed, we next build sentence (2) claiming that for *all* possible incoming parameter values that satisfy the pre-condition, there *exist* outgoing parameter values that satisfy the post-condition. Notice that the last two conjuncts in the post-condition are a direct result of the parameter modes, i.e., the value of r is restored to its incoming value, and the value of c is changed to an initial value for its type:

$$\forall \#r, \#u, \#c \ (pre\langle \#r, \#u, \#c\rangle \Rightarrow$$
$$\exists r, u, s, c \ (post\langle r, \#u, u, s, \#c, c\rangle \wedge (r = \#r) \wedge is\_initial(c))) \tag{2}$$

The variable r, introduced by the existential quantifier in sentence (2), is simply introducing a new name for #r. Thus, it can be removed from the existential quantifier by using the name r for both:

$$\forall r, \#u, \#c \ (pre\langle r, \#u, \#c\rangle \Rightarrow$$
$$\exists u, s, c \ (post\langle r, \#u, u, s, \#c, c\rangle \wedge is\_initial(c))) \tag{3}$$

If sentence (3) is valid then we have completed another of the specification admissibility checks introduced in [1]. Assuming the specification also passes this check, we now treat the updates-mode parameter u as if it were restores-mode and build sentence (4) claiming that the contract might be implemented by code that never modifies u:

$$\forall r, \#u, \#c \ (pre\langle r, \#u, \#c\rangle \Rightarrow$$
$$\exists u, s, c \ (post\langle r, \#u, u, s, \#c, c\rangle \wedge (u = \#u) \wedge is\_initial(c))) \tag{4}$$

Finally, we can simplify this to sentence (5):

$$\forall r, u, \#c \ (pre\langle r, u, \#c\rangle \Rightarrow \exists s, c \ (post\langle r, u, u, s, \#c, c\rangle \wedge is\_initial(c))) \tag{5}$$

Sentence (5) is the meaning of "the specification has a trivial-update defect." So, the validity of sentence (6) (the negation of sentence (5)) indicates the admissibility of the specification with respect to trivial-update defects:

$$\exists r, u, \#c \ (pre\langle r, u, \#c\rangle \wedge \forall s, c \ (\neg post\langle r, u, u, s, \#c, c\rangle \vee \neg is\_initial(c)))) \tag{6}$$

### 3.3 Examples Revisited

For the specification of IncreaseP, the sentence claiming there is a trivial-update defect is clearly valid:

$$\forall p, max : integer \ (p < max \Rightarrow p \geq p) \tag{7}$$

For the specification of RemoveAny, the sentence claiming there is a trivial-update defect is also valid, though it is hardly as obvious:

$$\forall s : \textit{finite set of Item} \ \ (s \neq \emptyset \Rightarrow \exists\, x : \textit{Item} \ \ ((x \in s) \wedge (s = s \cup \{x\}))) \quad (8)$$

The problem with the RemoveAny specification is that the second clause of the post-condition does not guarantee that $x$ has been removed from $s$. A correct specification replaces this clause with s = #s \ {x}.

In each example, the corrected specification results in the trivial-update defect sentence being invalid.

# 4   *SpecChec*: A Specification Analysis Tool

We created a specification analysis tool, *SpecChec*, that tries to prove both admissibility (sentences (1), (3), (6)) and inadmissibility (their negations) of specifications. The tool is implemented inside of the Modular Verification Environment (MVE), which is the foundation for the OSU RSRG RESOLVE tools [10].

Within the MVE framework, *SpecChec* is implemented as if it were a VC generator. Once its "VCs" (i.e., the six sentences mentioned above, only half of which are true) have been created, the system first sends each sentence to the automated theorem-prover SplitDecision. If that fails to prove it, the sentence is sent to Z3. The examples discussed in Section 3 can be accessed and tested with *SpecChec* via the website http://resolveonline.cse.ohio-state. edu/?r=NFM2014. At this site, the examples can be found by navigating to components in the tree along the left side of the page and then opened by clicking on the name of the specification. Clicking "Verify" at the top runs the *SpecChec* tool on the specification. After this step, the VCs that were generated for a given operation can be viewed by clicking on the large dot in the left margin on the line of specification associated with that set of VCs. A red dot indicates that the specification has an admissibility problem. Yellow indicates that *SpecChec* was unable to determine admissibility.

*SpecChec* is often able to discharge VCs associated with the admissibility checks, described earlier, when they involve only universal quantifiers or Presburger arithmetic. However, the trivial-update defect identification technique introduces an alternation of quantifiers that automated solvers generally cannot presently handle. When automated provers become more adept at handling various mathematical types and quantifier structures, even if just for $\forall\exists$- and $\exists\forall$-style quantifier alternation, more and more specifications will be automatically checkable for admissibility.

# 5   Conclusions

It will never be possible to prove that the formal specification of an operation captures its informally-stated requirements. However, the use of specification modes in RESOLVE or (to some extent) modifies clauses in other languages, introduces a small redundancy that provides an opportunity in principle to check whether a contract is self-consistent. The introduction of alternating quantifiers means that such admissibility checks often cannot be discharged automatically with current technology. Yet the fact that such a small degree of redundancy allows for any specification checks begs the open question of what other ways we might be able to leverage redundancy in contract specifications, e.g., perhaps by imposing other syntactic requirements for limited kinds of redundancy. JML, for example, optionally allows redundant clauses in post-conditions [8].

**Acknowledgment.** The authors thank all members of RSRG for their suggestions and support. This material is based upon work supported by the National Science Foundation under Grant No. CCF-1162331. Any opinions, findings, conclusions, or recommendations expressed here are those of the authors and do not necessarily reflect the views of the National Science Foundation.

# References

1. Tagore, A., Weide, B.W.: Automatically detecting inconsistencies in program specifications. In: Brat, G., Rungta, N., Venet, A. (eds.) NFM 2013. LNCS, vol. 7871, pp. 261–275. Springer, Heidelberg (2013)
2. Sitaraman, M., Adcock, B., Avigad, J., Bronish, D., Bucci, P., Frazier, D., Friedman, H., Harton, H., Heym, W., Kirschenbaum, J., Krone, J., Smith, H., Weide, B.: Building a push-button RESOLVE verifier: Progress and challenges. Formal Aspects of Computing 23(5), 607–626 (2011)
3. de Moura, L., Bjørner, N.S.: Z3: An efficient SMT solver. In: Ramakrishnan, C.R., Rehof, J. (eds.) TACAS 2008. LNCS, vol. 4963, pp. 337–340. Springer, Heidelberg (2008)
4. Adcock, B.M.: Working Towards the Verified Software Process. PhD thesis, The Ohio State University, Columbus, OH, USA (2010)
5. Westland, J.: The cost of errors in software development: evidence from industry. Journal of Systems and Software 62(1), 1–9 (2002)
6. Sitaraman, M., Weide, B.: Component-based software using RESOLVE. SIGSOFT Softw. Eng. Notes 19, 21–63 (1994)
7. Leino, K.R.M.: Dafny: An automatic program verifier for functional correctness. In: Clarke, E.M., Voronkov, A. (eds.) LPAR-16 2010. LNCS, vol. 6355, pp. 348–370. Springer, Heidelberg (2010)
8. Leavens, G.T., Leino, K.R.M., Poll, E., Ruby, C., Jacobs, B.: JML: Notations and tools supporting detailed design in Java. In: OOPSLA 2000 Companion, pp. 105–106. ACM (2000)
9. Barnett, M., Leino, K.R.M., Schulte, W.: The Spec# programming system: An overview. In: Barthe, G., Burdy, L., Huisman, M., Lanet, J.-L., Muntean, T. (eds.) CASSIS 2004. LNCS, vol. 3362, pp. 49–69. Springer, Heidelberg (2005)
10. Hoffman, D.: A Framework for Integrating Automated Software Verification Tools. Tech-Report (2012),
    ftp://ftp.cse.ohio-state.edu/pub/tech-report/2012/TR05.pdf

# Mechanized, Compositional Verification
# of Low-Level Code

Björn Bartels and Nils Jähnig

Technische Universität Berlin, Germany
{bjoern.bartels,nils.jaehnig}@tu-berlin.de

**Abstract.** For many safety-critical systems besides functional correctness, termination properties are especially important. Ideally, such properties are not only established for high-level representations of a system, but also for low-level representations.

In this paper, we therefore present a compositional semantics and a related proof calculus for possibly non-deterministic low-level languages. The calculus facilitates total correctness proofs about program representations given in a low-level language. We cope with the complexity inherent to such proofs by mechanizing the entire theory using the theorem prover Isabelle/HOL and exploiting the provers mechanisms for constructing well-founded relations.

## 1   Introduction

Many safety critical systems are composed of terminating components or tasks. In such a setting, not only functional correctness needs to be assured but also termination of the components. Furthermore, it is not sufficient to establish these properties on the level of a high-level programming language because transformations to low-level representations are complex and low-level code is often subject to manual optimizations. Therefore, the desired properties need to be established for the low-level implementation as well. However, proofs about low-level code are complicated by the unstructured nature of low-level code.

In [9] a compositional approach to the semantics of low-level languages and a related partial correctness logic is presented. In this paper, we build on this work and construct a compositional semantics and proof calculus for total correctness proofs about low-level languages. To obtain a formalization that can serve as a starting point for instantiations to a broad variety of concrete languages, we keep the low-level language as abstract as possible. The low-level language can be used to simulate advanced constructs like binary choice between commands and random assignment, for example. However, we need to account for the high level of abstraction when establishing soundness and completeness. For example, in the presence of unbounded non-determinism (as introduced by random assignment), the weakest precondition approach cannot be used anymore. To cope with these problems, we show that proof techniques targeting proof calculi for high-level languages [7] can be transferred to the level of low-level languages.

J.M. Badger and K.Y. Rozier (Eds.): NFM 2014, LNCS 8430, pp. 98–112, 2014.
© Springer International Publishing Switzerland 2014

Moreover, we provide a semantics and proof calculus that is polymorphic with respect to the notion of state and entirely mechanized [1] using the theorem prover Isabelle/HOL [6]. This facilitates the instantiation of our semantic framework to obtain mechanized verification environments for concrete low-level languages.

The paper is structured as follows. First, we introduce the syntax and the notion of state in Section 2. Based on these definitions, in Section 3 we define a small-step semantics for the basic low-level language. In Section 4, we present the compositional big-step semantics for which we define a total correctness calculus in Section 5 and establish soundness and completeness. Afterwards, we explain the usage of the logic using a small example in Section 6. Finally, we finish the paper with a discussion of related work in Section 7 and a conclusion in Section 8.

## 2   Syntax and State Definitions

We formalize the notion of state as a record with the name *state* that is parameterized over the type ($'a$):

**record** ($'a$) *state* $= R$  $::'a$   $PC$ ::*label*

In Isabelle/HOL records offer convenient selector functions for components of the record,i.e., we can refer to the components of a given state record $s$ using qualified names, i.e., $R$ $s$ or $PC$ $s$. Furthermore, components of a record can be updated in a similar fashion as we will explain in the next section. The low-level programming language that we consider operates on a store $R$ of type $'a$. Using the type variable $'a$ here expresses that we do not fix a concrete representation of the store. Our further definitions of instructions and semantics will be polymorphic over the type $'a$ as well. This implies that our formalization can later be used for concrete verification efforts by instantiating it with a convenient representation for the store, for example by using a simple function (as we do in the example later). The program counter $PC$ points to the instruction that is to be executed next and is of type *label* (which here is a type synonym for the HOL type *nat* of natural numbers). The low-level programming language is defined using the type of instructions $('a)instr$. Instructions are parameterized over the type of the store $'a$ as well:

**datatype** $('a)instr = do$ $('a \Rightarrow 'a$ $set)$   $|$   $br$ $label$   $|$   $brt$ $('a \Rightarrow bool)$ $label$ $label$

The instruction $do$ $f$ applies an arbitrary (HOL) function $f$ (of type $'a \Rightarrow 'a$ $set$) to the state. The function maps to a set of states and might thereby introduce non-determinism. The instructions $br$ and $brt$ are unconditional and conditional branch instructions and reflect the unstructured control flow of the language. The conditional branch instruction depends on a predicate of type $'a \Rightarrow bool$ that maps a given state to a boolean value.

---

[1] The theory files will soon be submitted to the Archive of Formal Proofs (AFP). For a preliminary version please contact the authors.

$$\frac{(l,\ do\ f) \in lis \qquad PC\ s = l \qquad x \in f\ (R\ s) \qquad t = s(\!|R := x,\ PC := PC\ s + 1|\!)}{(s,\ t) \in small\text{-}step}\ \text{DOF}$$

$$\frac{(l,\ br\ m) \in lis \qquad PC\ s = l \qquad t = s(\!|PC := m|\!)}{(s,\ t) \in small\text{-}step}\ \text{SMBR}$$

$$\frac{(l,\ brt\ bexp\ m\ n) \in lis \qquad PC\ s = l \qquad bexp\ (R\ s) \qquad t = s(\!|PC := m|\!)}{(s,\ t) \in small\text{-}step}\ \text{SMBRTT}$$

$$\frac{(l,\ brt\ bexp\ m\ n) \in lis \qquad PC\ s = l \qquad \neg\ bexp\ (R\ s) \qquad t = s(\!|PC := n|\!)}{(s,\ t) \in small\text{-}step}\ \text{SMBRTF}$$

**Fig. 1.** Rules of the Small Step Semantics

## 3 Small-Step Semantics

The rules of the small-step semantics are given in Figure 1. They refer to a fixed set of labeled instructions *lis* and are defined within a *locale* context [6]. In such a context assumptions can be fixed and referred to. For example, we require labeled instruction sets to contain no two tuples with the same label. In general, a state transition from a state $s$ to a state $t$ is possible, if the program counter in the state $s$ ($PC\ s$) points to the label of an instruction. For the individual instructions further conditions need to hold. If these are fulfilled, the state $t$ is obtained from $s$ by updating the respective components ($R$ and $PC$) of the state record. In our basic low-level language, we generalize the assignment instruction as used in [9] to a non-deterministic setting. This is reflected by the definition of the instruction *do f*. It is similar to the one used in [7] for a high-level language and formalizes the effect of an application of some HOL function $f$ to the state $s$. The function yields a set of states. Therefore, for every element of this set ($x \in f\ (R\ s)$) there is a possible state $t$, which can be reached from $s$. The program counter of this state $t$ is obtained by incrementing the program counter of $s$ by one. By allowing the function $f$ to be defined as an arbitrary HOL function, the instruction *do f* can be used to model a variety of instructions like single assignments and binary assignments. Furthermore, skip instructions (provided $f$ does not change the state), abortion (if $f$ yields the empty set) and non-deterministic instructions like non-deterministic choice and also random assignment can be modeled. The unconditional branch instruction *br m* updates the state $s$ by setting the program counter to the value $m$. The last two rules are concerned with the conditional branch *brt bexp m n* . Depending on the truth value of the the predicate *bexp*, evaluated with respect to the store $R$ in state $s$, the instruction either updates the state by setting the program counter to $m$ or $n$. Note that $f$ and *bexp* depend only on the store $R$ in a given state.

# 4    Big Step Semantics

Following [9], we define a compositional big step semantics by imposing a structure on sets of instructions. The central idea is that any unstructured set of labeled instructions can be viewed as being constructed from subsets of labeled instructions (which do not share labeled instructions with the same label) and that, if this implicit structure is made explicit, a compositional semantics can be obtained. Given some state $s$, the big-step semantics evaluates executions with respect to this structured set of instructions. Depending on the value of the program counter, a structured set of instructions may be entered at and exited to different labeled instructions. Evaluation solely depends on the instructions that the respective structured set is constructed from, i.e., no information about the possible effect of instructions outside of the respective structured set and its subcomponents is needed. This reflects the compositional nature of the semantics. We formalize structured code using the following inductively defined datatype:

**datatype** $('a)structuredCode = none \mid$
$\qquad\qquad\qquad\qquad one\ nat\ ('a)instr \mid$
$\qquad\qquad\qquad\qquad seq\ ('a)structuredCode\ ('a)structuredCode$

The constructor $none$ (which has the syntax abbreviation $\emptyset$) corresponds to the empty set, while the constructor $one$ (written as $label :: instruction$) corresponds to a set consisting of exactly one labeled instruction. The constructor $seq$ ($structuredCode \oplus structuredCode$) formalizes the intuition of set construction given above and is used for sequential composition in the big-step semantics. In general, a set of labeled instructions can be structured in many ways. However, the evaluations of the big-step semantics using the rules presented below are oblivious with respect to the actual fixed structure.

The rules of the big-step semantics are given in Figure 2. The rules for $do$, $br$ and $brt$ clearly correspond to the ones from the small-step semantics. However, for the branch instructions it is required that the destination of a jump does not equal its own label. In the inference rules, the labeled instructions are now defined with respect to a piece of structured code $sc$ that needs to be well-formed ( $wff_{sc}$ $sc$). Well-formedness here means that no constituent parts of a structured set of instructions share an instruction with the same label. The central part of the big-step semantics are the rules for sequential composition ($SEQ1$ and $SEQ2$), and the rule $TERM$ that is applicable if the program counter of a given state $s$ does not point into the structured piece of code. The intuition behind the rules for sequential composition is the following: if execution of a piece of structured code $sc1 \oplus sc2$ from a given state $s$ starts in the first part of the structured piece of code (because $PC\ s$ points to a label within $sc1$), then the code $sc1$ is executed from this state. After this, a state $s1$ with a program counter outside of $sc1$ is obtained. From this state both parts of the original structured code ($sc1 \oplus sc2$) are executed. The reason for considering both parts of the composition is that from $sc2$ there might be a jump back into $sc1$. This way of executing the

$$\frac{wff_{sc}\ sc \qquad sc = (l :: do\ f) \qquad (l,\ do\ f) \in lis}{PC\ s = l \qquad x \in f\ (R\ s) \qquad t = s(\!\!\!|\ R := x,\ PC := PC\ s + 1)\!\!\!|}{(s,\ sc,\ t) \in big\text{-}step}\text{DOF}$$

$$\frac{wff_{sc}\ sc \qquad sc = (l :: br\ m)}{(l,\ br\ m) \in lis \qquad PC\ s = l \qquad l \neq m \qquad t = s(\!\!\!|\ PC := m)\!\!\!|}{(s,\ sc,\ t) \in big\text{-}step}\text{BR}$$

$$\frac{wff_{sc}\ sc \qquad sc = (l :: brt\ bexp\ m\ n) \qquad (l,\ brt\ bexp\ m\ n) \in lis}{PC\ s = l \qquad bexp\ (R\ s) \qquad l \neq m \qquad t = s(\!\!\!|\ PC := m)\!\!\!|}{(s,\ sc,\ t) \in big\text{-}step}\text{BRTT}$$

$$\frac{wff_{sc}\ sc \qquad sc = (PC\ s :: brt\ bexp\ m\ n) \qquad (l,\ brt\ bexp\ m\ n) \in lis}{PC\ s = l \qquad \neg\ bexp\ (R\ s) \qquad l \neq n \qquad t = s(\!\!\!|\ PC := n)\!\!\!|}{(s,\ sc,\ t) \in big\text{-}step}\text{BRTF}$$

$$\frac{sc = (sc1 \oplus sc2) \qquad PC\ s \in_{sc} sc1}{wff_{sc}\ sc \qquad (s,\ sc1,\ s1) \in big\text{-}step \qquad (s1,\ sc1 \oplus sc2,\ t) \in big\text{-}step}{(s,\ sc,\ t) \in big\text{-}step}\text{SEQ1}$$

$$\frac{sc = (sc1 \oplus sc2) \qquad PC\ s \in_{sc} sc2}{wff_{sc}\ sc \qquad (s,\ sc2,\ s1) \in big\text{-}step \qquad (s1,\ sc1 \oplus sc2,\ t) \in big\text{-}step}{(s,\ sc,\ t) \in big\text{-}step}\text{SEQ2}$$

$$\frac{\neg\ (PC\ s \in_{sc} sc) \qquad wff_{sc}\ sc}{(s,\ sc,\ s) \in big\text{-}step}\text{TERM}$$

**Fig. 2.** Rules of the Bigstep Semantics

two pieces of code is done until a state is reached, in which the program pointer is outside of $sc1 \oplus sc2$.

The big-step semantics corresponds to the small-step semantics, i.e., for a given execution in the big-step semantics there exists a corresponding execution in the small-step semantics and for stuck executions of the small-step semantics ( i.e., if the program pointer does not point to a labeled instruction anymore) there exists a corresponding big-step execution. These simulation and reduction theorems enable the transfer of properties established on the level of the big-step semantics to the small-semantics. Thereby, the big-step semantics serves as a connection layer between the unstructured layer of the small-step semantics and the structured and more abstract layer of the proof calculus, which we present in the upcoming section.

# 5    Proof Calculus for Total Correctness

In this section, we present our proof calculus for total correctness. In our formalization assertions are defined using the extensional approach, i.e., we only fix the type of assertions but do not define an assertion language. We model auxiliary variables explicitly using an auxiliary state. Auxiliary variables are used to refer to the values of variables appearing in a precondition within the postcondition of a specification. The type of assertions is formalized as:

**type-synonym** $('aux, 'a) ass = 'aux \Rightarrow ('a) state \Rightarrow bool$

The definition is parameterized over the type of auxiliary state $'aux$ and the type of state $'a$ . The auxiliary state can therefore be instantiated conveniently when using the calculus. For example, in the completeness proof we instantiate the auxiliary state with the type of state.

The approach to total correctness proofs is similar to the way total correctness is realized in proof calculi for structured programming languages. The specification of a variant is required in the rule for sequential composition. Informally, for structured programming languages such a variant ensures that in every loop iteration a value of the state (or a combination of values) is decreased. If a lower bound is known for the values of the respective part of the state, execution of the loop must terminate at some point. Recall that the rule of sequential composition in our proof system for low-level code corresponds to both the rules for sequential composition and loops in Hoare calculi for high-level languages. In order to obtain a rule for sequential composition in our proof calculus, we can follow the approach used for structured languages. The rules of the total correctness calculus are given in Figure 3.

In contrast to the partial correctness case, the rule for $do\ f$ requires that the set of states yielded by $f$ is not empty. For the branch instructions it is required that they do not branch to their own label. Regarding sequential composition, a well-founded relation needs to be provided (condition $wf\ r$). A binary relation is well-founded iff it does not allow for infinitely descending chains. For example, the relation less-than on the natural numbers is a well-founded relation. Given such a relation, it needs to be established for both of the sub specifications that the state is decreased with respect to this relation. This is formalized by the term $s = s'$ in the precondition and the term $(s, s') \in r$ in the postcondition of the assumptions in the rule for sequential composition. The rule of consequence is similar to the one for partial correctness, but a conjunct for strengthening the auxiliary state in the precondition is added. This is required to achieve adaption completeness [10,8]. Informally, adaption completeness expresses that the auxiliary state can always be adjusted as required in order to express arbitrary valid specifications. This is of particular importance when extending a proof system to recursive function calls, for example. The treatment of recursion can be significantly simplified when using auxiliary variables [10].

Validity of a specification is defined similarly to validity in the context of partial correctness. Additionally, we require that if a state $s$ fulfills the precondition $p$, execution of the respective structured code terminates for *all* executions of *code* starting in $s$. This is formalized using the predicate $\downarrow$ defined by the rules in Figure 4 and reflected by the last conjunct in the following definition:

$$\left\langle \begin{array}{c} \lambda\ aux\ s.PC\ s = l \wedge f\ (R\ s) \neq \emptyset \wedge \\ \forall x \in f\ (R\ s).\ q\ aux\ (s(\!|R := x,\ PC := PC\ s + 1|\!)) \\ \vee\ PC\ s \neq l \wedge q\ aux\ s \end{array} \right\rangle l :: do\ f\ \langle q \rangle\ \text{HDOF}$$

$$\left\langle \begin{array}{c} \lambda\ aux\ s.PC\ s = l \wedge \\ q\ aux\ (s(\!|PC := m|\!)) \wedge m \neq l \\ \vee\ PC\ s \neq l \wedge q\ aux\ s \end{array} \right\rangle l :: br\ m\ \langle q \rangle\ \text{HBR}$$

$$\left\langle \begin{array}{c} \lambda\ aux\ s.PC\ s = l \wedge \\ (b\ (R\ s) \wedge q\ aux\ (s(\!|PC := m|\!)) \wedge m \neq l \vee \\ \neg\ b\ (R\ s) \wedge q\ aux\ (s(\!|PC := n|\!)) \wedge n \neq l) \\ \vee\ PC\ s \neq l \wedge q\ aux\ s \end{array} \right\rangle l :: brt\ b\ m\ n\ \langle q \rangle\ \text{HBRTF}$$

$$\dfrac{\begin{array}{c} wf\ r \\ \forall s'.\ \vdash_t \langle \lambda aux\ s.\ (PC\ s \in_{sc} sc1) \wedge i\ aux\ s \wedge s = s' \rangle\ sc1\ \langle \lambda aux\ s.\ i\ aux\ s \wedge (s, s') \in r \rangle \\ \forall s'.\ \vdash_t \langle \lambda aux\ s.\ (PC\ s \in_{sc} sc2) \wedge i\ aux\ s \wedge s = s' \rangle\ sc2\ \langle \lambda aux\ s.\ i\ aux\ s \wedge (s, s') \in r \rangle \end{array}}{\vdash_t \langle i \rangle\ sc1 \oplus sc2\ \langle \lambda aux\ s.\ \neg\ (PC\ s \in_{sc} sc1) \wedge \neg\ (PC\ s \in_{sc} sc2) \wedge i\ aux\ s \rangle}\ \text{HSEQ}$$

$$\dfrac{\begin{array}{c} \vdash_t \langle p' \rangle\ sc\ \langle q' \rangle \\ \forall s\ t.\ (\forall aux.\ p'\ aux\ s \longrightarrow q'\ aux\ t) \longrightarrow (\forall aux.\ p\ aux\ s \longrightarrow q\ aux\ t) \\ \forall s.\ (\exists aux.\ p\ aux\ s) \longrightarrow (\exists aux.\ p'\ aux\ s) \end{array}}{\vdash_t \langle p \rangle\ sc\ \langle q \rangle}\ \text{HCONS}$$

$$\vdash_t \langle p \rangle\ \emptyset\ \langle p \rangle\ \text{HNONE}$$

**Fig. 3.** Rules of the Total Correctness Calculus

## Definition 1 (Validity for total correctness)
$\models_t \langle p \rangle\ code\ \langle q \rangle \longleftrightarrow$
$\quad \forall aux\ s\ t.\ p\ aux\ s \wedge (s,\ code,\ t) \in big\text{-}step \longrightarrow q\ aux\ t \wedge$
$\quad \forall aux\ s.\ p\ aux\ s \longrightarrow code \downarrow s$

A specification is valid (abbreviated $\models_t \langle p \rangle\ code\ \langle q \rangle$) iff for all states that fulfill the precondition $p$ and from which $code$ is executed, the postcondition $q$ holds for the reached states and furthermore the execution of $code$ terminates. The axiomatization of termination using the predicate $\downarrow$ is necessary because in the presence of non-determinism the existence of a terminating execution is not sufficient to claim that all executions from a certain state terminate. The intuition behind the formalized rules is as follows. As mentioned in the introduction, the instruction $do\ f$ can be used to model an instruction that blocks execution given that the function $f$ yields an empty set. Therefore, the termination rule for $do\ f$ requires the set of states yielded by $f$ to be non-empty. For the branch instructions, it is obvious that they terminate if they do not target their own label. Any instruction terminates, if it is evaluated in a state where the instruction pointer does not point to the label of the respective instruction. The empty structured instruction $\emptyset$ terminates for any state because it contains no labeled instructions that the program counter might point to. The most interesting case is sequential composition, where termination behavior is defined inductively. A sequential composition terminates from a given state $s$,

$$\frac{f\ (R\ s) \neq \emptyset \vee PC\ s \neq l}{(l :: do\ f) \downarrow s}\text{DOF} \qquad \frac{m \neq l \vee PC\ s \neq l}{(l :: br\ m) \downarrow s}\text{BR}$$

$$\frac{b\ (R\ s) \wedge m \neq l \vee \neg\ b\ (R\ s) \wedge n \neq l \vee PC\ s \neq l}{(l :: brt\ b\ m\ n) \downarrow s}\text{BRTF}$$

$$\frac{\begin{array}{c}PC\ s \in_{sc} (sc1 \oplus sc2) \\ ((PC\ s \in_{sc} sc1) \wedge sc1 \downarrow s \wedge (\forall t.\ (s,\ sc1,\ t) \in big\text{-}step \longrightarrow (sc1 \oplus sc2) \downarrow t) \vee \\ (PC\ s \in_{sc} sc2) \wedge sc2 \downarrow s \wedge (\forall t.\ (s,\ sc2,\ t) \in big\text{-}step \longrightarrow (sc1 \oplus sc2) \downarrow t))\end{array}}{(sc1 \oplus sc2) \downarrow s}\text{SEQ}$$

$$\frac{\neg\ (PC\ s \in_{sc} (sc1 \oplus sc2))}{(sc1 \oplus sc2) \downarrow s}\text{SEQ2}$$

$$\emptyset \downarrow s\text{SNONE}$$

**Fig. 4.** Definition of the termination predicate

if execution of the first part of the structured code of the composition terminates from $s$ in a state $t$, and then the sequential composition terminates from this state or vice versa. If the program pointer in $s$ does not point into the sequential composition, it terminates as well.

**Theorem 1 (Soundness for total correctness)**
$\vdash_t \langle p \rangle\ code\ \langle q \rangle \longrightarrow \models_t \langle p \rangle\ code\ \langle q \rangle$

The proof is by induction on the rules of the proof logic. For the basic instructions, it is sufficient to unfold the definition of the respective rules from the big-step semantics and the termination predicate $\downarrow$. The most interesting case is sequential composition. The proof requires an induction over the rules of the big-step semantics. To establish that the termination predicate holds for sequentially composed code, we invoke well-founded induction over the induction predicate using the specified well-founded relation $r$.

We prove completeness using the most general triple approach [2] because the weakest precondition approach does not work in the presence of unbounded non-determinism. Formally, the most general triple is defined as follows:

**Definition 2 (Most general triple)**
$mgt\ code \equiv (\lambda z\ s.\ z = s \wedge code \downarrow s,\ code,\ \lambda z\ t.\ (z,\ code,\ t) \in big\text{-}step)$

The intuition behind the most general triple is that it reflects all possible executions from a state fulfilling the precondition by 'freezing' this state using the auxiliary state $z$, and then claiming in the postcondition that it holds for all states $t$ reachable via the big-step semantics. Since we deal with total correctness, it is also specified (using the termination predicate $\downarrow$) that execution from a state fulfilling the precondition needs to terminate. If it can be established that the rules of our calculus are sufficient to prove the most general triple, it follows that the proof system is complete (here *fst* refers to the first part of the mgt-tuple and *snd(snd(mgt code))* refers to the third part):

## Lemma 1 (Most general triple implies completeness)
*If* $wff_{sc}$ *code* **and** $\vdash_t \langle fst\ (mgt\ code)\rangle$ *code* $\langle snd\ (snd\ (mgt\ code))\rangle$ **then** $\models_t \langle P \rangle$ *code* $\langle Q \rangle \longrightarrow \vdash_t \langle P \rangle$ *code* $\langle Q \rangle$

The following theorem establishes that the rules of our proof system are sufficient to derive the most general triple:

## Lemma 2 (Derivation of the most general triple)
*If* $\cup_{sc}$ *code* $\subseteq$ *lis* **and** $wff_{sc}$ *code* **then** $\vdash_t \langle fst\ (mgt\ code)\rangle$ *code* $\langle snd\ (snd\ (mgt\ code))\rangle$

The proof is done by induction on *code* (which needs to be well-formed). We show the case for the instruction *do f* here and then focus on sequential composition. The other cases are similar. For *do f*, we need to show that the following triple holds:
$$\vdash_t \langle \lambda z\ s.\ z = s \wedge (l :: do\ f) \downarrow s\rangle\ l :: do\ f\ \langle \lambda z\ t.\ (z, l :: do\ f, t) \in big\text{-}step\rangle$$
Using the rule of consequence we strengthen the precondition to obtain the following triple:
$$\vdash_t \langle \lambda aux\ s.\ PC\ s = l\ \wedge f\ (R\ s) \neq \emptyset \wedge$$
$$\forall x{\in}f\ (R\ s).\ (aux, l :: do\ f, s(\!|R := x, PC := PC\ s + 1|\!)) \in big\text{-}step$$
$$\vee PC\ s \neq l \wedge (aux, l :: do\ f, s) \in big\text{-}step\rangle$$
$$l :: do\ f$$
$$\langle \lambda z\ t.\ (z, l :: do\ f, t) \in big\text{-}step\rangle$$
Using the proof rule for the instruction *do f*, we want to show that this triple can be derived in our proof system. In order to apply the rule, we first need to apply the rule of consequence. The application of the rule of consequence requires to show that the following holds:
**If** $(l :: do\ f) \downarrow s$ **and** $PC\ s = l \vee (s, l :: do\ f, s) \notin big\text{-}step$ **then**
$$PC\ s = l \wedge f\ (R\ s) \neq \emptyset \wedge$$
$$\forall x{\in}f\ (R\ s).\ (s, l :: do\ f, s(\!|R := x, PC := Suc\ (PC\ s)|\!)) \in big\text{-}step$$
The definition of termination in the first assumption $((l :: do\ f) \downarrow s)$ implies that the function $f$ must not yield the empty set ($f\ (R\ s) \neq \emptyset$). This already shows the second conjunction of our proof goal. The second assumption in this proof obligation states that either the program counter points to the instruction *do f* at label $l$, or that there exists no transition from $s$ to itself through the instruction *do f* at label $l$. It is easy to show that the latter can only be the case if the instruction pointer indeed points to $l$. It therefore remains to show that:
$$\forall x{\in}f\ (R\ s).\ (s, PC\ s :: do\ f, s(\!|R := x, PC := Suc\ (PC\ s)|\!)) \in big\text{-}step$$
This follows from the big-step rule for *do f*, since the program counter of $s$ points to the label of the *do f* instruction.

For sequential composition, we have the assumption that the following triples hold for the individual parts of the sequential composition:

$$\vdash_t \langle \lambda z\ s.\ z = s \wedge sc1 \downarrow s \rangle\ sc1\ \langle \lambda z\ t.\ (z,\ sc1,\ t) \in \text{big-step} \rangle \tag{1}$$

$$\vdash_t \langle \lambda z\ s.\ z = s \wedge sc2 \downarrow s \rangle\ sc2\ \langle \lambda z\ t.\ (z,\ sc2,\ t) \in \text{big-step} \rangle \tag{2}$$

and we have to establish the following triple:

$$\vdash_t \langle \lambda z\ s.\ z = s \wedge (sc1 \oplus sc2) \downarrow s \rangle \tag{3}$$
$$sc1 \oplus sc2$$
$$\langle \lambda z\ t.\ (z,\ sc1 \oplus sc2,\ t) \in \text{big-step} \rangle$$

In order to apply the appropriate proof rule for sequential composition, we need to find a suitable invariant and provide a well-founded relation for the composition. Both are based on the observation that execution of the sequential composition might alternate between the two pieces of structured code involved in the sequential composition. Therefore, we define the invariant based on the transitive closure of the set of state-pairs $(u, v)$, where the state $v$ can be reached from the state $u$ through $sc1$ or $sc2$. For a tuple of states $(z, t)$, the invariant then describes all the states $z$ visited after and between executing $sc1$ or $sc2$ in an alternating manner. Note that states visited 'within' the execution of either of the pieces of code are not captured. Furthermore, the invariant requires the alternating executions to terminate. Using the rule of consequence, we strengthen the precondition of the desired specification (3) to the following assertion, which exactly formalizes the invariant described above using the termination requirement:

$$\langle \lambda z\ t.\ (z, t) \in \{(u, v)\ |((PC\ u \in_{sc} sc1) \wedge (u, sc1, v) \in \text{big-step}\ \vee$$
$$(PC\ u \in_{sc} sc2) \wedge (u, sc2, v) \in \text{big-step})\}^* \wedge$$
$$(sc1 \oplus sc2) \downarrow z \rangle$$

We weaken the postcondition in a similar manner. Note that we need to add that the program counter does not point into the sequentially composed pieces of code anymore in order to apply the rule of consequence:

$$\langle \lambda z\ t.\ \neg\ (PC\ t \in_{sc} sc1) \wedge \neg\ (PC\ t \in_{sc} sc2) \wedge$$
$$(z, t) \in \{(u, v)\ |((PC\ u \in_{sc} sc1) \wedge (u, sc1, v) \in \text{big-step} \vee$$
$$(PC\ u \in_{sc} sc2) \wedge (u, sc2, v) \in \text{big-step})\}^* \wedge$$
$$(sc1 \oplus sc2) \downarrow z \rangle.$$

The desired specification (3) now has the form required to apply the rule for sequential composition as defined in our proof system. To apply the rule, we have to provide an appropriate well-founded relation. We use the following relation, which claims that the terminating executions of the sequential composition (which might 'circulate' through both parts of the composition) form a well-founded relation:

$$wf\{(t, s) \mid (sc1 \oplus sc2) \downarrow s \wedge PC\ s \in_{sc} (sc1 \oplus sc2) \wedge$$
$$(\ (PC\ s \in_{sc} sc1) \longrightarrow (s, sc1, t) \in \textit{big-step} \wedge$$
$$(PC\ s \in_{sc} sc2) \longrightarrow (s, sc2, t) \in \textit{big-step}\ )\}$$

To show that this relation is indeed well-founded, we use the following lemma, which specifies that if a sequential composition $sc1 \oplus sc2$ is executed starting in a state $f(k)$[2] and terminates, then for every possible execution path there exists an argument $i$ such that the program counter in the state $f(i)$ does not point into the sequential composition anymore and therefore the execution terminates. Clearly, this reflects the characterization of a well-founded relation, i.e., that there is no infinitely descending chain. The resulting lemma is the following:

**If** $(sc1 \oplus sc2) \downarrow f\ k$ **and**
$$(\forall i.\ PC\ (f\ i) \in_{sc} (sc1 \oplus sc2) \Longrightarrow$$
$$(PC\ (f\ i) \in_{sc} sc1) \longrightarrow (f\ i, sc1, f\ (Suc\ i)) \in \textit{big-step} \wedge$$
$$(PC\ (f\ i) \in_{sc} sc2) \longrightarrow (f\ i, sc2, f\ (Suc\ i)) \in \textit{big-step})$$
**then** $\exists i.\ \neg\ (PC\ (last\ (f\ i)) \in_{sc} sc1) \wedge \neg\ (PC\ (last\ (f\ i)) \in_{sc} sc2)$

The lemma is proved by induction on the termination predicate. Well-foundedness of the relation described above is then easily established. Now that the appropriate well-founded relation is specified, it needs to be shown that the preconditions of the triples (1) and (2) from the assumptions of our overall proof goal can be strengthened to yield the specified invariant. Moreover, we need to show that the postconditions can be weakened to yield the invariant and that furthermore the state is decreased with respect to the given well-founded relation. For (1) we need to show that we can obtain the following specification using the rule of consequence:

$\forall s' \langle \lambda aux\ s.PC\ s \in_{sc} sc1 \wedge$
$\qquad (aux, s) \in \{(u, v).(PC\ u \in_{sc} sc1) \wedge (u, sc1, v) \in \textit{big-step} \vee$
$\qquad\qquad\qquad\qquad (PC\ u \in_{sc} sc2) \wedge (u, sc2, v) \in \textit{big-step}\}^* \wedge$
$\qquad (sc1 \oplus sc2) \downarrow aux \wedge s = s' \rangle$
$sc1$
$\langle \lambda aux\ s.(aux, s) \in \{(u, v).(PC\ u \in_{sc} sc1) \wedge (u, sc1, v) \in \textit{big-step} \vee$
$\qquad\qquad\qquad\qquad (PC\ u \in_{sc} sc2) \wedge (u, sc2, v) \in \textit{big-step}\}^* \wedge$
$\qquad (sc1 \oplus sc2) \downarrow aux \wedge$
$\qquad ((sc1 \oplus sc2) \downarrow s' \wedge ((PC\ s' \in_{sc} sc1) \vee (PC\ s' \in_{sc} sc2)) \wedge$
$\qquad (PC\ s' \in_{sc} sc1) \longrightarrow (s', sc1, s) \in \textit{big-step} \wedge$
$\qquad (PC\ s' \in_{sc} sc2) \longrightarrow (s', sc2, s) \in \textit{big-step})\}\rangle$

Note that the precondition is a conjunction consisting of a predicate referring to the program pointer (as required by the respective rule of the proof system) and the invariant. It also connects the states of the precondition to the states of the postcondition via the universally quantified variable $s'$. The postcondition in turn is a conjunction of the invariant and the requirement that the states of the postcondition are related to the states of the precondition (via $s'$) with respect to the well-founded relation that we have given above. To prove that the specification can be derived from (1) we use the following auxiliary lemma:

---

[2] f is a function from the natural numbers into the states.

**Lemma 3 (Transitivity of termination)**
*If* $wff_{sc}$ $(sc1 \oplus sc2)$ *and* $\cup_{sc}$ $(sc1 \oplus sc2) \subseteq lis$ *and* $(sc1 \oplus sc2) \downarrow s$ *and* $s \neq s'$ *and* $PC \ s \in_{sc} (sc1 \oplus sc2)$ *and* $(s, s') \in \{(u, v) \mid (PC \ u \in_{sc} sc1) \wedge (u, sc1, v) \in big\text{-}step \vee (PC \ u \in_{sc} sc2) \wedge (u, sc2, v) \in big\text{-}step\}^*$ *then* $(sc1 \oplus sc2) \downarrow s'$

The lemma states that, if execution of a sequential composition $sc1 \oplus sc2$ terminates from a state $s$, and furthermore $s$ and $s'$ are related via the relation that describes the intermediate states of executions alternating between $sc1$ and $sc2$, then execution of $sc1 \oplus sc2$ terminates from $s'$ as well. Finally, the rule for sequential composition can be applied to establish that the desired specification (3) is indeed valid in our calculus. Once it is shown that the most general triple can be derived in the calculus, completeness follows directly (if the code is well-formed and fulfills the requirements for labeled instruction sets):

**Theorem 2 (Completeness for total correctness)**
*If* $\cup_{sc} c \subseteq lis$ *and* $wff_{sc} \ c$ *then* $\models_t \langle P \rangle \ c \ \langle Q \rangle \longrightarrow \vdash_t \langle P \rangle \ c \ \langle Q \rangle$

# 6 Example

As an example, we explain how the presented proof calculus can be used to verify the total correctness of low-level code resulting from the compilation of a high-level loop. The code and the related high-level code is given as follows:

```
reg1 = {1,2,3,4};          1 do set1t0
while (reg1 < 10)          2 brt sm10 3 5
    {reg1 := reg1 + 1}     3 do incr1
                          4 br 2
```

We use the following definitions to specify the initial non-deterministic assignment of a value from the set $\{1, 2, 3, 4\}$ to register 1 and the addition of 1 to the value residing in register 1 in line 3. Furthermore, the function $sm10$ defines the branch condition in line 2. Note that we use a function of type $nat \Rightarrow nat$ to model the registers here. The first two functions given below take such a function as an argument and perform pointwise updates. The value of the respective function for the argument 1 corresponds to the contents of the variable `reg1`.

$set1t0 \ regs = \{(regs(1{:=}1)),(regs(1{:=}2)),(regs(1{:=}3)),(regs(1{:=}4))\}$
$incr1 \ regs = \{regs(1 := (regs \ 1) + 1)\}$
$sm10 \ regs = (regs \ 1 < 10)$

We want to derive the following total correctness specification, which states that executed from a state where the program pointer PC points to label 1, execution ends in a state where the PC points to 5 and register 1 holds the value 10.

$\langle \lambda aux \ s. \ PC \ s = 1 \rangle$
$\quad (1 :: do \ set1t0) \oplus ((2 :: brt \ sm10 \ 3 \ 5) \oplus ((3 :: do \ incr1) \oplus (4 :: br \ 2)))$
$\langle \lambda aux \ s. \ PC \ s = 5 \wedge R \ s \ 1 = 10 \rangle$

$\langle \lambda aux\ s.\ (PC\ s \in_{sc} s3) \wedge Inv234\ aux\ s\ s'a \wedge s = s'b \rangle$
$3 :: do\ incr1$
$\langle \lambda aux\ s.\ Inv234\ aux\ s\ s'a \wedge (s,\ s'b) \in v3rela \rangle$

$\qquad\qquad\qquad\qquad\qquad \langle \lambda aux\ s.\ (PC\ s \in_{sc} s4) \wedge Inv234\ aux\ s\ s'a \wedge s = s' \rangle$
$\qquad\qquad\qquad\qquad\qquad 4 :: br\ 2$

$\qquad\qquad\qquad\qquad\qquad \langle \lambda aux\ s.\ Inv234\ aux\ s\ s'a \wedge (s,\ s') \in v3rela \rangle$
$\langle \lambda aux\ s.\ Inv234\ aux\ s\ s'a \rangle$
$s3 \oplus s4$
$\langle \lambda aux\ s.\ \neg (PC\ s \in_{sc} s3) \wedge \neg (PC\ s \in_{sc} s4) \wedge Inv234\ aux\ s\ s'a \rangle$
_____
$\langle \lambda aux\ s.\ (PC\ s \in_{sc} s34) \wedge Inv235\ aux\ s \wedge s = s' \rangle$
$s34$
$\langle \lambda aux\ s.\ Inv235\ aux\ s \wedge (s,\ s') \in cvrel \rangle \qquad \langle \lambda aux\ s.\ (PC\ s \in_{sc} s2) \wedge Inv235\ aux\ s \wedge s = s' \rangle$
$\qquad\qquad\qquad\qquad\qquad\qquad\qquad\qquad\qquad 2 :: brt\ sm10\ 3\ 5$

$\qquad\qquad\qquad\qquad\qquad\qquad\qquad\qquad\qquad \langle \lambda aux\ s.\ Inv235\ aux\ s \wedge (s,\ s') \in cvrel \rangle$
$\langle Inv235 \rangle$
$s2 \oplus s34$
$\langle \lambda aux\ s.\ \neg (PC\ s \in_{sc} s2) \wedge \neg (PC\ s \in_{sc} s34) \wedge Inv235\ aux\ s \rangle$
_____
$\langle \lambda aux\ s.\ (PC\ s \in_{sc} s234) \wedge Inv125\ aux\ s \wedge s = s' \rangle$
$s234$
$\langle \lambda aux\ s.\ Inv125\ aux\ s \wedge (s,\ s') \in cvrel \rangle \qquad \langle \lambda aux\ s.\ (PC\ s \in_{sc} s1) \wedge Inv125\ aux\ s \wedge s = s' \rangle$
$\qquad\qquad\qquad\qquad\qquad\qquad\qquad\qquad\qquad 1 :: do\ set1t0$

$\qquad\qquad\qquad\qquad\qquad\qquad\qquad\qquad\qquad \langle \lambda aux\ s.\ Inv125\ aux\ s \wedge (s,\ s') \in cvrel \rangle$
$\langle Inv125 \rangle$
$s1 \oplus s234$
$\langle \lambda aux\ s.\ \neg (PC\ s \in_{sc} s1) \wedge \neg (PC\ s \in_{sc} s234) \wedge Inv125\ aux\ s \rangle$
_____
$\langle \lambda aux\ s.\ PC\ s = 1 \rangle$
$(1 :: do\ set1t0) \oplus ((2 :: brt\ sm10\ 3\ 5) \oplus ((3 :: do\ incr1) \oplus (4 :: br\ 2)))$
$\langle \lambda aux\ s.\ PC\ s = 5 \wedge R\ s\ 1 = 10 \rangle$

**Fig. 5.** Proof tree for the example

The proof tree is given in Figure 5. We use the following abbreviations and definitions for structured code and assertions:

$s2 = 2 :: brt\ sm10\ 3\ 5$ $\qquad\qquad\qquad\qquad\qquad s3 = 3 :: do\ incr1$
$s4 = 4 :: br\ 2$ $\qquad\qquad\qquad\qquad\qquad\qquad\quad s34 = (3 :: do\ incr1) \oplus (4 :: br\ 2)$
$s234 = (2 :: brt\ sm10\ 3\ 5) \oplus ((3 :: do\ incr1) \oplus (4 :: br\ 2))$

$Inv125\ aux\ s = (\lambda aux s.((PC s = 1) \vee$
$\qquad\qquad\qquad\quad (PC\ s = 2 \wedge ((R\ s)\ 1) \geq 0 \wedge ((R\ s)\ 1) \leq 10) \vee$
$\qquad\qquad\qquad\quad (PC\ s = 5 \wedge ((R\ s)\ 1) = 10))) \ aux\ s$

$Inv235\ aux\ s = (\lambda aux s.((PC\ s = 2 \wedge ((R\ s)\ 1) \geq 0 \wedge ((R\ s)\ 1) \leq 10) \vee$
$\qquad\qquad\qquad\quad (PC\ s = 3 \wedge ((R\ s)\ 1) < 10) \vee$
$\qquad\qquad\qquad\quad (PC\ s = 5 \wedge ((R\ s)\ 1) = 10))) \ aux\ s$

$Inv234\ aux\ s\ s'a =$
$\qquad (\lambda aux\ s.((PCs = 3 \wedge ((R\ s)1) < 10 \wedge ((R\ s)1) \leq 10) \wedge v2def\ s = v2def\ s'a \vee$
$\qquad\quad (PCs = 4 \wedge ((R\ s)1) \leq 10) \wedge v2def\ s < v2def\ s'a \vee$
$\qquad\quad (PCs = 2 \wedge ((R\ s)1) \leq 10) \wedge v2def\ s < v2def\ s'a)) \ aux\ s$

When proving total correctness for structured code, a variant is specified, which is decreased by every execution of the loop body. The same technique can be used for low-level code, but here a variant needs to be specified here for every sequential composition. We use the following functions from the program state into the natural numbers in order to define suitable variants:

$v1def\ s = (if\ (PC\ s = 1)\ then\ 1\ else\ 0)$
$v2def\ s = (10 - (R\ s\ 1))$
$v3def\ s = (if\ (PC\ s \geq 1 \wedge PC\ s \leq 5)\ then\ (6 - PC\ s)\ else\ 0)$
$v4def\ s = (if\ (PC\ s = 3 \vee PC\ s = 4)\ then\ (5 - PC\ s)\ else\ 0)$
$cvdef\ s = ((v1def\ s), (v2def\ s), (v3def\ s))$
$cvrel = (inv\text{-}image\ (less\text{-}than <*lex*> less\text{-}than <*lex*> less\text{-}than)\ cvdef)$

Based on the given functions, we define well-founded relations $v1rela,v2rela,$ $v3rela$ using the function **measure** of Isabelle/HOL. The function yields relations, which are well-founded by construction. Note that we take the value of the register corresponding to the variable $reg1$ in the definition of $v2def$. We define the combined variant $cvrel$ for the given low-level code using the function $cvdef$, which maps a given state $s$ to a tuple consisting of the mappings of the previously defined functions to $s$. The well-founded relation $cvrel$ is then defined as the inverse image of the lexicographic product of the previously defined functions. The actual proof depicted in Figure 5 is carried out using backward reasoning. We use the combined variant $cvrel$ for the sequential compositions. An interesting situation arises in the last sequential composition in the upper right of the proof tree. To apply the rule of consequence, the invariant $Inv234$ needs to mention $v2def$ explicitly. This is due to the backward jump in line 4 and reflects the usage of the variant as known for total correctness proofs about high-level code in the setting of low-level code.

## 7   Related Work

Closely related to our work is of course the work of Saabas and Uustala on which our work builds [9]. The partial correctness calculus was mechanized in [1] using the theorem prover Coq and extended with a separation logic. Total correctness and non-determinism was not considered in this work. Regarding total correctness, [5] presents a logic for low-level code that is formalized using the theorem prover HOL. However, the assertion format used there is quite different from the one we use because it is not based on labels but uses multiple pre- and post-conditions. A further logic for low-level code extended with a separation logic is presented in [3].

## 8   Conclusions and Further Work

In this paper, we have presented a mechanized verification framework for total correctness of low-level code in the presence of non-determinism. We have built our development on the work presented in [9]. Our extensions required significant changes to the soundness and completeness proofs of the logic. To overcome these problems, we adopted an approach from [7] for high-level languages to the setting of low-level code. Furthermore, we have shown how the resulting verification environment can be used for concrete mechanized total correctness proofs by exploiting Isabelle/HOLs mechanisms for well-founded relations. This is especially useful to cope with the complexity inherent to proofs about unstructured low-level code and the further challenges of proving total correctness in this setting. As future work, we consider extending the formalization to a concurrent setting with shared variable concurrency. Because of the compositional nature of the presented logic, we expect that we can transfer techniques for rely-guarantee reasoning [4] to the setting of low-level code and obtain a mechanized and compositional verification environment for concurrent low-level code.

# References

1. Affeldt, R., Nowak, D., Yamada, K.: Certifying assembly with formal security proofs: The case of bbs, vol. 77, pp. 1058–1074. Elsevier North-Holland, Inc., Amsterdam (2012)
2. Gorelick, G.A.: A complete axiomatic system for proving assertions about recursive and non-recursive programs. Technical Report 75, Dept. of Computer Science,University of Toronto (1975)
3. Jensen, J.B., Benton, N., Kennedy, A.: High-level separation logic for low-level code. In: Proceedings of the 40th Annual ACM SIGPLAN-SIGACT Symposium on Principles of Programming Languages, POPL 2013, pp. 301–314. ACM, New York (2013)
4. Jones, C.B.: Specification and Design of (Parallel) Programs. In: IFIP Congress, pp. 321–332 (1983)
5. Myreen, M.O., Gordon, M.J.C.: Hoare logic for realistically modelled machine code. In: Grumberg, O., Huth, M. (eds.) TACAS 2007. LNCS, vol. 4424, pp. 568–582. Springer, Heidelberg (2007)
6. Nipkow, T., Paulson, L.C., Wenzel, M.T.: Isabelle/HOL — A Proof Assistant for Higher-Order Logic. LNCS, vol. 2283. Springer, Heidelberg (2002)
7. Nipkow, T.: Hoare logics for recursive procedures and unbounded nondeterminism. In: Bradfield, J.C. (ed.) CSL 2002 and EACSL 2002. LNCS, vol. 2471, pp. 103–119. Springer, Heidelberg (2002)
8. Olderog, E.-R.: On the notion of expressiveness and the rule of adaptation. Theoretical Computer Science 24(3), 337–347 (1983)
9. Saabas, A., Uustalu, T.: A compositional natural semantics and hoare logic for low-level languages. Electron. Notes Theor. Comput. Sci. 156(1), 151–168 (2006)
10. Schreiber, T.: Auxiliary variables and recursive procedures. In: Bidoit, M., Dauchet, M. (eds.) CAAP 1997, FASE 1997, and TAPSOFT 1997. LNCS, vol. 1214, pp. 697–711. Springer, Heidelberg (1997)

# Formally Verified Computation of Enclosures of Solutions of Ordinary Differential Equations

Fabian Immler*

Institut für Informatik, Technische Universität München
immler@in.tum.de

**Abstract.** Ordinary differential equations (ODEs) are ubiquitous when modeling continuous dynamics. Classical numerical methods compute approximations of the solution, however without any guarantees on the quality of the approximation. Nevertheless, methods have been developed that are supposed to compute enclosures of the solution.

In this paper, we demonstrate that enclosures of the solution can be verified with a high level of rigor: We implement a functional algorithm that computes enclosures of solutions of ODEs in the interactive theorem prover Isabelle/HOL, where we formally verify (and have mechanically checked) the safety of the enclosures against the existing theory of ODEs in Isabelle/HOL.

Our algorithm works with dyadic rational numbers with statically fixed precision and is based on the well-known Euler method. We abstract discretization and round-off errors in the domain of affine forms. Code can be extracted from the verified algorithm and experiments indicate that the extracted code exhibits reasonable efficiency.

**Keywords:** Numerical Analysis, Ordinary Differential Equation, Theorem Proving, Interactive Theorem Proving.

## 1 Introduction

Ordinary differential equations (ODEs) are used to model a vast variety of dynamical systems. In many cases there is no closed form for the solution, but one can resort to numerical approximations. They are usually given by "traditional" one-step methods like the Euler method or the more general family of Runge-Kutta methods, which approximate the solution in several discrete steps in time. However, especially in safety-critical applications, approximations are too vague in that they provide no rigorous connection to the solution.

To establish such a connection, in the area of "guaranteed integration", different approaches have been proposed. They have in common that they do not compute with approximate values, but with sets enclosing the solution. The most basic way to compute with sets is interval arithmetic, which suffers from the wrapping effect (i.e., large overapproximations when enclosing rotated boxes

---

* Supported by the DFG Graduiertenkolleg 1480 (PUMA)

J.M. Badger and K.Y. Rozier (Eds.): NFM 2014, LNCS 8430, pp. 113–127, 2014.
© Springer International Publishing Switzerland 2014

in a box) and cannot track dependencies between variables. The proposed approaches differ in the data structures that represent the sets as well as the algorithms that are used to compute them.

A well-studied family of algorithms is based on on Taylor series expansions and computing with interval arithmetic, surveyed e.g., by Nedialkov [18], and implemented in tools like AWA [15], ADIODES [25], VNODE [17], VNODE-LP[19]. Those overcome the wrapping effect with QR-decomposition. A different approach is based on Taylor models, which suffer from neither the wrapping effect nor the dependency problem and which were studied by Makino and Berz and implemented to solve ODEs in COSY [1]. A survey of Taylor model based methods is given by Neher *et al.* [20]. Tucker [26] uses the "traditional" Euler method with interval arithmetic and uses interval splitting to overcome the wrapping effect. Bouissou *et al.* [3] also use "traditional" methods, but they represent sets with affine forms [6] to overcome the wrapping effect and track linear dependencies.

Most of the aforementioned "guaranteed" methods have in common that the proofs that they actually compute enclosures of the solution are carried out on a relatively high level, without formal connection to the source code. Nedialkov [19] has been worried about this gap and responds with implementing VNODE-LP using literate programming, such that the correctness can be verified via code review by a human expert. The operations used in COSY are (manually) proved correct in [24] – but only for the basic operations on Taylor models, without a connection to ODEs.

Our work aims at narrowing the gap between implementation and proof even more by allowing for mechanical software verification. We formalize both proof and algorithm in an interactive theorem prover, namely Isabelle [22]. The theorem prover provides a formal language to express mathematical formulas and allows to prove theorems in a rigorous calculus, where every reasoning step is checked by the system. Isabelle/HOL implements higher-order logic, a subset of which can be seen as a functional programming language. Isabelle/HOL therefore allows to extract code from the formal specifications.

Our approach is to give a specification of a guaranteed method for ODEs in Isabelle/HOL. We verify that the computed enclosures are correct with respect to a formalization of ODEs in Isabelle/HOL. Our specified method is executable, we therefore extract code and compute enclosures for some examples.

The method we chose to formalize is based on the approach taken by Bouissou *et al.* [3]: they essentially let "traditional" methods operate on sets represented by affine forms. We liked the flexibility of their framework – the fact that it can be extended with different "traditional" methods, which are all well-studied and each known to be suited for particular kinds of ODEs. Moreover, we had already formalized a (rudimentary) numerical analysis of the Euler method.

## 1.1   Contributions

We contribute a formal and mechanically checked verification of a set-based Euler method. We therefore provide a formalization of affine forms, a formal specification of the Euler method based on affine forms and a formal correctness proof with respect to the formalized mathematical specification of ODEs. In the course, we discovered subtle issues in informal proofs given for other set-based methods (see also Section 2.4).

Note that every definition and theorem we explicitly display in the following text possesses a formally proved and mechanically checked counterpart. The development is available in the Archive of Formal Proofs [14,12].

## 1.2  Related Work

In addition to the already mentioned work on guaranteed integration, we would like to point to related work on differential equations in theorem provers: Spitters and Makarov [16] use the constructive proof of the existence of a unique solution to calculate solutions of ODEs in Coq. The local nature of the proof restricts their computations to short existence intervals. Boldo *et al.* [2] approximate the solution of one particular partial differential equation in Coq. A formal development of Taylor models is given by Brisebarre *et al.* [4]. Platzer [23] uses differential invariants to reason about dynamical systems in a proof assistant.

## 1.3  Overview

Let us start with a high-level overview of our "tool": We present the required mathematical background and the formalization thereof in Section 2. Formally verified approximations of ODEs will be obtained as follows:

1. The user needs to input a term $f$ for the right-hand side of the ODE.
2. A term for the derivative $Df$ of $f$ can then be obtained automatically via symbolic differentiation (Section 2.3).
3. Given $f$ and $Df$, we provide a method to automatically obtain affine arithmetic approximations $\hat{f}$ and $\hat{f}'$ of $f$ and $Df$. (Section 3)
4. Now $f$, $Df$ $\hat{f}$, and $\hat{f}'$ can be shown to satisfy the assumptions for numerical approximations with the Euler method (Section 4).
5. Code for the Euler method can then be extracted, compiled and executed in order to obtain a list of enclosures. Theorem 9 states the correctness of the method.

We conducted experiments with some concrete ODEs in Section 5.

## 2  Background

We work with the interactive theorem prover Isabelle [22], inside the logic Isabelle/HOL. Isabelle is an LCF-style theorem prover, i.e., every proposition passes through a small, trusted inference kernel.

In the following, we present the background theory we use in our formalization and the notation we use in this paper to refer to it. As a subset of Isabelle/HOL can be seen as a functional programming language, the notation we use in this presentation is inspired by functional programming languages: for a term $t$ we write $t :: \alpha$ if $t$ is of type $\alpha$. We write function application juxtaposition as in $f\ t$ and function abstraction $\lambda x.\ t$. Types are built from base types like $\mathbb{N}, \mathbb{Z}, \mathbb{R}, \mathbb{R}^n$ or via type constructors like $\alpha \Rightarrow \beta$ for functions from type $\alpha$ to $\beta$, $\alpha \times \beta$ for pairs, or $\alpha$ set respectively $\alpha$ list for sets respectively lists with elements of type $\alpha$. $\Rightarrow$ binds weaker than $\times$, which binds weaker than other type constructors. $\alpha$ option denotes the option type with constructors None and Some. For operations in the option monad we use Haskell-style **do**-notation. For $A :: \alpha$ set, $B :: \beta$ set we denote with $A \to B$ the function set $\{f \mid \forall a \in A.\ f\ a \in B\}$. We make use of standard functional programming functions like map, fold, filter, fst, snd and write appending (concatenating) lists with _@_ $:: \alpha$ list $\Rightarrow \alpha$ list $\Rightarrow \alpha$ list

We also make use of Isabelle's code generator [8]: it performs a (mostly syntactic) translation from equations in the logic to functions in functional programming languages like SML, OCaml, Haskell, or Scala. Worth noticing for our application is that we make use of a shallow embedding of integers $\mathbb{Z}$, i.e., operations on type $\mathbb{Z}$ are mapped to operations of the arbitrary-precision integers provided by the respective target languages.

In the remainder of this section, we present the notation of the mathematical formalization upon which we base our work.

## 2.1   Real Numbers

Isabelle/HOL provides a theory of real numbers $\mathbb{R}$, which does not directly allow for code generation. We formalize all of our algorithms in terms of real numbers, but in order to obtain an executable formalization, we make use of data refinement [7] and represent the type $\mathbb{R}$ with dyadic rational numbers:

We introduce (based on Obua's [21] construction of Floating point numbers) a "pseudo-constructor" Float $:: \mathbb{Z} \Rightarrow \mathbb{Z} \Rightarrow \mathbb{R}$ for dyadic rational numbers, i.e., Float $m\ e = m \cdot 2^e$. Isabelle's code generator can be instructed to translate $\mathbb{R}$ as a type with elements constructed by Float in the target language. Operations on real numbers then need to be given in terms of pattern matching on Float, e.g., (Float $m_1\ e_1$) $\cdot$ (Float $m_2\ e_2$) = Float $(m_1 \cdot m2)\ (e_1 + e_2)$.

For efficiency reasons we need to restrict the precision, i.e., the size of the mantissa, during computations. We therefore use $trunc^+$ and $trunc^-$ with the property $trunc^-\ p\ x \le x \le trunc^+\ p\ x$. Moreover, $trunc^+$ and $trunc^-$ make sure that the absolute value of the returned mantissa is smaller than $2^p$. When we speak of *precision*, we usually denote it with a value $p$ corresponding to the length of the mantissa as described above. We also give a function round, for which if round $p\ x = (y, e)$, then $y$ is rounded with precision $p$ and $|x - y| \le e$.

Some operations like division or transcendental functions cannot be computed exactly on dyadic rational numbers, for them we use approximating functions with precision $p$ like $div^-$ and $div^+$ with $div^-\ p\ x\ y \le \frac{x}{y} \le div^+\ p\ x\ y$.

## 2.2   Euclidean Space

Our work is based on Isabelle/HOL's Multivariate Analysis [11], which is an extension and generalization of a port of Harrison's formalization of Euclidean space in HOL Light [9].

Euclidean spaces $\mathbb{R}^n$ are formalized as types $\alpha$ with a set of base vectors *Basis* :: $\alpha$ *set* with the vector space operations addition $+$ :: $\alpha \Rightarrow \alpha \Rightarrow \alpha$, scalar multiplication $\cdot$ :: $\mathbb{R} \Rightarrow \alpha \Rightarrow \alpha$ and inner product $\bullet$ :: $\alpha \Rightarrow \alpha \Rightarrow \mathbb{R}$. Products of real numbers are Euclidean spaces, we therefore write for example $\mathbb{R} \times \mathbb{R}$ also as $\mathbb{R}^2$, and we have e.g., (*Basis* :: $\mathbb{R}^2$ *set*) $= \{(1,0),(0,1)\}$. Every element of the Euclidean space can be written as a sum of base vectors scaled with the respective coordinates. Coordinates can be extracted by taking the inner product with a base vector, so it holds that $x = \sum_{i \in Basis}(x \bullet i) \cdot i$.

For $a, b$ :: $\mathbb{R}^n$ write $a \le b$ if for all base vectors $i \in Basis$, $a \bullet i \le b \bullet i$. Then the interval $[a; b] = \{x \mid a \le x \wedge x \le b\}$ is the smallest box containing $a$ and $b$. We also define the absolute value $|a|$ :: $\mathbb{R}^n$ componentwise, i.e., for base vectors $i$, $|a| \bullet i = |a \bullet i|$.

## 2.3   Derivatives

The (ordinary) derivative of a function $g$ :: $\mathbb{R} \Rightarrow \mathbb{R}^n$ is written $g'$ :: $\mathbb{R} \Rightarrow \mathbb{R}^n$. For $f$ :: $\mathbb{R}^n \Rightarrow \mathbb{R}^m$, we denote by $Df$ :: $\mathbb{R}^n \Rightarrow \mathbb{R}^n \Rightarrow \mathbb{R}^m$ the Frechet (or total) derivative of $f$. $Df$ $x$ is the linear approximation of $f$ at $x$ (which can be represented with the Jacobian matrix). We use the notation for derivatives under the implicit assumption that they exist (which we prove or assume in the formal development).

Isabelle/HOL provides a set of rules allowing to symbolically compute derivatives. Together with the rewrite engine of Isabelle/HOL, this allows to automatically obtain a term for the derivative $Df$ of $f$.

## 2.4   Notes on Taylor Series Expansion in Euclidean Space

In the course of formally proving the correctness of our implementation, we even identified a subtle issue in the presentation of Bouissou *et al.* [3]: They develop (in Equation 8) a Taylor series expansion of a function $y$, where they assume the existence of a $\xi \in [t; t+h]$ with $y(t+h) = y(t) + \sum_{i=1}^{k} \frac{h^i}{i!} y^{(i)}(t) + \frac{h^{k+1}}{k!} y^{(k+1)}(\xi)$. Such a $\xi$ only exists for functions $y$ :: $\mathbb{R} \Rightarrow \mathbb{R}$. In the multivariate case, $y$ :: $\mathbb{R} \Rightarrow \mathbb{R}^n$ can be seen as a family of functions $y_i$ :: $\mathbb{R} \Rightarrow \mathbb{R}$ such that there exists a family of $\xi_i \in [t; t+h]$ for the remainders of $y_i$. The remainder of $y$ can then be written as $r := (y_i^{(k)} \xi_i)_{i \le n}$. But this element need not be a member of the set $A = \{y^{(k)}(t). t \in [t; t+h]\}$, which they overapproximate as enclosure of the remainder in their Equation 12. However, $r$ is an element of any box enclosing $A$ and they use such a box enclosure in their implementation, which keeps their method safe. Consider e.g., $y(t) = (t^3 + t, t^3)$ as example illustrating the issue.

## 2.5   Ordinary Differential Equations

In the following, we repeat standard results about ODEs, most of which have been formalized in [13]. A homogeneous first order ODE is an equation $x'\ t = f(x\ t)$ with an unknown function $x :: \mathbb{R} \Rightarrow \mathbb{R}^n$, the independent variable $t$ is usually denoted as time. We treat only this kind of ODE, as inhomogeneous ($f$ may depend on $t$) and higher-order ODEs (only the higher derivatives of $x$ are part of the ODE) can be reduced to the simple case. Constraining the ODE to an *initial value problem* (IVP) is crucial for the existence of a unique solution.

**Definition 1 (Initial Value Problem).** *An* initial value problem *ivp is a named tuple of elements* $f :: \mathbb{R}^n \Rightarrow \mathbb{R}^n$, $t_0 :: \mathbb{R}$, $x_0 :: \mathbb{R}^n$, $T :: \mathbb{R}$ *set,* $X :: \mathbb{R}^n$ *set ivp* $= (f, t_0, x_0, T, X)$.

**Definition 2 (Solution).** *A function* $x :: \mathbb{R} \Rightarrow \mathbb{R}^n$ *is a solution to an initial value problem ivp, if* $x'\ t = f(x\ t)$ *and* $x'\ t \in X$ *for all* $t \in T$ *and if* $x\ t_0 = x_0$.

If $X$ is bounded, the metric space of bounded continuous functions $T \to X$ is complete. Then the Banach fixed point theorem guarantees the existence of a unique fixed point of the Picard operator $P :: (\mathbb{R} \Rightarrow \mathbb{R}^n) \Rightarrow (\mathbb{R} \Rightarrow \mathbb{R}^n)$ with $P\ x\ t = x_0 + \int_{t_0}^{t} f\ (x\ s)\mathrm{d}s$, if $P$ is an endomorphism, i.e., maps functions from $T \to X$ onto $T \to X$.

**Theorem 3 (Existence of a unique solution).** *For* $T = [t_0; t_1]$, *if* $f$ *is Lipschitz continuous (i.e.,* $\exists L.\ \forall x_1, x_2 \in X.\ \|f\ x_1 - f\ x_2\| \leq L \cdot \|x_1 - x_2\|$) *on a compact set* $X$ *and if* $P$ *is an endomorphism on* $T \to X$, *then there exists a unique solution sol of the IVP ivp on* $T$.

Let us now present some results about numerical approximations of solutions. The Euler method naively approximates the solution with line segments in the direction given by the right-hand side of the ODE $(x(t+h) \in x\ t + h \cdot (f\ (x\ t)) + \mathcal{O}(h^2))$. Since the error in one step goes to zero with the stepsize $h$, the method is called *consistent*. We represent errors explicitly as sets, hence we give a formulation of consistency in terms of sets. We formalize enclosures of functions with the function set $X \to Y$.

**Theorem 4 (Consistency of Euler method).** *Assume a compact interval* $[t; t + h]$, *a convex and compact set* $X :: \mathbb{R}^n$ *set, and a function* $x \in T \to X$ *with derivative* $x'\ t = f(x\ t)$. *Further assume that* $f$ *is bounded by* $F$ ($f \in X \to F$) *and that the derivative* $Df$ *is bounded by a box* $[D_{\min}; D_{\max}]$ ($\forall x \in X.\ \forall y \in F.\ Df\ x\ y \in [D_{\min}; D_{\max}]$). *Then the Euler method is consistent:*
$$x(t+h) - x\ t + h \cdot (f(x\ t)) \in \left[\tfrac{h^2}{2} \cdot D_{\min}; \tfrac{h^2}{2} \cdot D_{\max}\right]$$

The proof makes use of the Taylor series expansion of $x$, which is why we assume $Df$ bounded by a box. This ensures that the remainder (which is represented with $Df$) is contained in that box (cf. the discussion in Section 2.4).

## 3  Affine Arithmetic

We are going to adapt the Euler method to compute with sets in order to obtain a guaranteed method. We represent sets by affine forms (as described in detail in [6]) $x_0 + \sum_{i=1}^{n} \varepsilon_i \cdot x_i$, where $x_0$ is called the center, the $x_i$ are coefficients and $\varepsilon_i$ formal variables or noise symbols. The set represented by such an affine form is the set of all elements given by the form when the $\varepsilon_i$ range in $[-1; 1]$.

We represent sets $\alpha$ *set* with affine forms of type $\alpha$ *affine*. In order to stay close to an efficient executable representation, we chose $\alpha$ *affine* $= \mathbb{N} \times \alpha \times (\mathbb{N} \times \alpha)$ *list*. For a tuple $(m, x_0, xs)$, $x_0 :: \mathbb{R}^n$ is the center, $xs :: (\mathbb{N} \times \mathbb{R}^n)$ *list* a list of indexed coefficients (distinct and sorted by the first component) where every index is smaller than the degree $m$. We write affine forms either with capital letters $X, Y$ or explicitly as tuples. *elem* $:: \mathbb{R}^n$ *affine* $\Rightarrow (\mathbb{N} \Rightarrow \mathbb{R}) \Rightarrow \mathbb{R}^n$ returns an element given by a valuation for the formal variables: *elem* $(m, x_0, xs)$ $e = \sum_{(i,x)\in xs}(e\ i) \cdot x$. *coeff* $:: (\mathbb{N} \times \mathbb{R}^n)$ *list* $\Rightarrow \mathbb{N} \Rightarrow \mathbb{R}^n$ returns the coefficient with a given index if it exists in the list and zero otherwise. The function *Affine* $:: \mathbb{R}^n$ *affine* $\Rightarrow \mathbb{R}^n$ *set* returns the set represented by an affine form: it is the set of all elements obtained via "valid" valuations: *Affine* $X = \{$*elem* $X\ e \mid e \in \mathbb{N} \to [-1; 1]\}$.

An important notion is that of the joint range of affine forms. Affine forms representing the same set may have different dependencies: $\varepsilon_i$ and $\varepsilon_j$ represent the same set $[-1; 1]$, but the subtraction $\varepsilon_i - \varepsilon_j$ represents either $\{0\}$ or $[-2; 2]$, depending on whether $i = j$. More general, when reasoning about some function $f$ taking two arguments $x \in$ *Affine* $X$ and $y \in$ *Affine* $Y$, $f$ is surely called only for arguments $(x, y) \in (Affine\ X) \times (Affine\ Y)$. But the Cartesian product discards dependencies that the affine forms are actually supposed to track: respecting the dependencies, we can be more precise and state that $(x, y)$ is contained in the set $\{(x, y) \mid x =$ *elem* $X\ e \wedge y =$ *elem* $Y\ e \wedge e \in \mathbb{N} \to [-1; 1]\}$, which is called the joint range of $X$ and $Y$. We generalize this to an arbitrary number of arguments by defining the joint range for lists of affine forms via *Affines* $:: \alpha$ *affine list* $\Rightarrow \alpha$ *list set*, where we have *Affines* $xs = \{$*map* $(\lambda x.$ *elem* $x\ e)\ xs \mid e \in \mathbb{N} \to [-1; 1]\}$.

The maximum deviation of an affine form $(m, x_0, xs)$ is the sum of the absolute values of all coefficients, we denote it by *rad* $xs :: \mathbb{R}^n$. We overapproximate *rad* with precision $p$ by safely rounding all additions: $rad^+\ p\ xs =$ *fold* $(\lambda(i, x)\ e_0.\ trunc^+\ p\ (|x| + e_0))\ xs\ 0$. This can be used to obtain a bounding box for an affine form with *box* $p\ (m, x_0, xs) = [x_0 - rad^+\ p\ xs; x_0 + rad^+\ p\ xs]$, where we have *Affine* $X \subseteq$ *box* $p\ X$.

To convert boxes to affine forms, distinct noise symbols are needed for every coordinate. $[a; b]$ is represented by the affine form $\frac{a+b}{2} + \sum_{i\in Basis} \varepsilon_i \cdot ((\frac{b-a}{2} \bullet i) \cdot i)$, for which we write *affine-of-ivl* $a\ b$.

The Minkowski sum $A \oplus B = \{a + b.\ a \in$ *Affine* $A \wedge b \in$ *Affine* $B\}$ discards dependencies between $A$ and $B$ and is used for example to add some uncertainty $B$ to a given affine form $A$. It can easily be implemented by adding the coefficients of $B$ as coefficients with fresh indices to $A$.

We define binary coefficientwise operations that accumulate round-off errors via *round-binop* $:: \mathbb{N} \Rightarrow (\alpha \Rightarrow \alpha \Rightarrow \alpha) \Rightarrow (\mathbb{N} \times \alpha)$ *list* $\Rightarrow (\mathbb{N} \times \alpha)$ *list* $\Rightarrow (\mathbb{N} \times \alpha)$ *list* $\times \alpha$. *round-binop* can be implemented efficiently thanks to the fact that lists of coefficients are sorted. For *round-binop* $p$ $f$ $xs$ $ys = (zs, err)$, the first essential property is that *round-binop* distributes a binary function $f$ rounded with precision $p$ over the coefficients: for all $i :: \mathbb{N}$, *coeff* $zs$ $i =$ *fst* (*round* $p$ ($f$ (*coeff* $xs$ $i$) (*coeff* $ys$ $i$))). The second property states that *err* overapproximates the sum of the absolute values of all rounding errors: $\sum_{i \in \mathbb{N}} |$*coeff* $zs$ $i - f$ (*coeff* $xs$ $i$) (*coeff* $ys$ $i$)$| \leq err$.

### 3.1 Reification of Expressions

The aim when using affine arithmetic is to replace operations in an expression on real numbers or Euclidean space by the corresponding operations on affine forms. This is similar to work by Hölzl [10] on approximations using interval arithmetic in Isabelle/HOL. This requires an explicit representation of expressions. A technique called *reification* allows to transform a term into an explicit data structure for expressions, evaluated by an interpretation function.

Let us start with expressions in real arithmetic *aexp*, for which we define an inductive datatype like in Figure 1. Elements of this datatype are interpreted recursively using the function $[\![\_]\!]_{vs}$ for an environment $vs :: \mathbb{R}^n$ *list* as given in Figure 2. The environment contains the list of free variables of the expression. They are of type $\mathbb{R}^n$ because ultimately we want to approximate functions $\mathbb{R}^n \Rightarrow \mathbb{R}^n$. *Var* $i$ $b$ allows to take the component indicated by a base vector $b$ of the $i$-th element of the environment.

$$aexp = Add\ aexp\ aexp$$
$$| \ Mult\ aexp\ aexp$$
$$| \ Minus\ aexp$$
$$| \ Inverse\ aexp$$
$$| \ Num\ \mathbb{R}$$
$$| \ Var\ \mathbb{N}\ \mathbb{N}$$

$[\![Add\ a\ b]\!]_{vs} = [\![a]\!]_{vs} + [\![b]\!]_{vs}$
$[\![Mult\ a\ b]\!]_{vs} = [\![a]\!]_{vs} \cdot [\![b]\!]_{vs}$
$[\![Minus\ a]\!]_{vs} = -[\![a]\!]_{vs}$
$[\![Inverse\ a]\!]_{vs} = 1/[\![a]\!]_{vs}$
$[\![Num\ r]\!]_{vs} = r$
$[\![Var\ i\ b]\!]_{vs} = (vs\ !\ i) \bullet b$

$$eexp = AddE\ eexp\ eexp$$
$$| \ Scale\ aexp\ \mathbb{R}^n$$

$[\![AddE\ x\ y]\!]_{vs} = [\![x]\!]_{vs} + [\![y]\!]_{vs}$
$[\![Scale\ a\ b]\!]_{vs} = [\![a]\!]_{vs} \cdot b$

**Fig. 1.** Inductive data type of arithmetic expressions

**Fig. 2.** Recursive interpretation of arithmetic expressions

**Fig. 3.** Datatype and interpretation of Euclidean space expressions

We make use of the automated method for reification by Chaieb [5], which, given a set of equations for the interpretation function and a term, proves a reification theorem. With the equations for $[\![\_]\!]$ from above and the fact that $x_2 = x \bullet b_2$ when $b_2$ is the second base vector, we get e.g., for the term $x_2 + 3$ the theorem $x_2 + 3 = [\![Add\ (Var\ 0\ b_2)\ (Num\ 3)]\!]_{[x]}$.

For functions between Euclidean spaces, every expression $\lambda(x_1, \ldots, x_n)$. $(f_1\ x_1\ \cdots\ x_n, \ldots, f_m\ x_1\ \cdots\ x_n)$ can be rewritten as $\lambda x.\ (f_1\ (x \bullet b_1)\ \cdots\ (x \bullet b_n)) \cdot b_1 + \cdots + (f_m\ (x \bullet b_1)\ \cdots\ (x \bullet b_n)) \cdot b_m$. We therefore define expression and interpretation for expressions on Euclidean space as given in Figure 3.

To give an example, the expression $(2, x_1)$ is first rewritten to $2 \cdot (1, 0) + (x \bullet b_1) \cdot (0, 1)$ and then reified to $[\![AddE\ (Scale\ (Num\ 2)\ (1, 0))\ (Scale\ (Var\ 0\ 1)\ (0, b_1))]\!]_{[x]}$

## 3.2   Approximation of Elementary Operations

For affine forms on real numbers, we support the arithmetic operations addition, multiplication, and their respective inverses. Note that, in essence, we work with a fixed, finite precision $p$, which means that we have to take rounding errors into account. The general approach is to round all "ideal" operations and summarize the encountered round-off errors in a fresh formal variable.

Let us illustrate this for the example of addition: We calculate the new center $z$ with rounding error $e_1$, the coefficientwise addition $zs$ of $xs$ and $ys$ with accumulated error $e_2$ and add a new coefficient (overapproximating the errors $e_1$ and $e_2$) for the formal variable with fresh index $l$ to the resulting affine form.

> *add-affine* $p\ (n, x_0, xs)\ (m, y_0, ys) =$
>    **let** $(z, e_1) =$ *round* $p\ (x_0 + y_0)$;
>       $(zs, e_2) =$ *round-binop* $p\ (\lambda x\ y.\ x + y)\ xs\ ys$;
>       $e =$ *trunc*$^{+}\ p\ (e_1 + e_2)$;
>       $l = \max\ n\ m$
>    **in** $(l + 1, z, zs@[(l, e)])$

Correctness of operations on affine forms states that if the arguments are members of affine sets, then the result from the "ideal" operation is in the affine set resulting from the operation on affine forms. Moreover the dependencies of the formal variables stay intact. In the example of addition:

**Theorem 5 (Correctness of Addition).** *If* $[x, y] \in$ *Affines* $[X, Y]$, *then* $[x, y, x + y] \in$ *Affines* $[X, Y,$ *add-affine* $p\ X\ Y]$

We proved similar correctness theorems for multiplication *mult-affine*. multiplicative inverse *inverse-affine* and unary minus, where we guided our implementation by the descriptions in [6].

## 3.3   Approximation of Expressions

The explicit representation of arithmetic expressions due to reification and the approximations of elementary operations allow to recursively define an approximation function *approx* :: $\mathbb{N} \Rightarrow$ *aexp* $\Rightarrow \mathbb{R}^n$ *affine list* $\Rightarrow \mathbb{N} \Rightarrow \mathbb{R}$ *affine option* in affine arithmetic. Below we give addition as example but refrain from a presentation of further cases. In order not to introduce wrong dependencies, $l$ is used as index of a fresh formal variable and needs to be threaded through the recursive calls. Approximation is performed inside the option monad, in order to handle failures like e.g., approximating the inverse of an affine form that contains zero.

> *approx* $p\ ($*Add* $a\ b)\ vs\ l =$
>    **do** $(n, x_0, xs) \leftarrow$ *approx* $p\ a\ vs\ l$
>       $(m, y_0, ys) \leftarrow$ *approx* $p\ b\ vs\ n$
>       *Some* $($*add-affine* $p\ (n, x_0, xs)\ (m, y_0, ys))$

Approximation *approx* :: $\mathbb{N} \Rightarrow$ *eexp* $\Rightarrow \mathbb{R}^n$ *affine list* $\Rightarrow \mathbb{N} \Rightarrow \mathbb{R}^n$ *affine* of expressions in Euclidean space is just coefficientwise scaling and addition.

Correctness for the approximation of an expression in Euclidean space can then be stated as follows: If the input variables $vs$ are in the joint range of the affine forms $VS$, then the approximated affine set is in the joint range with the interpreted expression. (We write $x \# xs$ for prepending the element $x$ to the list $xs$)

**Theorem 6 (Correctness of approximation).** *If $vs \in$ Affines $VS$, the maximum degree of the affine forms in $VS$ is $d$, and* approx $p$ expr $VS\ d =$ Some $X$, *then* $[\![expr]\!]_{vs} \# vs \in X \# VS$

### 3.4 Summarizing Noise Symbols

During longer computations, the approximations due to affine arithmetic (and rounding errors) will add more and more noise symbols to the affine form, which impairs performance in the long run. The number of noise symbols can be reduced by summarizing (or condensing) several noise symbols into a new one. This process obviously discards the correlation mediated by the summarized noise symbols, so a trade-off needs to be found.

Following [6], we summarize all symbols with an absolute value smaller than a given fraction $r$ (the *summarization threshold*) of the maximum deviation of the affine form. Note that we compare the coefficients in Euclidean space, that means when we summarize a noise symbol, the dependencies in all coordinates are small. We then extend the affine form consisting of the large coefficients $ys$ with a box enclosing all small deviations $zs$:

> summarize $p\ r\ (n, x_0, xs) =$
>      **let** $rad = rad^+\ p\ xs$
>      **let** $ys = filter\ (\lambda x.\ x \geq r \cdot rad)\ xs$
>           $zs = filter\ (\lambda x.\ \neg\ x \geq r \cdot rad)\ xs$
>      **in** $(n, x_0, ys) \oplus$ affine-of-ivl $(-rad^+\ p\ zs)\ (rad^+\ p\ zs)$

The necessary correctness theorem states that summarization returns a safe overapproximation: Affine $X \subseteq$ Affine (summarize $p\ r\ X$).

## 4    Approximation of ODEs

Our algorithm approximates ODEs in a series of discrete steps in time. We start the section by presenting the implementation and proofs for a single step, then show the extension to a series of steps.

The formalization of our algorithm and the correctness proof are generic in the ODE $f$, its derivative $Df$ and respective approximations in affine arithmetic $\hat{f}, \hat{f}'$, which we will assume for the remainder of this section:

$f :: \mathbb{R}^n \Rightarrow \mathbb{R}^n$
$\hat{f} :: \mathbb{N} \Rightarrow \mathbb{R} \Rightarrow \mathbb{R}^n$ affine $\Rightarrow \mathbb{R}^n$ affine option
$Df :: \mathbb{R}^n \Rightarrow \mathbb{R}^n \Rightarrow \mathbb{R}^n$
$\hat{f}' :: \mathbb{N} \Rightarrow \mathbb{R} \Rightarrow \mathbb{R}^n$ affine $\Rightarrow \mathbb{R}^n$ affine $\Rightarrow \mathbb{R}^n$ affine option

$\forall x.\ x \in \text{Affine } X \longrightarrow \hat{f}\ p\ t\ X = \text{Some } F \longrightarrow [x, f\ x] \in \text{Affines } [X, F]$

$\forall x\ y.\ [x, y] \in \text{Affines } [X, Y] \longrightarrow \hat{f}'\ p\ t\ X\ Y = \text{Some } F' \longrightarrow$

$\quad [x, y, Df\ x\ y] \in \text{Affines } [X, Y, F']$

$f$ has continuous derivative $Df$

## 4.1   Euler Step

ODEs are approximated in a series of discrete steps. A step consists of two phases, one for certification and one for approximation. In the first phase, we certify the existence of a unique solution and obtain an a-priori bound on the solution. In the second phase we use this a-priori bound to compute a tighter enclosure with a set-based Euler method. Let us assume a step size $h > 0$ at time $t_0 :: \mathbb{R}$. Further assume that the step starts at value $x_0 :: \mathbb{R}^n$, for which we assume an affine approximation $X_0$ with $x_0 \in \text{Affine } X_0$.

**Certification.** The idea is to certify the existence of a unique solution according to Theorem 3. One prerequisite is to show that the operator $P$ used for Picard iteration is an endomorphism, which can be shown by finding a post fixed point. Like Bouissou [3], we use the set-based overapproximation $Q\ X = X_0 + h \cdot (f\ X)$ of the operator $P$. For a box $X$ with $x\ t \in X$ for $t \in [t_0; t_0 + h]$, it holds that $P\ x\ t = x_0 + \int_{t_0}^{t} f\ (x\ s)\ ds \in Q\ X$.

We define a function $\hat{Q}$ using affine arithmetic to overapproximate $Q$. Then we iterate $\hat{Q}\ p\ r$, starting with **box** $p\ X_0$, until we find a post fixed point. That means when we encounter boxes $B$ and $C$ such that $\hat{Q}\ p\ r\ C = \text{Some } B$ and $B \subseteq C$. Since $Q$ is an overapproximation of $P$, it follows that for all $t \in T$ and $x \in T \to C$, $P\ x\ t \in C$, which certifies that $P$ is an endomorphism on $T \to C$.

Now that we have verified $P$ as an endomorphism, a unique solution exists according to Theorem 3, if $f$ is Lipschitz continuous, which follows from our assumption that $f$ is continuously differentiable.

The results of the certification phase can be summarized in the following theorem, which guarantees the existence of a unique solution for the current step size $h$ and also provides an a-priori bound for the evolution of the solution:

**Theorem 7 (Certification of Solution).** *If the iteration of $\hat{Q}$ started with $X_0$ yields a $C$ with $\hat{Q}\ p\ r\ C = \text{Some } B$ and $B \subseteq C$, then the ODE $f$ has a unique solution* sol *on $[t_0; t_0 + h]$ for the initial value $(t_0, x_0)$. Moreover, the solution is bounded by* sol $\in [t_0; t_0 + h] \to (\text{Affine } C)$.

Note that it is possible that the iteration of $Q$ does not reach a fixed point if the step size is too large – one can then repeat the phase with a smaller step size. It is also possible to accelerate the iteration with some sort of widening.

**Approximation.** The approximation phase aims to compute a tighter enclosure for the solution, making use of the a-priori enclosure from the previous phase. For this phase we assume that the previous phase returned for some step size $h :: \mathbb{R}$ an a-priori bound $C :: \mathbb{R}^n$ *affine*.

We work with a set-based Euler method and therefore use Theorem 4, which bounds the method error of one Euler step. We first overapproximate the Euler step $\psi\, x := x + h \cdot (f\, x)$ using an affine arithmetic function $\hat{\psi}$ and add to the resulting affine form the uncertainty given by the method error.

For the overapproximation of the Euler step $\psi\, x_0$, recall the assumption $x_0 \in X_0$. We can therefore overapproximate $\psi\, x_0$ with $\hat{\psi}\, p\, r\, X_0$.

Concerning the method error, we need to bound $Df$. We know from the a-priori bound of Theorem 7, that for all $t \in [t_0; t_0 + h]$, $sol\, t \in Affine\, C$. We can further bound $f$ on $C$ with $\hat{f}$, i.e., with $F := \hat{f}\, p\, r\, C$. With the assumption that $Df$ is bounded by $\hat{f}'$, we have for all $[x, y]$ in $Affines\, [C, F]$ that $[x, y, Df\, x\, y] \in Affine\, [C, F, \hat{f}'\, p\, r\, C\, F]$. If we set $[D_{\min}; D_{\max}] = box\, p\, (\hat{f}'\, p\, r\, C\, F)$, then Theorem 4 allows to prove that the solution is safely enclosed by an Euler step in affine arithmetic $\hat{\psi}\, p\, r\, X_0$, extended with the method error of one Euler step:

**Theorem 8.** $sol\, (t_0 + h) \in Affine\, (\hat{\psi}\, p\, r\, X_0 \oplus [\frac{h^2}{2} \cdot D_{\min}; \frac{h^2}{2} \cdot D_{\max}])$

### 4.2  Euler Series

We denote with the term "local" a solution certified by the fact that the certification phase of one Euler step succeeded. Taking the enclosure from the approximation phase (which is usually smaller, and can be made arbitrarily small with the step size) as initial enclosure $X_0$ for a subsequent Euler step and iterating the process, one gets a series of enclosures for local solutions. The respective step sizes are determined by the certification phase of the Euler step. Inductively, one can connect the proofs for the existence of local solutions to one theorem stating the existence of a unique global solution. The a-priori bounds can be used as bounds over local time intervals, and tight bounds can be given for discrete points in time. During computation, we accumulate several of the interval bounds and give back a list of time intervals, together with an enclosure of the solution on that interval and a tight enclosure at the end of the interval. We define the function that iterates and accumulates local steps as *euler-series* $p\, r$ for precision $p$ and summarizing threshold $r$ (Section 3.4), the final theorem then looks as follows:

**Theorem 9.** *If euler-series $p\, r\, t_0\, X_0$ returns $(t_1, xs)$, then there exists a unique solution on $[t_0; t_1]$. Moreover for all $(t_i, C_i, t_j, X_j) \in xs$, the solution is bounded by $C_i$ resp. $X_j$: for all $t \in [t_i; t_j]$, $sol\, t \in Affine\, C_i$ and $sol\, t_j \in Affine\, X_j$.*

## 5   Experiments

Our experiments do not aim for a thorough comparison of different approaches for guaranteed integration – this can and should be done for unverified code. We compare experiments using our extracted code with the experimental results of Bouissou *et al.* [3]. They run their experiments on a machine with two processors running with 2.33GHz and 2GB RAM, we perform our computations on an Intel® Core™2 Duo CPU T7700 at 2.40GHz and 4GB RAM.

**Table 1.** Experimental comparison for the oil reservoir problem (time interval $[0; 50]$)

| # | method | steps | time | error $y$ | error $z$ |
|---|--------|-------|------|-----------|-----------|
| 1 | *euler-series* 50 $2^{-7}$ | $13 \cdot 10^3$ | 280 s | $1.6 \cdot 10^0$ | $8.0 \cdot 10^{-2}$ |
| 2 | *euler-series* 50 $2^{-7}$ | $52 \cdot 10^3$ | 810 s | $2.5 \cdot 10^{-1}$ | $6.0 \cdot 10^{-3}$ |
| 3 | *euler-series* 50 $2^{-7}$ | $220 \cdot 10^3$ | 3100 s | $6.8 \cdot 10^{-2}$ | $1.6 \cdot 10^{-3}$ |
| 4 | Heun [3] | $220 \cdot 10^3$ | 141 s | $7 \cdot 10^{-5}$ | |
| 5 | ode45 [3] | $8 \cdot 10^3$ | 15 s | $1.7 \cdot 10^{-1}$ | |

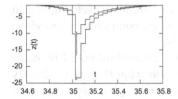

**Fig. 4.** Enclosures for $z$ in the oil reservoir problem

**Fig. 5.** Enclosures for $x$ in $f(t,x) = x^2 - t$ with $(t_0, x_0) = (0, 0.71875)$

One example they give is the oil reservoir problem $f(y, z) = (z, z^2 - \frac{3}{10^{-3}+y^2})$ for initial values $(y_0, z_0) = (10, 0)$. In Figure 4, we plot the enclosures from the list of verified bounds output by *euler-series* 50 $2^{-7}$ when extracted to SML (4500 lines of generated code) and compiled with PolyML 5.5.1. The values are therefore verified in the sense of Theorem 9. We experience similar behavior like Bouissou *et al.* [3] in that it is hard to integrate over the time around $t = 35$, i.e., very small step sizes are used there. But also note that the method gains accuracy later on. Note that this example is not trivial, as other packages like VNODE cannot integrate this ODE.

In Table 1, we cite experimental results from Bouissou and compare with our experiments. We give the number of steps, the time needed to integrate the problem and the error of the approximation at the end of the integration. Comparing experiments with comparable step sizes, namely lines 1 and 5 resp. 3 and 4, it can be seen that our method takes roughly a factor of 20 more time. Note that the method of Heun needs twice as many evaluations of $\hat{f}$ in one step and ode45 even more. So interpret the figures just as a rough estimate, suggesting that our method is currently between one or two orders of magnitude slower than comparable tools. We believe that this is still reasonable as e.g., our method does not use native floating point numbers, where we lose a large factor. With comparable step sizes our method is less accurate, which is not surprising, as the Euler method converges linearly with the step size, the method of Heun quadratic and ode45 cubic.

A second example we would like to give is a comparison with the numerical analysis given in previous work [13]. There we integrated the ODE $f(t, x) = x^2 - t$ on the time interval $t \in [0; 0.5]$ with an error $2 \cdot 10^{-2}$. We were unable to certify the existence of a solution for a longer time span. Now (with the same computational effort of around 2 seconds), we can give enclosures for the solution on an eight times larger time span $t \in [0; 4]$ with a smaller error of $3 \cdot 10^{-3}$ at $t = 0.5$, which we consider a significant improvement.

# 6   Conclusion

The experiments indicate that our method exhibits reasonable performance in comparison to unverified tools and great advances when compared to previous approaches to a formally verified treatment of ODEs.

Nevertheless, there is still room for improvement: our method could be compiled for native IEEE floating point numbers, a formalization thereof is already available in Isabelle/HOL [27]. Moreover we have not yet implemented approximations of e.g., trigonometric functions, square root or the exponential function in affine arithmetic. In order to achieve competitive accuracy, methods in addition to the Euler method need to be implemented and proved consistent.

**Acknowledgements.** I would like to thank Olivier Bouissou for discussions on the topic. Thanks are due to Johannes Hölzl and the anonymous reviewers for valuable comments on drafts of this paper.

# References

1. Berz, M., Makino, K.: Verified integration of ODEs and flows using differential algebraic methods on high-order Taylor models. Reliable Computing 4(4), 361–369 (1998)
2. Boldo, S., Clément, F., Filliâtre, J.C., Mayero, M., Melquiond, G., Weis, P.: Wave equation numerical resolution: A comprehensive mechanized proof of a C program. Journal of Automated Reasoning 50(4), 423–456 (2012)
3. Bouissou, O., Chapoutot, A., Djoudi, A.: Enclosing temporal evolution of dynamical systems using numerical methods. In: Brat, G., Rungta, N., Venet, A. (eds.) NFM 2013. LNCS, vol. 7871, pp. 108–123. Springer, Heidelberg (2013)
4. Brisebarre, N., Joldeş, M., Martin-Dorel, É., Mayero, M., Muller, J.-M., Paşca, I., Rideau, L., Théry, L.: Rigorous Polynomial Approximation Using Taylor Models in Coq. In: Goodloe, A.E., Person, S. (eds.) NFM 2012. LNCS, vol. 7226, pp. 85–99. Springer, Heidelberg (2012)
5. Chaieb, A.: Automated methods for formal proofs in simple arithmetic and algebra. Diss., Technische Universität, München (2008)
6. de Figueiredo, L.H., Stolfi, J.: Affine Arithmetic: Concepts and Applications. Numerical Algorithms 37(1-4), 147–158 (2004)
7. Haftmann, F., Krauss, A., Kunčar, O., Nipkow, T.: Data refinement in Isabelle/HOL. In: Blazy, S., Paulin-Mohring, C., Pichardie, D. (eds.) ITP 2013. LNCS, vol. 7998, pp. 100–115. Springer, Heidelberg (2013)

8. Haftmann, F., Nipkow, T.: Code generation via higher-order rewrite systems. In: Blume, M., Kobayashi, N., Vidal, G. (eds.) FLOPS 2010. LNCS, vol. 6009, pp. 103–117. Springer, Heidelberg (2010)

9. Harrison, J.: A HOL theory of Euclidean space. In: Hurd, J., Melham, T. (eds.) TPHOLs 2005. LNCS, vol. 3603, pp. 114–129. Springer, Heidelberg (2005)

10. Hölzl, J.: Proving inequalities over reals with computation in Isabelle/HOL. In: Reis, G.D., Théry, L. (eds.) Programming Languages for Mechanized Mathematics Systems (ACM SIGSAM 2009), pp. 38–45 (2009)

11. Hölzl, J., Immler, F., Huffman, B.: Type classes and filters for mathematical analysis in Isabelle/HOL. In: Blazy, S., Paulin-Mohring, C., Pichardie, D. (eds.) ITP 2013. LNCS, vol. 7998, pp. 279–294. Springer, Heidelberg (2013)

12. Immler, F.: Affine Arithmetic. Archive of Formal Proofs (February 2014), http://afp.sf.net/devel-entries/Affine_Arithmetic.shtml

13. Immler, F., Hölzl, J.: Numerical Analysis of Ordinary Differential Equations in Isabelle / HOL. In: Beringer, L., Felty, A. (eds.) ITP 2012. LNCS, vol. 7406, pp. 377–392. Springer, Heidelberg (2012)

14. Immler, F., Hölzl, J.: Ordinary differential equations. Archive of Formal Proofs (February 2014), http://afp.sf.net/devel-entries/Ordinary_Differential_Equations.shtml

15. Lohner, R.: Einschliessung der Lösung gewöhnlicher Anfangs- und Randwertaufgaben und Anwendungen. Dissertation, Universität Karlsruhe (1988)

16. Makarov, E., Spitters, B.: The Picard algorithm for ordinary differential equations in Coq. In: Blazy, S., Paulin-Mohring, C., Pichardie, D. (eds.) ITP 2013. LNCS, vol. 7998, pp. 463–468. Springer, Heidelberg (2013)

17. Nedialkov, N.S., Jackson, K.R.: The design and implementation of a validated object-oriented solver for IVPs for ODEs. Tech. rep., McMaster University (2002)

18. Nedialkov, N.S.: Interval tools for ODEs and DAEs. In: 12th GAMM-IMACS International Symposium SCAN. IEEE (2006)

19. Nedialkov, N.S.: Implementing a rigorous ODE solver through literate programming. In: Rauh, A., Auer, E. (eds.) Modeling, Design, and Simulation of Systems with Uncertainties. Mathematical Engineering, pp. 3–19. Springer (2011)

20. Neher, M., Jackson, K.R., Nedialkov, N.S.: On Taylor model based integration of ODEs. SIAM Journal on Numerical Analysis 45(1), 236–262 (2007)

21. Obua, S.: Flyspeck II: The basic linear programs. Diss., Technische Universität München, München (2008)

22. Paulson, L.C.: Isabelle: The next 700 theorem provers. In: Logic and Computer Science, pp. 361–386 (1990)

23. Platzer, A.: The complete proof theory of hybrid system. In: Logic in Computer Science (LICS), pp. 541–550 (2012)

24. Revol, N., Makino, K., Berz, M.: Taylor models and floating-point arithmetic: Proof that arithmetic operations are validated in COSY. The Journal of Logic and Algebraic Programming 64(1), 135–154 (2005)

25. Stauning, O.: Automatic validation of numerical solutions. Diss., Technical University of Denmark (1997)

26. Tucker, W.: A rigorous ODE solver and Smale's 14th problem. Foundations of Computational Mathematics 2(1), 53–117 (2002)

27. Yu, L.: A Formal Model of IEEE Floating Point Arithmetic. Archive of Formal Proofs (2013), http://afp.sf.net/entries/IEEE_Floating_Point.shtml

# On the Quantum Formalization of Coherent Light in HOL

Mohamed Yousri Mahmoud and Sofiène Tahar

Electrical and Computer Engineering Dept., Concordia University
1455 De Maisonneuve Blvd. W., Montreal, Canada
{mo_solim,tahar}@ece.concordia.ca
http://hvg.ece.concordia.ca

**Abstract.** During the last decade, formal methods, in particular theorem proving, have proven to be effective as analysis tools in different fields. Among them, quantum optics is a potential area of the application of theorem proving that can enhance the analysis results of traditional techniques, e.g., paper-and-pencil and lab simulation. In this paper, we present the formal definition of coherent light, which is typically a light produced by laser sources, using higher-order logic and show the effect of quantum operations on it. To this aim, we first present the formalization of underlying mathematics, in particular, finite/infinite summation over quantum states, then prove important theorems, such as uniqueness and the effect of linear operators. Thereafter, basic quantum states of light, called fock states, are formalized and many theorems are proved over such states, e.g., the effect of the quantum creation operation over fock states. Finally, the fundamental notions of coherent light are formalized and their properties also verified.

**Keywords:** Quantum optics, Fock states, Coherent states, Infinite summation, Theorem proving, HOL-Light.

## 1 Introduction

Classical physics has studied light from different points of view, i.e., ray and wave. Each corresponding theory exposed new optical properties, which later were used in developing several optical systems, such as cameras and high speed communications systems. In contrast, quantum optics treats light as a stream of particles, called *photons* [19]. It was started by Planck in 1900 when he explained the discrete nature of light energy based on the photon definition [2]. Light streams of a low number of photons are the best examples for applying quantum optics rules where non-classical optical properties appear, e.g., fluctuating absolute phase of a wave [12]. An important example is single-photon light streams which have wide applications in the area of quantum cryptography and quantum networks [17]. Quantum optics also introduces the most practical implementations of quantum computers, e.g., [9] and [8]. This application is quite important since it promises to solve "hard" computational problems [14].

J.M. Badger and K.Y. Rozier (Eds.): NFM 2014, LNCS 8430, pp. 128–142, 2014.

Despite the advantages of quantum optics, the analysis of quantum systems is not easy, and it poses many difficulties. Unlike regular systems, quantum ones cannot be simulated on ordinary computers, i.e., computers based on Turing machine [4]. Alternatively, a physical-lab simulation is being utilized for systems analysis. However, it is costly and not safe: every little optical element varies in cost from a few hundred to a few thousand of dollars [5]. In addition, scientists and engineers who carry out the simulation process should be well protected against the beams due to their harmful nature [15]. Another analysis method is using numerical tools (typically Matlab [18]) and CAS (typically Mathematica [3]) besides traditional paper-and-pencil based analytical approaches. However, such tools cannot completely replace paper-and-pencil analysis due to accuracy and expressiveness problems. In this paper, we propose to formalize a milestone in the vast theory of quantum optics using the HOL-Light theorem prover [6] in order to mechanize the paper-and-pencil reasoning process. Thus we can provide better and accurate results about the system subject to analyse.

An important notion of quantum mechanics is the *uncertainty principle*. It admits that performing a measurement on a quantum system affects the accuracy of the subsequent measurements. In 1926, Schrödinger discovered the notion of coherent states that achieve minimal measurement error [13]. Coherent states are of high interest in quantum optics analysis, as they are able to express the quantum systems in different states [12]. Therefore, their development allows the analysis of optical systems in several situations. Our formal development of coherent states is based on the formalization of quantum mechanics presented in [10]. Nevertheless, the formalization requires additional mathematical concepts, e.g., summation over infinite dimension vector spaces, which are presented here. The entire formalization presented in this paper is available at [11].

The rest of the paper is organized as follows: Section 2 briefly summarizes some basics of quantum optics and quantum-related mathematical definitions which are developed in [10]. Section 3 deals with the formalization of infinite summation over quantum states. Section 4 presents the development of fock and coherent states. Finally, we conclude the paper in Section 5 and give an overview of a potential application of coherent light.

## 2    Preliminaries

In this section we briefly present the basic knowledge of quantum optics, in particular coherent light. We then summarize the required mathematical notions for the coherent light formalization.

### 2.1    Quantum Physics

A quantum system is fully described with what is so-called *quantum states*, to which we refer as $|\psi\rangle$. Mathematically, it is a square integrable complex-valued function, and the set of all states forms an inner product space. The product function of such a space is the integration function. In addition, the square integration of each state is equal to one.

Usually, a system has a set of *pure quantum states* (or we can call them basis states, similar to the basis of a vector space). At any time, the system is described with a pure state or a mix of them:

$$|\psi\rangle = \sum |c_i| * |\psi\rangle_i \ i = 0, 1, 2, \dots \tag{1}$$

where $c_i$ is a complex number, $\sum |c_i| = 1$ and $|\psi\rangle_i$ is a pure state. A system is at a pure state $i$, if $c_i = 1$ and for any $j \neq i, c_j = 0$.

In quantum optics, light is considered as a stream of particles called photons, in contrast to the classical theory that considers light as an electromagnetic wave. As a quantum system, light has a set of pure states, called *fock states*. Light in a fock state $|n\rangle$, where $n = 0, 1, 2\dots$, means that the light stream exactly contains $n$ photons. Light is said to be coherent if the number of photons in the light stream (at any time instance) is probabilistically Poisson distributed. In other words, the probability of having (or observing) $n$ photons is:

$$P(N = n) = \frac{|\alpha|^n e^{|\alpha|}}{n!} \tag{2}$$

where $|\alpha|$ is the expected number of observed photons ($\alpha$ is a complex number). A coherent light with expected photons $|\alpha|$ is in the quantum state $|\alpha\rangle$. It is represented in terms of fock states as follows (see Equation (1)):

$$|\alpha\rangle = e^{-\frac{|\alpha|^2}{2}} \sum_{n=0} \frac{\alpha^n}{\sqrt{n!}} |n\rangle \tag{3}$$

Similar to classical physics, quantum mechanics physicists are interested in some information about the system, e.g., temperature, velocity, pressure,.etc. Classically, those quantities are expressed by *real* variables. However, they are complete functions (or operators) in quantum mechanics. Those functions operate on quantum states, i.e., they map complex-valued functions (i.e., quantum state space) onto complex-valued-functions. The important information we have to keep in mind is that a quantum operator (denoted as $\hat{O}$) is a linear transformation over the quantum states space.

In the case of optics, there are two basic quantum operators: *creator* and *annihilator* operators. Their names suggest how these operators affect a stream of photons. An annihilator $\hat{a}$ decreases the number of photons by one (i.e., destroys a photon):

$$\hat{a}|n\rangle = \sqrt{n}|n - 1\rangle \tag{4}$$

Note that the resulting state is not exactly the quantum state $|n-1\rangle$, it is scalar-multiplied by $\sqrt{n}$. Similarly, the creation $\hat{a}^\dagger$ increases the number of photons by one (i.e., creates a photon):

$$\hat{a}^\dagger|n\rangle = \sqrt{n + 1}|n + 1\rangle \tag{5}$$

It is important to mention here that the scalar-multiplication does not change the behavior of a quantum state. Thereby, the resulting states in (4) and (5) still have $n-1$ and $n+1$ photons, respectively.

By solving Equation (5) as a recurrence relation, we obtain a general representation of any fock state $|n\rangle$:

$$|n\rangle = \frac{(\hat{a}^\dagger)^n \, |0\rangle}{\sqrt{n!}} \tag{6}$$

where $|0\rangle$ is called vacuum state since it does not contain any photon. Note here that the power notation used in $(\hat{a}^\dagger)^n$ means the application of the creation operator $n$ times (recall that quantum operators are functions).

According to Equations (3) and (6), we can re-express coherent state in terms of the vacuum state and creation operator:

$$|\alpha\rangle = e^{-\frac{|\alpha|^2}{2}} \left( \sum_{n=0} \frac{(\alpha\hat{a}^\dagger)^n}{n!} \right) |0\rangle \tag{7}$$

Note that for a linear operator $a^\dagger$, $(\alpha\hat{a}^\dagger)^n = \alpha^n(\hat{a}^\dagger)^n$.

In a nutshell, formalizing quantum optics, in particular coherent states, requires different mathematical aspects: 1) Linear spaces of complex functions (i.e., quantum states), 2) Inner product space, 3) Linear transformation (i.e., quantum operators) over those spaces, and 4) infinite/finite summation of quantum states. The following section addresses the formalization of aspects (1-3) which were initially introduced in [10]. Infinite/finite summation and related aspects (e.g., notion of limit) will be covered in Section 3.

## 2.2   Quantum State Space Formalization

In order to reason about any quantum system, we first need to formalize the quantum space, which is mathematically an inner product space of square integrable complex-valued functions. In the following, we provide the most important definitions, for details see [10].

We start by defining a new HOL type for a quantum state, cfun : A → complex which stands for complex *function*. The type is a complex-valued function with an abstract domain. This type definition basically fits different systems. Before we go through the states space definition, we have to list the arithmetic operations allowed among quantum states. The following are the addition, scalar-multiplication, negation and subtraction:

**Definition 1.**
cfun_add $(v_1 : \text{cfun})$ $(v_2 : \text{cfun})$ : cfun $= \lambda x : A.\ v_1\ x + v_2\ x$
cfun_smul $(a : \text{complex})$ $v = \lambda x : A.\ a * v\ x$
cfun_neg $(v : \text{cfun})$ : cfun $= \text{cfun\_smul}\ (-Cx(1))\ v$
cfun_sub $(v_1 : \text{cfun})$ $(v_2 : \text{cfun})$ : cfun $= \text{cfun\_add}\ v_1\ (\text{cfun\_neg}\ v_2)$

where Cx is a function to cast real numbers to complex ones. Note that multiplication is not allowed (or meaningless) between two quantum states. A vector space of states is then defined as follows:

**Definition 2.**
is_cfun_subspace (spc : cfun → bool) ⇔
  ∀x y. x IN spc ∧ y IN spc ⇒
  x + y IN spc ∧ (∀a. a%x IN spc) ∧ cfun_zero IN spc

where cfun_zero = $\lambda$x : A. Cx(0) and it is the identity element of the space. To complete the states space definition, we have to define the inner product over the space. As previously mentioned, the inner product function of a quantum space is the integral function. However, in quantum mechanics, we are not interested in the operation itself but in the properties of the product function. Thus, we define the inner product function axiomatically as follows:

**Definition 3.**
is_inner_space ((s, inprod) : qs → bool × cfun → cfun → complex) ⇔
    is_cfun_subspace s ∧
    ∀x. x ∈ s ⇒
      real (inprod x x) ∧ 0 ≤ real_of_complex (inprod x x) ∧
      (inprod x x = Cx(0) ⇔ x = qs_zero) ∧
      ∀y. y ∈ s ⇒
      cnj (inprod y x) = inprod x y ∧
      (∀a. inprod x (a%y) = a ∗ (inprod x y)) ∧
      ∀z. z ∈ s ⇒
      inprod (x + y) z = inprod x z + inprod y z

where **real** x admits that the complex value x has no imaginary part, and **real_of_complex** is a function converting a complex number into a real one (if it is real).

Now we turn to quantum operators. Similar to the quantum state, we define a new type for an operator, cop : cfun → cfun. A quantum operator attains two main properties, first its linearity:

**Definition 4.**
is_linear_qop (op : cop) ⇔
  ∀x y. op (x + y) = op x + op y ∧ ∀a. op (a % x) = a % (op x)

and second its self-adjointness:

**Definition 5.**
is_self_adjoint (s, inprod) op$_1$ op$_2$ ⇔
  is_inner_space (s, inprod) ⇒
    is_closed_by s op ∧
    is_linear_cop op ∧
    ∀x y. inprod x (op y) = inprod (op x) y

where is_closed_by s op ⇔ ∀x. x ∈ s ⇒ op x ∈ s.

This concludes the preliminaries section where we acquired a basic knowledge of quantum optics, and how we can formalize some of its essential notions such as quantum states and quantum operators. In the next section, we will complete the formalization of the mathematical notions needed for the coherent states formalization.

# 3   Formalization of Quantum States Summation

In this section, we formalize the notion of infinite/finite summation over cfun. Being inspired by Harrison's formalization of summation over finite vector spaces [7], we develop ours for infinite complex space. The summation formalization goes through three major steps: 1) define the finite summation, 2) define the limit notion, then 3) extend the finite one to the infinite summation by applying the notion of limit.

## 3.1   Finite Quantum State Summation

HOL-Light supports the iterate function that accepts an operation and finite set of elements, then repeatedly applies the operation on the elements belonging to the set. Hence, iterate is the best way to define finite summation:

**Definition 6.**

cfun_sum = iterate cfun_add

where cfun_add is the addition operation between two quantum states. Now, cfun_sum is a new operation that accepts two parameters: a finite indexing set s (typically, but not limited to, a subset of natural numbers $\mathbb{N}$) and a function f : s → cfun. About 19 theorems have been proved for the finite summation over quantum states, we present here the most important ones.

In order to prove useful properties about cfun_sum, we first need to provide the following essential theorem, *sum clauses*:

**Theorem 1.**

$(\forall f.\ \text{cfun\_sum}\ \{\}\ f = \text{cfun\_zero}) \wedge$
$(\forall f\ n\ m.\ \text{FINITE}\ s \Rightarrow$
$\quad \text{cfun\_sum}\ (n..m)\ f = f(m) + \text{cfun\_sum}(n+1..m)\ f)$

Here, the theorem states that if the indexing set is empty then the summation is trivial and the result is cfun_zero. Or, given a set of natural numbers $\{x : x \geq n \wedge x \leq m\}$ then the summation can be divided into two terms as shown in the third line of Theorem 1. We can then prove many interesting results, such as *sum of constant*:

**Theorem 2.**

$\forall c\ s.\ \text{FINITE}\ s \Rightarrow \text{cfun\_sum}\ s\ (\lambda n.\ c) = (\text{CARD}\ s)\%c$

where CARD s returns the number of elements in s. Theorem 2 simply shows that a finite summation turns into a scalar multiplication whenever f is a constant function. The next theorem is about closure under cfun_sum:

**Theorem 3.**
∀g spc. is_cfun_subspace spc∧ (∀n. g n IN spc) ⇒
   ∀s. FINITE s ⇒ cfun_sum s g IN spc

The theorem describes that given a set of vectors which belong to a subspace spc, the resulting sum over those vectors belongs to the subspace spc, and hence it is a vector too. Another important theorem is linearity over summation:

**Theorem 4.**
∀f g s.is_linear_cop f ∧ FINITE s ⇒ (f(cfun_sum s g) = cfun_sum s (f o g))

The theorem states that linear functions are interchangeable with the summation operation, i.e., applying a linear function on a set of elements then doing the summation is equivalent to applying the summation of elements then doing the linear function. A known application of this theorem is exchanging the integration function with the summation operation.

### 3.2   Infinite Quantum State Summation

The infinite summation can be easily extended from the finite one as long as the notion of limit is provided. The latter is tightly coupled with the existence of a normed-space (i.e., a linear space augmented with a norm function which is defined over its elements). The quantum state space is a normed-space by definition: the square root of an inner product of a vector and itself yields the norm operation. Thus, the notion of limit can be implemented for quantum spaces:

**Theorem 5.**
cfun_lim (s, inprod) f l net ⇔
   is_inner_space (s, inprod) ∧ l IN s/ (∀x. (f x) IN s)∧
      (∀e. 0 ≤ e ⇒ eventually(λ x. cfun_dist inprod (f x) l < e) net)

where cfun_dist inprod x y = cfun_norm inprod (x − y) and
cfun_norm inprod x = $\sqrt{\text{inprod x x}}$. The definition starts by the guarding antecedents which assure that we have an inner space and all elements, we are dealing with, are inside this space. The limit comes as a predicate which ensures that the difference (or cfun_dist) between a vector f x and vector l is getting smaller, while x changes according to the net. An example of nets is sequential net for which the parameter x starts from 0 and increases gradually until infinity.

About 15 theorems have been proved for the notion of limit. Since limit is not the main interest of this section, we are presenting only one theorem as an example, which is believed to be the most important one, *uniqueness*:

**Theorem 6.**
∀ net f l l' innerspc.
   cfun_lim innerspc f l net ∧cfun_lim innerspc f l' net ⇒ (l = l')

We mean by uniqueness here that if it happens that a function $f : A \rightarrow cfun$ limits to a vector $l:cfun$, and at the same time to vector a $l':cfun$, then $l$ should be equal to $l'$.

Now, we can define infinite summation of cfun as follows:

**Definition 7.**
cfun_sums innerspc f l s $\Leftrightarrow$
   cfun_lim innerspc ($\lambda$n. cfun_sum (s INTER (0..n)) f) l sequentially

where INTER is the sets intersection operator. In order to easily understand the definition, let us assume s is equal to the set of natural numbers. Consequently, (s INTER (0..n))= 0..n. Then, the definition states that while $n$ increases, the finite summation cfun_sum coincides with (or limit to) l. However, this predicate definition does not help much in usual mathematical manipulation. Therefore, we develop another functional definition:

**Definition 8.**
cfun_infsum innerspc s f = @l. cfun_sums innerspc f l s

Here, the definition uses the Hilbert choice operator @ to get a vector that satisfies the cfun_sums predicate.

In order to proceed with proving theorems related to infinite summation, we have first to make sure that the series of vectors subject to summation is convergent, i.e., the limit exits. For this purpose, we define the summable predicate:

**Definition 9.**
cfun_summable innerspc s f = $\exists$l. cfun_sums innerspc f l s

It is important to know how cfun_infsum deals with arithmetic operations, i.e., addition and scalar multiplication. Thereby, we provide the following two essential theorems:

**Theorem 7.**
$\forall$ f g innerspc.
cfun_summable innerspc s f $\wedge$ cfun_summable innerspc s g $\Rightarrow$
   cfun_infsum innerspc s($\lambda$n.fn + gn) =
      cfun_infsum innerspc s f + cfun_infsum innerspc s g

**Theorem 8.**
$\forall$ f innerspc a. cfun_summable innerspc s f $\Rightarrow$
   cfun_infsum innerspc s($\lambda$n.a % f n) = a% cfun_infsum innerspc s f

Similar to the notion of limit, uniqueness of infinite summation is proved. Since we have already presented it, there is no need to re-express it here for infinite summation. Likewise, we prove the linearity theorem for cfun_infsum as it is developed for the finite summation. However, the linearity of a function is not enough to exchange it with infinite summation. It should be a bounded function too. Before we present the theorem of linearity, let us express the definition of boundness:

**Definition 10.**
is_bounded (s, inprod) h ⇔ is_inner_space (s, inprod)
  ⇒ is_closed_by s h ∧ ∃B. 0 < B∧
    (∀x. x IN s ⇒ cfun_norm inprod (h x))) ≤ B * cfun_norm inprod x)))

Here, a linear operator h is bounded if for all x the norm of h x is less than or equal to the norm of x multiplied by a scalar B, given that B does not depend on x. Now we can present the effect of a linear operator on the cfun_infsum operation:

**Theorem 9.**
∀f h s innerspc.
  cfun_summableinnerspcsf ∧ is_linear_cop h ∧ is_bounded innerspc h
    ⇒ cfun_infsum innerspc s(λn. h(f n)) = h(cfun_infsum innerspc s f)

The theorem shows that a linear bounded operator (or function) is exchangeable with the cfun_infsum operation.

We conclude this section by mentioning that about 50 theorems have been proved for the finite/infinite summation of over cfun. In the next section, we will describe the coherent states formalization where the notions presented in this section are being utilized.

# 4    Coherent Light Formalization

In this section, the formal definition of coherent states is presented, then we prove that coherent states are eigenvectors of the annihilation operator. The coherent light formal development is carried out in three steps: 1) quantum light formalization, 2) fock states formalization which are the basis of quantum optics states space, then finally 3) coherent states formalization.

## 4.1    Single Mode

Classically, light is consider as an electromagnetic field. Quantum physics restudies such a field according to quantum rules. Thereby, the first step towards quantum optics formalization is implementing the electromagnetic field quantization. Electromagnetic fields can be classified according to the number of resonance frequencies per field. Accordingly, there are single-mode fields, i.e., single resonance frequency and multi-mode fields for a higher number of frequencies. For simplicity, we are concerned with properties of single-mode field which can be extended for multi-mode fields. The first formal definition of quantum single-mode field is presented in [10]. We use it here with some changes: we fix the vacuum state of the field and add its properties to the definition itself (see the last two lines of the definition):

**Definition 11.**
is_sm $((sp, cs, H), w, vac) \Leftrightarrow$
    is_qsys $(sp, cs, H) \wedge 0 < w \wedge \exists q\ p.\ cs = [q; p]$
    $\wedge\ \forall t.$is_observable sp $(p\ t) \wedge$ is_observable sp$(q\ t)$
    $\wedge$ H $t = \frac{w^2}{2}\%((q\ t)$ pow 2$) +\quad \frac{1}{2}\%((p\ t)$ pow 2$)$
    $\wedge$is_qst sp vac $\wedge$ is_eigen_pair (H $t$) $(vac, \frac{planck*w}{2})$

The reason behind these changes is that quantum states spaces consist of equivalent classes of quantum states. In this way, we specify the representative of the vacuum state class, and hence of all other classes. The is_qst predicate ensures that the norm of the state is equal to unity and belongs to the space sp. According to the definition, we assume that vac is an eigenvector of the quantum operator H which is responsible for calculating the total energy inside the field. The corresponding eigenvalue is equal to $\frac{planck*w}{2}$. We can then prove that vac is an eigenvector of the photon number operator N which is responsible for calculating the number of photons inside the field. The corresponding eigenvalue is equal to zero:

**Theorem 10.**
$\forall$sp cs H omega vac.
    let sm $= (sp, cs, H),$ omega, vac in
        is_sm sm $\Rightarrow$ is_eigen_pair (n_of_sm sm)$(vac, 0)$

Before we tackle the notion of fock states, we have to consider two important theorems, which show the effects of creation and annihilation operators on eigenvectors of the photon number operator. Here is the creation operator effect:

**Theorem 11.**
$\forall$sp cs H omega vac.
    let sm $= (sp, cs, H),$ omega, vac in
    is_sm sm $\Rightarrow$
        $\forall v.$ (create_of_sm sm $v =$ cfun_zero) $\Rightarrow$
        $\forall n.$ is_eigen_pair (n_of_sm sm) $(v, n) \Rightarrow$
        is_eigen_pair (n_of_sm sm)(herma_of_sm sm $f, n + 1$))

where the last line shows that the number of photons is increased by one. Similarly, the annihilation operator affects the number of photons as follows:

**Theorem 12.**
$\forall$sp cs H omega vac.
    let sm $= (sp, cs, H),$ omega, vac in
    is_sm sm $\Rightarrow$
        $\forall v.$ (create_of_sm sm $v =$ cfun_zero) $\Rightarrow$
        $\forall n.$ is_eigen_pair (n_of_sm sm) $(v, n) \Rightarrow$
        is_eigen_pair (n_of_sm sm)(ann_of_sm sm $v, n - 1$))

Here, the number of photons is decreased by one. In the same context, it is important to know how annihilation operator affects the vacuum state, where there are no photons:

**Theorem 13.**
∀sp cs H omega vac.
  let sm = (sp, cs, H), omega, vac in
    is_sm sm ⇒ (a_of_sm sm) vac = cfun_zero

Note that the resulting state is a non-quantum state since the norm of cfun_zero is equal to zero.

## 4.2   Fock States

Recall that a single-mode field at a fock state $|n\rangle$ means that the light stream contains exactly $n$ photons. Such states are quite important since they form the basis of the single-mode quantum states space. Moreover, it is widely used in the development of single-photon devices which have direct applications in quantum cryptography. We start by giving the formal definition of a fock state:

**Definition 12.**
let (((s, inprod), cs, H), omega, vac) = sm in
  fock sm 0 = vac ∧ fock sm (SUC n) =
    get_qst inprod (creat_of_sm sm (fock sm n)))

As shown, it is recursively defined with vac state as the base case. Recall that we have proved before that vac is the eigenvector of the photon number operator with zero photons. Then, we can get any higher fock state by applying the creation operator. The function get_qst returns the normalized version of a vector, i.e., by dividing by the norm of the vector itself. This is to ensure that the norm of the resulting quantum state is equal to one. Here is the theorem that shows that a fock state is normalized:

**Theorem 14.**
∀s inprod cs H omega vac.
  let sm = ((s, inprod), cs, H), omega, vac in
    is_sm sm ⇒ ∀n. fock sm n ∈ s ∧ inprod (fock sm n) (fock sm n) = 1

Now, we provide the semantic of the fock definition by proving that it is an eigenvector of the photon number with n photons as an eigenvalue:

**Theorem 15.**
∀n sm.
  is_sm sm ∧ ((creat_of_sm sm (fock sm n)) = cfun_zero)
    ⇒ is_eigen_pair(n_of_sm sm) (fock sm n, n)

We also provide the effect of creation and annihilation operators on fock states. The following two theorems correspond to Equations (4) and (5) (See Section 2):

**Theorem 16.**
∀n sm.
  is_sm sm ∧ ((creat_of_sm sm (fock sm n)) = cfun_zero)
    ⇒ (anhh_of_sm sm) (fock sm (SUC n)) = $\sqrt{\text{SUC n}}$ % fock sm n

Since that the state number in the left hand side is SUC n, then the theorem is valid for all fock states except at zero, i.e., the vac state. Recall that we have proved that the left hand side is equal to zero_cfun for the vac state. However, the following theorem is valid for any state including the vac state:

**Theorem 17.**
∀n sm.
  is_sm sm ∧ ((creata_of_sm sm (fock sm n)) = cfun_zero)
    ⇒ (creat_of_sm sm) (fock sm n) = $\sqrt{\text{SUC n}}$ % fock sm (SUC n)

The above theorems are recurrence relations, if we are able to solve any of them, we can then get a non-recursive definition. The following provides the solution of the recurrence relation of Theorem 17:

**Theorem 18.**
∀s inprod cs H omega vac.
  let sm = ((s, inprod), cs, H), omega, vac in
  is_sm sm ∧ (∀n. (creat_of_sm sm) (fock sm n) = cfun_zero)
    ⇒ ∀m. fock sm m = $\frac{1}{\sqrt{m!}}$ % (creat_of_sm sm pow m) vac

This concludes the fock states formalization. In the next section, we will see how to formalize coherent states using the previously presented theorems and definitions.

### 4.3 Coherent States

Based on the fock states definition and infinite summation, a coherent state is defined as follows:

**Definition 13.**
 coherent sm α =
   let sm = ((s, inprod), cs, H), omega, vac in
     exp($-\frac{|\alpha|^2}{2}$))% cfun_infsum (s, inprod) (from 0) ($\lambda$n. $\frac{\alpha^n}{\sqrt{n!}}$%(focksmn))

where α is the state parameter. Recall that, the number of photons in a coherent stream is Poisson distributed with expectation $|\alpha|^2$. Note that Definition 13 corresponds to Equation (3).

Next, we need to make sure that the above definition is convergent. As illustrated in Section 3, we have handled a similar situation by defining the summable predicate:

**Definition 14.**
coherent_summable sm α ⇔
  let (((s, inprod), cs, H), omega, vac) = sm in
    cfun_summable (s, inprod) (from 0) ($\lambda$n. $\frac{\alpha^n}{\sqrt{n!}}$%(fock sm n))

Theorem 16 plays a crucial role in proving the relation between coherent states and the annihilation operator. However, it has a problem since it is only valid for fock states greater than zero (i.e., vac state). Consequently, we have to rewrite the coherent definition in a way that allows the application of Theorem 16:

**Theorem 19.**
$\forall$s inprod cs H omega vac $\alpha$.
  let sm $=$ ((s, inprod), cs, H), omega, vac in
  coherent_summable sm $\alpha \Rightarrow$
    coherent sm a $= \exp(-\frac{|\alpha|^2}{2})) $ %(vac$+$

cfun_infsum (s, inprod) (from 0) ($\lambda$n. $\frac{\alpha^{(SUC\ n)}}{\sqrt{(SUC\ n)!}}$%(fock sm (SUC n))))

It is important to mention here that vac is a coherent state with $\alpha = 0$. Although it is not covered by Definition 13, we can still prove this based on Theorem 13, by showing that the vac state is an eigenvector of the annihilator. We can appreciate the importance of the vac state since it acts as a coherent and a fock state at the same time. Fortunately, this allows us to use the properties of both notions which is very helpful.

Now, we can prove that coherent states are eigenvectors of the annihilation operator, with eigenvalue $\alpha$ based on Theorems 13, 16 and 19:

**Theorem 20.**
$\forall$sm $\alpha$.
  is_sm sm $\wedge$ ((creat_of_sm sm (fock sm n)) $=$ cfun_zero)
  $\wedge$ coherent_summable sm $\alpha \wedge$ is_bounded (s, inprod) (anhh_of_sm sm)
  $\wedge$ (coherent sm a $=$ cfun_zero) $\Rightarrow$
    is_eigen_pair(a_of_sm sm) (coherent sm $\alpha, \alpha$)

This concludes our HOL formalization of coherent light and the underlying mathematical and physical aspects which costs 1500 lines of HOL code. In the following section, we briefly present a potential application of our formalization in quantum computers as a future work.

## 5  Conclusion and Future Work

Quantum optics explores new and extremely useful phenomena and properties of light as a stream of photons. However, the analysis of quantum optical systems is complex. In particular, the traditional analysis techniques – simulation in optical laboratories, paper-and-pencil, numerical methods, and computer algebra systems – suffer from a number of problems: 1) Safety, 2) Cost, 3) Expressiveness and 4) Human Error. We believe that the proposed formalization of quantum optics can alleviate the limitations listed above.

Coherent light (or states) is an essential notion in quantum optics since it eases the analysis of many quantum systems. We have addressed the formal definition of coherent states, then we provided a theorem which proves that coherent states are eigenvectors of the creator operator. This development is handled in three major steps: 1) we started by formally defining fock states which represent the basis of quantum optics states space, then proved how the creation and annihilation operators affect the fock states, and finally derived a non-recursive definition for them. We also have proved that fock states are eigenvectors of the photon number operator; 2) since coherent states are formed by infinite summation of fock states, we have developed infinte/finite summation over quantum states in addition to the notion of limit; and 3) we were able to provide a formal definition of coherent light and show its relation with the annihilation operator.

One of the most interesting applications of coherent light is quantum computers, where coherent states are proposed to model quantum bits. Quantum computers firstly proposed in 1985 by Deutsch [1], after Feyman [4] had proved that quantum physics phenomena cannot be simulated over ordinary machines. They have the potential of solving certain problems exponentially faster than ordinary machines. Quantum bits and quantum gates are pillars of a quantum machine, as digital bits and gates for computers. $|0\rangle$ and $|1\rangle$ are the pure states of quantum computers. And hence, a quantum bit is equal to : $|Qbit\rangle = \delta|0\rangle + \beta|1\rangle$.

Coherent states are proposed to model quantum bits [16], where $|\alpha\rangle$ and $|-\alpha\rangle$ correspond to $|0\rangle$ and $|1\rangle$, respectively. Many quantum gates where implemented based on this model. For example, the quantum flip gate, which converts $\delta|0\rangle + \beta|1\rangle$ into $\beta|0\rangle + \delta|1\rangle$. Implementing such a gate requires to correlate coherent states with the so-called *displacement operator*, which can be physically implemented as a beam splitter and then cascade a phase conjugating mirror along with a beam splitter to form a quantum flip gate. In order to tackle such a gate in the future, it requires us to define a mirror and a displacement operator (or a beam splitter). The formalization of these devices can be handled using the foundations presented in this paper along with some additional mathematical concepts, such as summation over quantum operators and exponentiation of quantum operators. Thereby, the formalization and analysis of quantum flip gates is one of our essential future work.

# References

1. Deutsch, D.: Quantum theory, the church-turing principle and the universal quantum computer. Proceedings of the Royal Society 400(1818), 97–117 (1985)
2. Duck, I., Sudarshan, E.C.G.: 100 Years of Planck's Quantum. World Scientific (2000)
3. Feagin, J.M.: Quantum Methods with Mathematica. Springer (2002)
4. Feynman, R.: Simulating physics with computers. International Journal of Theoretical Physics 21, 467–488 (1982), doi:10.1007/BF02650179
5. Institute for Quantum Science and Technology at the University of Calgary. Introduction to an Optical lab (2014), http://old.rqc.ru/quantech/memo.php
6. Harrison, J.: HOL Light: A Tutorial Introduction. In: Srivas, M., Camilleri, A. (eds.) FMCAD 1996. LNCS, vol. 1166, pp. 265–269. Springer, Heidelberg (1996)
7. Harrison, J.: The HOL Light Theory of Euclidean Space. Journal of Automated Reasoning 50(2), 173–190 (2013)

8. Jennewein, T., Barbieri, M., White, A.G.: Single-photon device requirements for operating linear optics quantum computing outside the post-selection basis. Journal of Modern Optics 58(3-4), 276–287 (2011)
9. Li, Y., Browne, D.E., Ch, L.: Kwek, R. Raussendorf, and T. Wei. Thermal states as universal resources for quantum computation with always-on interactions. Physical Review Letter 107, 060501 (2011)
10. Mahmoud, M.Y., Aravantinos, V., Tahar, S.: Formalization of infinite dimension linear spaces with application to quantum theory. In: Brat, G., Rungta, N., Venet, A. (eds.) NFM 2013. LNCS, vol. 7871, pp. 413–427. Springer, Heidelberg (2013)
11. Mahmoud, M.Y.: On the Quantum Formalization of Coherent Light in HOL - HOL Light script, http://hvg.ece.concordia.ca/projects/qoptics/coh-light.php
12. Mandel, L., Wolf, E.: Optical Coherence and Quantum Optics. Cambridge University Press (1995)
13. Milonni, P., Nieto, M.M.: Coherent states. In: Compendium of Quantum Physics, pp. 106–108. Springer (2009)
14. Nielsen, M.A., Chuang, I.L.: Quantum Computation and Quantum Information: 10th Anniversary Edition. Cambridge University Press (2010)
15. Institute of Quantum Optics at Leibniz University of Hannover. General directives for safety in the institute of quantum optics (2014),
http://www.iqo.uni-hannover.de/fileadmin/institut/pdf/
job%20security/3._Sicherheitmerkblatt06012014_engl.pdf
16. Ralph, T.C., Gilchrist, A., Milburn, G.J., Munro, W.J., Glancy, S.: Quantum computation with optical coherent states. Physical Review A 68, 042319 (2003)
17. Santori, C., Fattal, D., Yamamoto, Y.: Single-photon Devices and Applications. Physics textbook. John Wiley & Sons (2010)
18. Tan, S.M.: A computational toolbox for quantum and atomic optics. Journal of Optics B: Quantum and Semiclassical Optics 1(4), 424 (1999)
19. Walls, D.F., Milburn, G.J.: Quantum Optics. Springer (2008)

# Refinement Types for TLA+

Stephan Merz[1] and Hernán Vanzetto[1,2]

[1] INRIA, Villers-lès-Nancy, France & LORIA
[2] Microsoft Research-INRIA Joint Centre, Saclay, France

**Abstract.** TLA+ is a specification language, mainly intended for concurrent and distributed systems. Its non-temporal fragment is based on a variant of (untyped) ZF set theory. Motivated by the integration of the TLA+ Proof System with SMT solvers or similar tools based on multi-sorted first-order logic, we define a type system for TLA+ and we prove its soundness. The system includes refinement types, which fit naturally in set theory. Combined with dependent function types, we obtain type annotations on top of an untyped specification language, getting the best of both the typed and untyped approaches. After implementing the type inference algorithm, we show that the resulting typing discipline improves the verification capabilities of the proof system.

## 1 Introduction

The specification language TLA+ [11] combines a variant of Zermelo-Fraenkel (ZF) set theory for the description of the data manipulated by algorithms and linear-time temporal logic for the specification of their behavior. The TLA+ Proof System (TLAPS) integrates different backends for automatic proving to provide proof support for TLA+. The work reported here is motivated by the development of an SMT backend through which users of TLAPS interact with standard SMT (satisfiability modulo theories) solvers for non-temporal reasoning in the set theory of TLA+.

In line with the foundations of classical mathematics, TLA+ is an untyped formalism [12]. On the other hand, it is generally accepted that strong type systems such as Martin-Löf type theory or HOL (Church's simple type theory) and its variants help provide semi-automatic proof support for highly expressive modeling languages. Automatic first-order theorem provers, including SMT solvers, are generally based on multi-sorted first-order logic that have interpreted operators over distinguished sorts, such as arithmetic operators over integers. Similarly, specification languages such as Z [19] or B [1] use typed variants of set theory that correspond naturally to multi-sorted first-order logic [5].

A sound way of encoding TLA+ in SMT-LIB [4], the de-facto standard input language for SMT solvers, described in our previous work [14], is to introduce a distinguished sort U corresponding to TLA+ values, with injections from existing sorts, such as $int2u$ : Int $\rightarrow$ U for integer values. To represent an operator such as addition, we declare a function $plus$ that takes arguments and returns results in U, but we relate it to the built-in addition operator $+$, over the image of $int2u$, by the axiom

$$\forall m, n : \mathsf{Int}.\ plus(int2u(m), int2u(n)) = int2u(m + n).$$

J.M. Badger and K.Y. Rozier (Eds.): NFM 2014, LNCS 8430, pp. 143–157, 2014.

1 declare $int2u$ : (Int) U
2 declare $plus$ : (U U) U
3 assert $\forall m, n$ : Int. $int2u(m) = int2u(n) \Rightarrow m = n$
4 assert $\forall m, n$ : Int. $plus(int2u(m), int2u(n)) = int2u(m + n)$
5 assert $\neg(\forall x$ : U. $(\exists n$ : Int. $x = int2u(n)) \Rightarrow plus(x, int2u(0)) = x)$

**Fig. 1.** Encoding of the proof obligation $\forall x.\ x \in Int \Rightarrow x + 0 = x$ in SMT-LIB

With this representation, the SMT backend will be unable to prove the TLA$^+$ formula $\forall x.\, x + 0 = x$ because the value of the bound variable $x$ is not known to be in the image of $int2u$. Indeed, this formula is not a theorem of TLA$^+$; for example, the expression $\{\} + 0$ is syntactically correct, but its value is unspecified. However, the TLA$^+$ formula $\forall x.\ x \in Int \Rightarrow x + 0 = x$ can be proved, based on the (pretty-printed) SMT-LIB encoding shown in Fig. 1. As can be seen from this example, this style of encoding requires a substantial number of quantified formulas that degrade the performance of SMT solvers. In particular, the hypothesis $x \in Int$ in the TLA$^+$ formula gives rise to the subformula $\exists n$ : Int. $x = int2u(n)$. If we could detect appropriate type information from the original TLA$^+$ formula, we could simply translate it to $\forall x$ : Int. $x + 0 = x$.

The above example motivates the definition of a type system and an associated type inference algorithm for TLA$^+$. Our previous work [14] contained a preliminary proposal in this direction. By necessity, type systems impose restrictions on the admissible formulas, and one can therefore not expect type inference to succeed for all TLA$^+$ proof obligations. If no meaningful types can be inferred, the translation can fall back to the "untyped" encoding described above. The question is then how expressive the type system should be in order to successfully handle a large class of TLA$^+$ formulas. The type system of [14] was fairly restricted and could in certain cases not express adequate type information. In particular, handling function applications in TLA$^+$ often requires precise type information, where it must be proved that the argument is in the domain of the function. For example, consider the TLA$^+$ formula[1]

$$\forall f \in [\{1, 2, 3\} \rightarrow Int].\, f[0] < f[0] + 1$$

This formula should not be provable: since 0 is not in the domain of $f$, we should not infer that $f[0]$ is an integer. In our previous work, we over-approximated the type of $f$ as a function from Int to Int, then generated a side condition that attempted to prove $0 \in \text{dom}\, f$. However, computing the domain of a function is not always as easy as in this example, leading to failed proof attempts. The design of an appropriate type system is further complicated by the fact that some formulas, such as $f[x] \cup \{\} = f[x]$, are actually valid irrespectively of whether $x \in \text{dom}\, f$ holds or not. This observation motivates the use of a more expressive type system. Using refinement types [7,20], the type of dom $f$ is $\{x$ : Int $\mid x = 1 \lor x = 2 \lor x = 3\}$. During type inference, the system will try to prove that $x = 0 \Rightarrow x \in \text{dom}\, f$, and this will fail, hence the translation

---

[1] In TLA$^+$, $[S \rightarrow T]$ denotes the set of functions with domain $S$ and co-domain $T$, and the application of function $f$ to argument $e$ is written $f[e]$.

will fall back to the untyped encoding (which will in turn fail to prove the formula, as it should). In many practical examples, the domain condition can be established during type inference, leading to shorter and simpler SMT proof obligations.

The main contribution of this paper is thus a novel use of refinement types for TLA$^+$ formulas. Since TLA$^+$ is very close to untyped Zermelo-Fraenkel set theory, we believe that our approach is more widely applicable for theorem proving in set-theoretic languages. A type system with refinement types is very expressive and actually quite close to set theory; it gives rise to proof obligations that are undecidable. Specifically, subtyping between two refinement types $\{x : \tau \mid \phi_1\}$ and $\{x : \tau \mid \phi_2\}$ reduces to prove $\phi_1 \Rightarrow \phi_2$. This is comparable to the use of predicate types in the PVS theorem prover [18] where type checking conditions may be generated that have to be discharged interactively. In our case, we divide the problem of type inference into constraint generation and constraint solving. Constraint generation rules are derived directly from type checking rules, and always succeed. For constraint solving, we again use SMT solvers, which may succeed or not. In case constraint solving fails, we fall back to the untyped encoding (restricted to the corresponding part of the proof obligation), which is comparable to dynamic type checking.

*Paper outline.* In Section 2 we present a formal definition of a fragment of TLA$^+$. Section 3 contains the definition of the type system, including the key concepts of typing hypothesis and safe types, the typing rules and finally the proof of soundness of the system. The typing rules give raise to the inference algorithm in Section 4. Next, we show some experimental results of a prototype implementation of the system in Section 5 and Section 6 concludes.

## 2    A Fragment of TLA$^+$

We now introduce a fragment of TLA$^+$, called $\mathcal{L}$, that represents the essential concepts of TLA$^+$. The main simplifications are: we restrict the discussion to unary operators and do not handle TLA$^+$'s CHOOSE operator, tuples, strings, records, or sequences. In order to adhere to a more standard presentation of ZF set theory, we also assume a distinction between terms (non-Boolean expressions) and formulas, whereas TLA$^+$ does not. However, in the "liberal interpretation" of TLA$^+$ [11] that underlies TLAPS, the results of Boolean connectives are always Boolean. Using a pre-processing step of "Boolification" that replaces all possibly non-Boolean arguments $e$ of Boolean operators by $e = \text{true}$, the distinction between terms and formulas can be recovered.

*Syntax.* We assume given non-empty, infinite, and disjoint sets $\mathcal{V}$ of variables and $\mathcal{O}$ of (unary) operator symbols, the latter subdivided into Boolean operators $w^b$ and non-Boolean operators $w$.[2] The set-theoretic kernel of $\mathcal{L}$ is given by the following grammar where for clarity we distinguish between different syntactic categories of expressions.

---

[2] TLA$^+$ operator symbols correspond to the standard function and predicate symbols of first-order logic but we reserve the term "function" for functional values in TLA$^+$.

**Language $\mathcal{L}$ grammar**

| | | |
|---|---|---|
| (terms) | $t$ | $::=\ v \mid w(e)$ |
| (sets) | $s$ | $::=\ t \mid \{\} \mid \{e, e\} \mid \mathbb{P}s \mid \cup s \mid \{v \in s : \phi\}$ |
| (expressions) | $e$ | $::=\ s$ |
| (formulas) | $\phi$ | $::=\ w^b(e) \mid \mathsf{false} \mid \phi \Rightarrow \phi \mid \forall v.\,\phi \mid e = e \mid e \in s$ |

A term is either a variable symbol $v$ in $\mathcal{V}$ or results from the application of an operator symbol $w$ in $\mathcal{O}$ to an expression. Since TLA$^+$ is a set-theoretic language, every term denotes a set. The language also contains explicit set constructors corresponding to the empty set, pairs, the powerset, the generalized union, and set comprehension. Initially, expressions are just sets. Formulas are built from the application of a Boolean operator symbol $w^b$ to an expression, from false, implication and universal quantification (from which the remaining first-order connectives can be defined), and from the binary operators $=$ and $\in$. This language, plus an object of infinity (the set of integer numbers $Int$ that we will add later), corresponds to MacLane set theory, which is a suitable fragment to formalize large parts of mathematics.

As a first extension of this purely set-theoretic language, we now introduce (total) functions. In standard set theory, functions are defined as binary relations (i.e., sets of pairs) restricted so that each element of the domain is mapped to a unique element in the range of the relation. TLA$^+$ instead introduces functions axiomatically using three primitive constructs. The expression $f[e]$ denotes the result of applying the function $f$ to the expression $e$, and $\mathrm{dom}\,f$ denotes the domain of $f$. The expression $\lambda x \in S.\ e$ denotes the function $f$ with domain $S$ such that $f[x] = e$, for any $x \in S$. For $x \notin S$, the value of $f[x]$ is unspecified. The expression $[S \to T]$ denotes the set of functions with domain $S$ and co-domain $T$. The characteristic predicate for a TLA$^+$ value being a function is defined as $IsAFcn(f) \triangleq f = \lambda x \in \mathrm{dom}\,f.\ f[x]$.

Furthermore, $\mathcal{L}$ also contains arithmetic expressions. Natural numbers are primitive symbols, $Int$ denotes the set of integer numbers, and the operators $+$, $-$, and $<$ denote the usual operations when applied to integers. For further reading, a more detailed presentation of the formal definition of TLA$^+$ appears in [11, Sec. 16].

**Extension with functions**

| | | |
|---|---|---|
| (terms) | $t$ | $::=\ \dots \mid f[e]$ |
| (sets) | $s$ | $::=\ \dots \mid \mathrm{dom}\,f$ |
| | | $\mid [s \to s]$ |
| (functions) | $f$ | $::=\ t \mid \lambda v \in s.\ e$ |
| (expressions) | $e$ | $::=\ \dots \mid f$ |

**Extension with arithmetic**

| | | |
|---|---|---|
| (sets) | $s$ | $::=\ \dots \mid Int$ |
| (numbers) | $n$ | $::=\ t \mid 0 \mid 1 \mid 2 \mid \cdots$ |
| | | $\mid n + n \mid n - n$ |
| (expressions) | $e$ | $::=\ \dots \mid n$ |
| (formulas) | $\phi$ | $::=\ \dots \mid n < n$ |

A many-sorted version of $\mathcal{L}$, written $\mathcal{L}^\tau$, is obtained by decorating variables with sorts, and by assigning a type $\langle \tau_1, \tau_2 \rangle$ to every operator where $\tau_1$ and $\tau_2$ denote the type of the argument and of the result. Our type system will be introduced in Section 3. In particular, we will write $\forall v : \tau.\ \phi$ for a quantified formula where the bound variable has sort $\tau$.

The definitions of free variables and substitution are the usual ones for first-order logic over the set of variables $\mathcal{V}$. We write $fv(\phi)$ for the set of free variables of $\phi$, and $e[y \leftarrow z]$ for the expression or formula $e$ where all occurrences of the free variable $y$ are substituted by $z$.

*Semantics.* A single-sorted *model* $\mathcal{M}$ is composed of a non-empty set $\mathcal{D}$ called the *domain*, a *valuation* function $\varphi : \mathcal{V} \rightarrow \mathcal{D}$ that assigns to each variable an element in the domain, and an *interpretation* function $\mathcal{I}$ that, in particular, assigns to each operator symbol $w$ a function $\mathcal{I}(w) : \mathcal{D} \rightarrow \mathcal{D}$. The definition of the interpretation continues in the standard way. In particular, models respect the extensionality and foundations axioms of ZF, functions are governed by the axiom

$$f = \lambda x \in s.\ e \ \Leftrightarrow \ \wedge \ IsAFcn(f)$$
$$\wedge \ \mathsf{dom}\ f = s$$
$$\wedge \ \forall y \in s.\ f[y] = e[x \leftarrow y]$$

and arithmetic expressions are interpreted in the standard way when arguments are integers. The semantics of the multi-sorted language $\mathcal{L}^\tau$ is analogous with the usual modifications corresponding to the presence of sorts [13].

A formula $\phi$ is *valid* (noted $\vdash \phi$) iff it holds in every model.

## 3   A Type System with Refinements

Types are given by the following grammar.

$$\tau ::= \mathsf{t}_1 \mid \mathsf{t}_2 \mid \ldots \mid \mathsf{Bool} \mid \mathsf{Int} \mid \alpha \mid \mathsf{Set}\,\tau \mid (v : \tau) \rightarrow \tau \mid \tau \uplus \tau \mid \{x : \tau \mid \phi\}$$

The basic types consist of a denumerable set of atomic types $\mathsf{t}_1, \mathsf{t}_2, \ldots$, as well as of types $\mathsf{Bool}$ for formulas and $\mathsf{Int}$ for integers. Further type constructors are directly correlated to set objects. For instance, the $\mathsf{Set}$ constructor determines the level of set strata for $\mathbb{P}$ and $\cup$. Type variables $\alpha$ are interpreted over the resulting Herbrand universe of types. A *ground assignment* $\sigma$ is a total function $\sigma$ of type variables to atomic types.

A refinement type $\{x : \tau \mid \phi\}$ is intended for representing set comprehension objects. It describes the set of values of type $\tau$ that satisfy the refinement predicate $\phi$, where $x$ is free in $\phi$. Refinement types have the property (3.1) that the refinement of a refinement type is also a refinement type. From this property, we know also that any type $\tau$ can be written as the (trivial) refinement type $\{x : \tau \mid \mathsf{true}\}$.

$$\{x : \{y : \tau \mid \phi_1\} \mid \phi_2\} = \{x : \tau \mid \phi_1[y \leftarrow x] \wedge \phi_2\} \tag{3.1}$$

The type of the empty set is defined as the type $\varnothing_\tau \triangleq \mathsf{Set}\,\{x : \tau \mid \mathsf{false}\}$, for any type $\tau$. A pair $\{a, b\}$ has the type $\tau_a \uplus \tau_b$, the logical union of the types of $a$ and $b$. The union type constructor $\uplus$ is an operation on refinements and sets and it is defined by:

$$\{x : \tau \mid \phi_1\} \uplus \{x : \tau \mid \phi_2\} = \{x : \tau \mid \phi_1 \vee \phi_2\} \tag{3.2}$$

$$(\mathsf{Set}\,\tau_1) \uplus (\mathsf{Set}\,\tau_2) = \mathsf{Set}\,(\tau_1 \uplus \tau_2) \tag{3.3}$$

A function $f$ has the dependent type $(x : \tau_1) \to \tau_2$ [2], where $\tau_1$ represents the domain of $f$ and the term $x$ may occur in the range type $\tau_2$. The variable $x$ of type $\tau_1$ is bound in type $\tau_2$. If $x$ does not occur in $\tau_2$, we can omit it from the syntax to obtain the standard function type $\tau_1 \to \tau_2$.

### 3.1  Typing Propositions and Typing Hypotheses

When encoding a multi-sorted language into a single-sorted one, the traditional method [6] is straightforward. For every sort $\tau$, it defines a characteristic proposition $\mathcal{P}_\tau$ that represents the set of values having sort $\tau$. For instance, the proposition associated to Set $\tau$ is derived from the axiom of power set. Then, it relativizes the quantifiers, that is, it replaces the sort annotations $x : \tau$ by new hypotheses $\mathcal{P}_\tau(x)$. This method is applied to formulas without type variables, therefore all types should be grounded. For each atomic type $t_i$, we introduce a new unary predicate symbol $t_i$ and an axiom stating that these predicates partition the universe of ground types in disjoint sets.

**Definition 1 (Typing propositions).** *Given a type assignment $x : \tau$, an encoding of it can be constructed into the formula $\mathcal{P}_\tau(x)$, defined as follows:*

$$\mathcal{P}_{t_i}(x) \triangleq t_i(x) \quad \mathcal{P}_{\mathsf{Bool}}(x) \triangleq x \in \{\mathsf{true}, \mathsf{false}\} \quad \mathcal{P}_{\mathsf{Int}}(x) \triangleq x \in Int$$

$$\mathcal{P}_{\mathsf{Set}\,\tau}(x) \triangleq \forall z \in x.\, \mathcal{P}_\tau(z) \quad \mathcal{P}_{\tau_1 \uplus \tau_2}(x) \triangleq \mathcal{P}_{\tau_1}(x) \vee \mathcal{P}_{\tau_2}(x)$$

$$\mathcal{P}_{\{y:\tau \mid \phi\}}(x) \triangleq \mathcal{P}_\tau(x) \wedge \phi[y \leftarrow x]$$

$$\mathcal{P}_{(x:\tau_1) \to \tau_2}(f) \triangleq \wedge\, f = \lambda x \in \mathrm{dom}\, f.\, f[x]$$
$$\wedge\, \forall z.\, z \in \mathrm{dom}\, f \Leftrightarrow \mathcal{P}_{\tau_1}(z)$$
$$\wedge\, \forall z.\, \mathcal{P}_{\tau_1}(z) \Rightarrow (\forall x.\mathcal{P}_{\tau_1}(x) \Rightarrow \mathcal{P}_{\tau_2}(f[z]))$$

For example, $\mathcal{P}_{\mathsf{Set}\,\{x:\mathsf{Int} \mid p(x)\}}(s) = \forall z \in s.\, z \in \mathsf{Int} \wedge p(z)$.

**Definition 2 (Relativization).** *A typed formula is relativized by recursively replacing the type annotations $x : \tau$ by a new hypothesis corresponding to the typing proposition $\mathcal{P}_\tau(x)$. The relevant transformation is $\forall x : \tau.\, \phi \rightsquigarrow \forall x.\, \mathcal{P}_\tau(x) \Rightarrow \phi$.*

**Lemma 1 (Relativization is sound).** $\vdash \forall x : \tau.\, \phi$ *implies* $\vdash \forall x.\, \mathcal{P}_\tau(x) \Rightarrow \phi$.

*Proof.* The proof follows [13] with the addition of the Set and refinement types.  □

Now suppose we want to annotate the formula $\forall x, y.\ \cup \{x, y\} = \cup\{y, x\}$. We can safely say that the type of $x$ and $y$ should be Set $t$, for some atomic type $t$. Semantically speaking, all values in the untyped universe $\mathcal{D}$ denote sets. And the stratification of sets using the Set constructor supports the key idea that a set must have a different type from its elements.

**Definition 3 (Safe types).** *A type is said to be* safe *if it is an atomic type $t_i$, for some $i$, or if it is Set $\tau_{safe}$, where $\tau_{safe}$ is safe.*

Since all values are sets and typing predicates are uninterpreted, safe types cannot introduce any unsoundness to a typed formula.

**Lemma 2.** *The relativization of the formula $\forall x : \tau_{safe}.\, \phi$ is equisatisfiable with $\forall x.\, \phi$.*

*Proof.* By the definitions of relativization and typing proposition of Set and atomic types.    □

In this paper we are going in the opposite direction, that is, from an unsorted to a many-sorted universe. We will obtain the type information from propositions that appear in the unsorted language in the form of *typing hypotheses*.[3]

**Definition 4 (Typing hypothesis).** *A typing hypothesis* $\mathcal{H}(x)$ *for variable the* $x$ *is a premise of the form* $x \in e$ *or* $x = e$, *for any expression* $e$ *where* $x$ *is not free in* $e$.

The type information that can be obtained from an untyped formula is almost directly taken from their typing hypotheses and can be captured with precision by refinement types. Suppose we want to annotate the invalid formula $\forall x. \ x + 0 = x$. It is incorrect to say that $x$ is an integer: that would make the formula valid. However, the formula $\forall x. \ x \in Nat \Rightarrow x + 0 = x$ contains a hypothesis from which we can soundly infer the type $\{y : \text{Int} \mid 0 \leq y\}$ for $x$. With this in mind, we define the typing rules.

### 3.2 Typing Rules

We start by declaring some conventional auxiliary definitions. A *typing context* $\Gamma$ : $\mathcal{V} \cup \mathcal{O} \to \tau$ is a finite partial function from variable and operator symbols to types. Its grammar is $\Gamma ::= x : \tau \mid \Gamma, x : \tau$. A triple $\Gamma \vdash \phi : \tau$ is a *pre-judgement*. It is a (valid) *judgement* if it can be derived from the typing rules. A pair $(\Gamma, \tau)$ is a *typing* of $\phi$ iff $fv(\phi) \subseteq dom(\Gamma)$ and $\Gamma \vdash \phi : \tau$ is valid. Likewise, the typing of a formula is just $\Gamma$. A formula $\phi$ is *typable* iff it admits a typing. Given an untyped formula $\phi \triangleq \forall x. \ \varphi$ such that $\Gamma \vdash \varphi : \text{Bool}$ is a judgment and $fv(\varphi) \subseteq dom(\Gamma)$, then the corresponding *annotated* (sorted) formula is $\phi' \triangleq \forall x : \Gamma(x). \ \varphi$.

The definition of the typing rules is similar to the standard rules for simple typed $\lambda$-calculus. The typing rules introduce many fresh type variables noted $\alpha, \alpha_1, \alpha_2, ...,$ etc. during a type derivation. In contrast to type inference in programming languages where type variables are unified throughout the whole derivation to obtain a most general type, here we just want to unify variables when deriving the typing hypotheses. In the rest of the formula, we just check that types are well-formed. The core of the typing rules lies in the definition of four binary relations on types. Equality $\equiv$ and subtyping $<:$ are used to unify type variables. They have their corresponding non-unifiable versions: equality checking $\approx$ and subtype checking $\prec:$. Unless explicitly noted, they are all interpreted in a context $\Gamma$, for example, as $\Gamma \vdash \tau_1 \equiv \tau_2$, to bind the free variables the refinement predicates may have.

The equality condition $\tau_1 \equiv \tau_2$ tries to unify both types when one of them is a type variable. The subtyping relation $<:$ is a pre-order on types (i.e., it is reflexive and transitive). For any ground types $\tau_1$ and $\tau_2$, $\tau_1 <: \tau_2$ iff $\forall x. \ \mathcal{P}_{\tau_1}(x) \Rightarrow \mathcal{P}_{\tau_2}(x)$; when at least one of $\tau_1$ and $\tau_2$ is a type variable, the types are unified, as explained

---

[3] TLA$^+$ was designed with the philosophy that the user should not think in terms of types when she writes the specifications and proofs. In practice, it is customary that the first thing the user does after declaring the variables in a TLA$^+$ module is to write a *type invariant* for every declared variable. Once proved, this invariant is used as a hypothesis in the other theorems.

**Typing rules for first-order formulas and set objects**

[T-FALSE]      [T-IMPLIES]
$$\dfrac{}{\Gamma \vdash \mathsf{false} : \mathsf{Bool}}$$

$$\dfrac{\Gamma \vdash \phi_1 : \mathsf{Bool} \quad \Gamma \vdash \phi_2 : \mathsf{Bool}}{\Gamma \vdash \phi_1 \Rightarrow \phi_2 : \mathsf{Bool}}$$

[T-QUANT]      [T-CHECK]
$$\dfrac{\Gamma, x : \alpha \vdash \phi : \mathsf{Bool}}{\Gamma \vdash \forall x.\, \phi : \mathsf{Bool}}$$

$$\dfrac{\Gamma, x : \tau \vdash \phi : \mathsf{Bool}}{\Gamma \vdash \forall x : \tau.\, \phi : \mathsf{Bool}}$$

[T-VAR]     [T-OP]
$$\dfrac{\Gamma(x) \equiv \alpha}{\Gamma \vdash x : \alpha}$$

$$\dfrac{\Gamma(w) \equiv \alpha_1 \to \alpha_2 \quad \Gamma \vdash e : \alpha_1}{\Gamma \vdash w(e) : \alpha_2}$$

[T-SETCOMP]
$$\dfrac{\Gamma \vdash s : \mathsf{Set}\,\alpha \quad \Gamma, x : \alpha \vdash \phi : \mathsf{Bool} \quad x \notin fv(s)}{\Gamma \vdash \{x \in s : \phi\} : \mathsf{Set}\,\{x : \alpha \mid \phi\}}$$

[T-EMPTY]        [T-PAIR]
$$\dfrac{}{\Gamma \vdash \{\} : \mathsf{Set}\,\varnothing_\alpha}$$

$$\dfrac{\Gamma \vdash e_1 : \alpha_1 \quad \Gamma \vdash e_2 : \alpha_2}{\Gamma \vdash \{e_1, e_2\} : \mathsf{Set}\,(\alpha_1 \uplus \alpha_2)}$$

[T-POWER]       [T-UNION]
$$\dfrac{\Gamma \vdash s : \mathsf{Set}\,\alpha}{\Gamma \vdash \mathbb{P}s : \mathsf{Set}\,\mathsf{Set}\,\alpha}$$

$$\dfrac{\Gamma \vdash s : \mathsf{Set}\,\mathsf{Set}\,\alpha}{\Gamma \vdash \cup s : \mathsf{Set}\,\alpha}$$

$$\dfrac{\Gamma \vdash e_1 : \alpha_1 \quad \Gamma \vdash e_2 : \alpha_2 \quad \Gamma \vdash \alpha_1 \prec: \alpha_3 \quad \Gamma \vdash \alpha_2 \prec: \alpha_3}{\Gamma \vdash e_1 = e_2 : \mathsf{Bool}} \text{ [T-EQ]}$$

$$\dfrac{\Gamma \vdash e_1 : \alpha_1 \quad \Gamma \vdash e_2 : \mathsf{Set}\,\alpha_2 \quad \Gamma \vdash \alpha_1 \prec: \alpha_2}{\Gamma \vdash e_1 \in e_2 : \mathsf{Bool}} \text{ [T-MEM]}$$

[TH-EQ]
$$\dfrac{\Gamma \vdash e : \alpha \quad \Gamma, x : \alpha \vdash \phi : \mathsf{Bool} \quad x \notin fv(e)}{\Gamma \vdash \forall x.\, x = e \Rightarrow \phi : \mathsf{Bool}}$$

[TH-MEM]
$$\dfrac{\Gamma \vdash e : \mathsf{Set}\,\alpha \quad \Gamma, x : \alpha \vdash \phi : \mathsf{Bool} \quad x \notin fv(e)}{\Gamma \vdash \forall x.\, x \in e \Rightarrow \phi : \mathsf{Bool}}$$

**Typing rules for function and arithmetic expressions**

$$\dfrac{\begin{array}{c}\Gamma \vdash f : \alpha_1 \quad \Gamma \vdash \alpha_1 \approx (x : \alpha_3) \to \alpha_4 \\ \Gamma \vdash e : \alpha_2 \qquad \Gamma \vdash \alpha_2 \prec: \alpha_3\end{array}}{\Gamma \vdash f[e] : [x \mapsto e] \cdot \alpha_4} \text{ [T-APP]}$$

$$\dfrac{\Gamma \vdash f : \alpha_1 \quad \Gamma \vdash \alpha_1 \approx (x : \alpha_2) \to \alpha_3}{\Gamma \vdash \mathsf{dom}\, f : \mathsf{Set}\,\alpha_2} \text{ [T-DOM]}$$

$$\dfrac{\Gamma \vdash s : \mathsf{Set}\,\alpha_1 \quad \Gamma, x : \alpha_1 \vdash e : \alpha_2}{\Gamma \vdash \lambda x \in s.\, e : (x : \alpha_1) \to \alpha_2} \text{ [T-FUN]}$$

$$\dfrac{\Gamma \vdash s : \mathsf{Set}\,\alpha_1 \quad \Gamma \vdash t : \mathsf{Set}\,\alpha_2}{\Gamma \vdash [s \to t] : \mathsf{Set}\,(\alpha_1 \to \alpha_2)} \text{ [T-FUNSET]}$$

$$\dfrac{}{\Gamma \vdash Int : \mathsf{Set}\,\mathsf{Int}} \text{ [T-INT]}$$

$$\dfrac{\Gamma \vdash e_i : \alpha_i \quad \Gamma \vdash \alpha_i \prec: \mathsf{Int} \quad i \in \{1,2\}}{\Gamma \vdash e_1 + e_2 : \{x : \mathsf{Int} \mid x = e_1 + e_2\}} \text{ [T-PLUS]}$$

$$\dfrac{n \in \{0,1,2,...\}}{\Gamma \vdash n : \{x : \mathsf{Int} \mid x = n\}} \text{ [T-NUM]}$$

$$\dfrac{\Gamma \vdash e_i : \alpha_i \quad \Gamma \vdash \alpha_i \prec: \mathsf{Int} \quad i \in \{1,2\}}{\Gamma \vdash e_1 < e_2 : \mathsf{Bool}} \text{ [T-LESS]}$$

**Rules for $\ll:$ (that is, $<:$ or $\prec:$) and $\approx$**

$$\dfrac{\Gamma \vdash e : \tau_1 \quad \Gamma \vdash \tau_1 \ll: \tau_2}{\Gamma \vdash e : \tau_2} \text{ [T-SUB]}$$

$$\dfrac{\Gamma \vdash \alpha_1 \equiv \tau_1 \quad \Gamma \vdash \alpha_2 \equiv \tau_2}{\Gamma \vdash (x : \tau_1) \to \tau_2 \approx (x : \alpha_1) \to \alpha_2} \text{ [MATCH-ARROW]}$$

[EQ-REF]
$$\dfrac{\Gamma, x : \tau \vdash \phi_1 \Leftrightarrow \phi_2}{\Gamma \vdash \{x : \tau \mid \phi_1\} \equiv \{x : \tau \mid \phi_2\}}$$

[EQ-ARROW]
$$\dfrac{\Gamma \vdash \tau_1 \equiv \tau_1' \quad \Gamma \vdash \tau_2 \equiv \tau_2'}{\Gamma \vdash (x : \tau_1) \to \tau_2 \equiv (x : \tau_1') \to \tau_2'}$$

[EQ-SET]
$$\dfrac{\Gamma \vdash \tau_1 \equiv \tau_2}{\Gamma \vdash \mathsf{Set}\,\tau_1 \equiv \mathsf{Set}\,\tau_2}$$

[SUB-REF]
$$\dfrac{\Gamma, x : \tau \vdash \phi_1 \Rightarrow \phi_2}{\Gamma \vdash \{x : \tau \mid \phi_1\} \ll: \{x : \tau \mid \phi_2\}}$$

[SUB-ARROW]
$$\dfrac{\Gamma \vdash \tau_1' \ll: \tau_1 \quad \Gamma, x : \tau_1' \vdash \tau_2 \ll: \tau_2'}{\Gamma \vdash (x : \tau_1) \to \tau_2 \ll: (x : \tau_1') \to \tau_2'}$$

[SUB-SET]
$$\dfrac{\Gamma \vdash \tau_1 \ll: \tau_2}{\Gamma \vdash \mathsf{Set}\,\tau_1 \ll: \mathsf{Set}\,\tau_2}$$

**Fig. 2.** Typing and subtyping rules

later by the rules of constraint solving. The condition $\tau_1 \prec: \tau_2$ is valid iff both types are ground types and $\tau_1 <: \tau_2$. That is, it checks that $\tau_1$ is a subtype of $\tau_2$, without unifying type variables. We use the symbol $\ll:$ as a shorthand for $<:$ and $\prec:$. The rules EQ-REF and SUB-REF yield type verification conditions on first-order formulas that have to be proved correct to satisfy the type property. Therefore, the verification of these conditions is an undecidable problem [17]. Well-formedness conditions on types reduce basically to check the type conditions.

The typing rules are given in Figure 2. As expected, once a formula has been Boolified (cf. Section 2), the rules for false and $\Rightarrow$ are trivial. Rule T-QUANT evaluates the body of $\forall x.\ \phi$ by adding $x$ to the context with a fresh type variable $\alpha$. We obtain the typing hypotheses by decomposing the assumptions present in a formula by elementary heuristics. The rules TH-EQ and TH-MEM, which are applied with higher priority than rule T-QUANT, encapsulate this requirement in a simplified way. However, the information provided by the typing hypotheses may not be completely captured by merely syntactic analysis. For example, the typing proposition $\mathcal{P}_{\text{Set Int}}(s)$ is equal to $\forall z \in s.\ z \in Int$, but the typing hypothesis may appear, for instance, as the equivalent formula $s \in \mathbb{P}Int$. The sub-expressions $x \in s$ in the rules T-SETCOMP and T-FUN are typing hypotheses and are therefore treated as such.

The precise type information of refinement types imposes a weak form of type equality (rule T-EQ). If we require the types of the arguments to be exactly equal, we would be ruling out many typable expressions. Instead, the rule requires them to a have common super-type. Suppose we want to type the expression $3 = 4$. It is false, but still typable because the types $\{x : \text{Int} \mid x = 3\}$ and $\{x : \text{Int} \mid x = 4\}$, which have the same base type Int, are both subtypes of $\{x : \text{Int} \mid x = 3 \vee x = 4\}$.

Functions are contravariant on their arguments while they are covariant on their result (rule SUB-ARROW). This has the effect of shrinking their domain while expanding their codomain. To extract the domain from a function type, as needed by rules T-APP and T-DOM, we use the condition $\tau_1 \approx \tau_2$ as a kind of pattern-matching for functions (MATCH-ARROW). When $\tau$ is a function type and $\alpha_1$ and $\alpha_2$ fresh variables, $\tau \approx (x : \alpha_1) \to \alpha_2$ obtains the domain of $\tau$ in $\alpha_1$ and the codomain in $\alpha_2$. Function applications (T-APP) have type $[x \mapsto e] \cdot \alpha_4$: it is the type $\alpha_4$ of the function's codomain, to which it is applied a substitution of the variable $x$ by expression $e$. The substitution has to be delayed until it is applied to a refinement type, when we can simplify it as:

$$[x \mapsto e] \cdot \{x' : \tau \mid \phi\} \quad \longrightarrow \quad \{x' : \tau \mid \phi[x \leftarrow e]\}$$

Literal integers and the set of integers have a constant type (T-NUM and T-INT). Rules T-PLUS and T-LESS require that their arguments to be integers with the condition $e_i \prec: \text{Int}$. The rule for $x - y$ is similar to the rule T-PLUS.

Finally, to type check an annotated formula, we use the same type system, except that the typing rules TH-MEM, TH-EQ and T-QUANT for quantifiers are no longer needed; they are replaced by the rule T-CHECK. This means that during type checking there are no derivations from typing hypotheses, and type annotations in quantifiers are passed directly to the body's context.

### 3.3 Soundness

Type annotations, as well as the typing hypotheses, restrict the domain of evaluation of the quantified variables. Suppose the formula $\phi$ is not valid. Then there exists some valuation in the universe $\mathcal{D}$ which makes the formula false. Still, there may exist some other valuation in $\mathcal{D}$ that makes $\phi$ true. Let us call $A$ the set of all valuations that make $\phi$ true. We want to show that the type system does not generate annotations for $\phi$, resulting in $\phi'$, such that those annotations restrict or confine the domain of evaluation of the variables to the set $A$ which would make $\phi'$ valid.

For example, consider $\forall x.\ x < x + 1$ which is false in some valuations of $x$, namely when $x \notin Int$. However, if we annotate $x$ incorrectly as an integer, $\forall x : \mathsf{Int}.\ x < x + 1$ would become valid, because $x$ would be evaluated precisely in those values that make $x < x + 1$ true. In essence, we need to prove that type assignments only follow from typing hypotheses.

**Theorem 1 (Soundness).** *If $x : \tau$ is a typing of $\phi$, then $\vdash \forall x.\ \phi$ iff $\vdash \forall x : \tau.\ \phi$.*

*Proof.* $\Rightarrow$) If $\phi$ is true in all models of the untyped universe, then in a sorted universe that restricts the domain of interpretation, $\phi$ will also be trivially true.

$\Leftarrow$) Assuming $\vdash \forall x : \tau.\ \phi$ (named $A_1$) we want to prove $\vdash \forall x.\ \phi$.

PROOF. We know that:

$\langle 1 \rangle 1.\ \ x : \tau \vdash \phi : \mathsf{Bool}$ is valid (i.e. there is a type derivation), by hypothesis.

$\langle 1 \rangle 2.\ \ \vdash \forall x.\ \mathcal{P}_\tau(x) \Rightarrow \phi$ (named $A_2$), by assumption $A_1$ and Lemma 1.

We need to show that $\mathcal{P}_\tau(x)$, derived from $x : \tau$, does not constraint the domain of evaluation of $x$ in $\phi$.

$\langle 1 \rangle 3.$ Suffices to prove that from $\vdash A_2$ we can prove $\vdash \forall x.\ \phi$, by step $\langle 1 \rangle 2$.

We proceed by a case analysis on the shape of $\phi$.

$\langle 1 \rangle 4.$ CASE 1. If there is no typing hypothesis for the variable $x$ in $\phi$, then $\vdash \forall x.\ \phi$.

PROOF.

$\langle 2 \rangle 1.$ The type derivation on $\phi$ yields the judgment $x : \alpha_x \vdash \phi : \mathsf{Bool}$, by step $\langle 1 \rangle 1$. Type variable $\alpha_x$ is fresh and after unification will be equal to $\tau$. The first applied rule is T-QUANT, the only possible one, since there are no typing hypotheses.

$\langle 2 \rangle 2.$ The type $\alpha_x$ can only be promoted to a safe type $\tau$.

PROOF. The TH (typing hypothesis) rules, where unification of type variables happens, do not apply, meaning that $\alpha_x$ cannot be unified with any non-safe type such as Bool, Int or functions. The only applicable rules that may promote $\alpha_x$ are the rules T-MEM, T-SETCOMP, T-PAIR, T-POWER or T-UNION, but these result in a safe Set type. For example, rule T-PLUS requires establishing $\alpha_x \prec:$ Int, which is impossible.

$\langle 2 \rangle 3.$ Finally, since $\tau$ is safe, it does not compromise the validity of $A_2$ when $x : \tau$ it is relativized to $\mathcal{P}_\tau(x)$, by Lemma 2.

$\langle 1 \rangle 5.$ CASE 2. If $\phi$ is of the form $\mathcal{H}(x) \Rightarrow \phi_1$, then $\vdash \forall x.\ \mathcal{H}(x) \Rightarrow \phi_1$.

PROOF.

$\langle 2 \rangle 1.$ Suffices to prove that $\mathcal{H}(x) \Rightarrow \mathcal{P}_\tau(x)$.

$\langle 2 \rangle 2$.  Suppose that $\mathcal{H}(x)$ is of the form $x \in s$. The first rule applied in the type derivation is necessarily TH-MEM, yielding

$$\vdash s : \mathsf{Set}\, \alpha_x \ (1) \qquad \text{and} \qquad x : \alpha_x \vdash \phi_1 : \mathsf{Bool} \ (2)$$

Here, we see that the fresh type variable $\alpha_x$ is the same in both sides of the derivation, which results in the unification of the types of $x$ and $s$. The TH rules are the only ones that share type variables in their different premises.

We apply induction on $fv(\mathcal{H}(x))$. For simplicity, we consider that $\mathcal{H}(x)$ does not include quantified formulas.

$\langle 3 \rangle 1$.  (Base case) There are no free variables, meaning that the type of $x$ does not depend on the type of any other variable. Therefore, it is trivially a constant type or an atomic type t. For instance, if $s$ is $Int$, the goal is to show that $x \in Int \Rightarrow \mathcal{P}_{\alpha_x}(x)$. So $\alpha_x$ is unified with $\mathsf{Int}$ and $\mathcal{P}_{\mathsf{Int}}(x) = x \in Int = \mathcal{H}(x)$.

$\langle 3 \rangle 2$.  (Inductive step) We proceed by a case analysis on the shape of $s$, which has to be necessarily a set, otherwise it would not match with $\mathsf{Set}\, \alpha_x$ in (1).

$\langle 4 \rangle 1$.  CASE $s \triangleq \mathbb{P}t$. The goal is to show that $x \in \mathbb{P}t \Rightarrow \mathcal{P}_{\alpha_x}(x)$. Given that $t : \alpha_t$, then $\alpha_x$ is unified with $\mathsf{Set}\, \alpha_t$. Then $\mathcal{P}_{\mathsf{Set}\, \alpha_t}(x) = \forall z \in x.\ \mathcal{P}_{\alpha_t}(z)$, by the inductive hypothesis $z \in t \Rightarrow \mathcal{P}_{\alpha_t}(z)$.

$\langle 4 \rangle 2$.  The other cases are proved in a similar way.

$\langle 2 \rangle 3$.  The case where $\mathcal{H}(x)$ is of the form $x = e$ is similar to the step $\langle 2 \rangle 2$.

$\langle 2 \rangle 4$.  QED , by $\langle 2 \rangle 1$, $\langle 2 \rangle 2$ and $\langle 2 \rangle 3$.

$\langle 1 \rangle 6$.  QED , by steps $\langle 1 \rangle 3$, $\langle 1 \rangle 4$ and $\langle 1 \rangle 5$. $\qquad\qquad\qquad\qquad\qquad\qquad$ $\square$

## 4  Type Inference Algorithm

The type inference algorithm takes a formula $\phi$ and returns a type assignment $\sigma$, that is, a function from type variables to types. The algorithm consists of a constraint generation phase followed by constraint solving.

Since the constraint-based algorithm is independent of the chosen type system we can adapt one originally introduced for a variant of ML by Knowles and Flanagan [10]. The main difference is in the constraint language, where we use two additional kinds of type checking conditions instead of only two for equality and subtyping. The constraint language grammar is defined following the notation of [16].

$$c ::= \tau \equiv \tau \mid \tau <: \tau \mid \tau \approx \tau \mid \tau \prec: \tau \mid \top \mid \bot \mid c \wedge c \mid \exists \bar{\alpha}.\, c \mid [x \mapsto e] \cdot c$$

In addition to the type constraints, there are the true and false constraints. Conjunction of constraints and existential quantification of type variables permit to replicate the structure of a type derivation in a single constraint formula. Delayed substitutions $[x \mapsto e] \cdot c$ replace variable $x$ by expression $e$ in constraint $c$.

A constraint $c$ is *satisfiable*, noted $\sigma \vdash c$, iff there exists a ground assignment $\sigma$ that satisfies $c$. Constraint judgements can be interpreted by the following rules, where $\sigma, \alpha \mapsto$ t is function $\sigma$ updated with a new assignment for $\alpha$ and t is fresh atomic type:

$$\frac{}{\sigma \vdash \top} \qquad \frac{\sigma \tau_1 \not\downarrow \sigma \tau_2}{\sigma \vdash \tau_1 \not\downarrow \tau_2} \ (\not\downarrow \in \{\equiv, \simeq, <:, \prec:\}) \qquad \frac{\sigma c_1 \quad \sigma c_2}{\sigma \vdash c_1 \wedge c_2} \qquad \frac{\sigma, \alpha \mapsto \mathsf{t} \vdash c}{\sigma \vdash \exists \alpha.\, c}$$

## 4.1  Constraint Generation

To a pre-judgement $\Gamma \vdash e : \tau$, where $fv(e) \subseteq dom(\Gamma)$, we associate a constraint $\langle\!\langle \Gamma \vdash e : \tau \rangle\!\rangle$. Constraint generation (CG) rules are essentially derived from their corresponding typing rules, with subsumption (rule T-SUB) distributed all through to make the rules syntax-directed. CG rules take as arguments an environment $\Gamma$, an expression $e$ and a type variable $\tau$. They are recursively defined on $e$. The resulting constraint has a linear size with respect to the size of the original formula. As an example, we show the CG rule obtained from the rule T-SETCOMP:

$$\langle\!\langle \Gamma \vdash \{x \in s : \phi\} : \alpha_r \rangle\!\rangle \triangleq \exists \alpha_1 \alpha_2. \wedge \langle\!\langle \Gamma \vdash s : \mathsf{Set}\, \alpha_1 \rangle\!\rangle$$
$$\wedge \langle\!\langle \Gamma, x : \alpha_2 \vdash \phi : \mathsf{Bool} \rangle\!\rangle$$
$$\wedge \Gamma \vdash \alpha_2 \prec: \alpha_1$$
$$\wedge \Gamma \vdash \alpha_r \equiv \mathsf{Set}\,\{x : \alpha_1 \mid \phi\}$$

Note that: (i) every free type variable that appears in the typing rule are existentially bounded by fresh type variables $\alpha_1$ and $\alpha_2$, (ii) the expected type for the expression in the second argument is unified to the type variable $\alpha_r$ passed as the third argument, and (iii) the subsumption rule is implicitly applied to the sub-formula $x \in s$.

The following theorem asserts that the soundness and completeness of the generated constraints, grounded by a type assignment $\sigma$.

**Theorem 2  (CG soundness and completeness).** $\sigma \vdash \langle\!\langle \Gamma \vdash \phi : \tau \rangle\!\rangle$ iff $\sigma\Gamma \vdash \phi : \sigma\tau$.

*Proof (idea).* By induction on $\phi$, using the typing rules, the CG definitions and the interpretation of constraints. For details, see [17].                                    $\square$

## 4.2  Constraint Solving

Constraint-based type inference for systems with subtyping is an extensive research topic. Pottier [16] and Odersky et al. [15] have developed Hindley-Milner systems parameterized by a subtyping constraint system. Broadly speaking, we specify a constraint solving algorithm following [9] as a non-deterministic system of constraint rewriting rules and first-order unification rules for subtyping constraints. The algorithm proceeds in one main step, that is repeated once, consisting of solving equality and subtyping constraints. Once the first execution is finished, the final typing we were searching for is $\Gamma$, but there are still some residual subtype checking constraints of the form $\tau_1 \prec: \tau_2$ to prove. The second step is to check that these constraints are satisfied, by converting them to the form $\tau_1 <: \tau_2$ and solving them by executing the main step again. If the remaining constraint is $\top$, the algorithm finishes successfully.

To solve the equality and subtyping constraints we proceed as follows. Given a context $\Gamma$ and a constraint $c$, we apply the rules 3.1, 3.2, 3.3 and MATCH-ARROW plus the following rules to eliminate the type variables introduced during constraint generation. Note that rule 4.2 has to be carefully applied to avoid recursive substitutions.

$$(\exists \alpha.\ c_1) \wedge c_2 \longrightarrow \exists \alpha.\ (c_1 \wedge c_2) \qquad \text{if } \alpha \notin fv(C_2) \qquad (4.1)$$
$$\exists \alpha.\ (\Gamma \vdash \alpha \equiv \tau \wedge c) \longrightarrow c[\tau \leftarrow \alpha] \qquad \text{if } \alpha \text{ does not occur in } \tau \qquad (4.2)$$

Subtype constraints $\Gamma \vdash \tau_1 <: \tau_2$ are solved by non-deterministically applying simplification rules SUB-REF, SUB-ARROW, and SUB-SET, or the unification rules:

$$\Gamma \vdash \mathsf{Set}\, \tau <: \sigma \cdot \alpha \;\rightsquigarrow\; \{\alpha \mapsto \mathsf{Set}\, \tau\}$$

$$\Gamma \vdash (x : \tau_1) \to \tau_2 <: \sigma \cdot \alpha \;\rightsquigarrow\; \{\alpha \mapsto (x : \alpha_1) \to \alpha_2\} \;(\alpha_1, \alpha_2 \text{ fresh variables})$$

$$\Gamma \vdash \{x : \tau \mid \phi\} <: \sigma \cdot \alpha \;\rightsquigarrow\; \{\alpha \mapsto \{x : \tau \mid \gamma\}\} \qquad (\gamma \text{ fresh placeholder})$$

$$\Gamma \vdash \{x : \tau \mid \phi_1\} <: \{x' : \alpha \mid \phi_2\} \;\rightsquigarrow\; \{\alpha \mapsto \{x : \tau \mid \phi_1\}\}$$

These four unification rules have their symmetric counterparts. They return a substitution $\{\alpha \mapsto \tau\}$ of a variable $\alpha$ by another type $\tau$, which are immediately applied to $\Gamma$ and $c$. Any other pair combination of set, function or refinement types will make the algorithm abort with a type error. The algorithm terminates when no rule can be applied. At this point, only subtype constraints $\alpha_1 <: \alpha_2$ between type variables remain in $c$. The type variables $\alpha_1$ and $\alpha_2$ can be set to a concrete ground type t, making the constraint valid by reflexivity. Placeholder symbols are introduced to defer the reconstruction of refinement predicates.

*Solving placeholders.* The final step in type inference algorithm is to find formulas to replace the placeholders while satisfying the typing conditions. The placeholders appear in conditions of the form $\Gamma \vdash \gamma \Rightarrow \phi$, $\Gamma \vdash \gamma_1 \Rightarrow \gamma_2$ or $\Gamma \vdash \phi \Rightarrow \gamma$. Our algorithm to calculate concrete refinement predicates is almost entirely based on a similar one developed in [10], which, in turn, is based on the intuition that implications can be analyzed as dataflow graphs.

## 5   Experimental Results

We have implemented a prototype of the type inference algorithm in TLAPS. In particular, the following table shows results for two case studies. They correspond to the invariant proofs of the $N$-process Peterson and Bakery algorithms for mutual exclusion, whose data structures are represented by functions ranging over the processes and they contain some basic arithmetic.

For each benchmark, we record the size of the proof, i.e. the number of non-trivial proof obligations generated by the proof manager, and the time in seconds required to verify those proofs on a standard laptop. The proof size corresponds to the number of proof obligations that are passed to the backend prover, which is proportional to the number of interactive steps and therefore represents the user effort for making TLAPS check the proof. We compare these figures for the SMT backend using the previous elementary type inference algorithm described in [14], and then for the SMT backend equipped with the new type system with refinement types. The results for the new type system includes three extra columns corresponding to the number of derived type verification conditions (non-trivial vs. total), total time in seconds to perform the type inference (including proving the type conditions), and number of initially generated constraints. The total time for the second system is the sum of the times required to do type inference and the time to actually prove the SMT encoding of the proof obligation. In all cases, the SMT solver used was CVC4 [3].

| | Simple Types | | Refinement Types | | | | |
| --- | --- | --- | --- | --- | --- | --- | --- |
| | size | time | size | time | tvc | type-inf | const |
| Peterson | 3 | 0.40 | 3 | 0.30 | 0/474 | 0.33 | 937 |
| Bakery | 15 | 9.52 | 3 | 1.51 | 6/1622 | 4.15 | 3317 |

The second case study, which is a significantly bigger specification than the first one, takes slightly less time than the previous backend, whereas the overall time taken is slightly longer for the Peterson case study. The size of the proof, i.e. the number of human interactions, is considerably reduced for the second case. The current prototypical implementation of the constraint solving algorithm may benefit from optimizations (see [16]) in order to speed up type inference.

In both examples, all non-trivial verification conditions were discharged almost instantly by the SMT solver. Consequently, no dynamic domain checkings were needed in the SMT-LIB encoding.

## 6   Conclusions

Beyond the recurring debates about using typed versus untyped languages for formalizing mathematics or software systems [12], we can observe that types, regarded just as a classification of the elements of a language, arise quite naturally in untyped set theory. In this paper, motivated by the use of powerful automatic provers for multi-sorted first-order logic, we have defined a sophisticated type system for a fragment of the TLA$^+$ specification language that captures with precision the values and semantics of sets and functions using refinement and dependent types. When type inference succeeds, we obtain type annotations on top of an untyped specification language, getting the best of both the typed and untyped approaches.

Inevitably, the resulting type system constrains the set of accepted TLA$^+$ expressions. Occasionally useful expressions that are not typable by the type system are, for example, enumerated sets whose elements are of different types. As we mentioned in the introduction, formulas for which type inference fails will still be translated according to the "untyped" encoding, and may thus be proved by the SMT solver. One advantage of doing type inference with constraints is that we can know exactly what part of the formula cannot be typed and can therefore restrict the use of the untyped encoding to these parts and produce useful type checking warnings and error messages [8].

Our experience so far with the implementation of this approach in TLAPS has been quite positive: types are successfully inferred for the vast majority of proof obligations that we have seen in practice. Since the new type system is a refinement of the previous one, it never fails when the old one succeeded, and it has been able to increase the number of proof obligations that the SMT backend can handle without human interaction. The improvements are particularly noticeable in specifications that contain a significant number of function applications, which are used quite frequently in TLA$^+$ specifications.

The type system is easily extended to accommodate TLA$^+$ constructs that we have not considered in this paper, such as tuples and records. Support for the CHOOSE operator (Hilbert's choice) is more challenging. It would be interesting to study the applicability of our type system to proofs of mathematical theorems in ZF set theory.

# References

1. Abrial, J.-R.: Modeling in Event-B - System and Software Engineering. Cambridge University Press (2010)
2. Aspinall, D., Compagnoni, A.B.: Subtyping dependent types. Theor. Comput. Sci. 266(1-2), 273–309 (2001)
3. Barrett, C., Conway, C.L., Deters, M., Hadarean, L., Jovanović, D., King, T., Reynolds, A., Tinelli, C.: Cvc4. In: Gopalakrishnan, G., Qadeer, S. (eds.) CAV 2011. LNCS, vol. 6806, pp. 171–177. Springer, Heidelberg (2011)
4. Barrett, C., Stump, A., Tinelli, C.: The Satisfiability Modulo Theories Library, SMT-LIB (2010), www.SMT-LIB.org
5. Déharbe, D.: Integration of SMT-solvers in B and Event-B development environments. Sci. Comput. Program. 78(3), 310–326 (2013)
6. Dowek, G.: Collections, sets and types. Mathematical. Structures in Comp. Sci. 9(1), 109–123 (1999)
7. Freeman, T., Pfenning, F.: Refinement types for ML. In: Proceedings of the ACM SIGPLAN 1991 Conference on Programming Language Design and Implementation, PLDI 1991, pp. 268–277. ACM, New York (1991)
8. Heeren, B., Hage, J., Swierstra, D.: Generalizing Hindley-Milner type inference algorithms. Technical report (2002)
9. Jouannaud, J.-P., Kirchner, C.: Solving equations in abstract algebras: A rule-based survey of unification. In: Computational Logic - Essays in Honor of Alan Robinson, pp. 257–321 (1991)
10. Knowles, K., Flanagan, C.: Type reconstruction for general refinement types. In: De Nicola, R. (ed.) ESOP 2007. LNCS, vol. 4421, pp. 505–519. Springer, Heidelberg (2007)
11. Lamport, L.: Specifying Systems: The TLA$^+$ Language and Tools for Hardware and Software Engineers. Addison-Wesley, Boston, Mass (2002)
12. Lamport, L., Paulson, L.C.: Should your specification language be typed? ACM Trans. Program. Lang. Syst. 21(3), 502–526 (1999)
13. Manzano, M.: Extensions of First-Order Logic, 2nd edn. Cambridge Tracts in Theoretical Computer Science. Cambridge University Press (2005)
14. Merz, S., Vanzetto, H.: Harnessing SMT Solvers for TLA $^+$ Proofs. ECEASST, 53 (2012)
15. Odersky, M., Sulzmann, M., Wehr, M.: Type inference with constrained types. In: Fourth International Workshop on Foundations of Object-Oriented Programming, FOOL (1997)
16. Pottier, F.: Simplifying subtyping constraints. In: Proceedings of the 1996 ACM SIGPLAN International Conference on Functional Programming, pp. 122–133. ACM Press (1996)
17. Pottier, F., Rémy, D.: The essence of ML type inference. In: Pierce, B.C. (ed.) Advanced Topics in Types and Programming Languages, ch. 10, pp. 389–489. MIT Press (2005)
18. Rushby, J., Owre, S., Shankar, N.: Subtypes for Specifications: Predicate Subtyping in PVS. IEEE Transactions on Software Engineering 24(9), 709–720 (1998)
19. Spivey, M.: The Z Notation: A Reference Manual. Prentice Hall (1992)
20. Xi, H., Pfenning, F.: Dependent types in practical programming. In: Appel, A.W., Aiken, A. (eds.) POPL, pp. 214–227. ACM (1999)

# Using Lightweight Theorem Proving in an Asynchronous Systems Context*

Matthew Danish and Hongwei Xi

Boston University Computer Science
111 Cummington Mall
Boston, MA 02215

**Abstract.** As part of the development of a new real-time operating system, an asynchronous communication mechanism, for use between applications, has been implemented in a programming language with an advanced static type system. This mechanism is designed to provide desired properties of asynchronicity, coherency and freshness. We used the features of the type system, including linear and dependent types, to represent and partially prove that the implementation safely upheld coherency and freshness. We believe that the resulting program code forms a good example of how easily linear and dependent types can be applied in practice to prove useful properties of low-level concurrent systems programming, while leaving no traces of runtime overhead.

## 1 Introduction

The Terrier [7] project focuses on doing low-level, OS-level systems programming while taking advantage of a dependently typed programming language named ATS [25]. The purpose of this project is to identify effective, practical means to create safer, more reliable systems through use of advanced type system features in programming languages. We are also interested in the implications of having powerful programming language tools available, and the effects on plausible system design. For example, Terrier moves much of the responsibility for program safety back out onto the programs themselves, rather than relying strictly on run-time checks or hardware protection mechanisms. For another, the Terrier program model is one in which asynchronous events play a central role in program design. These two shifts in thinking put more burden on the programmer—a burden that we expect to lighten through language-level assistance—but they also open up more flexibility in potential program design that we hope will enable higher performance and more naturally-written code in difficult problem domains.

ATS is a language with the goal of bringing together formal specification and practical programming. The core of ATS is an ML-like functional programming language which is compiled into C. The type system of ATS combines dependent and linear types to permit sophisticated reasoning about program behavior and

---

* This research is supported partly by NSF grant CCF-1018601.

J.M. Badger and K.Y. Rozier (Eds.): NFM 2014, LNCS 8430, pp. 158–172, 2014.

the safety of resource usage. The design of ATS provides close coupling of type-safe functional code and low-level C code, allowing the programmer to decide the balance between specification and speed. The ATS compiler can generate code which does not require garbage collection nor any other special run-time support, making it suitable for bare metal programming.

Using ATS, we have generated C code which links into our kernel to provide several critical components. We also encourage the use of ATS to help ensure the safety and correctness of programs that run under the OS. For example, programs that wish to communicate with one another are provided with libraries written in ATS which implement protocols that have been statically checked for safety and correctness.

One of those protocols that we implemented is Simpson's "four slot fully asynchronous communication mechanism" [20]. It is a shared memory communication protocol which was cleverly designed by its author to pack some desirable properties into just a few lines of code. It allows one-way, pool-based transmission of data without any synchronization delays between reader and writer. The communication medium is the normal shared memory that is found in most computer systems. The mechanism offers the properties of freshness and coherency, but not history. For example, you could imagine a bulletin board on which one person posts flyers while the other person reads, as shown in figure 1. This mechanism ensures that the reader only sees the latest, complete, coherent postings on the board.

The ATS implementation of the four slot mechanism is compact, efficient and shows how strongly specified types can provide useful assurances at a low-level without intruding into run-time performance of critical code or requiring voluminous quantities of proof-writing.

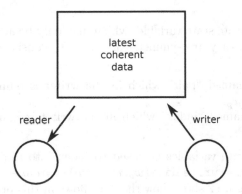

**Fig. 1.** Abstract depiction of four slot mechanism

## 1.1    The Four Slot Mechanism

The scenario for the four slot mechanism starts by assuming that there is a writer program which wishes to convey some information to a reader program. Furthermore, the information is able to be encoded into an arbitrary, fixed number of bytes, and there is a shared memory space large enough for at least four copies of the data to be stored, plus a few more bytes for state variables.

The four slot mechanism works by opening up space in memory for these four "slots" of data, usually in the form of an array. Coherency is ensured through program logic which keeps the reader and the writer apart: each has their own slot to operate upon, and further analysis will show that the mechanism prevents them from touching the same slot at the same time.

To achieve this property, the original four slot mechanism relies on several pieces of shared state, and it assumes that individual bits may be manipulated atomically. That is, all simultaneously accesses to a single bit will appear to have a definite ordering, either way [16]. In practice, atomic operations are offered at machine word sizes [2], not at the individual bit level, but the logic remains the same.

The shared state variables are used for coordination, by both reader and writer programs:

- The atomic bit variable named "reading" or $R$ is intended to roughly indicate which side of the mechanism the reader program is currently using.
- The atomic bit variable named "latest" or $L$ is intended to indicate which side of the mechanism was updated most recently.
- The bit array named "slot" further drills down on the specific slot of the array to be used. You could also choose to split this into two variables "slot0" and "slot1" for analysis purposes.
- Two bits are then used to index into the shared four-member array of data slots.

There are also private state variables which may only be accessed from within each program. Since they are symmetrical, we use a consistent naming scheme for them:

- A bit variable named "pair" which in the writer is named $w_p$ and in the reader is named $r_p$.
- A bit variable named "index" which in the writer is named $w_i$ and in the reader is named $r_i$.

Together, these private variables are used to index into the shared array, and that usage is denoted as write_data $(w_p, w_i, item)$ or $item \leftarrow$ read_data $(r_p, r_i)$.

The diagram in figure 2 shows how the data flows in this protocol. A program obtains its "pair" from either the "reading" or "latest" atomic variable. It then uses the "pair" to pick an "index" from the "slot" array. It then uses the "pair" and "index" to select one of the four slots to work on.

In example diagram you can see that the reader has selected 0, 1 and the writer has selected 1, 1. Visually, you can see that they are able to independently read and write without conflict.

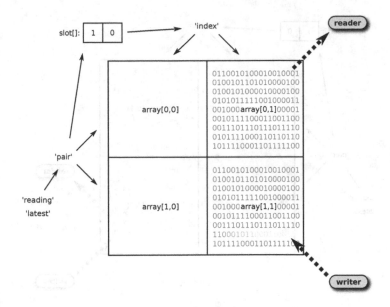

**Fig. 2.** Four Slot Mechanism

On the other hand, the diagram in figure 3 shows a case where the reader and writer are trampling over each other, likely causing data corruption. A properly working four slot mechanism will never allow this to occur.

The pseudocode for the four slot mechanism is shown in figure 4 and it is simple enough for a quick walk-through. For the first step of the writer, WS1, it reads the value of $R$, negates it, and stores it into the private variable $w_p$. For the second step, the writer reads a bit from the *slot* [] array, indexed by $w_p$, negates it, and then uses that as the value of $w_i$. With both $w_p$ and $w_i$, the writer is now ready to perform the actual write. Finally, the writer updates the shared state by writing its values of $w_i, w_p$ into *slot* [] and $L$ respectively.

The reader also takes 5 steps which are aimed at obtaining values of $r_p, r_i$ from shared state. However, the reader gets its value of $r_p$ from the $L$ variable, and it "stakes a claim" to that pair by writing it into the $R$ variable. Then it finds out which slot is most up-to-date, reads the data, and returns it.

## 2    Coherency

A cursory inspection of the pseudocode should reveal that it easily transmits a piece of data if the two programs run back-to-back with no overlap. But that is not very interesting. The real difficulty comes when you accept that the two programs may arbitrarily interleave with one another. Figure 5 is an annotated example of one possible interleaving, where writer and reader steps shown on the same line are happening in parallel:

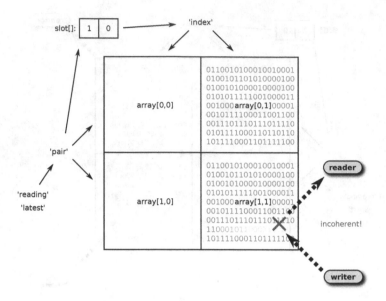

**Fig. 3.** Should not happen

| | |
|---|---|
| WS1 $w_p \leftarrow \neg R$ | RS1 $r_p \leftarrow L$ |
| WS2 $w_i \leftarrow \neg slot\,[w_p]$ | RS2 $R \leftarrow r_p$ |
| WS3 **write_data** $(w_p, w_i, item)$ | RS3 $r_i \leftarrow slot\,[r_p]$ |
| WS4 $slot\,[w_p] \leftarrow w_i$ | RS4 $item \leftarrow$ **read_data** $(r_p, r_i)$ |
| WS5 $L \leftarrow w_p$ | RS5 return $item$ |

**Fig. 4.** Four slot mechanism pseudocode

    – Suppose $L = 1$ and $R = 0$

WS1 $w_p \leftarrow \neg R$                    RS1 $r_p \leftarrow L$

    – Now $w_p = r_p$

WS2 $w_i \leftarrow \neg slot\,[w_p]$            RS2 $R \leftarrow r_p$

                                     RS3 $r_i \leftarrow slot\,[r_p]$

    – And $w_i \neq r_i$

WS3 **write_data** $(w_p, w_i, item)$     RS4 $item \leftarrow$ **read_data** $(r_p, r_i)$

    – ...

**Fig. 5.** Example of interleaving

You can see that when both programs reach their step 2, it is the case that $w_p = r_p$. But the design of the protocol, at this point, ensures that the writer picks the opposite index from the reader, so that $w_i \neq r_i$. Therefore the writer and the reader do not access the same data slot at the same time. This is just one case, and we needed to show that the mechanism always respects a coherency property. More specifically, we looked at the "dangerous" steps WS3 and RS4, where the real data transfers take place, and needed to show that those two steps would never conflict.

**Theorem 1 (Coherency).** *The writer and the reader do not access the same data slot at the same time. More precisely, this assertion must be satisfied at potentially conflicting program points* WS3 *and* RS4:

$$w_p \neq r_p \vee w_i \neq r_i$$

*or, the program points must be shown to be non-conflicting.*

Problem is, $w_p$ and $r_p$ (as well as $w_i$ and $r_i$) are private variables in separate programs. Therefore, dynamic or run-time checking was out of the question. So we turned to static checking encoded using dependent types. To find relevant properties, we looked at various "points of interaction" where the two programs might affect each other through atomic shared variables.

Recall that overlapping atomic operations will appear to occur in a definite ordering. Therefore, points of interaction involving atomic variables $R, L, slot\,[]$ can tell us facts about unseen state. Consider the orderings shown in figure 6.

$$\left.\begin{array}{ll} \text{RS2} & R \leftarrow r_p \\ \text{WS1} & w_p \leftarrow \neg R \end{array}\right\} w_p \neq r_p \text{ at WS1}$$

$$\left.\begin{array}{ll} \text{WS1} & w_p \leftarrow \neg R \\ \text{RS2} & R \leftarrow r_p \end{array}\right\} w_p \overset{?}{=} r_p \text{ at WS1}$$

**Fig. 6.** Two alternative orderings of WS1 and RS2

We do not know ahead of time whether WS1 or RS2 will occur first. But we do know the consequences of each ordering. In the first case, we can see that the writer will harmlessly pick the opposite value of "pair" from the reader. But in the second case, we have no idea what the values of $w_p, r_p$ are. That tells us an important property:

*Property 1.* If $w_p = r_p$ at WS1 then WS1 precedes RS2.

Further, by transitivity,

*Property 2.* If WS1 precedes RS2 then it also precedes RS3.

Recall that RS3 is the step where the reader obtains its value of $r_i$ by reading $slot\,[r_p]$. And as the data dependency graph of figure 7 shows, it is the writer which is in control of the value of $slot\,[r_p]$. Therefore, intuitively, the writer has enough knowledge of the value of $r_i$ to be able to pick a $w_i$ of the opposite value.

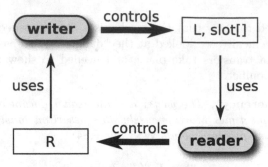

**Fig. 7.** Data dependencies

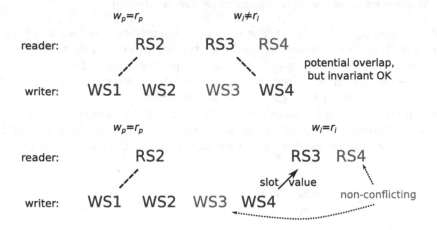

**Fig. 8.** Interaction between RS3 and WS4

This can be seen more precisely by examining the point of interaction between RS3 and WS4 via the *slot* [] array, as shown in figure 8, where the $w_p = r_p$ case is assumed. In this case, the only way that $w_i = r_i$ is if WS4 precedes RS3. By itself, it may seem to violate the coherency assertion but, in fact, the potentially conflicting program points WS3 and RS4 are non-conflicting because they are separated by an atomic operation with definite ordering. This is indicated on the diagram by the solid arrow.

## 3   Encoding the Proof

### 3.1   Write

Each step in the program is encoded into an ATS function prototype along with its types. The ATS code will be explained as we go.

WS1.

$$w_p \leftarrow \neg R$$

```
absview ws1_read_v (R: bit, rstep: int, rp: bit)

fun get_reading_state ():
  [rstep: nat]
  [R, rp: bit | R == rp || (R <> rp ==> rstep < 2)]
  (ws1_read_v (R, rstep, rp) | bit R)
```

For WS1 we have a kind of datatype definition as well as a function prototype. The datatype is abstract which means it does not have a real form in the output. That works because it is intended to be just a property which is erased by compilation. In ATS, properties which are linear are called "views" [26] and that just means that the property, after being introduced, must be consumed once and exactly once. They behave like a "resource" [24].

In this case, the ws1_read_v is an abstract view intended to represent the concept that we have observed the value of $R$ at this particular moment, and this point of interaction tells us a certain fact about the reader, that is true until consumed.

The function simply reads the value of $R$ and returns it, but it also gives us some properties about $R$ which exist in the so-called "static" world [6] as opposed to the "dynamic" world. In ATS, there is a syntactic division between the static world and the dynamic world, represented by the vertical bar in concrete syntax. The static world can be more abstract, where you may encode relations that you do not want to appear in the final output, while the dynamic world is the practical side which will eventually be formed into the C output of the compiler.

The two are connected through use of indexed types. Here we see various type indices: rstep, R, rp. The index R represents the shared state variable $R$, rp represents the hidden private state variable $r_p$, and rstep represents the program counter of the reader program in an abstract form.

ATS allows some specifications about the values of these indices to be made in a convenient, set-like notation. In this case, we have made the following static assertion: that R is equal to rp, or, if R is not equal to rp, then rstep is less than 2.

Then we have returned the linear property indexed by these three, and on the dynamic side we have returned the actual bit value which is linked to the index R.

## WS2.

$$w_i \leftarrow \neg slot\,[w_p]$$

```
absview ws2_slot_v (s: bit, rp: bit, ri: bit)

fun get_write_slot_index {R, wp, rp: bit} {rstep: nat} (
    pfr: !ws1_read_v (R, rstep, rp) | wp: bit wp
  ): [s, ri: bit | (rstep < 3 && wp == rp) ==> s == ri)]
    (ws2_slot_v (s, rp, ri) | bit s)
```

Again, we need a linear property—which here represents the value found in the slot array as well as some facts learned from that point of interaction. In this case, s represents the slot value in memory $s$, rp is a stand-in for $r_p$, and ri for $r_i$.

In order to call this function for step 2, we need evidence that the reading state has been examined, and that evidence is provided by the ws1_read_v view. By default, a linear property like this is consumed and not usable again, but we want this particular property to be reproduced for later use, because we will want to make some statements about $R$ in later steps. Now, one way to reproduce the property would be to explicitly return it again, but ATS provides the ! operator as a bit of syntactic sugar to help make that common case convenient.

On the dynamic side, we need to pass the value of wp because that is used as an index into the slot array.

The return value is a view of the value of the slot that we received, as well as the actual value itself, combined with another fact about the relationship between the variables: if rstep was less than 3 and wp was equal to rp, then we know that s will be equal to ri.

The assertion wp == rp ==> s == ri is a simple statement about array access. The reader program performs $r_i \leftarrow slot\,[r_p]$, and if $w_p = r_p$ then the writer program will see the slot value $s$ which is the same as $r_i$.

The reason why we have to check if rstep was less than 3 is because it might be possible for the reader to get to step 3 and then block for a long time. If the reader is blocking for a long time, it could have a stale value of $r_i$ sitting around, a potentially conflicting value. By guarding against that, we know that the reader has yet to pick a value of $r_i$, and so when it does, it will be equal to the value of $s$.

### WS3.

$$write\_data\,(w_p, w_i, item)$$

```
fun{a: t@ype} write_data
  {R, s, wp, wi, rp, ri: bit | wp <> rp || wi <> ri} {rstep: nat} (
    pfr: !ws1_read_v (R, rstep, rp),
    pfs: !ws2_slot_v (s, rp, ri) |
    wp: bit wp, wi: bit wi, item: a
  ): void
```

Armed with the facts that we have learned about $w_p, w_i, r_p, r_i$ from the points of interaction, we are ready to use the function which does the actual work of writing data into memory. This function has theorem 1 (Coherency) encoded into its type: wp <> rp || wi <> ri, and therefore can only be called if this assertion can be statically proven, or else it results in a type error.

The ATS typechecker uses the Z3 SMT solver [8] on the facts that it has learned about these variables, and can discharge this assertion without further work by the programmer.

### WS4.

$$slot\,[w_p] \leftarrow w_i$$

**absview** ws4_fresh_v (p: bit)

```
fun save_write_slot_index {s, wp, wi, rp, ri: bit | wi <> s} (
    pfs: ws2_slot_v (s, rp, ri) | wp: bit wp, wi: bit wi
): (ws4_fresh_v wp | void)
```

After the write is complete, we need to update the shared state variables so that subsequent reads will obtain the new value. This is a somewhat more minor concern than coherency, but still encoded enough to be sure that it is done properly. This step consumes the ws2_slot_v resource which is no longer valid or needed. It returns a new view which I have labeled ws4_fresh_v, which acts as an obligation to update the remaining shared state.

## WS5.

$$L \leftarrow w_p$$

```
fun save_latest_state
    {R, rp, wp: bit | wp <> R} {rstep: nat} (
    pfr: ws1_read_v (R, rstep, rp),
    pff: ws4_fresh_v wp |
    wp: bit wp
): void
```

The final step cleans up, consuming both remaining views, as they will both become invalid after this step. A final check is added to ensure that the new value of $L$ will not be equal to the old value of $R$.

**Putting it Together.** The code for the **write** operation, alongside the pseudocode, is shown in figure 9. The real code is largely similar to the pseudocode, and each line is implemented through ATS's close integration with a small amount of C code which performs the low-level atomic operations and memory copying.

```
val (pfr | R) = get_reading_state ()          WS1  wp ← ¬R
val wp = not R

val (pfs | s) = get_write_slot_index (pfr | wp)   WS2  wi ← ¬slot[wp]
val wi = not s

val _ = write_data (pfr, pfs | wp, wi, item)     WS3  write_data(wp, wi, item)

val (pff | _) = save_write_slot_index (pfs | wp, wi)   WS4  slot[wp] ← wi

val _ = save_latest_state (pfr, pff | wp)        WS5  L ← wp
```

**Fig. 9.** write

## 3.2   Read

Again, each step in the program is encoded along with a type.

**RS1.**

$$r_p \leftarrow L$$

**absview** rs1_latest_v (L: bit)

**fun get_latest_state** (): [L: bool] (rs1_latest_v L | **bit** L)

The value of $L$ is returned along with a linear proposition stating that it was seen.

**RS2.**

$$R \leftarrow r_p$$

**absview** rs2_read_v (R: bit)

**fun save_reading_state** {L, rp: bit | L == rp} (
    pf: rs1_latest_v L | **rp: bit** rp
): [R: bit | R == rp] (rs2_read_v R | **void**)

With the proposition in hand, we show that we are saving the correct value in the $R$ shared variable. In return, we learn the fact that $r_p = R$ now.

**RS3.**

$$r_i \leftarrow slot\,[r_p]$$

**absview** rs3_slot_v (s: bit, wp: bit, wi: bit)

**fun get_read_slot_index** {R, rp: bit} (
    pf: rs2_read_v R | **rp: bit** rp
): [s, wp, wi: bool | wp == rp ==> s == ~wi]
    (rs3_slot_v (s, wp, wi) | **bit** s)

The rs2_read_v is consumed to prove that we are using the pair corresponding to $R$. In return, we gain a property with a constraint based on simple facts about arrays as well as the behavior of the **write** program. It stipulates that if both reader and writer access $slot\,[r_p]$ when $r_p = w_p$, then the writer's $w_i$ will be the opposite of whatever value is found in $slot\,[r_p]$.

**RS4.**

$$item \leftarrow \text{read\_data}\,(r_p, r_i)$$

**fun**{a: t@ype} **read_data** {rp, ri, wp, wi: bool | wp <> rp || ri <> wi} (
    pf: rs3_slot_v (ri, wp, wi) | **p: bit** rp, **i: bit** ri
): a

Finally, the last interesting step of **read** is the one that requires the coherency theorem to be satisfied, wp <> rp || ri <> wi.

**Putting it Together.** Figure 10 shows the code and much like before, it is close to the pseudocode, and yet compiles down into efficient C. The ATS typechecker is powerful enough to automatically solve the constraints.

```
val (pfl | rp) = get_latest_state ()              RS1  r_p ← L

val (pfr | _) = save_reading_state (pfl | rp)     RS2  R ← r_p

val (pfs | ri) = get_read_slot_index (pfr | rp)   RS3  r_i ← slot [r_p]

val item = read_data (pfs | rp, ri)               RS4  item ← read_data (r_p, r_i)
```

**Fig. 10.** read

# 4 Related Work

## 4.1 The Four Slot Mechanism

Simpson developed a technique called "role model analysis" [21] and then applied it to his four slot mechanism [22] to verify properties of coherency and freshness. Henderson and Paynter [12] created a formal model of the four slot mechanism in PVS and used it to show that it was atomic under certain assumptions about interleaving. Rushby [19] used model checking to verify coherency and freshness in the four slot mechanism but also found the latter can only be shown if the control registers are assumed to be atomic. Our approach has been to encode pieces of the desired theorems into the type system, apply it to working code, and then allow the typechecker to verify consistency. If a mistake is made, it will be caught prior to compilation. Or, if the typechecker is satisfied, then the end result is efficient C code that may be compiled and linked and used directly by applications.

## 4.2 Operating System Verification

The seL4 project is based on a family of microkernels known as L4 [15]. In that work, a refinement proof was completed that demonstrates the adherence of a high-performance C implementation to a generated executable specification, created from a prototype written in Haskell, and checked in the Isabelle [17] theorem proving system. The prototype itself is checked against a high-level design. One difference with our work is that we seek to eliminate the phase of manual translation from high to low level language. Another difference is that, while the seL4 approach can certainly bring many benefits, we feel that the cost associated with it is too high for ordinary use. For example, it may turn out to be intractably difficult to apply this technique to a multiprocessor kernel. That is currently an open problem [9].

Singularity [14] is a microkernel OS written in a high-level and type-safe language that employs language properties and software isolation to guarantee memory safety and eliminate the need for hardware protection domains in many cases. In particular, it makes use of a form of linear types in optimizing communication channels. Singularity was an inspiration for Terrier, although several goals are different. For instance, Terrier seeks to avoid, as much as possible, the overhead associated with high-level languages. Terrier's design is more explicitly geared towards embedded devices responding to real-time events. And inter-program communication in Terrier is left open enough to accommodate multiple approaches, tailored to the particular application domain.

House [11] is an operating system project written primarily in the Haskell functional programming language. It takes advantage of a rewrite of the GHC [18] run-time environment that eliminates the need for OS support, and instead operates directly on top of PS/2-compatible hardware. Then a foreign function interface is used to create a kernel written in Haskell. There is glue code written in C that glosses over some of the trickiness. For example, interrupts are handled by C code which sets flags that the Haskell code can poll at safe points. This avoids potentially corrupting the Haskell heap due to interruptions of the Haskell garbage collector while it is an inconsistent state. The Hello Operating System [10] is an earlier than and similar project to House which features a kernel written and compiled using Standard ML of New Jersey [4], bootstrapped off of Linux [23]. SPIN [3] is a pioneering effort along these lines which used the Modula-3 language [5] to provide a protection model and extensibility. In general, these types of systems do not tackle the problem of high-level language overhead, generally do not handle multiprocessing well if at all, and only offer guarantees as good as their type system can handle.

Both VFiasco [13] and Verisoft [1] take a different approach to system verification. Verisoft relies upon a custom hardware architecture that has itself been formally verified, and a verified compiler to that instruction set. VFiasco claims that it is better to write the kernel in an unsafe language such as C++ and then mechanically generate theorems from that source code, to be discharged by an external proof engine.

## 5    Conclusion

Our challenge was to take the four slot mechanism and encode at least some of reasoning behind it into dependent types that would compose into a safety theorem. We found this to be feasible, as well as an illuminating example of using a lightweight approach with a dependently typed language to prove useful properties in a non-traditional, concurrent systems programming environment. The code shown in this paper is not a toy example. It is adapted from the actual implementation which is used for inter-program communication in Terrier. The only difference between this and the actual ATS code is the omission of a "handle" parameter which threads state through the functions, and would only complicate the explanation of the proof without adding any strength to it.

To be utterly clear, we are not claiming a full verification of the safety or freshness of the four slot mechanism here. Instead, this approach is a hybrid, based on an advancement in type system power, allowing the programmer to decide what constitutes a sufficient level of assurance. In this case, the types are strong enough that they are able to catch most slight variations. Errors that common type systems would not catch are caught by the ATS typechecker; for example, failing to negate a bit value appropriately, or swapping the order of two seemingly interchangeable statements. These are changes that would break the four slot mechanism but cannot be protected against by a type system without the help of dependent and linear types.

This style of development, intertwining program and proof, with an incremental approach, is the basis of the Terrier project. The four slot mechanism is one example of a component which applies those principles to achieve reliability and efficiency. More complex mechanisms are layered on top of this library, with the confidence that the type system enforces the correct usage of the interface, while the ATS compiler strips away the overhead in the end.

**Acknowledgment.** We thank Richard West for his guidance on the topics related to operating systems.

# References

1. Alkassar, E., Hillebrand, M.A., Leinenbach, D., Schirmer, N.W., Starostin, A.: The Verisoft Approach to Systems Verification. In: Shankar, N., Woodcock, J. (eds.) VSTTE 2008. LNCS, vol. 5295, pp. 209–224. Springer, Heidelberg (2008)
2. ARM Limited. ARM Architecture Reference Manual, ARMv7-A and ARMv7-R edition (2011)
3. Bershad, B.N., Savage, S., Pardyak, P., Sirer, E.G., Fiuczynski, M., Becker, D., Eggers, S., Chambers, C.: Extensibility, Safety and Performance in the SPIN Operating System. In: Proceedings of the Fifteenth ACM Symposium on Operating Systems Principles, pp. 267–284 (1995)
4. Blume, M., et al.: Standard ML of New Jersey (2009), http://www.smlnj.org/
5. Cardelli, L., et al.: Modula-3 report (revised). Technical report, Digital Equipment Corp. (now HP Inc.) (November 1989),
   http://www.hpl.hp.com/techreports/Compaq-DEC/SRC-RR-52.html
6. Chen, C., Xi, H.: Combining Programming with Theorem Proving. In: ICFP 2005: Proceedings of the Tenth ACM SIGPLAN International Conference on Functional Programming, pp. 66–77. ACM Press (2005)
7. Danish, M.: Terrier OS, http://www.github.com/mrd/terrier
8. de Moura, L., Bjørner, N.: Z3: An Efficient SMT Solver. In: Ramakrishnan, C.R., Rehof, J. (eds.) TACAS 2008. LNCS, vol. 4963, pp. 337–340. Springer, Heidelberg (2008)
9. Elphinstone, K., Heiser, G.: From L3 to seL4 What Have We Learnt in 20 Years of L4 Microkernels? In: Proceedings of the Twenty-Fourth ACM Symposium on Operating Systems Principles, SOSP 2013, pp. 133–150. ACM, New York (2013)
10. Fu, G.: Design and Implementation of an Operating System in Standard ML. Master's thesis, University of Hawaii (August 1999),
    http://www2.hawaii.edu/~esb/prof/proj/hello/

11. Hallgren, T., Jones, M.P., Leslie, R., Tolmach, A.: A principled approach to operating system construction in Haskell. SIGPLAN Not. 40(9), 116–128 (2005)
12. Henderson, N., Paynter, S.E.: The formal classification and verification of Simpson's 4-slot asynchronous communication mechanism. Springer, Heidelberg (2002)
13. Hohmuth, M., Tews, H.: The VFiasco approach for a verified operating system. In: Proceedings of the 2nd ECOOP Workshop on Programming Languages and Operating Systems (2005),
    http://www.cs.ru.nl/H.Tews/Plos-2005/ecoop-plos-05-letter.pdf
14. Hunt, G.C., Laru, J.R.: Singularity: Rethinking the Software Stack. In: ACM SIGOPS Operating System Review, vol. 41, pp. 37–49. Association for Computing Machinery (April 2007)
15. Klein, G., Elphinstone, K., Heiser, G., et al.: seL4: Formal verification of an OS kernel. In: Proceedings of the 22nd ACM Symposium on Operating Systems Principles, Big Sky, MT, USA (October 2009)
16. Lamport, L.: On interprocess communication. Distributed Computing 1-2, 77–101 (1986)
17. Paulson, L.C.: Isabelle. LNCS, vol. 828. Springer, Heidelberg (1994)
18. Peyton-Jones, S., Marlow, S., et al.: The Glasgow Haskell Compiler,
    http://www.haskell.org/ghc/
19. Rushby, J.: Model checking Simpson's four-slot fully asynchronous communication mechanism. Computer Science Laboratory–SRI International, Tech. Rep. Issued (2002)
20. Simpson, H.R.: Four-slot fully asynchronous communication mechanism. In: IEE Proceedings, vol. 137, Pt. E, No. 1. IEE (January 1990)
21. Simpson, H.R.: Correctness analysis for class of asynchronous communication mechanisms. IEE Proceedings E (Computers and Digital Techniques) 139, 35–49 (1992)
22. Simpson, H.R.: Role model analysis of an asynchronous communication mechanism. In: Computers and Digital Techniques, IEE Proceedings, vol. 144, pp. 232–240. IET (1997)
23. Torvalds, L., et al.: Linux, http://www.linuxfoundation.org/
24. Wadler, P.: A taste of linear logic. In: Borzyszkowski, A.M., Sokolowski, S. (eds.) MFCS 1993. LNCS, vol. 711, pp. 185–210. Springer, Heidelberg (1993),
    http://dx.doi.org/10.1007/3-540-57182-5_12
25. Xi, H., et al.: The ATS language, http://www.ats-lang.org/
26. Zhu, D., Xi, H.: Safe Programming with Pointers through Stateful Views. In: Hermenegildo, M.V., Cabeza, D. (eds.) PADL 2004. LNCS, vol. 3350, pp. 83–97. Springer, Heidelberg (2005)

# JKelloy: A Proof Assistant for Relational Specifications of Java Programs*

Aboubakr Achraf El Ghazi, Mattias Ulbrich, Christoph Gladisch,
Shmuel Tyszberowicz, and Mana Taghdiri

Karlsruhe Institute of Technology, Germany
{elghazi,ulbrich,christoph.gladisch,tyshbe,mana.taghdiri}@kit.edu

**Abstract.** Alloy is a relational specification language with a built-in
transitive closure operator which makes it particularly suitable for writing concise specifications of linked data structures. Several tools support
Alloy specifications for Java programs. However, they can only check the
validity of those specifications with respect to a bounded domain, and
thus, in general, cannot provide correctness proofs. This paper presents
JKelloy, a tool for deductive verification of Java programs with Alloy
specifications. It includes automatically-generated coupling axioms that
bridge between specifications and Java states, and two sets of calculus rules that (1) generate verification conditions in relational logic and
(2) simplify reasoning about them. All rules have been proved correct.
To increase automation capabilities, proof strategies are introduced that
control the application of those rules. Our experiments on linked lists
and binary graphs show the feasibility of the approach.

**Keywords:** first-order relational logic, relational specification, Alloy,
Java, theorem proving, KeY.

## 1 Introduction

The efficiency of specifying and verifying a linked data structure depends to
a large extent on both the level of abstraction of that data structure and the
conciseness of expressing a property over its reachable elements. A suitable formalism for expressing such properties that can also be utilized in the context
of theorem proving is relational logic with a transitive closure operator. In this
logic, the links of the data structures can be modeled as binary relations, and
thus reachability can be expressed using transitive closure. Furthermore, relational specifications allow the user to easily abstract away from the exact order
and connection of elements in a data structure by viewing it as a set. This reduction of precision, when applicable, pays off in simplification of proofs as well
as in better readability of the specifications and the intermediate verification
conditions, which is important for user interaction.

In this paper we describe JKelloy, our extension of the deductive Java verification tool KeY [3], to support specifications written in the relational specification

---

* This work has been partially supported by GIF (grant No. 1131-9.6/2011).

J.M. Badger and K.Y. Rozier (Eds.): NFM 2014, LNCS 8430, pp. 173–187, 2014.

language Alloy [10]—a first-order relational logic with built-in operators for transitive closure, set cardinality, integer arithmetic, and set comprehension. To the best of our knowledge, this work is the first attempt in this direction; other related approaches either restrict the analysis to bounded domains (e.g. [1,7,19,21]) or focus only on the Alloy models of systems without considering their implementations (e.g. [2,15,18]). In our previous work [18] we formalized a translation from Alloy specifications into the KeY first-order logic, with the aim of full (i.e., *unbounded*) verification of declarative models of systems that are specified in Alloy. This, however, is not sufficient for handling Alloy as a specification language for Java programs since it has no explicit model of program state change.

JKelloy assumes a *relational view* of the Java heap: classes are modeled as Alloy signatures and fields as binary relations. To evaluate Alloy expressions in different program states, e.g. pre- and post-state of a method, we translate Alloy relations into functions which take the heap (representing the program state) as an argument. We define the relationship between Alloy relations and Java program states using pre-defined *coupling axioms*. This eliminates the need for the user to provide coupling invariants manually. Changes to program states are aggregated as heap expressions. We introduce an automatic transformation of those heap expressions to relational expressions using a set of *heap resolution rules* that normalize all intermediate heap expressions. The transformation allows us to reason about verification conditions in the relational logic. To simplify the reasoning process, we further introduce a set of *override simplification rules* that exploit the specific shape of the resulting conditions. To increase the degree of automation, we have developed two *proof strategies* that control the application of our rules. We have proved the correctness of all rules using KeY.

Given a Java program, JKelloy can also generate an *Alloy context* that maps the class hierarchy of the program to a semantically equivalent Alloy type hierarchy. This allows the user to check the consistency of the specifications using the automatic, lightweight Alloy Analyzer before starting the full, possibly interactive verification process. Building on top of KeY enables the user to take advantage of the supported SMT solvers to prove simpler subgoals. It also lets the user provide additional lemmas. Complex lemmas, e.g. those that contain transitive closure over update expressions, can be proved by using induction in side-proofs, and then be reused to automatically prove non-trivial verification conditions without requiring induction.

## 2   Overall Framework

Our verification tool JKelloy extends KeY [3], a deductive verification engine that supports both automatic and interactive verification of Java programs. Figure 1 presents the general structure of JKelloy as well as the user's workflow. The input of the tool is a Java program together with its specification written in Alloy [10]. JKelloy follows the *design-by-contract* [14] paradigm in which every method is specified individually with pre- and post-conditions. Verification is performed method by method, in a modular way. For simpler programs and properties, the

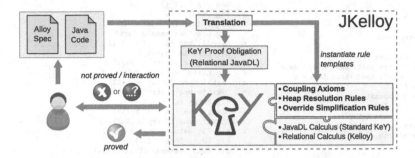

**Fig. 1.** Overall Framework. Contributions highlighted in a boldface font

verification may run through automatically. In other cases, some user interaction may be required, in which the user guides the steps taken by the prover.

JKelloy extends KeY with a translation front-end that converts Alloy specifications of Java methods to *Java Dynamic Logic (JavaDL)*, the input logic of KeY. Our previous work, Kelloy [18], embedded general Alloy expressions into JavaDL (thus called *relational JavaDL*) and provided a basic relational calculus. JKelloy augments Kelloy with heap-dependent relations for modeling Java classes and fields. Furthermore, JKelloy introduces a set of calculus rules that facilitates verification of relational specifications. Some of these rules are program-dependent, and are generated for each program during the translation by instantiating pre-defined templates. The verification process for a method contract typically proceeds as follows:

1. The Alloy pre- and post-conditions are translated to relational JavaDL. The relations in the conditions become relational symbols depending on a heap-state. Their evaluation in a heap state is defined by *coupling axioms*.
2. The code of the Java method is symbolically executed, computing the post-heap-state in relation to the pre-heap.
3. *Heap resolution rules* are applied to normalize the resulting heap-dependent expressions so that all heap arguments become constant.
4. The resulting proof obligation is relational and can be discharged using the relational calculus. *Override simplification rules* simplify this process by providing additional lemmas in relational logic.

## 3   Alloy Specifications for Java Programs

Alloy is a first-order relational logic, which is well-suited for concisely specifying properties of linked data structures. Properties of object-oriented programs can be specified in Alloy using the relational view of the heap. Given a Java program, JKelloy automatically generates an *Alloy context* [6] which encodes the type hierarchy of that program, and declares all the relations accessible to the user for writing the specifications. The user can then add the specifications to this context

```
1    class List {
2      Entry head;
3
4      /*@ requires true;
5        @ ensures self.head'.*next'.data'
6        @ = self.head.*next.data + d;
7        @*/
8      void prepend(Data d) {
9        Entry oldHead = head;
10       head = new Entry();
11       head.next = oldHead;
12       head.data = d;
13     }
14   }
15
16   class Entry {
17     Data data;
18     Entry next;
19   }
20
21   interface Data {..}
22   class ID implements Data {..}
23   class Name implements Data {..}
```

```
1    one sig Null {}
2    sig Object' {}
3    sig Object in Object' {}
4    sig List' extends Object' {
5      head': one (Entry' + Null) }
6    sig List in Object {
7      head: one (Entry + Null) }
8    sig Entry' extends Object' {
9      data': one (Data' + Null),
10     next': one (Entry' + Null) }
11   sig Entry in Object {
12     data: one (Data + Null),
13     next': one (Entry + Null) }
14   sig ID' extends Object' {..}
15   sig ID in Object {..}
16   sig Name' extends Object' {..}
17   sig Name in Object {..}
18   sig Data' in Object' {..}
19   sig Data in Object {..}
20   fact { List = List' & Object
21          Entry = Entry' & Object
22          ID = ID' & Object
23          Name = Name' & Object
24          Data' = Name' + ID'
25          Data = Name + ID }
26   pred pre[self: one List, d: one (Data + Null)] {}
27   pred post[self: one List, d: one (Data + Null)] {
28     self.head'.*next'.data' = self.head.*next.data + d}
```

(a)                                    (b)

**Fig. 2.** (a) Sample code (b) Alloy context along with pre- and post-conditions

in order to check their consistency using the Alloy Analyzer before starting the verification process using JKelloy. Although the Alloy Analyzer checks Alloy models only for bounded domains, it helps users detect flaws automatically.

Figure 2(a) provides a sample Java program and its Alloy specification. It implements a singly linked list that stores **Data** objects. The method **prepend** adds a **Data** object to the beginning of the list. Figure 2(b) presents the corresponding Alloy context. A signature declaration **sig A{}** declares A as a top-level type (set of atoms); **sig B in A{}** declares B as a subtype (subset) of A. The **extends** keyword has the same effect as the keyword **in** with the additional constraint that extensions of a type are mutually disjoint. An attribute f of type B declared in signature A represents a relation $f \subseteq A \times B$. The multiplicity keyword **one**, when followed by a set, constrains that set to be a singleton, and when used as a type qualifier of a relation, constrains that relation to be a total function.

The generated Alloy context always contains a singleton **Null** (Fig. 2(b) Line 1) which represents the Java **null** element. Every Java class C is represented by two signatures, C and C', that give the set of atoms corresponding to the allocated objects of type C in the pre- and post-state, respectively. **Object** is constrained to be a subset[1] of **Object'** (Line 3)[2] and any other signature C is constrained to be the intersection of C' and **Object** (e.g. Lines 20–23). If a Java class B extends a class A (immediate parent), the signature B' will be an extension of A', and B a subset of A[3]. A Java field f of type T declared in a

---

[1] Object creation is possbile, but deallocation (garbage collection) is not considered.

[2] The top-level class **Object** is always included.

[3] It is easy to show that subclasses of a class are disjoint in the pre-state, too.

class C is represented by two functional relations f: C → (T ∪ Null) for the pre-state, and f': C' → (T' ∪ Null) for the post-state (e.g. Lines 5, 7).

Specifications must be legal Alloy formulas. Basic formulas are constructed using subset (in) and equality (=) operators over Alloy expressions, and are combined using the usual logical connectives as well as universal (all) and existential (some) quantifiers. Alloy expressions evaluate to relations. Sets are unary relations and scalars are singleton unary relations. The operators +, -, and & denote union, difference, and intersection, respectively. For relations r and s, relational join (forward composition), Cartesian product, and transpose are denoted by r.s, r -> s, and ~r, respectively. The relational override r++s contains all tuples in s, and any tuples of r whose first element is not the first element of a tuple in s. The transitive closure ^r denotes the smallest transitive relation that contains r, and *r denotes the reflexive transitive closure of r. The expressions s<:r and r:>s give domain and range restriction of r to s, respectively.

Figure 2(a) gives the pre- and post-condition of prepend using the requires and ensures clauses, respectively (Lines 4-7). Specifications can access receiver object (self) and method arguments (Lines 26-28 of Fig. 2(b)). Post-conditions can also access the method's return value (ret) if any exists. The post-condition of prepend specifies that the set of Data objects stored in the receiver list in the post-state augments that of the pre-state with the prepended data[4].

# 4   Relational Java Dynamic Logic

## 4.1   Background

JavaDL, the verification logic of KeY, extends typed first-order logic with dynamic logic [9] operators over Java program fragments. Besides propositional connectives and first-order quantifiers, it introduces modal operators. The formula $\{p := t\}\varphi$ in which $p$ is a constant symbol, $t$ is a term whose type is compatible with that of $p$, and $\varphi$ is a JavaDL formula, is true iff $\varphi$ is true after the assignment of $t$ to $p$. The modal operator $\{p := t\}$ is called an *update*. The formula $[\pi]\varphi$ in which $\pi$ is a sequence of Java statements and $\varphi$ is a formula, is true iff $\varphi$ is true in the post-state (if any exists) of the program $\pi$. The formula $\langle\pi\rangle\varphi$ additionally requires $\pi$ to terminate.[5]

JavaDL is based on an *explicit heap model* [20]: a dedicated program variable *heap* of type *Heap* stores the current heap state. A read access o.f in Java is encoded as *select(heap, o, f)*, abbreviated as *heap[o.f]*. Heap modifications are modeled using *heap constructors*, as defined in Fig. 3. The *store* function is used to encode changes to a field other than ⟨created⟩. The boolean field ⟨created⟩ is implicitly added to the class Object to distinguish between created and uncreated objects. A Java assignment of a variable $v$ to a field f of a non-null object $o$ can be interpreted as an update:

$$[\text{o.f} = \text{v};]\varphi \ \leftrightarrow \ \{heap := store(heap, \text{o}, \text{f}, \text{v})\}\varphi \tag{1}$$

---

[4] As shown by this example, the specifications can be arbitrarily partial.

[5] $[\pi]\varphi$ and $\langle\pi\rangle\varphi$ correspond to $wlp(\pi, \varphi)$ and $wp(\pi, \varphi)$ in the wp-calculus [4].

$store(h, p, g, v)[o.f] = (\text{if } o = p \wedge f = g \wedge g \neq \langle\texttt{created}\rangle \text{ then } v \text{ else } h[o.f])$

$create(h, p)[o.f] = (\text{if } o = p \wedge f = \langle\texttt{created}\rangle \text{ then } \textbf{true} \text{ else } h[o.f])$

$anon(h_1, l, h_2)[o.f] = (\text{if } (o, f) \in l \wedge f \neq \langle\texttt{created}\rangle \vee o \in free(h_1) \text{ then } h_2[o.f] \text{ else } h_1[o.f])$

**Fig. 3.** Definitions of heap constructors

The *create* function is used to set the $\langle\texttt{created}\rangle$ field of an object to **true**. The *anonymizing* function *anon* modifies a set of locations rather than a single location. The heap denoted by the term $anon(h_1, l, h_2)$ coincides with $h_2$ (the anonymous heap) in all fresh locations and those in the location set $l$, and coincides with $h_1$ (the base heap) on the remaining ones.

JavaDL's type system includes the hierarchy of Java reference types, with the root type *Object* which denotes an infinite set of objects (including the **null** object), whether or not created. The expression $free(h) = \{o : Object \mid \neg h[o.\langle\texttt{created}\rangle] \wedge o \neq \textbf{null}\}$ gives the set of all uncreated objects of $h$. The types *Boolean* and *Integer* have their usual meanings, the type *Field* consists of all Java fields declared in the verified program, and *LocSet* consists of sets of locations, which are binary relations between *Object* and *Field*. For a type $T$, the type predicate $x \sqsubseteq T$ evaluates to true iff $x$ is of type $T$.

KeY performs *symbolic execution* [11] of the given Java code. The effects of this execution on the program state are recorded as JavaDL updates. The equivalence (1), for instance, is used to encode the effect of the Java assignment o.f=v. Similar equivalences are used for other Java statements. Branching statements cause the proof obligation to split into cases; corresponding path conditions are assumed in each case. Consequently, symbolic execution resolves the original proof obligation $pre \rightarrow [p]post$ of a program $p$ into a conjunction of formulas of the form $pre \wedge path \rightarrow \{\mathcal{U}\}post$, in which $path$ stands for the accumulated path condition, and $\mathcal{U}$ for the accumulated state updates in an execution path.

In [18] we presented an embedding of Alloy into JavaDL (thus called *relational JavaDL*). This included new JavaDL types, namely *Atom* for elements of relations, and a $Rel_n$ type for all $n$-ary relations (for each $n$). New function symbols for Alloy operators were introduced and defined using axioms. The integers in JavaDL were used to axiomatize transitive closure as it is not axiomatizable in pure first-order logic. We use $\cup$, $\setminus$, $\oplus$, $\times$, $\triangleleft$, $\bullet$, $^*$, $^+$ (ascending precedence order) to denote the symbols in relational JavaDL that correspond to the Alloy operators +, -, ++, ->, <:, ., *, ^, respectively.

## 4.2 Coupling Axioms

The embedding of Alloy into relational JavaDL is not sufficient for verifying Java programs as it lacks a model of program state. To encode a relational view of the heap, we translate relations for Java classes and fields as heap-dependent function symbols. A Java class C is translated to a function symbol $C_{rel} : Heap \rightarrow Rel_1$ such that the expression $C_{rel}(h)$ gives the set of all created objects of type $C$ in the heap $h$, as given by the first coupling axiom:

$$C_{rel}(h) := \{o \mid h[o.\langle\texttt{created}\rangle] \wedge o \sqsubseteq C \wedge o \neq \textbf{null}\} \tag{2}$$

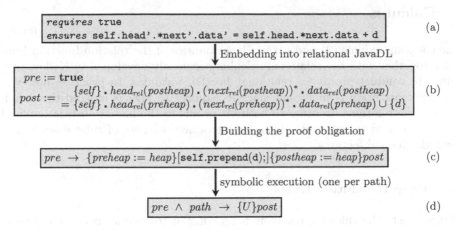

**Fig. 4.** The verification process for the method List.prepend as running example

It should be noted that, without loss of generality, we make *Atom* a supertype of *Object* to let Java objects be elements of relations as in Axiom 2. A Java field f of type R declared in a class C is translated to a function symbol $f_{rel} : Heap \rightarrow Rel_2$ where $f_{rel}(h)$ gives the set of all pairs $(o_1, o_2)$ such that, in heap $h$, the created object $o_1$ points to the object $o_2$ via f, as given by the second coupling axiom:

$$f_{rel}(h) := \{(o_1, o_2) \mid o_1 \in C_{rel}(h) \wedge (o_2 = \texttt{null} \vee o_2 \in R_{rel}(h)) \wedge o_2 = h[o_1.\texttt{f}]\} \quad (3)$$

Following the design-by-contract paradigm, Alloy specifications can access only the pre- and post-state. Thus we provide two sets of relations (unprimed for pre- and primed for post-state) instead of introducing an explicit notion of state. Heap arguments are introduced when Alloy specifications are translated into JavaDL: references to C and f are translated to $C_{rel}(preheap)$ and $f_{rel}(preheap)$, respectively, referring to the heap in the pre-state; references to C' and f' are translated to $C_{rel}(postheap)$ and $f_{rel}(postheap)$, referring to the heap in the post-state. Null signature is translated as $Null_{rel}(h) := \{\texttt{null}\}$ for every heap $h$.

Figure 4 shows how JKelloy processes the example of Fig. 2. Figure 4(a) is the original Alloy specification, Fig. 4(b) gives its translation into relational JavaDL, and Fig. 4(c) the relational JavaDL proof obligation for List.prepend. In addition to the program modality [self.prepend(d);], two updates {*preheap* := *heap*} and {*postheap* := *heap*} are used to store the respective current heap. Symbolic execution then resolves the code of the method. Several formulas of the form shown in Fig. 4(d) are produced for various execution paths of the code. The example is continued in Section 5.

The above coupling axioms are defined such that they preserve the meaning of the Alloy relations used in the specifications. For instance, relation head' in the example of Fig. 2 is a total binary relation containing the references from all created List objects to Entry objects (or null) after the method call. Axiom (3) ensures that $head_{rel}(postheap)$ contains precisely those elements.

# 5  Calculus

The coupling axioms (2) and (3) fix the semantics of the relation function symbols. Together with the relational calculus previously developed in Kelloy, they suffice to conduct proofs for relational JavaDL formulas. In practice, however, this axiomatization is inefficient since it requires to always expand the definitions of the relations. In order to both lift proofs to the higher abstraction level of relations and to automate them, we introduce two sets of rules described in the following subsections.

## 5.1  Heap Resolution Rules

Figure 5 lists the rules for resolving heap constructor occurrences as argument of field relations ($R_1$–$R_3$) and class relations ($R_4$–$R_6$). All rules reduce relational expressions over composed heaps to expressions over their heap argument. They are applied to the verification conditions after symbolic execution and eliminate all heap constructors from arguments of relational function symbols. Rules $R_1$, $R_2$ and $R_5$, for instance, make case distinctions between the cases when the relation needs to be updated and when it remains untouched. $R_3$ is special since it updates a set of elements and not only one element in the relation. See [6] for an extensive explanation of the rules. All rules were proved correct with respect to the coupling axioms.

We explain the idea of heap resolution using the example in Fig. 4. The update $U$ in Fig. 4(d) encodes the successive heap modifications performed by the program. After some simplifications, the heap modification of the method body is encoded as

$$
\begin{array}{ccccc}
h_5 & h_4 & h_3 & h_2 & h_1 \\
\downarrow & \downarrow & \downarrow & \downarrow & \downarrow
\end{array}
$$
$$
postheap := store\,(\,store\,(\,store\,(\,create\,(\,preheap\,,e),
$$
$$
self, \mathbf{head}, e),
$$
$$
e, \mathbf{next}, preheap[self.\mathbf{head}]),
$$
$$
e, \mathbf{data}, d)
$$

where $h_1, \ldots, h_5$ are abbreviations for the intermediate heap expressions and $e$ is a reference to the freshly created Entry object. In Fig. 4(b), some of the field relations take $postheap$ as argument (like $head_{rel}(postheap)$) in which, under the influence of $U$, $postheap$ is replaced by the nested term $h_5$. Heap modifications in $h_5$ affect the value of $head_{rel}(h_5)$ only if they are related to the field $\mathbf{head}$. Rule $R_1$, which is responsible for the resolution of this term, translates the $store$ expression into an if-then-else term resulting either in an overridden relation $(f_{rel}(h) \oplus \{o_1\} \times \{o_2\})$ or in the original relation $f_{rel}(h)$. The relations $head_{rel}(h_5)$, $head_{rel}(h_4)$ and $head_{rel}(h_3)$, for instance, are equivalent as the modified Java fields $\mathbf{data}$ and $\mathbf{next}$ are different from $\mathbf{head}$. But the $store$ expression of $h_3$ modifies the field $\mathbf{head}$; hence, the relation $head_{rel}$ must be updated for the arguments of $store$ and we obtain

$$
head_{rel}(h_3) = head_{rel}(store(h_2, self, \mathbf{head}, e)) = head_{rel}(h_2) \oplus \{self\} \times \{e\} \ . \quad (4)
$$

$\mathbf{R_1}$: $f_{rel}(store(h, o_1, g, o_2)) \rightsquigarrow$ if $g = \mathbf{f} \wedge h[o_1.created] \wedge o_1 \sqsubseteq C \wedge o_1 \neq \mathbf{null}$
then $f_{rel}(h) \oplus \{o_1\} \times \{o_2\}$ else $f_{rel}(h)$

assuming $wellformed(store(h, o_1, g, o_2))$

$\mathbf{R_2}$: $f_{rel}(create(h, o)) \rightsquigarrow$ if $o \neq \mathbf{null} \wedge o \sqsubseteq C$ then $f_{rel}(h) \oplus \{o\} \times \{h[o.\mathbf{f}]\}$ else $f_{rel}(h)$

$\mathbf{R_3}$: $f_{rel}(anon(h_1, l, h_2)) \rightsquigarrow f_{rel}(h_1) \oplus (((l \centerdot \{\mathbf{f}\}) \cup free(h_1)) \lhd f_{rel}(h_2))$

$\mathbf{R_4}$: $C_{rel}(store(h, o_1, g, o_2)) \rightsquigarrow C_{rel}(h)$

$\mathbf{R_5}$: $C_{rel}(create(h, o)) \rightsquigarrow$ if $o \neq \mathbf{null} \wedge o \sqsubseteq C$ then $C_{rel}(h) \cup \{o\}$ else $C_{rel}(h)$

$\mathbf{R_6}$: $C_{rel}(anon(h_1, ls, h_2)) \rightsquigarrow C_{rel}(h_1) \cup C_{rel}(h_2)$

**Fig. 5.** Heap Resolution Calculus. The term rewrite relation "$\rightsquigarrow$" represents an equivalence transformation. In $R_1$ and $R_2$ the field $\mathbf{f}$ is defined in class $C$.

Relation $head_{rel}(h_2)$ is finally simplified to $head_{rel}(h_1)$ by rule $R_2$ since the creation of the $\mathtt{Entry}$ element $e$ does not affect the relation $head_{rel}$ for the field $\mathtt{head}$ declared in class $\mathtt{List}$. Equation (4) shows the main idea of the heap resolution calculus: the heap state changes are transformed into relational operations. In particular, an assignment $\mathtt{o1.f=o2}$ in Java resolves into a relational override of the form $f_{rel}(heap) \oplus \{o_1\} \times \{o_2\}$.

Applying these rules exhaustively leads to a normal form where all heap arguments are constants. JKelloy extends KeY with a proving strategy that always achieves this task automatically. The final result of applying the heap resolution rules to the post-condition of the running example (Fig. 4(b)) is the following relational verification condition:

$$\{self\} \centerdot (head_{rel}(h_1) \oplus \{self\} \times \{e\})$$
$$\centerdot (next_{rel}(h_1) \oplus \{e\} \times \{self\} \centerdot head_{rel}(h_1))^* \centerdot (data_{rel}(h_1) \oplus \{e\} \times \{d\})$$
$$= \{self\} \centerdot head_{rel}(h_1) \centerdot next_{rel}(h_1)^* \centerdot data_{rel}(h_1) \cup \{d\} \tag{5}$$

After all heap terms have been resolved, further reasoning can proceed on the relational level.

## 5.2 Override Simplification Rules

The normalized proof obligations that result from applying heap resolution rules can be proved on the relational level using our previous Kelloy tool. However, Kelloy only provides definition axioms for relational operators and a set of lemmas for general relational expressions. To make proofs easier and to increase the automation level, we introduce a set of lemma rules which exploit the shape of the relational expressions that result from verifying Java programs. These lemmas do not increase the power of the calculus but ease the verification by reducing the need for expanding the definitions of relational operators. That is particularly costly for the transitive closure as it leads to quantified integer formulas that generally require user interaction in form of manual induction. Out

$R_7$:  $\{a\} \centerdot (R \oplus \{a\} \times \{b\}) \rightsquigarrow \{b\}$

$R_8$:  $S_1 \centerdot (R \oplus S_2 \times S_3) \rightsquigarrow$ if $S_2 = \emptyset$ then $S_1 \centerdot R$ else $S_1 \centerdot (S_2 \times S_3) \cup (S_1 \setminus S_2) \centerdot R$

$R_9$:  $S_1 \centerdot (R \oplus \{a\} \times S_2)^+ \rightsquigarrow$ if $S_2 = \emptyset \vee a \notin S_1$ then $S_1 \centerdot R$

$\qquad\qquad\qquad\qquad\qquad\qquad$ else $S_2 \cup ((S_2 \setminus \{a\}) \centerdot R^+) \cup (S_1 \centerdot R^+)$

assuming $R \centerdot \{a\} = \emptyset$

$R_{10}$: $\{a\} \centerdot (R \oplus \{b\} \times \{c\})^+ \rightsquigarrow$ if $b \in \{c\} \centerdot R^+ \vee b = c$ then $(\{a\} \centerdot R^+ \cup \{c\} \cup \{c\} \centerdot R^+) \setminus \{b\} \centerdot R^+$

$\qquad\qquad\qquad\qquad\qquad\qquad$ else $(\{a\} \centerdot R^+ \setminus \{b\} \centerdot R^+) \cup \{c\} \cup \{c\} \centerdot R^+$

assuming $parFun(R)$, $acyc(R)$ and $b \in a \centerdot R^+$

$R_{11}$: $S_1 \centerdot f_{rel}(h) \centerdot (R_1 \oplus S_2 \lhd R_2) \rightsquigarrow S_1 \centerdot f_{rel}(h) \centerdot R_1$ $\qquad\qquad$ assuming $S_2 \subseteq free(h)$

$R_{12}$: $S_1 \centerdot f_{rel}(h) \centerdot (g_{rel}(h) \oplus S_2 \lhd R)^+ \rightsquigarrow S_1 \centerdot f_{rel}(h) \centerdot g_{rel}(h)^+$ $\qquad$ assuming $S_2 \subseteq free(h)$

$R_{13}$: $(f_{rel}(h) \oplus S_2 \lhd R)^+ \rightsquigarrow f_{rel}(h)^+ \oplus S_2 \lhd R$ $\qquad\qquad\qquad$ assuming $S_2 \subseteq free(h)$

**Fig. 6.** A sampling of our override driven calculus rules

of more than 220 new lemmas we have introduced, we present the subset that is most relevant to the examples of Fig. 2 and Section 6; not all of them are used in the presented examples. All lemmas have been proved correct using KeY.

Equation (5) is typical for our approach: its right-hand side (RHS) refers to the base relations of the pre-state, whereas its left-hand side (LHS) refers to the post-state and thus includes override-updates on the field relations. To prove such formulas, we bring the LHS closer to the shape of the RHS by resolving or pulling out the override operations that occur below other operators such as join and transitive closure.

Figure 6 lists a number of lemmas dealing with this override resolution to give an idea of the process. The most simple case is $R_7$ which says that retrieving a value $a$ from a relation which has been overridden at the very same $a$ results precisely in the updated value $b$. In other, more composed cases, the resolution is not as simple. Rules $R_9$ and $R_{10}$, e.g., allow us to resolve the override beneath a transitive-closure operation under certain conditions at the cost of larger replacement expressions without override. Rules $R_{11}$–$R_{13}$ resolve override operations which only modify objects not yet created in the base heap ($S_2 \subseteq free(h)$). For a more detailed account on the presented rules, see the extended version [6].

In the example, the subexpression $\{self\} \centerdot (head_{rel}(h_1) \oplus \{self\} \times \{e\})$ in (5) can be simplified to $\{e\}$ using $R_7$ as the left argument $\{self\}$ of the join equals the domain of the overriding relation $\{self\} \times \{e\}$. After this simplification, the LHS contains the subexpression

$$\{e\} \centerdot (next_{rel}(h_1) \oplus \{e\} \times \{self\} \centerdot head_{rel}(h_1))^* \ .$$

To resolve the override operation in this expression, we first transform reflexive transitive closure to transitive closure using the equality $S.R^* = S \cup S.R^+$, and then apply rule $R_9$. Further simplifications result in:

$$\{e\} \cup \underline{\{self\} \centerdot head_{rel}(h_1)} \cup \underline{\{self\} \centerdot head_{rel}(h_1) \centerdot next_{rel}(h_1)^+}$$

---

$\mathbf{R}_{14}$: ⊢ $parFun(f_{rel}(h))$
$\mathbf{R}_{15}$: ⊢ $parFun(R) \rightarrow parFun(R \oplus \{a\} \times \{b\})$
$\mathbf{R}_{16}$: ⊢ $parFun(R_1) \wedge parFun(R_2) \rightarrow parFun(R_1 \oplus R_2)$

$\mathbf{R}_{17}$: ⊢ $acyc(R) \wedge R \cdot \{a\} = \emptyset \wedge a \neq b \rightarrow acyc(R \oplus \{a\} \times \{b\})$
$\mathbf{R}_{18}$: ⊢ $acyc(R) \wedge \{b\} \cdot R = \emptyset \wedge a \neq b \rightarrow acyc(R \oplus \{a\} \times \{b\})$
$\mathbf{R}_{19}$: ⊢ $acyc(R) \wedge a \notin \{b\} \cdot R^+ \wedge a \neq b \rightarrow acyc(R \oplus \{a\} \times \{b\})$

$\mathbf{R}_{20}$: $S_2 \in S_1 \cdot R^+ \rightsquigarrow$ **false**                                    assuming $S_1 \cdot R = \emptyset$
$\mathbf{R}_{21}$: $\{a\} \in R \cdot \{b\} \rightsquigarrow$ **true**                                    assuming $\{a\} \cdot R = \{b\}$
$\mathbf{R}_{22}$: $\{a\} \in R \cdot \{b\} \rightsquigarrow$ **false**                  assuming $parFun(R)$ and $\{a\} \cdot R \neq \{b\}$

---

**Fig. 7.** A selection of auxiliary rules for the override simplification

The underlined subexpression is equivalent to $\{self\} \cdot head_{rel}(h_1) \cdot next_{rel}(h_1)^*$ which also appears on the RHS of (5). We have thus reached our goal of resolving the override and bringing the LHS closer to the RHS.

The simplification rules focus on resolving override operations, yet further rules are required to reason about expressions that occur in the rules' assumptions, if-conditions, and results. Fig. 7 shows such rules divided into three categories. The first involves partial functionality of relations: every relation corresponding to a field is a partial function by construction ($\mathbf{R}_{14}$); $\mathbf{R}_{15}$ and $\mathbf{R}_{16}$ allow the propagation of this property over the override operator. Similarly, the second propagates the acyclicity of relations over the override operator. The last category lists some rules for handling reachability between objects effectively.

# 6    Evaluation

Proofs in KeY are conducted by applying calculus rules either manually or automatically, using KeY's proof search strategy. We extend the existing strategy by incorporating two new strategies that assign priorities to heap resolution rules and override simplification rules, and apply them consecutively. The `List.prepend` example[6] verifies fully automatically within 5.4 seconds[7] using 1546 rule applications although its post-condition involves transitive closure.

We have also verified a slightly different example (`List.append`) where the **Data** argument is added to the end of the list. The proof contains a total of 2850 rule applications out of which 28 are interactive. These include 6 applications of proof-branching rules, and 6 rule applications to establish the assumptions for rule $\mathbf{R}_{10}$. Automatic rule applications take 20.3 seconds. The **append** method is more complex than **prepend** as it contains a loop that traverses the list to the end, thus requires handling loop invariants. The proof requires the more complex transitive closure rule $\mathbf{R}_{10}$ since the code updates already-created objects.

---

[6] All examples and proofs can be found at http://i12www.ira.uka.de/~elghazi/jkelloy/
[7] On an Intel Core2Quad, 2.8GHz with 8GB memory.

```
1    public class Graph {
2      NodeList nodes;
3      /*@ requires acyc(next);
4       @ requires not n = null;
5       @ ensures self.nodes'.first'.*next' = self.nodes.first.*next - n;
6       @ ensures Object <: left' = left ++ ((left.n & self.nodes.first.*next) -> null);
7       @ ensures Object <: right' = right ++ ((right.n & self.nodes.first.*next) -> null); @*/
8      void remove(Node n) {
9        if (nodes != null) {
10         Node curr = nodes.first;
11         /*@ loop_invariant
12          @   curr in self.nodes.first.*next and
13          @   Object<:left' = left ++ ((left.n & (self.nodes.first.*next - curr.*next)) -> null) and
14          @   Object<:right' = right ++ ((right.n & (self.nodes.first.*next - curr.*next)) -> null)
15          @ assignable
16          @   (self.nodes.first.*next -> left) + (self.nodes.first.*next -> right); @*/
17         while (curr != null) {
18           if (curr.left == n)  { curr.left = null; }
19           if (curr.right == n) { curr.right = null; }
20           curr = curr.next;
21         }
22         nodes.remove(n);
23    } } }
24    class NodeList { Node first;  void remove(Node n) { ... } }
25    class Node { Node next, left, right; }
```

**Fig. 8.** Specification and implementation of the graph remove example

We illustrate that JKelloy can be used to verify programs which manipulate rich heap data structures using the example of Fig. 8. This example also illustrates that structurally complex specifications can be concisely expressed by exploiting combinations of relational operators in Alloy. The **Graph** class implements a binary graph[8] where each node stores its two (possibly **null**) successors (**left** and **right**, Line 25). The graph keeps a linked list of its nodes (Line 2) using the **next** field (Line 25). The method **Graph.remove** removes a node n from the receiver graph by removing all of its incoming edges (Lines 17–21), and then removing n (and thus its outgoing edges) from the node list (Line 22).

The method requires the node list to be acyclic (Line 3) and the argument node n to be non-null (Line 4). It ensures that n is removed from the graph's node list (Line 5), and that the **left** and **right** fields of all nodes in this list that used to point to n, point to **null** at the end of the method (Lines 6 and 7). This example also illustrates that structurally complex specifications can be concisely expressed by exploiting combinations of relational operators in Alloy. In particular, sets of nodes with a particular property can be easily expressed using Alloy operators. For example, using the join operator from the right side of a field relation, the expression **left.n** concisely gives the set of all nodes whose **left** field points to n. The domain restriction to **Object** restricts the relation in the post-state to those objects already existing in the pre-state. The relational override operator denotes exactly what locations are modified and how, thus also implicitly specifies which locations do not change.

The example requires additional intermediate specifications which are not part of the contract. This includes a *loop specification* (Lines 11–16) describing the state after the execution up to the current loop iteration. Primed relations in

---

[8] A directed graph with an outgoing degree of at most two for every node.

the loop invariant refer to the state of the heap after the current loop iteration, whereas unprimed relations refer to the pre-state of the method. The assignable clause specifies the set of heap locations which may be modified by the loop. `Graph.remove` calls `NodeList.remove` which removes n from the linked list; the call is abstracted by the callee's contract which is omitted here for space reasons.

Though the specification in the example is concise, it extensively combines relational operators including, in particular, transitive closure. In the code, the nested method call and the loop result in complex composed heap expressions after symbolic execution. Brought together, these two technical points make this example difficult to verify. The proof required 6973 rule applications distributed over 157 subgoals, where 1201 of the rule applications were interactive. Amongst them, 309 apply override simplification rules and 224 general relational rules. Our rules for handling transitive closure proved to be very effective; they were applied 43 times, and allowed us to conduct the proof without any explicit induction. Induction was needed only to prove the soundness of the rules themselves. Relational operations were never expanded to their definitions. Thus the proof was completely conducted in the abstraction level of relations. The rules introduced with JKelloy made up 37% of all rule applications; the rest were default KeY rules. The whole proof, including specification adjustments, was conducted by an Alloy and KeY expert in one week; the total time spent by the automatic rule applications was 6.3 minutes. Other comparable examples in KeY (using the JML specification language) require $50k$ to $100k$ proof steps (see e.g. [8]).

## 7  Related Work

Several approaches (e.g. [5,17,19]) support Alloy as a specification language for Java programs. To check the specifications, however, they bound the analysis domain by unrolling loops and limiting the number of elements of each type. Thus although they find non-spurious counterexamples automatically, they cannot, in general, provide correctness proofs. JForge specification language [21] is another lightweight language for specifying object-oriented programs. It is a behavioral interface specification language with a relational view of the heap, that allows some Alloy operators. So far it has been used only for bounded program checking.

Galeotti [7] introduced a bounded, automatic technique for the SAT-based analysis of JML-annotated Java sequential programs dealing with linked data structures. It incorporates (i) DynAlloy [1], an extension of Alloy to better describe dynamic properties of systems using actions, in the style of dynamic logic; (ii) DynJML, an intermediate object-oriented specification language; and (iii) TACO, a prototype tool which implements the entire tool-chain.

A few approaches [2,15,18] support full verification of Alloy models. Since they do not model program states, they cannot be readily applied for verifying code with Alloy specifications. DYNAMITE [15], for example, extends PVS to prove Alloy assertions, and incorporates Alloy Analyzer for checking hypotheses.

Other approaches (e.g. [8,16,22]) also verify properties of linked data structure implementations. In contrast to ours, in [22], for example, specifications are written in classical higher-order logic (including set comprehension, $\lambda$-expressions, transitive closure, set cardinality) and are verified using Jahob which integrates several provers. A decision procedure based on inference rules for a quantifier-free specification language with transitive closure is presented in [16]. In [8] the focus is to write specifications in JML so that they can be used for both deductive program verification and runtime checking.

Similar to our approach, [12, 13] handle reachability of linked data structures using a first-order axiomatization of transitive closure. Their general idea, however, is to use a specialized induction schema for transitive closure, to provide useful lemmas for common situations. [12] focuses on establishing a relatively complete axiomatization of reachability, whereas [13] focuses on introducing as complete schema lemmas as possible and adding their instantiations to the original formula. The main difficulty of schema rules is to find the right instantiation (analogous to induction hypothesis).

## 8   Conclusions

We have presented an approach for verifying Java programs annotated with Alloy specifications. Alloy operators (e.g. relational join, transitive closure, set comprehension, and set cardinality) let users specify properties of linked data structures concisely. Our tool, JKelloy, translates Alloy specifications into relational Java Dynamic Logic and proves them using KeY. It introduces coupling axioms to bridge between specifications and Java states, and two sets of calculus rules and strategies that facilitate interactive and automatic reasoning in relational logic. Verification is done on the level of abstraction of the relational specifications. JKelloy lets relational lemmas be proved beforehand, and reused to gain more automation. Our calculus rules are proved lemmas that exploit the shape of the relational expressions that occur in proof obligations.

Although our automatic proof strategies can still be improved, our examples show the advantages of the approach. They illustrate how the liberal combinations of transitive closure and relational operators in Alloy can be exploited for concise specifications of linked data structures. The sizes of proofs are an order of magnitude smaller compared to other similar proofs using standard KeY.

KeY supports JML, a behavioral specification language for Java. A combination of the specification concepts of JML and Alloy has the potential to bring together the best of both paradigms. Furthermore, the symbolic execution engine of KeY along with our calculus rules can produce relational summaries of Java methods which can be checked for bugs using the Alloy Analyzer before starting a proof attempt. Investigating these ideas is left for future work.

## References

1. Aguirre, N.M., Frias, M.F., Ponzio, P., Cardiff, B.J., Galeotti, J.P., Regis, G.: Towards abstraction for DynAlloy specifications. In: Liu, S., Araki, K. (eds.) ICFEM 2008. LNCS, vol. 5256, pp. 207–225. Springer, Heidelberg (2008)
2. Arkoudas, K., Khurshid, S., Marinov, D., Rinard, M.: Integrating model checking and theorem proving for relational reasoning. In: Berghammer, R., Möller, B., Struth, G. (eds.) RelMiCS 2003. LNCS, vol. 3051, pp. 21–33. Springer, Heidelberg (2004)

3. Beckert, B., Hähnle, R., Schmitt, P.H. (eds.): Verification of Object-Oriented Software: The KeY Approach. Springer (2007)
4. Dijkstra, E.W.: Guarded commands, nondeterminacy and formal derivation of programs. Communications of the ACM 18(8), 453–457 (1975)
5. Dolby, J., Vaziri, M., Tip, F.: Finding bugs efficiently with a SAT solver. In: FSE, pp. 195–204 (2007)
6. El Ghazi, A.A., Ulbrich, M., Gladisch, C., Tyszberowicz, S., Taghdiri, M.: On verifying relational specifications of Java programs with JKelloy. Technical Report 2014-03, KIT, Department of Informatics (2014)
7. Galeotti, J.P.: Software Verification using Alloy. PhD thesis, Universidad de Buenos Aires (2010)
8. Gladisch, C., Tyszberowicz, S.: Specifying a linked data structure in JML for formal verification and runtime checking. In: Iyoda, J., de Moura, L. (eds.) SBMF 2013. LNCS, vol. 8195, pp. 99–114. Springer, Heidelberg (2013)
9. Harel, D., Tiuryn, J., Kozen, D.: Dynamic Logic. MIT Press (2000)
10. Jackson, D.: Software Abstractions: Logic, Language, and Analysis. MIT Press (2012)
11. King, J.C.: Symbolic execution and program testing. Communications of the ACM 19(7), 385–394 (1976)
12. Lahiri, S.K., Qadeer, S.: Verifying properties of well-founded linked lists. In: Proceedings of POPL, pp. 115–126. ACM (2006)
13. Lev-Ami, T., Immerman, N., Reps, T.W., Sagiv, M., Srivastava, S., Yorsh, G.: Simulating reachability using first-order logic with applications to verification of linked data structures. Logical Methods in Computer Science 5(2) (2009)
14. Meyer, B.: Applying "design by contract". IEEE Computer 25(10), 40–51 (1992)
15. Moscato, M.M., López Pombo, C.G., Frias, M.F.: Dynamite 2.0: New features based on UnSAT-core extraction to improve verification of software requirements. In: Cavalcanti, A., Deharbe, D., Gaudel, M.-C., Woodcock, J. (eds.) ICTAC 2010. LNCS, vol. 6255, pp. 275–289. Springer, Heidelberg (2010)
16. Rakamarić, Z., Bingham, J.D., Hu, A.J.: An inference-rule-based decision procedure for verification of heap-manipulating programs with mutable data and cyclic data structures. In: Cook, B., Podelski, A. (eds.) VMCAI 2007. LNCS, vol. 4349, pp. 106–121. Springer, Heidelberg (2007)
17. Taghdiri, M.: Automating Modular Program Verification by Refining Specifications. PhD thesis. MIT (2008)
18. Ulbrich, M., Geilmann, U., El Ghazi, A.A., Taghdiri, M.: A proof assistant for Alloy specifications. In: Flanagan, C., König, B. (eds.) TACAS 2012. LNCS, vol. 7214, pp. 422–436. Springer, Heidelberg (2012)
19. Vaziri, M.: Finding Bugs in Software with Constraint Solver. PhD thesis. MIT (2004)
20. Weiß, B.: Deductive Verification of Object-Oriented Software: Dynamic Frames, Dynamic Logic and Predicate Abstraction. PhD thesis. KIT (2010)
21. Yessenov, K.T.: A Lightweight Specification Language for Bounded Program Verification. Master's thesis. MIT (2009)
22. Zee, K., Kuncak, V., Rinard, M.: Full functional verification of linked data structures. In: PLDI, pp. 349–361 (2008)

# Verifying Hybrid Systems
# Involving Transcendental Functions

Paul Jackson[1], Andrew Sogokon[1], James Bridge[2], and Lawrence Paulson[2]

[1] School of Informatics, University of Edinburgh, UK
pbj@inf.ed.ac.uk, a.sogokon@sms.ed.ac.uk
[2] Computer Laboratory, University of Cambridge, UK
{jpb65,lp15}@cam.ac.uk

**Abstract.** We explore uses of a link we have constructed between the KeYmaera hybrid systems theorem prover and the MetiTarski proof engine for problems involving special functions such as sin, cos, exp, etc. Transcendental functions arise in the specification of hybrid systems and often occur in the solutions of the differential equations that govern how the states of hybrid systems evolve over time. To date, formulas exchanged between KeYmaera and external tools have involved polynomials over the reals, but not transcendental functions, chiefly because of the lack of tools capable of proving such goals.

## 1  Introduction

KeYmaera is an interactive prover which makes use of external tools such as computer algebra systems for simplification, solving differential equations and proving quantified formulas involving real arithmetic. MetiTarski is a prover specifically tailored for reasoning with transcendental functions. It eliminates transcendental functions from inequalities by applying polynomial and continued-fraction bounds and employs external provers to discharge goals involving these approximations. In this section we will give an overview of the context which motivates the integration of these two systems.

### 1.1  Hybrid Systems

Hybrid systems generalise both transition systems and continuous dynamical systems. The state of a hybrid system has both discrete- and continuous-valued components. Together, the values of the discrete components specify the mode of the system. Within each mode the evolution of the state is governed by differential equations. Transitions between between modes usually have guards describing when they are enabled and specify how the continuous components might jump in value when the transitions are taken. Figure 1 shows an example hybrid system, described using the *hybrid automaton* formalism.

Hybrid systems are very useful for creating models of cyber-physical systems, systems which involve computers or some kind of discrete control logic interacting with a physical environment [7]. Cyber-physical systems are found in many

J.M. Badger and K.Y. Rozier (Eds.): NFM 2014, LNCS 8430, pp. 188–202, 2014.
© Springer International Publishing Switzerland 2014

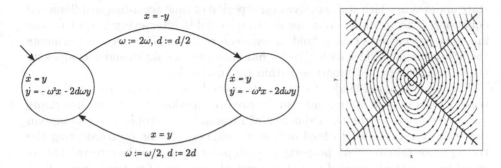

**Fig. 1.** Switched damped oscillator (**left**) and a possible phase portrait (**right**)

industrial sectors, including transport, energy and health-care automation. They are frequently safety-critical, so there is much interest in improved verification techniques for them.

### 1.2  Formal Verification of Hybrid Systems

In the past two decades a variety of techniques have been explored for the formal verification of hybrid systems. Many have involved a bounded approach where one computes an over-approximation of the state space reachable after some number of interleaved time evolutions within modes and jumps between modes [8,5,15,6]. The primary verification goal has been to show that no unsafe states are reached. Depending on the hybrid system considered, the chosen bound and the approximation methods, the state space exploration might reach a fixed-point, in which case verification of safety is sound. Otherwise, there's the possibility that there is an unsafe reachable state which has not yet been explored.

Since the early work there has been much improvement in the methods for representing and computing the over-approximations of the reachable state sets. Often these approaches have placed restrictions on the form of the differential constraints in modes and the jumps, requiring them to be linear or to be bounded by constants, for example. In these cases, systems with more general non-linear differential equations, perhaps involving transcendental functions, can be approximated with piecewise linear equations.

With KeYmaera [13] a different approach is investigated.

### 1.3  KeYmaera

KeYmaera mechanises a deductive calculus for reasoning about hybrid systems. The base calculus is *differential dynamic logic* (d$\mathcal{L}$) [12]. It extends first-order logic with modalities $[\alpha]\phi$ and $\langle\alpha\rangle\phi$, where $\alpha$ is a *hybrid program* and $\phi$ is a d$\mathcal{L}$ formula. Hybrid programs are described in a simple compositional language that includes conditional statements, loops, discrete state updates, and continuous state updates in which states evolve over a period of time according to differential equations. The modality $[\alpha]\phi$ asserts that $\phi$ holds after every run of $\alpha$, the modality $\langle\alpha\rangle\phi$ asserts that $\phi$ holds after some run of $\alpha$. The calculus augments the first-order logic rules with rules for handling the modalities and decomposing the structure of hybrid programs within the modalities.

The most common kinds of statements proved concern invariants of the systems. Proofs of such statements usually involve creation of inductive invariants and *differential invariants*. A differential invariant is a property of the system that can be established to hold over some interval of time by considering the truth of a certain auxiliary property at each point in time in the interval. Differential invariants are related to the concept of Lyapunov functions, generalised energy functions whose decrease in value over a state space region of interest is used to argue for stability in the theory of dynamical systems. Previous work in safety verification of hybrid systems introduced *barrier certificates* [14] which impose Lyapunov-like conditions on the time derivative of differentiable functions in order to prove safety properties. Differential invariants in turn generalise barrier certificates to formulas with boolean connectives [12] and thus allow one to work with a much larger class of invariants.

Proofs in KeYmaera can be guided interactively or can be automated using tableau-based strategies. KeYmaera includes heuristics for guessing simpler forms of inductive and differential invariants. The KeYmaera logic implements directly very little reasoning concerning expressions of real arithmetic and constraints on the derivatives of the real-valued state components. Instead, use is made of procedures in external tools such as the Mathematica computer algebra system and QEPCAD-B [2] for simplification of real expressions, solution of differential equations and proving goals involving real arithmetic.

To date the interface to these external tools has limited the expression language to real-valued polynomials, and has not permitted the use of transcendental functions such as sine, cosine, logarithm and exponentiation. This was primarily because there had been no effective techniques for proving goals that involved inequalities over expressions including transcendental functions. Such goals can arise in several ways. For example, transcendental functions can be used in the descriptions of hybrid systems. They are also commonly found in the solutions of linear differential equations. And there are examples of Lyapunov functions in the dynamical systems literature where transcendental functions are required.

The deductive approach taken in KeYmaera is harder to apply than the bounded automated approaches described in Section 1.2, as interaction and human-directed creative steps are needed. Its advantages include the possibility of proving richer properties, the lack of a restriction of analyses to some bound, and often better capabilities for exploring parameterised systems.

## 1.4   MetiTarski and Goals of Work

For several years, Paulson and others have been developing MetiTarski, an automatic proof engine specifically tailored for proving goals involving inequalities over transcendental functions [11,10]. In the work reported here we are interested in exploring how MetiTarski could support reasoning about hybrid systems in KeYmaera. We are also hoping that transcendental problems generated from the hybrid systems domain can help steer the future development of MetiTarski.

Previously MetiTarski has been used for the verification of analog circuits, modeled as dynamical systems or hybrid systems [4]. The computer algebra system Maple was used to analyse continuous behaviours of the systems, to solve linearisations of the differential equations describing their time evolution, for example. A systematic partly-manual process was then used to set up the relevant goals for MetiTarski to solve. In the work reported here, KeYmaera provides a significantly richer, more automated framework for the top-level reasoning about hybrid systems and the coordination of external reasoning services.

The core of MetiTarski is a first-order resolution theorem prover Metis and a database of axioms specifying polynomial and rational function bounds on transcendental functions. Weights that guide the resolution are tailored so as to employ the axioms to reduce problems involving inequalities over transcendental functions to problems involving inequalities over real polynomial expressions. MetiTarski augments the resolution calculus with extra rules for handling real polynomial expressions. These rules make use of external tools for proving goals involving polynomial expressions, for example the Z3 SMT solver [9], QEPCAD-B [2], and the quantifier-elimination procedure provided by the Mathematica computer algebra system.

## 2  KeYmaera-MetiTarski Interface

KeYmaera implements a plugin architecture (shown in Figure 2) in which the user may choose a backend tool to perform particular tasks, such as solving differential equations, simplifying arithmetic expressions and performing quantifier elimination.

The primary purpose of quantifier elimination is to prove goals involving quantified arithmetic expressions by reducing them to "true". In KeYmaera, it is sometimes also useful to have quantifier elimination produce quantifier-free expressions involving variables that are free in the goals, as these quantifier-free expressions can suggest missing assumptions.

In our work we have added MetiTarski as a new quantifier elimination backend tool, handling the common case of when quantifier-elimination is expected to return "true". The link is implemented in Scala and Java and uses a file-level interface in which first-order goals from KeYmaera are translated into MetiTarski's input format (a variation on the TPTP format that allows infix notation) and stored in temporary files. These files are passed as arguments to the MetiTarski binary along with command-line options which the KeYmaera user selects in KeYmaera's GUI. This link from KeYmaera to MetiTarski is now part of standard KeYmaera releases.

The diagram in Figure 2 labels with ∀ the interfaces where KeYmaera goals are universally closed and the quantifier-elimination procedure is only ever expected

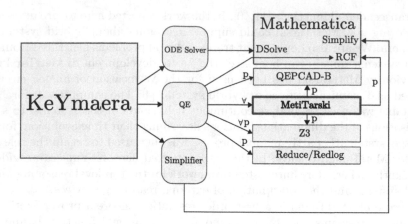

**Fig. 2.** KeYmaera plugin architecture

to return "true" when it succeeds. Label **p** is used for interfaces that handle purely polynomial problems, problems without special functions.

MetiTarski itself relies on decision procedures for real arithmetic and is able to call QEPCAD-B, Z3 and Mathematica to access this functionality. KeYmaera users may select the appropriate tool for MetiTarski by setting the pertinent option in KeYmaera. The problems sent to these external tools are purely polynomial, as shown in Figure 2.

In Figure 2, Mathematica is shown to provide more functionality than any of the other tools. In particular, it is able solve systems of differential equations. The user has to trust these solutions, but in certain cases this may introduce unsoundness.

The simplifier offered by Mathematica is very powerful and it may often be necessary to simplify complicated expressions before any further progress can be made on a problem using either Mathematica itself or MetiTarski. Once more, one needs to be aware of the potential soundness issues in performing this step.

While MetiTarski may use Mathematica's decision procedure for real closed fields (RCF), which it trusts to be sound, it will not make use of other potentially unsound computer algebra functionality, such as the simplifier.

## 3    Examples of How Transcendental Functions Arise

We review here three ways in which transcendental functions can arise during formal verification of continuous and hybrid systems.

### 3.1    Systems with Closed Form Solutions

Some systems admit closed-form solutions to the initial value problem; however, these tend to be much more complicated than the differential equations themselves and will often involve special functions.

KeYmaera offers inference rules which allow reasoning about safety and liveness properties by considering closed form solutions when they exist. Using this facility tends to generate first-order goals involving transcendental functions, which are delegated to an external solver.

We consider here a safety verification scenario where the solution is available in closed form and the safety property is ensuring boundedness of oscillation. The motion of a damped oscillator, such as that shown in Figure 3, can be

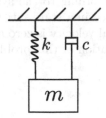

**Fig. 3.** Damped oscillator

described by the linear second-order differential equation

$$\ddot{x} + 2d\omega\dot{x} + \omega^2 x = 0,$$

where $\omega = \sqrt{\frac{k}{m}}$ is the frequency, $d = \frac{c}{2\sqrt{km}}$ is the damping factor and $x$ is the displacement from the point of equilibrium. We can convert this into a state space model by setting $x_1 = \dot{x}$ and $x_2 = x$. For a concrete example, let us choose $\omega = 2$ and $d = \frac{3}{5}$.

$$\dot{x}_1 = -\frac{3}{5} \cdot 2 \cdot 2 \cdot x_1 - 2^2 \cdot x_2,$$

$$\dot{x}_2 = x_1$$

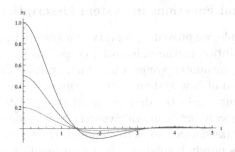

**Fig. 4.** $x_2$-component of solutions with $x_2(0) = \{1, \frac{1}{2}, \frac{1}{5}\}$, $x_1(0) = 0$

It is intuitively obvious that a damped oscillator will lose energy and eventually come to a halt, assuming there is no input. Consider proving that an initial displacement $x_2$ will never result in that displacement subsequently being exceeded. We could phrase this property using differential dynamic logic as

$$t \geq 0, \ x_1 = 0, \ x_2 \leq b, \ x_2 \geq a \vdash [\dot{x} = f(x)] \ x_2 \leq b.$$

Here the *box modality* [ ] expresses the property that $x_2 \leq b$ is necessarily true after the system evolves according to the system of differential equations $\dot{x} = f(x)$ whenever it is initialised in a state satisfying the antecedent.

Consider the case where initial velocity is zero and the initial displacement is in the interval $[0, 1]$. A formalisation of this problem in KeYmaera is shown in Figure 5.

```
\programVariables{
  R x1;
  R x2;
}

\problem {
  (x2<=1 & x2>=0 & x1=0) ->
   \[ {x1' = -((3/5)*2*2*x1 + 2^2*x2), x2' = x1 } \]
   (x2<=1)
}
```

**Fig. 5.** Proving boundedness of displacement of a damped oscillator using KeYmaera

Computing the solution, this amounts to proving

$$t \geq 0, \ x_2 \leq 1, \ x_2 \geq 0 \vdash \frac{1}{4} e^{-\frac{6}{5}t} x_2 \left( 4\cos(\frac{8}{5}t) + 3\sin(\frac{8}{5}t) \right) \leq 1.$$

This goal is difficult to prove, with Mathematica being unable to handle it in reasonable time; MetiTarski can solve this in under a second.

### 3.2   Transcendental Functions in System Description

In the previous example, we proved a property of a system by proving a property of the closed form solution to the differential equations governing evolution. It is not uncommon to encounter systems in which transcendental functions are used in the description of how system state continuously evolves. Transcendental functions can occur too in the description of the guards and state updates associated with mode switches in hybrid systems. Sometimes the descriptions of such systems can be transformed so as to eliminate the transcendental functions and have descriptions purely involving polynomial functions. In general though it is desirable to work directly with the transcendental functions.

It is rare that closed form solutions can be found for the continuous state evolution of systems described using transcendental functions. Indeed, it is also not possible to find closed form solutions for most systems described using non-linear polynomials. To address these cases, a number of related methods have been developed that allow the proof of properties of interest by referring directly to the differential equations governing state evolution and not requiring solution of the equations. These methods use such concepts as *Lyapunov function*, *barrier certificate* and *differential invariant* (we refer the reader to the Appendix).

We give an example here of a simple dynamical system which involves transcendental functions in its description and sketch how an invariance property can be proven using differential invariants.

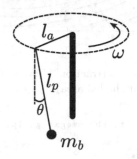

**Fig. 6.** Whirling pendulum

Consider a whirling pendulum (i.e. one which is itself suspended from a rod of radius $l_a$, moving with an angular velocity $\omega$). Its equations of motion are given by the following non-polynomial system:

$$\dot{x}_1 = x_2,$$
$$\dot{x}_2 = -\frac{k_f}{m_b}x_2 + \omega^2 \sin(x_1)\cos(x_1) - \frac{g}{l_p}\sin(x_1),$$

where the state $x_1$ is the pendulum's angle with the vertical and $x_2$ is the rate of change of this angle, $k_f$ is the friction coefficient, $l_p$ is the length of the rigid arm, and $m_b$ is its mass (see [3] for a detailed description of the model). A possible Lyapunov function for this system suggested by Chesi [3] is

$$V(\boldsymbol{x}) = x_1^2 + x_1 x_2 + 4x_2^2.$$

In KeYmaera we might formulate the property of time-evolution being confined to sub-level sets for $a$ in the range $0 \ldots b$ for some constant $b$ using the sequent

$$0 \le a,\ a \le b,\ V(\boldsymbol{x}) \le a \vdash [\dot{\boldsymbol{x}} = f(\boldsymbol{x})]\, V(\boldsymbol{x}) \le a\ .$$

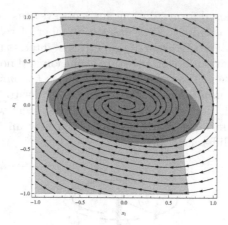

**Fig. 7.** Estimate to the domain of attraction $V(x) \leq 0.69$ (dark shaded area) and states where $\nabla V \cdot f(x) < 0$ (light shaded area)

```
\programVariables { R x1, x2, kf, mb, omega, g, lp, a; }

\problem {
   kf    = 0.2 & /* FRICTION */
   mb    = 1   & /* MASS OF RIGID ARM */
   omega = 0.9 & /* ROTATING ANGULAR VELOCITY */
   g     = 10  & /* GRAVITY ACCELERATION */
   lp    = 10  & /* LENGTH OF RIGID ARM */

(x1^2 +x1*x2 +4*(x2^2)) <= a   & a>=0   /* LYAPUNOV FUNCTION */ ->

   \[ { x1' = x2,
        x2' = -(kf/mb)*x2 + (omega^2)*Sin(x1)*Cos(x1) - (g/lp)*Sin(x1) &
        (x1^2 +x1*x2 +4*(x2^2)) <= 0.69929971
      }
   \] (x1^2 +x1*x2 +4*(x2^2)) <= a
}
```

**Fig. 8.** Lyapunov function $V(x) = x_1^2 + x_1 x_2 + 4x_2^2$ is non-increasing within the domain of attraction $V(x) \leq 0.69929971$

This is most easily proved in KeYmaera by first rephrasing it as

$$0 \leq a, \; V(x) \leq a \;\vdash\; [\dot{x} = f(x) \wedge V(x) \leq b] \, V(x) \leq a \quad .$$

Taking $k_f = 0.2$, $m_b = 1$, $\omega = 0.9$, $l_p = 10$, gravity $g = 10$ and $b = 0.69929971$, we can formalise this property in KeYmaera as shown in Figure 8.

The number $0.69929971$ defines the bound on the sub-level set of $V(x)$, which is used as a conservative estimate to the domain of attraction of the whirling pendulum.

Explicitly the subgoal we get in KeYmaera in applying the differential induction rule is

$$k_f = 0.2, \ m_b = 1, \ \omega = 0.9, \ g = 10, \ l_p = 10, \ x_1^2 + x_1 x_2 + 4x_2^2 \leq a, \ a \geq 0 \vdash$$

$$\forall x_{21}, x_{11} \in \mathbb{R}. \ x_{11}^2 + x_{11}x_{21} + 4x_{21}^2 \leq 0.69929971 \implies$$

$$2x_{11}x_{21} + x_{21}^2$$

$$+ x_{11}\left(-\frac{k_f}{m_b}x_{21} - \frac{g}{l_p}\sin(x_{11}) + \omega^2\cos(x_{11})\sin(x_{11})\right)$$

$$+ 8x_{21}\left(-\frac{k_f}{m_b}x_{21} - \frac{g}{l_p}\sin(x_{11}) + \omega^2\cos(x_{11})\sin(x_{11})\right) \leq 0.$$

MetiTarski solves this problem in under 10 minutes.

### 3.3 Non-polynomial Invariant Candidates

A further use case for the link between the two systems concerns the handling of invariant candidates which are non-polynomial.

Unlike in the previous example, where transcendental functions were used to define the dynamics of the system and the invariant candidate was polynomial, one may instead have a polynomial vector field and an invariant candidate featuring transcendental functions. An simple example is shown in Figure 9.

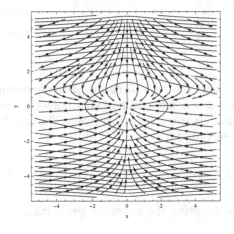

**Fig. 9.** Invariant sub-level sets of a non-polynomial Lyapunov function $V(x,y) = \ln(1 + x^2) + y^2$ [1]

Recently it has been shown that even for purely polynomial vector fields that are *globally asymptotically stable* it may be impossible to find a Lypaunov function which is of polynomial form [1].

Generally, allowing special functions in the description of invariant candidates enlarges the class of invariant assertions amenable to verification (given the right tools).

## 4   Performance and Discussion

At present, MetiTarski and Mathematica are the only tools that are able to handle problems involving special functions which appear in KeYmaera proofs. Table 1 compares them on some of the problems featuring transcendental functions which arose during proof attempts in KeYmaera. The table shows the run-time in milliseconds of several tool configurations on the problems. Time here is wall-clock time on an Intel i5-2520M CPU @ 2.50GHz. A '-' character indicates that no result was obtained after running for 10 minutes. There are three columns for the MetiTarski results, each using a different external tool for proving polynomial problems. The name of the external tool is shown in parentheses in each case. The right-hand column shows how Mathematica performs when we pass it directly the problems with special functions.

**Table 1.** Problems involving transcendental functions in KeYmaera proofs

| Problem | Functions | MetiTarski (Z3) | (QEPCAD-B) | (Mathematica) | Mathematica |
|---|---|---|---|---|---|
| Damped oscillator | exp, sin, cos | 430 | 850 | 2,403 | - |
| Whirling pendulum | sin, cos | 419,340 | 3,849 | 14,182 | - |
| Domain of attraction | exp, cos | - | 2,161 | 3,899 | - |
| Drill string | sin, cos | 17,441 | 30,270 | 48,944 | - |
| Local Lyapunov | exp | - | - | - | - |
| Diffcut 1 | exp | 45 | 154 | 956 | 33 |
| Diffcut 2 | exp | - | - | - | 59 |
| Heater Simple | exp | 144 | 376 | 1,427 | 68 |
| Tunnel diode 1 | exp | - | - | - | 84,171 |
| Tunnel diode 2 | exp | 227 | 370 | 1,587 | 18,444 |

MetiTarski handles well the first three problems featuring inequalities over trigonometric functions or a combination of trigonometric and exponential functions, whereas Mathematica times out on all these. The goal for the first problem, shown also earlier in Section 3.1, is

$$t \geq 0 \wedge x_2 \leq 1 \wedge x_2 \geq 0 \vdash \frac{1}{4} e^{-\frac{6}{5}t} x_2 \left( 4 \cos(\frac{8}{5}t) + 3 \sin(\frac{8}{5}t) \right) \leq 1.$$

MetiTarski proves this by using the bounding properties

$$0 \leq x \Rightarrow \sin(x) \leq x$$
$$\cos(x) \leq 1 - \frac{x^2}{2} + \frac{x^4}{24}$$
$$x \leq 0 \Rightarrow e^x \leq \frac{2304}{(-x^3+6x^2-24x+48)^2}.$$

MetiTarski's performance on the problems involving just the exponential function is more mixed. Consider the *diffcut 2* goal:

$$x > 15, \ t \geq 0 \vdash 25e^t + e^{t/2}(x - 40) > 0.$$

MetiTarski's strategy of substituting polynomial or rational function bounds for exponential function occurrences is not so appropriate here, as the goal's validity depends on the relationship between $e^t$ and $e^{t/2}$ for all $t \geq 0$. In general, polynomial or rational function bounds are accurate and best used for special function with bounded arguments, although we happened to have success with them in the *damped oscillator* example above where $t$ is also unbounded. For *diffcut 2*, a simple solution strategy involves replacing $e^{t/2}$ with a new variable, and we are considering introducing such substitutions if we observe a significant number of further examples where they would be useful.

The *tunnel diode 1* and *tunnel diode 2* goals are

$$t \geq 0 \; \vdash \; -a_1 e^{-k_1 t} + a_2 e^{-k_2 t} - a_3 e^{k_3 t} \leq 0,$$
$$t \geq 0 \; \vdash \; -a_1 e^{-k_1 t} + a_2 e^{-k_2 t} + a_4 e^{k_3 t} \geq 0$$

respectively, where $a_1, a_2, a_3, a_4, k_1, k_2$ and $k_3$ are all positive constants. The constants $a_3$ and $a_4$ are both significantly larger than $a_1$ and $a_2$, and so the inequalities can be seen as obviously true from just basic bounding properties of the exponential function. MetiTarski has problems with the *tunnel diode 1* because the constants are not just rationals, but constant expressions involving square roots. For example $a_1$ is $1104311 - 34469\sqrt{254841}$. MetiTarski currently works with such constants by breaking them down and using bounding lemmas for the square root. MetiTarski has an interval constraint solver that can work with bounded interval approximations for constants, and it would easily handle such constants as above if we were to extend this facility to handle square roots.

The differences in MetiTarski's performance with different real polynomial arithmetic proof procedures appears primarily due to the differences in the procedures themselves and the interfaces to them. With virtually all the problems considered, the proof found by MetiTarski does not vary with the proof procedure selected. The lower performance of MetiTarski with Mathematica as the proof procedure for real arithmetic is due in part to the performance overhead incurred from contacting the Mathematica license server. KeYmaera keeps an open TCP connection with Mathematica, whereas MetiTarski needs to establish a new connection for each problem.

## 5   Conclusion

We have presented here some preliminary experiments with an interface between the KeYmaera and MetiTarski tools. The results are encouraging and we are now seeking more complex examples that bear a closer relationship to practical hybrid systems verification problems and that produce interesting problems for MetiTarski.

One issue is that often readily available examples have been reformulated or simplified so as to allow working only with polynomials. To this end we are finding we are having to develop expertise in how problems are first represented in KeYmaera and how KeYmaera is then guided to solving verification problems of interest. We are also trying to build closer ties with current users of KeYmaera. For example, we know of at least two groups applying KeYmaera to autonomous car problems that involve transcendental functions and we are hoping for fruitful collaboration with these groups.

**Acknowledgements.** This research was supported by EPSRC grants EP/I011005/1, EP/I010335/1. We would like to thank the anonymous reviewers for their feedback and helpful suggestions. We extend special thanks to Grant Passmore at the LFCS, University of Edinburgh, for offering his expert advice.

# References

1. Ahmadi, A.A., Krstic, M., Parrilo, P.A.: A globally asymptotically stable polynomial vector field with no polynomial Lyapunov function. In: CDC-ECE, pp. 7579–7580 (2011)
2. Brown, C.W.: Qepcad b: a program for computing with semi-algebraic sets using cads. SIGSAM Bull. 37(4), 97–108 (2003),
   http://doi.acm.org/10.1145/968708.968710
3. Chesi, G.: Estimating the domain of attraction for non-polynomial systems via LMI optimizations. Automatica 45(6), 1536–1541 (2009)
4. Denman, W., Akbarpour, B., Tahar, S., Zaki, M., Paulson, L.: Formal verification of analog designs using metitarski. In: Formal Methods in Computer-Aided Design, FMCAD 2009, pp. 93–100 (2009)
5. Fränzle, M., Herde, C.: Hysat: An efficient proof engine for bounded model checking of hybrid systems. Formal Methods in System Design 30(3), 179–198 (2007)
6. Frehse, G., Le Guernic, C., Donzé, A., Cotton, S., Ray, R., Lebeltel, O., Ripado, R., Girard, A., Dang, T., Maler, O.: Spaceex: Scalable verification of hybrid systems. In: Gopalakrishnan, G., Qadeer, S. (eds.) CAV 2011. LNCS, vol. 6806, pp. 379–395. Springer, Heidelberg (2011)
7. Heemels, W., Lehmann, D., Lunze, J., De Schutter, B.: Introduction to hybrid systems. In: Lunze, J., Lamnabhi-Lagarrigue, F. (eds.) Handbook of Hybrid Systems Control – Theory, Tools, Applications, ch. 1, pp. 3–30. Cambridge University Press, Cambridge (2009)
8. Henzinger, T.A., Ho, P.H., Wong-Toi, H.: Hytech: A model checker for hybrid systems. STTT 1(1-2), 110–122 (1997)
9. de Moura, L., Bjørner, N.S.: Z3: An efficient SMT solver. In: Ramakrishnan, C.R., Rehof, J. (eds.) TACAS 2008. LNCS, vol. 4963, pp. 337–340. Springer, Heidelberg (2008)
10. Paulson, L.C.: MetiTarski: Past and Future. In: Beringer, L., Felty, A. (eds.) ITP 2012. LNCS, vol. 7406, pp. 1–10. Springer, Heidelberg (2012)
11. Paulson, L.C.: University of Cambridge (2013),
    http://www.cl.cam.ac.uk/~lp15/papers/Arith/
12. Platzer, A.: Logical Analysis of Hybrid Systems: Proving Theorems for Complex Dynamics. Springer, Heidelberg (2010)
13. Platzer, A.: Carnegie Mellon Uniersity (2013),
    http://symbolaris.com/info/KeYmaera.html

14. Prajna, S., Jadbabaie, A.: Safety verification of hybrid systems using barrier certifi-
    cates. In: Alur, R., Pappas, G.J. (eds.) HSCC 2004. LNCS, vol. 2993, pp. 477–492.
    Springer, Heidelberg (2004)
15. Ratschan, S., She, Z.: Safety verification of hybrid systems by constraint
    propagation-based abstraction refinement. ACM Trans. Embedded Comput.
    Syst. 6(1) (2007)

# Appendix: Direct Methods and Safety Verification

Historically, Lyapunov was perhaps one of the first to observe that in the study
of stability, closed form solutions are rarely revealing and that it is possible to
work with the differential equation *directly* to prove properties of interest. This
observation led to what has become known as Lyapunov's direct method, which
introduced the concept of Lyapunov functions.

Informally, a Lyapunov function $V$ is a continuously-differentiable *positive-
definite* function of the system state, whose time-derivative along the vector
field is never greater than zero. More precisely, given a system $\dot{x} = f(x)$ which
is defined on some state space $X \subseteq \mathbb{R}^n$, if one can find a $V : X \to \mathbb{R}$ such that

$$V(x) > 0 \quad \forall x \in X \setminus 0,$$
$$\nabla V \cdot f(x) \leq 0 \quad \forall x \in X,$$

then one can conclude that the origin is stable.

A set $\{x \mid V(x) \leq a\}$ is known as an $a$ sub-level set of $V$ and if $V$ is a Lyapunov
function, then each sub-level set of $V$ is a system invariant (in forward time);
that is, once a solution enters the set, it cannot escape.

The method of barrier certificates [14] uses Lyapunov-like conditions to argue
for safety, rather than stability. Given a system $\dot{x} = f(x)$ as before, a set of
initial states $X_i \subseteq X$ and a set of unsafe states $X_u \subseteq X$, if one can find a
continuously-differentiable function $B : X \to \mathbb{R}$ such that

$$B(x) > 0 \quad \forall x \in X_u,$$
$$B(x) \leq 0 \quad \forall x \in X_i,$$
$$\nabla B \cdot f(x) \leq 0 \quad \forall x \in X,$$

then the system is guaranteed to be safe.

The problem of safety verification with barrier certificates is essentially that
of finding a $B$ which satisfies the above conditions.

The $d\mathcal{L}$ calculus used by KeYmaera provides a proof rule called *differential
induction* (henceforth called DI; see Platzer [12] for a thorough exposition),
which allows one to reason about invariance of sets defined by quantifier-free
formulas,

$$\text{DI} \frac{X \to \dot{F}}{F \to [\dot{x} = f(x) \wedge X]F}.$$

In DI, $F$ is a quantifier-free first-order formula in the theory of real arithmetic, $X$ is the evolution domain constraint and the *differential formula* $\dot{F}$ is defined using the derivation operator $D$ [12] which is given as follows:

$$D(r) = 0 \quad \text{for real numbers,}$$
$$D(x) = \dot{x} \quad \text{for real variables,}$$
$$D(a + b) = D(a) + D(b),$$
$$D(a \cdot b) = D(a) \cdot b + a \cdot D(b),$$
$$D(F \wedge G) \equiv D(F) \wedge D(G),$$
$$D(F \vee G) \equiv D(F) \wedge D(G), \quad (\wedge \text{ here is important for soundness})$$
$$D(a \leq b) \equiv D(a) \leq D(b), \quad \text{accordingly for } \geq, >, <, = .$$

The differential formula $\dot{F}$ is shorthand for $D(F)_{\dot{x}}^{f(x)}$, where each $\dot{x}$ in $D(F)$ is replaced with the corresponding right hand side in the differential equation. Formulas $F$ provable using DI are called *differential invariants*.

Safety verification with differential invariants is similar to the method of barrier certificates, i.e., given a formula $F_i$ which is satisfied by the initial states and a formula $F_u$ satisfied by the unsafe states, one requires a differential invariant $F$ such that

$$F_i \rightarrow F,$$
$$F \rightarrow [\dot{x} = f(x) \wedge X]F,$$
$$F \rightarrow \neg F_u.$$

Indeed, if one succeeds in finding a $F \equiv B(x) \leq 0$, then this is equivalent to a proof of safety using barrier certificates. Differential invariants thus include barrier certificates as a special case [12].

# Verifying Nonpolynomial Hybrid Systems by Qualitative Abstraction and Automated Theorem Proving

William Denman

Computer Laboratory, University of Cambridge, UK
william.denman@cl.cam.ac.uk

**Abstract.** Few methods can automatically verify nonlinear hybrid systems that are modelled by nonpolynomial functions. Qualitative abstraction is a potential alternative to numerical reachability methods for formally verifying these systems. The QUANTUM abstracter is shown to be competitive at verifying several benchmark nonpolynomial hybrid systems.

## 1 Introduction

Examples of *hybrid systems* include self-driving cars and autonomous drones. As these complex systems are becoming prevalent, fast and efficient methods for safety verification are now more important than ever. The formal verification of hybrid systems is inherently computationally intractable. This is due to the interplay of continuous variables, which vary over the infinite field $\mathbb{R}$, and discrete variables, which introduce nondeterminism. Consequently, determining whether the system can reach an unsafe state is extremely difficult.

Since hybrid systems lie at the interface of the physical world, transcendental and special functions naturally arise in modelling their behaviour. Angular measurements might involve sine, cosine, tangent and related transcendental functions. Several types of friction or drag can involve the exponential function. However, there is no clear choice as to which method is best suited for formally verifying such nonpolynomial hybrid systems.

One approach is to iteratively compute over-approximations of reachable states [1], while another is to abstract the state space [2] or transition relation [3]. Though significant advancements have been made, most tools, even state-of-the-art ones, have difficulty dealing with hybrid systems that contain transcendental functions in the definition of the vector field (system of differential equations) or in the transition guards. Moreover, the tools that do support transcendental functions are restricted to techniques such as interval differential equation solving [4], bounded model checking [3] or linearization [5].

This short paper describes an enhanced qualitative abstraction method, which uses the automated theorem prover MetiTarski [6] to discretize nonpolynomial hybrid systems, while performing an on-the-fly reachability analysis. Preliminary results indicate that this verification method is competitive on several nonlinear

J.M. Badger and K.Y. Rozier (Eds.): NFM 2014, LNCS 8430, pp. 203–208, 2014.

nonpolynomial hybrid system problems and demonstrates that MetiTarski is powerful enough to discharge theorems arising from the abstraction process.

The initial work on using qualitative abstraction to verify hybrid systems was done by Tiwari [7] and implemented in the original HybridSAL tool. However, the problems analysable by HybridSAL were restricted to linear and nonlinear polynomial differential equations. The QUANTUM abstracter[1] that is used in this paper implements a modified algorithm for performing qualitative abstraction. Firstly, MetiTarski is used to remove infeasible abstract states and to validate abstract transitions through analysis of the nonpolynomial vector field. Secondly, QUANTUM performs a *lazy* abstraction that will immediately terminate if a predefined safety property is invalidated (by transitioning into an unsafe state). An important improvement over the original version of QUANTUM is distributing the calls to MetiTarski across several processes. This has significantly decreased the abstraction times in case studies from those previously reported [8].

## 2    Modelling Hybrid Systems

The input to the QUANTUM abstracter is a *hybrid automaton*, which is one of the more common formalisms used to model hybrid systems. It has been well studied, its limitations are well understood and it is the standard input to several verification tools.

**Definition 1 (Hybrid Automata [2]).** *A hybrid system (HS) is defined by the tuple (Q, X, Init, Inv, t, G, U, f). Q is the finite set of discrete modes and* **Q** *is the finite set of all valuations of Q. X is the set of continuous real variables and* $\mathbf{X} = (X \to \mathbb{R})$ *is the set of all valuations of X . The state of the hybrid system is* $(q, x) \in \mathbf{Q} \times \mathbf{X}$. *Init* $\subseteq \mathbf{Q} \times \mathbf{X}$ *is the set of initial states. Inv is the set of invariants that restrict the range of the real variables X in each state. A transition relation,* $t \subset (\mathbf{Q} \times \mathbf{X}) \times (\mathbf{Q} \times \mathbf{X})$ *defines potential transitions between states. The transitions between states of the hybrid system are controlled by guards* $g \in G$. *A transition will occur from state* $(q, x)$ *to* $(q, x)'$ *if g evaluates to True. During a transition, the continuous variables X can be updated from values in U (if it is non-empty). f is the set of differential equations governing the flow of the continuous variables for each discrete state* $q \in \mathbf{Q}$.

*Example 1 (Bouncing Ball on a Sine Curve, adapted from Ishii et al. [9]).* The hybrid automaton in Fig. 1a models a ball bouncing on a sine shaped curve. Fig. 1b is a single simulated trajectory of the system. $Q = \mathbf{Q} = \{falling\}$, X $= \{px, py, vx, vy, t\}$. $px$ and $py$ are the position of the ball, $vx$ and $vy$ are the respective velocities. Inv $= \{py > -1\}$. G $= \{\sin(px) - py = 0\}$. The guard evaluates to True when the ball hits the curve. The values of $vx$ and $vy$ are updated according to the equations defined by the ':=' operator. The assignments make up the set U.

---

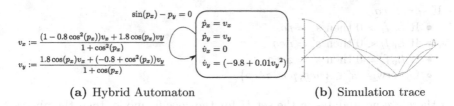

(a) Hybrid Automaton                    (b) Simulation trace

**Fig. 1.** Bouncing Ball Example

# 3 Qualitative Abstraction of Hybrid Systems

The abstraction algorithm implemented in QUANTUM is based on that of HybridSAL [7]. For brevity, this paper focuses on abstracting only the continuous part of the hybrid system. The basic idea is to use a finite set $F = \{f_1, f_2, ..., f_k\}$ of k smooth functions $f_i : \mathbb{R}^n \to \mathbb{R}$, to discretize the infinite state space into qualitatively distinct regions. There are several automatic and manual methods that can be used to choose the functions to include in F. One strategy is to start with the guards, invariants and vector field as a source of functions.

Taking $Sign = \{zero, pos, neg\}$, the abstract state space is $Sign^k$. The abstraction function is defined as $\alpha : \mathbb{R}^n \to Sign^k$ where $\alpha(x) = (s_1, ..., s_k)$ for $i = 1..k$ where $s_i = pos$ if $f_i(x) > 0$, $s_i = zero$ if $f_i(x) = 0$, $s_i = neg$ if $f_i(x) < 0$. Each abstract state s can be associated with the predicate $P_s(x) = \bigwedge_{i=1..k} f_i(x) \sim_{s_i} 0$, where $\sim_{pos}$ is >, $\sim_{zero}$ is = and $\sim_{neg}$ is <.

The first step of the abstraction algorithm is to delete all infeasible states. That is we need to prove for each abstract state the first order formula $\exists x : P_s(x)$ evaluates to True, indicating that the abstract state s is indeed feasible. The second step of the abstraction algorithm is to determine all potential next abstract states. For continuous transitions this is done by analysing the sign of the Lie derivative of abstraction functions with respect to the vector field.

**Definition 2.** *The Lie derivative of f along the vector field v is*

$$L_v f = \sum_{j=1}^{n} \frac{\partial f}{\partial x_j} v_j \tag{1}$$

The sign of the Lie derivative constrains the possible signs of the discretizing functions $f_i$ in the next abstract state $s'$ according the following rules. There is a transition from state s to $s'$ iff for all $i = 1..k$

- If $s_i = pos$
  - If $L_v f_i \geq 0$ then $s'_i = pos$
  - Otherwise $s'_i \in \{pos, zero\}$
- If $s_i = neg$
  - If $L_v f_i \leq 0$ then $s'_i = neg$
  - Otherwise $s'_i \in \{neg, zero\}$

– If $s_i = zero$
  - If $L_v f_i > 0$ then $s'_i = pos$
  - If $L_v f_i < 0$ then $s'_i = neg$
  - If $L_v f_i = 0$ then $s'_i = zero$
  - Otherwise $s'_i \in \{neg, pos, zero\}$

If there are no updates in the set $U$ for the specific mode, then the abstract discrete transition is automatically taken as long as the next state $s'$ is feasible. If there are updates to the continuous variables, determining the set of possible next states for discrete transitions is performed similarly to that above. The sign of the Lie derivative of the system is checked with respect to the vector field with the sign of the updated continuous variables.

Once the signs of the abstraction functions in the next state are determined, the process repeats. Each newly reachable state is checked to determine if it is feasible and the next states from that new state are also computed. This continues until no new states are found.

*Example 2 (Abstracting the Bouncing Ball).* One simple safety property of this system is that if the ball is dropped from rest inside a trough, then it will remain there for all time. The set of abstraction functions F is chosen to include the continuous variables, the guards, the invariants, the functions that describe the initial state of the system and the unsafe states.

$$F = \left\{ vx, vy, py - \sin(px), py + 1, py - 1, px - \frac{\pi}{2}, px - (2\pi + \frac{\pi}{2}) \right\}$$

QUANTUM generates the proper input format to MetiTarski to check feasibility of abstract states. To prove that a particular abstract state is infeasible, that is $\nexists x : P_s(x)$ is True, the equivalent universally quantified logical sentence $\forall x : \neg P_s(x)$ is sent to MetiTarski. Below is a sample input for feasibility checking of an abstract state of the bouncing ball problem. MetiTarski uses the TPTP syntax format, where *fof* indicates a first order formula, ! is equivalent to $\forall$ and $\tilde{}$ is equivalent to $\neg$. Variables must be uppercase.

```
fof(checkFeasibility, conjecture, (![PY,VY,VX,PX] :
  (~(PY - 1<0 & VY=0 & VX=0 & PY + 1=0 & PY>0 & PX<0 &
    PX - pi/2<0 & PX - (2*pi+pi/2)=0 & -PY + sin(PX)<0)))).
```

To determine abstract transitions, QUANTUM will symbolically calculate the Lie derivative of each $f_i$ in turn and generate and send the problems to MetiTarski. Below, the equation to the right of the implication is the Lie derivative of $f_i = -PY + \sin(PX)$.

```
fof(checkTransition, conjecture, (![PY,VY,VX,PX] :
  (PY - 1<0 & VY=0 & VX=0 & PY + 1>0 & PY=0 & PX<0 &
   PX - (2*pi+pi/2)=0 & -PY + sin(PX)<0
   => (VX*cos(PX) - VY >= 0))))
```

**Theorem 1 (Tiwari [2]).** *The discrete state abstraction of a hybrid automaton obtained by qualitative reasoning based on analysis of the Lie derivative is sound.*

Theorem 1 guarantees that any state not reachable in an abstraction created by QUANTUM is not reachable in the original hybrid automaton. The abstraction process provides a guaranteed over-approximation of the reachable states of the system.

## 4    Experimental Results

The qualitative abstracter QUANTUM has been tested on several nonpolynomial hybrid systems including the bouncing ball on sine curve, two tanks and steering car. The three examples are taken from the hydlogic [9] and iSat-ODE [4] tool-sets, that use bounded model checking for verification. Bounded model checking only guarantees a bounded safety result by unrolling the transition relation a limited number of times.

The bouncing ball (bounce-ball-sin)$^2$ is an interesting case study because there are nonpolynomial functions in the transition guards. To verify that the bouncing ball does not exit a trough of the sine curve, QUANTUM constructs the abstraction and searches the abstract state space for a violation of the safety property $G\neg(PY > 1)$.

The two tanks system (twotanks-1) [4] is defined by a system of differential equations that contain the square root function. The model is of two cascaded vessels, one placed above the other. The top vessel fills with water from an inlet, and subsequently empties into the second vessel below, which empties at a different rate. The property to be verified is whether the system reaches an unsafe elliptical instability region that leads to either vessel overflowing.

The steering problem (steering-2) [9] consists of a 6 state hybrid automaton modelling the control of an autonomous vehicle. The property to be verified is whether a car performing a curved turn on a road, will avoid falling into the adjacent river. The system of differential equations in this case contain the sine function.

Keeping in mind that hydlogic and iSat-ODE only perform bounded verification, the run-times in Table 1 are reported to highlight that qualitative abstraction is a competitive alternative. QUANTUM distinguishes itself by verifying unbounded safety properties. QUANTUM and hydlogic run-times are from a 2.4 GHz Intel Core 2 Duo processor. iSat-ODE results are from a slightly faster, yet same processor generation, 2.6 GHz AMD Opteron processor. All use 4 GB of RAM. The number in parenthesis is the corresponding number of transition relation unwindings for bounded model checking. An **unknown** result indicates that the model checker could not verify the safety property to the specified number of unwindings.

---

$^2$ The labels in parenthesis are the experiment file-names located in the *examples* directory of the QUANTUM distribution.

**Table 1.** Experimental run-times in seconds

| experiment | hydlogic | iSat-ODE | quantum |
|---|---|---|---|
| bounce-ball-sin | 29.15 (10) | unknown (10) | 42.82 |
| twotanks-1 | 20.5 (40) | 33.49 (40) | 40.80 |
| steering-2 | 198.30 (3) | 200.1 (11) | 197.10 |

## 5    Conclusion

A direct comparison between the verification times by QUANTUM and the tools mentioned above to support a claim that one is superior to the other would be unreasonable. However, the results do indicate that QUANTUM is at least competitive at verifying benchmark nonpolynomial hybrid system problems. This result is promising.

Qualitative reasoning has generally not been considered powerful enough to reason about complex dynamical systems. The combination of qualitative reasoning and the automated theorem prover MetiTarski has the potential to prove this notion wrong.

**Acknowledgments.** This research was supported by the Engineering and Physical Sciences Research Council [grant numbers EP/I011005/1, EP/I010335/1]. Further support was provided by the Natural Sciences and Engineering Research Council of Canada.

## References

1. Frehse, G., et al.: SpaceEx: Scalable verification of hybrid systems. In: Gopalakrishnan, G., Qadeer, S. (eds.) CAV 2011. LNCS, vol. 6806, pp. 379–395. Springer, Heidelberg (2011)
2. Tiwari, A.: Abstractions for hybrid systems. Form. Methods Syst. Des. 32(1), 57–83 (2008)
3. Tiwari, A.: HybridSAL relational abstracter. In: Madhusudan, P., Seshia, S.A. (eds.) CAV 2012. LNCS, vol. 7358, pp. 725–731. Springer, Heidelberg (2012)
4. Eggers, A., Ramdani, N., Nedialkov, N., Fränzle, M.: Improving SAT modulo ODE for hybrid systems analysis by combining different enclosure methods. In: Barthe, G., Pardo, A., Schneider, G. (eds.) SEFM 2011. LNCS, vol. 7041, pp. 172–187. Springer, Heidelberg (2011)
5. Dang, T., Maler, O., Testylier, R.: Accurate hybridization of nonlinear systems. In: Hybrid Systems: Computation and Control, pp. 11–20. ACM (2010)
6. Akbarpour, B., Paulson, L.C.: MetiTarski: An automatic theorem prover for real-valued special functions. Journal of Automated Reasoning 44, 175–205 (2010)
7. Tiwari, A., Khanna, G.: Series of abstractions for hybrid automata. In: Tomlin, C.J., Greenstreet, M.R. (eds.) HSCC 2002. LNCS, vol. 2289, pp. 465–478. Springer, Heidelberg (2002)
8. Denman, W.: QUANTUM: Qualitative abstractions of non-polynomial models. In: Qualitative Reasoning (August 2013)
9. Ishii, D., Ueda, K., Hosobe, H.: An interval-based SAT modulo ODE solver for model checking nonlinear hybrid systems. Int. J. Softw. Tools Technol. Transf. 13(5), 449–461 (2011)

# Combining PVSio with Stateflow*

Paolo Masci[1,**], Yi Zhang[2], Paul Jones[2], Patrick Oladimeji[3], Enrico D'Urso[4],
Cinzia Bernardeschi[4], Paul Curzon[1], and Harold Thimbleby[3]

[1] School of Electronic Engineering and Computer Science
Queen Mary University of London, United Kingdom
{p.m.masci,p.curzon}@qmul.ac.uk
[2] Center for Devices and Radiological Health
U.S. Food and Drug Administration, Silver Spring, Maryland, USA
{yi.zhang2,paul.jones}@fda.hhs.gov
[3] Future Interaction Technology Lab (FITLab)
Swansea University, United Kingdom
{p.oladimeji,h.thimbleby}@swansea.ac.uk
[4] Dipartimento di Ingegneria dell'Informazione
Universitá di Pisa, Italy
e.durso@studenti.unipi.it, c.bernardeschi@unipi.it

**Abstract.** An approach to integrating PVS executable specifications
and Stateflow models is presented that uses web services to enable a
seamless exchange of simulation events and data between PVS and Stateflow. Thus, it allows the wide range of applications developed in Stateflow
to benefit from the rigor of PVS verification. The effectiveness of the approach is demonstrated on a medical device prototype, which consists of
a user interface developed in PVS and a software controller implemented
in Stateflow. Simulation on the prototype shows that simulation data
produced is exchanged smoothly between in PVSio and Stateflow.

**Keywords:** Simulation, PVSio, Stateflow.

## 1 Introduction

Model based engineering is being increasingly adopted to develop complex control systems that demand high assurance of safety and quality. Designing a
complex system often requires a combination of modeling and verification tools,
such as PVS and Simulink. Reasons include: (i) different modeling tools have
their own strengths and limitations, making them suitable for different tasks;
(ii) one modeling tool might have been used to develop legacy models that are
reused in a new project that depends on another tool; (iii) different development
teams may prefer different tools, based on their expertise.

PVS [9] and MathWorks Simulink [2] are two modeling frameworks widely
used in both industry and academia, each of which has a native simulation environment for model animation. PVSio [7] is the simulation environment of PVS.

---

* The rights of this work are transferred to the extent transferable according to title
  17 U.S.C. 105.
** Corresponding Author.

J.M. Badger and K.Y. Rozier (Eds.): NFM 2014, LNCS 8430, pp. 209–214, 2014.

Simulink enables the simulation of system models with mixed discrete and continuous control logic; its Stateflow component [3] models the discrete control of these systems.

The integration of PVS and Simulink environments can benefit system designers, allowing them to model part of the system in PVS and the rest in Simulink. However, in reality, PVSio and Simulink (and Stateflow in particular) are not interoperable. That is, PVS specifications and Stateflow models that correspond to different parts of a system cannot be simulated together. As a result, designers have to sacrifice freedom and flexibility, and model the discrete control of the entire system in either PVS higher-order logic or Stateflow.

**Contributions.** We present a new, flexible approach for integrating PVSio with Stateflow. Specifically, our approach establishes web services to create a communication infrastructure between these two frameworks. An illustrative example is presented that applies the approach to a non-trivial medical device prototype, with a user interface specified in PVS and a software controller developed in Stateflow. Simulation of the prototype demonstrates that the PVSio and Stateflow components can interoperate effectively. The tools and example models are available at http://www.pvsioweb.org .

**Related Work.** Research on integration of Stateflow with other modeling tools is generally based on the idea of performing a translation between Stateflow models and another formal specification. For example, in [5], a formal semantics of Stateflow is developed to enable the translation of Stateflow models into SAL (Symbolic Analysis Laboratory) specifications. Similarly, in [12], a tool is presented that translates Stateflow models into Lustre specifications. In [11], Stateflow models are generated from formal specifications based on Event-B semantics. A good overview of similar approaches can be found in [4, 10]. Such approaches have the advantage of allowing formal verification of whole systems.

## 2   The Approach for Integrating PVSio with Stateflow

The most significant challenge in integrating PVS with Stateflow is the lack of a publicly available formal semantics for Stateflow. As argued in [5], a formal operational semantics can be defined only for a subset of Stateflow. It is therefore not possible to faithfully translate Stateflow models that use constructs outside of the formalized subset. Similarly, Stateflow models translated from other models can use only the formalized subset of its semantics. In contrast, our approach alleviates this issue by enabling communication between PVSio and Stateflow models, rather than performing model translation. This offers designers more freedom and reliability, since no restricted translation is involved.

Our approach establishes two web services, PVSio-web [8] and Stateflow-web, to create a communication protocol between PVSio and Stateflow (see figure 1). Each model runs in parallel, sending data and events (when they occur) the other needs to continue the simulation. The protocol is "tool-neutral" in the sense that it enables seamless exchange of events and data between PVSio and Stateflow

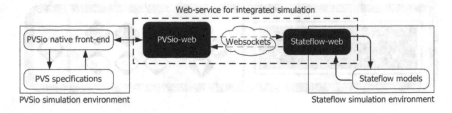

**Fig. 1.** The developed approach for integrated simulation

during simulation, without changing either of these environments. Thus, it preserves the underlying semantics of PVSio and Stateflow environments.

PVSio-web, our web-server for PVSio, comprises a *tool-specific* communication interface to connect to the PVS environment, and a *tool-neutral* communication interface to exchange simulation events with Stateflow-web. The former is tailored to the PVSio environment, while the latter utilizes the Websocket standard (a low-latency communication protocol) and encodes simulation events in the widely-used open-standard format JSON (JavaScript Object Notation). Handlers defined within PVSio-web programmatically intercept and inject simulation events, thus enabling interaction with the Stateflow environment.

Handlers in PVSio-web are implemented as JavaScript functions, which interact with PVSio by submitting PVS higher-order logic expressions to the PVSio command prompt and then reading PVSio responses. The handlers also convert PVS expressions into simulation events that can be exchanged with and understood by Stateflow-web. To ease the conversion, PVS expressions are specified as transition functions over a PVS record type `state`. Each field of `state` specifies data or commands that need to be exchanged with the Stateflow model. The original PVS theory is kept unchanged.

Stateflow-web has a similar design to PVSio-web. Its handlers are specified as either Statechart diagrams (i.e., state machines) or C++ classes. Statechart diagram handlers are used to trigger transitions in the Stateflow model based on the commands received from PVSio-web, and to update simulation data in the Stateflow model accordingly. These handlers also intercept simulation events and data produced by Stateflow and translate them into the format that PVSio-web understands. C++ handlers are responsible for exchanging simulation events with PVSio-web based on a Websocket communication library.

## 3  Example: A Patient Controlled Analgesia (PCA) Device

The effectiveness of the approach is illustrated using a medical device prototype: the Generic Patient Controlled Analgesia (PCA) pump [1]. PCA infusion pumps are widely used for delivering pain-relief drugs to patients. PCA pumps offer a patient-controlled feature ("bolus") to briefly boost drug delivery on demand.

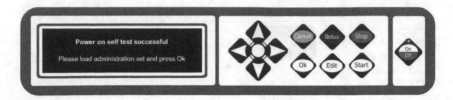

**Fig. 2.** The visual appearance of the GPCA user interface

Bolus features are controlled, so a patient cannot voluntarily give themselves too high a dose.

The aim of the Generic PCA (GPCA) pump is to capture functionalities shared by existing commercial PCA pumps and provide a common basis for healthcare stakeholders to discuss and assess their safety.

### 3.1   The Generic Patient Controlled Analgesia (GPCA) Model

The two primary software components of the GPCA pump are the *user interface* and *software controller*. While the user interface manages the interaction with the users (nurse or patient), the software controller regulates the drug infusion process and handles alarms and warnings. These two components exchange information (events and data) during model execution to simulate typical infusion scenarios. The information exchanged can be divided into four categories: *infusion parameters*, including the infusion volume and rate programmed by the user through the user interface; *user actions*, which are commands (such as start or stop infusion) that the user issues through the user interface; *current state*, the current operational status of the software controller; and *infusion status*, the status of currently active infusion, including bolus dosage, infusion rate, and the volumes of drug delivered and to be infused.

A model of the GPCA was previously developed in Stateflow, in which a naïve user interface was implemented for demonstration purposes. For this paper, we replaced this naïve user interface with a more sophisticated one [6], which was implemented as a PVS executable specification. This sophisticated user interface has been verified in PVS for basic safety properties (see [6] for details).

The objective of this study, then, is to use the presented approach to connect the PVS-based user interface with the Stateflow-based software controller, and perform a simulation over the entire GPCA pump model.

### 3.2   Simulation of GPCA Model

We were able to run simulations over the integrated GPCA model using our approach. During the simulation, users interact with the PVS-based user interface by pressing buttons and reading display elements of the graphical front-end shown in figure 2. Each user interaction is captured by PVSio-web handlers, which in turn send PVS expressions to PVSio for model animation. PVSio-web

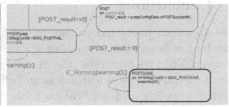

(a) PVSio simulation of the user interface    (b) Stateflow simulation of the controller

**Fig. 3.** Close-up view of the simulator's output during an execution of the GPCA

links with Stateflow-web to exchange simulation events generated by the software controller simulated in parallel within Stateflow. For example, figures 3(a) and 3(b) respectively demonstrate the simulation state in PVSio and Stateflow for the scenario where a pump successfully passes the power-on self test.

To allow the GPCA to be simulated, dedicated handlers were implemented in PVSio and in Stateflow to enable communication of events and data. On the PVSio-web side, three Javascript functions were defined:

- **Create a connection:** *gipConnect* establishes a Websocket connection with Stateflow-web on a given port. It calls functions provided by Node.js[1].
- **Messages from Stateflow-web:** *gipReceive* is invoked every time a message is received over the Websocket connection. It receives tool-neutral simulation events and data from Stateflow-web. These events and data specify the current state of the software controller and the infusion status. They are converted into PVS expressions that can be evaluated in PVSio.
- **Messages to Stateflow-web:** *gipSend* parses predefined fields of the state returned by PVSio after it has evaluated a PVS expression. The values of these fields are used to generate tool-neutral messages containing simulation events and data to be sent to the software controller.

On the Stateflow-web side, two Stateflow blocks were defined:

- **Communicating with PVSio-web:** *Websocket communication bridge* is a System Function block implemented in C++. A standard communication library is used to send and receive messages over Websocket connections. Two input buses are used to intercept the state variables of the software controller and thus generate tool-neutral simulation events and data for the user interface. Three output buses are used to inject simulation events and data received from the user interface software.
- **Driving Stateflow model:** *UI Commands dispatcher* is a Statechart block that forwards simulation events and data to appropriate blocks in the Stateflow model. This Statechart has one input line that receives commands originated from the user interface; 21 output lines for redirecting received commands to the appropriate components in the GPCA Stateflow model. The number of output lines would of course vary for different Stateflow models.

---

[1] Node.js, a popular scalable network framework, is the Javascript runtime environment used to implement PVSio-web

## 4   Conclusions

The approach presented in this paper for integrating PVS and Simulink uses standard web services to connect PVSio (the simulator of the theorem proving system PVS) and Stateflow (the discrete modeling component of Simulink). The approach thus provides a seamless and effective way to integrate these two mainstream modeling and verification tools. In this way, the hazards of translating design models composed in different tools are avoided, and fast and realistic prototyping becomes possible for designs modeled with multiple tools.

In the case study, a model written in Stateflow was connected to a formally verified user interface implemented in PVS. The success of this case study suggests an alternative way to verify Stateflow models: for example, the correctness of Stateflow models can be evaluated through PVS using methods like black-box testing (guided by PVSio) and assume-guarantee reasoning (supported by PVS).

**Acknowledgments.**   This   work   is   part   of   CHI+MED   (EPSRC   grant EP/G059063/1).

## References

1. GPCA project, http://rtg.cis.upenn.edu/medical/gpca/gpca.html
2. Mathworks Simulink, http://www.mathworks.com/products/simulink
3. Mathworks Stateflow, http://www.mathworks.com/products/stateflow
4. Chen, C., Dong, J.S., Sun, J.: A formal framework for modeling and validating Simulink diagrams. Formal Aspects of Computing 21(5), 451–483 (2009)
5. Hamon, G., Rushby, J.: An operational semantics for Stateflow. In: Wermelinger, M., Margaria-Steffen, T. (eds.) FASE 2004. LNCS, vol. 2984, pp. 229–243. Springer, Heidelberg (2004)
6. Masci, P., Ayoub, A., Curzon, P., Lee, I., Sokolsky, O., Thimbleby, H.: Model-Based Development of the Generic PCA Infusion Pump User Interface Prototype in PVS. In: Bitsch, F., Guiochet, J., Kaâniche, M. (eds.) SAFECOMP. LNCS, vol. 8153, pp. 228–240. Springer, Heidelberg (2013)
7. Muñoz, C.: Rapid prototyping in PVS. Technical Report NIA Report No. 2003-03, NASA/CR-2003-212418, National Institute of Aerospace (2003)
8. Oladimeji, P., Masci, P., Curzon, P., Thimbleby, H.: PVSio-web: A tool for rapid prototyping device user interfaces in PVS. In: 5th International Workshop on Formal Methods for Interactive Systems, FMIS 2013 (2013), Tool and application examples available at http://www.pvsioweb.org
9. Owre, S., Rushby, J.M., Shankar, N.: PVS: A Prototype Verification System. In: Kapur, D. (ed.) CADE 1992. LNCS, vol. 607, pp. 748–752. Springer, Heidelberg (1992)
10. Roy, P., Shankar, N.: SimCheck: a contract type system for Simulink. Innovations in Systems and Software Engineering 7(2), 73–83 (2011)
11. Satpathy, M., Ramesh, S., Snook, C., Singh, N.K., Butler, M.: A mixed approach to rigorous development of control designs. In: IEEE Multi-Conference on Systems and Control (MSC 2013) (August 2013)
12. Scaife, N., Sofronis, C., Caspi, P., Tripakis, S., Maraninchi, F.: Defining and translating a safe subset of Simulink/Stateflow into Lustre. In: 4th ACM International Conference on Embedded Software. ACM (2004)

# Qed. Computing What Remains to Be Proved

Loïc Correnson

CEA, LIST, Software Safety Laboratory
PC 174, 91191 Gif-sur-Yvette France
`firstname.lastname@cea.fr`

**Abstract.** We propose a framework for manipulating in a efficient way terms and formulæ in classical logic modulo theories. Qed was initially designed for the generation of proof obligations of a weakest-precondition engine for C programs inside the Frama-C framework, but it has been implemented as an independent library. Key features of Qed include on-the-fly strong normalization with various theories and maximal sharing of terms in memory. Qed is also equipped with an extensible simplification engine. We illustrate the power of our framework by the implementation of non-trivial simplifications inside the Wp plug-in of Frama-C. These optimizations have been used to prove industrial, critical embedded softwares.

## 1 Introduction

In the context of formal verification of critical softwares, the recent fantastic improvement of automated theorem provers and SMT solvers[1] opens new routes. Inside the Frama-C [2] platform, we have developed the Wp plug-in to implement an efficient *weakest precondition calculus* to formally prove a C program against its specification. The specification is written in terms of the "ANSI-C Specification Language" (ACSL) [3], which is a first-order logic system with dedicated constructs to express C properties such as pointer validity and floating point operations.

The Wp plug-in actually compile C and ACSL constructs into an internal logic representation that is finally exported to SMT solvers and other theorem provers. Thus, we need an internal system to represent and manipulate first-order logical formulæ. This is exactly what Qed has been designed for.

Designing such a library is not difficult in itself. Some datatype is needed for expressing terms and properties, combined with pretty-printing facilities to export them into several languages. This is what we implemented in our early prototypes.

However, experimental results shown that a formula can not be naively build then translated and finally sent to an external back-end prover. We actually observed limitations of such a naive approach on real life examples from critical embedded software:

- SMT solvers are quite efficient, but they are sensitive to the amount of hypotheses they receive. Having a proof for $A \to B$ does not mean you will have a proof for $A \wedge A' \to B$.

J.M. Badger and K.Y. Rozier (Eds.): NFM 2014, LNCS 8430, pp. 215–229, 2014.

- The generated formulæ are huge and deep. Without extra precautions, you often face an exponential blow-up when dumping them to disk.
- On the contrary, few transformations of the generated formulæ reduce their size and complexity in a dramatic way.

These reasons drive us in the direction of designing a dedicated system for representing and simplifying formulæ in an efficient way. We use classical techniques inspired by *preprocessing* optimizations found in various SMT solvers. However, in practice, it is not possible to rely on external preprocessors. One reason is that not all SMT solvers are equipped with such techniques. But most importantly, without on-the-fly preprocessing, the generation of proof obligations simply doesn't terminate in practice.

Moreover, applying these preprocessing facilities on-the-fly allows for non-trivial optimizations during the *weakest precondition calculus* [4], by pruning out useless branches for instance. Moreover, it allows for *domain specific preprocessing*: we designed Qed to be equipped with an extensible simplification engine, and we made it available to the end-user of Wp [5, §2.3.10].

This paper is first (§ 2) a tour and a formal presentation of the Qed framework, as a pure first-order logic system equipped with built-in theories for equality, arithmetic, arrays, records and unspecified functions. Second (§ 3), we illustrate how Qed improves in a very significant way the results of Wp plug-in inside Frama-C. We finally conclude with future research directions.

# 2    The Qed Engine

Our logical framework allows for defining and manipulating formulæ in first-order classical logic modulo theories. The key concept that drives the design of Qed is to implement only *fast* and *non-local* simplifications. This is of course incomplete, but more complex resolution techniques are left for back-end solvers.

The framework actually consists in three parts: a formally defined algebra of *term normal forms*, a collection of *smart constructors* to build *terms*, and an extensible *simplification engine*. The three components are tiedly coupled with each others.

The framework is implemented as an OCaml library, with additional features for exporting Qed formulæ to foreign systems, like Coq [6], Alt-Ergo [7] and Why-3 [8]. The efficiency of the framework relies (although not only) on a compact representation of *terms* into memory. Especially, *hash-consing* [9] is used to maximize memory sharing of equal terms. Hence, we benefit from constant-time equality and hashing over terms. Moreover, hash-consing allows for the identification of each term by an unique integer. This can be used to implement sets and maps of terms based on Patricia-trees [10], which provides the end-user of Qed with $O(n)$ unions, intersections and merges instead of the usual $O(n \log n)$ ones.

We do not present the implementation details in this article. The code is freely available under open source license together with the Frama-C distribution.[1]

In this paper, we present formally the three coupled components of the Qed framework and how they work with each others. We first introduce the internal representation of formulæ, the *term* algebra. Then, we define the *smart constructors* for building *terms*, with the associated normalization algorithms. Finally, we present the extensible *simplification engine*.

## 2.1 Terms Algebra

The internal representation of *terms* consists in an inductive datatype quotiented by normalization invariants. The Qed *smart constructors* are then especially designed to enforce those invariants.

The datatype of *terms* ($a \in \mathcal{L}$) is presented in Figure 1. It is parametrized by datatypes for the symbols identifying variable names ($x \in \mathcal{X}$), record's field names ($\mathtt{f} \in \mathtt{Fd}$) and user-defined or unspecified functions ($f \in \mathcal{F}$). The notation $\overline{a}$ stands for finite lists of terms, that is, $\overline{a} = a_1, \ldots, a_n$ for some $n \geq 0$.

$$a \in \mathcal{L} ::=$$

| | | |
|---|---|---|
| *Equality* | *Quantifiers* | *Functions* |
| $\mid a = a \mid a \neq a$ | $\mid x \mid \forall x.a \mid \exists x.a$ | $\mid f(\overline{a})$ |

| *Logic* | |
|---|---|
| $\mid \mathsf{true} \mid \mathsf{false}$ | Booleans |
| $\mid \wedge \overline{a} \mid \vee \overline{a}$ | Conjunction, Disjunction |
| $\mid \wedge \overline{a} \rightarrow a$ | Implication |
| $\mid \neg a$ | Negation |
| $\mid a\,?\,a:a$ | If-then-else |

| *Arithmetic* | |
|---|---|
| $\mid k \in \mathbf{Z} \mid q \in \mathbf{Q}$ | Constants |
| $\mid a \leq a \mid a < a$ | Inequalities |
| $\mid k.a \mid \Sigma\,\overline{a} \mid \Pi\,\overline{a}$ | Factors, Sums & Products |

| *Arrays & Records* | |
|---|---|
| $\mid a[a]$ | Access |
| $\mid a[a \mapsto a]$ | Updates |
| $\mid a.\mathtt{f}$ | Field Access |
| $\mid \{\mathtt{f} \mapsto a\,;\ldots\}$ | Records |

**Fig. 1.** Qed Terms Algebra

---

[1] From `http://frama-c.com/download/frama-c-Fluorine-20130601.tar.gz`, Qed sources are provided in the self-contained sub-directory `src/wp/qed`.

In the flow of the text, we would write Qed formulæ within quotes, like «$a \leq b$», to distinguish the *terms* from their *semantics*. For instance, we must read $0 < x$ as the usual math property that $x$ is positive, and «$0 < x$» as a term in $\mathcal{L}$ where variable «$x$» is compared to zero. Conversely, we denote by $[\![\, a\,]\!]$ the semantics in usual mathematics of formulæ «$a$».

We assume all symbols to be equipped with total orders such that there is an induced total order $a \preceq b$. The constant-time structural equality $a \equiv b$ on terms is provided by hash-consing. To summarize our notations:

| | | | |
|---|---|---|---|
| «$a$» | Term in $\mathcal{L}$ | $[\![\, a\,]\!]$ | Semantics of $a \in \mathcal{L}$ |
| $a \preceq b$ | Total order | $a \equiv b$ | Structural (and physical) equality |

The strict order $a \prec b$ defined by $(a \preceq b \wedge a \not\equiv b)$ is also used. For maintaining the normalization invariants of terms, we introduce $\mathsf{ac}(\overline{a})$ and $\mathsf{ac}^*(\overline{a})$ to denote non-empty sorted lists with or without repetitions:

$$\mathsf{ac}(a_1 \ldots a_n) \quad \Leftrightarrow \quad 0 < n \wedge \forall i, j \in 1..n, \ i < j \Rightarrow a_i \prec a_j$$
$$\mathsf{ac}^*(a_1 \ldots a_n) \quad \Leftrightarrow \quad 0 < n \wedge \forall i, j \in 1..n, \ i < j \Rightarrow a_i \preceq a_j$$

We now investigate the various normal forms of $a \in \mathcal{L}$ and the associated invariants.

*Equality.* Terms «$a = b$» and «$a \neq b$» are quotiented by $a \prec b$ and $[\![\, a\,]\!] \neq [\![\, b\,]\!]$ when the built-in theories of Qed applies. For instance, «$1 = 2$» is *not* a Qed normal term.

*Quantifiers.* Terms «$\forall x.a$» and «$\exists x.a$» can only be formed if $x$ appears free in $a$. Structural equality ($\equiv$) in $\mathcal{L}$ is *not* quotiented by $\alpha$-conversion. This is a choice we made because in practice such equalities are rare and $\alpha$-conversion can be costly [11]. For instance, using De-Bruijn indices requires lambda liftings [12] which are *not* local transformations.

*Logic.* Boolean connectives are $n$-ary operators quotiented with $\mathsf{ac}^*$ arguments. Moreover, there are never two-arguments $a$ and $b$ of logical connectives such that we can decide $[\![\, a\,]\!] \Leftrightarrow \neg [\![\, b\,]\!]$ with Qed. Moreover, there is no duplication of *boolean* term operators and logical connectives for *properties* as usual in first-order logic. Rather, we use a two-sorted typing system to recover this distinction when it is required, for instance, to send a Qed formula to a SMT-solver.

*Arithmetic.* We choose $n$-ary sums and products operators quotiented by $\mathsf{ac}$ arguments. Linear forms are maximally flattened and factorized. For instance, it is not possible to have formula «$1 - x \leq x - y$», but we would have «$y < 2.x$» instead (provided $x$ and $y$ are integers). These operators apply to both integer and real values, which case can be disambiguated by typing when necessary.

*Arrays.* The theory of functional arrays [13] is built-in in Qed. Access-updates are reduced whenever equality can be decided with Qed. Hence, «$m[a \mapsto v][b]$» is reduced into «$m[b]$» or «$v$» whenever $[\![\, a = b\,]\!]$ can be decided.

*Records.* The theory of records is built-in in Qed. We do not choose to represent field-update terms, since they can always be represented by extensive reconstruction of the record. This choice makes the computation of normal forms for records more local.

*Unspecified Functions.* We decided to never inline a *definition* of a function symbol $f \in \mathcal{F}$. Although, this can be done using the extensible simplification engine. However, function symbols $f \in \mathcal{F}$ can be attributed with *algebraic* properties, such as injectivity, commutativity, associativity, neutral elements and such. This leads to many normalizations and simplifications that will be discussed with the associated *smart constructors*.

## 2.2 Smart Constructors and Normalizations

To build formulæ with the Qed framework, one must use the provided *smart constructors* listed in Figure 2. Thus, it is not possible to forge arbitrary terms $a \in \mathcal{L}$ that would violate the expected invariants. Moreover, since all the simplifications in the framework are *local*, we always obtain fully normalized terms on-the-fly.

| Equality | | Arithmetic | | Logic | |
|---|---|---|---|---|---|
| eq : | $a, a \to a$ | int : | $\mathbf{Z} \to a$ | true : | $a$ |
| neq : | $a, a \to a$ | real : | $\mathbf{Q} \to a$ | false : | $a$ |
| | | add : | $a, a \to a$ | not : | $a \to a$ |
| **Variables** | | sub : | $a, a \to a$ | and : | $a, a \to a$ |
| var : | $x \to a$ | times : | $\mathbf{Z}, a \to a$ | or : | $a, a \to a$ |
| forall : | $x, a \to a$ | mul : | $a, a \to a$ | imply : | $a, a \to a$ |
| exists : | $x, a \to a$ | leq : | $a, a \to a$ | equiv : | $a, a \to a$ |
| | | lt : | $a, a \to a$ | ite : | $a, a, a \to a$ |
| **Functions** | | **Arrays** | | **Records** | |
| call : | $f, \overline{a} \to a$ | get : | $a, a \to a$ | field : | $a, \mathbf{f} \to a$ |
| | | set : | $a, a, a \to a$ | record : | $(\mathbf{f}_i, a_i)_i \to a$ |

**Fig. 2.** Qed Smart Constructors (API)

In this section, we investigate the normalizations computed by the smart constructors of Qed framework. We first discuss boolean normalizations and arithmetic ones. Then, functions, arrays and records will be discussed in turn. Each theory $\mathcal{T}$ will define smart constructors $\mathsf{eq}_{\mathcal{T}}$ and $\mathsf{neq}_{\mathcal{T}}$ for equalities, which will be finally merged together into the smart constructor for equality on the entire algebra $\mathcal{L}$.

**Logic.** The normalization of logical connectives is based on list of literals packed with their negation, like $(a, \neg a)$. Equipped with a suitable order, such a representation allows for fast detection of $a$ and $\neg a$ among arguments of logical connectives. This leads to frequent calls to the smart constructor $\mathsf{not}(a)$ and, in the OCaml implementation, we use a cache to amortize this cost.

We use recursive definitions to extract list of literals from terms. But thanks to invariants in the term algebra, it is always limited at 2-depth recursive calls. We also use an exception (denoted by $\bot_{\mathsf{Absorbing}}$) to handle absorbing elements. This leads to the following flattening accumulative functions (in Haskell flavor):

$$
\begin{array}{ll}
\mathsf{lit}_\vee \; \ll \vee \, \bar{a} \gg \; l = \mathsf{fold} \; \mathsf{lit}_\vee \; \bar{a} \; l & \qquad \mathsf{lit}_\wedge \; \ll \wedge \, \bar{a} \gg \; l = \mathsf{fold} \; \mathsf{lit}_\wedge \; \bar{a} \; l \\
\mathsf{lit}_\vee \; \ll \mathsf{true} \gg \; l = \bot_{\mathsf{Absorbing}} & \qquad \mathsf{lit}_\wedge \; \ll \mathsf{false} \gg \; l = \bot_{\mathsf{Absorbing}} \\
\mathsf{lit}_\vee \; \ll \mathsf{false} \gg \; l = l & \qquad \mathsf{lit}_\wedge \; \ll \mathsf{true} \gg \; l = l \\
\mathsf{lit}_\vee \quad a \qquad l = (a, \mathsf{not}\; a) : l & \qquad \mathsf{lit}_\wedge \quad a \qquad l = (a, \mathsf{not}\; a) : l
\end{array}
$$

For instance, given the formula $a = \mathsf{and}(b, \mathsf{not}\, c)$, we obtain the list of and-literals $\mathsf{lit}_\wedge \; a \; [] = [b, \mathsf{not}\; b; \mathsf{not}\; c, \mathsf{not}(\mathsf{not}\; c)]$. Remark here that the double negation will be simplified on-the-fly by the $\mathsf{not}$ smart-constructor.

These lists of literals are then sorted in order for $a$ and $(\neg a)$ to appear side by side. For this purpose, we use a tricky relation $(\mathcal{R}_{\mathsf{id}})$ based on the hash-consed unique identifiers of terms computed during hash-consing:

$$
(a, a') \; \mathcal{R}_{\mathsf{id}} \; (b, b') \; \Leftrightarrow \; \min(a_{\mathsf{id}}, a'_{\mathsf{id}}) \leq \min(b_{\mathsf{id}}, b'_{\mathsf{id}})
$$

The relation $\mathcal{R}_{\mathsf{id}}$ is clearly a total order on pairs of terms. Thus we can sort list of literals with it. Moreover, we have $(a, b) \; \mathcal{R}_{\mathsf{id}} \; (b, a)$ for all terms $a$ and $b$, such that pairs $(a, \neg a)$ and $(\neg a, a)$ are equal modulo $\mathcal{R}_{\mathsf{id}}$. Thus, opposite literals will be placed side-by-side in the sorted list.

Reducing lists of literals is surprisingly the same algorithm for conjunctions and disjunctions. The normalizations are based on the fact that, for any boolean property $\varphi$, both $(\varphi \vee \neg\varphi)$ and $(\varphi \wedge \neg\varphi)$ simplify to their associated absorbing elements, respectively $\mathsf{true}$ and $\mathsf{false}$. The dual normalization uses the simplification of both $(\varphi \vee \varphi)$ and $(\varphi \wedge \varphi)$ into $\varphi$. For this purpose, we define weak versions of $(a \Leftrightarrow b)$ and $(a \Leftrightarrow \neg b)$, respectively defined as follows:

$$
\begin{array}{l}
\mathsf{eqv}_{\mathsf{lit}} \; (a, a') \; (b, b') = (a \equiv b) \\
\mathsf{neq}_{\mathsf{lit}} \; (a, a') \; (b, b') = (a \equiv b') \vee (a' \equiv b)
\end{array}
$$

Then, provided $[\![a']\!] = \neg[\![a]\!]$ and $[\![b']\!] = \neg[\![b]\!]$ (which is the case for literals), the two following properties hold:

$$
\begin{array}{lll}
\mathsf{eqv}_{\mathsf{lit}} \; (a, a') \; (b, b') & \Rightarrow & [\![a]\!] \Leftrightarrow [\![b]\!] \\
\mathsf{neq}_{\mathsf{lit}} \; (a, a') \; (b, b') & \Rightarrow & [\![a]\!] \Leftrightarrow \neg[\![b]\!]
\end{array}
$$

The reduction of both conjunction and disjunction of literals is then implemented by one single function $\mathsf{group}$, as follows:

$$
\begin{array}{ll}
\mathsf{group} \; \varphi : \psi : l \mid \mathsf{eqv}_{\mathsf{lit}} \; \varphi \; \psi = \mathsf{group} \; (\psi : l) & \qquad \mathsf{group} \; \varphi : l = \varphi : \mathsf{group} \; l \\
\mathsf{group} \; \varphi : \psi : l \mid \mathsf{neq}_{\mathsf{lit}} \; \varphi \; \psi = \bot_{\mathsf{Absorbant}} & \qquad \mathsf{group} \; [] \quad = []
\end{array}
$$

Putting every ingredient together, we define the smart constructors and and or in terms of a generic function $\mathsf{connective}_{\otimes,1,0}$ for connective $\otimes$ with neutral $\mathbf{1}$ and absorbing element $\mathbf{0}$:

$$\mathsf{and} = \mathsf{connective}_{\wedge,\mathsf{true},\mathsf{false}} \qquad \mathsf{or} = \mathsf{connective}_{\vee,\mathsf{false},\mathsf{true}}$$

The generic function $\mathsf{connective}_{\otimes,1,0}$ is in turn defined by flattening, sorting and grouping the $\otimes$-literals as follows:

$$\mathsf{connective}_{\otimes,1,0}(a,b) =$$
$$\mathsf{try\ let}\ p = \mathsf{group} \circ \mathsf{sort}\ \mathcal{R}_{\mathsf{id}}\ (\mathsf{lit}_\otimes\ a\ (\mathsf{lit}_\otimes\ b\ [\,]))\ \mathsf{in}$$
$$\mathsf{if}\ p = [\,]\ \mathsf{then}\ \mathbf{1}\ \mathsf{else}$$
$$\mathsf{let}\ \bar{a} = \mathsf{sort}\ (\preceq) \circ \mathsf{map\ fst}\ p\ \mathsf{in}\ «\otimes \bar{a}»$$
$$\mathsf{with}\ \bot_{\mathsf{Absorbing}} \to \mathbf{0}$$

The smart constructor for implication is more direct. Recall that the normal form of implication is $«\wedge \bar{a} \to a»$. We only need to filter out the list of hypotheses on the left of $(\to)$ against the conclusion and its negation. Below are two examples of the reduction rules implemented for the imply smart constructor:

$$\mathsf{imply}\ «\wedge \bar{a}»\ b\ \mid\ (\exists i, a_i \equiv b) = «\mathsf{true}»$$
$$\mathsf{imply}\ «\wedge \bar{a}»\ b = «\wedge [a_j | a_j \not\equiv \mathsf{not}\ b] \to b»$$

Equivalence is the same than equality in the boolean theory. The contribution of boolean theory to equality smart constructors is defined below:

$$\mathsf{eq}_\mathcal{B}\ «\mathsf{true}»\ a = a \qquad \mathsf{eq}_\mathcal{B}\ «\mathsf{false}»\ a = \mathsf{not}\ a$$
$$\mathsf{eq}_\mathcal{B}\ a\ b\ \mid\ (a \equiv \mathsf{not}\ b) = «\mathsf{false}»$$

Finally, we define the smart constructor for negation recursively with all the other connectives. We do not present all the rules here by lack of place. Let us just mention the transformation of $\mathsf{not}\,(a \neq b)$ into $(a = b)$, $\mathsf{not}\,(a \leq b)$ into $(b < a)$, among many other similar or dual patterns.

**Arithmetic.** The normalization of arithmetic terms relies on computing with linear forms of terms:

$$\mathsf{linear}(a) = c + \sum_{i=1}^{n} k_i.a_i \quad \mathsf{with}\ c, k_i \in \mathbf{Z}$$

Maximal linear forms of terms are easy to compute in an efficient way with lists of monoms $(k, a)$, in the same spirit than for logical connectives. For linear complexity, we use an accumulative variant of linear, denoted by lin, such that:

$$\mathsf{lin}\ k\ a\ L = k.\,\mathsf{linear}(a) + L$$

Conversely, it is easy to inject linear forms into well-formed terms as follows:

$$\mathsf{inj}_\Sigma \left( c + \sum_{i=1}^{n} k_i.a_i \right) = «\Sigma \bar{s}» \quad \mathsf{where} \quad \begin{cases} s_0 = «c» \\ s_i = «k.a_i», i \in 1..n \end{cases}$$

With list implementation, $\mathsf{inj}_\Sigma$ relies on sorting and compacting the list of monoms to obtain a normalized linear form. Smart constructors for arithmetic are then straightforward definitions:

$$
\begin{array}{l}
\mathsf{add}(a,b) = \mathsf{inj}_\Sigma(\mathsf{lin}\ 1\ a\ (\mathsf{lin}\ 1\ b\ [])) \\
\mathsf{sub}(a,b) = \mathsf{inj}_\Sigma(\mathsf{lin}\ 1\ a\ (\mathsf{lin}\ \text{-}1\ b\ [])) \\
\mathsf{times}(k,a) = \mathsf{inj}_\Sigma(\mathsf{lin}\ k\ a)
\end{array}
$$

Comparisons, including equalities and inequalities, are also performed with linear forms using a generic comparison function $\mathsf{cmp}_\mathcal{R}$ for relation $\mathcal{R}$:

$$
\mathsf{leq} = \mathsf{cmp}_\leq \quad \mathsf{lt} = \mathsf{cmp}_< \quad \mathsf{eq}_\mathcal{A} = \mathsf{cmp}_= \quad \mathsf{neq}_\mathcal{A} = \mathsf{cmp}_{\neq}
$$

For the definition of this generic comparison function, we first introduce a dispatching function that takes a linear form $L$ and separate positive from negative factors:

$$
\mathsf{dispatch}\left(c + \sum_{i=1}^n k_i.a_i\right) = \left(c^\oplus + \sum_{i=1}^n k_i^\oplus.a_i\ ,\ c^\ominus + \sum_{i=1}^n k_i^\ominus.a_i\right)
$$

where $c^\oplus = \max(c,0)$ and $c^\ominus = \max(-c,0)$. Then, we lift any arithmetic comparison $\mathcal{R}$ to linear forms with:

$$
\mathsf{lift}_\mathcal{R}(L^\oplus, L^\ominus)\ =\ \ll L^\oplus\ \mathcal{R}\ L^\ominus \gg \quad \text{where typically} \quad L^\oplus, L^\ominus = \mathsf{dispatch}(L)
$$

When linear forms are reduced to constants $c$ and $c'$, we compute the boolean result of $(c\mathcal{R}c')$ and turn it into « true » or « false ». We also introduce few additional simplifications when both $L^\oplus$ and $L^\ominus$ are in $\mathbf{Z}$ (rather than in $\mathbf{R}$) in order to catch off-by-one comparisons ; typically $1 + a < b$ reduces to $a \leq b$.

Finally, the generic comparison operator $\mathsf{cmp}_\mathcal{R}$ is defined by:

$$
\mathsf{cmp}_\mathcal{R}(a,b) = \mathsf{lift}_\mathcal{R} \circ \mathsf{dispatch} \circ \mathsf{inj}_\Sigma(\mathsf{lin}\ 1\ a\ (\mathsf{lin}\ \text{-}1\ b\ []))
$$

Product are conducted in a similar, although simpler way. The simplification is here based on generalized products rather than linear forms:

$$
\mathsf{product}(a) = k.\prod_{i=1}^n a_i \quad \text{and, conversely:} \quad \mathsf{inj}_\Pi\left(k.\prod_{i=1}^n a_i\right) = \ll k.\Pi\ \overline{a} \gg
$$

Their implementation with lists are straightforward. We introduce an accumulative variant of product, named prod such that:

$$
\mathsf{prod}\ a\ (k,l) = k.\mathsf{product}(a) \times l
$$

Finally, the smart constructor for multiplication is:

$$
\mathsf{mul}(a,b) = \mathsf{inj}_\Pi \circ \mathsf{sort}\ (\preceq)\ (\mathsf{prod}\ a\ (\mathsf{prod}\ b\ []))
$$

**Arrays and Records.** The theories for arrays and records are similar and we present them together. For arrays, we need to decide whether two indices $a$ and $b$ are equal. Qed is not able to decide equality in all case, so we rely on a weak decision instead, *ie.* a sound but incomplete approximation of $[\![\,a = b\,]\!]$. Let us define:

$$a =_{\text{true}} b \quad \Leftrightarrow \quad \text{eq}(a, b) \equiv \text{«\,true\,»}$$
$$a =_{\text{false}} b \quad \Leftrightarrow \quad \text{eq}(a, b) \equiv \text{«\,false\,»}$$

The simplifications rules used by the smart constructors for arrays are then:

$$
\begin{array}{ll}
\text{get «}\, a[b \mapsto c]\, \text{»}\ b' & | \ (b =_{\text{true}} b') = c \\
\text{get «}\, a[b \mapsto c]\, \text{»}\ b' & | \ (b =_{\text{false}} b') = \text{get } a\ b' \\
\text{set «}\, a[b \mapsto c]\, \text{»}\ b'\ c' & | \ (b =_{\text{true}} b') = \text{«}\, a[b \mapsto c']\, \text{»}
\end{array}
$$

Records are more complete since we can always decide for field equality. But there is no mystery in them. We omit here the details of the normalization algorithms.

There is no special equalities for arrays. For records, we rely on the fact that two records are equal if and only they have equal field entries. More precisely, given $r = (\mathbf{f}_i, a_i)_{i \in 1..n}$ and $r' = (\mathbf{f}'_j, a'_j)_{j \in 1..m}$, we introduce:

$$
\begin{array}{ll}
\text{eq}_{\text{Fd}}\, \text{«}\, \{r\}\, \text{»}\ \text{«}\, \{r'\}\, \text{»} & \\
\quad = \text{«\,false\,»} & \text{when } n \neq m \ \vee\ \exists k,\ \mathbf{f}_k \neq \mathbf{f}'_k \\
\quad = \text{and}(\,\overline{e}\,) & \text{otherwise, where } \forall k,\ e_k = \text{eq}(a_i, a'_i)
\end{array}
$$

**Function Properties.** We enrich the standard theory of unspecified functions by attributing function symbols $f \in \mathcal{F}$ with algebraic properties. The structural equality ($\equiv$) over terms $a \in \mathcal{L}$ implements directly the general equality for unspecified functions. We enrich it with additional equalities when $f$ is injective and when it is a constructor of an abstract datatype.

Sometimes, the function $f$ is just the $n$-ary notation for some unspecified operator ($\odot$), that is, $f(\overline{x}) = x_1 \odot \ldots \odot x_n$. In this case, $f$ can be attributed with groupoid properties like associativity and such.

The available properties, for operators, injections and constructors, are listed in Figure 3. Each function can be attributed with zero, one or several properties, although you can not mix operator properties with non-operator ones.

Smart constructors for functions take into account those properties in two ways. Groupoid properties are used to flatten the list of arguments (associativity), to sort them with respect to ($\preceq$) (commutativity) and to filter out absorbing and neutral elements, whenever each case applies. The other properties are used to simplify equalities between terms $\text{«}\, f(\overline{a})\, \text{»}$ and $\text{«}\, f'(\overline{a}')\, \text{»}$. Implementation is based on list manipulations similar to linear forms and logical connectives.

**Equalities.** The built-in theories of Qed define specific smart constructors for equality, that we need to merge into a single one. Moreover, equality as an equivalence relation also requires general normalizations to be applied. This is

Properties for unspecified function $f$:

| | |
|---|---|
| injective: | $f(\overline{x}) = f(\overline{y}) \Leftrightarrow \forall i,\, x_i = y_i$ |
| constructor: | $f(\overline{x}) = g(\overline{y}) \Leftrightarrow f = g \,\wedge\, \forall i,\, x_i = y_i$ |

Properties for unspecified operator $f(\overline{x}) = x_1 \odot \ldots \odot x_n$:

| | |
|---|---|
| commutative: | $x \odot y = y \odot x$ |
| associative: | $x \odot (y \odot z) = (x \odot y) \odot z$ |
| neutral($e$): | $e \odot x = x \odot e = x$ |
| absorbant($e$): | $e \odot x = x \odot e = e$ |
| inversible: | $x \odot y = x \odot z \Leftrightarrow y = z \Leftrightarrow y \odot x = z \odot x$ |

**Fig. 3.** Properties for unspecified functions

performed by smart constructor $\mathsf{eq}_{\mathcal{E}}$ which simplifies equal terms modulo ($\equiv$) and ensures that in « $a = b$ », we get ($a \prec b$).

Combining equalities from all theories is achieved by applying each specific smart constructors in a staged way. Starting with the smart constructor of theory $\mathcal{T}$, if $\mathsf{eq}_{\mathcal{T}}(a, b) = $ « $a' = b'$ », we pass the residual equality through the next theory $\mathsf{eq}_{\mathcal{T}'}(a', b')$, and so on.

In this process, several optimizations are performed to avoid unnecessary calls to dedicated smart constructors. The global stack is: first, use pure equality $\mathsf{eq}_{\mathcal{E}}$; then, solve arithmetic with $\mathsf{eq}_{\mathcal{A}}$ or solve boolean equalities with $\mathsf{eq}_{\mathcal{B}}$; finally, depending on which theory applies, use $\mathsf{eq}_{\mathsf{Fd}}$ for records or $\mathsf{eq}_{\mathcal{F}}$ for functions.

## 2.3    Extensible Simplifier

One of the non-common features of Qed framework is its ability to be extended with user-supplied simplification routines. We have designed three possible entry points for additional normalizations, based on unspecified functions $f \in \mathcal{F}$:

- when applying a function « $f(\overline{a})$ » ;
- for simplifying equalities « $a = f(\overline{a})$ » and « $f(\overline{a}) = a$ » ;
- or inequalities « $a \leq f(\overline{a})$ » and « $f(\overline{a}) \leq a$ ».

Restricting these entry points to terms with a function symbol $f$ at head is a design choice. It reduces the cost of finding routine, try to run them, and fallback to default implementation. In a similar way, we allow only *one* simplification routine per function symbol $f$ and entry point. If several routines are desired, packing them with priorities and other features is left to the end-user of the framework, while keeping Qed simple and robust.

Regarding the implementation, calls to user-supplied simplification routines are staged *after* the default normalization routines and *before* hash-consing is performed. Although user-supplied simplification routines can be arbitrary OCaml code, there are some design rules to consider. We investigate them in turn.

*Result.* Simplification routines build terms using only the Qed smart constructors. A partial simplification routine may raise an exception $\perp_{\mathsf{Default}}$ to interrupt the simplification and makes Qed fallback to the default smart-constructor.

*Recursion.* To avoid infinite loops, Qed enforces a fallback to default smart constructors after a given depth of recursion with the same routine (2 in practice). This is consistent with the local complexity of all normalizers in the framework.

*Decisions.* Whenever a simplification needs to decide between several cases, it is recommended to build a Qed term instead, and decide upon its normalized form. For instance, to decide whether a sub-term $a$ is positive, simply build the term leq «$0$» $a$ and compare its normal form «true» and «false». This allows for several simplification routines to cooperate with each others.

*Example.* For instance, assume the symbol $f_{\mathsf{abs}}$ is specified to compute the absolute value of real and integral numbers. One may implement the following routine for simplifying $f_{\mathsf{abs}}$ expressions:

$$
\begin{aligned}
\mathsf{call}_{\mathsf{abs}}\ a \ = \ &\mathsf{match}\ (\mathsf{leq}\ «\,0\,»\ a)\ \mathsf{with} \\
&|\ «\,\mathsf{true}\,» \ \to \ a \\
&|\ «\,\mathsf{false}\,» \ \to \ \mathsf{times}\ «\,\text{-}1\,»\ a \\
&|\ \quad\_\quad \ \to \ \perp_{\mathsf{Default}}
\end{aligned}
$$

To simplify notations, let us introduce $\mathsf{abs}(a) = \mathsf{call}(f_{\mathsf{abs}}, [a])$. This makes $\mathsf{abs}(«\,\text{-}1\,»)$ to simplify into «$1$» as expected. If we now add a routine for simplifying comparisons with symbols $f_{\mathsf{abs}}$:

$$
\begin{aligned}
\mathsf{leq}_{\mathsf{abs}}\ «\,0\,»\ «\,f_{\mathsf{abs}}(a)\,» \ &= \ \mathsf{true} \\
\mathsf{leq}_{\mathsf{abs}}\ «\,f_{\mathsf{abs}}(a)\,»\ «\,0\,» \ &= \ \mathsf{eq}\ a\ «\,0\,» \\
\mathsf{leq}_{\mathsf{abs}}\ a\ b \ &= \ \perp_{\mathsf{Default}}
\end{aligned}
$$

Then we get the simplification of $\mathsf{abs}(\mathsf{abs}(a))$ into $\mathsf{abs}(a)$ for free by mutual interaction of the two simplification routines.

# 3   Experimental Results

In this section, we illustrate how Qed has been used to successfully empower the efficiency of the Wp plug-in of Frama-C. Recall from the introduction that Wp computes *weakest preconditions* on C programs annotated by ACSL contracts. The primary outcome of Wp is *proof obligations*, that are first-order logic formulæ. If one succeed in *proving* all those formulæ, then weakest precondition calculus entails that the C program is correct with respect to its specification.

The introduction of Qed as the internal implementation for building and managing the proof obligations has leverage the efficiency of Wp in many ways. First, it allows up to implement effectively a *linear* [14] weakest precondition calculus with on-the-fly *maximal memory sharing*. On programs with a lot of paths in the

| | Goals | Alt-Ergo | Coq | | Goals | Qed | Alt-Ergo |
|---|---|---|---|---|---|---|---|
| A | 13 | 13 | - | | 11 | 11 | - |
| B | 35 | 14 | 17 | | 22 | 18 | 3 |
| C | 54 | 24 | 30 | | 25 | 25 | - |
| D | | Memory out | | | 172 | 116 | 56 |
| Case Study | | Without Qed | | | | After Qed | |

**Fig. 4.** Impact of Qed on Wp

control flow graph, like successive conditionals, this is absolutely necessary to avoid an exponential growth of proof obligations. Second, surprisingly, normalizations makes "not-so-few" proof obligations to simplifies into «true». Hence, Qed became our primary back-end solver in practice.

An experiment conducted before and after the introduction of Qed is depicted in Figure 4. It depicts four simple case studies, that are small C routines from industrial embedded systems, and our attempts to discharge the generated proof obligations (goals). The figures show that introduction of Qed actually avoid exponential growth and demonstrate its capability to discharge proofs. Without Qed, hardly 50% of the goals must be discharged by hand with the Coq proof assistant. For case-study named 'D', Wp is not even capable of generating the proof obligations. Introducing Qed solves most of these issues, however one proof obligation is still not discharged in the 'B' case study.

We then conducted a much larger experiment on a full bench of real industrial codes from avionics and energy industries. These case studies can not be disclosed here because of industrial agreements. The bench consists of 15 case studies, cumulating 60,000 lines of code and specifications which generates up to 10,000 proof obligations to be discharged. Of course, on such a large-scale experiment, we encountered non-generated goals and non-discharged ones. This can be the consequence of bugs, inefficiencies and over-complicated goals.

The results of the experiment on different variants of Wp and Qed are depicted in Figure 5. The graphics shows the number of proof obligations actually generated, and those discharged by Qed and Alt-Ergo. The graphics also provides the number of goals where Alt-Ergo has been interrupted, and those where it returns without deciding the validity of the proof obligation.

The various versions we experimented with this bench illustrate the benefit from non-trivial optimizations implemented in Wp thanks to the Qed framework:

WP. The base version of Wp with Qed (beginning of the experiment).
VAR. Transformation of equalities introduced by Wp into substitutions.
CST. Addition of simplification routines for machine-integer computations.
LET. Correction of an inefficiency issue with in-memory sharing.
LIT. Propagation of literals by substitutions.
CUT. Pruning proof obligations by eliminating irrelevant chunks of code.

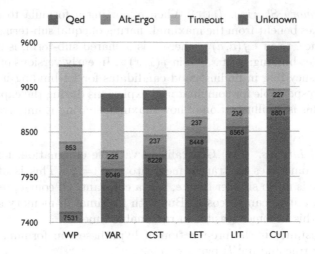

**Fig. 5.** Impact of Wp optimizations based on Qed

As illustrated by the results over the bench, each version improves the results in several ways. The number of generated proof obligations is lower when different control-flow paths can be merged thanks to simplifications during the weakest precondition calculus. On the other hand, inefficiency bugs may prevent Wp from generating proof obligations, leaving part of the specifications unproved. More goals are discharged by Qed after each optimization we introduced. And sometimes, residual goals are more efficiently discharged by Alt-Ergo, meaning that Qed has simplified them.

We now investigate in more details the experimented optimizations, and how they take benefit from the Qed framework.

*Turning Equalities into Substitutions.* (VAR) During linear weakest precondition calculus, the side effects of the program are transformed into a kind of static single assignment form. This generates a huge number of intermediate variables, each receiving a small expression. This leads to many $(x = e)$ hypotheses in the formulæ to prove. But, formula $\forall x, x = e \to \varphi$ can be transformed into $\varphi[x := e]$ by substitution (provided $x$ does not appear free in $e$). This is a well known transformation named variable elimination. But from the Qed point of view, this introduces many opportunities to perform aggressive normalization. For instance, $\forall x, x = 4 \to 0 \le x$ does not simplifies locally in Qed, but simplifies into true after substitution.

*Simplification Routines.* (CST) To model the semantics of C machine integers, the Wp introduces unspecified symbols with suitable properties in order for SMT solvers to reason with. However, in many cases, these symbols are fed with constant integer values. Hence, we can compute on-the-fly the resulting values. For instance, when converting constants from one integer type into another. Together with variable elimination, this makes significant improvements.

*Exploiting Memory Sharing.* (LET) When exporting a formula to an external solver, Qed takes benefit from the maximal sharing of equal sub-terms into memory. For instance, term « $f(a,a)$ » where $a$ is a shared sub-term, is rendered by introducing a let-binding: « let $x = a$ in $f(x,x)$ ». In early versions of Qed, there was an inefficiency bug in finding good candidates for let-binding introduction. This bug was responsible for combinatorial explosions during the export of proof obligations. This is an illustration of how maximal sharing is important in practice.

*Propagation of Literals.* (LIT) Generalizing variable elimination, formula $(e = c) \rightarrow \varphi$ may sometimes be transformed into $\varphi[e := c]$. This is of particular interest when $c$ is much simpler than $e$, say, a constant. Of course, recognizing a sub-expression $e$ in $\varphi$ can be costly. But with maximal in-memory sharing and hash-consing, this becomes feasible in reasonable time.

A special instance is the propagation of hypotheses: in formula $l \rightarrow \varphi$, we substitute $l$ by true and not($l$) by false in $\varphi$.

Moreover, we also propagate consequences inequalities: $a < b$ also propagates $a \leq b$ and $a \neq b$. Finally, we also detect both $a \leq b$ and $b \leq a$ and turn them into $a = b$. This combines well with the normalization of inequalities performed by Qed, since this makes variants of the same literal to be equal and substituted. For instance, it is often the case that at the end of a loop, the loop counter will be replaced with its final value, which introduces more opportunities for further variable eliminations.

However, in $\psi \rightarrow l \rightarrow \varphi$, we only propagate $l$ from left-to-right, in $\varphi$ only, because propagation in both directions is exponential.

*Pruning Contradictory Branches.* (CUT) A typical program has many conditionals statements to detect error cases that shortcuts normal computations. When proving a property of such a program, we generally have a specification such as "*unless an error condition is raised, some property $\varphi$ holds.*" This leads to formulæ with the following form:

$$(d ? \psi^+ : \psi^-) \rightarrow (e \rightarrow \varphi)$$

There are two opportunities for simplifications in this formula. First, we can put $e$ in head of the goal, such that forward propagation of literals described above has a chance to filter out non relevant cases. Then, we may investigate whether $(e \wedge d \wedge \psi^+)$ or $(e \wedge \neg d \wedge \psi^-)$ leads to a contradiction by simplification with Qed. Whenever it is the case, the corresponding branch can be removed.

This is effective in practice, as shown by our experiments. However, it must be pointed out that this only occurs because Qed performs many normalizations in the background.

## 4    Conclusion

Our primary objective was to statically prove program properties with SMT solvers. For this purpose, we generate first-order logic formulæ relying on several domain specific theories. Naive approaches lead to generating huge formulæ that are tremendously difficult for SMT solvers to discharge. We have tackled this problem by introducing the Qed framework, an efficient library for managing formulæ modulo built-in and domain specific theories. This provides us with a mean of simplifying on-the-fly the generation of the formulæ to prove. Our rationale is that simplifications that are fast and local should be done in the early stage of the process, while only the difficult residual goals are sent to state-of-the art SMT solvers for deep exploration. Future research includes the simplification of terms by abstract interpretation and the usage of Qed in other tool chains.

# References

1. Barrett, C.W., de Moura, L., Stump, A.: Smt-comp: Satisfiability modulo theories competition. In: Etessami, K., Rajamani, S.K. (eds.) CAV 2005. LNCS, vol. 3576, pp. 20–23. Springer, Heidelberg (2005)
2. Cuoq, P., Kirchner, F., Kosmatov, N., Prevosto, V., Signoles, J., Yakobowski, B.: Frama-c: A software analysis perspective. In: Eleftherakis, G., Hinchey, M., Holcombe, M. (eds.) SEFM 2012. LNCS, vol. 7504, pp. 233–247. Springer, Heidelberg (2012)
3. Baudin, P., Filliâtre, J.C., Hubert, T., Marché, C., Monate, B., Moy, Y., Prevosto, V.: ACSL Specification Language (2013), http://frama-c.com/acsl.html
4. Barnett, M., Leino, K.R.M.: Weakest-precondition of unstructured programs. SIG-SOFT Softw. Eng. Notes 31(1), 82–87 (2005)
5. Baudin, P., Correnson, L., Dargaye, Z.: WP User Manual, v0.7 (2013), http://frama-c.com/download/frama-c-wp-manual.pdf
6. Coq Development Team: The Coq Proof Assistant (2011), http://coq.inria.fr
7. Conchon, S., et al.: The Alt-Ergo Automated Theorem Prover, http://alt-ergo.lri.fr
8. Bobot, F., Filliâtre, J.C., Marché, C., Melquiond, G., Paskevich, A.: The Why3 platform 0.81
9. Filliâtre, J.C., Conchon, S.: Type-safe modular hash-consing. In: Proceedings of the 2006 Workshop on ML 2006, pp. 12–19. ACM, New York (2006)
10. Okasaki, C., Gill, A.: Fast mergeable integer maps. In: Workshop on ML (1998)
11. Gordon, A., Melham, T.: Five axioms of alpha-conversion. In: von Wright, J., Harrison, J., Grundy, J. (eds.) TPHOLs 1996. LNCS, vol. 1125, pp. 173–190. Springer, Heidelberg (1996)
12. Johnsson, T.: Lambda lifting: Transforming programs to recursive equations. In: Jouannaud, J.-P. (ed.) Functional Programming Languages and Computer Architecture. LNCS, vol. 201, pp. 190–203. Springer, Heidelberg (1985)
13. de Moura, L.M., Bjorner, N.: Generalized, efficient array decision procedures. In: IEEE FMCAD, pp. 45–52 (2009)
14. Leino, K.R.M.: Efficient weakest preconditions (2003) (unpublished manuscrit), http://research.microsoft.com/en-us/um/people/leino/papers/krml114a.pdf

# Warps and Atomics: Beyond Barrier Synchronization in the Verification of GPU Kernels*

Ethel Bardsley and Alastair F. Donaldson

Imperial College London
{emb2009,afd}@imperial.ac.uk

**Abstract.** We describe the design and implementation of methods to support reasoning about data races in GPU kernels where constructs other than the standard barrier primitive are used for synchronization. At one extreme we consider kernels that exploit implicit, coarse-grained synchronization between threads in the same *warp*, a feature provided by many architectures. At the other extreme we consider kernels that reduce or avoid barrier synchronization through the use of *atomic* operations. We discuss design decisions associated with providing support for warps and atomics in GPUVerify, a formal verification tool for OpenCL and CUDA kernels. We evaluate the practical impact of these design decisions using a large set of benchmarks, showing that warps can be supported in a scalable manner, that a coarse abstraction suffices for efficient reasoning about most practical uses of atomic operations, and that a novel, refined abstraction captures an important design pattern where atomic operations are used to compute unique array indices. Our evaluation revealed two previously unknown bugs in publicly available benchmark suites.

## 1 Introduction

The rise of the use of graphics processing units (GPUs) for general purpose programming allows for high-throughput massively parallel problems to be accelerated on relatively cheap commodity hardware. This throughput is achieved on GPUs by running thousands of threads in parallel. GPUs are thus suited to a variety of parallel tasks ranging from graphics and imaging to simulation, medical imaging, and computational finance.

The massively parallel nature of graphics cards gives rise to concurrency bugs, such as data races and deadlocks. Data races lead to non-determinism, incorrect computation and undefined behavior. There has been recent interest in the program analysis community on methods for formal or semi-formal analysis of GPU kernels, leading to methods for finding bugs in [14,5] or proving correctness properties of [13,3,8,12] GPU kernels, principally focused on data races.

The main GPU programming models, OpenCL [10] and CUDA [16] organize threads into multiple, independent work groups, and provide a *barrier* operation for synchronizing threads within the same work group. When a thread reaches a barrier it must wait for every thread in its work group to arrive at the barrier. The barrier ensures that all

---

* This work was supported by the EU FP7 STREP project CARP (project number 287767), and EPSRC project EP/K011499/1, and the Imperial College London UROP scheme.

J.M. Badger and K.Y. Rozier (Eds.): NFM 2014, LNCS 8430, pp. 230–245, 2014.
© Springer International Publishing Switzerland 2014

memory accesses issued before the barrier have completed on barrier exit. The threads in the work group then continue execution beyond the barrier. From the perspective of race analysis tools, barriers allow analysis to be restricted to separate *barrier intervals* [14], and each barrier interval can be checked for data races with respect to a *single* thread schedule [13,14,3,5]. However, the runtime overhead of barrier synchronization is high [16, §5.4.3] and there are instances where ensuring race-freedom using barriers is cumbersome or impossible without destroying parallelism. Two features of modern GPU designs allow these problems to be reduced to some extent: *warps*, where implicit synchronization is guaranteed due to lock-step execution of threads, and *atomic* read-modify-write operations, which enable memory locations to be updated asynchronously and lock-free synchronization to be implemented. Because concurrent atomic operations on a memory location are not considered racy, atomics allow acceptable non-determinism to arise from the order of thread interleavings within a barrier interval, thus it is no longer sound to consider a single thread schedule during race analysis.

In this paper, we discuss design decisions associated with providing support for warps and atomics in GPUVerify, an existing verification technique and tool for OpenCL and CUDA kernels [3]. For warps we present a *two-pass* approach where intra- and inter-warp analyses are performed separately, and a *re-sync* approach where intra-warp synchronization at the instruction level is accounted for in a general analysis. In contrast to a recent method for bug-finding in the presence of atomics which heuristically explores thread interleavings [4], we employ abstraction to enable verification of data race-freedom. For kernels that use atomics merely for asynchronous shared state updates we show that a coarse abstraction, where shared memory reads yield arbitrary values, suffices for analysis. This coarse abstraction yields false positives when atomics are used to ensure non-interference between threads. We have identified an important use case where threads atomically increment a counter to compute a successive series of unique indices, and present a novel refined abstraction to efficiently capture this use case.

We evaluate the precision and performance of our methods using a set of 199 CUDA and 190 OpenCL kernels. Warp-aware analysis allows verification of 7 kernels whose race-freedom depends on inter-warp synchronization; GPUVerify previously reported false positives for these examples. Atomics are used by 22 kernels, making verification tools inapplicable to these examples prior to this work. We discovered two previously unknown bugs in these kernels, in the ParBoil [18] and CUDA 5.0 SDK [16] suites, one directly related to use of atomics, which we have reported to the developers concerned. After fixing these bugs, we were able to verify 15 of the kernels that used atomics.

In summary, our main contributions are:

- Two methods for supporting warps when reasoning about races in GPU kernels;
- A coarse abstraction for accommodating atomic operations and a novel refined abstraction to capture an important atomic-based synchronization pattern;
- An implementation of our methods in the open source GPUVerify tool, and an experimental evaluation over a large set of publicly available kernels.

## 2   Background

We briefly review important aspects of the GPU kernel programming model (Section 2.1), discuss warps and atomics in more detail (Section 2.2), and summarize the GPUVerify verification method on which we build (Section 2.3).

### 2.1   GPU Kernel Programming Model

A conventional modern GPU (e.g. a design from NVIDIA or AMD) consists of many *processing elements* (PEs) organized into *compute units*. Each PE is equipped with a portion of private memory, each compute unit includes a portion of shared memory accessible to the PEs of the compute unit, and there is a global memory available to all PEs on the GPU. The OpenCL [10] and CUDA [16] programming models roughly mirror this structure; we discuss the OpenCL case. On OpenCL, a *kernel* is executed in parallel by a number of *work groups*, each of which runs on a compute unit. A work group consists of a number of *work items* (often, and in this paper, referred to as threads), each of which executes on a PE. Thread-private variables are stored in PE private memory, and threads in a work group share data stored in the memory space of the compute unit. Data in GPU global memory is shared among all threads executing a kernel.

Behavior of the kernel is specified by a single kernel function, a template describing the behavior of each thread. A thread has access to a thread id which it can use to behave in an individual manner. Threads in the same work group synchronize via the *barrier* primitive. When a thread reaches a barrier the thread stalls until all threads in its work group have reached the same barrier. The barrier enforces memory ordering, guaranteeing that memory accesses issued before the barrier will have completed before threads commence execution beyond the barrier. Barriers allow synchronization only between threads in the same work group.

The GPU kernel programmer must carefully place barriers to avoid *data races*:

**Definition 2.1 (Warp- and atomic-oblivious data race).** *An execution of a GPU kernel has a data race if two distinct threads access a common memory location, at least one of the accesses modifies the location, and no barrier synchronization between the threads separates these accesses.*

The behavior of a kernel with a data race is undefined according to the OpenCL specification. In practice data races lead to non-determinism, and expose re-orderings of loads and stores due to relaxed underlying memory models.

Figure 1a shows a simple OpenCL kernel[1] that exhibits data races between adjacent threads. There is a race, for example, between threads 0 and 1 because thread 0 reads from $A[1]$ (via A[(tid + 1)% N]), thread 1 writes to $A[1]$ (via A[tid]) and there is no guarantee on the order in which these accesses will occur. Figure 1b shows how a barrier can be used to eliminate this race: all threads must reach the barrier until any can proceed past the barrier, thus the conflicting accesses allowed by the kernel of Figure 1a cannot be simultaneous in the kernel of Figure 1b.

---

[1] OpenCL supports multi-dimensional arrangements of work groups and threads. For ease of presentation all our example kernels are one-dimensional, and we use tid and N to abbreviate the OpenCL syntax for the id of a thread and the total number of threads, respectively.

```
kernel void add(local float *A)        kernel void add(local float *A)
{                                      { float temp = A[(tid + 1)%N];
  A[tid] = A[tid] +                      barrier();
         A[(tid + 1)%N];                 A[tid] = A[tid] + temp;
}                                      }
```

    **(a)** OpenCL kernel with data race          **(b)** Data race eliminated via barrier

**Fig. 1.** OpenCL kernels illustrating data races and the use of barriers

## 2.2 Warps and Atomics

*Warps and Implicit Synchronization.* GPU architectures from NVIDIA and AMD provide a degree of implicit synchronization between threads. On NVIDIA hardware, threads are divided into power-of-two-sized subgroups of at least size 32, known as *warps* [16, §4.1]. AMD designs provide a similar notion of a *wavefront* [1] of threads. We use the term *warp* to denote this feature in general. Threads in the same warp execute in lock-step, sharing a program counter. Threads in the warp cannot simultaneously execute distinct instructions (*predicated execution* [16, §5.4.2] is used to handle non-uniform execution of conditional code by a warp), thus the scope for data races and non-determinism within a warp is reduced. This mode of execution is termed *SIMT* (Single Instruction, Multiple Thread) by NVIDIA, and is analogous to SIMD (Single Instruction Multiple Data).

Warp-level synchronization guarantees can allow expensive barrier synchronizations to be omitted. If the kernel of Figure 1a is executed by 32 threads on an NVIDIA GPU, these threads will be scheduled as a single warp. Every thread will read from `A[(tid + 1)%N]` before *any* thread writes to `A[tid]`, making a data race impossible. Intra-warp races can only occur when two threads in a warp attempt to simultaneously update the same location, for example via a statement such as `A[0] = tid`.

Exploitation of warps is recommended in the CUDA programming guide [16], and efficient algorithms have been developed that depend on this feature: Sengupta et al show the number of barrier synchronization operations required during a parallel scan can be reduced from $\log_2(N)$ to $\log_{32}(N)$, where $N$ is the number of threads, by first scanning within warps, using implicit synchronization, and then aggregating across warps [17]. The OpenCL programming model aims to be general purpose and thus does not acknowledge the existence of warps, so relying on platform-specific warp behavior leads to non-portable code. However, the new OpenCL 2.0 extension specification [9, §9.17, p133] contains an optional extension for *subgroups*, which allow the behavior of warps to be captured. Furthermore, since many OpenCL kernels are ported from CUDA versions, a warp-sensitive analysis for OpenCL can aid in distinguishing between data races preserved by the porting process, and data races introduced by porting due to assumptions about warps which are not valid in OpenCL.

*Atomic Operations.* OpenCL and CUDA are equipped with a set of atomic *read-modify-write* intrinsics. Concurrent atomic operations on the same memory location are *not* considered racy, thus atomics allow a memory location to be updated asynchronously

```
kernel void histo(local int* A,          kernel void histo(local int* A,
                  local int* B) {                          local int* B) {
                                            int t = A[tid];
                                            for (int j = 0; j < N; j++) {
  int t = A[tid];                             if (tid == j)
  atomic_inc(&B[t]);                            B[t]++;
                                              barrier();
                                          } }
}
```

(a) Efficient histogram implementation using an atomic operation

(b) Without atomics, a race-free histogram is not efficient

**Fig. 2.** An illustration of the advantages brought by atomic operations

by multiple threads in a manner that is considered race-free. Such updates can lead to non-determinism due to the order in which threads are scheduled. The example kernel of Figure 2a uses the OpenCL `atomic_inc` intrinsic to implement a histogram: A is an array of data values, and B is an array of buckets; on finding that value t is present in A, a thread increments the bucket at offset t from B. Using an atomic operation ensures that buckets are incremented consistently, and because increment operations are commutative, the order in which threads interleave is not important. If `atomic_inc(&B[t])` in Figure 2a was changed to a non-atomic increment, `B[t]++`, there could be data races on buckets, leading to an insufficient number of increments at best, and memory corruption at worst. It is not feasible to safely implement this kind of kernel without atomics; the kernel of Figure 2b shows how barrier synchronization can be used to serialize bucket updates, but this destroys parallelism by effectively serializing the kernel as a whole. Atomics can also be used for communication between threads in distinct work groups, to ensure race-freedom. In Section 4.2 we show how atomics can be used to compute disjoint array indices across multiple work groups.

*Data Races in the Presence of Warps and Atomics.* We refine Definition 2.1 to take account of warps and atomics. If two threads are in the same warp then a *warp synchronization* occurs between the threads on execution of every instruction. The new parts of the definition are emphasized:

**Definition 2.2 (Warp- and atomic-aware data race).** *An execution of a GPU kernel has a data race if two distinct threads access a common memory location, at least one of the accesses modifies the location,* **at least one of the accesses is non-atomic,** *and no barrier* **or warp** *synchronization between the threads separates these accesses.*

### 2.3 Race Analysis Using GPUVerify

The GPUVerify tool [3] takes as input an OpenCL or CUDA kernel, optionally annotated with loop invariants and procedure specifications. GPUVerify uses the Clang/LLVM framework to process the kernel, translating it into a sequential program expressed in the Boogie verification language [11]. This transformation encodes race checks using assertions such that if the sequential program can be proven correct[2] (i.e. free from assertion failures) then the kernel is guaranteed to be free from data races. The sequential program is checked using the Boogie verifier [2].

GPUVerify scales to large thread counts by encoding in the sequential program the execution of the kernel by an arbitrary distinct *pair* of threads [3]. This pair of threads are considered to execute in lock-step, so that they execute exactly the same sequence of instructions. Uniform execution of conditionals and loops is enforced in the sequential program via *predicated execution* [3]. This fixed schedule eliminates thread interleavings. However, data race analysis with respect to arbitrary thread interleavings is possible by maintaining read and write sets for shared arrays. Let $(s, t)$ denote the pair of threads under consideration, and associate with each array $A$ a set $\mathcal{R}_A$ of read offsets and $\mathcal{W}_A$ of written offsets. Execution of a write instruction where $s$ and $t$ write to $A$ at offsets $o_s$ and $o_t$, respectively, is modelled by adding $o_s$ to $\mathcal{W}_A$ and then checking that $o_t$ does not belong to $\mathcal{R}_A \cup \mathcal{W}_A$. Read operations are handled similarly, with the check relaxed to allow read sharing. At a barrier, $\mathcal{R}_A$ and $\mathcal{W}_A$ are set to be empty for every array $A$. This transformation is valid in the context of race checking, as a correct kernel is deterministic for a given input, and threads cannot communicate aside from barriers, between which there is no guaranteed schedule. The effects of the other threads are thus abstracted.

Consider again the example of Figure 1a. GPUVerify reasons that this kernel is racy by selecting an arbitrary pair of threads $s$ and $t$, and introducing read and write sets, $\mathcal{R}_A$ and $\mathcal{W}_A$, for the array $A$, which are initially empty. The reads from A[tid] and A[(tid + 1)%N] are first checked by adding $s$ and $(s+1)\%N$ to $\mathcal{R}_A$ and checking that $t$ and $(t+1)\%N$ do not belong to $\mathcal{W}_A$; this holds trivially because $\mathcal{W}_A$ is empty. The write to A[tid] is then checked by adding $s$ to $\mathcal{W}_A$ and checking that $t \notin \mathcal{R}_A \cup \mathcal{W}_A$. This logging and checking is encoded using a set of constraints, and races between specific threads are detected by solving for $s$ and $t$. In the case $t = (s+1)\%N$, we have $t \in R_A \cup W_A$, so a race is reported.

For the two-thread reduction used by GPUVerify to be sound it is necessary to over-approximate the effects of additional threads. The simplest solution is to make *no* assumptions about the behavior of additional threads, assuming that these threads may update the shared state arbitrarily. This can be achieved in two ways [3]:

- **Adversarial abstraction**: shared arrays are removed altogether, and every read from a shared array instead returns a non-deterministic value
- **Equality abstraction**: shared arrays are updated non-deterministically (havocked) each time a barrier is reached

Adversarial abstraction is sufficient for checking race-freedom of many kernels and avoids the need to reason about arrays. Equality abstraction (so called because both threads have an equal but arbitrary view of the shared state) is more refined, and is necessary when race-freedom of a kernel requires agreement between threads on the contents of a shared memory location, such as a flag.

The soundness of the two-thread abstraction is argued in [3], and of race analysis via a single schedule in [14,19].

---

[2] We use *correct* to mean *partially correct*; GPUVerify does not perform termination analysis.

# 3  Warp-Aware Race Analysis

We considered two approaches to supporting intra-warp synchronization during race analysis, which we call the *re-sync* method and the *two-pass* method.

## 3.1  Re-sync Method

In the re-sync method (so called because threads synchronize at barriers, and analogously threads in the same warp *re*-synchronize after each instruction), intra- and inter-warp races are checked simultaneously. Race analysis works as described in Section 2.3, but after each uniform read and write instruction with associated array $A$, the sets $\mathcal{R}_A$ and $\mathcal{W}_A$ are set to be empty if the threads under consideration belong to the same warp.

Consider the example of Figure 1a with 64 threads, i.e. $N = 64$, and suppose that these threads are organized into two warps, each of size 32. No races will be detected between threads $s$ and $t$ in the same warp, i.e. if $s, t \in \{0, \ldots, 31\}$ or $s, t \in \{32, \ldots, 63\}$: the read set $\mathcal{R}_A$ is cleared immediately before the write to A[tid] is analyzed. On the other hand, races will be detected for the cases $s = 31, t = 32$ and $s = 63, t = 0$; we explain the $s = 31, t = 32$ case. After the read operations we have $\mathcal{R}_A = \{s, s + 1\} = \{31, 32\}$; because $s$ and $t$ are in different warps $\mathcal{R}_A$ is *not* made empty; the write is then analyzed by adding $s$, i.e. 31, to $\mathcal{W}_A$ and checking whether $t$, i.e. 32, belongs to $\mathcal{R}_A$. This is the case, so a data race is reported.

This is sufficient to maintain soundness in the uniform case, where the threads follow the same path, as for some racy code A[o] = ..., $o_s$ will still be in $W_A$ when $o_t \notin W_A$ is checked, and thus the assertion failure will still be reported. For the divergent case (referred to by [14] as a "porting race"), this reset is predicated, such that, for threads $s, t$, with enabled predicates $p_s, p_t$, the reset is predicated by $p_s \wedge p_t$. For example, in the racy code if (tid < 16) {A[o] = 1} else {A[o] = 2}, if $s$ follows the *then* branch and $t$ takes the *else*, the reset won't occur until the threads re-converge, and so the case $o_s = o_t$ will report assertion failure as per the regular GPUVerify method.

## 3.2  Two-Pass Method

The two-pass method involves two independent analyses that can run in parallel, one checking exclusively for inter-warp data races, the other exclusively for intra-warp data races. Inter-warp data race analysis proceeds according to the method outlined in Section 2.3, except that the arbitrary threads $s$ and $t$ are constrained to reside in different warps. For intra-warp race analysis, $s$ and $t$ are constrained to reside in the same warp, and for each write instruction we check that the offsets $o_s$ and $o_t$ being written to are different; there is no need to maintain read and write sets or analyze read instructions.

With respect to the running example of Figure 1a, with 64 threads organized as two warps of size 32, the intra-warp case of the two-pass method determines that the write A[tid] leads to disjoint accesses for any distinct threads $s, t$, thus there are no intra-warp races. The inter-warp case detects the races between threads 31 and 32 and threads

0 and 63 in the manner described for the re-sync method, except that there is no need to consider setting the read/write sets for $A$ to be empty between instructions.

This is implemented as, when thread paths are uniform, altering the log mechanism such that, for writes, $W_A := \{o_s\}$ instead of $W_A := W_A \cup \{o_s\}$, and making it the empty set otherwise. This maintains soundness, as the write set will contain the current instruction's offset for the unified case, and in the non-unified case the technique behaves as without this modification.

It is clear that the re-sync and two-pass methods achieve the same goal. Our hypothesis was that the two-pass method might lead to faster verification by decomposing analysis into two simpler cases that can be checked in parallel. Our experiments in Section 5 validate this hypothesis with respect to a 215 example kernels: the two-pass method outperforms the re-sync method in many cases.

### 3.3  Inter-warp Synchronization and Shared State Abstraction

Recall from Section 2.3 that the two-thread reduction used by GPUVerify depends on an accompanying abstraction of the shared state. Adversarial abstraction provides no guarantees about the contents of the shared state and thus combines directly with our approaches to warp-based synchronization. Combining warp-level synchronization with equality abstraction requires some care. With equality abstraction, shared arrays are havocked at every barrier. Consider the following code snippet, which is incorrect when executed by a single warp of at least three threads:

```
if(tid == 0) {
  A[0] = 1; A[1] = 1; A[2] = 1;
}
// At this point, A = { 1, 1, 1, ... }
A[tid] = 0;
// Now A = { 0, 0, 0, ... }
if(tid == 0) {
  // The assertion should thus fail
  assert(A[0] == 1 || A[1] == 1 || A[2] == 1);
}
```

Suppose we analyze this example using the two-thread reduction with straightforward equality abstraction. Consider the pair of threads 0, 1. After execution of the first conditional there are no data races and the threads' view of $A$ is $\{1,1,1,1,\ldots\}$. The assignment $A[\text{tid}] = 0$ by threads 0 and 1 leads to a state where $A = \{0,0,1,1,\ldots\}$. This is incomplete: it does not take into account the actions of additional threads. Hence the pair 0, 1 erroneously conclude, at the assertion, that at least one of $A[0], A[1]$ and $A[2]$ is equal to 1, namely $A[2]$.

To rectify equality abstraction in the presence of warps it is necessary to perform additional havocking: after a write instruction to array $A$, the array $A$ must be havocked to reflect the fact that *other* unmodelled threads in the warp have also modified $A$. With respect to the above example this means that the threads' view of $A$ is arbitrary after each instruction, leading (as desired) to states in which the assertion fails.

## 4   Race Analysis and Abstraction for Atomic Operations

As discussed in Section 2.2, atomic operations relax the definition of what constitutes a data race, reflected in Definition 2.2. This allows designated memory locations to be updated concurrently in manner that is considered non-racy. Such concurrent updates are a valid source of non-determinism, violating the assumption on which race analysis in GPUVerify and other methods rests: that a race-free kernel behaves deterministically. As a result, it is not sound in general to restrict analysis to a single thread schedule in the presence of atomic operations.

For a precise analysis geared towards bug-finding this is problematic: to accurately find bugs arising from atomic manipulation it is necessary to resort to exploring thread interleavings. This has been investigated in the context of the GKLEE bug-finding tool for CUDA [4], where delay bounding [7] is used to limit schedule explosion.

We have observed that in practice most GPU kernels that use atomics do so for simple purposes, such as updating shared data asynchronously or computing unique array indices. We focus here on using abstraction to prove race-freedom for these sorts of kernels, without resorting to exploration of thread interleavings.

### 4.1   Over-Approximating Atomics with Adversarial Abstraction

Suppose we wish to analyze a kernel that updates elements of an array $A$ atomically.[3] If we handle $A$ using adversarial abstraction, so that every read from $A$ yields a non-deterministic result, then there is no need to explicitly consider thread interleavings arising from non-determinism introduced by atomic updates to $A$: adversarial abstraction encodes *at least* the non-determinism that could arise from such updates.

Under adversarial abstraction we can adapt the race analysis procedure described in Section 2.3 as follows. For a shared array $A$, in addition to read and write sets $\mathcal{R}_A$ and $\mathcal{W}_A$ we introduce an *atomic* set $\mathcal{A}_A$ recording offsets from $A$ that have been accessed atomically. Suppose the threads under consideration are $s$ and $t$, and that an instruction $\iota$ causes $s$ and $t$ to access offsets $o_s$ and $o_t$ of a shared array $A$, respectively. We log the access made by $s$ by adding $o_s$ to $\mathcal{R}_A$, $\mathcal{W}_A$, or $\mathcal{A}_A$ depending on whether $\iota$ is a read, write or atomic operation. We then check the access made by $t$, reporting a data race if:

- $o_t \in \mathcal{W}_A \cup \mathcal{A}_A$ in the case where $\iota$ is a non-atomic read
- $o_t \in \mathcal{R}_A \cup \mathcal{W}_A \cup \mathcal{A}_A$ in the case where $\iota$ is a non-atomic write
- $o_t \in \mathcal{R}_A \cup \mathcal{W}_A$ in the case where $\iota$ is an atomic operation

This extension of our method is sufficient for analysis of kernels where the return values of atomic operations do not influence whether or not data races occur. An example is the histogram kernel of Figure 2a: array $B$ is updated atomically, thus $B$ must be adversarially abstracted. However, because no data is subsequently read from $B$, this coarse abstraction of $B$ cannot lead to false positive data race reports. Our approach thus allows for sound race analysis of this simple example. In Section 5 we report on a data race we detected in one of the ParBoil benchmarks [18], where both atomic and

---

[3] In practice atomics are often used to update single memory locations, such as counters; we can regard these as single-element arrays.

```
private int i = atomic_inc(c);
while(i < MAX) {
  out[i] = compute(in, i);
  i = atomic_inc(&c);
}
```

**Fig. 3.** Using atomic increment to compute disjoint array indices

non-atomic operations are used to manipulate the same array without adequate synchronization.

It is *not* sound in general to use equality abstraction for an array that is atomically updated: atomics allow non-determinism between barriers, so multiple reads from an atomically-manipulated memory may yield different results.

## 4.2 A Refined Abstraction for Repetition-Free Atomic Operations

The example of Figure 3 demonstrates how atomic operations can be used to compute disjoint indices for array accesses. In the figure, in and out are distinct shared arrays of length MAX, and c is a pointer to a shared counter, initialized to zero. The unspecified compute procedure performs some computation on the i-th element of in, returning a value. The atomic_inc operation atomically increments the shared memory location pointed to by its argument and returns the previous value of this location.

This design pattern is useful in parallel processing of data where the computation time per data element may vary in an unpredictable manner. Such variance means that it is not possible to achieve high performance by statically allocating a fixed chunk of data elements to each thread. A classic example of this is fractal image computation, where time to convergence for a pixel varies dramatically across the image, and we have seen the above design pattern used (in a more sophisticated form) for lock-free division of work in optimized Mandelbrot fractal kernels that ship with the CUDA SDK.

The basic atomic support described in Section 4.1 would report a false positive data race for the above example. This is due to adversarial abstraction of the counter, which allows two distinct threads to see common values returned by atomic_inc, leading to write-write data races on A. The example is in fact race-free when executed by multiple threads. This is because, although the sequence of values a thread obtains by calling atomic_inc is dependent on the thread schedule, the sequences of values obtained by two distinct threads must be disjoint—the counter only ever increases and thus (assuming the counter does not overflow) it will never contain the same value twice.

If we can identify that a location $l$ is accessed exclusively via atomic_inc operations then we can refine adversarial abstraction to take advantage of the "repetition-free" nature of this operation. Suppose we have a set used($l$) recording all the values that have been read from $l$ so far during the program. Initially used($l$) is empty. We can model an application of atomic_inc to location $l$ by returning a non-deterministically chosen value that does *not* belong to used($l$), and then adding this value to used($l$) so that it is not returned again in future. This refined abstraction thus knows nothing about the location $l$ *except* that its current value is different from any other value previously returned by `atomic_inc`. This additional knowledge is sufficient to capture the case where `atomic_inc` is used to derive a unique array index.

More generally, we can compute this refined abstraction for a location $l$ if we can determine that $l$ is manipulated exclusively using a single, *repetition-free* function.

**Definition 4.1 (Repetition-free function).** *Let $S$ be a set and $f : S \to S$ a function, with $f^k : S \to S$ denoting $f$ applied $k$ times. We say that $f$ is repetition-free if for every $x \in S$ and $m, n \geq 0$ with $m \neq n$, $f^m(x) \neq f^n(x)$. That is, $f$ has no periodic points.*

The `atomic_inc` operation can be viewed as updating a location storing value $v$ to store $f(v)$, where $f$ is the repetition-free function defined by $f(x) = x + 1$. We can consider the `atomic_add` operation, which takes a location and a non-negative integer argument $n$, similarly in the case where $n$ is positive: applying `atomic_add` to a location holding value $v$ updates the location to store $f^n(v)$, where $f(x) = x + 1$. The operations `atomic_dec` and `atomic_sub` can be treated analogously using the repetition-free function $g$ defined by $g(x) = x - 1$.

This abstraction is technically unsound because it does not take into account the possibility of overflow, which may cause a location to yield the same value twice if an operation such as increment is called an extremely large number of times. Our aim in this work is to provide pragmatic support for reasoning about kernels that use atomics, thus we use the abstraction without regard for overflow. If overflow is a concern then soundness can be restored through the addition of overflow checks (with a corresponding increase in verification burden).

### 4.3 Implementation Issues for Atomics

Supporting atomic operations using adversarial abstraction (Section 4.1) is straightforward: we adapted GPUVerify to determine statically those arrays that may be manipulated atomically and force adversarial abstraction of these arrays. We used the existing encoding of read and write sets, described in [3], to add sets recording atomic accesses, and implemented atomic-aware race checks as described in Section 4.1.

To support the refined atomic abstraction of Section 4.2 we made GPUVerify aware of the repetition-free atomic operations `atomic_inc` and `atomic_dec`, and implemented an analysis that determines whether an array is only ever accessed using a single repetition-free atomic operation; we say that such an array is *repetition-free*. A call to `atomic_add` or `atomic_sub` with a positive numeric argument is regarded as consisting of a series of increments or decrements respectively.

For each repetition-free array $A$ we introduce in the Boogie program generated by GPUVerify a map $used_A : \mathsf{Int} \times \mathsf{Int} \to \mathsf{Bool}$. If $used_A(x, v)$ holds, this indicates that offset $x$ of $A$ has previously yielded the value $v$, and thus will not yield $v$ when accessed again using the repetition-free operation. When translating an atomic operation on repetition-free array $A$ in the context of threads $s$ and $t$, suppose that the threads access array offsets $o_s$ and $o_t$ and store the operation results into private variables $z_s$ and $z_t$, respectively. We generate the following sequence of Boogie statements (presented here using mathematical syntax) to model the atomic operation:

$\mathcal{A}_A := \mathcal{A}_A \cup \{o_s\};$      Log the atomic access made by thread $s$

assert $o_t \notin \mathcal{R}_A \cup \mathcal{W}_A;$      Ensure the atomic access made by thread $t$ does not race

havoc $z_s, z_t;$      The threads receive values that are arbitrary, except:

assume $\neg \text{used}_A(o_s, z_s);$      neither value has been used

assume $\neg \text{used}_A(o_t, z_t);$      previously at this offset, and

assume $z_s \neq z_t$      the threads receive different values

$\text{used}_A(o_s, z_s) := \text{true};$      The values are now marked as used up

$\text{used}_A(o_t, z_t) := \text{true};$

Thus, $o_s$ and $o_t$ are guaranteed unique, and subsequent use of them to index into some array will be correctly found race-free.

In Section 5 we evaluate the overhead in terms of verification time of using this refined abstraction over regular adversarial abstraction.

## 5 Experimental Evaluation

To evaluate our implementation of warp and atomic support in the GPUVerify tool [3] we considered the following benchmark suites:

- CUDA 5.0 SDK benchmarks (171 CUDA kernels)
- CUDA 2.0 SDK benchmarks (8 CUDA kernels do not appear in the 5.0 SDK)
- C++ AMP samples, translated into CUDA, from [3] (20 CUDA kernels)
- AMD APP SDK (78 OpenCL kernels)
- ParBoil benchmarks (25 OpenCL kernels)
- SHOC benchmarks (87 OpenCL kernels)

Of the 199 CUDA and 190 OpenCL kernels, 6 and 16 use atomic operations, respectively. The benchmarks and our tool chain, with instructions on how to re-run our experiments, are available online.[4]

Experiments were performed on a PC with a 3.4GHz Intel i7-2600 and 16GB RAM running Ubuntu 13.04, using GPUVerify revision 988 (2013-11-25), and Z3 4.3.1. A time limit of 900 seconds (15 minutes) per kernel was used for analysis.

*Impact of Warp-Level Synchronization.* We ran GPUVerify with warp-level synchronization enabled (warp size 32) across the 199 CUDA kernels. We found 7 cases where verification succeeded with warp-level synchronization enabled but failed without. GPUVerify is thus able to provide precise results for these kernels where before it would report false positives. We were surprised to find one case (dwtHaar1D) where verification succeeded with the two-pass method but failed with re-sync. In this case re-sync requires a loop invariant that makes reference to whether the threads under consideration are in the same warp, which GPUVerify does not infer. With the two-pass method the intra-warp case is trivial to verify, and a simpler loop invariant which *is* inferred suffices for the inter-warp case.

Figure 4 compares verification times across the CUDA benchmarks with respect to the re-sync and two-pass methods. A point at coordinates $(x, y)$ represents a benchmark

---

[4] http://multicore.doc.ic.ac.uk/tools/GPUVerify/NFM2014

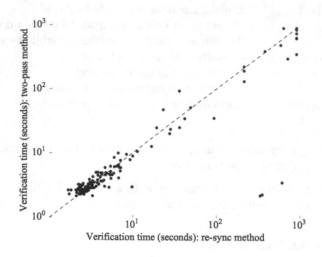

**Fig. 4.** Verification times for two-pass vs. re-sync methods over 199 CUDA kernels

for which analysis (successful verification, or the report of a failed proof attempt) took $x$ seconds using the re-sync method and $y$ seconds using the two-pass method. The figure shows that the two-pass method is faster in many cases, sometimes dramatically. We attribute this to the fact that the two-pass method involves solving two simpler verification problems which are solved in parallel. We also compared verification time using the re-sync method to verification time without warp-level synchronization, for the CUDA kernels where the verification result was not affected by warp-awareness. We observed some fluctuation in verification times between examples, but overall the performance difference was negligible: verification using the re-sync method was 1.043 times slower than with verification without support for warps. Thus warp-awareness does *not* compromise verification speed.

*Impact of Support for Atomic Operations.* Prior to this work, GPUVerify (nor any other *verification* tool for GPU kernels) was applicable to the 22 kernels in our suite that use atomic operations. Using GPUVerify we found two bugs in these kernels.

In a CUDA 5.0 SDK Mandelbrot kernel, where atomic operations are used for work distribution in a manner similar to the example of Figure 3, we found a read-write data race arising due to a missing barrier. The race was not due to misuse of atomics, but the kernel was not amenable to analysis prior atomic support. We reported this race to engineers at NVIDIA who confirmed and subsequently fixed the issue.

We discovered an atomic/non-atomic race in a sophisticated histogram implementation kernel in the ParBoil suite (`tpacf/gen_hists`). In this example, work groups share histogram buckets in group-shared memory. Threads first initialize this memory to zero, then repeatedly update histogram buckets atomically. No barrier was issued between bucket initialization and bucket update, leading to races between these phases. This race was confirmed by the maintainers of the Parboil suite.

These bugs *cannot* be found directly using GKLEE, a bug-finding tool for CUDA kernels [14] that has been extended with support for atomics [4]. This is because the kernels manipulate floating point data which GKLEE does not support. Floating point operators are approximated by GPUVerify through the use of uninterpreted functions [3].

We also found what is strictly a read/atomic race in the histo/histo_main Par-Boil example. A non-atomic read is used to retrieve the value of a histogram bucket before an atomic update is applied. We do not regard this as a programmer error: we believe the intention is that the read should be an atomic read operation, which OpenCL 1.2 does not directly provide. However, atomic read *is* provided by the recently announced OpenCL 2.0, so the kernel should be re-written accordingly in due course.

After fixing these bugs, we were able to verify race-freedom for 15 of the 22 kernel that use atomics. In 13 cases verification was fully automatic: GPUVerify was able to automatically generate loop invariants required to prove race-freedom. In 2 cases it was necessary to provide loop invariant annotations for verification to succeed. These invariants were unrelated to the use of atomics – they were necessary to capture disjointness of the data access patterns associated with non-atomic arrays. The invariants are available in our online set of benchmarks.

Of the 7 kernels for which verification failed, 4 were kernels used in the implementation of breadth-first-search graph algorithms in the ParBoil and SHOC suites. These kernels are only correct with respect to non-trivial, quantified preconditions on input arrays, beyond the limited support for precondition annotations currently provided by GPUVerify, thus the tool reports a write-atomic race for each of these kernels.

Two of the CUDA 5.0 Mandelbrot kernels use an atomic counter to compute disjoint indices into shared arrays as discussed in Section 4.2. However, in each thread block only the "master" thread, thread 0, is responsible for updating the global index counter, obtaining a base index used by all threads in the block. In this setting the two-thread reduction does not allow a proof of race-freedom for a pair of non-master threads $s$ and $t$ in different thread blocks. Even with our refined atomic abstraction, in the absence of concrete knowledge about master thread behavior, $s$ and $t$ cannot deduce that their base indices are distinct. In future work we plan to solve this issue by extending the two-thread reduction to allow specific threads, such as master threads, to be concretely represented. To evaluate our refined atomic abstraction we created a simplified Mandelbrot fractal generator, capturing all the behavior of the more complex of the two Mandelbrot examples, but simplified so that each thread directly computes its array indices from a global counter, eliminating the role of a master thread. After this simplification, we were able to verify the example using the refined abstraction of Section 4.2.

The final kernel using atomics that we could not verify is the histo/histo_main kernel discussed above: after we fixed the read/atomic race, GPUVerify reported possible races on other, non-atomic arrays; we have yet to find strong enough loop invariants to eliminate these false positives.

# 6   Related Work

Several recent works have focused on GPU kernel verification using SMT solving [13,3], combined static and dynamic analysis [12] and separation logic with permissions [8].

The closest work to GPUVerify is the PUG technique and tool [13], and the methods have been compared qualitatively and experimentally [3]. To our knowledge, ours is the first work to present support for either warps or atomics in a verification technique.

Dynamic symbolic execution is used by the GKLEE [14] and KLEE-CL [5] tools to find bugs in CUDA and OpenCL kernels, respectively. The GKLEE tool accurately models warp-based execution and thus can find bugs in CUDA kernels precisely, without reporting false positive data races that are impossible due to warp scheduling constraints. An extension to the GKLEE tool considers analysis of CUDA kernels that use atomic operations [4]. On discovering a potential conflict involving atomic accesses, thread schedules are enumerated to try to find a concrete counterexample to correctness. Delay bounding [7] is used to limit schedule explosion. This method has proven effective in finding bugs, but cannot be used to verify *absence* of defects. As noted in Section 5, application of GKLEE is limited due to lack of support for floating point operations. A proposal for extending the KLEE-CL method with support for atomics, via a symbolic encoding of schedules, is proposed as future work in [6], but has not been implemented.

The two-thread reduction employed by GPUVerify is also used in other methods for GPU kernel analysis [13,15], and that several methods exploit the fact that race analysis can be performed with respect to a single thread schedule [13,14,5].

## 7   Conclusions and Future Work

We have presented methods for extending a GPU kernel verification technique with support for two additional inter-thread communication mechanisms: warps and atomics. Our experimental evaluation shows that these extensions, implemented in the GPUVerify tool, allow a larger set of kernels to be successfully analyzed.

Our main direction for future work will be the investigation of more sophisticated abstractions for reasoning about atomic operations: extending the two-thread reduction so that manipulation of atomic variables by master threads can be precisely handled, as discussed in Section 5, and designing custom abstractions to capture further design patterns associated with the use of atomics. We also plan to investigate the use of verification methods for kernel optimization. For example, warp divergence [14], where threads in the same warp simulate different control flow paths through predicated execution, is often regarded as a performance bug. By combining support for reasoning about warps with prior work on barrier divergence [3], we can investigate the use of verification to prove absence of warp divergence in complex kernels.

## References

1. AMD, Inc.: AMD graphics cores next (GCN) architecture, white paper (2012)
2. Barnett, M., Chang, B.-Y.E., DeLine, R., Jacobs, B., Leino, K.R.M.: Boogie: A modular reusable verifier for object-oriented programs. In: de Boer, F.S., Bonsangue, M.M., Graf, S., de Roever, W.-P. (eds.) FMCO 2005. LNCS, vol. 4111, pp. 364–387. Springer, Heidelberg (2006)
3. Betts, A., Chong, N., Donaldson, A.F., Qadeer, S., Thomson, P.: GPUVerify: a verifier for GPU kernels. In: OOPSLA (2012)

4. Chiang, W.-F., Gopalakrishnan, G., Li, G., Rakamarić, Z.: Formal analysis of GPU programs with atomics via conflict-directed delay-bounding. In: Brat, G., Rungta, N., Venet, A. (eds.) NFM 2013. LNCS, vol. 7871, pp. 213–228. Springer, Heidelberg (2013)
5. Collingbourne, P., Cadar, C., Kelly, P.H.J.: Symbolic testing of OpenCL code. In: Eder, K., Lourenço, J., Shehory, O. (eds.) HVC 2011. LNCS, vol. 7261, pp. 203–218. Springer, Heidelberg (2012)
6. Collingbourne, P.C.: Symbolic Crosschecking of Data-Parallel Floating Point Code. Ph.D. thesis, Imperial College London (2012)
7. Emmi, M., Qadeer, S., Rakamaric, Z.: Delay-bounded scheduling. In: POPL (2011)
8. Huisman, M., Mihelčić, M.: Specification and verification of GPGPU programs using permission-based separation logic. In: BYTECODE (2013)
9. Khronos Group: The OpenCL extension specification, version 2.0 (2013)
10. Khronos Group: The OpenCL specification, version 2.0 (2013)
11. Leino, K., Rustan, M.: This is Boogie 2 (2008), manuscript KRML 178 (2008)
12. Leung, A., Gupta, M., Agarwal, Y., Gupta, R., Jhala, R., Lerner, S.: Verifying GPU kernels by test amplification. In: PLDI (2012)
13. Li, G., Gopalakrishnan, G.: Scalable SMT-based verification of GPU kernel functions. In: FSE (2010)
14. Li, G., Li, P., Sawaya, G., Gopalakrishnan, G., Ghosh, I., Rajan, S.P.: GKLEE: concolic verification and test generation for GPUs. In: PPoPP. ACM (2012)
15. Li, P., Li, G., Gopalakrishnan, G.: Parametric flows: automated behavior equivalencing for symbolic analysis of races in CUDA programs. In: SC (2012)
16. NVIDIA Corporation: CUDA C programming guide, version 5.5 (2013)
17. Sengupta, S., Harris, M., Garland, M.: Efficient parallel scan algorithms for GPUs. Tech. Rep. NVR-2008-003, NVIDIA (2008)
18. Stratton, J.A., et al.: Parboil: A revised benchmark suite for scientific and commercial throughput computing. Tech. Rep. IMPACT-12-01, UIUC (2012)
19. Collingbourne, P., Donaldson, A.F., Ketema, J., Qadeer, S.: Interleaving and lock-step semantics for analysis and verification of GPU kernels. In: Felleisen, M., Gardner, P. (eds.) ESOP 2013. LNCS, vol. 7792, pp. 270–289. Springer, Heidelberg (2013)

# Testing-Based Compiler Validation
# for Synchronous Languages*

Pierre-Loïc Garoche[1], Falk Howar[2], Temesghen Kahsai[2],
and Xavier Thirioux[3]

[1] ONERA
[2] NASA Ames / CMU
[3] IRIT

**Abstract.** In this paper we present a novel lightweight approach to validate compilers for synchronous languages. Instead of verifying a compiler
for all input programs or providing a fixed suite of regression tests, we
extend the compiler to generate a test-suite with high behavioral coverage and geared towards discovery of faults for every compiled artifact.
We have implemented and evaluated our approach using a compiler from
Lustre to C.

## 1 Introduction

In the safety critical domain it is common to verify (safety) properties of systems.
Usually proofs for these properties are established at the level of source code or
formal models. Source code and/or models are compiled to executables for some
target platform. This compilation may invalidate already established verification
results. It is thus of utmost importance to have a *trustworthy compilation process*. Existing approaches to trusted compilation fall into two categories. Either
they aim at verifying the compiler itself (e.g., [7]), or they aim at validating
the compiled output using a verified validator (e.g., [8]). Both exist in weaker
variants, where verification is replaced by testing. There exists a body of work
on generating test suites for verifying the correctness of a compiler (c.f., [3]).
Testing the correctness of a compiled artifact is usually done by some form of
specification-based testing (e.g., [9]).

The more rigorous approaches come at a high cost. Establishing the correctness of a compiler takes a lot of effort. Developing and verifying a validator is
not less of an effort. Also, to be successful, a shared semantic basis is needed
between the source and the target language. Testing the correctness of a compiler is difficult because the set of potential input programs to a compiler is
potentially infinite and hard to sample in an automated fashion. Specification-
based testing, on the other hand, is well understood and cheap (compared to
the other approaches). It will, however, in many cases not uncover errors in a
compiler: test-suites are geared towards finding violations of a specification and
not towards uncovering faults in the translation of a program.

* Acknowledgement for the projects ANR INS CAFEIN and NSF Craves.

J.M. Badger and K.Y. Rozier (Eds.): NFM 2014, LNCS 8430, pp. 246–251, 2014.

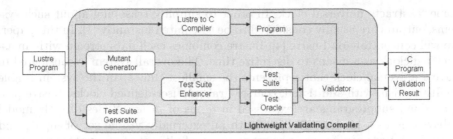

**Fig. 1.** Schematic view of a testing-based validating compiler from Lustre to C

In this paper, we present a *lightweight* approach to compiler validation. We build our validating compiler upon specification-based testing, which we augment with a method for generating test cases targeting potential bugs in a compiler. Fig. 1 illustrates an overview of the developed framework. The lightweight validating compiler from Lustre to C consists of five main components: A modular *compiler* from Lustre to C, a *test suite generator* for Lustre programs, a grammar-based *mutant generator* for Lustre programs, a *test suite enhancer* – extends test suites with test cases for killing mutants – and a *validator*, which will execute the test suite on the compiled C program. The validator will use the input Lustre program as a test oracle. Test results are provided as output along with the compiled C program.

The central idea of this approach is twofold. On one hand, we verify that the compiler did not introduce any difference between the source program (Lustre) and the compiled version (C). We do this by generating automatically test suites from the source program (Lustre) based on MC/DC coverage criterion. On the other hand, we use mutations of the source program to simulate bugs in the compiler, and that test cases that differentiate mutations from the original program are likely to uncover errors in the translation of this program. We have implemented a prototypical version of such a lightweight validating compiler from Lustre to C. In this paper, we discuss the different components of our approach and present some results from a preliminary evaluation of our technique.

**Outline.** The paper is structured as follows: The next section, introduces the synchronous language Lustre and outlines our coverage-based test synthesis using bounded model checking (BMC). Section 3 presents how we reinforce test suites using mutants. Finally, Section 4 presents our preliminary experimental evaluations.

## 2   MC/DC Test Suites for Lustre Programs

*Synchronous languages* are a class of languages proposed for the design of "reactive systems" – systems that maintain a permanent interaction with a physical environment. Such languages are based on the theory of synchronous time, in which the system and its environment are considered to both view time with some "abstract" universal clock. In order to simplify reasoning about such systems, outputs are usually considered to be calculated instantly [1]. In this paper, we will concentrate on Lustre [4]. Lustre combines each data stream with an associated clock as a means to discretize time. The overall system is considered to have a universal clock that represents the smallest time span the system is able to distinguish, with additional, coarser-grained, user-defined clocks. Lustre programs and subprograms are expressed in terms of *nodes*. Nodes directly model subsystems in a modular fashion, with an externally visible set of inputs and outputs. A *node* can be seen as a mapping of a finite set of input streams (in the form of a tuple) to a finite set of output streams (also expressed as a tuple). At each instant $t$, the node takes in the values of its input streams and returns the values of its output streams. Operationally, a node has a cyclic behavior: at each cycle $t$, it takes as input the value of each input stream at position or instant $t$, and returns the value of each output stream at instant $t$. Lustre nodes have a limited form of memory in that, when computing the output values they can also look at input and output values from previous instants, up to a finite limit statically determined by the program itself. Figure 2 describes a simple Lustre program: a node that every four computation steps activates its output signal, starting at the third step. The **reset** input reinitializes this counter.

```
node counter(reset: bool) returns (active: bool);
var a, b: bool;
let
  a = false -> (not reset and not (pre b));
  b = false -> (not reset and pre a);
  active = a and b;
tel
```

**Fig. 2.** A simple Lustre program

Lustre programs can be compiled to main stream languages such as C or Java. Whereas initial compilation schemes of Lustre were computing a global automaton of the system [4], the approach of [2] relies on an object-like compilation of the program: each Lustre node call is seen as an instance of the generic declaration of the node. Our compiler from Lustre to C follows the latter approach.

A traditional technique to verify safety properties of synchronous languages is to use *SMT-based model checking* [6]. Such technique requires a predicate $\mathrm{M}[\tilde{s}, \tilde{in}, \tilde{s}', \tilde{out}]$[1] describing the relationship between input flows $\tilde{in}$, output flows $\tilde{out}$ as well as internal states $\tilde{s}$ for the model $M$ it represents. It also requires a predicate over initial states $\mathrm{M}_{init}[\tilde{s}]$ as well as a condition $\mathrm{C}[\tilde{s}, \tilde{in}, \tilde{out}]$ we are trying to meet at some time. A valid finite trace of length $n$ for $M$ would satisfy the following expression:

$$\mathrm{M}_{init}[\tilde{s}_0] \wedge \bigwedge_{i=0}^{n-1} \mathrm{M}[\tilde{s}_i, \tilde{in}_i, \tilde{s}_{i+1}, \tilde{out}_i] \wedge \mathrm{C}[\tilde{s}_n, \tilde{in}_n, \tilde{out}_n]$$

---

[1] We refer to the traditional definition of transition system in model checking techniques. A detailed description of a transition system for Lustre programs can be found in [5].

A satisfiability check using an SMT solver over this expression for a given $n$ will produce a set of values for $\tilde{in}_i$, $\tilde{s}_i$ and $\tilde{out}_i$ for $i \in [0..n]$. In practice, tools unroll the transition relation one step at a time trying to meet the specific $C$ condition. This can be done efficiently with an SMT solver by reusing previously computed states. We denote by $\mathsf{bmc}(M_{init}, M, C)$ such a typical BMC algorithm.

We generate test suites using Modified Condition/Decision Coverage (MC/DC) coverage criterion. The latter has been used as a test adequacy metrics for decades specially when testing critical software. We express MC/DC criteria as a predicates $\mathsf{C}[\tilde{s}, \tilde{in}, \tilde{out}]$ and use BMC to find test cases that satisfy these predicates. From a decision $P(c_1, \ldots, c_n)$ where the $c_i$'s are a set of atomic conditions over the variables $\tilde{s}$, $\tilde{in}$ and $\tilde{out}$, we have to exert the value of each condition $c_i$ with respect to the global truth value of $P$, the other conditions $c_{j \neq i}$ being left untouched. Precisely, we have to find two test cases for which, in the last element of the trace, $c_i$ is respectively assigned to *False* and *True*.

**Remark:** Bounded model checking may not be able to find a test case for some condition within an acceptable time limit[2]. In such cases, we conclude that the generated test suite does not reach the MC/DC coverage.

## 3   Reinforcing Test Suites via Mutation Testing

In the following, we denote by a *mutant* a mutated model or implementation where a single mutation has been introduced. The considered mutation, which is grammar based, does not change the control flow graph or the structure of the semantics but could either: (i) perform arithmetic, relational or boolean operator replacement; or (ii) introduce additional delay (*pre* operator in Lustre)[3], or (iii) negate boolean variables or expressions; or (iv) replace constants. Such generation of mutants has been implemented as an extension of our Lustre to C compiler. Once mutants are generated and the coverage-based test suite is computed, we can evaluate the number of mutants killed by the test suite. This evaluation is performed at the binary level, once the C code has been obtained from the compilation of the mutant. In this setting, the original Lustre model acts as an oracle, i.e., a reference implementation. Any test that shows a difference between a run of the original model compiled and a mutation of it, allows to kill this mutant.

In the literature, mutants are mainly used to evaluate the quality of a test suite. In our case, the motivation is different, we aim at providing the user with a test suite related to its input model. This test suite covers the model behavior in order to show that the compiler doesn't introduce bugs. We conjecture that a test suite achieving a good coverage of the code but unable to kill many mutants would not certify that the compiler did a good job. We thus introduce new tests to kill the un-killed (or resistant) mutants by the initial MC/DC-based test suite.

---

[2] In our experiments the timeout for BMC was set to 100 secs.

[3] Note that, introducing additional delay could produce a program with initialization issues.

*(1)* **proc** genNewTest($M_{init}, M, M'_{init}, M'$) $\equiv$
*(2)*     $M'' := $ gen_mcdc_conds($M_{init}, M$);
*(3)*       $test := $ bmc($M_{init}[\tilde{x}] \wedge M'_{init}[\tilde{y}]$,
*(4)*                 $M[x_{\tilde{k}-1}, in_{\tilde{k}-1}, \tilde{x}_k, out_{\tilde{k}-1}] \wedge M'[y_{\tilde{k}-1}, in_{\tilde{k}-1}, \tilde{y}_k, out'_{\tilde{k}-1}]$,
*(5)*                 $\neg(out = out')$)
*(6)*     **print** $test$

**Fig. 3.** A procedure to introduce new test cases in order to kill previously un-killed mutants

Figure 3 illustrates the procedure to generate new test cases that allow to kill previously un-killed mutants. If the call to BMC (Line 3) does not terminate within the timeout (100 sec in our experiments), we don't introduce a new test case.

# 4   Experimental Evaluation

We have implemented a prototypical version of the lightweight validating compiler from Lustre to C using the PKind model checker [6] and have performed a preliminary evaluation[4]. We ran the lightweight validating compiler on a set of 330 Lustre benchmarks. For every benchmark, we use MC/DC conditions to generate basic test suites. We then automatically generate a set of mutants (160 on average) for each benchmark.

Test suite generated via BMC guided by MC/DC conditions were able to achieve 100% MC/DC coverage on 10% of the overall benchmark. On the remaining 90% benchmarks, 87% of the MC/DC conditions could be satisfied, while 13% could not be satisfied. On average, test cases generated using BMC guided by the MC/DC conditions were able to kill 25.12% of the generated mutants (with a standard derivation of 0.26). Test cases generated using the procedure highlighted in Figure 3 increased the performance of these basic test suites by 56% (std. dev. of 1.06). In absolute terms, the combined test suites killed 34% of the mutants (std. dev. of 0.31). Figure 4 shows a view on this results. For every experiment we show the percentages of mutants killed by MC/DC generated test cases and additional mutants killed by test cases generated using genNewTest. The data set was sorted by the overall number of killed mutants.

Considering these results, the number of mutants that could not be killed is strikingly high. We believe that this is due to many behaviorally equivalent mutants being generated. This is supported by the relatively high number of cases for which we could not satisfy MC/DC conditions, indicating the existence of dead code in the examples. This will have to be substantiated in a future investigation.

---

[4] The prototypical implementation, benchmarks and results can be found at https://bitbucket.org/lememta/nfm-14

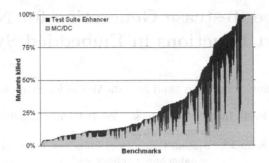

**Fig. 4.** Killed mutants per Benchmark. Ordered by percentage of mutants killed

## 5 Future Work

As a next step we plan to assess the fault finding capabilities of the generated test suites and compare these to other methods for generating test suites (e.g., random testing). A more recent work by Whalen et. al extended MC/DC with a notion of *observability* (OMC/DC) [9]. Our approach is orthogonal to such, in principle any coverage criterion can be used to generate the initial test case. We plan to integrate the OMC/DC technique in our validating compiler. Moreover, we plan to perform experiments with seeded bugs in the Lustre to C compiler to confirm that the mutations that we selected on Lustre programs mimic the effects of potential bugs in a compiler. We also plan to investigate how the validation results can be quantified and provide an estimate for the trustworthiness of the compiler. Finally, we plan to extend this work to object oriented languages.

## References

1. Benveniste, A., Berry, G.: The synchronous approach to reactive and real-time systems. In: Proceedings of the IEEE, pp. 1270–1282 (1991)
2. Biernacki, D., Colaço, J.L., Hamon, G., Pouzet, M.: Clock-directed modular code generation for synchronous data-flow languages. In: Flautner, K., Regehr, J. (eds.) LCTES, pp. 121–130. ACM (2008)
3. Boujarwah, A., Saleh, K.: Compiler test case generation methods: a survey and assessment. Information and Software Technology 39(9), 617–625 (1997)
4. Caspi, P., Pilaud, D., Halbwachs, N., Plaice, J.: Lustre: A declarative language for programming synchronous systems. In: POPL 1987, pp. 178–188. ACM Press (1987)
5. Hagen, G., Tinelli, C.: Scaling up the formal verification of Lustre programs with SMT-based techniques. In: FMCAD 2008, pp. 109–117. IEEE (2008)
6. Kahsai, T., Tinelli, C.: PKind: a parallel k-induction based model checker. In: PDMC. EPTCS, vol. 72, pp. 55–62 (2011)
7. Leroy, X.: Formal verification of a realistic compiler. Communications of the ACM 52(7), 107–115 (2009)
8. Necula, G.C.: Translation validation for an optimizing compiler. SIGPLAN Not. 35(5), 83–94 (2000)
9. Whalen, M., Gay, G., You, D., Heimdahl, M.P.E., Staats, M.: Observable modified condition/decision coverage. In: ICSE 2013, pp. 102–111. IEEE Press (2013)

# Automated Testcase Generation for Numerical Support Functions in Embedded Systems

Johann Schumann[1] and Stefan-Alexander Schneider[2]

[1] SGT, Inc./ NASA Ames, Moffett Field, CA 94035
Johann.M.Schumann@nasa.gov
[2] Schneider System Consulting, München, Germany
sahschneider@gmx.de

**Abstract.** We present a tool for the automatic generation of test stimuli for small numerical support functions, e.g., code for trigonometric functions, quaternions, filters, or table lookup. Our tool is based on KLEE to produce a set of test stimuli for full path coverage. We use a method of iterative deepening over abstractions to deal with floating-point values. During actual testing the stimuli exercise the code against a reference implementation. We illustrate our approach with results of experiments with low-level trigonometric functions, interpolation routines, and mathematical support functions from an open source UAS autopilot.

## 1 Introduction

Modern aircraft, spacecraft, or cars contain a large amount of software that is required to function properly for safe system operation and to accomplish the mission. It is estimated that a modern mid-size car is running more than 100 millions lines of code [1] on potentially more than 100 individual processing units. With the increase of software size and complexity, model-based approaches have found their way into safety-relevant applications in the aerospace and automotive domain. Although extensive analyses can be performed on the model level, a large percentage of the overall development cost for safety-critical software is spent on Verification and Validation (V&V) of the actual code and has become a huge challenge for system integrators and subsystem vendors.

Several prominent standards have been developed that require testing with a specific coverage metric depending on the safety-criticality of the code. For example, *ISO 26262 Road Vehicles* [2] requires testing according to MC/DC (Modified Condition Decision Coverage) for code belonging to Automotive Safety Integrity Level (ASIL) D. For levels A and B, only statement coverage is "highly recommended". Similarly, DO 178-C [3] defines levels A–E, where level A concerns the most critical software that has to be tested to 100% MC/DC coverage.

The application software, in particular, when generated using a model-based tool, requires a large number of low level support routines, which typically include advanced floating point operations (like trigonometric functions, matrices, vectors, or quaternions) as well as support functions for the auto-generated code (e.g., table look-up, interpolation, filters, or integrators). Many embedded

J.M. Badger and K.Y. Rozier (Eds.): NFM 2014, LNCS 8430, pp. 252–257, 2014.
© Springer International Publishing Switzerland 2014

system use the Netlib[1] mathematical library, or parts thereof like FDLIBM.[2] Also, John Hauser's SoftFloat[3] is being widely used. Most underlying algorithms, approximations, and tables are based on well-known algorithms [4]. Often such routines are part of the compiler or operating system package. Therefore, they are assumed to be given and correct and their proper testing tends to be ignored.

Because testing of such routines is essential, but manual test case generation is cumbersome and time consuming, we have developed a tool for the automatic generation of test stimuli for small numerical subroutines. In the following, we will first give a description of testcase generation using symbolic execution with KLEE. We then describe our tool architecture and discuss iterative deepening of abstractions. To illustrate advantages and limitations of our tool, we present results of experiments on trigonometric subroutines, table lookup, and a set of low-level mathematical support functions for an open source autopilot.

## 2  Automatic Testcase Generation

The input to our tool is a support function $o = f(x_1, \ldots, x_m)$ implemented[4] in C or C++. The tool generates test stimuli, i.e., a set of vectors with concrete values $\langle x_1^i, \ldots, x_m^i \rangle$ that, when given as parameters to $f$, will fully cover the code of $f$. For testing, we use the test stimuli to exercise $f$, compare the calculated result $o$ against a reference implementation and measure the code coverage according to the required coverage metric using an external tool.

Since we test against a reference implementation and do not use the output of our tool as an oracle, soundness of stimulus generation tool is not required. Tool unsoundness, however, can lead to an increased number of unnecessary test stimuli, decreasing testing performance.

Due to the requirement of handling floating-point values, the testcase generation has to be incomplete in general. Our tool architecture uses iterative deepening over abstractions to accomplish a reasonably complete set of test stimuli. We obtain the actual coverage by using an external trusted tool.

For the testcase generation, we use KLEE,[5] which is a symbolic execution engine based upon the LLVM framework.[6] It exhaustively explores all paths of the code; variables of interest (in our case, $x_i$) are treated as symbolic values, and each path is represented by a path constraint. For example, the code fragment `if (x<0 || x>10) A; else B;` produces three distinct path constraints: $\langle [x < 0] : A \rangle$ means that A can be reached by making the first condition true; similarly for $\langle [x > 10] : A \rangle$, the second condition must be true. Finally, the path constraint $\langle [\neg(x < 0) \land \neg(x > 10)] : B \rangle$ reaches B. Solving each path constraint leads to a set of test stimuli, for example, $\{-1, 11, 5\}$. Here, 3 test cases are needed for full

---

[1] http://netlib.org
[2] http://www.netlib.org/fdlibm
[3] http://jhauser.us/arithmetic/SoftFloat.html
[4] This code can also include calls to initialize objects or data structures.
[5] klee.llvm.org or [5]
[6] http://www.llvm.org

path coverage; statement coverage only requires two stimuli, e.g., $\{-1, 5\}$. KLEE uses the powerful STP[7] solver to find solutions for the path constraints. However, KLEE only provides very little support for floating point numbers; in most cases, KLEE silently instantiates the variable with a random value. KLEE-FP [6] has been designed to reason about equivalence of floating point numbers and is not suitable for this task. Yet, we chose to use KLEE, because it can handle the full C/C++ syntax and provides support for bitwise operations, which is essential for our purposes.

Our tool architecture and process is depicted in Figure 1. Starting with code under test $P$, which implements the function $o = f(\cdot)$ in one or more syntactic procedures, and an initial set of parameters $d = 0$, a parameterized abstraction is generated and applied to $P$. In this abstraction, all variables of type `float` or `double` are converted to integers. Each floating point constant $c$ is represented as $sign(c)\lfloor\min(maxint, |c| \times 10^d)\rfloor$. We chose a base of 10 because then the abstraction can be done on the source code by simply moving decimal points. Embedded function calls to other low-level routines (e.g., sqrt, sin) are abstracted by simple Taylor series or table lookup. Since most of the results of floating point operations in $P$ do not show up in equality comparisons in conditional statements, our abstraction is often successful by using this fixed-point abstraction with $d$ decimal places. Additional abstraction parameters define, how often $P$ is invoked during each test—an important step for testing reentrant functions like filters. The abstracted code $P_A$ is processed by KLEE, which returns a set of (abstracted) test stimuli $T_A$. They might cover all paths in $P_A$ or only a subset if KLEE timed out. We translate $T_A$ into actual test stimuli and use them to exercise $P$; coverage is measured on the original code $P$. If we are not satisfied with the results, the parameters controlling the abstraction are incremented and the iterative deepening loop starts again.

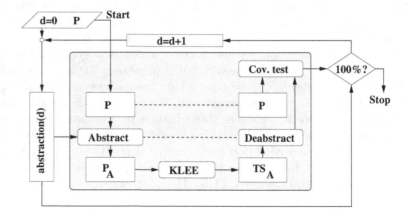

**Fig. 1.** Tool architecture

―――――――――
[7] http://people.csail.mit.edu/vganesh/STP_files/stp.html

# 3  Experiments

In this section, we describe selected experiments with this tool and discuss findings, advantages, and limitations of our approach.

**Trigonometric Functions.** Functions to calculate trigonometric functions are often considered part of the operating system or compiler. However, for small embedded systems, such functions must be provided externally and must be tested accordingly. As an example, consider a standard implementation (e.g., [8]) of the trigonometric function `double sin(double x)`. In a first step,[8] the input $x$ is broken down into its components (exponent, mantissa, and sign) according to IEEE 754 [7] using a C union and bit-fields. After handling cases for infinity, NaN, and very small argument values, $x$ is normalized to $[0 \ldots \pi/2]$, and the quadrant is determined. Finally, the function value is approximated by a 7th order polynomial. A complex algorithm for multiplication without loss of accuracy is used (see [8], [9]). Multiple macro definitions are used to handle machine-dependent issues. Although there are no loops in this code, there is a substantially complex control flow with 10 nested if-then-elses and one switch statement with 4 cases and an empty default label. Such a code structure makes a manual development of test cases hard.

With our tool, we generated a total of 44 test stimuli in less than 10s CPU time on an Intel Macbook Pro. This set of stimuli also contain NaN and Inf, which are encoded according to IEEE 754 by specific settings of mantissa and exponent bits. Several iterations of abstractions resulted in $d = 7$. Due to technical restrictions of KLEE, it also was necessary to pass two 32bit integer values instead of one 64bit double to the function.

When executing the generated test stimuli, two interesting observations could be made: (1) a comparison of the calculated values against the standard Mac OSX implementation revealed that, while the error between this code and the reference was in general between $10^{-11}$ and $10^{-18}$, two test stimuli caused errors that were larger than $3 \times 10^{-6}$, which might give raise to some concern. (2) a detailed analysis of the results with the industry-standard testing and coverage tool LDRA[9] revealed that this piece of code, which is actually a part of a commercial distribution, contains dead code. The empty default label in the switch statement can never be reached due to the range of the argument. Thus no test set can produce 100% MC/DC coverage, a fact which makes one wonder if that routine was ever tested according to that metric.

**Interpolation Table.** One of the most common block types in model-based systems like Simulink is the table lookup or 1-D interpolation block. Given an input $u$, it calculates an approximation of $f(u)$, whereby values of $f(x)$ for monotonically increasing values of $x$ are given statically as a table (see Figure 2A for a code sketch). We have analyzed a generic version of an 1-D table lookup, which is somewhat similar to Mathworks' `rt_look.c`.[10] After checking for boundary cases, a binary search is used to find the appropriate indices into the table.

---

[8] See suppl. material `ti.arc.nasa.gov/profiles/schumann/publications/nfm2014`
[9] `http://ldra.com`
[10] `rtw_demos/rt_look.c` is found in Mathworks' distribution of RealTime Workshop.

We used our tool to generate test stimuli for two relevant scenarios: (1) given a concrete lookup table $\langle x, f(x) \rangle_{1..len}$, find values for $u$ such that all paths are covered. E.g., for $x = \langle -2, 0, 3, 5, 8 \rangle$, and $f$ the identity function, the following six test cases for $u$ are generated in less than 0.1s: $u \in \{-2147483648, -1, 0, 2, 4, 6, 8\}$. Here, $d = 1$ was sufficient to obtain full coverage. In general, the necessary value of $d$ depends on the minimal difference $\Delta = x_{i+1} - x_i$. In the abstracted program $\Delta$ must be at least 2 in order to trigger the divide-and-conquer algorithm. This requires that $d \geq \log_{10} \lceil \min_i (x_{i+1} - x_i) \rceil$. In scenario (2), given the desired length $len$ of the interpolation table, triples $(\langle x, f(x) \rangle, u)$ with $length(x) = len$ are generated such that the code is fully covered. Note that the values of $x$ must be increasing monotonically. Therefore, the additional constraint $x_1 < x_2 \ldots$ must be specified in the test driver. Figure 2B shows, for different values of $len$, the number $C_0$ of all generated stimuli and the number $C$ of stimuli that obey our constraint and can be used as proper test stimuli.

```
double lookup(double *x, double *f, int len, double u){
if (u <= x[0]) return f[0];        // outside the table (left)
else if (u >= x[len-1]) return f[len-1]; // outside (right)
else
   for (;;){    // do binary search
   _assert( (x[bot] < u) && (u < x[top]));
   ind = (bot + top)/2;    // find middle
   if (...)
      top = ...; bot = ...
   else
      return f[ind];
   } }
```

| $len$ | $C_0$ | $C$ | t[s] |
|-----|-----|-----|------|
| 5   | 15  | 11  | 0.3  |
| 10  | 32  | 9   | 1.2  |
| 20  | 66  | 19  | 4.6  |
| 30  | 96  | 29  | 10.2 |
| 100 | 330 | 231 | 130  |

**Fig. 2.** A: code sketch of interpolation routine, B: number of generated test stimuli

All results have been obtained with the assertion _assert (Fig. 2A) turned off. When activated, it is textually replaced by a conditional statement that aborts the execution if the condition is not met. Interestingly, KLEE could still find a full coverage test set. This indicates that there exist stimuli $u$, which, for a given table $x$, cause the abortion of the execution. In an embedded system, such a behavior could have disastrous consequences. A closer look at the code reveals that the actual binary search loop is correct, but the assertion in rt_look.c is wrong (R2014a and earlier).

**ArduPilot.** ArduPilot[11] is an open source project aiming to provide high quality code for a simple autopilot for small fixed wing or rotorcraft UAVs, RC cars, or model boats. Ardupilot is implemented in C++ and runs on the Arduino platform.[12] Its mathematical libraries contain numerous functions dealing with trigonometric functions (via table lookup), vectors, matrices, quaternions, and filters. We used our tool to generate test stimuli for a number of those functions, leveraging the fact that KLEE can work on C++ code with templates. Although the code for each function is short and usually does not contain any loops, the presence of (nested) conditional statements makes our tool convenient for the task of testcase generation. In our experiments, we generated between 2 and

---

[11] http://code.google.com/ardupilot-mega
[12] http://arduino.cc

more than a hundred test stimuli (e.g., 116 for a function, which determines if a point is inside or outside a closed polygon with 7 edges).

## 4  Conclusions and Future Work

We have presented a tool for the automatic generation of test stimuli for small numeric support functions. Based upon KLEE, it uses iterative deepening over abstractions to deal with floating point operations. Because in practically all examples we analyzed so far, the results of floating point operations in $P$ do not show up in equality comparisons, our abstraction is often successful in producing a sufficient set of test stimuli. Although our tool has been able to conveniently and automatically generate test stimuli for a number of small, but often "tricky" numerical support routines, our approach still has several shortcomings. For example, configuration parameters and #define macros or template parameters (e.g., length of a filter buffer) currently cannot be treated symbolically and thus cannot be varied by our tool. Furthermore, preparation and abstraction of the code has not been fully automated yet, and support for writing test drivers and test scripts with symbolic variables is still very primitive. Obviously, scalability is an issue with larger programs, or programs, which contain nested loops (e.g., matrix operations). There, the restriction to MC/DC coverage to substantially reduce number of explored paths and generated stimuli and an abstraction for loops or the ability to modify KLEE's behavior on generating path conditions should be investigated.

## References

1. Charette, R.: This car runs on code (2009),
   http://spectrum.ieee.org/green-tech/advanced-cars/
   this-car-runs-on-code
2. Intl. standard ISO 26262 Road Vehicles – functional safety 1st edn. (2011)
3. RTCA: DO-178C: Software considerations in airborne systems and equipment certification (2011)
4. Hart, J.F., Cheney, E.W., Lawson, C.L., Maehly, H.J., Mesztenyi, C.K., Rice, J.R., Thacher, J.H.G., Witzgall, C.: Computer Approximations. SIAM Series in Applied Mathematics. John Wiley and Sons (1968)
5. Cadar, C., Dunbar, D., Engler, D.R.: KLEE: Unassisted and automatic generation of high-coverage tests for complex systems programs. In: 8th USENIX Symp. on Operating Systems Design and Implementation, OSDI, pp. 209–224 (2008)
6. Collingbourne, P., Cadar, D., Kelly, P.: Symbolic Crosschecking of Floating-Point and SIMD Code. In: EuroSys (2011)
7. IEEE standard 754 for floating-point arithmetic (2008)
8. Overton, M.L.: Numerical computing with IEEE floating point arithmetic - including one theorem, one rule of thumb, and 101 exercises. SIAM (2001)
9. Huckle, T., Schneider, S.A.: Numerische Methoden: Eine Einführung für Informatiker, Naturwissenschaftler, Ingenieure und Mathematiker. Springer (2006)
10. Giannakopoulou, D., Bushnell, D.H., Schumann, J., Erzberger, H., Heere, K.: Formal testing for separation assurance. Annals of Mathematics and Artificial Intelligence 63, 5–30 (2011)

# REFINER: Towards Formal Verification
# of Model Transformations

Anton Wijs and Luc Engelen

Department of Mathematics and Computer Science
Eindhoven University of Technology
P.O. Box 513, 5600 MB, Eindhoven, The Netherlands
{A.J.Wijs,L.J.P.Engelen}@tue.nl

**Abstract.** We present the REFINER tool, which offers techniques to define behavioural transformations applicable on formal models of concurrent systems, reason about semantics preservation and the preservation of safety and liveness properties of such transformations, and apply them on models. Behavioural transformations allow to change the potential behaviour of systems. This is useful for model-driven development approaches, where systems are designed and created by first developing an abstract model, and iteratively refining this model until it is concrete enough to automatically generate source code from it. Properties that hold on the initial model and should remain valid throughout the development in later models can be maintained, by which the effort of verifying those properties over and over again is avoided. The tool integrates with the existing model checking toolsets MCRL2 and CADP, resulting in a complete model checking approach for model-driven system development.

## 1 Introduction

REFINER[1] is a tool to verify so-called *behavioural* transformations of formal models of concurrent systems. Such transformations allow to manipulate the potential behaviour of the processes in a model. The ability to verify them opens up the possibility to step-wise develop complex concurrent systems, while preserving important system properties. Step-wise system development allows a developer to start the design phase with an abstract model, and making it more and more concrete through small, manageable transformations, until a model has been obtained with sufficient information to generate source code from it.

With REFINER, a developer can construct behavioural transformations, which the tool can efficiently analyse to determine if it preserves the semantics of models it is applied on, and if it preserves given safety or liveness properties. To the best of our knowledge, this is the first tool that can automatically check property preservation of user-defined model transformations, independent of source models. The topic is related to refinement checking. However, tools such as RODIN [1], FDR2,[2]

---

[1] Available at http://www.win.tue.nl/~awijs/refiner
[2] http://www.fsel.com/documentation/fdr2/html

J.M. Badger and K.Y. Rozier (Eds.): NFM 2014, LNCS 8430, pp. 258–263, 2014.

CSP-CASL-PROVER [2] can establish refinements between given models, but not verify transformation rules. ATELIER B[3] uses a notion comparable to transformation rules, but verifies resulting models instead of the rules themselves.

Semantics and property preservation checking is done by a single analysis technique. The first case is useful for refactoring and restructuring of models, while the second one allows for behaviour refinements. The technique is independent of the input and output models; it does not involve the state space of either of them, hence it usually works many orders of magnitude faster than repeated verification of the models through standard model checking, and it allows to build a repository of verified transformations. The tool integrates with the action-based, explicit-state model checking toolsets CADP [3] and MCRL2 [4]. These tools can be used to model concurrent systems in process algebras and automata, and to verify that the models satisfy functional properties. The semantics of the processes in such models can be represented by *Labelled Transition Systems* (LTSs), and the process LTSs can be combined using synchronisation composition. In REFINER, transformations are formalised as LTS transformations, defining which patterns in the LTSs need to be transformed into particular new patterns.

The theoretical basis has been published as [5–7]. Since then, a prototype implementation has been further developed to a complete tool, with a graphical user interface and multi-core computation capability.

## 2  Models and Model Transformations

REFINER uses a compositional action-based formalisation of system behaviour, i.e. LTSs are used to define the potential behaviour of individual processes and of systems as a whole. Its techniques are therefore applicable on any model with an LTS semantics, e.g. expressed in a process algebra. An LTS is a quadruple $\mathcal{G} = \langle \mathcal{S_G}, \mathcal{A_G}, \mathcal{T_G}, \underline{s}_\mathcal{G} \rangle$, with $\underline{s}_\mathcal{G}$ the initial state, $\mathcal{S_G}$ the (finite) set of states reachable from $\underline{s}_\mathcal{G}$, $\mathcal{A_G}$ a set of actions used to identify events, $\tau \notin \mathcal{A_G}$ being a special action representing internal events, and $\mathcal{T_G} : \mathcal{S_G} \times \mathcal{A_G} \cup \{\tau\} \times \mathcal{S_G}$ a relation expressing which actions can be performed in which states, and what the resulting state is. With $s \xrightarrow{a}_\mathcal{G} s'$, we express that $\langle s, a, s' \rangle \in \mathcal{T_G}$.

Process LTSs can be combined into a system. This is formalised as a *network of* LTSs [8]. In the following, given an integer $n > 0$, $1..n$ is the set of integers ranging from 1 to $n$. A vector $\overline{v}$ of size $n$ contains $n$ elements indexed by $1..n$. For $i \in 1..n$, $\overline{v}[i]$ denotes element $i$ in $\overline{v}$.

**Definition 1 (Network of LTSs).** *A network of LTSs $\mathcal{M}$ of size $n$ is a pair $\langle \Pi, \mathcal{V} \rangle$, where*

- *$\Pi$ is a vector of $n$ (process) LTSs. For each $i \in 1..n$, we write $\Pi[i] = \langle \mathcal{S}_i, \mathcal{A}_i, \mathcal{T}_i, \mathcal{I}_i \rangle$, and $s_1 \xrightarrow{b}_i s_2$ is shorthand for $s_1 \xrightarrow{b}_{\Pi[i]} s_2$;*
- *$\mathcal{V}$ is a finite set of synchronisation laws. A synchronisation law is a tuple $\langle \overline{t}, a \rangle$, where $a$ is an action label, and $\overline{t}$ is a vector of size $n$ called a synchronisation vector, in which for all $i \in 1..n$, $\overline{t}[i] \in \mathcal{A}_i \cup \{\bullet\}$, where $\bullet$ is a special symbol denoting that $\Pi[i]$ performs no action.*

---

[3] http://www.atelierb.eu

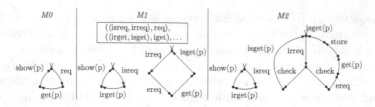

**Fig. 1.** Three versions of a network modelling an agent fetching pages

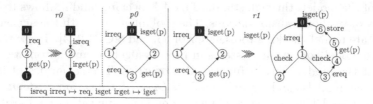

**Fig. 2.** Rules $r_0$, $p_0$ of rule system $R_0$, and $r_1$ of rule system $R_1$

The synchronous composition LTS($\mathcal{M}$) defined by a network $\mathcal{M}$ represents the state space of $\mathcal{M}$, and is an LTS with $\underline{s} = \langle \underline{s}_1, \ldots, \underline{s}_n \rangle$, $\mathcal{A} = \{a \mid \langle \bar{t}, a \rangle \in \mathcal{V}\}$, $\mathcal{S} = \mathcal{S}_1 \times \ldots \times \mathcal{S}_n$, and $\mathcal{T}$ is the smallest relation satisfying:

$$\langle \bar{t}, a \rangle \in \mathcal{V} \wedge (\forall i \in 1..n) \left( \begin{array}{c} (\bar{t}[i] = \bullet \wedge \bar{s}'[i] = \bar{s}[i]) \\ \vee \, (\bar{t}[i] \neq \bullet \wedge \bar{s}[i] \xrightarrow{\bar{t}[i]}_i \bar{s}'[i]) \end{array} \right) \implies \bar{s} \xrightarrow{a} \bar{s}'.$$

We formalise behavioural model-to-model transformations from networks of LTSs to new networks of LTSs as *rule systems*, containing a finite number of LTS *transformation rules*. Such a rule consists of a pair of LTSs $\mathcal{L} \to \mathcal{R}$. The used transformation mechanism is the *double-pushout* method from graph transformation [9]: $\mathcal{L}$ defines a pattern, to be found and replaced in a given LTS $\mathcal{G}$ (for this, a *match*, i.e. an injective homomorphism, $m : \mathcal{L} \to \mathcal{G}$ must be established), and $\mathcal{R}$ defines the pattern that should replace all occurrences of $\mathcal{L}$ in $\mathcal{G}$. Apart from some conditions that need to hold in order to have a valid match of $\mathcal{L}$ on an LTS $\mathcal{G}$,[4] a subset of so-called *glue-states* $S \subseteq \mathcal{S}_\mathcal{L} \cap \mathcal{S}_\mathcal{R}$ is defined, which indicates how $\mathcal{L}$ relates to $\mathcal{R}$. When applying transformation on a match $m : \mathcal{L} \to \mathcal{G}$, resulting in a new LTS $T(\mathcal{G})$, first, all states matched on $\mathcal{S}_\mathcal{L} \setminus S$ and all related transitions are removed, and second, each state in $\mathcal{S}_\mathcal{R} \setminus S$ (and related transitions) leads to a new state in $\mathcal{S}_{T(\mathcal{G})}$ (and new related transitions in $\mathcal{T}_{T(\mathcal{G})}$).

Rules are applied on process LTSs of a network to transform it, but rule systems also include left and right synchronisation laws, expressing how behaviour in the left and right rule patterns, respectively, should synchronise with each other and the outside world. In order for a rule system $R$ to be applicable on a network $\mathcal{M}$, the left laws of $R$ must be compatible with those of $\mathcal{M}$, and if so, then the right laws of $R$ are introduced when transforming.

---

[4] The interested reader is referred to [6,9].

Figs. 1 and 2 show a small, but illustrative example of the approach. In Fig. 1, network $M_0$ is an abstract specification of an agent, for instance a web browser, which can request a page ($req$), receive a page $p$ ($get(p)$), and display it ($show(p)$). Initial states of LTSs are marked with an incoming arrowhead. Actually, $M_0$ is still very abstract, and we wish to specify that the communication with the outside world is handled by an additional component. This is added in $M_1$, and we have two new laws expressing the need for synchronisation between the two components over actions internal to the system (these actions are prefixed by '$i$'). We can obtain $M_1$ from $M_0$ by transforming the latter using a rule system $R_0$ defined in Fig. 2. There, black states are glue-states, and square black states are glue-states with the added condition that states matched on them do not have outgoing transitions that are not covered by the left pattern. Rule $r_0$ rewrites the component we already had in $M_0$, and $p_0$ is a special kind of rule called a *process adding* rule, which adds a new component. It can be interpreted as a rule with an empty left pattern. Finally, it introduces two new laws, expressed without using vectors, since the rules have no fixed order. When transforming, these are matched on the input network to derive concrete new laws for the new network.

Likewise, $M_1$ can be transformed to $M_2$ with the motivation that the communication component should have a local buffer, and check for each request whether that page is already in the buffer before attempting communication with the outside world. Rule $r_1$ of Fig. 2 can be applied on $M_1$ to obtain $M_2$.

In this example, the networks are not much larger than the rule systems, but in practice, they usually are, and rules are often applicable in multiple places.

*Verification of Transformations.* REFINER can check whether a rule system $R$ is confluent, i.e. leads to a unique target model, and verify whether it is semantics preserving and/or correctness preserving, i.e. that it preserves a desired system property. In both cases, it identifies, based on the left and right laws of $R$, which transformation rules are dependent on each other. Two rules $r = \mathcal{L}_r \rightarrow \mathcal{R}_r$, $r' = \mathcal{L}_{r'} \rightarrow \mathcal{R}_{r'}$ are dependent iff in $\mathcal{L}_r$ (or $\mathcal{R}_r$), there is at least one transition that needs to synchronise with a transition in $\mathcal{L}_{r'}$ (or $\mathcal{R}_{r'}$). This partitions the set of rules in $R$ into sets of dependent rules. For each set $D$ of dependent rules,[5] the left patterns and the right patterns of all the elements are combined into two new networks $D_L$ and $D_R$. For semantics preservation, it is checked if LTS($D_L$) and LTS($D_R$) are *(strongly) bisimilar*, i.e. whether they can be considered equivalent.

A more general approach is required to check the preservation of particular properties. In order to allow the semantics to be altered, $D_L$ and $D_R$ should be compared w.r.t. a given property, instead of the entire semantics. For this, we move the LTS($D_L$) and LTS($D_R$) to an appropriate level of abstraction before the analysis, using the *maximal hiding* technique [10]. For any property $\varphi$ written in the $\mu$-calculus fragment $L_\mu^{dsbr}$ [10], maximal hiding hides all actions in an LTS, i.e. renames them to $\tau$, that are not crucial for the truth-value of $\varphi$. Furthermore, it is shown in [10] that if $\varphi$ is satisfied by an LTS $\mathcal{G}_1$, and $\mathcal{G}_1$ is *divergence-sensitive*

---

[5] In addition to each $D$, also all their subsets are involved in the analysis, the latter representing situations with unsuccessful synchronisation. For the details, see [6].

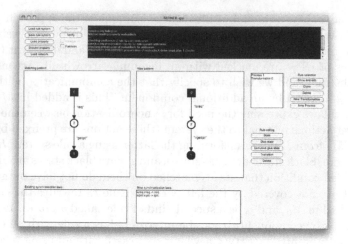

**Fig. 3.** The graphical user interface of REFINER

*branching bisimilar* [11] (DSBB)[6] to an LTS $\mathcal{G}_2$, then also $\mathcal{G}_2$ satisfies $\varphi$. This allows comparing LTSs w.r.t. $\varphi$. We apply maximal hiding w.r.t. a given $\varphi$ to the LTS($D_L$) and LTS($D_R$), before checking that they are DSBB. If the checks pass for all $D_L$ and $D_R$, then $R$ preserves $\varphi$. Semantics preservation checking is actually the special case in which maximal hiding has no effect.

Consider again the example rule systems of Fig. 2, and the $L_\mu^{dsbr}$ property $\varphi = [\text{true}^*][\tau^*.req]([(\neg get(p))^*]\neg \text{deadlock} \wedge [\neg get(p)] \dashv)$, where 'deadlock' is a formula expressing the presence of a deadlock. This property expresses that after every *req*, eventually a *get(p)* will occur (for the semantics of $L_\mu^{dsbr}$, see [10]). Based on this, maximal hiding will hide all transition labels, except for *req* and *get(p)*. Combining the left- and right-patterns of $r_0$ and $p_0$, constructing the synchronous compositions, and applying this hiding, leads to DSBB LTSs. This is also the case for $r_1$ in isolation. Hence, both rule systems preserve $\varphi$.

## 3   Implementation

REFINER has been implemented in PYTHON 3, and consists of about 5,000 lines of code. It is platform-independent, and has a graphical user interface (Fig. 3), implemented using the TKINTER module, but it can also be run from the command line. It provides the functionality to create and edit rule systems, load and save them, apply them on models, and verify them in various ways. The tool does not focus on creating and verifying models; instead, this can be done using the model checker toolsets CADP and mCRL2. With these tools, REFINER shares file formats for LTSs, networks of LTSs, and $L_\mu^{dsbr}$ properties.

For verification, REFINER allows to check semantics preservation of rule systems, model-independent preservation of properties, and property preservation

---

[6] DSBB is, like weak and branching bisimilarity [11], sensitive to $\tau$-transitions, but also to divergences, i.e. the ability to perform infinite sequences of $\tau$-transitions [11]. As such, it preserves safety and liveness properties.

w.r.t. particular models. Besides this, there are the fine-tuning options 'fairness', by which divergences in a rule system will be ignored (useful for safety properties), and 'divergency', by which the divergences already present in an input network will be taken into account, allowing for a more relaxed check.

Finally, REFINER has multi-core computation capability. Verifying a rule system may involve many DSBB checks. Since these can be done independently, parallelisation is straight-forward. Experiments have shown that this scales linearly [7]. As demonstrated in [6], REFINER can, through model transformation verification, determine in mere seconds that transformed networks with state spaces of multiple billions of states satisfy a particular property. Model checking those networks would take many orders of magnitude more time. For future work, we plan to support timing [12], and directed search techniques [13].

# References

1. Abrial, J.R., Butler, M., Hallerstede, S., Hoang, T., Mehta, F., Voisin, L.: RODIN: An Open Toolset for Modelling and Reasoning in EVENT-B. STTT 12(6), 447–466 (2010)
2. Kahsai, T., Roggenbach, M.: Property Preserving Refinement for CSP-CASL. In: Corradini, A., Montanari, U. (eds.) WADT 2008. LNCS, vol. 5486, pp. 206–220. Springer, Heidelberg (2009)
3. Garavel, H., Lang, F., Mateescu, R., Serwe, W.: CADP 2010: A Toolbox for the Construction and Analysis of Distributed Processes. In: Abdulla, P.A., Leino, K.R.M. (eds.) TACAS 2011. LNCS, vol. 6605, pp. 372–387. Springer, Heidelberg (2011)
4. Cranen, S., Groote, J., Keiren, J., Stappers, F., de Vink, E., Wesselink, W., Willemse, T.: An Overview of the mCRL2 Toolset and Its Recent Advances. In: Piterman, N., Smolka, S.A. (eds.) TACAS 2013. LNCS, vol. 7795, pp. 199–213. Springer, Heidelberg (2013)
5. Engelen, L., Wijs, A.: Incremental Formal Verification for Model Refining. In: MoDeVVa 2012, pp. 29–34. ACM (2012)
6. Wijs, A., Engelen, L.: Efficient Property Preservation Checking of Model Refinements. In: Piterman, N., Smolka, S.A. (eds.) TACAS 2013. LNCS, vol. 7795, pp. 565–579. Springer, Heidelberg (2013)
7. Wijs, A.: Define, Verify, Refine: Correct Composition and Transformation of Concurrent System Semantics. In: Xue, J., Fiadeiro, J.L., Liu, Z. (eds.) FACS 2013. LNCS, Springer (2013) (to appear)
8. Lang, F.: EXP.OPEN 2.0: A Flexible Tool Integrating Partial Order, Compositional, and On-the-Fly Verification Methods. In: Romijn, J.M.T., Smith, G.P., van de Pol, J. (eds.) IFM 2005. LNCS, vol. 3771, pp. 70–88. Springer, Heidelberg (2005)
9. Heckel, R.: Graph Transformation in a Nutshell. In: FoVMT 2004. ENTCS, vol. 148, pp. 187–198. Elsevier (2006)
10. Mateescu, R., Wijs, A.: Property-Dependent Reductions for the Modal Mu-Calculus. In: Groce, A., Musuvathi, M. (eds.) SPIN 2011. LNCS, vol. 6823, pp. 2–19. Springer, Heidelberg (2011)
11. van Glabbeek, R., Weijland, W.: Branching Time and Abstraction in Bisimulation Semantics. Journal of the ACM 43(3), 555–600 (1996)
12. Fokkink, W., Pang, J., Wijs, A.: Is Timed Branching Bisimilarity an Equivalence Indeed? In: Pettersson, P., Yi, W. (eds.) FORMATS 2005. LNCS, vol. 3829, pp. 258–272. Springer, Heidelberg (2005)
13. Wijs, A.: What To Do Next?: Analysing and Optimising System Behaviour in Time. PhD thesis, VU University Amsterdam (2007)

# Designing a Deadlock-Free Train Scheduler: A Model Checking Approach*

Franco Mazzanti, Giorgio Oronzo Spagnolo, and Alessio Ferrari

Istituto di Scienza e Tecnologie dell'Informazione "A.Faedo",
Consiglio Nazionale delle Ricerche, ISTI-CNR, Pisa, Italy

**Abstract.** In this paper we present the approach used in the design of
the scheduling kernel of an Automatic Train Supervision (ATS) system.
A formal model of the railway layout and of the expected service has been
used to identify all the possible critical sections of the railway layout in
which a deadlock might occur. For each critical section, the prevention of
the occurrence of deadlocks is achieved by constraining the set of trains
allowed to occupy these sections at the same time. The identification of
the critical sections and the verification of the correctness of the logic
used by the ATS is carried out by exploiting a model checking verification
framework locally developed at ISTI-CNR and based on the tool UMC.

## 1 Introduction

The current trend in the design of metropolitan railway systems is to provide
fully automated platforms, where trains move in driverless mode, and are moni-
tored by a centralized component, normally called Automatic Train Supervision
system (ATS). The main role of an ATS system is to automatically coordinate
the progress of the trains. In absence of delays, an ATS ensures a perfect adherence to the planned time table. In presence of delays, the ATS system must
perform the correct train scheduling choices in order to guarantee that every
train will still reach its destination. In particular, this means that the ATS
should necessarily avoid the occurrence of *deadlock* situations, i.e., situations
where a group of trains block each other, preventing in this way the completion
of their missions.

The Italian project "Train Control Enhancement via Information Technology" (TRACE-IT) is a project funded by the Tuscany Region which sees the
cooperation of an industrial partner active in the field of railway signaling and
academic partners among which the ISTI institute of the CNR. One of the goals
of the TRACE-IT project is the design, development and experimentation of a
Communications Based Train Control system (CBTC) [1]. ISTI is involved in
the specification and development of the ATS component of the CBTC system,
and this task includes the development of a demonstrative prototype of an ATS
system for a simple but not trivial railway yard layout and a simple but not
trivial service plan.

---

* This work was partially supported by the PAR FAS 2007-2013 (TRACE-IT) project.

J.M. Badger and K.Y. Rozier (Eds.): NFM 2014, LNCS 8430, pp. 264–269, 2014.
© Springer International Publishing Switzerland 2014

Our approach starts with the construction of a formal model of the railway layout and of the expected service. By performing exhaustive model checking of the system, we identify all the possible critical sections of the railway layout in which the given set of running trains might lead to the generation of deadlocks. For each critical section, the prevention of deadlocks is achieved in a simple but efficient way, by constraining the set of trains allowed to occupy the section at the same time. The scheduling kernel of the ATS is designed to take into account this information while performing its scheduling choices. The overall correctness of the behavior of the ATS in presence of delays is finally verified by proving that the adopted design guarantees that the supervised traffic is deadlock-free. The formal verification of the full railway yard is performed by decomposing it into several regions, which are analyzed separately, and by proving that the adopted decomposition allows to extend the results to the full layout. The modeling and verification of the system has been carried out using the UML model checker UMC (accessible at http://fmt.isti.cnr.it/umc/ together with the examples of the paper) developed at ISTI. UMC is an abstract, on-the-fly, state-event based, verification environment working on UML-like state machines [2].

## 2   The Initial Model of the System

In UMC a system is described as a set of communicating UML-like state machines. In our particular case, the kernel of the ATS system is modeled by a unique state machine. The state machine has a local status describing the current progress of the trains in the railway yard. Moreover, it makes the appropriate scheduling choices among the trains according to the structure of their missions. At our level of analysis the basic elements which are the subject of the scheduling are the request for itineraries. An itinerary consists of a sequence of track circuits (i.e., independent line segments) which must be traversed for arriving to a station platform from an external entry point, or for leaving from a station platform towards an external exit point.

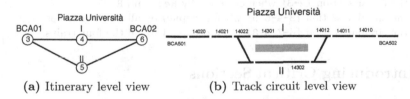

(a) Itinerary level view          (b) Track circuit level view

**Fig. 1.** The itinerary and track circuit level view of a station

In Figure 1 we show the two levels of abstraction of the train movement, namely the itinerary level view and the track circuit level view. Notice that, at the interlocking management level, we would be interested in the more detailed track circuit level view, because we have to deal with the setting of signals and commutation of switches for the preparation of the requested itineraries. These elements are not visible at the itinerary level view, which is our level of observation of the system for the deadlock-freedom problem.

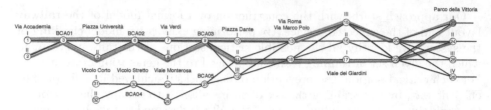

**Fig. 2.** The yard layout and the missions for the trains of the green and red line

In our case, the overall map of the railway yard which describes the various interconnected station platforms and station exit/entry points (itinerary endpoints) is shown in Figure 2. Given our map, the mission of a train can be seen as a sequence of itinerary endpoints. In our case, the service consists of eight trains which start their missions at the extreme points of the layout and traverse the whole layout in one direction. For example, the missions of the four trains providing the green-line and red-line service shown in Figure 2, are represented by the following data:

```
Green1: [1,3,4,6,7,9,10,13,15,20,23] Green2: [23,22,17,18,11,9,5,8,6,5,3,1]
Red1: [2,3,4,6,7,8,10,13,15,20,24]    Red2: [24,22,17,18,11,9,5,8,6,5,3,2]
```

Initially, in order to discover all the possible basic deadlock situations, trains are allowed to move from one point to the next only if the destination point is not occupied. Given the set of train missions, and given their current point of progress, UMC can deduce which trains can advance and compute all the possible successive states of the system. In particular, we verify a logic formula that specifies that every system evolution leads to the completion of all the missions. In UMC, we verify the CTL-like formula *AF completed*, where *completed* is a predicate that is true when all trains are in their final destination. The UMC analysis of the model, even with just the four trains shown above, reveals that deadlocks (i.e., violations of the formula) occur in four sections of the layout:

a) In the linear section [1-3] when occupied by Green1 and Green2.
b) In the linear section [2-3] when occupied by Red1 and Red2.
c) In the circular section [3-4-6-5] when occupied by all the four trains.
d) In the circular section [6-7-9-8] when occupied by all the four trains.

## 3   Introducing Critical Sections

For each case of deadlock identified at the previous step, we can build a countermeasure to avoid it by associating a "critical section" to the set of points on which it the deadlock occurred, and by constraining the set of trains allowed to occupy the section at the same time. For example, with respect to the four cases of deadlocks shown before, we can set up the following set of critical sections and corresponding constraints:

a) Section A=[1-3] : at most 1 train among Green1 and Green2.
b) Section B=[2-3] : at most 1 train among Red1 and Red2.
c) Section C=[3-4-6-5] : at most 3 among all the four trains.
d) Section D=[6-7-9-8] : at most 3 among all the four trains.

**Fig. 3.** Deadlock situations over the composition of basic critical sections

A second version of the model of our system can now be built by taking into consideration the discovered set of critical sections and by enriching the mission definitions with information of which critical sections we are entering/exiting when we move from one point to the next one. In this way our ATS model, before allowing the train to advance, can first check whether the movement of the train would violate the constraints of some critical section. With respect to our four trains on the layout shown on Figure 2, the ATS strategy is described by the following sections constraints and mission enriched data:

```
Sections: [A max 1,B max 1,C max 3,D max 3]
Green1: [1,(enter C),3,(exit A),4,(enter D),6,(exit C),7,9,(exit D),10,13,15,20,23]
Green2: [23,22,17,18,11,(enter D),9,5,8,(enter C),6,(exit D),5,(enter A),3,(exit C),1]
Red1: [2,(enter C),3,(exit B),4,(enter D),6,(exit C),7,9,(exit D),10,13,15,20,24]
Red2: [24,22,17,18,11,(enter D),9,5,8,(enter C),6,(exit D),5,(enter B),3,(exit C),2]
```

## 4   From Simple to Composite Critical Sections

Whenever we have critical sections that partially overlap (sharing some common points of the layout), the introduction of the rules for entering a section may reveal less evident cases of deadlocks. Therefore additional rounds of model checking are needed to complete the analysis of the system. In the case of four trains in the layout of Figure 2, the model checking reveals the new deadlock situations that are illustrated in Figure 3. Notice that, in the left case, train Green2 cannot exit from critical section C because it is not allowed to enter critical section A. Moreover, train Green1 is not allowed to leave critical section A because it is not allowed to enter critical section C. To solve these situations, we can introduce an additional composite critical section E over points [1-2-3-4-6-5], which is allowed to contain at most three of the trains Green1, Green2, Red1, Red2. At the end of these further rounds of model checking the situation has become as shown below:

```
Sections: [A max 1,B max 1,C max 3,D max 3,E max 3]
Green1:[1,(enter C),3,(exit A),4,(enter D),6,(exit C,E),7,9,(exit D),10,13,15,20,23]
Green2:[23,22,17,18,11,(enter D),9,5,8,(enter C,E),6,(exit D),5,(enter A),3,(exit C),1]
Red1:[2,(enter C),3,(exit B),4,(enter D),6,(exit C,E),7,9,(exit D),10,13,15,20,24]
Red2:[24,22,17,18,11,(enter D),9,5,8,(enter C,E),6,(exit D),5,(enter B),3,(exit C),2]
```

A final verification of the model with four trains confirms that the traffic is now deadlock free and therefore that these section definitions and extended mission data can be safely used by the ATS for its train scheduling.

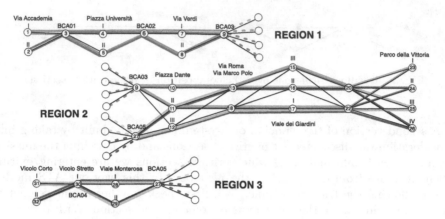

**Fig. 4.** The three regions partitioning the full layout

## 5  Partitioning the Full Model

Sometimes the scheduling problem might be too complex to be handled by the model checker. In these cases, it is useful to split the overall layout into subregions to be analyzed separately. In particular, in the system actually employed in our project, we have four other trains moving along the yellow-line and blue-line service, with eight trains possibly occupying the right side of the layout at the same time. Our model checker is not able to perform an exhaustive analysis of the full network (32M states need to be generated, and this leads to verification time problems), therefore we have to split the overall layout. For example, we can partition the system as shown in Figure 4. The analysis of region 1 has been performed following the approach outlined in the previous sections, and has led to the introduction of five critical sections.

The analysis of region 3 is similar to the previous one, and leads to the introduction of further four critical sections. The analysis of region 2 is more complex, being bigger and with eight trains inside it. The analysis reveals two other circular sections in which a deadlock might occur (shown in Figure 5). After the introduction of the appropriate critical sections and corresponding constraints, also region 2 can be proved to be deadlock free.

In general, it is not true that the separate analysis of the single regions in which a layout is partitioned actually reveals all the possible deadlocks of the full system. For this being true it is necessary that the adopted partitioning does not cut (hiding it from the analysis) any critical section that overlaps two regions. In our case, this property of the partitioning is guaranteed by two facts. First, the set of borderline points in common between each region and its "external world" consists of a single point. This guarantees that the partitioning does not cut any circular critical section, because that would have created at least two points in the border. Secondly, the (unique) borderline point does not belong to a critical section in each side of the border. In fact, should this have happened, it might have led to an undiscovered composite critical section composed by the union of the two confining critical sections of the two regions.

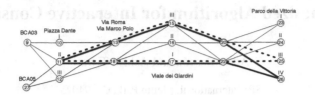

**Fig. 5.** Two critical sections in region 2

# 6 Conclusions

The development of solutions to the problem of deadlock avoidance in train scheduling is a complex and still open task [3]. Many studies have been carried out on the subject since the early '80s, but most of them are related to normal railway traffic, and not to the special case of driverless metropolitan systems. Automatic metro systems indeed may express some original properties, e.g., the difficulty of changing the station platform on which a train should stop, or the fact that all trains keep moving continuously, which makes the problem rather different from the classical railway case. Formal methods have been widely and successfully used in the railway context [4], but usually they are applied only to their safety critical components. The ATS, despite its functional relevance, is not considered a safety critical component and we are not aware of other experiences in formally designing it.

The project under which this study has been carried out is still in progress, and the actual ATS prototype in under development. There are many directions in which this work might proceed. For example, it would be interesting to see if the model checking phase for the detection of critical regions could be included as part of the ATS behavior instead of being done at a previous pre-configuration phase. This would allow to perform automatically and in a safe way also the dynamic change of the itinerary of the trains. Currently the data discovered by the model checker must be manually analyzed, and the ATS configuration data must be manually created. This task might be a source of errors; we are currently working on approaches to automatically generate the ATS configuration data from the results of the system model checking.

# References

1. IEEE: Standard for CBTC Performance and Functional Requirements. IEEE Std 1474.1 (2004)
2. Gnesi, S., Mazzanti, F.: An abstract, on the fly framework for the verification of service-oriented systems. In: Wirsing, M., Hölzl, M. (eds.) SENSORIA Project. LNCS, vol. 6582, pp. 390–407. Springer, Heidelberg (2011)
3. Törnquist, J.: Computer-based decision support for railway traffic scheduling and dispatching: A review of models and algorithms. In: Proc. of ATMOS 2005 (2006)
4. Fantechi, A., Fokkink, W., Morzenti, A.: Some trends in formal methods applications to railway signaling. In: Formal Methods for Industrial Critical Systems: A Survey of Applications, pp. 61–84. John Wiley & Sons (2013)

# A Synthesized Algorithm for Interactive Consistency

Adrià Gascón and Ashish Tiwari

SRI International, Menlo Park, CA 94025

**Abstract.** We revisit the interactive consistency problem introduced by Pease, Shostak and Lamport. We first show that their algorithm does not achieve interactive consistency if faults are transient, even if faults are non-malicious. We then present an algorithm that achieves interactive consistency in the presence of non-malicious, asymmetric and transient faults, but only under an additional guaranteed delayed ack assumption. We discovered our algorithm using an automated synthesis technique that is based on bounded model checking and QBF solving. Our synthesis technique is general and simple, and it is a promising approach for synthesizing distributed algorithms.

## 1 Introduction

Distributed consensus is a fundamental problem in Computer Science. The goal is to reach agreement in a distributed system in the presence of faults. Depending on the formulation of the problem, it has been called the distributed agreement, distributed consensus, or interactive agreement.

Consider a distributed system composed of $n$ processes that can communicate with each other only by means of two-party messages. Each process has a local Boolean value that it wishes to share with all other processes. Eventually we want all the processes to know each other's local value. Achieving this desired final configuration is complicated by the presence of faults.

We will assume a synchronous timinig model; that is, there are known bounds on the time required for executing one step of a process and on the time required for a message to reach its destination. Formally, we will assume that execution times are negligible. So, the distributed agreement protocol can work in *rounds*: in each round, every process receives the messages its neighbors had sent in the previous round and it sends out a new message to each of its neighbors.

A key challenge in achieving agreement is to do so in the presence of faults. In our presentation, we assume that processes can be faulty, but the communication channel is reliable. As it will become clear to the reader later, we can also formulate our results in a way that makes the processes reliable and the channels faulty. Moreover, every pair of processes communicate through a dedicated channel and hence the receiver of a message always knows which process has sent that message.

So, what do we assume about the nature of a fault? First, let us define some attributes of faults. A fault is *transient* if the identity of the faulty process is not fixed; that is, a process that is faulty in the current step can become non-faulty in the next step and vice versa. In contrast, a fault is *permanent* if the same set of processes remain faulty at every synchronous step.

J.M. Badger and K.Y. Rozier (Eds.): NFM 2014, LNCS 8430, pp. 270–284, 2014.

A fault is *benign or non-malicious or fail-silent* if every faulty process either behaves exactly as a non-faulty process or sends just *nil* messages to other processes. Note that this kind of fault is equivalent to a fault where "messages are dropped by the communication channel" or where "a process does not send or forward a message it was supposed to send or forward" because, due to the synchronous nature of the timing model, a receiver can identify unsent or dropped messages. In contrast, a fault is *malicious* if the faulty process can send any message to its neighbors, including false messages. A fault is *asymmetric* if a faulty process is not forced to send the same information to each of its neighbors. In contrast, in a *symmetric fault*, a faulty process sends the same (possibly wrong) message to all neighbors. In other words, faulty processes lie consistenly to all other processes.

As mentioned above, we assume that processes can only communicate by means of two-party messages, that is, we assume a fully connected topology for the processes. In other words, the neighbor set of a process contains all other $n - 1$ processes.

One key assumption we make about the behavior of faulty process is that a faulty process always updates its local state correctly (just like a non-faulty process). The faulty behavior of a process is manifest only through the possibly faulty messages it sends to its neighbors. There are many different ways to motivate this assumption. One way is to view the processes as non-faulty and the communication channels (specifically, all outgoing channels from a faulty process) to be faulty. A second way is to note that this assumption makes no difference in case of permanent faults. It is relevant only for transient faults, and in a transient fault, a faulty process could become non-faulty and hence it could update its internal state correctly.

Rather than working with an arbitrary number $n$ of processes out of which some $f$ are faulty, we will work with concrete instances in this paper. Specifically, we will focus on $n = 4$ or $n = 3$ processes out of which $f = 1$ will be faulty.

Finally, in our faulty distributed system setting, we have to appropriately redefine our desired "agreeement state". Note that, in the scenario where a certain process is always faulty and never shares its correct local value, the other processes can not ever know the correct value of such faulty process and hence never reach agreement on the correct internal values of all processes. The notion of "interactive consistency" was, therefore, introduced to describe a final agreement configuration where all nonfaulty processes know the correct internal value of all (other) nonfaulty processes, and agree on the same (maybe wrong) value for the faulty processes. When faults are transient, the identity of the faulty process keeps changing. Therefore, we adapt the definition of interactive consistency so that it does not mention faulty and non-faulty processes and instead just talks about the number of processes that are in agreement (Definition 1).

Our main result is an algorithm for achieving interactive consistency in the presence of non-malicious, transient, and asymmetric faults. Our algorithm achieves interactive consistency in three rounds, *and then preserves it forever thereafter*, and allows one (possibly different) process to be faulty in each round. If our algorithm is run for $f \geq 3$ rounds, we tolerate a total of $f$ faults in $f$ rounds. We overcome the impossibility result (which says that $f + 1$ rounds are needed for tolerating $f$ faults) by introducing a *guaranteed delayed ack* assumption. Our algorithm was synthesized automatically. We also describe our synthesis approach in this paper, which is a generic approach for synthesis, and is particularly promising for synthesizing distributed algorithms.

## 1.1 Formalization and Notation

We assume there are $n$ processes. Formally, a process is just an element of the set $\bar{n} = \{1, \ldots, n\}$. Each process $i$ has a private Boolean value. Each process (say, Process $i$) is assumed to maintain a local *consistency vector* $\mathrm{cv}^{(i)} := (v_1, \ldots, v_n)$ where $v_j$ is Process $i$'s estimate of Process $j$'s private value and belongs to the set *Vals* := $\{\texttt{true}, \texttt{false}, \texttt{nil}\}$. For every $i$, the component $v_i$ of the consistency vector of Process $i$ is the private Boolean value for Process $i$. Processes do not change their own private value in their consistency vector, but do update their estimate of the private value of other processes in their local consistency vector.

A *message* is a tuple $(s, v)$, where $s$ is a finite string over the alphabet $\bar{n}$; that is, $s \in \bar{n}^*$, where $A^* = \cup_i A^i$, and $v \in$ *Vals* is a value. The length of the string $s$ is at least 2. The tuple $(12, \texttt{true})$ denotes the message sent by Process 2 to Process 1 informing Process 1 that Process 2's private value is $\texttt{true}$. If the length of $s$ is greater-than 2, then the meaning of the message $(s, v)$ is defined inductively. The tuple $(12s, v)$ denotes the message that is forwarded by Process 2 to Process 1 informing Process 1 that Process 2 had received the message $(2s, v)$ in the previous round. For example, $(123, \texttt{true})$ is the message forwarded by Process 2 to Process 1 which Process 2 had received from Process 3 in the previous round (containing the value $\texttt{true}$). Note that if Process 1 receives $(123, \texttt{true})$, then Process 1 receives the string 123 as well as the value $\texttt{true}$.

We remark here about the implicit assumption being made above. We are assuming that nodes have an "identity" and processes know which process sent what message to it. So, for example, the scenario "Process 1 receives the messages $(12, \texttt{true})$ and $(13, \texttt{false})$" is different from the scenario "Process 1 receives the messages $(12, \texttt{false})$ and $(13, \texttt{true})$". If Process 1 could not distinguish between the different senders, then the two scenarios would look identical to Process 1: in both cases, Process 1 receives one $\texttt{true}$ and one $\texttt{false}$ message.

We assume that processes are *deterministic*. In each round, Process $i$ receives messages (sent to it by the other processes in the previous round), and updates its local consistency vector using some deterministic function of its old consistency vector and the received messages. Furthermore, Process $i$ also generates, and then sends, messages to other processes. As we will later see, on most occassions, these messages are just *forwarded* messages.

**Definition 1 (Interactive Consistency).** *A set of $n$ processes, out of which at most $f$ can be faulty in any given round, are said to have achieved interactive consistency if the local consistency vector of some $n - f$ processes are identical.*

The definition of interactive consistency given above is a generalization of the definition given by Pease, Shostak and Lamport [14] to the case when faults can be transient. Their definition used the identity of the faulty process, and makes sense when faults are permanent.

Interactive consistency is the *agreement* requirement. Distributed consensus algorithms additionally are required to satisfy *validity* and *termination* requirements.

**Table 1.** Formal characterization of the fault attributes used in this paper

| Fault attribute | Characterization |
|---|---|
| Permanent | $\forall r : \texttt{fault}(r) = \texttt{fault}(1)$ |
| Transient | Does not satisfy constraint for permanent fault |
| Benign | $\forall \texttt{msg}(\texttt{ij}, \texttt{v}) : v = \texttt{nil} \lor v = \texttt{cv}^{(j)}[j]$ |
| Malicious | $\forall \texttt{msg}(\texttt{ij}, \texttt{v}) : v \in \textit{Vals}$ |
| Symmetric | $\forall \texttt{msg}(\texttt{ij}, \texttt{v}_1), (\texttt{kj}, \texttt{v}_2) : v_1 = v_2$ |
| Asymmetric | Faulty node $j$ need not satisfy above constraint |

Validity is implicitly present in our formulation via the assumption that (a) processes are not allowed to change their private value, combined with the assumption that (b) Process $i$'s consistency vector stores its private value at vector's $i$-th component.

*Fault Attributes.* Let $r \in \{1, 2, \ldots\}$ denote the round number and let $\texttt{fault}(r)$ denote the set of processes that are faulty in Round $r$. Table 1 contains the formal characterization of the different fault attributes used in this paper.

*Problem Statement.* We wish to find an algorithm for achieving interactive consistency in presence of transient, non-malicious, and asymmetric faults. By achieving we mean (a) the system should reach an interactive consistent state after a finite number of rounds (termination property), and
(b) the interactive consistency property is preserved ad infinitum thereafter.

Part (b) of the requirement above is usually not included in classic distributed consensus. For permanent faults, it is irrelevant, but for transient faults, it is an important requirement. In linear temporal logic, the two parts together define an *eventually-always* (FG) property, but with the difference that the $F$ operator is a "bounded-$F$" operator.

## 2  Non-transient, Malicious and Asymmetric Faults

Pease, Shostak, and Lamport presented in [14] an algorithm to achieve interactive consistency among $n$ processes with a synchronous timing model and a permanent, malicious, and asymmetric fault model. Their algorithm is based on rounds of message exchanges and can withstand $f$ faulty processes, as long as $n \geq 3f + 1$ holds. In this section we informally present Pease, Shostak, and Lamport's algorithm for the particular case when $n = 4$ and $f = 1$, and show that it does not work if we allow faults to be transient, even if we restrict them to be non-malicious.

In the particular case where $n = 4$ and $f = 1$, Pease, Shostak, and Lamport's algorithm achieves interactive consistency after two rounds of information exchange. In the first round, each non-faulty process sends its private value to every other process and, in the second round, the processes exchange the information obtained in the first round. Hence, for instance, process 1 receives messages $(12, v_2)$, $(13, v_3)$, $(14, v_4)$ in the first round, and messages $(123, v_{23})$, $(124, v_{24})$, $(132, v_{32})$, $(134, v_{34})$, $(142, v_{42})$, $(143, v_{43})$ in the second round. Then, each process $i$ updates the $j$th component of its consistency vector, with $j \neq i$, according to the *three* received messages that report about $j$'s value: if two of the values in these three messages coincide then $i$ updates $cv^{(1)}[2]$ to that common value. Otherwise, $i$ sets $cv^{(i)}[j]$ to nil. For example, process 1, would determine the value of $cv^{(1)}[2]$ using the values $v_2, v_{42}, v_{32}$ of the received messages shown above.

To informally argue about the correctness of the algorithm, let us represent graphically, as a directed acyclic graph, the exchanges of messages that are relevant for Process 1 (left) and Process 3 (right) to determine the private value of 2.

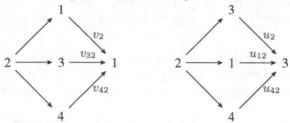

The paths starting from a root node of the DAG represent messages. The path 231 in the left DAG represents the message $(132, v_{32})$ where Process 3 says to Process 1 in Round 2 that it received value $v_{32}$ from Process 2 in Round 1. The path 211 in the left DAG denotes that, after Round 2, Process 1 has access to the value $v_2$ that Process 2 had sent to Process 1 in Round 1.

Assume that 1 and 3 are not faulty and let us first consider the case where 2 is faulty. Note that, in that case, $v_{42} = u_{42}$, $v_2 = u_{12}$, and $v_{32} = u_2$ hold, and hence 1 and 3 update $cv^{(1)}[2]$ and $cv^{(3)}[2]$ to the same value. Now consider the case where 2 is not faulty and thus 4 is the faulty node. In this case we have that $v_2 = u_{12} = v_{32} = u_2 = cv^{(2)}[2]$ holds, and both 1 and 3 update $cv^{(1)}[2]$ and $cv^{(3)}[2]$ to 2's private value. Note that, although we argued about processes 1 and 3 for clarity, we actually showed that every pair of non-faulty processes agree on a value for a faulty one and correcly infer the private value of a non-faulty one and hence the algorithm achieves interactive consistency.

We now show that Pease, Shostak, and Lamport's algorithm fails to achieve interactive consistency if faults are transient, even if the fault model is non-malicious. We give a counterexample using the same dag representation that we used above. However, in the transient case we must specify which process $i \in \{1, 2, 3, 4\}$ is faulty at each round. We denote such faulty process as $\bar{i}$. In our counterexample 2 is faulty in the first round and 1 is faulty in the second round. Note that, since the fault model is non-malicious, the private value of 2 must be true and, after the first two rounds, 3 and 4 will agree on the value of 2 to be nil, while 2 and 1 will agree on it to be true, which violates the interactive consistency property.

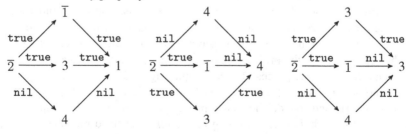

The reader might wonder: if 2 is non-faulty in Round 2, then if we start a new instance of the Pease, Shostak and Lamport's algorithm in Round 2 (so that the new instance's Round 1 will happen along with Round 2 of the first instance in Step 2), then in Step 3 we would likely reach agreement. This is true, but in this case, there is another scenario in which agreement is not guaranteed after any fixed number of rounds. Consider the case when Process 2 is faulty in the first $k$ steps, and in the $k + 1$-th step, Process 1 becomes faulty (as shown above). In this case, the interactive consistency property holds in steps $2, 3, \ldots, k$, but is violated in Step $k + 1$. Since $k$ can be arbitrary, at no step can the processes know that they have achieved interactive consistency *from hereon*.

The above observation is not surprising: our formulation of the problem under the transient fault model can be viewed as there being $f$ faults in $f$ rounds (for $n = 4$ processes). It is known that tolerating $f$ faults requires at least $f + 1$ rounds (so that existence of at least one fault-free round is guaranteed); see Theorem 6.33 in [11]. Our goal is to tolerate $f$ faults in $f$ rounds, but under an additional assumption. Note that Pease, Shostak and Lamport's algorithm tolerates 2 faults in 2 rounds, but *it assumes that the same process is faulty in both rounds*.

Our assumption, which we call the *guaranteed delayed ack* assumption, is as follows: whenever Process $i$ sends a value (or a message) to Process $j$ in Round $r$, then, in Round $r + 2$, it knows the value (or message) Process $j$ received from it in Round $r + 1$. Intuitively, after 2 rounds, the sender gets a confirmation about whether its message was delivered or dropped. Formally, for every $i$, we define a function $\text{conf}_i$ that given a message path $iji$ returns value $v$ if $(ji, v)$ was a message that was seen in the previous round:

$$\text{conf}_i(iji) = v \text{ if } (ji, v) \text{ was a message sent in previous round}$$

We assume that Process $i$ has access to function $\text{conf}_i$ in Round 3 of our protocol.[1]

## 3  Algorithm for Interactive Consistency under Non-malicious, Asymmetric, and Transient Faults

In this section we present an algorithm for interactive consistency in presence of transient, non-malicious, and asymmetric faults for the case where $n = 4$ and $f = 1$. The algorithm was synthesized with the help of automated synthesis techniques described in the next section. In this section, we just describe the algorithm and present an informal proof for its correctness.

Similar to Pease, Shostak, and Lamport's algorithm, our algorithm is based on rounds of message exchanges. However, we use three rounds instead of two to reach a state that satisfies the interactive consistency property. We present our procedure as a nonterminating procedure that preserves interactive consistency in every step after the first three

---

[1] Note that the Pease, Shostak and Lamport's algorithm is not designed to benefit from such an assumption. Even if the assumption is made stronger and we let a faulty process know *in the next round* (that it was faulty in the previous round), the Pease, Shostak and Lamport algorithm can not use this fact since the faulty process does not participate in the message exchanges that are used to decide on it's local value.

steps. Note that the preservation property is not trivial: since the fault model is transient, different processes can become faulty in different rounds and can potentially cause violation of interactive consistency.

Our algorithm is presented in Figure 1. Our algorithm exchanges the same messages as the Pease, Shostak and Lamport algorithm in the first two rounds. The third round is introduced to add a redundant channel of communication thanks to the *guaranteed delayed ack* assumption introduced in the previous section.

Recall the notation about messages: the message $(ji, v)$ represents that Process $j$ receives value $v$ from Process $i$ in this round, and the messages $(jjji, v)$ and $(jji, v)$ represent that Process $j$ receives the value $v$ from Process $i$ two and one rounds back, respectively. Note that $(ji, v)$ involves a message exchange, but $(jji, v)$ does not involve any message exchanges and is just a convenient notation for describing information from one round back.

In the algorithm in Figure 1, at each step, every process first receives messages (containing information from up to three rounds back), then updates its consistency vector, and then sends messages. Every process sends information refering to one, two, and three steps back; that is, messages of the form $(s, v)$, with $s$ of lengths 2, 3, and 4.

The rule that Process $i$ uses for updating its consistency vector is as follows: $\text{cv}^{(i)}[i]$ is left unchanged; and for all $j \neq i$, $\text{cv}^{(i)}[j]$ is set to a *non-nil* value $v$ if either
(1) Process $i$ receives a message $(iiij, v)$, or
(2) Process $i$ receives a message $(ixxj, v)$ for some $x$ different from $i$ and $j$, or
(3) Process $i$ receives a message $(ijxj, v)$ for some $x$ different from $i$ and $j$.

Apart from the messages of the form $(ijxj, v)$, all other messages have the usual meaning. This becomes clear from the code in Figure 1 that constructs the messages to be sent. Specifically, the value $v$ in the message $(ijxj, v)$ is not equal to the value of the message path $jxj$, but it is equal to $\text{conf}_j(jxj)$. The notation $\tilde{v}$ in Figure 1 denotes $v$ *if* the process sending (or forwarding) value $v$ is non-faulty, and it denotes a non-deterministically picked element from the set $\{v, \text{nil}\}$ *if* the process is faulty.

*Example 1.* Let us consider an example where Processes $1, 3, 4$ are trying to learn the local value $l_2$ of Process 2. First assume no process in faulty in any of the rounds. In this case, Process 2 sends $l_2$ to all three processes in Round 1; that is, in Round 0, we have

$$\forall i : (i2, l_2) \in S_1, \quad S_2 = S_3 = S_{\text{conf}} = \emptyset$$

After Round 1 (focusing only on value sent by Process 2), we have

$$\forall i, j : (ji2, l_2) \in S_2, \quad S_3 = S_{\text{conf}} = \emptyset$$

After Round 2 (focusing only on value sent by Process 2), we have

$$\forall i, k : \forall j \neq 2 : (kji2, l_2) \in S_3, \quad \forall i, k : (k2i2, l_2) \in S_{\text{conf}}$$

So, in Round 3, every Process $i$ updates its consistency vector to have value $l_2$ in $\text{cv}^{(i)}[2]$ – since, for example, $(iii2, l_2)$ is received by every Process $i$.

As a more interesting example, consider the scenario where Process 2 is faulty in Round 0 and sends its local value $l_2$ to only Process 3 (and nil's to others); and moreover, Process 3 becomes faulty in Round 1 and does not forward the correct message

**Inputs:** local value $l_i$ for each $i \in \overline{n}$
**Global:** consistency vector $\mathbf{cv}^{(i)}$; Initialized such that $\forall i: \mathbf{cv}^{(i)}[i] = l_i \wedge \forall j \neq i : \mathbf{cv}^{(i)}[j] = \mathtt{nil}$
**Output:** consistency vector $\mathbf{cv}^{(i)}$ that always satisfies the invariant
$\quad \exists i \in \overline{n}$ s.t. $\mathbf{cv}^{(j)}$'s are identical for all $j \neq i$.

---

$\mathrm{IC}_{4,1}$:                    // Describing a round for Process $i$
$\quad R = \mathtt{receiveMessages}()$
$\quad$For $j \in \overline{n}, \ j \neq i \quad$ Do
$\qquad D := \{v \mid (iiij, v) \in R\} \cup \{v \mid \exists x \neq i, x \neq j : (ixxj, v) \in R \vee (ijxj, v) \in R\}$
$\qquad$If $\exists v \in D : v = \mathtt{true}$ Then $\mathbf{cv}^{(i)}[j] = \mathtt{true}$
$\qquad$ElseIf $\exists v \in D : v = \mathtt{false}$ Then $\mathbf{cv}^{(i)}[j] = \mathtt{false}$
$\qquad$Else $\mathbf{cv}^{(i)}[j] = \mathtt{nil}$
$\quad S_1 := \{(ji, \widetilde{l_i}) \mid j \in \overline{n}\}$
$\quad S_2 := \{(jix, \widetilde{v}) \mid (ix, v) \in R \wedge i, x \in \overline{n}\}$
$\quad S_3 := \{(jixy, \widetilde{v}) \mid (ixy, v) \in R \wedge y \neq i \wedge x, y, j \in \overline{n}\}$
$\quad S_{conf} = \{(jixi, \widetilde{v}) \mid \mathtt{conf}_i(ixi) = v \wedge x, y, j \in \overline{n}\}$
$\quad \mathtt{sendMessages}(S_1 \cup S_2 \cup S_3 \cup S_{conf})$
$\quad$where $\widetilde{v} = v$ if $i$ is not faulty and $\widetilde{v} \in \{v, \mathtt{nil}\}$ if $i$ is faulty

**Fig. 1.** Algorithm for interactive consistency ($n$=4, $f$=1)

it received from Process 2 to others. In Round 2, if Process 2 is non-faulty, then it will send the message $(i232, l_2)$ to all processes $i$ (these messages will belong to the set $S_{conf}$ is Round 2). Consequently, in Round 3, all processes $i$ will update $\mathbf{cv}^{(i)}[2]$ to $l_2$. But, what if Process 2 becomes faulty in Round 2? In that case, Process 3 is not faulty, and hence it forwards correctly; that is, $(i332, l_2)$ is in the set $S_3$ of sent messages in Round 2. Consequently, in Round 3, all processes $i$ will again update $\mathbf{cv}^{(i)}[2]$ to $l_2$.

We will argue informally about the correctness of the algorithm of Figure 1 using again the DAG representation introduced in the previous section. It is easy to see that if all processes execute the algorithm of Figure 1 and a faulty process, say 2, does not reveal its local value to any other process for the first $k > 0$ steps, i.e. sends messages $(j2, \mathtt{nil})$ to every process $j \neq 2$, then $\mathbf{cv}^{(j)}[2] = \mathtt{nil}$ holds in steps $k, k+1$, and $k+2$, for every process $j \neq 2$. Hence, note that it suffices to get convinced that, if in step $k+1$ Process 2 sends its local value to some process, say Process 3, then $\mathbf{cv}^{(j)}[2] = l_2$ will hold in step $k + 4$, for every process $j$. Consider the following two DAGs representing the exchanges of messages that are relevant for processes 3 and 1 to decide about the value of Process 2 and assume that 2 sends $(32, l_2)$.

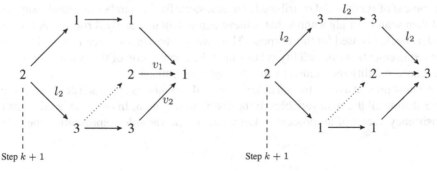

Step $k + 1$                                          Step $k + 1$

Note that, due to the *guaranteed delayed ack* assumption, either $v_1 = l_2$ or 2 is faulty in round $k + 3$ and $v_2 = l_2$. In any case, Process 1 updates $\text{cv}^{(1)}[2]$ to $l_2$ in round $k + 4$. Moreover, note that Process 4 also updates $\text{cv}^{(4)}[2]$ to $l_2$ in the same round by a symmetric argument. Finally, Process 3 updates $\text{cv}^{(3)}[2]$ to $l_2$ in round $k + 4$ because it receives the message $(3332, l_2)$.

# 4   A General Synthesis Approach for $FG$ Properties

In this section, we will outline the synthesis approach we used to arrive at the (variants of the) algorithms presented in the previous section.

All modern synthesis tools work by enumerating the space of possible solutions and checking if one of these solutions satisfies the requirement. Checking if a synthesized solution satisfies a requirement is a formal verification problem. Broadly speaking, synthesis is performed as a loop over the formal verification tool. Our approach to synthesis is simpler and can be viewed as a generalization of the idea of bounded model checking to synthesis. Just as bounded model checking turns a verification problem into a *existential* contraint that encodes a *weaker* version of the verification problem, we turn synthesis into a *forall-exists* constraint that encodes a *weaker* version of the synthesis problem.

The key step that makes automated synthesis effective is the step that defines the weaker version. A simpler version of the synthesis problem is obtained by
(a) restricting the universe of possible algorithms that will be searched and
(b) replacing the verification step by an approximate step.

In particular, we make the search space of possible solutions finite. In the context of synthesis of distributed consensus, this is achieved by first fixing the number of processes (to a small number such as 4). Then, we fix the *type of messages* that are exchanged in different rounds: in our case, we fix the component $s$ of the messages $(s, v)$ that are exchanged in a round and we even fix the computation of the value $v$ of the message in most cases. We then just need to synthesize the *deterministic function* that is used to update the local consistency vector and generate the value $v$ for the messages (if they are not already fixed) for the next round. The domain and range of the function is finite. Hence, there are only finitely many, but a huge number nonetheless, of such functions.

We also make the verification problem simple – instead of performing full verification, we just perform bounded model checking (checking up to some fixed bound). In the context of synthesis of distributed consensus, we fix the number of rounds (say, to 3) and then search for algorithms that achieve agreement in exactly 3 rounds. A bounded model checker is used for this purpose. Thus, we synthesize for agreement and termination requirements, while validity is built-in in the formulation of the synthesis problem. We ignore stability requirement while performing synthesis.

We now present a more formal description of the synthesis approach described above. Let x denote all the state variables of the distributed system. In our case, x contains the consistency vector of all processes. Let y denote the variables representing the *values* of the messages that are exchanged in any round. Let $\phi(x)$ be the formula that encodes the property that x is the desired final state (that is, x is an interactive-consistent state.) The following *verification constraint*, generated by a bounded model checker, says that there is a sequence of 4 states of the system that follows the consensus algorithm, but does not end in an agreement state (it is the negation of the what we want to prove):

$$\exists x_0, x_1, x_2, x_3, y_0, y_1, y_2 :$$
$$I(x_0) \wedge T(x_0, y_0, x_1) \wedge T(x_1, y_1, x_2) \wedge T(x_2, y_2, x_3) \wedge \neg\phi(x_3) \quad (1)$$

Here $I(x)$ is a predicate that is true if x is a valid initial state and $T(x, y, x')$ is a predicate that is true if y are the messages that are generated in state x and $x'$ is the next state generated from current state x and these messages.

For a given deterministic consensus algorithm, the predicate $T(x, y, x')$ is a function from $(x, y)$ to $x'$, but it is not a function from x to $(y, x')$ since different manifestation of the faults can cause different messages to be generated from the same state x. So, the verification constraint says that consensus algorithm does not achieve agreement in 3 steps for some choice of initial state and fault behavior.

When we synthesize the consensus algorithm, the predicate $T$ is not fully known. It is, in fact, parameterized by some additional *synthesis variables* z such that the new relation $T(x, y, z, x')$ is a function from $(x, y, z)$ to $x'$. So, the *bounded synthesis constraint* is defined as

$$\forall z : \exists x_0, x_1, x_2, x_3, y_0, y_1, y_2 :$$
$$I(x_0) \wedge T(x_0, y_0, z, x_1) \wedge T(x_1, y_1, z, x_2) \wedge T(x_2, y_2, z, x_3) \wedge \neg\phi(x_3) \quad (2)$$

The synthesis constraint says that forall choices of the synthesis variables z, the resulting consensus algorithm does not achieve agreement in 3 steps (for some initial state and fault behavior). If we do not want to fix *a priori* the function that determines what message values y are generated in a state x (for a fixed choice of faulty nodes), then we can also synthesize that function by including additional parameters in z that are used to define that function.

In our case, the domain of all variables in Formula 2 have finite cardinality. Hence, the formula can be written as a quantified ($\forall\exists$) Boolean formula (2-QBF). Bounded model checkers (such as the SAL bounded model checker we used) already generate a Boolean satisfiability (SAT) formula for the verification constraint (Formula 1).

Our synthesis approach implementation consists of a script that glues together different tools as follows:

1. We model the consensus algorithm in SAL [15,2]. The model includes synthesis variables z to define the transition relation.
2. We use the SAL bounded model checker to generate the SAT formula for the verification constraint (Formula 1). The SAT formula implicitly existentially quantifies all variables, including the synthesis variables z.
3. We modify the SAT formula and convert it into a QBF formula by universally quantifying the synthesis variables. (This step uses the mapping from the original SAL variables to the Boolean SAT variables.)

4. We use off-the-shelf QBF solvers (and QBF preprocessors) to check satisfiability of the ∀∃ formula.
5. If the QBF solver returns Unsat, then the synthesis is declared *successful*, and if the QBF solver returns Sat, then the synthesis process is *unsuccessful*.
6. If synthesis is successful, the QBF solver outputs a valuation for the synthesis variables z, which is used to obtain a concrete consensus algorithm.
7. The synthesized algorithm is formally verified: the property that "after 3 steps, the property $\phi$ is always true" is verified using $k$-induction.

In many cases when synthesis was successful, the valuation for the synthesis variables z returned by the QBF solver was not easy to describe; that is, the resulting update function did not have a concise description. This happens because QBF solver would instantiate "don't care" variables arbitrarily. These algorithms were not suitable for describing in this paper. Hence, in such cases, we used our intuition to modify the synthesized function so that it had a concise description, and then formally verified the resulting algorithm and presented it here. Let us remark that, in our approach, once we instantiate the synthesis variables in the SAL model, we immediately get a SAL model that is ready for formal verification using SAL tools.

## 5  Synthesis Problem Formulation and Experimental Results

As mentioned in the previous section, we restricted the space of possible algorithms to be searched by the synthesis tool to a finite set. The major restriction, apart from fixing $n$ to be 4, is only considering algorithms based on rounds of message exchanges. Distributed algorithms that are based on other schemas, such as, where a fixed process acts as the leader, are not included in our synthesis search space.

Hence, while the dynamics of the messages exchanges are fixed, the task of the synthesis tool is to decide how to update the consistency vector depending on the messages received at each step. Note that this corresponds to the For-Do loop of Figure 1. More specifically, the goal of our tool was to synthetize a deterministic function $f_{i,j}^k$, which corresponds to the algorithm executed by Process $i$ to update $\text{cv}^{(i)}[j]$ given the messages received in the last $k$ rounds reporting about the value of $j$. Hence, each function $f_{i,j}^k$ in this family of functions parameterized by $k$ has the following signature:

$$f_{i,j}^k : \{i, j, k, l\}^{k-1} \times \Sigma \mapsto \Sigma$$

where $\Sigma = \{\text{true}, \text{false}, \text{nil}\}$ and $k$ is the number of rounds of message exchanges to be considered by the synthesized interactive consensus algorithm. The synthesis of $f_{i,j}^k$ is subject to the constraint that the resulting algorithm achieves interactive consistency. Such constraint, as well as the fault model were very naturally encoded as an LTL property and part of a SAL model, as explained in the previous section. For example, assuming $k = 2$, as in the Pease, Shostak and Lamport's algorithm, our synthesis problem consists on deciding how Process $i$ must update $\text{cv}^{(i)}[j]$ given messages $(iij, v_1), (ijj, v_2), (ikj, v_3), (ilj, v_4)$, for every possible value of $v_1, v_2, v_3, v_4 \in \{\text{true}, \text{false}, \text{nil}\}$ and assuming that $i, j, k, l$ are pairwise disjoint. Using this approach we could easily synthesize Pease, Shostak and Lamport's algorithm for $n = 4$. Similarly, we could prove that there is no interactive consistency algorithm for the non-malicious, asymmetric, and transient case that uses just two rounds of message exchanges, even if we assume guaranteed delayed ack.

Note that the domain of $f_{i,j}^k$, although finite, has exponential size with respect to $k$. In fact, in the case where $k = 3$, it has size 48, which corresponds to a synthesis search space of size $3^{48}$. However, to speed up the synthesis process, we reduced the size of the image of $f_{i,j}^3$ by

(a) not considering combinations of messages that are not possible due to the characteristics of the fault model (note that Process $i$ cannot receive messages reporting $j$'s local value to be both true and false since faults are non-malicious), and

(b) not considering some messages that intuitively seemed to be unnecesary for the algorithm (for example, the message $(ijij, v)$, is clearly useless in our setting).

In fact, although the version of the algorithm presented in Section 3 uses only the five messages corresponding to the paths $iiij, ikkj, illj, ijkj, ijlj$, our first synthetized version used also $iikj$ and $iilj$, which intuitively correspond to Processes $k$ and $l$, respectively, telling Process $i$ in the second round the value that they got from $j$ in the first round. Later on we realized that these messages were indeed unnecesary, and we could synthetize a solution that ignores them.

With respect to impossibility results, we could use our tool to prove some particular cases of Theorem 6.33 in [11] that arise from fixing a particular message exchange dynamics, such as variants on the idea of running two overlapping instances of Pease, Shostak and Lamport's algorithm as commented in Section 2.

In all our experiments we used the QBF solver DepQbf [10] and the QBF preprocessor Bloqqer [1] and obtained the results in the order of minutes. Moreover, all our synthetized algorithms were verifiable using $k$-induction, which was proven much more effective than symbolic model checking. The sal model used to obtain our main result, as well as the corresponding QBF formula are available online [4].

# 6  Discussion

Distributed algorithms are difficult to design because of the enourmous number of scenarios generated due to the faults. We found our synthesis tool to be extremely useful in the process of identifying existence of algorithms of a certain form that achieve a certain goal.

We were able to synthesize the original Pease, Shostak and Lamport's algorithm for $n = 4$ processes and $f = 1$ fault, where the fault was permanent (across the two rounds) and asymmetric – irrespective of whether the fault was malicious or not. The synthesis tool declared "synthesis unsuccessful" when we changed the fault model to transient – both when the fault was malicious and when it was not malicious. We also tried to perform synthesis under slightly different fault models. For instance, when Process 1 receives a message $(123, \mathtt{nil})$, then we allowed Process 1 to know if 2 was faulty in the previous round, or if 3 was faulty in the round before (akin to *manifest* faults). However, synthesis failed in most of such minor variants on the fault model.

*Generalizing to $n > 4$.* Our synthesized algorithm, presented in Section 3, is easy to generalize for larger values of $n$, but keeping the assumption that in each round at most one process is faulty. In fact, for any value of $n$ larger than one, exactly the same algorithm generalizes and three rounds suffice to reach interactive consistency. The case when more than one process is faulty in every round is not yet known to us. The synthesized algorithm does not naturally generalize to a working algorithm for this case.

*Message Complexity.* In our description of the algorithm, we assumed that arbitrary messages of the form $(ijkl, v)$ are exchanged. However, Process $i$ uses only *five* messages in the end to decide on a value for Process $j$: the values corresponding to the message paths $iiij, ikkj, illj, ijkj, ijlj$: these involve only a total of $1 + 2 + 2 + 3 + 3 = 11$ messages (across all three rounds) for each pair $i, j$ of nodes. We are counting every use of the $\text{conf}_j$ function as a message exchange.

*Tolerating Malicious Faults with Authentication.* The algorithm that works for non-malicious faults can also work for malicious faults, if we assume the processes authenticate their communications using digital signatures. Even though a faulty process is now allowed to send arbitrary messages, the receiver can check if a non-nil value was really sent by the originator and discard it (treat it as a nil value) if the check fails. This forces the faulty process to only possibly behave like a non-malicious faulty process.

*Extensions.* The results described in this paper are just a first step in application of synthesis technology for discovering fault-tolerant distributed algorithms. There are plenty of avenues to explore for future work. First, there are asymmetric architectures that can provide same level of fault tolerance with less hardware resource. For example, the Draper Laboratory's Fault Tolerant Processor (FTP) [7,9] is an asymmetrical design that uses *interstages* to relay messages from a process to it's neighbors. Second, one can also consider hybrid fault models [9] in distributed consensus. Finally, one can also consider problems in distributed algorithms for automated synthesis that have requirements other than the consensus property. An interesting possibility is to capture all such possible extensions in a common framework, such as the one presented in [13].

*Synthesis for Fault-Tolerance.* Automated synthesis was first considered in the context of synthesizing from LTL specification [12]. Later, Kulkarni et al. [6] started with a fault-intolerant distributed algorithm and showed how to automatically transform it into a fault-tolerant program. The technique was based on refining the given program by removing states and transitions that lead to violation of agreement in presence of faults. Our formulation of the synthesis problem is inspired by recent work on Sketching [16,17,5] where the starting point is an incomplete sketch that is filled in by automated tools; in particular, by solvers for $\exists \forall$ formulas [5]. The use of sophisticated constraint solvers (SMT solvers, SAT and QBF solvers) allows our approach to discover completely unexpected algorithms from a huge search space.

# 7  Conclusion

We used automated synthesis to discover an algorithm for achieving interactive consistency in the presence of transient, non-malicious and asymmetric faults. Our algorithm can be seen as filling a known gap in the literature. One the one hand, it is known that there is no $f$ round algorithm that achieves agreement in the presence of $f$ non-malicious, asymmetric and transient faults. On the other hand, it is known that there is one such algorithm that achieves agreement in $f + 1$ rounds. Our algorithm achieves agreement in $f$ rounds, but uses an extra assumption that we have called the guaranteed delayed ack assumption. The assumption allows a sender to know the value the receiver received from it, but only after an extra intermediate round of message exchanges.

Our synthesis approach for discovering distributed algorithms is based on bounded model checking and quantified boolean formula (QBF) solving, and has been an indispensable tool in our effort to obtain the above positive result, and also for showing the non-existence of a consensus algorithm for various other cases.

**Acknowledgments.** We are greatly thankful to Patrick Lincoln (SRI International), John Rushby (SRI International) and Paul Miner (NASA) for providing useful guidance through various stages in this work. We also thank the reviewers for their comments and suggestions.

This work was partly supported by the NASA contract NNL10AB32T and NSF grant SHF:CSR-1017483. Any opinions, findings, and conclusions or recommendations expressed in this material are those of the authors and do not necessarily reflect the views of the funding agencies.

# References

1. Biere, A., Lonsing, F., Seidl, M.: Blocked clause elimination for QBF. In: Bjørner, N., Sofronie-Stokkermans, V. (eds.) CADE 2011. LNCS (LNAI), vol. 6803, pp. 101–115. Springer, Heidelberg (2011)
2. de Moura, L., Owre, S., Rueß, H., Rushby, J., Shankar, N., Sorea, M., Tiwari, A.: SAL 2. In: Alur, R., Peled, D.A. (eds.) CAV 2004. LNCS, vol. 3114, pp. 496–500. Springer, Heidelberg (2004)
3. Fischer, M.J., Lynch, N.A., Paterson, M.S.: Impossibility of distributed consensus with one faulty process. JACM 32(2), 374–382 (1985)
4. Gascon, A., Tiwari, A.: Webpage: Synthesis of fault-tolerant distributed algorithms (2013), http://www.csl.sri.com/users/tiwari/softwares/synth_distributed/
5. Gulwani, S., Jha, S., Tiwari, A., Venkatesan, R.: Synthesis of loop-free programs. In: Proc. PLDI (2011)
6. Kulkarni, S.S., Arora, A., Chippada, A.: Polynomial time synthesis of byzantine agreement. In: 20th Symp. on Reliable Distributed Systems, SRDS (2001)
7. Lala, J.H.: A Byzantine resilient fault tolerant computer for nuclear power applications. In: Fault Tolerant Computing Symposium, pp. 338–343 (1986)
8. Lamport, L., Shostak, R.E., Pease, M.C.: The byzantine generals problem. ACM Trans. Program. Lang. Syst. 4(3), 382–401 (1982)

9. Lincoln, P., Rushby, J.: Formal verification of an interactive consistency algorithm for the Draper FTP architecture under a hybrid fault model. In: Proc. 9th Conf. on Computer Assurance, COMPASS (1994)

10. Lonsing, F., Biere, A.: DepQBF: A Dependency-Aware QBF Solver. JSAT 7(2-3), 71–76 (2010)

11. Lynch, N.A.: Distributed Algorithms. Morgan Kaufmann (1996)

12. Manna, Z., Wolper, P.: Synthesis of communicating processes from temporal logic specifications. ACM Trans. on Programming Languages and Systems 6, 68–93 (1984)

13. Miner, P., Geser, A., Pike, L., Maddalon, J.: A Unified Fault-Tolerance Protocol. In: Lakhnech, Y., Yovine, S. (eds.) FORMATS/FTRTFT 2004. LNCS, vol. 3253, pp. 167–182. Springer, Heidelberg (2004)

14. Pease, M., Shostak, R., Lamport, L.: Reaching agreement in the presence of faults. JACM 27(2), 228–234 (1980)

15. The SAL intermediate language. Computer Science Laboratory, SRI International, Menlo Park, CA (2003), http://sal.csl.sri.com/

16. Solar-Lezama, A., Rabbah, R., Bodík, R., Ebcioglu, K.: Programming by sketching for bit-streaming programs. In: PLDI (2005)

17. Solar-Lezama, A., Tancau, L., Bodík, R., Saraswat, V., Seshia, S.: Combinatorial Sketching for Finite Programs. In: ASPLOS (2006)

# Energy-Utility Quantiles

Christel Baier, Marcus Daum, Clemens Dubslaff,
Joachim Klein, and Sascha Klüppelholz*

Institute for Theoretical Computer Science
Technische Universität Dresden, Germany

**Abstract.** The concept of quantiles is well-known in statistics, but its
benefits for the formal quantitative analysis of probabilistic systems have
been noticed only recently. To compute quantiles in Markov decision processes where the objective is a probability constraint for an until (i.e.,
constrained reachability) property with an upper reward bound, an iterative linear-programming (LP) approach has been proposed in a recent
paper. We consider here a more general class of quantiles with probability or expectation objectives, allowing to reason about the trade-off
between costs in terms of energy and some utility measure. We show how
the iterative LP approach can be adapted for these types of quantiles and
propose another iterative approach that decomposes the LP to be solved
into smaller ones. This algorithm has been implemented and evaluated in
case studies for quantiles where the objective is a probability constraint
for until properties with upper reward bounds.

## 1 Introduction

The concept of quantiles is well-known in statistics (see, e.g., [21]) and used there
to reason about the cumulative distribution function of a random variable $R$.
Quantiles are defined as maximal values $r$ such that the probability for the event
$R > r$ is beyond a given threshold. Although quantiles can provide very useful
insights in the interplay of various cost functions and other system properties,
they have barely obtained attention in the context of formal algorithmic system
analysis. Quantiles for probabilistic operational models, such as Markov chains or
Markov decision processes, can be defined using parameterized state properties
$\Phi[r]$ or $\Psi[r]$, where $r$ is a parameter for some cost or reward function and $\Phi[r]$ is
increasing in $r$, whereas $\Psi[r]$ is decreasing in $r$. The notion "increasing" means
that $s \models \Phi[r]$ implies $s \models \Phi[i]$ for all $i > r$ ("decreasing" has an analogous
meaning). Quantiles for objectives $\Phi[r]$ and $\Psi[r]$ in state $s$ of the given model are
defined as $\min\{ r : s \models \Phi[r] \}$ resp. $\max\{ r : s \models \Psi[r] \}$. We formalize $\Phi[r]$ and
$\Psi[r]$ by PRCTL-like constraints that assert lower or upper bounds either for the
probabilities for reward-bounded path formulas or for the expected accumulated

* This work was partly funded by the DFG through the CRC 912 HAEC, the cluster
  of excellence cfAED, the project QuaOS, and the DFG/NWO-project ROCKS and
  partially by Deutsche Telekom Stiftung, the ESF young researcher groups IMData
  100098198 and SREX 100111037, and the EU-FP-7 grant 295261 (MEALS).

J.M. Badger and K.Y. Rozier (Eds.): NFM 2014, LNCS 8430, pp. 285–299, 2014.
© Springer International Publishing Switzerland 2014

rewards until reaching a certain target. Typical examples are formulas of the form $\Phi_u[e]$ for fixed $u$ and $\Psi_e[u]$ for fixed $e$ asserting that the probability for

$$\lambda_{e,u} = \Diamond\big((\text{energy} \leqslant e) \wedge (\text{utility} \geqslant u)\big)$$

is, e.g., at least 0.8. (We use LTL notations where the temporal operator $\Diamond$ stands for "eventually".) The quantile $e_{\min} = \min\{e \in \mathbb{N} : s \models \Phi_u[e]\}$ is the minimal initial energy budget required to achieve the utility value $u$ with probability at least 0.8, while $u_{\max} = \max\{u \in \mathbb{N} : s \models \Psi_e[u]\}$ is the maximal utility that can be achieved with probability at least 0.8, when the energy budget is $e$. The curve for $\lambda_{e,u}$ on the left of the figure below illustrates how the probability increases when the utility value $u$ is fixed and the energy budget $e$ tends to $\infty$. The curve on the right shows how the probability for $\lambda_{e,u}$ decreases when the energy budget $e$ is fixed and the demanded degree of utility tends to $\infty$.

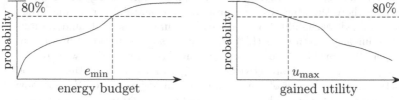

State properties $\Phi[r]$ or $\Psi[r]$ can also impose a constraint on the expected value of a random variable. For example, one might ask for the minimal initial energy budget $e$ that is needed to ensure that the expected degree of utility is at least some predefined utility threshold $u$. Vice versa, an expectation quantile might specify the maximal degree of utility that can be achieved when the expected energy consumption is required to be less or equal some fixed value $e$.

In probabilistic models with nondeterminism (e.g., for modeling concurrency by interleaving) such as Markov decision processes (MDPs), quantiles can be defined either in an existential or in a universal version, depending on whether the quantile is used in a worst-case analysis (where all possible resolutions of the nondeterminism are taken into account) or whether the task is to synthesize a control mechanism that schedules actions in an optimal way.

As the above examples suggest, quantiles can be seen as a concept to reason about the trade-off between different quantitative aspects, such as energy and utility. Thus, they yield an alternative to *multi-objective reasoning* for MDPs by means of Pareto optimal schedulers for multiple objectives given as Boolean combinations of constraints on the probabilities for certain events and/or expected accumulated costs [11,12]. The demand for algorithms to compute quantiles in Markovian models occurred to us during case studies with resource management protocols [3]. However, in various case studies with probabilistic model checkers carried out by other researchers, quantiles have been used implicitly in diagrams illustrating the evaluation results of the experimental studies.

Model-checking algorithms for various types of properties with *fixed* reward bounds have been proposed for discrete Markovian models and implemented in tools, see, e.g., [1,18,15]. The task to compute quantiles is, however, more challenging since it requires to compute an *optimal* reward bound for parameterized objectives. Our recent paper [4] briefly considers quantiles for discrete and continuous-time Markov chains, as an example for nonstandard multi-objective reasoning. To the best of our knowledge, [22] is the only paper where the computation of quantiles has been addressed for MDPs. It considers quantiles in MDPs with a nonnegative reward function for the states where the objective is a probability constraint for a reachability property with an upper reward bound $r$, formalized using the temporal reward-bounded until operator $U^{\leqslant r}$. The above mentioned quantile $\min\{e : s \models \Phi_u[e]\}$ appears as a special case since $\Phi_u[e]$ can be seen as a probability constraint for the path property $\lambda_{e,u} = \Diamond^{\leqslant e}(utility \geqslant u) = true\, U^{\leqslant e}(utility \geqslant u)$. In [22], polynomial-time algorithms for qualitative constraints where the probability bounds are 0 or 1 and an iterative linear-programming (LP) approach for probability bounds $p$ with $0 < p < 1$ has been presented. The minimal or maximal probabilities for a path property $A\, U^{\leqslant r}\, B$ for $r = 0, 1, 2, \ldots$ is calculated until the probability bound $p$ is reached, where the extrema are taken over all resolutions of nondeterminism. This approach appears to be naïve, but the computation of quantiles is known to be computationally hard (at least NP-hard already for Markov chains by the results of [19]). This is reflected in the exponential upper bound in [22] for the number of iterations and the size of the LPs to be solved.

**Contribution.** First, we generalize the approach of [22] by introducing general notions of quantiles in MDPs where the objective can either be a probability constraint or a constraint on an expectation (Sec. 3). Second, we revisit the iterative LP approach suggested by [22] and discuss refinements that make the approach feasible in practice. The core idea is an iterative method that propagates intermediate results as much as possible and follows the dynamic-programming scheme with embedded LPs to deal with zero-reward cycles (Sec. 4.2). We implemented this approach into PRISM [14] and study its performance by means of an energy-aware job-scheduling system (Sec. 6). Third, we present new algorithms for the computation of quantiles in MDPs where the objective is (a) either a probability constraint for reachability conditions with lower reward bounds (Sec. 4.3), or (b) a constraint on the expected accumulated reward (Sec. 5). These algorithms also rely on an iterative LP approach and the propagation principle is applicable as well (Sec. 4). Although we are not aware that expectation quantiles in MDPs have been addressed before, the presented algorithm for (b) shares some similarities with algorithms that have been proposed for stochastic shortest path problems [6] and to maximize/minimize the expected cost to reach a target [10].

## 2   Preliminaries

We provide a brief summary of the relevant concepts of MDPs and specifications given as formulas in probabilistic computation tree logic with reward-bounded modalities (PRCTL). Further details can be found, e.g., in [20,9,5].

**Markov Decision Processes (MDPs).** An MDP is a tuple $\mathcal{M} = (S, Act, P)$, where $S$ is a finite set of states, $Act$ a finite set of actions, $P : S \times Act \times S \to [0, 1]$ such that $\sum_{s' \in S} P(s, \alpha, s') \in \{0, 1\}$ for all states $s \in S$ and actions $\alpha \in Act$. The tuples $(s, \alpha, s') \in S \times Act \times S$ with $P(s, \alpha, s') > 0$ are called *steps* and we then say that state $s'$ is an $\alpha$-successor of $s$. We write $Act(s)$ for the set of actions $\alpha$ that have an $\alpha$-successor from state $s \in S$ and require that $Act(s) \neq \varnothing$ for all states $s$. Intuitively, if the current state of $\mathcal{M}$ is $s$, then first there is a nondeterministic choice to select one of the enabled actions $\alpha$. Then, $\mathcal{M}$ behaves probabilistically and moves with probability $P(s, \alpha, s')$ to some state $s'$. *Markov chains* are purely probabilistic instances of MDPs, i.e., where the action set is a singleton.

Paths in an MDP $\mathcal{M}$ can be seen as sample runs with resolved nondeterminism. Formally, paths are finite or infinite sequences $\pi = s_0 \, \alpha_0 \, s_1 \, \alpha_1 \, s_2 \, \alpha_2 \ldots \in (S \times Act)^* S \cup (S \times Act)^\omega$ that are built by consecutive steps, i.e., $\alpha_i \in Act(s_i)$ and $P(s_i, \alpha_i, s_{i+1}) > 0$ for all $i$. $\pi[k]$ denotes the $(k+1)$-st state in $\pi$ and $pref(\pi, k)$ the prefix of $\pi$ consisting of the first $k$ steps, ending in state $\pi[k] = s_k$. We write $FPaths(s)$ for the set of finite paths and $IPaths(s)$ for the set of infinite paths starting in $s$.

**Reward Structure.** A reward structure $\mathcal{R}$ for $\mathcal{M}$ consists of finitely many reward functions $rew : S \times Act \to \mathbb{N}$. If $\pi = s_0 \, \alpha_0 \, s_1 \, \alpha_1 \ldots \alpha_{n-1} \, s_n$ is a finite path, then the accumulated reward $rew(\pi)$ is the sum of the rewards for the state-action pairs, i.e., $rew(\pi) = \sum_{0 \leqslant i < n} rew(s_i, \alpha_i)$.

**Schedulers and Induced Probability Space.** Reasoning about probabilities for path properties in MDPs requires the selection of an initial state and the resolution of the nondeterministic choices between the possible transitions. The latter is formalized via *schedulers*, often also called policies or adversaries, which take as input a finite path and select an action to be executed. A (deterministic) scheduler is a function $\mathfrak{S} : FPaths \to Act$ such that $\mathfrak{S}(\pi) \in Act(s_n)$ for all finite paths $\pi = s_0 \, \alpha_0 \ldots \alpha_{n-1} \, s_n$. An $\mathfrak{S}$-*path* is any path that arises when the nondeterministic choices in $\mathcal{M}$ are resolved using $\mathfrak{S}$, i.e., $\mathfrak{S}(pref(\pi, k)) = \alpha_k$ for all $0 \leqslant k < n$. Infinite $\mathfrak{S}$-paths are defined accordingly. Given some scheduler $\mathfrak{S}$ and state $s$ (viewed as the initial state), the behavior of $\mathcal{M}$ under $\mathfrak{S}$ is purely probabilistic and can be formalized by a tree-like (infinite-state) Markov chain $\mathcal{M}_s^{\mathfrak{S}}$. One can think of the states in $\mathcal{M}_s^{\mathfrak{S}}$ as finite $\mathfrak{S}$-paths $\pi = s_0 \alpha_0 \ldots \alpha_{n-1} s_n$ starting in state $s$, where the probability to move from $\pi$ to $\pi \, \alpha \, s'$ is simply $P(s_n, \alpha, s')$. Using standard concepts of measure and probability theory, a sigma-algebra and a probability measure $\mathsf{Pr}_s^{\mathfrak{S}}$ for measurable sets of the infinite paths in the Markov chain $\mathcal{M}_s^{\mathfrak{S}}$, also called *(path) events* or *path properties*, is defined and can be transferred to maximal $\mathfrak{S}$-paths in $\mathcal{M}$ starting in $s$. For further details, we refer to standard text books such as [13,16,20].

For a worst-case analysis of a system modeled by an MDP $\mathcal{M}$, one ranges over all initial states and all schedulers (i.e., all possible resolutions of the nondeterminism) and considers the minimal or maximal probabilities for $\varphi$. If $\varphi$ represents a desired path property, then $\mathsf{Pr}_s^{\min}(\varphi) = \inf_{\mathfrak{S}} \mathsf{Pr}_s^{\mathfrak{S}}(\varphi)$ is the probability for $\mathcal{M}$ satisfying $\varphi$ that can be guaranteed even for worst-case scenarios, i.e., when ranging over all schedulers. Similarly, if $\varphi$ stands for a bad (undesired) path property, then $\mathsf{Pr}_s^{\max}(\varphi) = \sup_{\mathfrak{S}} \mathsf{Pr}_s^{\mathfrak{S}}(\varphi)$ is the least upper bound that can be guaranteed for the bad behaviors.

**State and Path Properties.** Let $s$ be a state, $p \in [0, 1]$ a probability bound, $\bowtie \in \{<, \leqslant, \geqslant, >\}$ and $\varphi$ a path property. We write $s \models \exists \mathsf{P}_{\bowtie p}(\varphi)$ if there exists a scheduler $\mathfrak{S}$ with $\mathrm{Pr}_s^{\mathfrak{S}}(\varphi) \bowtie p$. Similarly, $s \models \forall \mathrm{P}_{\bowtie p}(\varphi)$ if $\mathrm{Pr}_s^{\mathfrak{S}}(\varphi) \bowtie p$ for all schedulers $\mathfrak{S}$. Given a reward structure $\mathcal{R}$ with reward function $rew$, sets $A$, $B \subseteq S$, and $r \in \mathbb{N}$, then $A\,\mathrm{U}((rew \bowtie r) \wedge B)$ stands for the set of infinite paths $\tilde{\pi}$ such that there is some $k \in \mathbb{N}$ with $rew(\mathit{pref}(\tilde{\pi}, k)) \bowtie r$ and $\tilde{\pi}[k] \in B$, $\tilde{\pi}[i] \in A$ for $0 \leqslant i < k$. If $rew$ is clear from the context (e.g., if the reward structure $\mathcal{R}$ is a singleton), we briefly write $A\,\mathrm{U}^{\bowtie r} B$ rather than $A\,\mathrm{U}((rew \bowtie r) \wedge B)$. We often use the notation $\pi \models A\,\mathrm{U}^{\bowtie r} B$ instead of $\pi \in A\,\mathrm{U}^{\bowtie r} B$. As usual, we derive the release operator R by $A\,\mathrm{R}^{\bowtie r} B = \neg(\neg A\,\mathrm{U}^{\bowtie r} \neg B)$, where $\neg B$ denotes the complement of $B$. The temporal modalities $\Diamond$ (eventually) and $\Box$ (always) with or without reward-bounds are derived as usual, e.g., $\Diamond^{\bowtie r} B = \mathit{true}\,\mathrm{U}^{\bowtie r} B$ and $\Box^{\bowtie r} B = \neg\Diamond^{\bowtie r} \neg B$, where $\mathit{true}$ stands for the full state space.

Reward-bounded path properties such as $\varphi[r] = A\,\mathrm{U}^{\leqslant r} B$ are called *increasing* as $\tilde{\pi} \models \varphi[r]$ implies $\tilde{\pi} \models \varphi[r+1]$. The dual path properties $\psi[r] = \neg\varphi[r]$ are called *decreasing* as $\tilde{\pi} \models \psi[r+1]$ implies $\tilde{\pi} \models \psi[r]$. Analogously, a state property $\Phi[r]$ is called increasing if $s \models \Phi[r]$ implies $s \models \Phi[r+1]$. Examples for increasing state properties are $\exists \mathrm{P}_{>p}(\varphi[r])$, $\forall \mathrm{P}_{>p}(\varphi[r])$, $\exists \mathrm{P}_{<p}(\psi[r])$ and $\forall \mathrm{P}_{<p}(\psi[r])$. Decreasing state properties are defined accordingly.

**Sub-MDPs, End Components.** We use the notion *sub-MDP* of $\mathcal{M}$ for any pair $(T, \mathfrak{A})$ where $T \subseteq S$ and $\mathfrak{A} : T \to 2^{Act}$ such that for all $t \in T$: (1) $\mathfrak{A}(t) \subseteq Act(t)$ and (2) if $\alpha \in \mathfrak{A}(t)$ and $P(t, \alpha, t') > 0$ then $t' \in T$. An *end component* of $\mathcal{M}$ is a sub-MDP $(T, \mathfrak{A})$ of $\mathcal{M}$ where $\mathfrak{A}(t)$ is nonempty for all $t \in T$ and the underlying directed graph with node set $T$ and the edge relation $t \to t'$ iff $P(t, \alpha, t') > 0$ for some $\alpha \in \mathfrak{A}(t)$ is strongly connected. An end component is said to be *maximal* if it is not contained in any other end component.

# 3   Quantiles

As stated in the introduction, quantiles in MDPs can be defined for arbitrary objectives given by increasing or decreasing parameterized state properties. We now provide general definitions for quantiles in MDPs where the state properties impose either a probability or an expectation constraint, and identify the instances for which we present algorithms in the next two sections.

**Quantiles for Probability Objectives.** Let $\mathcal{M} = (S, Act, P)$ be an MDP as in Sec. 2 and $rew : S \times Act \to \mathbb{N}$ a distinguished reward function in its reward structure. Given an increasing path property $\varphi[r]$ where parameter $r \in \mathbb{N}$ stands for some bound on the accumulated reward, we define the following types of *existential quantiles*, where $\psi[r] = \neg\varphi[r]$, $\trianglerighteq \in \{\geqslant, >\}$ and $p \in [0,1] \cap \mathbb{Q}$:

$$\mathrm{Qu}_s\big(\exists \mathrm{P}_{\trianglerighteq p}(\varphi[?])\big) = \min\big\{r \in \mathbb{N} : s \models \exists \mathrm{P}_{\trianglerighteq p}(\varphi[r])\big\}$$

$$= \min\big\{r \in \mathbb{N} : \mathrm{Pr}_s^{\max}(\varphi[r]) \trianglerighteq p\big\}$$

$$\mathrm{Qu}_s\big(\exists \mathrm{P}_{\trianglerighteq p}(\psi[?])\big) = \max\big\{r \in \mathbb{N} : s \models \exists \mathrm{P}_{\trianglerighteq p}(\psi[r])\big\}$$

$$= \max\big\{r \in \mathbb{N} : \mathrm{Pr}_s^{\max}(\psi[r]) \trianglerighteq p\big\}$$

Similarly, we can define the corresponding types of *universal quantiles*:

$$Qu_s\big(\forall P_{\trianglerighteq p}(\varphi[?])\big) \;=\; \min\big\{\, r \in \mathbb{N} : Pr_s^{\min}\big(\varphi[r]\big) \trianglerighteq p \,\big\}$$

$$Qu_s\big(\forall P_{\trianglerighteq p}(\psi[?])\big) \;=\; \max\big\{\, r \in \mathbb{N} : Pr_s^{\min}\big(\psi[r]\big) \trianglerighteq p \,\big\}$$

From each of these quantiles we can derive three more quantiles by applying duality arguments, e.g., $Pr_s^{\max}(\varphi[r]) = 1 - Pr_s^{\min}(\psi[r])$, and the fact that $\min\{r \in \mathbb{N} : s \models \Phi[r]\}$ equals $\max\{r \in \mathbb{N} : s \not\models \Phi[r-1]\}$ when $\Phi[r]$ is an increasing state property. For example:

$$
\begin{aligned}
\min\{r \in \mathbb{N} : Pr_s^{\max}\big(\varphi[r]\big) > p\} \;&=\; \min\big\{\, r \in \mathbb{N} : Pr_s^{\min}\big(\psi[r]\big) < 1-p \,\big\} \\
&=\; \max\big\{\, r \in \mathbb{N} : Pr_s^{\min}\big(\psi[r-1]\big) \geqslant 1-p \,\big\} \\
&=\; \max\big\{\, r \in \mathbb{N} : Pr_s^{\max}\big(\varphi[r-1]\big) \leqslant p \,\big\}
\end{aligned}
$$

This observation yields groups of four quantiles that are derivable from each other. See [2] for the list of quantile dualities. For the above example we have:

$$
\begin{aligned}
Qu_s\big(\exists P_{>p}(\varphi[?])\big) \;&=\; Qu_s\big(\forall P_{<1-p}(\psi[?])\big) \\
&=\; Qu_s\big(\forall P_{\geqslant 1-p}(\psi[?])\big) + 1 \;=\; Qu_s\big(\exists P_{\leqslant p}(\varphi[?])\big) + 1
\end{aligned}
$$

The quantiles studied in [22] are obtained by considering $\varphi[r] = A\,U^{\leqslant r} B$ and $\psi[r] = (\neg A)\,R^{\leqslant r}(\neg B)$. Additionally, we address until-properties with lower reward bounds, i.e., $\varphi[r] = A\,U^{\geqslant r} B$ and $\psi[r] = (\neg A)\,R^{\geqslant r}(\neg B)$. To investigate the interplay of two reward functions (such as one for energy and one for utility) we also address path formulas where instead of the sets $A$ and $B$, constraints for some other reward function are imposed. For instance:

$$\lambda_{e,u} \;=\; \Diamond\big(\,(energy \leqslant e) \wedge (utility \geqslant u)\,\big),$$

where $e, u \in \mathbb{N}$ and *energy* and *utility* stand for the accumulated reward along finite paths of reward functions $erew : S \times Act \to \mathbb{N}$ (for the energy) and $urew : S \times Act \to \mathbb{N}$ (for the utility). For an infinite path $\tilde{\pi}$, we have $\tilde{\pi} \models \lambda_{e,u}$ iff $\tilde{\pi}$ has a finite prefix $\pi$ with $erew(\pi) \leqslant e$ and $urew(\pi) \geqslant u$. Likewise, $\lambda_{e,u}$ can be interpreted as an instance of an until-property with an upper or a lower reward bound. For fixed utility threshold $u$, the path property $\varphi[e] = \lambda_{e,u} = \Diamond^{\leqslant e}(utility \geqslant u)$ is increasing, while $\psi[u] = \lambda_{e,u} = \Diamond^{\geqslant u}(energy \leqslant e)$ is decreasing for fixed energy budget $e$. The task to compute the existential quantiles

$$Qu_s\big(\exists P_{>p}(\lambda_{?,u})\big) \;=\; \min\big\{\, e \in \mathbb{N} : Pr_s^{\max}(\lambda_{e,u}) > p \,\big\}$$

$$Qu_s\big(\exists P_{>p}(\lambda_{e,?})\big) \;=\; \max\big\{\, u \in \mathbb{N} : Pr_s^{\max}(\lambda_{e,u}) > p \,\big\}$$

corresponds to the problem of constructing a scheduler that minimizes the energy ensuring that the achieved utility is at least $u$ with probability $> p$ or to maximize the achieved degree of utility for a given energy budget $e$. Analogously, universal quantiles provide the corresponding information on the energy-utility characteristics in worst-case scenarios.

**Quantiles for Expectation Objectives.** We also consider quantiles where the objective is the minimal or maximal expected value of a random variable

$f[r] : IPaths \rightarrow \mathbb{N} \cup \{\infty\}$. For instance, if $f[r]$ is increasing in $r$ and $\theta$ some rational threshold, then an expectation quantile can be defined as the least $r \in \mathbb{N}$ such that the expected value of $f[r]$ is larger than $\theta$ for all or some scheduler(s). As an example for quantiles with expectation objectives, we consider a Boolean condition $cond$ for finite paths and the random variable $f[e] = utility|_{cond} :$ $IPaths \rightarrow \mathbb{N} \cup \{\infty\}$ that returns the utility value that is earned along finite paths where $cond$ holds. Formally:

$$utility|_{cond}(\tilde{\pi}) = \sup \{ urew(pref(\tilde{\pi}, k)) : k \in \mathbb{N}, pref(\tilde{\pi}, k) \models cond \}$$

That is, if $\tilde{\pi}$ is an infinite path with $\tilde{\pi} \models \Diamond cond$ (i.e., $pref(\tilde{\pi}, k) \models cond$ for some $k \in \mathbb{N}$) then $utility|_{cond}(\tilde{\pi}) = urew(\pi)$, where $\pi$ is the longest prefix of $\tilde{\pi}$ with $\pi \models cond$. If $\tilde{\pi} \models \Box cond$ (i.e., $pref(\tilde{\pi}, k) \models cond$ for all $k \in \mathbb{N}$) then $utility|_{cond}(\tilde{\pi})$ can be finite or infinite, depending on whether there are infinitely many positions $i$ with $urew(s_i, \alpha_i) > 0$. Given a scheduler $\mathfrak{S}$ and a state $s$ in $\mathcal{M}$, the *expected utility* for condition $cond$ is the expected value of the random variable $utility|_{cond}$ under the probability measure induced by $\mathfrak{S}$ and $s$:

$$\mathsf{ExpUtil}_s^{\mathfrak{S}}(cond) = \sum_{r \in \mathbb{N}} r \cdot \Pr_s^{\mathfrak{S}} \{ \tilde{\pi} \in IPaths : utility|_{cond}(\tilde{\pi}) = r \}$$

Note that $\mathsf{ExpUtil}_s^{\mathfrak{S}}(cond) = \infty$ is possible if $\Pr_s^{\mathfrak{S}}(\Diamond \Box (cond)) > 0$. We define

$$\mathsf{ExpUtil}_s^{\max}(cond) = \sup_{\mathfrak{S}} \mathsf{ExpUtil}_s^{\mathfrak{S}}(cond).$$

$\mathsf{ExpUtil}_s^{\min}(cond)$ is defined accordingly, taking the infimum over all schedulers rather than the supremum. Expectation energy-utility quantiles can be formalized by dealing with conditions $cond[e]$ that are parameterized by some energy value $e \in \mathbb{N}$. Examples are the following quantiles that fix a lower bound $u$ for the extremal expected degree of utility and ask to minimize the required energy:

$$\mathsf{Qu}_s(\exists \mathsf{ExpU}_{>u}(energy \leqslant ?)) = \min \{ e \in \mathbb{N} : \mathsf{ExpUtil}_s^{\max}(energy \leqslant e) > u \}$$

$$\mathsf{Qu}_s(\forall \mathsf{ExpU}_{>u}(energy \leqslant ?)) = \min \{ e \in \mathbb{N} : \mathsf{ExpUtil}_s^{\min}(energy \leqslant e) > u \}$$

where $\pi \models (energy \leqslant e)$ iff $erew(\pi) \leqslant e$. Analogous definitions can be provided for quantiles that ask to maximize the achieved utility if an upper bound $e$ for the expected consumed energy is given.

## 4   Computing Probability Quantiles

We now present algorithms for the computation of the quantitative quantiles introduced in Sec. 3. We start in this section with quantiles where the objective is a constraint on the extremal probability for a reward-bounded until formula. As stated before, quantiles that refer to reward-bounded release formulas are dual and can be computed using the same techniques.

Recently, a linear-programming (LP) approach for computing quantiles for (constrained) reachability properties with upper reward bounds (briefly called minimize $\sum_{(s,i)\in S[r]} x_{s,i}$ where $S[r] = S \times \{0, 1, \ldots, r\}$, subject to

$$x_{s,i} = 0 \qquad\qquad\qquad \text{if } s \not\models \exists(A \cup B) \text{ and } 0 \leqslant i \leqslant r$$

$$x_{s,i} = 1 \qquad\qquad\qquad \text{if } s \in B \text{ and } 0 \leqslant i \leqslant r$$

$$x_{s,i} \geqslant \sum_{t \in S} P(s, \alpha, t) \cdot x_{t, i-rew(s,\alpha)} \quad \text{if } s \notin B,\, s \models \exists(A \cup B) \text{ and } \alpha \in Act(s)$$
$$\text{such that } rew(s, \alpha) \leqslant i \leqslant r$$

**Fig. 1.** Linear program $\mathbb{LP}_r$ with the unique solution $p_{s,i} = \Pr_s^{\max}(A \cup^{\leqslant i} B)$

$U^{\leqslant?}$-quantiles) in MDPs with state rewards has been suggested [22]. We first recall this approach for quantitative $U^{\leqslant?}$-quantiles (Sec. 4.1) and then provide an efficient computation scheme that relies on an iterative back-propagation procedure including several heuristics (Sec. 4.2). In Sec. 4.3, we briefly show how to adapt these methods for reachability properties with lower reward bounds.

### 4.1 Iterative Linear-Programming Based Approach

We recall the approach of [22], focusing on existential $U^{\leqslant?}$-quantiles with strict probability bounds. Other $U^{\leqslant?}$-quantiles can be treated similarly (see [22]).

The idea for computing $Qu_s(\exists P_{>p}(A \cup^{\leqslant?} B))$ is to first apply standard methods for computing the maximum probability $p_s = \Pr_s^{\max}(A \cup B)$ for the unbounded until formula $A \cup B$. If $p_s$ does not meet the probability bound $p$, i.e., $p_s \leqslant p$, the quantile is infinite for state $s$. For $p_s > p$, the idea of [22] is to compute the maximal probabilities $p_{s,r} = \Pr_s^{\max}(A \cup^{\leqslant r} B)$ for increasing reward bound $r$, until $p_{s,r} > p$. For this purpose, [22] provides an LP with variables $x_{s,i}$ for $(s, i) \in S[r] = S \times \{0, 1, \ldots, r\}$ and the unique solution $(p_{s,i})_{(s,i)\in S[r]}$, where $p_{s,i} = \Pr_s^{\max}(A \cup^{\leqslant i} B)$. Fig. 1 shows the LP of [22], adapted for the case of state-action rewards (rather than state rewards). This LP-based computation scheme can be solved in exponential time, as shown in [22] by establishing an upper bound $r_{\max}$ for the smallest (finite) quantile. A naïve approach thus could first compute $r_{\max}$, generate the LP with variables $x_{s,i}$ for $(s, i) \in S[r_{\max}]$ and then use general-purpose linear- or dynamic-programming techniques to solve the constructed LP (e.g., the Simplex algorithm, ellipsoid methods or value or policy iteration). However, since the upper bound $r_{\max}$ is exponential in the size of $\mathcal{M}$ and depends on the number of states in $\mathcal{M}$, the transition probabilities and rewards in $\mathcal{M}$ and the probability bound $p$, this approach turns out to be intractable when $\mathcal{M}$ or the reward values are large.

### 4.2 Back-Propagation Approach

The main bottleneck of the LP approach for computing quantitative quantiles is the possibly exponential size of the LP. We propose an iterative approach that computes the values $p_{s,i} = \Pr_s^{\max}(A \cup^{\leqslant i} B)$ successively for $i = 0, 1, 2, \ldots$ by decomposing the LP in Fig. 1 into smaller ones and propagating already computed values as much as possible. Due to the reuse of already computed values, we call this approach *back-propagation (BP) approach*.

Given that the solution $(p_{s,j})_{0 \leqslant j < i}$ for $\mathbb{LP}_{i-1}$ is known when considering $\mathbb{LP}_i$, the constraints for variable $x_{s,i}$ in the third case of Fig. 1 (i.e., if $s \notin B$, $s \models \exists (A \cup B)$ and $\alpha \in Act(s)$) can be rewritten as follows:

$$x_{s,i} \geqslant c_{s,i} \stackrel{\text{def}}{=} \max \Big\{ \sum_{t \in S} P(s, \alpha, t) \cdot p_{t, i - rew(s,\alpha)} : \alpha \in Act(s), rew(s, \alpha) > 0 \Big\}$$

$$x_{s,i} \geqslant \sum_{t \in S} P(s, \alpha, t) \cdot x_{t,i} \quad \text{if } rew(s, \alpha) = 0$$

We can now use standard methods to solve $\mathbb{LP}'_i$ with variables $(x_{s,i})_{s \in S}$ consisting of the above linear constraints together with the terminal cases $x_{s,i} = 0$ if $s \not\models \exists (A \cup B)$ and $x_{s,i} = 1$ if $s \in B$, where the objective is to "minimize $\sum_{s \in S} x_{s,i}$". $\mathbb{LP}'_i$ has indeed a unique solution which agrees with the (unique) solution $(p_{s,i})_{s \in S}$ of $\mathbb{LP}_i$ for the variables $x_{s,i}$.

Suppose the task is to compute $q_s = \mathsf{Qu}_s(\exists P_{>p}(A \cup^{\leqslant ?} B))$ for all states $s$. Let $n = |S|$, $m = \sum_{s \in S} |Act(s)|$ and $z$ be the number of state-action pairs $(s, \alpha)$ for which $s \in S$, $\alpha \in Act(s)$ and $rew(s, \alpha) = 0$. Then, with the proposed back-propagation approach, $(q_s)_{s \in S}$ is obtained by first computing $\mathsf{Pr}_s^{\max}(A \cup B)$ for all states $s$ (which can be done in time polynomial in the size of $\mathcal{M}$ [7,5] and serves to identify the states $s \in S$ where $q_s = \infty$) and then solving the LPs $\mathbb{LP}'_0, \mathbb{LP}'_1, \ldots, \mathbb{LP}'_r$ (where $r \in \max\{q_s : \mathsf{Pr}_s^{\max}(A \cup B) > p\}$) with $n$ variables and $z + |S|$ linear constraints each.

**Reward Window.** To reduce the memory requirements, we can use the observation that the constants $c_{s,i}$ in $\mathbb{LP}'_i$ are obtained from the values $p_{t, i - rew(s,\alpha)}$ where $\alpha \in Act(s)$ and $rew(s, \alpha) > 0$. As a consequence, the solution $(p_{t,i})_{t \in S}$ for $\mathbb{LP}'_i$ can be discarded as soon as $\mathbb{LP}'_{i+w}$ has been solved for the maximal reward value $w = \max\{ rew(s, \alpha) : s \in S, \alpha \in Act(s) \}$ in $\mathcal{M}$. A further improvement considers the maximum reward of all incoming transitions per state. That is, the value of $p_{t,i}$ is not needed any more as soon as $\mathbb{LP}'_{i+w}$ has been solved where $w$ equals the maximal reward of the state-action pairs $(s, \alpha)$ with $P(s, \alpha, t) > 0$.

**Linear Programs for Zero-Reward Sub-MDP.** The back-propagation approach can yield a major speed-up compared to the naïve approach with a single LP. However, if the number of state-action pairs with zero reward is large compared to the full set of actions in $S$, $\mathbb{LP}'_i$ needs still to be solved for several $i$. The idea then is to decompose $\mathbb{LP}'_i$ and treat the sub-LPs in a specific order. Let $\mathcal{G}$ be the directed graph with node set $S$ and the edge relation $\rightarrow \subseteq S \times S$ given by $s \rightarrow t$ iff $P(s, \alpha, t) > 0$ for some action $\alpha \in Act(s)$ with $rew(s, \alpha) = 0$. Applying standard graph algorithms, we compute the strongly connected components in $\mathcal{G}$ and a topological sorting $C_1, \ldots, C_k$ for them. Then the SCCs $C_1, \ldots, C_k$ are the finest partition of $S$ such that: if $s \in C_h$, $t \in C_j$, $P(s, \alpha, t) > 0$ and $rew(s, \alpha) = 0$, then $h \leqslant j$. Thus, we can decompose $\mathbb{LP}'_i$ into LPs $\mathbb{LP}'_{i,1}, \ldots, \mathbb{LP}'_{i,k}$, where $\mathbb{LP}'_{i,h}$ consists of the linear constraints $x_{s,i} \geqslant c_{s,i}$ and

$$x_{s,i} \geqslant \sum_{t \in C_h} P(s, \alpha, t) \cdot x_{t,i} + \sum_{u \in C_{>h}} P(s, \alpha, u) \cdot p_{u,i}$$

for $s \in C_h$, $\alpha \in Act(s)$, $rew(s, \alpha) = 0$. Here, $C_{>h} = C_{h+1} \cup \ldots \cup C_k$ and $(p_{u,i})_{u \in C_j}$ denotes the solutions of $\mathbb{LP}'_{i,j}$. The objective of $\mathbb{LP}'_{i,h}$ is to minimize the sum $\sum_{s \in C_h} x_{s,i}$.

Assuming that the sub-MDP $\mathcal{M}|_{rew=0}$ of $\mathcal{M}$ resulting by removing all actions $\alpha$ from $Act(s)$ with $rew(s,\alpha) > 0$ is acyclic, no LP has to be solved within our approach. In this case, the sets $C_1, \ldots, C_k$ are singletons, say $C_h = \{s_h\}$, and the solution $(p_{s,i})_{s \in S}$ is obtained directly when processing the states in reversed topological order $s_k, s_{k-1}, \ldots, s_1$.

**Other Improvements.** Several other heuristics can be integrated to speed up the computation time or to decrease the memory requirements. For instance, zero-reward self-loops can be removed by a quantile-preserving transformation $\mathcal{M} \rightsquigarrow \mathcal{M}'$. The MDP $\mathcal{M}'$ has the same state space $S$ as $\mathcal{M}$ and the same rewards for all state-action pairs. The transition probability function $P'$ of $\mathcal{M}'$ is given by $P'(s,\alpha,t) = P(s,\alpha,t)/(1-P(s,\alpha,s))$ if $rew(s,\alpha) = 0$, $t \neq s$ and $0 < P(s,\alpha,s) < 1$ and $P'(s,\alpha,t) = P(s,\alpha,t)$ in all other cases (see [2]). Another heuristic, which is however not yet realized in our implementation, is the aggregation method proposed in [8]. This approach permits to collapse all states belonging to the same maximal end components in the sub-MDP $\mathcal{M}|_{rew=0}$ into a single state.

## 4.3   Lower Reward Bounds

The approach for computing $U^{\leqslant?}$-quantiles can be adapted to compute quantiles for (constrained) reachability formulas with lower reward bounds, i.e., $A \, U^{\geqslant?} \, B$. For simplicity, we sketch only the treatment of reachability $(\lozenge^{\geqslant?} B)$ with a lower reward bound. More details and proofs can be found in [2]. We start with the universal quantile:

$$\mathrm{Qu}_s\big(\forall P_{<p}(\lozenge^{\geqslant?} B)\big) \;=\; \min\big\{r \in \mathbb{N} : \mathrm{Pr}_s^{\max}(\lozenge^{\geqslant r} B) < p\big\}$$

Clearly, if $\mathrm{Pr}_s^{\max}(\lozenge B) < p$ then the quantile for state $s$ is 0. Furthermore:

$$\mathrm{Qu}_s\big(\forall P_{<p}(\lozenge^{\geqslant?} B)\big) = \infty \quad \text{iff} \quad \mathrm{Pr}_s^{\max}\big(\lozenge(C \wedge \lozenge B)\big) \geqslant p,$$

where $C$ consists of all states $t$ that are contained in a maximal end component $(T, \mathfrak{A})$ with $rew(t',\alpha) > 0$ for some state $t' \in T$ and an action $\alpha \in \mathfrak{A}(t')$. Intuitively, when entering $C$ one can stay in $C$ until the accumulated reward is greater or equal than $r$, before entering $B$. Otherwise, we apply the same idea as before and compute the values $p_{s,r} = \mathrm{Pr}_s^{\max}(\lozenge^{\geqslant r} B)$ for increasing $r$ until $p_{s,r} < p$. The values $p_{s,r}$ are obtained as the unique solution of the following LP with variables $x_{s,i}$ for $(s,i) \in S[r]$ and the following constraints for $s \in S$ and $1 \leqslant i \leqslant r$:

$$x_{s,0} \;=\; \mathrm{Pr}_s^{\max}(\lozenge B)$$

$$x_{s,i} \;\geqslant\; 0$$

$$x_{s,i} \;\geqslant\; \sum_{t \in S} P(s,\alpha,t) \cdot x_{t,\ell} \quad \text{if } \alpha \in Act(s) \text{ and } \ell = \max\{0, i - rew(s,\alpha)\}$$

The objective is to minimize $\sum_{(s,i) \in S[r]} x_{s,i}$. To speed up the computation, one can add the following constraints: $x_{s,i} = 1$ if $\mathrm{Pr}_s^{\max}\big(\lozenge(C \wedge \lozenge B)\big) = 1$ for $s \in S$.

The existential quantile

$$\mathsf{Qu}_s\big(\exists\mathsf{P}_{<p}(\Diamond^{\geqslant ?}B)\big) \quad = \quad \min\big\{\,r \in \mathbb{N} : \mathsf{Pr}_s^{\min}(\Diamond^{\geqslant r}B) < p\,\big\}$$

can then be computed by an analogous approach, using the fact that the values $p_{s,r} = \mathsf{Pr}_s^{\min}(\Diamond^{\geqslant r}B)$ are the greatest solutions in $[0,1]$ of the linear constraints

$$x_{s,0} \;=\; \mathsf{Pr}_s^{\min}(\Diamond B)$$

$$x_{s,i} \;=\; 0 \qquad\qquad\qquad \text{if } \mathsf{Pr}_s^{\min}(\Diamond B) = 0 \text{ and } i \geqslant 1$$

$$x_{s,i} \;\leqslant\; \sum_{t \in S} P(s,\alpha,t)\cdot x_{t,\ell} \quad \text{if } \mathsf{Pr}_s^{\min}(\Diamond B) > 0,\, i \geqslant 1,\, \alpha \in \mathit{Act}(s)$$
$$\text{and } \ell = \max\{0, i - \mathit{rew}(s,\alpha)\}.$$

Then, $\mathsf{Qu}_s\big(\exists\mathsf{P}_{<p}(\Diamond^{\geqslant ?}B)\big) = \infty$ iff $\mathsf{Pr}_s^{\min}\big(\Box\Diamond B \wedge \Box\Diamond\mathit{posR}\big) \geqslant p$, where $\mathit{posR} \subseteq S \times \mathit{Act}$ is the set of state-action pairs $(s,\alpha)$ with $\mathit{rew}(s,\alpha) > 0$. Again, one could add the following constraints: $x_{s,i} = 1$ if $\mathsf{Pr}_s^{\min}(\Box\Diamond B \wedge \Box\Diamond\mathit{posR}) = 1$ for $s \in S$. Obviously, the back-propagation approach (cf. Sec. 4.2) is applicable for the existential and universal quantiles with lower bounds as well.

## 4.4   Energy-Utility Quantiles

The energy-utility quantile $\mathsf{Qu}_s\big(\exists\mathsf{P}_{>p}(\lambda_{?,u})\big)$ as introduced in Sec. 3 can be computed using the same techniques as explained for quantiles of the form $\mathsf{Qu}_s\big(\exists\mathsf{P}_{>p}(\Diamond^{\leqslant ?}B)\big)$. For this purpose, we might use an automaton $\mathcal{U}_u$ with states $q_0, q_1, \ldots, q_{u-1}, q_u$ representing the accumulated utility value. The goal state $q_u$ represents that the achieved utility is at least $u$. The transitions of $\mathcal{U}_u$ are given by $q_i \to q_j$ for $j \geqslant i$. We put $\mathcal{M}$ and $\mathcal{U}_u$ in parallel to obtain an MDP $\mathcal{M} \otimes \mathcal{U}_u$ with a single reward function for the energy and synchronous transitions that capture the meaning of $\mathcal{U}_u$'s states. Formally, $\mathcal{M} \otimes \mathcal{U}_u = (S \times \{q_0, \ldots, q_u\}, \mathit{Act}, P')$ where

$$P'(\langle s, q_i\rangle, \alpha, \langle t, q_j\rangle) \;=\; P(s,\alpha,t) \quad \text{if } j = \min\{u, i + \mathit{urew}(s,\alpha)\}$$

and $P'(\cdot) = 0$ in all other cases. The reward structure of $\mathcal{M} \otimes \mathcal{U}_u$ consists of the energy reward function $\mathit{erew}$ lifted to the product. That is, we deal with the reward function $\mathit{erew}'$ for $\mathcal{M} \otimes \mathcal{U}_u$ given by $\mathit{erew}'(\langle s, q_i\rangle, \alpha) = \mathit{erew}(s,\alpha)$ for all $s \in S$, $0 \leqslant i \leqslant u$ and $\alpha \in \mathit{Act}$. With $B = S \times \{q_u\}$, we then have

$$\mathsf{Pr}_{\mathcal{M},s}^{\max}\big(\Diamond((\mathit{energy} \leqslant e) \wedge (\mathit{utility} \geqslant u))\big) \;=\; \mathsf{Pr}_{\mathcal{M}\otimes\mathcal{U}_u,\langle s,q_0\rangle}^{\max}\big(\Diamond^{\leqslant e}B\big)$$

and therefore $\mathsf{Qu}_s^{\mathcal{M}}\big(\exists\mathsf{P}_{>p}(\lambda_{?,u})\big) = \mathsf{Qu}_{\langle s,q_0\rangle}^{\mathcal{M}\otimes\mathcal{U}_u}\big(\exists\mathsf{P}_{>p}(\Diamond^{\leqslant ?}B)\big)$.

The quantile $\mathsf{Qu}_s\big(\exists\mathsf{P}_{>p}(\lambda_{e,?})\big)$ is computable by an analogous automata-based approach, but now using the LP approach suggested for lower reward bounds (Sec. 4.3). Various other energy-utility quantiles can be computed using reductions to the case of reward-bounded until formulas or derived path properties. It is obvious that an analogous automata-based approach is applicable for quantiles where the objective is a probability constraint on path properties of the form $\Diamond((\mathit{rew} \bowtie r) \wedge \kappa)$, where $\kappa$ is a Boolean combination of constraints of the form $\mathit{rew}_i \bowtie_i r_i$ for multiple reward functions $\mathit{rew}_1, \ldots, \mathit{rew}_k$ (other than $\mathit{rew}$).

## 5   Computing Expectation Quantiles

We now discuss how to compute the expectation quantiles in MDPs with two reward functions *erew* and *urew* for modeling the energy requirements and the achieved utility (see Sec. 3). Let us exemplify the approach computing

$$E_s^\exists \;=\; \mathsf{Qu}_s\big(\exists\,\mathsf{ExpU}_{>u}(energy \leqslant ?)\big) \text{ and } E_s^\forall \;=\; \mathsf{Qu}_s\big(\forall\,\mathsf{ExpU}_{>u}(energy \leqslant ?)\big).$$

Using known results for standard MDPs, we obtain that $\mathsf{ExpUtil}_s^{\max}(energy \leqslant e)$ is finite, provided that $\mathsf{Pr}_s^{\min}(\Diamond(energy > e)) = 1$. If, however, $\mathcal{M}$ contains end components where all the state-action pairs have zero energy reward then $\mathsf{Pr}_s^{\min}(\Diamond(energy > e)) < 1$ and $\mathsf{ExpUtil}_s^{\max}(energy \leqslant e) = \infty$ is possible.

Let us first make the simplifying assumption that all end components are both energy- and utility-divergent, i.e., whenever $(T, \mathfrak{A})$ is an end component of $\mathcal{M}$ then there exist state-action pairs $(t, \alpha)$ and $(v, \beta)$ with $t, v \in T$ and $\alpha \in \mathfrak{A}(t)$, $\beta \in \mathfrak{A}(v)$ such that $erew(t, \alpha)$ and $urew(v, \beta)$ are positive. This assumption yields that $\mathsf{Pr}_s^{\min}(\Diamond(energy > e)) = 1$ and hence, $\mathsf{ExpUtil}_s^{\max}(energy \leqslant e)$ and $\mathsf{ExpUtil}_s^{\min}(energy \leqslant e)$ are finite for all states $s \in S$ and all energy bounds $e \in \mathbb{N}$. Moreover, $\lim_{e\to\infty} \mathsf{ExpUtil}_s^{\mathfrak{S}}(energy \leqslant e) = \infty$ for each scheduler $\mathfrak{S}$. This yields the finiteness of the expectation quantiles $E_s^\exists$ and $E_s^\forall$. The computation of $E_s^\exists$ and $E_s^\forall$ can be carried out using an iterative approach as for probability quantiles. For $E_s^\exists$, we compute iteratively the values $u_{s,e} = \mathsf{ExpUtil}_s^{\min}(energy \leqslant e)$ until $u_{s,e} > u$, in which case $E_s^\exists = e$. It remains to explain how to compute $u_{s,e}$. Again, we can use an LP-based approach and characterize the vector $(u_{s,i})_{(s,i)\in S[e]}$ as the unique solution of the LP with variables $x_{s,i}$ for $(s, i) \in S[e] = S \times \{0, 1, \ldots, e\}$ and the objective to maximize the sum of the $x_{s,i}$'s subject to:

$$x_{s,i} \;\leqslant\; urew(s, \alpha) + \sum_{t \in S} P(s, \alpha, t) \cdot x_{t, i - erew(s,\alpha)}$$

if $\alpha \in Act(s)$ and $erew(s, \alpha) \leqslant i \leqslant e$. For computing $E_s^\forall$, the values $v_{s,e} = \mathsf{ExpUtil}_s^{\max}(energy \leqslant e)$ can be computed by a similar schema, using the fact that the vector $(v_{s,i})_{(s,i)\in S[e]}$ is the least solution in $[0, 1]^{S[e]}$ of the linear constraints

$$x_{s,i} \;\geqslant\; urew(s, \alpha) + \sum_{t \in S} P(s, \alpha, t) \cdot x_{t, i - erew(s,\alpha)}$$

if $\alpha \in Act(s)$ and $erew(s, \alpha) \leqslant i \leqslant e$. Obviously, the back-propagation approach is applicable as well.

The computation of expectation quantiles for the general case, where no assumptions on the end components are imposed, are detailed in [2]. Basically, this computation relies on an analogous LP approach, but requires a preprocessing step to identify the states where $\mathsf{ExpUtil}_s^{\max}(energy \leqslant e) = \infty$, respectively $\mathsf{ExpUtil}_s^{\min}(energy \leqslant e) = \infty$ and computing those states where the quantile is infinite. The main feature for this preprocessing is an analysis of end components, similar as in [10,12].

# 6    Implementation and Case Studies

In this section, we deal with our implementation of the algorithms for computing $U^{\leqslant ?}$-quantiles presented in Sec. 4.1 and 4.2 and demonstrate its usability within case studies. Our implementation relies on the computation of extremal probabilities for upper *reward-bounded* until properties on top of the explicit engine of the prominent probabilistic model checker PRISM version 4.1 [14], which have not yet been supported within PRISM so far. We compute quantiles either by solving the LP of [22] (see Fig. 1) directly using the LP-solver LPSOLVE[1] or with our back-propagation approach (BP). Our first case study is taken from PRISM's benchmark suite [17], showing the applicability of our implementation on relatively small models and compare the performance of the LP and BP approach. Then, we turn to computing energy-utility quantiles for an energy-aware job-scheduling protocol. All calculations were carried out on a computer with two Intel E5-2680 8-core CPUs at 2.70 GHz with 384GB of RAM. More detailed information and further case studies can be found in [2].

**Self-stabilization.** The self-stabilizing protocol by Israeli and Jalfon is modeled[2] as an MDP for $N$ equal processes organized in a ring, each having a token at the beginning and aiming to randomly send and receive tokens until the ring is in a stable state, i.e., only one process has a token. We used our quantile algorithms to compute the minimal number of steps required for reaching a stable state with probability of at least $p$ for some schedulers (existential quantile) or all schedulers (universal quantile). The latter problem also has been answered in

**Table 1.** Results for randomized self-stabilizing (existential and universal quantile)

| | | model | | existential quantile | | | universal quantile | | |
|---|---|---|---|---|---|---|---|---|---|
| $N$ | $p$ | states | build | result | LP | BP | result | LP | BP |
| 10 | 0.1 | 1,023 | 0.24$s$ | 18 | 118.38$s$ | 0.03$s$ | 26 | 403.36$s$ | 0.16$s$ |
| | 0.5 | " | " | 38 | 1,066.64$s$ | 0.05$s$ | 43 | 1,388.15$s$ | 0.09$s$ |
| | 0.99 | " | " | 117 | 11,552.55$s$ | 0.14$s$ | 130 | 19,794.61$s$ | 0.15$s$ |
| 15 | 0.1 | 32,767 | 1.56$s$ | 42 | timeout | 1.85$s$ | 61 | timeout | 3.78$s$ |
| | 0.5 | " | " | 89 | timeout | 3.85$s$ | 100 | timeout | 4.10$s$ |
| | 0.99 | " | " | 270 | timeout | 11.42$s$ | 305 | timeout | 12.18$s$ |

the referred PRISM case study, but by iteratively increasing the step bound until the probability bound $p$ was met. Our approach is more elegant by implicitly computing the probability values and answering only one (quantile) query. Table 1 shows our results for the LP and BP approach, with a timeout of 12 hours. The time for BP covers the entire computation of the quantile value $r$. For LP, we report the time for solving the linear program $\mathbb{LP}_r$. As it can be seen, the LP approach turns out to be infeasible already for relatively small models, whereas the BP implementation performs well. Table 1 also reveals that especially within

---

[1] http://lpsolve.sourceforge.net, we used version 5.5.2, presolving deactivated.

[2] http://www.prismmodelchecker.org/casestudies/self-stabilisation.php#ij

**Table 2.** Results for energy-aware job scheduling (quantiles $e_{\min}$ and $u_{\max}$)

| | | model | | quantile $e_{\min}$ | | | | model | | quantile $u_{\max}$ | |
|---|---|---|---|---|---|---|---|---|---|---|---|
| $N$ | $p$ | states | build | result | time | $N$ | $p$ | states | build | result | time |
| 4 | 0.1 | 368,521 | 14.67$s$ | 179 | 37.43$s$ | 4 | 0.1 | 872,410 | 14.47$s$ | 7 | 173.71$s$ |
| | 0.5 | " | " | 198 | 37.02$s$ | | 0.5 | " | " | 7 | 173.22$s$ |
| | 0.99 | " | " | 225 | 42.69$s$ | | 0.99 | " | " | 7 | 155.66$s$ |
| 5 | 0.1 | 6,079,533 | 377.95$s$ | 242 | 1,058.48$s$ | 5 | 0.1 | 3,049,471 | 65.69$s$ | 9 | 812.19$s$ |
| | 0.5 | " | " | 266 | 1,135.65$s$ | | 0.5 | " | " | 9 | 812.93$s$ |
| | 0.99 | " | " | 301 | 1,261.89$s$ | | 0.99 | " | " | 9 | 736.93$s$ |

the LP approach the time spent for evaluating the quantile increases significantly when the probability bound $p$ is high (and hence, also the quantile value is high).

**Energy-Aware Job Scheduling.** We now turn to an energy-aware job-scheduling protocol modeled as an MDP, for which we compute energy-utility quantiles. Assume a system of $N$ processes which need to enter a critical section in order to perform tasks, each within a given deadline. Access to the critical section is exclusively granted by a scheduler, which selects processes only if they have requested to enter. When a process states such a request, a deadline counter is set and decreased over time even if the process did not enter the critical section yet. Since computing a task also requires a certain amount of time in the critical section, deadlines can be exceeded. Utility is hence provided in terms of tasks finished without exceeding their deadline. Each process consumes energy, especially if it is in the critical section, and the global energy consumption equals the sum of energy consumed by all processes. Additional dependencies between utility and energy arise as the scheduler can activate a turbo mode for the critical section, doubling the computation speed but tripling energy consumption. As motivated in the introduction, we are now interested in the following energy-utility quantiles, both illustrating the trade-off between energy and utility w.r.t. several probability bounds $p$. We consider the quantile for the minimal energy $e_{\min}$ required to guarantee $u$ successfully finished tasks, and the quantile for the maximal number $u_{\max}$ of tasks successfully finished by one process requiring not more than $e$ energy. Our experiments solving these quantiles used the BP implementation with parameters $u=N$, $e=50 \cdot N$. The results shown in Table 2 illustrate that even for large model sizes with millions of states, our implementation of the BP algorithm is feasible. As expected, none of the quantile computations for $e_{\min}$ and $u_{\max}$ finished within 12 hours when we used the LP approach instead of our BP implementation.

## 7    Conclusion

We introduced a general notion of (energy-utility) quantiles for MDPs and extended the LP schema from [22] to compute quantitative quantiles with lower and upper reward bounds, where the objective can be a probability constraint or a constraint on an expectation. We implemented a BP approach for quantitative quantiles with upper reward bounds, which can significantly speed up quantile computations, and demonstrated its performance by means of case studies.

# References

1. Andova, S., Hermanns, H., Katoen, J.-P.: Discrete-time rewards model-checked. In: Larsen, K.G., Niebert, P. (eds.) FORMATS 2003. LNCS, vol. 2791, pp. 88–104. Springer, Heidelberg (2004)
2. Baier, C., Daum, M., Dubslaff, C., Klein, J., Klüppelholz, S.: Energy-Utility Quantiles. Technical report, TU Dresden (2014), http://wwwtcs.inf.tu-dresden.de/ALGI/PUB/NFM14/
3. Baier, C., et al.: Waiting for locks: How long does it usually take? In: Stoelinga, M., Pinger, R. (eds.) FMICS 2012. LNCS, vol. 7437, pp. 47–62. Springer, Heidelberg (2012)
4. Baier, C., Dubslaff, C., Klein, J., Klüppelholz, S., Wunderlich, S.: Probabilistic Model Checking for Energy-Utility Analysis. Festschrift (to appear 2014)
5. Baier, C., Katoen, J.-P.: Principles of Model Checking. MIT Press (2008)
6. Bertsekas, D., Tsitsiklis, J.: An analysis of stochastic shortest path problems. Mathematics of Operations Research 16(3), 580–595 (1991)
7. Bianco, A., de Alfaro, L.: Model checking of probabilistic and non-deterministic systems. In: Thiagarajan, P.S. (ed.) FSTTCS 1995. LNCS, vol. 1026, pp. 499–513. Springer, Heidelberg (1995)
8. Ciesinski, F., Baier, C., Größer, M., Klein, J.: Reduction techniques for model checking Markov decision processes. In: QEST 2008, pp. 45–54. IEEE (2008)
9. de Alfaro, L.: Formal Verification of Probabilistic Systems. PhD thesis, Stanford University, Department of Computer Science (1997)
10. de Alfaro, L.: Computing minimum and maximum reachability times in probabilistic systems. In: Baeten, J.C.M., Mauw, S. (eds.) CONCUR 1999. LNCS, vol. 1664, pp. 66–81. Springer, Heidelberg (1999)
11. Etessami, K., Kwiatkowska, M., Vardi, M., Yannakakis, M.: Multi-objective model checking of Markov decision processes. Logical Methods in Computer Science 4(4) (2008)
12. Forejt, V., Kwiatkowska, M., Norman, G., Parker, D.: Automated verification techniques for probabilistic systems. In: Bernardo, M., Issarny, V. (eds.) SFM 2011. LNCS, vol. 6659, pp. 53–113. Springer, Heidelberg (2011)
13. Haverkort, B.: Performance of Computer Communication Systems: A Model-Based Approach. Wiley (1998)
14. Hinton, A., Kwiatkowska, M., Norman, G., Parker, D.: PRISM: A tool for automatic verification of probabilistic systems. In: Hermanns, H., Palsberg, J. (eds.) TACAS 2006. LNCS, vol. 3920, pp. 441–444. Springer, Heidelberg (2006)
15. Katoen, J.-P., Zapreev, I., Hahn, E., Hermanns, H., Jansen, D.: The ins and outs of the probabilistic model checker MRMC. Perform. Eval. 68(2) (2011)
16. Kulkarni, V.: Modeling and Analysis of Stochastic Systems. Chapman & Hall (1995)
17. Kwiatkowska, M., Norman, G., Parker, D.: The PRISM benchmark suite. In: QEST 2012. IEEE Computer Society (2012)
18. Kwon, Y., Agha, G.: A Markov reward model for software reliability. In: IPDPS 2007, pp. 1–6. IEEE (2007)
19. Laroussinie, F., Sproston, J.: Model checking durational probabilistic systems. In: Sassone, V. (ed.) FOSSACS 2005. LNCS, vol. 3441, pp. 140–154. Springer, Heidelberg (2005)
20. Puterman, M.: Markov Decision Processes: Discrete Stochastic Dynamic Programming. Wiley (1994)
21. Serfling, R.J.: Approximation Theorems of Mathematical Statistics. Wiley (1980)
22. Ummels, M., Baier, C.: Computing quantiles in Markov reward models. In: Pfenning, F. (ed.) FOSSACS 2013. LNCS, vol. 7794, pp. 353–368. Springer, Heidelberg (2013)

# Incremental Verification of Compiler Optimizations*

Grigory Fedyukovich[1], Arie Gurfinkel[2], and Natasha Sharygina[1]

[1] University of Lugano, Switzerland
{grigory.fedyukovich,natasha.sharygina}@usi.ch
[2] SEI/CMU, USA
arie@cmu.com

**Abstract.** Optimizations are widely used along the lifecycle of software. However, proving the equivalence between original and optimized versions is difficult. In this paper, we propose a technique to incrementally verify different versions of a program with respect to a fixed property. We exploit a safety proof of a program given by a safe inductive invariant. For each optimization, such invariants are adapted to be a valid safety proof of the optimized program (if possible). The cost of the adaptation depends on the impact of the optimization and is often less than an entire re-verification of the optimized program. We have developed a preliminary implementation of our technique in the context of Software Model Checking. Our evaluation of the technique on different classes of industrial programs and standard LLVM optimizations confirms that the optimized programs can be re-verified efficiently.

## 1 Introduction

Program verification is necessary for building reliable software intensive systems. One challenge in using verification is deciding on the right level of abstraction. On one hand, verifying the source code (or a high-level compiler representation) before optimizations gives meaningful verification results to the user. On the other, verifying the binary (or a low-level compiler representation) after optimizations takes compiler out of the trusted computing base. Our experience with the UFO [1] indicates that verification results at both levels are desired.

There are two common techniques for adapting verification results from an original program $P$ to an optimized program $Q$: (1) complete re-verification of $Q$; (2) establish property preserving equivalence (typically a form of a simulation) between $P$ and $Q$. Re-verification is computationally expensive. Establishing a simulation between $P$ and $Q$ often requires manual instrumentation of the

* This material is based upon work funded and supported by the Department of Defense under Contract No. FA8721-05-C-0003 with Carnegie Mellon University for the operation of the Software Engineering Institute, a federally funded research and development center. Any opinions, findings and conclusions or recommendations expressed in this material are those of the author(s) and do not necessarily reflect the views of the United States Department of Defense. This material has been approved for public release and unlimited distribution. DM-0000784

J.M. Badger and K.Y. Rozier (Eds.): NFM 2014, LNCS 8430, pp. 300–306, 2014.

compiler which is hard to do and maintain [6]. In this paper, we propose an alternative solution that combines the advantages of the two approaches.

We assume that the original program $P$ comes with a property $G$, and that $P$ satisfies $G$ (i.e., $P \models G$). Instead of showing an equivalence between $P$ and $Q$, we show that $Q$ satisfies $G$. First, by adapting the proof of $P \models G$, given by an inductive invariant, to $Q$, and then strengthening it by re-verification as needed. Our technique can be seen as a *property-specific equivalence*: $P$ and $Q$ are equivalent iff they both satisfy $G$.

We evaluate our approach on the `instcombine` optimization of LLVM that does local optimizations (such as turning x = 1 + 1 into x = 2). Our experiments show that the approach is very effective. In many cases, the complete safety proof can be transferred between the original and the optimized programs. Whenever re-verification was required, it was insignificant.

## 2    From Optimization to Evolution

In this section, we formally define the problem of *incremental property-directed verification of optimizations*. We begin with formal definitions of programs, safety proofs, and admissible optimizations. A "large-block" representation of a *program* is a tuple $P = (V, en, err, E, \tau_P)$, where $V$ is a set of cutpoints (i.e., locations which represent heads of some loops); $en, err \in V$ are designated entry and error locations, respectively; $E \subseteq V \times V$ is the control-flow relation (represent a loop-free program fragments), $\tau_P : E \to Stmt^*$ maps control edges to loop-free program fragments. An example of a program is shown in Fig. 1a. We call the graph $(V, E)$ the Cut-Point Graph (CPG) which collapses the more fine grained Control-Flow Graph (CFG).

We write $\vdash X$ to mean that $X$ is valid. Let $Expr$ be a set of expressions over program variables, $pre, post \in Expr$ and $S$ a loop-free program fragment. We write $\vdash \{pre\}\ S\ \{post\}$ to mean that $pre$ and $post$ are pre- and post-conditions of $S$, i.e., whenever $S$ starts in a state satisfying $pre$, if $S$ terminates, it ends in a state satisfying $post$. A *safety proof* of $P$ is a mapping $\psi : V \to Expr$ such that

$$\forall (u, v) \in E \cdot\ \vdash \{\psi(u)\}\ \tau_P(u, v)\ \{\psi(v)\} \qquad\qquad \psi(err) \to \bot \qquad (1)$$

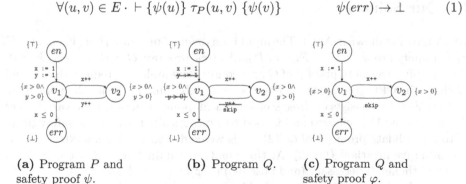

(a) Program $P$ and safety proof $\psi$.      (b) Program $Q$.      (c) Program $Q$ and safety proof $\varphi$.

**Fig. 1.** A simple program and an optimization

---

**Algorithm 1:** OPTVERIFY$(P, \psi, Q)$

**Input:** *Original* program $P$, safety proof $\psi$ of $P$, *new* program $Q$
**Output:** A pair $\langle res, \varphi \rangle$ s.t. $res \rightarrow \varphi$ is safety proof of $Q$

1  $\sigma \leftarrow$ GUESSMAP$(P, Q)$            ▷ Guess a map between variables of $P$ and $Q$
2  $\pi \leftarrow$ MKIND$(\psi\sigma, Q, P)$       ▷ Weaken candidate $\psi\sigma$ until it is inductive for $Q$
3  $res, \varphi \leftarrow$ VERIFY$(Q, \pi)$      ▷ Strengthen $\varphi$ until it is SAFE for $Q$
4  **return** $\langle res, \varphi \rangle$

---

An *optimization* of $P$ is a program $Q = (V, en, err, E, \tau_Q)$, that differs from $P$ only in the labeling of the edges of the CPG. Note that this definition limits optimizations to changes that do not affect the loop-structure of $P$ (i.e., loops cannot be added or removed). However, since we deal with "large-blocks", loop unrolling is admissible. At the same time, we do not put any other restrictions on $Q$. In particular, we do not require for $Q$ to simulate $P$. An example of optimization $Q$ of $P$ is shown at the Fig. 1b in which the variable y was removed

The problem of incremental property-directed verification is: Given a program $P$, a safety proof $\psi$ of $P$, and an optimization $Q$ of $P$, *adapt* a safety proof $\psi$ to a safety proof $\varphi$ of $Q$, or show that $Q$ does not admit a safety proof (i.e., has a counterexample).

Thus, we view the problem as a variant of *upgrade checking* (as opposed to verification). The key concept in upgrade checking is adapting verification results from one program to another. We extend this concept to safety proofs. Let $P$, $\psi$, and $Q$ be as above. An adaptation $\pi$ of $\varphi$ to $Q$ is a weakening of $\psi$ such that

$$\forall w \in V \cdot \psi(w) \rightarrow \pi(w) \tag{2}$$

$$\forall (u, v) \in E \cdot \vdash \{\pi(u)\} \, \tau_Q(u, v) \, \{\pi(v)\} \tag{3}$$

Intuitively, (2) says that $\pi$ is a weakening of $\psi$, and (3) says that $\pi$ is inductive. Note that if $\pi(err) = \bot$, then $\pi$ is a safety proof of $Q$. Otherwise, $\pi$ is simply an inductive invariant.

## 3   Our Solution

OPTVERIFY is shown in Alg. 1. The input is an *original* program $P = (V, en, err, E, \tau_P)$, a safety proof $\psi : V \rightarrow Expr$ of $P$ and a *new* program $Q = (V, en, err, E, \tau_Q)$. The output is a safety proof $\varphi$ of $Q$ or a counter-example. We require that $P$ and $Q$ share the CPG (i.e., same loop-heads), and differ only in the labeling of edges.

OPTVERIFY consists of three steps: (1) a mapping $\sigma$ between the variables of $P$ and $Q$ (line 1) is guessed and is used to syntactically transfer the safety proof $\psi$ to a candidate proof $\psi\sigma$ of $Q$. (2) $\psi\sigma$ is weakened to $\pi$ using MKIND until $\pi$ is an inductive invariant (line 2). At this point, $\pi$ is inductive, but not safe. (3) $\pi$ is strengthened if necessary (and possible) to $\varphi$ by a standalone verifier (line 3).

In our implementation, $\sigma$ is guessed by syntactically matching variable names: a variable v of $P$ is mapped to a variable v of $Q$ if v exists in $Q$, and to a

---

**Algorithm 2:** MKIND($\psi, Q, P$)

   **Input**: Candidate invariant $\psi$, *new* program $Q$, *original* program $P$

   **Output**: Inductive invariant $\pi : V \to Expr$ of $Q$

1  $\pi \leftarrow \psi$; $W \leftarrow \{(u,v) \in E \mid \tau_P(e) \neq \tau_Q(e)\}$;

2  **while** $W \neq \emptyset$ **do**

3     $(u,v) \leftarrow$ GETWTOSMALLESTEDGE($W$);        // according to the WTO

4     $pre \leftarrow \pi(u)$ ; $post \leftarrow \pi(v)$;

5     **if** ($\vdash \{pre\}\, \tau_Q(u,v)\, \{post\}$) **then** $W \leftarrow W \setminus \{(u,v)\}$;  // use SMT-solver

6     **else**

7       $\pi(v) \leftarrow$ WEAKPOST($pre, \tau_Q(u,v), post$);        // see Alg 3

8       $W \leftarrow (W \setminus \{(u,v)\}) \cup \{(v,x) \in E \mid x \in V\}$

9  **return** $\pi$

---

fresh symbol otherwise. To implement VERIFY, we use UFO [1] that iteratively strengthens the given inductive invariant. In particular, if $\pi$ is already safe, UFO returns immediately and $\varphi \equiv \pi$. A verifier that cannot work by strengthening a given invariant would be useless as it would amount to verifying $Q$ from scratch. Our key contribution is an algorithm MKIND for weakening a candidate invariant. We describe it in details in the rest of this section.

MKIND is shown in Alg. 2. The input is a candidate invariant $\psi$, a *new* program $Q$ and an *original* program $P$. The output is an inductive weakening $\pi$ of $\psi$ (i.e., $\pi$ satisfies (2) and (3)) for $Q$. MKIND maintains a work-list $W \subseteq E$ that is initialized with all the edges $(u,v) \in E$ on which $P$ and $Q$ disagree (i.e., $\tau_P(u,v) \neq \tau_Q(u,v)$). In each iteration of the main loop, first, an edge $(u,v) \in W$ that is least in the Weak Topological Ordering (WTO) [2] (in which inner loops are traversed before outer loops) is picked. Second, an SMT-solver is used to check whether the current values of $\pi(u)$ and $\pi(v)$ form a valid Hoare-triple for the corresponding loop-free code fragment $\tau_Q(u,v)$. If this is not the case, the post-condition $\pi(v)$ is weakened until the triple becomes valid and all outgoing edges of $v$ are added to $W$. Soundness of MKIND is immediate – the work-list is empty only if every edge is annotated with a valid pre- and post-condition pair. Termination follows from the fact that at each iteration either the work-list is reduced, or a post-condition is weakened, and, our implementation of WEAKPOST allows only for finitely many weakening steps.

WEAKPOST is shown in Alg. 3. The input is a pre-condition *pre*, a post-condition *post* and a loop-free program fragment $S$. The output is a weakening $post'$ of *post* such that $\{pre\}\, S\, \{post'\}$ is valid. We assume that the post-condition *post* is given as a conjunction of lemmas, i.e., $post = \bigwedge_i \ell_i$. The algorithm computes the (possibly empty) subset of $\{\ell_i\}$ that forms a valid post-condition.

The naive implementation of WEAKPOST iteratively checks whether each $\ell_i$ is a post-condition. Instead, we use an incremental SMT solver to do this enumeration efficiently. We assume that in addition to the SMTSOLVE API, an SMT solver has the method SMTASSERT to add constraints to the current context. First, we compute an SMT-formula that encodes the verification condition (VC) of $S$. We use helper method MKVC that implements VC-generation from [5].

---

**Algorithm 3:** WEAKPOST($pre, S, post$)

**Input**: $pre, post \in Expr$; $post = \bigwedge_{i=0}^{n} \ell_i$; $S \in Stmt^*$

**Output**: $post' \in Expr$, such that $\vdash \{pre\}\ S\ \{post'\}$ is valid

1  let $\{x_i \mid 0 \le i \le n\}$ be fresh Boolean variables; $U \leftarrow \{0, \ldots, n\}$;
2  $vc \leftarrow pre \wedge \text{MKVC}(S) \wedge \neg(\bigwedge_{i=0}^{n}(x_i \rightarrow \ell_i))$;
3  SMTASSERT($vc$);
4  **while** SMTSOLVE( ) = SAT **do**
5      $M \leftarrow$ SMTMODEL( );
6      **foreach** $\{0 \le i \le n \mid M \models x_i\}$ **do** SMTASSERT($\neg x_i$); $U \leftarrow U \setminus \{i\}$;
7  $post' \leftarrow \wedge\{\ell_i \mid i \in U\}$;
8  **return** $post'$

---

Second, we construct $vc$ that determines the validity of pre- and post-condition by conjoining the pre-condition and negation of the post-condition (line 2) to the VC. Note that the post-condition is asserted under assumptions, encoded by Boolean variables $x_i$ such that lemma $\ell_i$ is active iff $x_i$ is true. We then iteratively check the validity of $vc$. In each iteration, if $vc$ is satisfiable, we assert $\neg x_i$ to disable the corresponding lemma(s). This terminates eventually since there are finitely many lemmas and at least one is disabled at every iteration. The conjunction of all active lemmas is returned as $post'$.

To summarize we illustrate MKIND on an example from Figs. 1a-1b. Given $P$, its safety proof $\psi$ and $Q$, MKIND first checks the validity of the edge $en \rightarrow v_1$, i.e., $\{\top\}$ x:=1 $\{x > 0 \wedge y > 0\}$. It is clearly invalid, thus WEAKPOST is used to weaken $\pi(v_1)$ to $x > 0$. Next, the validity of the triple for the edge $v_1 \rightarrow v_2$ is checked, i.e., $\{x > 0\}$ x++ $\{x > 0 \wedge y > 0\}$. Note that the post-condition constructed in the previous step is now used as the pre-condition. Again, the triple is invalid and the post-condition is weakened to $x > 0$. Finally, the edges $v_2 \rightarrow v_1$ and $v_1 \rightarrow err$ are checked, and MKIND terminates. The final inductive invariant $\pi$ of $Q$ is shown in Fig. 1c. In this case, $\pi$ is also a safety proof ($\pi(err) \rightarrow \bot$, and, therefore, $\varphi \equiv \pi$), so no further strengthening is required.

## 4    Evaluation

We have implemented OPTVERIFY in the UFO framework, and evaluated it on the Software Verification Competition (SVCOMP'13) benchmarks and `instcombine` optimization of LLVM. For each benchmark (300 - 5000 lines of source code), we measured the verification time OV, time of OPTVERIFY (MKIND + VERIFY), and time to re-verify from scratch (UV). Out of 397 safe benchmarks, we chose 108 that had non-trivial original verification time (OV > 1s). Due to lack of space, results are available at http://www.inf.usi.ch/phd/fedyukovich/optVerify.pdf .

In all but 6 cases, re-verification (VERIFY) was insignificant ($< 1s$). Furthermore, in 67 cases the candidate invariant was already safe and no strengthening was needed. In 52 cases, OPTVERIFY was at least an order of magnitude faster than re-verification (UV). This highlights the benefit of the approach. In

34 cases, `instcombine` dramatically reduced verification time (from minutes to < 1s). This shows that sometimes it is better to verify the optimized program first and then adapt the results to the original one. While this can be done using OPTVERIFY, we have not done so yet.

# 5   Related Work

There is a large body of related work on incremental verification, verifying compilers, and translation validation. Here, we only survey some of the most relevant techniques. Our algorithm is inspired by recent advancements in upgrade checking [3] and witnessing compiler transformations [6].

The goal of upgrade checking is to adapt a verification result from an original program $P$ to an *upgraded* program $Q$, where $Q$ is obtained from $P$ by changing some of its functions. Current techniques [3] apply to bounded programs with functions, and work by adapting function summaries (i.e., relationship between function's inputs and outputs) from $P$ to $Q$. In contrast, we work on unbounded programs without functions and adapt safety proofs (i.e., safe inductive invariants). Extending our approach to deal with functions is an interesting direction for future work.

The goal of witnessing compiler transformations is to formally establish equivalence (namely, stuttering simulation) between an original program $P$ and its optimization $Q$. Current technique [6] works by instrumenting every optimization pass to output a witness relating its input and output. In contrast, we are interested in an automated solution. In that, our work is more similar to translation validation [7]. However, we only require equivalence with respect to a given property. At the technical level, our use of CPGs makes the approach less sensitive to many restructuring optimizations such as loop unrolling. We expect that in practice the two approaches can be combined, extending our algorithm, for example, to handle optimizations changing CPG structure.

At its core, our solution is similar to Houdini [4] inference algorithm that constructs inductive invariant out of a set of candidate formulas. However, there are many technical differences. One being our use of incremental SMT solver to speed up the search. More importantly, we need to adapt candidates from one program to another. Since based on discarding some candidate lemmas, our current adaptation strategy is rather rough and might be replaced by a more accurate one which weakens formulas on logical level and guided by results on analysis of concrete optimizations. This remains a challenge for future work.

# References

1. Albarghouthi, A., Li, Y., Gurfinkel, A., Chechik, M.: UFO: A Framework for Abstraction- and Interpolation-Based Software Verification. In: Madhusudan, P., Seshia, S.A. (eds.) CAV 2012. LNCS, vol. 7358, pp. 672–678. Springer, Heidelberg (2012)

2. Bourdoncle, F.A.: Efficient Chaotic Iteration Strategies with Widenings. In: Pottosin, I.V., Bjorner, D., Broy, M. (eds.) FMP&TA 1993. LNCS, vol. 735, pp. 128–141. Springer, Heidelberg (1993)
3. Fedyukovich, G., Sery, O., Sharygina, N.: eVolCheck: Incremental Upgrade Checker for C. In: Piterman, N., Smolka, S.A. (eds.) TACAS 2013. LNCS, vol. 7795, pp. 292–307. Springer, Heidelberg (2013)
4. Flanagan, C., Leino, K.R.M.: Houdini: An Annotation Assistant for ESC/Java. In: Oliveira, J.N., Zave, P. (eds.) FME 2001. LNCS, vol. 2021, pp. 500–517. Springer, Heidelberg (2001)
5. Gurfinkel, A., Chaki, S., Sapra, S.: Efficient Predicate Abstraction of Program Summaries. In: Bobaru, M., Havelund, K., Holzmann, G.J., Joshi, R. (eds.) NFM 2011. LNCS, vol. 6617, pp. 131–145. Springer, Heidelberg (2011)
6. Namjoshi, K.S., Zuck, L.D.: Witnessing program transformations. In: Logozzo, F., Fähndrich, M. (eds.) SAS 2013. LNCS, vol. 7935, pp. 304–323. Springer, Heidelberg (2013)
7. Necula, G.C.: Translation validation for an optimizing compiler. In: PLDI (2000)

# Memory Efficient Data Structures for Explicit Verification of Timed Systems

Peter Gjøl Jensen, Kim Guldstrand Larsen, Jiří Srba,
Mathias Grund Sørensen, and Jakob Haar Taankvist

Department of Computer Science, Aalborg University,
Selma Lagerlöfs Vej 300, 9220 Aalborg East, Denmark

**Abstract.** Timed analysis of real-time systems can be performed using continuous (symbolic) or discrete (explicit) techniques. The explicit state-space exploration can be considerably faster for models with moderately small constants, however, at the expense of high memory consumption. In the setting of timed-arc Petri nets, we explore new data structures for lowering the used memory: PTries for efficient storing of configurations and time darts for semi-symbolic description of the state-space. Both methods are implemented as a part of the tool TAPAAL and the experiments document at least one order of magnitude of memory savings while preserving comparable verification times.

## 1 Introduction

Semantics of real-time systems can be defined via real-valued time delays (continuous semantics) or integral time delays (discrete semantics). It is a folklore knowledge (see e.g. [2]) that both semantics coincide up to reachability as long as the formal model uses only closed (non-strict) clock guards. Continuous state-spaces are usually explored via zone-based abstractions (using the DBM data structure [8]), giving us a finite approximation of the model behaviour. Alternatively, we can explore the discrete state-space in an explicit manner, assuming a suitable extrapolation operator that guarantees termination of the search.

Explicit model checking is less studied even though it can successfully compete with zone-based methods on models without too large constants [3,12,10,1]. One of the main criticisms of explicit model checking is a high memory usage. We shall study possible solutions for saving memory in explicit model checking using BDDs [4], time darts data structure [10] and a new data-structure PTrie. We provide a realistic comparison of their performance on several case-studies from the literature. We base our study on the formal model of timed-arc Petri nets (TAPN) and the associated model checker TAPAAL [7] where the above mentioned techniques were implemented and made publicly available.

An example of a timed-arc Petri net, describing a researcher submitting papers for peer-reviewed conferences, is given in Figure 1. The net consists of places (circles), transitions (rectangles) and arcs (arrows). Places contain tokens, each with a real-time age, forming a marking of the net. In our example the initial

J.M. Badger and K.Y. Rozier (Eds.): NFM 2014, LNCS 8430, pp. 307–312, 2014.
© Springer International Publishing Switzerland 2014

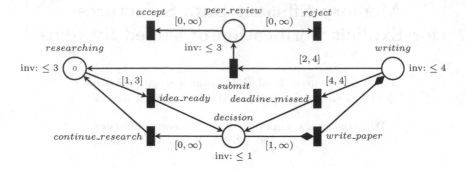

**Fig. 1.** A timed-arc Petri net describing a publication process

marking contains just one token of age 0 in the place *researching*. The place *researching* contains the age invariant $\leq 3$, meaning that the token in this place cannot be older than 3. The net can so delay up to 3 time units (months) and once the age of the token is at least 1, the transition *idea_ready* gets enabled as the token's age fits into the interval [1,3]. The transition can now fire, consuming the token from the place *researching* and adding a new token of age 0 to the place *decision*. Now a decision whether to continue the research or write a paper must be taken within one month. If the researcher decides to write a paper, the token of age 1 is moved from the place *decision* to the place *writing* while preserving its age 1 due to the use of transport arcs (with diamond-shaped arrow-tips). Hence the time of the decision counts into the total number of months used for writing the paper. After writing for at least 1 month, the researcher can submit the paper while producing two new tokens of age 0 into the places *researching* and *peer_review*. By repeating the process, it is possible to have two publications under peer-review at the same time, though the timing constraints imply that having submitted three publications concurrently is impossible. As the net is bounded, this can be verified using the model checker TAPAAL [7] that supports also other primitives like weights, inhibitor arcs, urgent transitions, constants and components with interfaces.

## 2    PTries and Time Darts

The basic reachability algorithm based on explicit state-space search is given in Figure 2 where $\varphi$ is a propositional formula over the number of tokens in the places of the net, and $M \xrightarrow{t} M'$ and $M \xrightarrow{1} M'$ represent transition firing resp. a delay of one time unit. The function *cut* is an extrapolation of token ages that exceed their maximum relevant bounds, yielding a canonical representative for each marking. This guarantees finiteness of the state-space for bounded nets (see [1]). A fragment of the state-space for our running example is shown in Figure 2; here e.g. $(r, 0)$ stands for a token of age 0 in place *researching*.

The algorithm utilizes two data structures, the *passed* and *waiting* sets that store the discovered state-space. The size of these sets (in particular the *passed*

**Input:** A closed TAPN $N$ with initial marking $M_0$, proposition $\varphi$ and a bound $k$.
**Output:** True if $M_0 \to^* M$ via $k$-bounded markings and $M \models \varphi$, False otherwise.

$Passed := \emptyset; \ Waiting := \emptyset;$
AddToPW($M_0$);
**while** $Waiting \neq \emptyset$ **do**
    | Remove $M$ from $Waiting$;
    | $Passed := Passed \cup \{M\};$
    | **foreach** $M \xrightarrow{t} M'$ or $M \xrightarrow{1} M'$
    | **do** AddToPW($cut(M')$)
**return** False;

AddToPW($M$): **begin**
    **if** $M \notin Passed \cup Waiting \ \wedge$
    $size(M) \leq k$ **then**
       **if** $M \models \varphi$ **then**
          | **return** True and **exit**;
       $Waiting := Waiting \cup \{M\};$

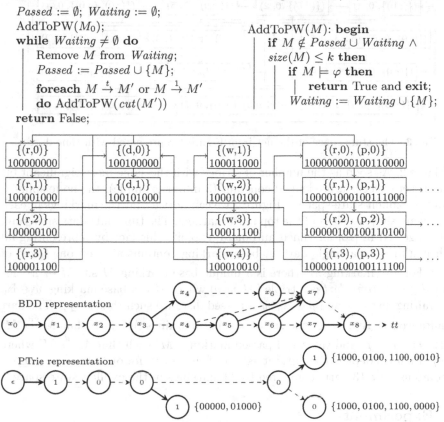

**Fig. 2.** Explicit reachability algorithm and the initial fragment of the state-space for the net from Figure 1. Places are abbreviated by their first letters and the full state-space contains 29 markings. The markings include their binary encodings and the first three columns of the state-space are stored using BDD and PTrie.

one) can be large and we need an efficient way to store them. For this purpose, we represent each marking as a binary string (in an arbitrary but fixed manner) as shown in Figure 2. An obvious way to store the binary encodings of markings is using BDDs. However, the repeated additions to the sets make this approach inefficient as BDDs are normalized after each insertion. We suggest instead a new data structure Partial Trie or *PTrie* (based on Trie [9]) that stores the binary values in the path through the decision tree rather than in the nodes. As the cost of storing a single node in the PTrie exceeds one bit, using a fully unfolded tree may not necessarily preserve any memory. For this purpose we introduce buckets at different levels of the tree that contain suffixes of the binary encodings after the initial prefix that is encoded in the path leading to the bucket, as demonstrated

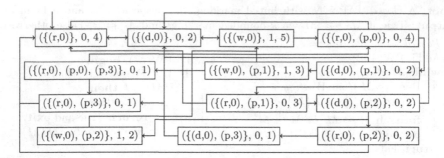

**Fig. 3.** The state-space of the net from Figure 1 represented with time darts

in Figure 2. As soon as the number of strings with the same most-significant bit in a bucket exceeds a predefined constant (3 in our example), the node splits.

In the explicit state-space in Figure 2 we can notice that the markings in each column are simply delays of the top most marking. The time dart data structure, first suggested in [10] for timed automata, exploits this fact by representing all such markings in a single dart. A base marking contains at least one token of age 0. For any marking $M'$ there is a unique base marking $M$ s.t. $M \xrightarrow{d} M'$ for some $d \geq 0$. A *time dart* is a triple $(M, w, p)$ where $M$ is a base marking, $w \in \mathbb{N}_0$ is a waiting distance and $p \in \mathbb{N}_0^\infty$ is a passed distance such that $w \leq p$. The dart simultaneously represents the set of waiting markings $M'$ such that $M \xrightarrow{d} M'$ where $w \leq d < p$, and the set of passed markings $M'$ such that $M \xrightarrow{d} M'$ where $d \geq p$. Figure 3 depicts the full state-space of time darts for our running example. It contains only 13 darts compared to 29 markings in the explicit state-space.

## 3    Experiments

We report on four case studies of Alternating Bit Protocol [13] (ABP), Business Activity with Participant Completion [11] (BAwPC), Patient Monitoring System [6] (PMS) and MPEG-2 video encoder [14]. The reachability queries for all models require a complete state-space search. All TAPAAL models are available at http://www.tapaal.net and the experimental data can be reproduced by using TAPAAL 2.4.1. The experiments (run on a Macbook Pro 2.7GHz Intel Core i7) were terminated once the memory usage exceeded 6GB (OOM) or the verification took longer than one hour (☺); for the BDD-based engine we allowed a two-hour timeout. The TAPAAL column refers to the verification performed by the DBM-based continuous engine of TAPAAL, while the UPPAAL column reports on the best automatic translation [5] from TAPAAL to UPPAAL timed automata. The remaining columns deal with explicit state-space exploration using BDDs, combination of time-darts with PTries, time darts and PTries separately, and no memory optimization (Basic); all efficiently implemented in C++.

The aim of this paper is not to compare the zone-based vs. explicit methods as this largely depends on the concrete models (see e.g. [2,3,12])—we see that while the explicit methods are faster on the first three models, the zone-based

| | Zone-based | | Explicit | | | | |
|---|---|---|---|---|---|---|---|
| Scale | TAPAAL | UPPAAL | BDD | Darts+PTries | Darts | PTries | Basic |
| **Alternating Bit Protocol (ABP)**, scaled by the number of messages | | | | | | | |
| 15 | 116.8 s 278 MB | 4.0 s 32 MB | 2701.2 s 8 MB | 3.1 s 6 MB | 2.4 s 23 MB | 7.6 s 12 MB | 5.4 s 77 MB |
| 16 | 328.4 s 501 MB | 5.6 s 34 MB | 4057.7 s 9 MB | 3.9 s 7 MB | 3.1 s 34 MB | 9.7 s 15 MB | 7.1 s 105 MB |
| 17 | 1233.7 s 979 MB | 7.6 s 41 MB | 5929.2 s 10 MB | 5.0 s 8 MB | 3.9 s 34 MB | 12.4 s 18 MB | 9.0 s 132 MB |
| 30 | ⏲ | 182.2 s 288 MB | ⏲ | 46.3 s 53 MB | 38.8 s 377 MB | 120.2 s 139 MB | 91.0 s 1107 MB |
| 40 | ⏲ | 1063.0 s 920 MB | ⏲ | 151.2 s 155 MB | 120.8 s 1088 MB | 390.3 s 410 MB | 288.6 s 3465 MB |
| 50 | ⏲ | ⏲ | ⏲ | 378.2 s 362 MB | 298.3 s 2593 MB | 1018.4 s 962 MB | OOM |
| **Business Activity Protocol (BAwPC)**, scaled by the number of messages | | | | | | | |
| 2 | 2.9 s 30 MB | 7.8 s 9 MB | 635.0 s 23 MB | 4.4 s 35 MB | 6.8 s 50 MB | 8.3 s 10 MB | 7.5 s 66 MB |
| 3 | 14.3 s 114 MB | 19.6 s 55 MB | 4529.6 s 57 MB | 25.0 s 23 MB | 22.2 s 162 MB | 26.2 s 25 MB | 24.1 s 197 MB |
| 4 | 60.4 s 392 MB | 84.0 s 116 MB | ⏲ | 66.7 s 52 MB | 62.9 s 415 MB | 71.5 s 55 MB | 67.5 s 502 MB |
| 8 | OOM | ⏲ | ⏲ | 861.9 s 501 MB | 770.8 s 4934 MB | 918.3 s 490 MB | 846.5 s 5198 MB |
| **Patient Monitoring System (PMS)**, scaled by the sampling frequency | | | | | | | |
| 18 | 22.2 s 52 MB | ⏲ | 158.0 s 5 MB | 0.9 s 3 MB | 0.6 s 18 MB | 0.8 s 4 MB | 0.4 s 19 MB |
| 12 | 399.6 s 215 MB | ⏲ | 578.5 s 9 MB | 3.0 s 8 MB | 2.0 s 51 MB | 2.5 s 7 MB | 1.4 s 54 MB |
| 10 | 2315.3 s 635 MB | ⏲ | 1537.8 s 17 MB | 7.4 s 15 MB | 5.0 s 122 MB | 6.4 s 16 MB | 3.6 s 112 MB |
| 6 | ⏲ | ⏲ | ⏲ | 94.4 s 149 MB | 68.0 s 1482 MB | 82.5 s 154 MB | 51.6 s 1665 MB |
| 5 | ⏲ | ⏲ | ⏲ | 671.9 s 826 MB | OOM | 575.6 s 815 MB | OOM |
| **MPEG2 Encoder (MPEG2)**, scaled by the number of B frames | | | | | | | |
| 3 | 0.1 s 2 MB | 0.1 s 10 MB | ⏲ | 0.6 s 4 MB | 0.3 s 13 MB | 19.9 s 117 MB | 19.7 s 665 MB |
| 4 | 0.1 s 2 MB | 0.2 s 14 MB | ⏲ | 5.2 s 22 MB | 3.7 s 95 MB | 156.7 s 880 MB | 165.3 s 4811 MB |
| 5 | 0.1 s 3 MB | 0.2 s 18 MB | ⏲ | 46.7 s 147 MB | 40.4 s 870 MB | 1104.8 s 5162 MB | OOM |

methods will eventually outperform any explicit search on models with large enough constants as demonstrated on MPEG2 (the constants here are in thousands of nanoseconds). We instead aim at comparing the memory performance of the different data structures. The first observation is that the BDD encoding, while memory efficient, has an unacceptable runtime performance. On the other hand PTries cause only 20-30% slowdown compared to the basic algorithm and still provide similar memory savings as BDDs. The time dart method usually provides both time and memory improvements; this is most visible on models with large constants like in MPEG2. The combination of PTries and time darts gives the largest memory savings with a very acceptable performance.

## 4 Conclusion

The general data structure PTrie provides significant memory savings at marginal runtime overhead and can be directly employed by any explicit model checker. The semi-symbolic method of time darts requires a more substantial adaptation but it gives in general both time and memory improvements, especially for models with larger constants. Both data structures have been implemented within an open source, publicly available tool TAPAAL, and show promising experimential results.

## References

1. Andersen, M., Gatten Larsen, H., Srba, J., Grund Sørensen, M., Haahr Taankvist, J.: Verification of liveness properties on closed timed-arc Petri nets. In: Kučera, A., Henzinger, T.A., Nešetřil, J., Vojnar, T., Antoš, D. (eds.) MEMICS 2012. LNCS, vol. 7721, pp. 69–81. Springer, Heidelberg (2013)
2. Asarin, E., Maler, O., Pnueli, A.: On discretization of delays in timed automata and digital circuits. In: Sangiorgi, D., de Simone, R. (eds.) CONCUR 1998. LNCS, vol. 1466, pp. 470–484. Springer, Heidelberg (1998)
3. Bozga, M., Maler, O., Tripakis, S.: Efficient verification of timed automata using dense and discrete time semantics. In: Pierre, L., Kropf, T. (eds.) CHARME 1999. LNCS, vol. 1703, pp. 125–141. Springer, Heidelberg (1999)
4. Bryant, R.E.: Graph-based algorithms for boolean function manipulation. IEEE Transactions on Computers C-35(8), 677–691 (1986)
5. Byg, J., Jacobsen, M., Jacobsen, L., Jørgensen, K.Y., Møller, M.H., Srba, J.: TCTL-preserving translations from timed-arc Petri nets to networks of timed automata. In: TCS (2013), http://dx.doi.org/10.1016/j.tcs.2013.07.011
6. Cicirelli, F., Furfaro, A., Nigro, L.: Model checking time-dependent system specifications using time stream Petri nets and UPPAAL. Applied Mathematics and Computation 218(16), 8160–8186 (2012)
7. David, A., Jacobsen, L., Jacobsen, M., Jørgensen, K.Y., Møller, M.H., Srba, J.: TAPAAL 2.0: Integrated development environment for timed-arc Petri nets. In: Flanagan, C., König, B. (eds.) TACAS 2012. LNCS, vol. 7214, pp. 492–497. Springer, Heidelberg (2012)
8. Dill, D.L.: Timing assumptions and verification of finite-state concurrent systems. In: Sifakis, J. (ed.) CAV 1989. LNCS, vol. 407, pp. 197–212. Springer, Heidelberg (1990)
9. Fredkin, E.: Trie memory. Communications of the ACM 3(9), 490–499 (1960)
10. Jørgensen, K.Y., Larsen, K.G., Srba, J.: Time-darts: A data structure for verification of closed timed automata. In: SSV 2012. EPTCS, vol. 102, pp. 141–155. Open Publishing Association (2012)
11. Marques Jr., A.P., Ravn, A.P., Srba, J., Vighio, S.: Model-checking web services business activity protocols. International Journal on Software Tools for Technology Transfer (STTT) 15(2), 125–147 (2013)
12. Lamport, L.: Real-time model checking is really simple. In: Borrione, D., Paul, W. (eds.) CHARME 2005. LNCS, vol. 3725, pp. 162–175. Springer, Heidelberg (2005)
13. Lynch, W.C.: Computer systems: Reliable full-duplex file transmission over half-duplex telephone line. Communications of the ACM 11, 407–410 (1968)
14. Pelayo, F.L., Cuartero, F., Valero, V., Macia, H., Pelayo, M.L.: Applying timed-arc Petri nets to improve the performance of the MPEG-2 encoding algorithm. In: MMM 2004, pp. 49–56. IEEE Computer Society (2004)

# The Gradual Verifier

Stephan Arlt[1,*], Cindy Rubio-González[2], Philipp Rümmer[3,**], Martin Schäf[4],
and Natarajan Shankar[4,***]

[1] Université du Luxembourg
[2] University of California, Berkeley
[3] Uppsala University
[4] SRI International

**Abstract.** Static verification traditionally produces yes/no answers. It
either provides a proof that a piece of code meets a property, or a
counterexample showing that the property can be violated. Hence, the
progress of static verification is hard to measure. Unlike in testing, where
coverage metrics can be used to track progress, static verification does
not provide any intermediate result until the proof of correctness can
be computed. This is in particular problematic because of the inevitable
incompleteness of static verifiers.

To overcome this, we propose a *gradual verification* approach, GraVy.
For a given piece of Java code, GraVy partitions the statements into
those that are unreachable, or from which exceptional termination is
impossible, inevitable, or possible. Further analysis can then focus on the
latter case. That is, even though some statements still may terminate
exceptionally, GraVy still computes a partial result. This allows us to
measure the progress of static verification. We present an implementation
of GraVy and evaluate it on several open source projects.

## 1 Introduction

Static verification is a powerful technique to increase our confidence in the quality
of software. If a static verifier, such as VCC [6] provides us a proof that a piece
of code is correct, we can be sure beyond doubt that this code will not fail for
any specified input. If the static verifier fails to compute a proof, we end up with
one counterexample. This counterexample may reveal a bug or may be spurious
in which case we have to provide annotations to help the verifier. This process
is repeated until no new counterexample can be found.

---

[*] Supported by the Fonds National de la Recherche, Luxembourg (FNR/P10/03).
[**] Supported by the Swedish Research Council.
[***] This work was supported by NSF Grant CNS-0917375, NASA Cooperative Agreement NNA10DE73C, and by United States Air Force and the Defense Advanced
Research Projects Agency under Contract No. FA8750-12-C-0225. The views and
conclusions contained herein are those of the authors and should not be interpreted
as necessarily representing the official policies or endorsements, either expressed
or implied, of NSF, NASA, US Air Force, DARPA, or the U.S. Government.

J.M. Badger and K.Y. Rozier (Eds.): NFM 2014, LNCS 8430, pp. 313–327, 2014.
© Springer International Publishing Switzerland 2014

Unfortunately, the process of eliminating counterexamples one by one is not suitable for assessing software quality. Certainly, eliminating one bug improves the quality of software, but the static verification does not provide us with any information on how much we have verified already or how many bugs might still be in there.

Ultimately, static verification is incomplete and thus the proof we are looking for might not exist. In this case we end up with nothing. Static verification does only provide yes/no answers, but to obtain partial results manual effort is needed.

Testing, on the other hand, only delivers such partial results in the form of coverage data. Each test case increases the confidence in the application under test. Progress can be measured using different kinds of coverage metrics. That is, from an economic point of view, testing is more predictable. The more time we invest in testing the more we can observe the coverage (and thus our confidence) increase.

In this paper we present a *gradual verification* approach, *GraVy*. Gradual verification is an extension to existing static verification techniques such as VCC [6] or Smack [16] that helps us quantify the progress of the verification. Instead of computing just one counterexample, gradual verification computes an over-approximation of all counterexamples to identify the subset of statements that provably cannot terminate exceptionally anymore. That is, beyond the counterexample indicating that the program is not yet verified, gradual verification gives a percentage of statements that are already guaranteed to be safe.

Gradual verification results can be integrated into existing testing workflows. Each time gradual verification is executed on an application under test, it returns the subset of statements for which it can already prove that exceptional termination is impossible. This provides a metric of progress of the verification process and allows the verification engineer to focus on the remaining statements.

Gradual verification is *not* a new static verification technique. It is an extension that can be applied to any existing static verification techniques to provide additional information to the verification engineer. Thus, issues, such as handling of loops or aliasing are not addressed in this paper. These are problems related to sound verification, but gradual verification is about how to make the use of such verification more traceable and quantifiable.

In gradual verification, we consider programs as graphs, where nodes correspond to a *control location* in the program and edges represent *transition relations* between these control locations. Further, we assume that sink nodes in this graph either are *exceptional sink nodes* where the execution of the program ends exceptionally, or *normal sink nodes* where executions terminate normally.

A statement in a programming language such as Java may be represented by more than one edge if, for example, the statement throws an exception when executed on certain inputs. In order to verify that a statement never terminates exceptionally, we need to show that none of the edges representing this statement goes into an exceptional sink. That is, either the statement is not represented by edge going into an exceptional sink node, or this edge has no feasible execution in the program.

On this graph, we perform a two-phase algorithm: in phase one, we identify all edges that may occur on a feasible execution terminating in a normal sink. For the remaining edges we have a guarantee that they are either unreachable or only occur on feasible executions into exception sinks.

In the second phase we check which of these remaining edges occur on *any* feasible execution. That is, we identify edges that are unreachable and edges that must flow into an exceptional sink. This allows us to categorize program statements depending on the edges that they are represented by: a statement is *unreachable* if it is represented by no feasible edge, *safe* if it is represented only by feasible edges terminating in normal sinks (and reachable), *strictly unsafe* if it is represented only by feasible edges terminating in exceptional sinks (and not unreachable), and *possibly unsafe* otherwise.

That is, a program is safe, if all its statements are safe. However, if we cannot show that all statements are safe, our algorithm still can provide a subset of statements that are guaranteed to be safe, helping the programmer to focus on those parts of the program that still need work. gradual verification can be applied to full programs as well as to isolated procedures. It can be applied in a modular way and also incorporate assertions generated by other tools.

We evaluate an implementation of our gradual verification technique, GraVy, on several large open source projects. Our experimental results show that even using a coarse abstraction of the input program, GraVy can still prove that a large percentage of statements can never throw exceptions.

*Related Work.* GraVy is based on modular static verification as known from VCC [6], Smack [16], or ESC/Java [12]. These tools translate an application under test "procedure by procedure" into SMT formulas that are valid if this procedure is safe w.r.t. a desired property. A counterexample to this formula can be mapped back to an execution of the (abstract) procedure that violates the property. The problem of these approaches is that they only produce one counterexample at a time which makes it hard to estimate the progress of the verification. To overcome this, GraVy uses techniques that detect contradictions in programs [5,10,19] to identify the subset of statements that never (or always) occur on a counterexample.

Gradual verification can also be compared with symbolic execution techniques as found in program analysis tools like Frama-C [9], Java Pathfinder [14], or Pex [18]. These techniques compute an over-approximation of the set of states from which a program statement can be executed. A program statement is considered safe if this set of states does not contain any state from which the execution of the statement is not defined. Gradual verification can be seen as a lightweight alternative to these approaches: like static verification, it can be applied locally even on isolated code fragments, but it still can identify individual statements that will never terminate exceptionally. Hence, gradual verification does not provide the precision of other symbolic execution techniques, but it is still sufficient to visualize the progress of verification to its user.

Recently, approaches have been presented that generate information during the verification process that go beyond simple yes/no answers. Clousot [8, 11], for example, infers a precondition for each procedure that is sufficient to guarantee the safe execution of this procedure. Compositional may-must analysis, such as [13], can be used to distinguish between possibly and strictly unsafe statements. GraVy can be seen as a lightweight mix of both approaches. It detects a subset of statements that cannot throw exceptions (but does not provide preconditions), and categorizes statements that may, or must throw exceptions (but does not provide the precision of a may-must analysis.)

## 2    Example

We illustrate our approach with the toy example shown in Figure 1. The Java procedure `toyexample` takes a variable x of type `Obj` as input and first sets `x.a` to 1 and then sets `x.b` to 2. An execution of the first statement `x.a = 1` terminates with a `NullPointerException` if `toyexample` is called with `x==null`. Otherwise it terminates normally. Note that the second statement `x.b = 2` can never throw a `NullPointerException`, because the first statement already ensures that x cannot be `null` at this point.

```
1  void toyexample (Obj x) {
2     x.a = 1;
3     x.b = 2;
4  }
```

**Fig. 1.** Java source code of a toy example

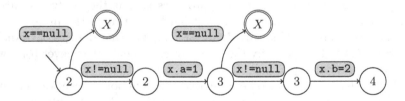

**Fig. 2.** Program graph of the procedure `toyexample`. Edges are labeled with transition relations, and nodes are labeled with line numbers, where the label $X$ refers to the point in the program that is reached when an exception is thrown.

Suppose that we are interested in verifying that, for any input, the procedure does not terminate with an exception. First, we create a graph representation of our program as shown in Figure 2. In this graph, nodes are labeled with line numbers, where the label $X$ refers to the point in the program that is reached when an exception is thrown. This labeling is simplified for demonstration. Two different nodes might still share the same line number. Each statement of our original program from Figure 1 is associated with one or more edges in this graph, starting in the nodes labeled with the respective line number. For example, the statement x.a in Figure 1 is represented by the three edges in Figure 2 starting in nodes labeled with 2: $(2, \boxed{\text{x==null}}, X)$, stating that, if x is null, the execution terminates exceptionally; $(2, \boxed{\text{x!=null}}, 2)$, stating that execution moves on if x is initialized; and $(2, \boxed{\text{x.a=1}}, 3)$ which is the actual assignment if x is initialized.

Now it is time to check if our procedure does not terminate exceptionally. Existing techniques would easily come up with a counterexample to this property that shows that for the input x==null the procedure will throw a NullPointerException. However, this is a very pessimistic answer, and, given that we do not know in which context toyexample will be called, it may even be a useless answer if there is no calling context such that x==null. Hence, we propose to give a different, optimistic, answer when checking if our procedure does not terminate exceptionally:

$$x.b = 2 \textit{ never throws an exception.}$$

There are a few things to notice: First, our answer gives proofs instead of a simple counterexample. Second, our answer holds in any context (but might be too weak), whereas the counterexample may turn out to be infeasible. Third, in our answer, our verifier verifies; existing techniques just complain.

To get to this answer, we start a two-phase algorithm. In phase one we try to cover all edges that occur on any feasible path of the program that terminate normally. That is, in our example, we try to find feasible complete paths ending in the sink labeled with 4. One such path exists:

$$(2, \boxed{\text{x!=null}}, 2)(2, \boxed{\text{x.a=1}}, 3)(3, \boxed{\text{x!=null}}, 3)(3, \boxed{\text{x.b=2}}, 4)$$

That is, the only two edges that cannot be covered during that process are $(2, \boxed{\text{x==null}}, X)$ and $(3, \boxed{\text{x==null}}, X)$. For these edges we know that either they are unreachable, or their execution leads to an exceptional termination. Note that in this example, both edges happen to be immediately connected to the error location $X$. However, in general, there might be other edges, not directly connected to a sink, that can only be executed if normal termination is not possible.

For the uncovered edges we start the second phase of our algorithm, where we try to find *any* feasible complete path. From the first phase, we know that no path through the remaining edges exists that terminates in 4, hence we are only interested in paths terminating in $X$. For our example, this reveals one more feasible path:

$$(2, \boxed{\text{x==null}}, X)$$

That is, the other edge, $(3, \boxed{\text{x==null}}, X)$, provably does not have any feasible execution. Now, we have a proof that x.b=2 in line 3 never throws a

`NullPointerException` in `toyexample`. We can further report that `x.a=1` in line 2 may throw a `NullPointerException` if `x` is `null`.

From here, the verification engineer knows that she has to focus on `x.a=1`, and either guard the code with a conditional choice or strengthen the precondition under which `toyexample` can be called. Then, gradual verification can be re-run for the modified code. This is repeated until all statements are safe or a desired percentage of statements is safe.

## 3    Statement Safety and Gradual Verification

In this section we give a precise definition of our gradual verification methodology. We assume a piece $P$ of sequential program code (in case of Java, the body of a method), containing the set $Stmt$ of statements. The control-flow of $P$ can be represented as a finite directed graph $CFG_P = (\mathcal{L}, \ell_0, \mathcal{L}_{exit}, \mathcal{L}_{exc}, \delta, stmt)$, where $\mathcal{L}$ represents control locations, $\ell_0 \in \mathcal{L}$ is the unique entry point, $\mathcal{L}_{exit} \subseteq \mathcal{L}$ is a set of exit locations representing regular termination, and $\mathcal{L}_{exc} \subseteq \mathcal{L}$ is a set of error locations representing termination due to a runtime exception. Further, we assume that $\mathcal{L}_{exit} \cap \mathcal{L}_{exc}$ is empty. An edge $(\ell, Tr, \ell') \in \delta$ is labeled with a transition formula $Tr(\bar{v}, \bar{v}')$ over unprimed and primed variables describing program state.

A statement in our sequential program $P$ is represented by possibly multiple transitions, some of which may lead into error locations $\mathcal{L}_{exc}$. The latter case models runtime exceptions. For instance, a Java statement `a.x = 1` could be translated into two edges: one that assumes that `a` is allocated and `a.x` is assigned to 1, and one where `a` is not allocated and control passes to an appropriate error location. Throughout the paper, we use the partial function $stmt : \delta \rightharpoonup Stmt$ mapping edges to statements in the program code $P$. Conditional choice of the form `if (c) A else B` is represented by at least two transitions, one assuming $c$ and one assuming $\neg c$, and all other transitions that are necessary to represent $c$. The transitions representing the blocks `A` and `B` are not considered as part of the conditional choice.

A *complete path* in a program is a finite sequence of control locations and transition formulas $\pi = \ell_0 Tr_0 \ell_1 Tr_1 \ell_2 Tr_2 \ldots Tr_{n-1} \ell_n$, where $\ell_0$ is the entry point, $\ell_n \in \mathcal{L}_{exit} \cup \mathcal{L}_{exc}$ is an exit location, and for each $i \in \{0, \ldots, n-1\}$ it is the case that $(\ell_i, Tr_i, \ell_{i+1}) \in \delta$. A complete path $\pi$ is called a *regular path* if $\ell_n \in \mathcal{L}_{exit}$, and an *error path* if $\ell_n \in \mathcal{L}_{exc}$. A path is *feasible* if the composition $Tr_0 \circ Tr_1 \circ \cdots \circ Tr_{n-1}$ is satisfiable. An edge $(\ell, Tr, \ell') \in \delta$ is called *feasible* if it occurs on a complete feasible path.

We use $\delta_{reg} \subseteq \delta$ to denote the subset of edges that occur on regular paths (i.e., on paths that end in a location in $\mathcal{L}_{exit}$). Further we use $\delta_{bad} = \delta \setminus \delta_{reg}$ to denote all edges that inevitably lead into an error location. With the help of $\delta_{reg}$ and $\delta_{bad}$, Figure 3 defines safety categories for a statement $s \in Stmt$ in $P$ considered in gradual verification, which correspond to the four possible combinations of regular or error transitions being feasible. For instance, a statement $s$ is considered *safe* if all transitions representing $s$ are in $\delta_{reg}$.

| | | ∃ feasible $e \in \delta_{reg}$ with $s = stmt(e)$ | |
| :---: | :---: | :---: | :---: |
| | | Yes | No |
| ∃ feasible $e \in \delta_{bad}$ with $s = stmt(e)$ | Yes | $s$ is *possibly unsafe* | $s$ is *strictly unsafe* |
| | No | $s$ is *safe* | $s$ is *unreachable* |

**Fig. 3.** Safety categories of statements

# 4 The Analysis Procedure

---

**Algorithm 1.** Gradual verification algorithm.

---

**Input**: $CFG_P = (\mathcal{L}, \ell_0, \mathcal{L}_{exit}, \mathcal{L}_{exc}, \delta, stmt)$ : control-flow graph
**Output**: $\delta_{bad}$: set of edges that never occur on feasible regular paths;
$\quad\quad\quad\;\; \delta_{inf}$: set of edges that do not occur on any feasible path
**begin**
$\quad S \leftarrow \delta$ ;
$\quad$**for** *regular path* $\pi$ *in* $CFG_P$ **do**
$\quad\quad$**if** $isFeasible(\pi)$ **then**
$\quad\quad\quad$**for** $(\ell, Tr, \ell')$ *in* $\pi$ **do**
$\quad\quad\quad\quad| \quad S \leftarrow S \setminus \{(\ell, Tr, \ell')\}$ ;
$\quad\quad\quad$**end for**
$\quad\quad$**end if**
$\quad$**end for**
$\quad \delta_{bad} \leftarrow S$ ;
$\quad$**for** *error path* $\pi$ *in* $CFG_P$ **do**
$\quad\quad$**if** $isFeasible(\pi)$ **then**
$\quad\quad\quad$**for** $(\ell, Tr, \ell')$ *in* $\pi$ **do**
$\quad\quad\quad\quad| \quad S \leftarrow S \setminus \{(\ell, Tr, \ell')\}$ ;
$\quad\quad\quad$**end for**
$\quad\quad$**end if**
$\quad$**end for**
$\quad \delta_{inf} \leftarrow S$ ;
**end**

---

To check whether a statement is *safe, strictly unsafe, unreachable,* or *possibly unsafe*, we determine for each edge in the control-flow graph whether it can be part of a feasible regular path, and if a statement is represented by a feasible transition into an error location. We introduce Algorithm 1 to this end. The algorithm takes a control-flow graph $CFG_P = (\mathcal{L}, \ell_0, \mathcal{L}_{exit}, \mathcal{L}_{exc}, \delta, stmt)$ as input and returns two sets $\delta_{bad}$ and $\delta_{inf}$. $\delta_{bad}$ contains all edges of the control-flow graph that do not occur on any feasible regular path. $\delta_{inf} \subseteq \delta_{bad}$ is the set of edges that do not occur on any feasible path (regular, or error paths).

The algorithm uses a local variable $S$ to track the edges in $\delta$ that have not been covered yet. In a first loop, Algorithm 1 covers edges that occur on feasible regular paths. That is, all edges that remain in $S$ after the loop terminates can either only be executed on error paths or are unreachable. This set is stored in $\delta_{bad}$. In the second loop, our algorithms checks which of the remaining edges can be covered with feasible error paths and removes them from $S$. That is, any edge covered in the second loop has a feasible path into an error location. All uncovered edges are stored in $\delta_{inf}$ because they have no feasible execution at all.

With the resulting sets $\delta_{bad}$ and $\delta_{inf}$, we can check the above properties as follows: given a statement $st$ and the set of edges $\delta_{st} = \{(\ell, Tr, \ell')|(\ell, Tr, \ell') \in \delta \wedge stmt((\ell, Tr, \ell')) = st\}$. The statement $st$ is unreachable if $\delta_{st} \setminus \delta_{inf}$ is empty and $\delta_{inf}$ is not empty. It is safe if $\delta_{st} \cap (\delta_{bad} \setminus \delta_{inf})$ is empty and $\delta_{st} \setminus \delta_{inf}$ is not empty. In other words, $st$ is safe if it is not represented by any feasible edge into an error location and has at least one feasible edge. We say, $st$ is strictly unsafe if $\delta_{st} \setminus \delta_{bad}$ is empty and $\delta_{bad} \setminus \delta_{inf}$ is not empty. In any other case, we say $st$ is possibly unsafe.

Algorithm 1 terminates only if the control-flow graph $CFG_P$ has a finite number of paths (i.e., is loop-free). For programs with looping control-flow, abstraction is necessary. We will discuss one possible abstraction in Section 5 together with other implementation details.

We say an abstraction of a control-flow graph $CFG_P$ is sound, if for any feasible (regular and error) path $CFG_P$, there exists a corresponding path in the abstraction. That is, an abstraction is sound if it over-approximates the set of feasible control-flow paths.

Given a program $CFG_P$ and an abstraction of it, and, given a statement $st$ that exists in the program and its abstraction (but may be represented by a different set of edges in the control-flow graph), the following properties hold if the abstraction is sound:

- If $st$ is *safe* in the abstraction then it is *safe* or *unreachable* in $CFG_P$.
- If $st$ is *strictly unsafe* in the abstraction then it is *strictly unsafe* or *unreachable* in $CFG_P$.
- If $st$ is *unreachable* in the abstraction then it is *unreachable* in $CFG_P$.
- If $st$ is *possibly unsafe* in the abstraction then it is *safe, strictly unsafe, unreachable,* or *possibly unsafe* in $CFG_P$.

That is, for any sound abstraction, our algorithm guarantees that any statement that may transition into an error location will be declared as either *possibly unsafe* or *strictly unsafe*. Hence, if all statements in our program are either *safe* or *unreachable*, we have a proof that the program will never terminate exceptionally.

To be useful in practice, an implementation of our algorithm has to make sure that it does not report overly many *possibly unsafe* in the abstraction, as we cannot say much about them in the original program. Further, it would be useful if *unreachable* statements in the original program are not reported as *strictly unsafe* in the abstraction. Even though we are of the opinion that unreachable code should be avoided at all cost, a user may be alienated if unreachable code is reported as error. In the following we evaluate our approach.

# 5   Implementation

We have implemented our technique in a static verifier for Java bytecode called GraVy. Our analysis automatically checks for the following types of exceptions: `NullPointerException`, `ClassCastException`, `IndexOutOfBoundsException`, and `ArithmeticException`. Other exceptions and arbitrary safety properties can be encoded using `RunTimeExceptions`.

An error location in GraVy is an exceptional return of a procedure with one of the above exceptions, unless this exception is explicitly mentioned in the `throws`-clause of this procedure. Hence, if GraVy proves a statement to be safe, it only means that none of the above exceptions may be thrown.

GraVy analyzes programs using the bytecode analysis toolkit Soot [20]. It translates the bytecode into the intermediate verification language Boogie [4] as described in [2]. In this step we add guards for possible runtime exceptions: for each statement that may throw a runtime exception, we add a conditional choice with an explicit throw statement before the actual statement. Further, we add a local helper variable `ex_return` to each procedure which is `false` initially. For any of the exceptions that we are looking for which is not in the `throws` clause and not caught, we add a statement that assigns this variable to `true`. This variable is used later on by the prover to distinguish between normal and exceptional termination of a procedure.

*Abstraction.* Our algorithm from Section 4 requires a loop-free program as input. Hence, we first need to compute loop-free abstractions of programs. To this end we use a simple loop elimination as discussed in [1]: for each loop, we compute a conservative approximation of the variables that may be modified within the loop body. Then, we add statements that assign non-deterministic values to these variables at the beginning and at the end of the loop body. Finally, we redirect all looping control-flow edges of the loop body to the loop exit.

This way, we simulate an arbitrary number of loop iterations: the non-deterministic assignments allow the loop body to be executed from any possible initial state and allow the variables modified within the loop to have any possible value after the loop. This is a very coarse abstraction which also loses all information about possible non-termination. However, if a statement can be proved safe in this approximation, it will be safe in the original program, as the abstraction over-approximates the program's executions.

GraVy does not perform any inter-procedural analysis. Like in the case of loops, we first compute an over-approximation of the set of variables that may be modified by the called procedure and then replace the call statement by a non-deterministic assignment to these variables. In our translation into Boogie, exceptions are treated as return values of a procedure and are thus included in this abstraction. Again, this is an over-approximation of the program's executions, and thus, any statement that can be proved safe in this abstraction will be safe in the original program.

All these abstractions can be refined to increase the precision of GraVy.

*Gradual Verification.* On the loop-free program without procedure calls, we can apply our algorithm from Section 4 to each procedure in a straightforward manner (e.g., [1]) by translating the loop-free program into a SMT formula that is satisfiable only by models that can be mapped to a feasible path in the program. In the first pass of our analysis, GraVy adds an assertion to the SMT formula such that the helper variable `ex_return` is `false`, in order to only allow paths that do not terminate with unwanted exceptions. We use the theorem prover Princess [17] to check for the satisfiability of this formula. For each model returned by Princess, we extract an enabling clause to ensure that another path must be picked in the next query. This process is repeated until the formula becomes unsatisfiable. Then, GraVy pops the assertion that `ex_return` must be `false` and continues until the formula becomes unsatisfiable again.

Using the information obtained during this process, GraVy prints a report for each procedure that pigeonholes its bytecode instructions into the categories unreachable, safe, strictly unsafe, and possibly unsafe as described in Section 3.

*Soundness.* GraVy is **neither sound nor complete**. Here, *soundness* means that if a statement is reported to be safe, it is always safe. *Completeness* means that any statement that is safe will be reported to be safe. GraVy has several sources of unsoundness: e.g., Java integers are modeled as natural numbers (i.e., over- and under-flows are ignored). Furthermore, we ignore the use of reflection (i.e., `InvokeDynamic`), and we do not consider parallel executions.

However, note that the unsoundness is specific to our prototype implementation. Gradual verification is always as sound as its underlying static verification algorithm. Thus, there is much room for improvement by combining GraVy with more advanced static verifiers.

# 6    Evaluation

The motivation of gradual verification is to make static verification predictable by providing a progress metric. That is, to be of practical use, GraVy must identify a reasonable percentage of statements to be safe, so that the verification engineer can focus on the remaining code. Further, it must be fast enough to be applicable in an incremental verification process. That is, it must not be significantly slower than existing static verifiers such as VCC. This leads us to the following two research questions:

**Q1.** Is GraVy precise enough to show that a reasonable percentage of statements are safe in well-tested applications?

**Q2.** Is GraVy fast enough to be applied to real-world software?

*Experimental Setup.* To answer these questions we evaluate GraVy on several open source programs. For each application under test (AUT), we analyzed the JAR files of the latest stable (and thus hopefully tested) release from the official websites. All experiments were carried out on a standard notebook with an i7 CPU and 8 GB RAM (the Java VM was started with initially 4 GB). GraVy tried to analyze each procedure of the AUTs for at most 10 seconds. If no result is reached after 10 seconds, the procedure is skipped and a timeout is reported. We ran the analysis two times for each AUT: once with gradual verification, and once with a weakest-precondition-based static verifier [15]. For the weakest-precondition-based static verifier we implemented a simple verifier inside GraVy that reused large parts of the GraVy infrastructure. Instead of repeatedly querying the theorem prover, the static verifier only sends one query. The result to this query is either a proof that no statement in the procedure may throw an exception of the previously mentioned types, or a counterexample that represents an execution of the abstract procedure that leads to exceptional termination.

In addition to the results returned by GraVy about which statements are unreachable, safe, strictly unsafe, or possibly unsafe, we collected the following information: the total time for analyzing a procedure including the time for printing the report, and the total number of procedures for which GraVy returns a timeout.

To compare the gradual static verification with the weakest-precondition-based static verification, we also stopped the time that both approaches spent inside the SMT solver. We compared the time inside the prover rather than actual computation time, because the overhead for both approaches is the same, and thus, the time spent in the prover is the only relevant time difference.

*Discussion.* Table 1 shows the report computed by GraVy for each AUT. By comparing the columns *# stmts* and *safe*, GraVy is able to prove more than 80% of the analyzed statements to be safe for all AUTs. For *Args4j* and *Log4j*, GraVy can even prove over 86% percent of the statements to be safe. If we only

**Table 1.** Results of applying GraVy to several AUTs. *# stmts* is the number of analyzed statements per AUT. *# throwing stmts* is the number of statements that is represented by at least one edge into an error location.

| AUT | # stmts | safe | # throwing stmts | possibly unsafe | strictly unsafe | unreachable |
|---|---|---|---|---|---|---|
| Args4j | **2,322** | **2,011** | 820 | 311 | 0 | 0 |
| GraVy | **20,372** | **16,522** | 15,516 | 3,844 | 0 | 6 |
| Hadoop | **209,683** | **177,373** | 109,758 | 32,249 | 7 | 54 |
| Log4j | **25,128** | **22,381** | 11,007 | 2,746 | 0 | 1 |

consider the statements that are represented by edges into an error location (i.e., by comparing the columns *# throwing stmts* and *possibly unsafe*), GraVy proves 62% of the statements to be safe in *Args4j*, and 75% in *Log4j*.

For *Hadoop*, which is also widely used and well-tested, we only achieve 84% to be safe (and 70% of statements represented by edges into error locations). This is because Hadoop makes heavy use of multithreading which is not handled by GraVy. The use of multithreading is also the cause of the reported unreachable and strictly unsafe statements. None of these statements is actually unreachable or strictly unsafe, they rather exhibit situations where a thread is waiting for another thread to initialize an object.

GraVy applied to itself can only prove 81% to be safe (and 75% of the statements represented by edges into error locations). This supports the idea that the percentage of safe statements relates to the maturity of the code: GraVy is currently under development and represents a rather prototypical implementation.

Hence, we can give a positive answer to our research question **Q1**. GraVy can, even on a coarse abstraction, prove a large percentage of statements safe. Further, experiments indicate that the percentage of safe statements may correlate with code quality.

What remains open is what useful thresholds for the percentage of safe statements are. Many statements in Java bytecode can never throw any of the considered exceptions and thus are always safe. Therefore it is hard to define a lower bound for the percentage of safe statements. Our experiments cannot say anything about an upper bound either, because we did not try to improve the AUTs and rerun GraVy as this would exceed the scope of this paper. For the future of GraVy we plan a case study on how to apply gradual static verification, e.g., by using specification languages such as JML [7].

Table 2 shows the performance results of our experiments. For all AUTs the average time needed per method is significantly below one second ($< 0.4s$). The number of procedures that reach a timeout is below 2.1% for all AUTs. Experimenting with timeouts larger than 10 seconds did not significantly improve this number. Most procedures that timeout contain large amounts of initialization code (e.g., constructors), or GUI related code.

Before running gradual verification we run a constant propagation to eliminate all possible exceptions that can be ruled out trivially. We are able to eliminate

**Table 2.** Performance and number of timeouts of GraVy on the different AUTs. The column # timeouts states the number of procedures that could not be analyzed within the time limit. The last column states the percentage of exceptions that could be removed using constant propagation.

| AUT | # procedures | time (s) | time per procedure (s) | # timeouts | removed exceptions |
|---|---|---|---|---|---|
| Args4j | 361 | 57 | **0.16** | 2 | 6.7% |
| GraVy | 2,044 | 668 | **0.33** | 33 | 8.3% |
| Hadoop | 18,728 | 6,459 | **0.34** | 391 | 8.4% |
| Log4j | 3,172 | 704 | **0.22** | 40 | 13.0% |

**Table 3.** Theorem proving time for gradual static verification (GSV) and weakest-precondition-based static verification (SV) for the AUTs. Only the time spent in the theorem prover is measured as the overhead for transformation, etc. is identical for both approaches. The last row states how many procedures can be proven safe by both approaches (i.e., only contain safe statements).

|      | Args4j | GraVy | Hadoop | Log4j |
|------|--------|-------|--------|-------|
| GSV  | 45s    | 346s  | 4,425s | 294s  |
| SV   | 7s     | 33s   | 689s   | 41s   |
| Safe | 32.6%  | 40.8% | 40.2%  | 40.3% |

between 6.7% and 13.0% of the exceptions. That is, a significant percentage of the statements proved safe by GraVy need non-trivial reasoning.

In summary, GraVy can produce meaningful results within a reasonable time (less than 0.4s per procedure) and with few timeouts.

Table 3 compares the computation time of GraVy and a normal non-gradual verifier. For this purpose we built our own weakest-precondition based static verification following the idea from [15]. As both approaches require the same program transformation, we only compare the time spent by the theorem prover.

The first row shows the theorem proving time for gradual verification (GSV), the second row shows the theorem proving time for non-gradual verification (SV), and the last row shows the percentage of the procedures that can be proven safe by both approaches (i.e., procedures that only contain safe statements). For each AUT, the extra time needed for gradual static verification is less than a factor of 10. Most procedures still can be analyzed within few seconds. We believe that, by further improving the reuse of theorem prover results as suggested in [3], we can reduce these extra costs even further.

Non-gradual verification alone is able to verify between 30% and 40% of the procedures (excluding timeouts) for the desired property for all AUTs. Most of these procedures are generated by the Java compiler, such as default constructors. For all remaining procedures, non-gradual verification only returns a counterexample. Here, gradual static verification provides additional information by ruling out those statements that are already safe within the remaining procedures.

In conclusion, we can also give a positive answer to research question **Q2**: GraVy takes less than a second per procedure for real-world software. Although it is (naturally) slower than non-gradual verification, it is still fast enough to be usable in practice.

*Threats to Validity.* The main and by far most important threat to validity is our unsoundness. For example, in Hadoop, where we prove 177,373 statements to be safe, it is not possible to manually inspect if they are subject to unsoundness or not. To get a sense of how our abstraction affects the precision of GraVy, we investigated roughly a hundred statements from different AUTs and different categories (i.e., safe, unreachable, etc.). We found several cases where code was reported to be unreachable or strictly unsafe in the abstraction but safe in the original program. We did not find statements that are reported safe in the abstraction but unsafe in the original program.

Another threat to validity is the subset of exceptions that we consider in our analysis. There are many more exceptions that can cause unexpected program behavior. However, from manual data-flow inspection we can see that `NullPointerException` is by far the most common exception that can be thrown. Thus, we believe that adding more classes of exceptions to GraVy will certainly increase the usefulness of our approach, but will only have a limited influence on the results presented in this paper.

Finally, the used tools are a threat to validity. Using Java bytecode as input allows us to use a much simpler memory model than, e.g., for C. It is not clear if our approach can be applied to C programs equally well. For example, we allow arbitrary aliasing between variables when analysing a procedure. This would, most likely, be too coarse for analyzing C programs and further analysis would be required.

## 7  Conclusion

We have presented a technique for gradual static verification. Gradual verification extends existing static verification which provides yes/no answers (i.e., either a proof or a counterexample) by a notion of the verification progress. That is, even if a full correctness proof is impossible (e.g., because there are some cubic formulas in the code), we can still report how many statements can be "verified".

Gradual verification blends nicely with existing best practices in testing, where a test coverage metric is used to measure progress, and to decide when to stop testing. Therefore, we believe that gradual verification can make the use of formal methods in industrial software development more acceptable.

Our experiments show that GraVy is reasonably fast and that it can already prove a convincingly high percentage of statements to be safe, even using a coarse abstraction. Further, the experiments indicate that verification coverage may be a good indicator for the maturity of code.

We are convinced that gradual static verification is a useful addition to existing static verification tools and a nice and cheap alternative to verifiers based on symbolic execution such as Frama-C.

## References

1. Arlt, S., Liu, Z., Schäf, M.: Reconstructing paths for reachable code. In: Groves, L., Sun, J. (eds.) ICFEM 2013. LNCS, vol. 8144, pp. 431–446. Springer, Heidelberg (2013)
2. Arlt, S., Rümmer, P., Schäf, M.: Joogie: From java through jimple to boogie. In: SOAP. ACM (2013)
3. Arlt, S., Rümmer, P., Schäf, M.: A theory for control-flow graph exploration. In: Van Hung, D., Ogawa, M. (eds.) ATVA 2013. LNCS, vol. 8172, pp. 506–515. Springer, Heidelberg (2013)

4. Barnett, M., Chang, B.-Y.E., DeLine, R., Jacobs, B., Leino, K.R.M.: Boogie: A modular reusable verifier for object-oriented programs. In: de Boer, F.S., Bonsangue, M.M., Graf, S., de Roever, W.-P. (eds.) FMCO 2005. LNCS, vol. 4111, pp. 364–387. Springer, Heidelberg (2006)

5. Bertolini, C., Schäf, M., Schweitzer, P.: Infeasible code detection. In: Joshi, R., Müller, P., Podelski, A. (eds.) VSTTE 2012. LNCS, vol. 7152, pp. 310–325. Springer, Heidelberg (2012)

6. Cohen, E., Dahlweid, M., Hillebrand, M., Leinenbach, D., Moskal, M., Santen, T., Schulte, W., Tobies, S.: VCC: A practical system for verifying concurrent C. In: Berghofer, S., Nipkow, T., Urban, C., Wenzel, M. (eds.) TPHOLs 2009. LNCS, vol. 5674, pp. 23–42. Springer, Heidelberg (2009)

7. Cok, D.R.: OpenJML: JML for java 7 by extending openJDK. In: Bobaru, M., Havelund, K., Holzmann, G.J., Joshi, R. (eds.) NFM 2011. LNCS, vol. 6617, pp. 472–479. Springer, Heidelberg (2011)

8. Cousot, P., Cousot, R., Fähndrich, M., Logozzo, F.: Automatic inference of necessary preconditions. In: Giacobazzi, R., Berdine, J., Mastroeni, I. (eds.) VMCAI 2013. LNCS, vol. 7737, pp. 128–148. Springer, Heidelberg (2013)

9. Cuoq, P., Kirchner, F., Kosmatov, N., Prevosto, V., Signoles, J., Yakobowski, B.: Frama-c - a software analysis perspective. In: Eleftherakis, G., Hinchey, M., Holcombe, M. (eds.) SEFM 2012. LNCS, vol. 7504, pp. 233–247. Springer, Heidelberg (2012)

10. Engler, D., Chen, D.Y., Hallem, S., Chou, A., Chelf, B.: Bugs as deviant behavior: A general approach to inferring errors in systems code. In: SOSP (2001)

11. Fähndrich, M., Logozzo, F.: Static contract checking with abstract interpretation. In: Beckert, B., Marché, C. (eds.) FoVeOOS 2010. LNCS, vol. 6528, pp. 10–30. Springer, Heidelberg (2011)

12. Flanagan, C., Leino, K.R.M., Lillibridge, M., Nelson, G., Saxe, J.B., Stata, R.: Extended static checking for java. SIGPLAN Not., 234–245 (2002)

13. Godefroid, P., Nori, A.V., Rajamani, S.K., Tetali, S.: Compositional must program analysis: Unleashing the power of alternation. In: POPL, pp. 43–56 (2010)

14. Khurshid, S., Păsăreanu, C.S., Visser, W.: Generalized symbolic execution for model checking and testing. In: Garavel, H., Hatcliff, J. (eds.) TACAS 2003. LNCS, vol. 2619, pp. 553–568. Springer, Heidelberg (2003)

15. Leino, K.R.M.: Efficient weakest preconditions. Inf. Process. Lett., 281–288 (2005)

16. Rakamarić, Z., Hu, A.J.: A scalable memory model for low-level code. In: Jones, N.D., Müller-Olm, M. (eds.) VMCAI 2009. LNCS, vol. 5403, pp. 290–304. Springer, Heidelberg (2009)

17. Rümmer, P.: A constraint sequent calculus for first-order logic with linear integer arithmetic. In: Cervesato, I., Veith, H., Voronkov, A. (eds.) LPAR 2008. LNCS (LNAI), vol. 5330, pp. 274–289. Springer, Heidelberg (2008)

18. Tillmann, N., Schulte, W.: Parameterized unit tests. In: ESEC/SIGSOFT FSE, pp. 253–262 (2005)

19. Tomb, A., Flanagan, C.: Detecting inconsistencies via universal reachability analysis. In: ISSTA, pp. 287–297 (2012)

20. Vallée-Rai, R., Hendren, L., Sundaresan, V., Lam, P., Gagnon, E., Co, P.: Soot - A Java Optimization Framework. In: CASCON 1999, pp. 125–135 (1999)

# Synthesizing Predicates from Abstract Domain Losses

Bogdan Mihaila and Axel Simon

Technical University of Munich, Garching b. München, Germany
{firstname.lastname}@in.tum.de

**Abstract.** Numeric abstract domains are key to many verification problems. Their ability to scale hinges on using convex approximations of the possible variable valuations. In certain cases, this approximation is too coarse to verify certain verification conditions, namely those that require disjunctive invariants. A common approach to infer disjunctive invariants is to track a set of states. However, this easily leads to scalability problems. In this work, we propose to augment a numeric analysis with an abstract domain of predicates. Predicates are synthesized whenever an abstract domain loses precision due to convexity. The predicate domain is able to recover this loss at a later stage by re-applying the synthesized predicates on the numeric abstract domain. This symbiosis combines the ability of numeric domains to compactly summarize states with the ability of predicate abstraction to express disjunctive invariants and non-convex spaces. We further show how predicates can be used as a tool for communication between several numeric domains.

## 1 Introduction

Verification by means of a reachability analysis is based on abstract domains that over-approximate the possible concrete states that a program can reach. The forte of abstract domains is their ability to synthesize new invariants that are not present in the program. However, their inherent approximation may mean that the invariant required to verify a program cannot be deduced. On the contrary, the strength of predicate abstraction used in software model checking is that predicates precisely partition the state space of a program. The challenge here is to synthesize new predicates that eventually suffice to verify a program. This work combines the benefits of both approaches: we synthesize new predicates by observing the precision loss in numeric domains and refine the precision of the numeric domains using the predicates. Our technique is particularly useful for expressing non-convex invariants that are commonly lost when using off-the-shelf numeric abstract domains that are based on convex approximations.

The importance of non-convex invariants is illustrated by the C code in Fig. 1. Here, line 1 computes a flag f that is true if the divisor d of the expression in line 5 is non-zero. Assuming that the initial value of d lies in $[-2, 2]$, the possible values when evaluating the conditional are shown in Fig. 1b). Abstracting this set of discrete points using, say, the abstract domain of intervals yields the state

J.M. Badger and K.Y. Rozier (Eds.): NFM 2014, LNCS 8430, pp. 328–342, 2014.

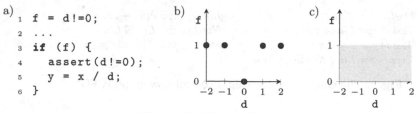

**Fig. 1.** Avoiding a division by zero

in Fig. 1c). This state space is too imprecise to deduce that d is non-zero if f is one. As a consequence, testing that $f$ is one in line 3 does not restrict the abstract state sufficiently to show that the assertion holds.

Interestingly, analyzing the same example using predicate abstraction does not suffer from this imprecision as non-convex spaces can naturally be represented using disjuncts. In the example, a predicate $p_f \equiv d \neq 0$, which is equivalent to the disjunction $d \leq -1 \vee d \geq 1$, suffices to verify the assertion since testing f in line 3 results in $p_f$ being true.

A common approach to enriching numeric abstract domains to allow expressing non-convex states is to use disjunctive completion [4], that is, a set of states. In particular, several works have proposed to some variant of a binary decision-diagram (BDD) where decision nodes are labeled with predicates and the leaves are abstract domains [10,14]. A similar effect is obtained by duplicating the control flow graph (CFG) for each subset of satisfied predicates [6,15,17]. In both settings, the number of numeric domains that are tracked may be exponential in the number of predicates. Our work improves over this setup by combining classic predicate abstraction [1] with a single numeric domain, thereby avoiding this exponential duplication of the numeric state. In particular, we present a generic *combinator domain* that is parameterized over any numeric abstract domain and allows any predicate expressible by the abstract domain. We thereby also generalize over bespoke domains that explicitly track specific disjunctive information, such as disequalities [16]. Overall, we make the following contributions:

- We propose an abstract domain that tracks implications between two predicates. By combining this domain with a single numeric state, we retain the performance and simplicity of the numeric state transformers.
- We present an effective reduction mechanism that refines a numeric state based on the implications in the predicate domain.
- By observing precision losses in the numeric domain, relevant predicates are synthesized that preempt a loss of precision during the computation of a join. This novel mechanism addresses precision losses due to convexity without a costly replication of the numeric state.

The remainder of this paper is organized as follows: after presenting the setup of our domains and necessary notation, Sect. 3 defines the transfer functions of the predicate domain and the reduction with numeric states. Section 4 details the lattice operations and shows how new implications can be synthesized by the numeric domain. Section 5 presents experiments, related work and conclusions.

$$
\begin{array}{llll}
Pred & ::= Test & Lin & ::= c_1x_1 + \ldots + c_nx_n \\
Test & ::= Lin \bowtie Lin & NonLin & ::= Lin \boxtimes Lin \\
Assign & ::= x = Expr & \bowtie & ::= \leq \,|\, \nleq \,|\, < \,|\, \nless \,|\, = \,|\, \neq \\
Expr & ::= Lin \,|\, NonLin \,|\, Test & \boxtimes & ::= \times \,|\, / \,|\, \% \,|\, \hat{}
\end{array}
$$

**Fig. 2.** The grammar decorating a control flow graph (CFG)

## 2   Preliminaries

Our analysis operates on the control flow graph (CFG) of a program. The CFG is represented by a set of vertices labeled $v_1, v_2, \ldots$ and a set of directed edges representing the transfer functions. The transfer functions are either assignments $v_i \xrightarrow{Assign} v_j$ or assumptions $v_i \xrightarrow{Pred} v_j$ where $Assign$ and $Pred$ are given by the grammar in Fig. 2. Additionally, we use assertions in programs, e.g. `assert(x == 0)` that correspond to edges $v_i \xrightarrow{x \neq 0} v_e$ to a designated error node $v_e$. We associate each vertex $v_i$ with an abstract state $d_i \in \mathcal{D}$ where $\mathcal{D}$ is the universe of a lattice $\langle \mathcal{D}, \sqsubseteq_{\mathcal{D}}, \sqcup_{\mathcal{D}}, \sqcap_{\mathcal{D}}, \top_{\mathcal{D}}, \bot_{\mathcal{D}} \rangle$. Initially the states are $d_0 = \top_{\mathcal{D}}$ and $d_i = \bot_{\mathcal{D}}$ for $i \neq 0$. The solution to the program analysis problem is characterized by a set of constraints $d_j \sqsupseteq_{\mathcal{D}} [\![l_i^j]\!]^{\mathcal{D}}(d_i)$, each constraint corresponding to an edge $v_i \xrightarrow{l_i^j} v_j$. It can be inferred using chaotic iteration which picks indices $i, j$ for which the constraint is not satisfied and, for the edge from $v_i$ to $v_j$ updates $d_j$ to $d_j := d_j \sqcup_{\mathcal{D}} [\![l_i^j]\!]^{\mathcal{D}}(d_i)$. In general, the lattice $\mathcal{D}$ may have infinite ascending chains. We therefore assume that each cycle in the CFG contains at least one application of the widening operator $\nabla$ in order to ensure termination [4].

### 2.1   The *Predicate* Abstract Domain

We present our predicate domain as a co-fibered domain [20], that is, as a domain that is parameterized by another domain. Due to an implementation [3] in OCaml, such a domain is also called a functor domain. A co-fibered domain $\mathcal{D}$ is parameterized by a child domain $\mathcal{C}$ that it controls. Their combination is written as $\mathcal{D} \triangleright \mathcal{C}$ and a state as a tuple $\langle d, c \rangle \in \mathcal{D} \triangleright \mathcal{C}$. A transfer function on $\mathcal{D} \triangleright \mathcal{C}$ may apply any number of transfer functions on its child $c \in \mathcal{C}$ before returning a result. Co-fibered domains may be nested. For instance, we combine the predicate domain $\mathcal{P}$ with a co-fibered affine equality domain $\mathcal{A}$ [18] and a plain interval domain $\mathcal{I}$, yielding a stack of domains $\mathcal{P} \triangleright \mathcal{A} \triangleright \mathcal{I}$ where a state $\langle \bar{\iota}, \langle a, i \rangle \rangle$ contains the individual domain states $\bar{\iota} \in \mathcal{P}$, $a \in \mathcal{A}$ and $i \in \mathcal{I}$. The predicate domain is given by the lattice $\langle \mathcal{P} \triangleright \mathcal{C}, \sqsubseteq_{\mathcal{P}}, \sqcup_{\mathcal{P}}, \sqcap_{\mathcal{P}} \rangle$ where the universe $\mathcal{P} : \wp(Pred \times Pred)$ is a finite set of implications $p_1 \rightarrow p_2$ over predicates $p_i \in \mathcal{L}(Pred)$ as defined in Fig. 2. Predicates relate linear expressions over the program variables $X$ using a comparison operator $\bowtie$. Note that the set of operators is closed under negation so that the universe of predicates is closed under negation. The choice of implications between only two predicates allows for a simple yet effective propagation of information, as detailed in the next section.

$\llbracket x = a \bowtie b \rrbracket^{\mathcal{P}} \langle \bar{\iota}, c \rangle = \langle \bar{\iota}', \llbracket x = a \bowtie b \rrbracket^{\mathcal{C}} c \rangle$
  where $\bar{\iota}' = \{ p \to q \in \bar{\iota} \mid x \notin vars(p) \cup vars(q) \}$
  $\cup \{ x = 1 \to a \bowtie b, x = 0 \to a \not\bowtie b, a \bowtie b \to x = 1, a \not\bowtie b \to x = 0 \}$
$\llbracket x = NonLin \rrbracket^{\mathcal{P}} \langle \bar{\iota}, c \rangle = \langle \bar{\iota}', \llbracket x = NonLin \rrbracket^{\mathcal{C}} c \rangle$
  where $\bar{\iota}' = \{ p \to q \in \bar{\iota} \mid x \notin vars(p) \cup vars(q) \}$
$\llbracket x = Lin \rrbracket^{\mathcal{P}} \langle \bar{\iota}, c \rangle = \langle \bar{\iota}', \llbracket x = Lin \rrbracket^{\mathcal{C}} c \rangle$
  where $\bar{\iota}' = \{ p \to q \in \bar{\iota} \mid x \notin vars(p) \cup vars(q) \}$
  $\cup \{ transform(p \to q) \mid p \to q \in \bar{\iota} \}$ and $\sigma = [x/Lin]$

  and $transform(p \to q) = \begin{cases} \sigma^{-1}(p) \to \sigma^{-1}(q) & \text{if } \sigma^{-1}(p) \wedge \sigma^{-1}(q) \text{ exists} \\ true \to true & \text{otherwise} \end{cases}$

$\llbracket a \bowtie b \rrbracket^{\mathcal{P}} \langle \bar{\iota}, c \rangle = \langle \bar{\iota}, fixapply(\{a \bowtie b\}, \emptyset, c) \rangle$
  where $fixapply(\bar{p}, \bar{u}, c') = $ if $\bar{p} \subseteq \bar{u}$ then $c'$ else
  let $t \in \bar{p} \setminus \bar{u}$ and $\bar{n} = \{t\} \cup consequences^{\mathcal{C}}(t, c')$
  and $\bar{n}' = \{ q \mid p \to q \in \bar{\iota} \wedge n \in \bar{n} \wedge n \vdash p \} \cup \{ \neg p \mid p \to q \in \bar{\iota} \wedge n \in \bar{n} \wedge n \vdash \neg q \}$
  in $fixapply(\bar{p} \cup \bar{n}', \bar{u} \cup \{t\}, \llbracket t \rrbracket^{\mathcal{C}} c')$

**Fig. 3.** Assignments and branch transfer functions for the predicates domain. The comparison operator $\bowtie$ in a predicate is one of $\leq, \not\leq, <, \not<, =, \neq$.

# 3   Transfer Functions and Reductions

This section details the transfer functions and presents the flow of information between the predicate domain and the numeric child domains.

## 3.1   Transfer Functions

The transfer functions of the combined domain state $\langle \bar{\iota}, c \rangle \in \mathcal{P} \triangleright \mathcal{C}$ are given in Fig. 3. In general, a transfer function $\llbracket l \rrbracket^{\mathcal{P}} \langle \bar{\iota}, c \rangle$ applies the corresponding transfer function on the child domain $c \in \mathcal{C}$, yielding $\langle \bar{\iota}', \llbracket l \rrbracket^{\mathcal{C}} c \rangle$ where $\bar{\iota}'$ is the new state of the predicate domain. We distinguish three forms of assignments. The first, $\llbracket x = a \bowtie b \rrbracket^{\mathcal{P}}$, assigns the result of a comparison to a variable $x$. Here, the predicate domain removes any predicate that mentions $x$ and adds new predicates based on the comparison. We assume that $x$ is set to one if test $a \bowtie b$ holds and to zero otherwise. Thus, the predicates $x = 0$ and $x = 1$ are used to encode the value of $x$ in the implications. Specifically, the two outcomes $x = 1 \leftrightarrow a \bowtie b$ and $x = 0 \leftrightarrow a \not\bowtie b$ are stored using four implications.

The transfer function $\llbracket x = NonLin \rrbracket^{\mathcal{P}}$ for non-linear assignment removes all implications in the predicate domain containing $x$. An assignment $\llbracket x = Lin \rrbracket^{\mathcal{P}}$ of a linear expression to $x$ tries to transform implications containing $x$ if $Lin$ contains $x$, e.g. x=x+1. For example, consider the predicates state $\bar{\iota} = \{ f = 0 \to x \leq 5, x \not\leq 10 \to y = 10 \}$ and the assignment x=x+1 mentioned above. Given the substitution $\sigma = [x/x + 1]$ that describes the change of the state space, we compute $\sigma^{-1} = [x/x - 1]$ that describes how predicates can be transformed so that they are valid in the new state. In the example, applying $\sigma^{-1}$ to the implications yields $\bar{\iota}' = \{ f = 0 \to x \leq 6, x \not\leq 11 \to y = 10 \}$. In all three assignments, more predicates can be retained by testing if they are still valid after the assignment.

We now consider the transfer function for an assumption $[\![a \bowtie b]\!]^{\mathcal{P}}$. The information from the test $a \bowtie b$ is used by the predicate domain to gather further facts about the state. The process of applying these facts to the child domain is called reduction [4]. The reduction is performed as a fixpoint computation and can be seen as an instance of Granger's framework for reduction by local iteration [8]. Specifically, the function *fixapply* gathers a set of deduced predicates $\bar{p}$ and a set of predicates $\bar{u}$ that have already been used. In each iteration a predicate $t \in \bar{p} \setminus \bar{u}$ is applied to the child state $c'$, yielding $[\![t]\!]^{\mathcal{C}} c'$. Furthermore, a set of new predicates that are implied by $t$ are computed in two steps. First, $t$ is combined with a set $\bar{n}$ of semantic consequences which is computed by *consequences*$^{\mathcal{C}}$ as detailed below. Second, a set of syntactically implied predicates $\bar{n}'$ is computed from $\bar{n}$ by inspecting the implications in the predicate domain. We use modus ponens resolution to deduce $q$ from an implication $p \rightarrow q \in \bar{\iota}$ where $t \vdash p$ and deduce $\neg p$ if $t \vdash \neg q$. Here, the syntactic entailment $\vdash$ is defined as follows:

**Definition 1 (Syntactic Predicate Entailment $\vdash$).** *A predicate $q$ is entailed by another predicate $p$, written as $p \vdash q$, if $p \equiv q$ or if $p$ describes a weaker condition that subsumes the condition of $q$. We use the following syntactic entailment rules (analogous definitions for the negations of the comparison operators $\nleq, \nless$):*

$$p \vdash x \neq c \quad \text{if} \quad p \in \{x = c' \mid c' \neq c\} \cup \{x \leq c' \mid c' < c\} \cup \{x < c' \mid c' \leq c\}$$
$$p \vdash x \leq c \quad \text{if} \quad p \in \{x = c' \mid c' \leq c\} \cup \{x \leq c' \mid c' \leq c\} \cup \{x < c' \mid c' - 1 \leq c\}$$
$$p \vdash x < c \quad \text{if} \quad p \in \{x = c' \mid c' < c\} \cup \{x \leq c' \mid c' < c\} \cup \{x < c' \mid c' \leq c\}$$

The set of syntactically implied predicates $\bar{n}'$ is added to $\bar{p}$ and, hence, eventually applied to the child state. Since at most two predicates for each implication in $\bar{\iota}$ can be added to $\bar{p}$, this iterative reduction terminates.

Although not strictly necessary, the *consequences*$^{\mathcal{C}}$ function allows information to flow from the child domain to the predicate domain. The function synthesizes new predicates that become valid after applying the test $t$. It is different for each child domain. An implementation for the interval domain $\mathcal{I}$ is as follows:

$$consequences^{\mathcal{I}}(t, c) = \text{ let } c' = [\![t]\!]^{\mathcal{I}} c \text{ in } \{x = l \mid c(x) \neq c'(x) \wedge c'(x) \in [l, l]\}$$

Here, $c(x)$ is the interval of the variable $x$ in the state $c$. The insight in this definition is that the only additional information inferable by the interval domain is that a variable $x$ may have become constant due to a test such as $x \leq c$. Returning these equality predicates may allow additional deductions in the predicate domain. Note that other child domains may deduce different facts.

## 3.2    Example for the Reduction after Executing Assumptions

We illustrate the reduction when applying an assumption $[\![a \bowtie b]\!]^{\mathcal{P}}$ using an example. Consider applying the test $f < 1$ to the state $s = \langle \bar{\iota}, c \rangle$ that consists of the predicates $\bar{\iota} \in \mathcal{P}$ and the intervals $c \in \mathcal{I}$ as child domain. Let $\bar{\iota} = \{f = 0 \rightarrow x \leq 0\}$ and $c = \{f \in [0, 1], x \in [-1, 1]\}$. The first step in the transfer function is to infer the consequences of the test: $\bar{n} = consequences^{\mathcal{I}}(f < 1, c)$. As the child state becomes $c' = \{f \in [0, 0], x \in [-1, 1]\}$, the consequences are

$\bar{n} = \{f = 0\}$. The synthesized predicate in $\bar{n}$ syntactically entails the left-hand side of the implication $f = 0 \rightarrow x \leq 0$ that is tracked in the predicate domain. Thus, *fixapply* calls itself recursively with the new predicate $x \leq 0$ which results in a call to *consequences*$^{\mathcal{I}}(x \leq 0, c') = \emptyset$. Now, the set of implied predicates $\bar{n}'$ is empty and a fixpoint is reached since $\bar{p} = \bar{u} = \{f < 1, x \leq 0\}$. Thus, the result of the transfer function is $[\![f < 1]\!]^{\mathcal{P}}s = \langle\{f = 0 \rightarrow x \leq 0\}, \{f \in [0,0], x \in [-1,0]\}\rangle$. This recursive reduction mechanism implements all required reductions between the predicate and the child domain. The next section illustrates how this reduction mechanism is used to preempt the loss of precision due to convexity.

### 3.3   Application to Non-convex Spaces

Reconsider the example in Fig. 1 where a division by zero is prevented by a guard. The problem here is that the state space for $d$ is non-convex and cannot be expressed with the intervals domain $\mathcal{I}$. However, using the predicate domain $\mathcal{P}$ we are able to prove the invariant at program point 4 even though the interval value for $d$ at that point is $d \in [-2, 2]$. We illustrate an analysis of the program for an initial state where the interval domain tracks $d$ with the value $d \in [-2, 2]$. By executing line 1, the four implications for the assignment of a comparison are added to the predicate domain, yielding the state $\bar{\imath} = \{f = 1 \rightarrow d \neq 0, f = 0 \rightarrow d = 0, d \neq 0 \rightarrow f = 1, d = 0 \rightarrow f = 0\}$. On entering the **then**-branch, the test $f = 1$ in line 3 restricts the variable $f$ in the interval domain to $f \in [1, 1]$. The predicate domain uses the first implication to deduce $d \neq 0$, which is also applied to the child domain. However, the child domain $\mathcal{I}$ is not able to express the disjunction $d \in [-2, -1] \vee [1, 2]$ thus the state after applying $d \neq 0$ remains $d \in [-2, 2]$. The assertion in line 4 translates to an edge to the dedicated error node that is labelled with the test $d = 0$. Hence, the assertion fails if $d = 0$ is satisfiable. The predicate domain observes that the right-hand side $d \neq 0$ of the implication $f = 1 \rightarrow d \neq 0$ is *false* and thus adds the negated left-hand side $f \neq 1$ to $\bar{n}'$. Once the predicate domain applies $f \neq 1$ to the child state $c = \{f \in [1, 1], d \in [-2, 2]\}$, the result is $\bot$, the unreachable state. Thus, the error node is not reachable in the program and the assertion is verified even though the convex numeric domain is not precise enough to express $d \neq 0$. The reduction mechanism is able to exploit the information in the implications for verifying assertions without requiring more complex (i.e. non-convex) numeric domains.

In general, observing predicates from assignments is only a syntactic technique that may fail for more complex disjunctive invariants. The next section therefore illustrates how the reduction mechanism implemented by *fixapply* naturally combines with a more sophisticated way of inferring new implications.

## 4   Lattice Operations and Predicate Synthesis

We present entailment test, join and widening operations of the predicate domain. Moreover, we introduce a novel *synth* function that synthesizes new implications between predicates that counteract the loss of precision in numeric domains.

$\langle \bar{\iota}_1, c_1 \rangle \sqsubseteq_{\mathcal{P}} \langle \bar{\iota}_2, c_2 \rangle = c_1 \sqsubseteq_{\mathcal{C}} c_2 \wedge entailed(\bar{\iota}_2, \bar{\iota}_1, c_1) = \bar{\iota}_2$

$\quad$ where $entailed(\bar{\iota}', \bar{\iota}, c) = \{ p' \rightarrow q' \in \bar{\iota}' \mid (\exists p \rightarrow q \in \bar{\iota}.p' \vdash p \wedge q \vdash q') \vee (\llbracket p' \rrbracket^{\mathcal{C}} c \vDash q') \}$

$\langle \bar{\iota}_1, c_1 \rangle \sqcup_{\mathcal{P}} \langle \bar{\iota}_2, c_2 \rangle = \langle join(\bar{\iota}_1, \bar{\iota}_2) \cup synth^{\mathcal{C}}(c_1, c_2), c_1 \sqcup_{\mathcal{C}} c_2 \rangle$

$\quad$ where $join(\bar{\iota}_1, \bar{\iota}_2) = entailed(\bar{\iota}_1, \bar{\iota}_2, c_2) \cup entailed(\bar{\iota}_2, \bar{\iota}_1, c_1)$

**Fig. 4.** Lattice operations for the predicate domain

## 4.1   Lattice Operations

We commence by detailing the entailment test $\langle \bar{\iota}_1, c_1 \rangle \sqsubseteq_{\mathcal{P}} \langle \bar{\iota}_2, c_2 \rangle$ in Fig. 4. It performs the entailment test $c_1 \sqsubseteq_{\mathcal{C}} c_2$ on the child domain and tests if all the implications in the right argument $\bar{\iota}_2$ are entailed by the left argument by calling the function $entailed(\bar{\iota}', \bar{\iota}, c)$. The latter function returns an implication $p' \rightarrow q' \in \bar{\iota}'$ if it is either syntactically entailed in $\bar{\iota}$ or semantically entailed in the state $c$. Semantic entailment $\vDash$ is defined as follows:

**Definition 2 (Semantic Predicate Entailment $\vDash$).** *A predicate $q$ is entailed in a state $c$, written $c \vDash q$, if testing $\neg q$ in $c$ yields an empty state, i.e., $\llbracket \neg q \rrbracket^{\mathcal{C}} c = \bot$.*

By this definition, the test $\llbracket p' \rrbracket^{\mathcal{C}} c \vDash q'$ in *entailed* reduces to checking whether $\llbracket \neg q' \rrbracket^{\mathcal{C}} (\llbracket p' \rrbracket^{\mathcal{C}} c) = \bot$. Thus, if the predicate $p'$ on the left-hand side of the implication $p' \rightarrow q'$ is false in $c$ then $\llbracket \neg q' \rrbracket^{\mathcal{C}} \bot = \bot$ follows and the implication is entailed in $c$. The two tests $\llbracket \cdot \rrbracket^{\mathcal{C}}$ on the child domain $c$ can be avoided if the implication is syntactically entailed by an implication in $\bar{\iota}$. Here, the implication $p \rightarrow q \in \bar{\iota}$ entails $p' \rightarrow q'$ if the premise $p'$ is stronger and the conclusion $q'$ is weaker which is expressed by $p' \vdash p \wedge q \vdash q'$. Note that neither the syntactic nor the semantic entailment test subsumes the other as both approximate the test differently.

The join $\langle \bar{\iota}_1, c_1 \rangle \sqcup_{\mathcal{P}} \langle \bar{\iota}_2, c_2 \rangle$ independently computes a join on the predicate domain and on the child domain. In oder to join the implication sets $\bar{\iota}_1$ and $\bar{\iota}_2$, we define a function *join* that keeps all implications that hold in the respective other state using the *entailed* function described above. Note that the semantic entailment test in *entailed* is particularly important for the join as one of the predicate domain states may be empty so that the syntactic entailment would discard all implications. The semantic join is able to retain newly inferred predicates in, for example, loop bodies as illustrated later.

In addition to the predicates returned by the *join* function, new implications are synthesized from the child domain states using the $synth^{\mathcal{C}}$ function. The idea is to synthesize implications that characterize the approximation that occurred as part of the $\sqcup_{\mathcal{C}}$ operation. Which synthesized implications are generated depends on the numeric domain. If the predicate language is sufficiently expressive, a domain could potentially characterize all precision losses that occur during a join. The following $synth^{\mathcal{I}}$ function for the interval domain is an example that generates implications for all changing bounds. Moreover, by relating changes of interval bounds between different variables, it generates relational information that cannot be expressed within the interval domain itself. It is defined as follows:

$synth^{\mathcal{I}}(c_1, c_2) = $ let $c = c_1 \sqcup_{\mathcal{I}} c_2$
     and $\bar{m} = \{x \in vars(c_1) \cap vars(c_2) \mid c_1(x) \neq c_2(x)\}$ and $i \in \{1, 2\}$
     and $\bar{u}_i = \{u_{xi} \mid x \in \bar{m} \wedge c_i(x) \in [l_{xi}, u_{xi}] \wedge c(x) \in [l_x, u_x] \wedge u_{xi} < u_x\}$
     and $\bar{l}_i = \{l_{xi} \mid x \in \bar{m} \wedge c_i(x) \in [l_{xi}, u_{xi}] \wedge c(x) \in [l_x, u_x] \wedge l_x < l_{xi}\}$
     in $\{u_{x1} < x \rightarrow l_{y2} \leq y, u_{y1} < y \rightarrow l_{x2} \leq x \mid x, y \in \bar{m} \wedge u_{xi}, u_{yi} \in \bar{u}_i \wedge l_{xi}, l_{yi} \in \bar{l}_i\}$

Let $vars(c)$ return all the variables $\bar{x} \subseteq X$ tracked in the state $c$ and let $c(x)$ denote the interval of the variable $x$. The set of variables $\bar{m}$ that are not equal in both states are those whose joined value is an approximation of the input intervals. For these variables we compute a set of changing lower and upper bounds $\bar{l}_i$ and $\bar{u}_i$ whose indices indicate the variable and origin of the bound. For example, when joining $c_1(x) \in [0, 5]$ with $c_2(x) \in [10, 15]$, resulting in $c(x) \in [0, 15]$, the upper bound $u_{x1} = 5$ of $c_1(x)$ and the lower bound $l_{x2} = 10$ of $c_2(x)$ are lost whereas the other bounds are retained in $c(x)$. These changing bounds are used for generating implications. Specifically, each implication correlates a lost upper bound $u_{xi}$ from $c_i$ with a lost lower bound $l_{y(2-i)}$ from $c_{2-i}$ where $i = 1, 2$. For the example above $x = y$, thus the only generated implication is $u_{x1} < x \rightarrow l_{x2} \leq x$, that is, $5 < x \rightarrow 10 \leq x$. The implication allows that a test such as $7 < x$ is refined to $10 \leq x$, thereby recovering the precision loss in the join that is due to the convexity of the interval domain. In general, the bounds of several variables can be related, thereby even generating relational information.

One drawback of the definition above is that implications are added for each pair of variables from $\bar{m}$, thus, the returned set of implications is quadratic in $|\bar{m}|$. This quadratic growth can be avoided by not generating a redundant implication $a \rightarrow c$ if both $a \rightarrow b$ and $b \rightarrow c$ are already present. Specifically, by sorting $\bar{m}$ using some total ordering, we only emit implications over variables that are adjacent in this ordering, as well as an implication relating the largest variable with the smallest. As the predicate domain performs a transitive closure on application of a test predicate (through *fixapply*), adding only implications between adjacent variables is sufficient to recover all information expressed in a chain of implications. Using this optimization, we are able to reduce the number of synthesized implications to be linear in the number of changed variables $|\bar{m}|$.

Before we consider further examples, we consider the widening operation, defined by, say, $\langle \bar{\iota}_1, c_1 \rangle \nabla_{\mathcal{P}} \langle \bar{\iota}_2, c_2 \rangle = \langle join(\bar{\iota}_1, \bar{\iota}_2) \cup synth^{\mathcal{C}}(c_1, c_2), c_1 \nabla_{\mathcal{C}} c_2 \rangle$. This definition is analogous to the join operation but applies widening on the child states $c_1, c_2$. One caveat of this definition is that termination is not guaranteed. Consider an implication $p' \rightarrow q'$ at a loop head and assume that a conditional in the loop refines the child state by using the $[\![a \bowtie b]\!]^{\mathcal{P}}$ transformer in Fig. 3 which, in turn, may use the information in $p' \rightarrow q'$. Suppose that joining the two branches of the conditional creates a new implication $p \rightarrow q$ by means of the $synth^{\mathcal{C}}$ function that is syntactically weaker than $p' \rightarrow q'$. If $[\![p']\!]^{\mathcal{C}} c_1 \nvDash q'$ (the previous implication cannot be shown to hold in the new state) then the loop is not stable. If furthermore $[\![p]\!]^{\mathcal{C}} c_2 \vDash q$ (the new implication holds in the previous state), the loop is analyzed with the new implication. Thus, one implication may be replaced by another one, possibly indefinitely so. In order to ensure termination, standard widening techniques can be used, such as eventually

| | $c_1$ | $c_2$ | $synth^{\mathcal{I}}(c_1, c_2)$ | $c_1 \sqcup_{\mathcal{I}} c_2$ |
|---|---|---|---|---|
| $x \in$ | $[0, 5]$ | $[10, 15]$ | $\{5 < x \to 2 \leq y,$ | $[0, 15]$ |
| $y \in$ | $[-5, -1]$ | $[2, 3]$ | $-1 < y \to 10 \leq x\}$ | $[-5, 3]$ |

**Fig. 5.** The join of two states in the intervals domain $\mathcal{I}$ and the synthesized implications correlating the bounds lost due to the convex approximation

disallowing new implications [15]. This can be implemented by using the definition $\langle \bar{\iota}_1, c_1 \rangle \nabla_{\mathcal{P}} \langle \bar{\iota}_2, c_2 \rangle = \langle entailed(\bar{\iota}_1, \bar{\iota}_2, c_2), c_1 \nabla_{\mathcal{C}} c_2 \rangle$ after $k$ iterations. So far, we were unable to find examples that exhibit this non-terminating behavior.

### 4.2 Recovering Precision Using Relational Information

One strength of our $synth^{\mathcal{I}}$ function is that it creates relational information, that is, it generates implications between different variables. This relational information enables *fixapply* to deduce, from a test of one variable, more precise ranges for other variables. In particular, a test $t$ that separates two states, i.e. $\llbracket t \rrbracket^{\mathcal{I}} c_1 = c_1$ and $\llbracket t \rrbracket^{\mathcal{I}} c_2 = \bot$ is enriched by the relational implications so that all losses due to convexity are recovered, that is, $\llbracket t \rrbracket^{\mathcal{P}}(\langle \bar{\iota}_1, c_1 \rangle \sqcup_{\mathcal{P}} \langle \bar{\iota}_2, c_2 \rangle) = \langle \bar{\iota}_1', c_1 \rangle$.

We illustrate this ability using two states $s_1 = \langle \emptyset, \{x \in [0, 5], y \in [-5, -1]\} \rangle$ and $s_2 = \langle \emptyset, \{x \in [10, 15], y \in [2, 3]\} \rangle$. The joined state $s = s_1 \sqcup_{\mathcal{P}} s_2$ is given by $s = \langle \{5 < x \to 2 \leq y, -1 < y \to 10 \leq x\}, \{x \in [0, 15], y \in [-5, 3]\} \rangle$. This operation is illustrated in Fig. 5 where the bounds in bold are those that are lost and the arrows indicate which bounds are related by the generated implications. We now show how applying the test $0 < y$ on $s$ recovers the numeric state in $s_2$ and, analogously, that applying $y \leq 0$ recovers the numeric state of $s_1$. Specifically, when applying the test $0 < y$ on state $s$, the left-hand side of the implication $-1 < y \to 10 \leq x$ is syntactically entailed, so that $10 \leq x$ is also applied to the child state, yielding the precise value $[10, 15]$ for $x$. The predicate $10 \leq x$ syntactically entails the other implication $5 < x \to 2 \leq y$. Thus, the predicate $2 \leq y$ is applied to the child state, yielding the precise value $[2, 3]$ for $y$. After that no new predicates are entailed and the recursive predicate application in the function *fixapply* stops with the state $s_2' = \langle \{5 < x \to 2 \leq y, -1 < y \to 10 \leq x\}, \{x \in [10, 15], y \in [2, 3]\} \rangle$. Observe that the interval domain is identical to that of $s_2$. Analogously, we get a state $s_1'$ in which the interval for $x$ is $[0, 5]$ and for $y$ is $[-5, -1]$ after applying the opposing condition $y \leq 0$.

In summary, the predicate domain improves the precision of a child domain tracking precision losses that are reported by the child. In particular, the domain-specific $synth^{\mathcal{C}}$ function can generate predicates that cannot be expressed in the domain itself. This allows the predicate domain to maintain enough disjunctive information to recover the state before the join whenever a test is able to separate the two states. Note though that there exist cases when this is not completely possible, namely when the value of $x$ in one state overlaps the value in the other state. Consider $c_1(x) \in [0, 4]$ and $c_2(x) \in [2, 8]$. A test $x < 3$ does not separate the two states. However, any test outside the overlapping range $[2, 4]$ is able to separate the two states which, in turn, leads to the refinement of other bounds.

## 4.3  Application to Path-Sensitive Invariants

This section illustrates how our domain can verify an example taken from [5]. The challenge of analyzing the code in Fig. 6a) is that the join of different paths loses precision and the invariant that a file is only accessed if it was opened before cannot be proved. For the sake of presentation, we use *open* to denote the value of out->is_open. Note that the assertion in line 3 can be proved by using the interval domain alone, as *open* is $[1,1]$ due to line 2. However, the assertion in line 10 cannot be proved by using intervals alone: observe that *open* is set to $[0,0]$ in line 4 and that the join of this value with the value $[1,1]$ from line 7 yields the convex approximation of $[0,1]$ in line 10 of the assertion. As a consequence, the assertion cannot be proved since the edge to the error state with assumption *open* $= 0$ is satisfiable. Now consider analyzing the example using the predicate domain with the interval domain as child. Then the join of the **then** branch in line 7 and the state before line 6 creates an implication $0 < \mathit{flag} \rightarrow 1 \leq \mathit{open}$. When applying the branch condition $\mathit{flag} = 1$ of line 9, the implied predicate $1 \leq \mathit{open}$ is used to reduce the state, yielding $\mathit{open} \in [1,1]$ in the interval domain. Thus, the assertion can be proved since the edge to the error state with assumption *open* $= 0$ is unreachable. The example illustrates how numeric domains may lose precision when joining paths and, thus, may fail to express a path-sensitive invariant which is crucial to prove assertions in the branch of a conditional.

Fischer et al. [5] prove the assertion in line 10 by not joining the states after the conditional in line 6, thus keeping the states where *open* $= 0$ and *open* $= 1$ separate. They associate a predicate with a numeric state and join numeric states only if they are associated with the same predicate. Thus, their abstract state before the conditional in line 9 is $\{\langle \mathit{flag} = 0, \mathit{open} \in [0,0]\rangle, \langle \mathit{flag} = 1, \mathit{open} \in [1,1]\rangle\}$ which reduces to $\{\langle \mathit{flag} = 1, \mathit{open} \in [1,1]\rangle\}$ inside the conditional. Although their approach is able to prove the assertion, it is more costly as it tracks several numeric states. Although using sharing can reduce the resource overhead of tracking multiple states [11] the cost of tracking several states is generally higher [14]. Our approach retains the conciseness of a single convex numeric state and merely adds the implications necessary to express certain disjunctive information. In particular, we only infer disjunctive information for variables that actually differ in the join of two numeric states rather than duplicating the information on all variables.

## 4.4  Application to Separation of Loop Iterations

A particularly challenging example from the literature [12] requires that variable values of certain loop iterations are distinguished. The example in Fig. 6b) is prototypical for a loop that frees a memory region in its last iteration. The assertion in line 4 expresses that the memory region pointed-to by p has not yet been deallocated. In order to prove this assertion, an analysis needs to separate the value of the pointer p in the last loop iteration from its value in all previous iterations. In particular, the example is difficult to prove using convex numeric

a)
```
1   FILE *out;
2   out->is_open = 1;
3   assert(out->is_open == 1);
4   out->is_open = 0;
5   ...
6   if (flag)
7      out->is_open = 1;
8   ...
9   if (flag)
10     assert(out->is_open == 1);
```

b)
```
1   p = &some_var;
2   n = 5;
3   while (n >= 0) {
4      assert(p != 0);
5      // dereference p
6      ...
7      if (n == 0)
8         p = 0;
9      n--;
10  }
```

**Fig. 6.** Two challenging examples from the literature: a) accessing a file only if it was already opened and b) freeing a pointer in the last loop iteration

domains due to a precision loss that occurs when joining the point $\langle p, n \rangle = \langle 0, -1 \rangle$ at line 10 of the last loop iteration with the earlier states where $p \neq 0$ and $n \geq 0$.

However, using the simple interval numeric domain and our predicate domain, the example is proved using the fixpoint computation detailed in Fig. 7. In step 1 of the table, p is initialized to a non-zero address of a variable, which we illustrate by using the value 99. After initializing the loop counter n in step 2, the loop is entered as the loop condition n >= 0 is satisfied. In step 5, it is determined that the **then**-branch in line 8 is not reachable. After decrementing n, the state is propagated to the loop head via the back-edge in step 8. At this point, widening is applied. Additional heuristics [15] ensure that the interval $[-1, 5]$ is tried for $n$, rather than widening $n$ immediately to $[-\infty, 5]$. By applying the loop condition n >= 0, a new state for the loop body is obtained in step 9. In step 12, it is observed that the **then**-branch in line 8 is reachable. In the next step in line 9 the states of both branches are joined and the interval domain approximates p with $[0, 99]$. In the same step, the implications $0 < n \rightarrow 99 \leq p, 0 < p \rightarrow 0 \leq n$ are synthesized. In step 14 these predicates are transformed using $\sigma^{-1} = [n/n + 1]$. This state is joined with the previous state at the loop header at step 15. Our widening heuristic suppresses widening since a new branch in the program has become live [15]. Since the resulting numeric state has changed due to the new value of p, the fixpoint computation continues. Note that during the join in step 15, both implications $-1 < n \rightarrow 99 \leq p, 0 < p \rightarrow -1 \leq n$ are semantically entailed in the current state at the loop head (as computed in step 8') and therefore kept in the joined state. Evaluating the loop condition in step 16 enforces that $n \geq 0$, that is, $0 \leq n$. The latter predicate syntactically entails the predicate $-1 < n$. Thus, the *fixapply* function deduces that $99 \leq p$ holds, yielding $p \in [99, 99]$. The assertion holds since intersecting the state at step 16 with $p = 0$ yields $\bot$. Thus, at line 4, p cannot be 0 and the assertion holds. Continuing the analysis of the loop observes a fixpoint in step 22. Note that the assertion can also be shown when using standard widening that sets $n$ to $[-\infty, 0]$ in step 8'. However, for the sake of presentation, we illustrated the example with the more precise states.

| step | line | | intervals $p$ | $n$ | implications |
|---|---|---|---|---|---|
| 1 | 2 | | $[99,99]$ | | |
| 2 | 3 | | $[99,99]$ | $[5,5]$ | |
| 3 | 4 | | $[99,99]$ | $[5,5]$ | |
| ... | | | ... | | ... |
| 5 | 7 | | $[99,99]$ | $[5,5]$ | |
| 6 | 9 | | $[99,99]$ | $[5,5]$ | |
| 7 | 10 | | $[99,99]$ | $[4,4]$ | |
| 8 | 3 | $\sqcup$ | $[99,99]$ | $[4,5]$ | |
| 8' | 3' | $\triangledown$ | $[99,99]$ | $[-1,5]$ | |
| 9 | 4 | | $[99,99]$ | $[0,5]$ | |
| ... | | | ... | | ... |
| 12 | 8 | | $[99,99]$ | $[0,0]$ | |
| 13 | 9 | $\sqcup$ | $\mathbf{[0,99]}$ | $[0,5]$ | $\{0 < \mathbf{n} \to 99 \leq \mathbf{p}, 0 < \mathbf{p} \to 0 \leq \mathbf{n}\}$ |
| 14 | 10 | | $[0,99]$ | $[-1,4]$ | $\{-1 < n \to 99 \leq p, 0 < p \to -1 \leq n\}$ |
| 15 | 3 | $\sqcup$ | $[0,99]$ | $[-1,5]$ | $\{-1 < n \to 99 \leq p, 0 < p \to -1 \leq n\}$ |
| 16 | 4 | | $\mathbf{[99,99]}$ | $[0,5]$ | $\{-1 < n \to 99 \leq \mathbf{p}, 0 < p \to -1 \leq n\}$ |
| ... | | | ... | | ... |
| 22 | 3 | $\sqsubseteq$ | $[0,99]$ | $[-1,5]$ | $\{-1 < n \to 99 \leq p, 0 < p \to -1 \leq n\}$ |

**Fig. 7.** States during the analysis of the loop example in Fig. 6b)

| benchmark suite | programs | lines | lines avg. | time avg. | time avg. (P) | time avg. (D) |
|---|---|---|---|---|---|---|
| literature | 9 | 9–17 | 14 ms | 38 ms | 99 ms | 381 ms |
| test | 8 | 66–274 | 115 ms | 393 ms | 1658 ms | - |

**Fig. 8.** Evaluation of our implementation. Due to technical reasons, the "test" benchmark suite could not be analyzed using the disjunctive domain (D).

# 5  Related Work and Evaluation

The Predicate abstract domain was inspired by a weaker domain that tracked bi-implications of the form $f \leftrightarrow x \leq c$ [18]. This domain is useful in the analysis of machine code where conditional branches are encoded using two separate instructions. The first instruction is a comparison that stores the result of $x \leq c$ in a processor flag $f$. The second instruction is a branch instruction that determined the jump target based on $f$. By tracking an association between the comparison result $f$ and the predicate $x \leq 0$, the edge of the jump with the assumption $f = 1$ can be made more precise by also assuming $x \leq 0$ and analogously for $f = 0$. However, the use of simple bi-implications only states additional invariants rather than predicates that hold conditionally. Hence, disjunctive information cannot be described by using only bi-implications.

We evaluated our combined predicate/numeric domain on several examples in the literature, including the ones presented in this paper, shown as "literature" in Fig. 8. We also evaluated larger examples shown as "test". All examples from the literature required the predicate domain to verify except for the example in Fig. 1 that our weaker predicate domain [18] already handles. The times are shown when running without and with the predicate domain "(P)". The last column shows the running time with a disjunctive domain "(D)" that tracks different numeric states depending on the index ranges of a loop [6,15]. Due to this, only one example in the "literature" benchmark suite could possibly profit. A precision comparison of our disjunctive and the predicate domain can therefore not be conclusive for the various disjunctive domains in the literature [11,14].

## 5.1   Related Work

The idea of abstracting a system relative to a set of predicates was first applied by Graf and Saïdi to state graphs created during model checking [7]. This approach has later been generalized to software model checking by Ball et al. [1]. Here, an abstraction tool C2BP translates a C program to a program over Boolean variables. The value of a Boolean variable is true if the corresponding predicate holds in the input C program. The universe of possible predicates is very large as the semantics of each assignment and test is expressed by predicates. For scalability, C2BP abstracts the input C program only with respect to a few predicates. The idea of counter-example driven refinement is to increase this set of predicates by deducing which additional predicates are needed to discharge a verification condition. This deduction is performed on a path through the program on which the current Boolean abstraction is insufficient to prove a verification condition. There are two ways in which this refinement may fail: Firstly, the translation of C statements and tests into predicates may be inaccurate or the logic of the predicates may be insufficient to represent the C semantics precisely. Secondly, a set of predicates that suffices to discharge the verification condition on the chosen path may be insufficient when considering the whole program.

An abstract interpretation over domains that lose precision due to convexity is naturally improved by avoiding the computation of joins. This approach is commonly known as disjunctive completion [4]. In practice, the disjunctions are qualified by a set of predicates and are stored in a binary decision-diagram (BDD) where decision nodes are labeled with predicates and the leaves are convex numeric abstract domains [11,14]. The challenge in implementing these domains is that evaluation of transfer functions in one leaf may lead to a result that has to be propagated to many other leaves. A particular challenge is the widening operator and the reduction between predicates and states [10,15]. One drawback of using a BDD as state is that computing a fixpoint of a loop will perform all operations on each leaf of the BDD, even those that are stable within, say, the current loop. This can be avoided by lifting the fixpoint computation from tracking a map $P \to S$ to $P \times C \to S$ where $P$ are program points, $S$ are states and $C$ is a context. By using the predicates on a path in the decision diagram as context, the whole decision tree can be encoded by using one context per path. The advantage of this encoding is that stable leaves in the original decision tree are no longer propagated since they are each checked for stability by the fixpoint engine [17]. Using predicates as context can be seen as an elegant way of duplicating the CFG which is a technique often used to improve widening [6].

Beyer et al. combine abstract domains with predicates [2]. Their framework associates a precision level $\Pi$ with each domain that can be adjusted based on observed values in the program. A value-set analysis, for instance, may specify that only variables with less than five values are tracked while a predicate domain will store the set of possible predicates in $\Pi$. They propose to change this precision level during the analysis, so that a precision loss in one domain can be met with a precision increase in another. They instantiate their framework by an analysis that switches from tracking value sets to tracking predicates once the former becomes too expensive. Their states are tuples of the precision levels and the domain states so that a different domain state is tracked for each precision level. Their approach thereby resembles the disjunctive completion approaches discussed earlier. Interestingly, they propose the use of a function *abstract* to synthesize predicates from an abstract state. However, in their implementation it only returns predicates occurring in the current program.

Further afield are techniques to refine abstract interpretations based on counter examples [13,9]. The idea here is to re-run the abstract interpretation once a verification condition cannot be discharged. An improved precision of the abstract interpreter is obtained by improving the widening or the abstract state based on the path of the counter example. Our work can be seen as dual to counterexample-driven refinement as we employ predicates to avoid a precision loss rather than to refine a state that is too coarse. An approach that uses counterexample-driven refinement and which is seemingly close to ours is that of Fischer et al. [5] who propose a domain containing a map from a predicate to a numeric abstract domain. Like our setup, their construction is a reduced cardinal power domain [4] or, more generally, a co-fibered domain [20]. However, since they track one numeric abstract domain for each predicate, there is no bound on the number of states that they infer. Future work should address if their techniques can be incorporated into our abstract domain, that is, if new predicates can be synthesized without duplicating the numeric state.

Interestingly, when state spaces are bounded, disjunctive invariants can be encoded using integral polyhedra [19]. However, since even rational polyhedra are expensive, storing disjunctive information explicitly seems to be preferable.

## 5.2 Conclusion

We presented a co-fibered domain that tracks implications between predicates. This domain takes a single numeric abstract domain as child and thereby avoids tracking several child domains which is the most prominent way to encode disjunctive information. We illustrated that our domain solves challenging verification examples form the literature while using a simple deduction and reduction mechanism in form of the two novel functions *synth* and *fixapply*, respectively.

**Acknowledgements.** This work was supported by DFG Emmy Noether program SI 1579/1.

## References

1. Ball, T., Majumdar, R., Millstein, T., Rajamani, S.K.: Automatic Predicate Abstraction of C Programs. In: Programming Languages, Design and Implementation, pp. 203–213. ACM (2001)
2. Beyer, D., Henzinger, T., Théoduloz, G.: Program analysis with dynamic precision adjustment. In: Automated Software Engineering (2008)
3. Blanchet, B., Cousot, P., Cousot, R., Feret, J., Mauborgne, L., Miné, A., Monniaux, D., Rival, X.: A Static Analyzer for Large Safety-Critical Software. In: Programming Language Design and Implementation, San Diego, USA. ACM (June 2003)

4. Cousot, P., Cousot, R.: Systematic Design of Program Analysis Frameworks. In: Principles of Programming Languages, San Antonio, Texas, USA, pp. 269–282. ACM (1979)
5. Fischer, J., Jhala, R., Majumdar, R.: Joining Dataflow with Predicates. In: Wermelinger, M., Gall, H. (eds.) European Software Engineering Conference, vol. 30, pp. 227–236. ACM (September 2005)
6. Gopan, D., Reps, T.: Guided Static Analysis. In: Riis Nielson, H., Filé, G. (eds.) SAS 2007. LNCS, vol. 4634, pp. 349–365. Springer, Heidelberg (2007)
7. Graf, S., Saidi, H.: Construction of abstract state graphs with PVS. In: Grumberg, O. (ed.) CAV 1997. LNCS, vol. 1254, pp. 72–83. Springer, Heidelberg (1997)
8. Granger, P.: Improving the Results of Static Analyses of Programs by Local Decreasing Iterations. In: Shyamasundar, R.K. (ed.) FSTTCS 1992. LNCS, vol. 652, pp. 68–79. Springer, Heidelberg (1992)
9. Gulavani, B.S., Rajamani, S.K.: Counterexample Driven Refinement for Abstract Interpretation. In: Hermanns, H., Palsberg, J. (eds.) TACAS 2006. LNCS, vol. 3920, pp. 474–488. Springer, Heidelberg (2006)
10. Gurfinkel, A., Chaki, S.: Boxes: A Symbolic Abstract Domain of Boxes. In: Cousot, R., Martel, M. (eds.) SAS 2010. LNCS, vol. 6337, pp. 287–303. Springer, Heidelberg (2010)
11. Gurfinkel, A., Chaki, S.: Combining Predicate and Numeric Abstraction for Software Model Checking. Software Tools for Techn. Transfer 12(6), 409–427 (2010)
12. Heizmann, M., Hoenicke, J., Podelski, A.: Software Model Checking for People Who Love Automata. In: Sharygina, N., Veith, H. (eds.) CAV 2013. LNCS, vol. 8044, pp. 36–52. Springer, Heidelberg (2013)
13. Leino, K.R.M., Logozzo, F.: Loop Invariants on Demand. In: Yi, K. (ed.) APLAS 2005. LNCS, vol. 3780, pp. 119–134. Springer, Heidelberg (2005)
14. Mauborgne, L., Rival, X.: Trace Partitioning in Abstract Interpretation Based Static Analyzers. In: Sagiv, M. (ed.) ESOP 2005. LNCS, vol. 3444, pp. 5–20. Springer, Heidelberg (2005)
15. Mihaila, B., Sepp, A., Simon, A.: Widening as Abstract Domain. In: Brat, G., Rungta, N., Venet, A. (eds.) NFM 2013. LNCS, vol. 7871, pp. 170–184. Springer, Heidelberg (2013)
16. Péron, M., Halbwachs, N.: An Abstract Domain Extending Difference-Bound Matrices with Disequality Constraints. In: Cook, B., Podelski, A. (eds.) VMCAI 2007. LNCS, vol. 4349, pp. 268–282. Springer, Heidelberg (2007)
17. Sankaranarayanan, S., Ivančić, F., Shlyakhter, I., Gupta, A.: Static Analysis in Disjunctive Numerical Domains. In: Yi, K. (ed.) SAS 2006. LNCS, vol. 4134, pp. 3–17. Springer, Heidelberg (2006)
18. Sepp, A., Mihaila, B., Simon, A.: Precise Static Analysis of Binaries by Extracting Relational Information. In: Pinzger, M., Poshyvanyk, D. (eds.) Working Conference on Reverse Engineering, Limerick, Ireland. IEEE (October 2011)
19. Simon, A.: Splitting the Control Flow with Boolean Flags. In: Alpuente, M., Vidal, G. (eds.) SAS 2008. LNCS, vol. 5079, pp. 315–331. Springer, Heidelberg (2008)
20. Venet, A.: Abstract Cofibered Domains: Application to the Alias Analysis of Untyped Programs. In: Cousot, R., Schmidt, D.A. (eds.) SAS 1996. LNCS, vol. 1145, pp. 366–382. Springer, Heidelberg (1996)

# Formal Verification of kLIBC with the WP Frama-C Plug-in

Nuno Carvalho[1], Cristiano da Silva Sousa[1],
Jorge Sousa Pinto[1], and Aaron Tomb[2]

[1] HASLab/INESC TEC & Universidade do Minho, Portugal
[2] Galois, Inc., Portland, Oregon, USA

**Abstract.** This paper presents our results in the formal verification of kLIBC, a minimalistic C library, using the Frama-C/WP tool. We report how we were able to completely verify a significant number of functions from <string.h> and <stdio.h>. We discuss difficulties encountered and describe in detail a problem in the implementation of common <string.h> functions, for which we suggest alternative implementations. Our work shows that it is presently already viable to verify low-level C code, with heavy usage of pointers. Although the properties proved tend to be shallower as the code becomes of a lower-level nature, it is our view that this is an important direction towards real-world software verification, which cannot be attained by focusing on deep properties of cleaner code, written specifically to be verified.

## 1 Introduction

The state-of-the-art in program verification tools based on deduction has seen great advances in recent years. This has been motivated in part by the popularity of the Design-by-Contract [1] principles, according to which program units are annotated with behavior specifications called *contracts*, that provide appropriate interfaces for *compositional* verification. On the other hand, developments in Satisfiability Modulo Theories (SMT) solvers have complemented these advances with sophisticated tools for automated theorem proving, which have made possible the automatic verification of intricate algorithms that previously required very demanding interactive proofs.

The Frama-C deductive verification plug-in WP is a tool for compositional verification of C code based on contracts. It starts with C programs annotated with behavior specifications written in a language called ACSL, and then generates a collection of *verification conditions* (VCs): proof obligations that must be valid in order for each program unit to meet its specification. A variety of back-end provers can then be used to attempt to discharge these VCs. If all VCs are shown to be valid, then the program is correct (given that the contract specified correctly covers the functional properties of the program).

An ACSL-annotated program is shown in the straightforward example of Listing 1: the swap C function is annotated with a precondition requiring the two

J.M. Badger and K.Y. Rozier (Eds.): NFM 2014, LNCS 8430, pp. 343–358, 2014.

```
/*@
   requires \valid(a) && \valid(b);
   ensures A: *a == \old(*b);
   ensures B: *b == \old(*a);
   assigns *a,*b;
@*/
void swap(int *a,int *b){
  int tmp = *a;
  *a = *b;
  *b = tmp;
  return;
}
```

**Listing 1.** Swap basic example

pointers to be *valid* (in the sense that it can be safely accessed), which is necessary for the safe execution of the operations involving dereferencing. The postconditions on the other hand ensure the functional behavior expected of swap, and the *frame condition* states which elements of the global state are assigned during its execution.

With the development of tools such as Frama-C it is to be expected that where one would previously resort to extensive testing of code, one will now increasingly use tools to *statically verify* it. Initial applications have focused on algorithmically complex examples that are rich in 'deep' properties, but there is a clear absence in the literature of work on the verification of real-world code (initial steps in this direction with WP are reported in [2]). One class of code that could largely benefit from static verification is the code in the standard libraries of various programming languages, since more and more people depend on many widely used applications based on them.

In this paper we present our results in the formal verification of kLIBC, a minimalistic C library, using the WP plug-in of Frama-C. With this kind of verification we are treading new ground: the tools are very recent and under continued development. As such, our results should be seen as a snapshot of the state-of-the art in program verification and its applicability to real-world code.

*Organization of the Paper.* Section 2 describes the verification and proof tools (including the underlying memory models) used in our experiments, as well as the subset of kLIBC considered. Sections 3 and 4 are the core sections of the paper, where the results obtained in the verification of functions from <string.h> and <stdio.h> are respectively reported. The verification was done bottom-up, starting with the leaf functions and then working our way up to the callers. The human effort consisted essentially in finding appropriate annotations; after that the VCs were automatically discharged. Where problems are detected, we also provide suggested corrections to the implementation of the relevant library functions. Section 5 summarizes our results and discusses the difficulties faced, and Section 6 concludes the paper. A full list of the functions analyzed can be found in Appendix A.

## 2    Experimental Environment

**ACSL.** ANSI/ISO C Specification Language (ACSL) [3] is a Behavioral Interface Specification Language (BISL) [4] for C programs, which adds a layer of first-order logic constructs on top of the well-known C syntax. As with other BISLs, such as JML [5], building on top of the programming language's syntax for boolean expressions makes it possible for programmers to easily start adding specification annotations to their programs.

All annotations are written as comments, using one of the notations //@ ... or /*@ ... @*/, for single- and multi-line annotations, respectively. The pre- and postconditions of functions are written as \requires and \ensures clauses, respectively. The memory locations that can be modified within a function call can be specified with an \assigns annotation (usually known as *frame condition*). Loop annotations include loop invariant, loop variant and loop assigns. The return value of a function can be accessed (in particular in the function's postcondition) with the \result clause.

All of the above annotations are fairly standard in BISLs used for deductive verification; ACSL also includes many other annotations that specifically target aspects of the C programming language. A particularly important one is the \valid predicate, which takes a memory location or region as argument. The intended meaning is that the content of that memory regions has been properly allocated and can thus be safely accessed. This predicate is crucial for verifying (statically) the absence of runtime memory safety violations.

Finally, the \at operator can be used for accessing the value of an expression at a given program state, identified by a label. As an example, the expression \at(p, Pre) denotes the value of the variable p in the pre-state of the current function. The special label Pre is predefined, and this expression can in fact be written equivalently as \old(p). The operator can however be used with any C program label present in the program.

**Frama-C and WP.** Frama-C [6] is a platform dedicated to the static analysis of C source code. It has a collaborative and extensible approach that allows plug-ins to interact with each other. The most common use of Frama-C is probably as a bug-finding tool that alerts the user about dangerous code and highlights locations where errors could occur during runtime. The kind of bug-finding implemented by Frama-C aims at being correct: if there is a location in the code where an error could be generated, it should be properly reported. Users provide functional specifications written in ACSL, and Frama-C then aids them in proving that the source code is in accordance with these specifications.

Frama-C plug-ins include among others tools for calculating common source code metrics; value analysis based on abstract interpretation; program slicing; and of course deductive verification. In fact Frama-C has *two* plug-ins for deductive verification: Jessie [7] and WP [8,9]. Both plug-ins function in the same way: they convert the annotated code to a set of VCs, which are then submitted to a choice of external tools, comprising both automatic and interactive theorem provers.

In this paper we focus on the WP plug-in, since Jessie is clearly not targeted at the verification of properties of low-level code such as the code found in library functions. Moreover, WP is very actively maintained, with new versions being regularly released (for the work reported in this paper several major versions of Frama-C were used, including Oxygen and Fluorine 1, 2 and 3). We will see that a feature that has been included in the latest releases (to cope with unsafe casts) was crucial in the verification of <stdio.h> functions.

**WP Memory Models.** A memory model consists of a set of data types, operations and properties that are used to construct an abstract representation of the values stored in the heap during execution of a program. The WP plug-in of Frama-C makes available to the user a number of different memory models, the simplest of which, present in every release of the plug-in, is the Hoare model, based on the core weakest precondition calculus. This is a very simple model that does not support pointer operations, and is thus not suitable for our aim in this paper. The Store model was available in the Oxygen release but is not included in the more recent Fluorine releases. The heap values were stored as logical values in a global array. Support for pointer operations was fairly limited, and therefore heterogeneous type casts were not supported. Integers, floats, and pointers had to be 'boxed' into the global array and then 'unboxed' from it in order to implement read and write operations. All this boxing-unboxing was preventing automatic provers from making maximal usage of their native array theories. The Runtime model was the most powerful model included in Oxygen; it has equally been discontinued in the Fluorine release. This model was intended to be used for low-level operations, representing the heap as a wide array of bits. It was a very precise model but the price to pay for using it was high, since it generated huge VCs.

In the Fluorine releases a new model, called Typed, was introduced to replace both Store and Runtime. It makes better usage of the theories built into automated provers. The heap is represented by three memory variables, respectively holding arrays of integers, floats and addresses. This data is now indexed directly by addresses, which avoids all boxing-unboxing operations.

Very importantly, the "unsupported casts" feature of this model allows for the usage of unsafe casts, as long as they are never used to store data through a modification of the aliased memory data layout, as illustrated in Listing 2.

**RTE Plug-in.** The runtime error plug-in of Frama-C automatically generates annotations that can later be discharged by more powerful plug-ins such as Jessie or WP, even though it can also be used on its own to just guard against runtime errors [10]. It is worth noting that the generated annotations may not be easily discharged, even if they can be easily generated. RTE generates annotations for:

- common runtime errors, such as division by zero, signed integer overflow or invalid memory accesses;

```
int *p = ... ;
char *q1 = (char *)p;
char *q2 = (char *)p;
if(q1 == q2){ ... }    // CORRECT
if(*q1 == *q2){ ... }  // CORRECT
q1[2] = 0xFF;          // STILL CORRECT BUT ...
if(*p == ...)          // INCORRECT, because q1 is aliased to internal representation of p
```

**Listing 2.** Unsafe casts usage

- unsigned integer overflows, which are considered well-defined behaviors in the C language but which complicate other proofs;
- function contracts at call sites (for functions with an ACSL specification).

RTE assumes that all signed integers have a two's complement representation since it is a common implementation choice. The annotations generated are dependent on the machine where Frama-C is being executed.

**Theorem Provers.** The VCs generated by WP can be submitted to an interactive or automatic theorem prover. Frama-C natively supports two provers: the Alt-Ergo automatic prover and the Coq proof assistant. Other provers are supported through the Why platform[1]. In the experiments reported in this paper the following provers were used:

- Alt-ergo 0.95.1
- CVC3 2.4.1 (through the Why platform)
- Z3 4.3.1 (through the Why platform)

**kLIBC** kLIBC is intended to be a minimalist subset of libc, to be used with the *initramfs* file system. It is mainly used during the Linux kernel startup because at that point there is no access to the standard glibc library. It is designed for small size, minimal confusion and portability. The experiments reported in this paper focus on string-related functions from <string.h> and on the file API present in <stdio.h>. The version of kLIBC used was 2.0.2, which was released on October 5, 2012.

## 3   Verification of <string.h>

The <string.h> header file defines several functions to manipulate C strings and arrays. It also includes various memory handling functions. Most of these functions follow the same formula: they iterate on the string, using pointer arithmetics or an integer variable, for n bytes or until '\0' is found, performing some operation on each position.

For the functions that iterate until the end of the string is found, having access to the actual length of the string at the logical level is useful. For this

---

[1] http://why3.lri.fr

```
/*@
  predicate Length_of_str_is{L}(char *s, integer n) =
    n >= 0 && \valid(s+(0..n)) && s[n] == 0 &&
      \forall integer k ; (0 <= k < n) ==> (s[k] != 0) ;

  axiomatic Length{
    logic integer Length{L}(char *s) reads s[..];

    axiom string_length{L}:
      \forall integer n, char *s ; Length_of_str_is(s, n) ==> Length(s) == n ;
  }
@*/
```

**Listing 3.** Valid string predicate and length axiom

```
/*@
    requires \exists integer i; Length_of_str_is(s,i);
    assigns \nothing;
    ensures \result == Length(s);
@*/
int strlen(const char *s) {
    const char *ss = s;

    /*@
        loop invariant BASE: \base_addr(s) == \base_addr(ss);
        loop invariant RANGE: s <= ss <= s+Length(s);
        loop invariant ZERO:
            \forall integer i; 0 <= i < (ss-s) ==> s[i] != 0;
        loop assigns ss;
        loop variant Length(s) - (ss-s);
    @*/
    while (*ss) ss++;

    //@ assert END: Length_of_str_is(s,ss-s);
    return ss - s;
}
```

**Listing 4.** strlen implementation and annotations

we define a predicate `Length_of_str_is` as shown in Listing 3. The formula `Length_of_str_is{L}(s,n)` is true in the state identified by L, for nonnegative n, when all memory positions from 0 to n are valid; the final character is the null terminator '\0' (note that this character is present even when n is zero); and no other character in the string is the null terminator. Observe that the formula `\exists integer i; Length_of_str_is{L}(s,i)` holds exactly when s is a valid string in state L. With this definition, we can quickly verify the function that calculates the length of a string. Note that a logical function `Length` is also introduced, as well as an axiom linking its result to the values of n that satisfy the `Length_of_str_is` predicate for a given string (this enforces the existence of a single such value).

**strlen.** kLIBC's implementation of `strlen` and its annotations are shown in Listing 4. The contract is quite straightforward. The precondition states that only valid strings are expected by this function (this precondition is present in

```
int memcmp(const void *s1, const void *s2, size_t n){
    const unsigned char *c1 = s1, *c2 = s2;
    int d = 0;

    while (n--) {
        d = (int)*c1++ - (int)*c2++;
        if (d) break;
    }
    return d;
}
```

**Listing 5.** Original memcmp implementation

almost all functions from `<string.h>`). The postcondition guarantees that the result of the function is equal to the length of the string.

The implementation is not the triviality one could expect. Instead, pointer arithmetic is used for loop control, where ss-s is the number of iterations executed. Because of this we need to define the loop invariant RANGE in order to guarantee that the pointer ss never goes out of bounds. Also, WP requires that pointers that are used in a comparison have the same base pointer, which is stated by the loop invariant BASE. Finally, The loop invariant ZERO is the one that actually allows for the contract to be proved. It states that whenever the loop condition holds, all memory positions of the array previously visited by the loop must be different from the null terminator.

The loop assigns and variant clauses are straightforward. The final assertion END is necessary in the Fluorine release of Frama-C: without it the contract could not be proven. What this assertion states is that, after the loop, the length of string s is the difference between the pointers ss and s. The resulting annotated function is fully verified with both Alt-Ergo and CVC3.

**memcmp.** This function compares two byte strings with at least n bytes of length. The implementation is shown in Listing 5 (the original implementation includes in-line assembly, which is ignored here). Just verifying the run-time execution guards uncovered an underflow in the variable n. This error is in fact present in multiple functions from `<string.h>`; we will now explain in detail its particular occurrence in memcmp.

The parameter variable n is declared as having type size_t, which is a typedef for an unsigned long, meaning the value of n is always larger than or equal to 0. However, in the loop's final iteration, when n is zero, the condition is evaluated to false but the variable is still decremented, causing an underflow. Although this underflow does not affect execution of the function, it still causes confusion, and prevents the assertion generated by WP -rte from being proven.

A proposed correction of the implementation, with the appropriate annotations, is shown in listing 6. By moving the decrement operation inside the loop, we avoid the underflow in the final iteration. The resulting annotated function is fully verified with both Alt-Ergo and CVC3.

```
/*@
    requires n >= 0;
    requires \valid(((char*)s1)+(0..n-1));
    requires \valid(((char*)s2)+(0..n-1));
    requires \separated(((char*)s1)+(0..n-1), ((char*)s2)+(0..n-1));

    assigns \nothing;
    behavior eq:
        assumes n >= 0;
        assumes \forall integer i;
            0 <= i < n ==> ((unsigned char*)s1)[i] == ((unsigned char*)s2)[i];
        ensures \result == 0;
    behavior not_eq:
        assumes n > 0;
        assumes \exists integer i;
            0 <= i < n && ((unsigned char*)s1)[i] != ((unsigned char*)s2)[i];
        ensures \result != 0;

    complete behaviors;   // at least one behavior applies
    disjoint behaviors;   // at most one behavior applies
@*/
int memcmp(const void *s1, const void *s2, size_t n)
{
    const unsigned char *c1 = s1, *c2 = s2;
    int d = 0;
    /*@
        loop invariant N_RANGE: 0 <= n <= \at(n, Pre);
        loop invariant C1_RANGE: c1 == (unsigned char*)s1+(\at(n,Pre) - n);
        loop invariant C2_RANGE: c2 == (unsigned char*)s2+(\at(n,Pre) - n);
        loop invariant COMPARE: \forall integer i;
            0 <= i < (\at(n, Pre) - n) ==> ((unsigned char*)s1)[i] == ((unsigned
                char*)s2)[i];
        loop invariant D_ZERO: d == 0;
        loop assigns n, d, c1, c2;
        loop variant n;
    @*/
    while (n){
        d = (int)*c1++ - (int)*c2++;
        if (d) break;
        n--; //inserted code
    }
    return d;
}
```

**Listing 6.** Corrected memcmp implementation and annotations

The specification of this function requires that the memory areas pointed by s1 and s2 must not overlap, as otherwise the behavior would be undefined. ACSL provides the \separated clause for this purpose, which is here included in the precondition. Furthermore both memory areas must be valid (with length n bytes). Observe that, depending on the contents of the two byte strings, the result may or may not be zero. By encoding this as two different ACSL behaviors we can cover both executions.

Similarly to strlen, the loop invariants N_RANGE, C1_RANGE and C2_RANGE guarantee that the pointers never go out of bounds. The difference here is that we can specifically assert the values of the pointers c1 and c2 by using n. The loop invariants COMPARE and D_ZERO are the crucial ones for our contract, specifying that all previously iterated positions contain pairwise equal values. This

```
struct _IO_file {
    int _IO_fileno;    /* Underlying file descriptor */
    _Bool _IO_eof;     /* End of file flag */
    _Bool _IO_error;   /* Error flag */
};
typedef struct _IO_file FILE;

/*@
    predicate valid_FILE(FILE *f) = \valid(f) && f->_IO_fileno >= 0;
@*/
```

**Listing 7.** FILE structure definition

```
struct _IO_file_pvt {
    struct _IO_file pub; /* Data exported to inlines */
    struct _IO_file_pvt *prev, *next;
    char *buf;    /* Buffer */
    char *data;   /* Location of input data in buffer */
    unsigned int ibytes; /* Input data bytes in buffer */
    unsigned int obytes; /* Output data bytes in buffer */
    unsigned int bufsiz; /* Total size of buffer */
    enum _IO_bufmode bufmode; /* Type of buffering */
};

#define offsetof(t,m) ((size_t)&((t *)0)->m)
#define container_of(p, c, m) ((c *)((char *)(p) - offsetof(c,m)))
#define stdio_pvt(x) container_of(x, struct _IO_file_pvt, pub)
```

**Listing 8.** Encapsulating FILE structure and stdio_pvt macro

implicitly means that d==0 must always hold (otherwise the strings are not equal).

## 4  Verification of <stdio.h>

The <stdio.h> header file provides many functions to handle I/O operations. We aim here at verifying file functions such as fopen, fclose, and fgetc, i.e. the *file* API. Almost all functions in this API resort to system calls, which act like black boxes, and it is thus difficult or impossible to specify what the output will be on a given input. Due to this fact, contracts tend to be quite weak. Note that even though the properties that can be verified are shallower than those considered in the previous section, they can still be extremely important – in particular, we have been able to prove various *memory safety* properties.

Since we will be working with the file API, it makes sense to start by defining a predicate that establishes the validity of a FILE structure. kLIBC's definition of this structure and the corresponding validity predicate are shown in Listing 7. A FILE structure is considered valid when both the area pointed by the pointer and the file descriptor are valid.

In reality a slightly more complex encapsulating FILE structure is used, see Listing 8. The FILE structure is kept in the field pub of the _IO_file_pvt structure. The set of all _IO_file_pvt structs is organized as a circular linked

```
/*@
predicate valid_IO_file_pvt(struct _IO_file_pvt *f) =
    \valid(f) && f->bufsiz == 16384 && 0 <= f->ibytes < f->bufsiz
    && 0 <= f->obytes < f->bufsiz
    && valid_FILE(&(f->pub))
    && stdio_pvt(&(f->pub)) == f
    && \separated(f, f->next, f->prev, f->buf+(0..(f->bufsiz+32-1)))
    && \valid(f->buf+(0..(f->bufsiz+32-1)))

    && f->buf <= f->data < f->buf + f->bufsiz + 32
    && \base_addr(f->data) == \base_addr(f->buf)

    && valid_IO_file_pvt_norec(f->next)
    && f->next->prev == f
    && valid_IO_file_pvt_norec(f->prev)
    && f->prev->next == f;
@*/
```

**Listing 9.** valid IO_file_pvt predicate

list. The buf pointer points to an area of fixed size, and data points to somewhere in this area, representing the current input data location in the buffer. The function fdopen allocates the memory necessary for this structure: memory for the structure itself, the buffer, and some extra bytes for the input buffer, as in f = zalloc(bufoffs + BUFSIZ + _IO_UNGET_SLOP) (kLIBC defines BUFSIZE as 16384 and _IO_UNGET_SLOP as 32).

The valid_IO_file_pvt predicate is defined in Listing 9. In addition to the expected safety conditions, it is stated that the values of both ibytes and obytes cannot exceed the actual buffer size. The separated clause guarantees that no memory overlapping exists between the actual file structure and its fields. This is essential to ensure that the buffer is separated from the field structure. Since they are used in a comparison operation, data and buf must have the same base address, to guarantee that the data pointer always points somewhere in the allocated area, as mentioned in Section 3. In order to guarantee that the circular linked list is correctly constructed, we can specify that "the next node of the previous node", and "the previous node of the next node" are both the node itself. We could use the valid_IO_file_pvt predicate to check the validity of the neighboring nodes. This however, would recursively check each neighboring node and WP does not support recursive predicates. Instead, we define an auxiliary predicate, similar to valid_IO_file_pvt, but that *does not check its neighboring nodes*. This way, whenever we check the validity of a _IO_file_pvt structure, its immediate neighbors are also checked. This is sufficient because all functions that require access to the linked list, only access the direct neighbors of a given _IO_file_pvt structure.

Functions that receive a FILE structure, but need to access the encapsulating _IO_file_pvt structure, may obtain it by resorting to the stdio_pvt macro, also shown in Listing 8 (the -pp-annot flag instructs Frama-C to process the define macros). This macro was the source of various problems when using Frama-C releases prior to Fluorine. The cast from FILE* to char* was not supported in those versions. However, the new unsafe casts option seems

```
/*@
    requires valid_IO_file_pvt(stdio_pvt(file));
    requires -128 <= c <= 127;

    behavior fail:
        assumes stdio_pvt(file)->obytes || stdio_pvt(file)->data <= stdio_pvt(file)->buf;
        assigns \nothing;
        ensures \result == EOF;
    behavior success:
        assumes stdio_pvt(file)->obytes == 0 && !(stdio_pvt(file)->data <=
            stdio_pvt(file)->buf);
        assigns stdio_pvt(file)->ibytes, stdio_pvt(file)->data,
            *(\at(stdio_pvt(file)->data, Pre)-1);
        ensures stdio_pvt(file)->ibytes == \at(stdio_pvt(file)->ibytes, Pre) + 1;
        ensures stdio_pvt(file)->data == \at(stdio_pvt(file)->data, Pre) -1;
        ensures *(stdio_pvt(file)->data) == c == \result;

    complete behaviors; disjoint behaviors;
@*/
int ungetc(int c, FILE *file) {
    struct _IO_file_pvt *f = stdio_pvt(file);

    if (f->obytes || f->data <= f->buf) return EOF;

    *(--f->data) = c;
    f->ibytes++;

    return c;
}
```

**Listing 10.** ungetc implementation and specification

to handle this very well. This was crucial for the success of our efforts, since in our verification of functions from <stdio.h>, the valid_IO_file_pvt predicate was commonly used in ACSL annotations with the stdio_pvt macro, as in valid_IO_file_pvt(stdio_pvt(file)), since almost every function in the file API receives a FILE* pointer as argument, instead of the encapsulating structure, which is what is actually needed.

We will now consider in detail the verification of two functions from this API.

**ungetc.** This is a very simple function: it accesses some fields of the file structure, and then assigns a character back to the buffer, properly updating the ibytes counter. A detailed contract can be specified, because the function does not resort to system calls. The annotated function and its implementation are shown in Listing 10. Since the output of the function depends on the outcome of the conditional clause, it is adequate to define two behaviors fail and success. This function is easily verifiable in the Fluorine release with Z3, but it requires the unsafe casts option to be activated.

**__fflush.** Many functions in the file API rely on the __fflush function for actually modifying (and then flushing) a file structure. Its annotated implementation is shown in Listing 11. The instruction inserted before the while loop was necessary in order to be able to specify an interval for the variable rv in the

```
/*@
    requires valid_IO_file_pvt(f);
    assigns f->ibytes, f->pub._IO_eof, f->pub._IO_error, f->obytes, errno;
    ensures \result >= -1;
@*/
int __fflush(struct _IO_file_pvt *f){
    ssize_t rv;
    char *p;

    if (__unlikely(f->ibytes)) return fseek(&f->pub, 0, SEEK_CUR);

    p = f->buf;
    rv = -1; // inserted code
    /*@
        loop invariant 0 <= f->obytes;
        loop invariant \base_addr(p) == \base_addr(f->buf);
        loop invariant -1 <= rv <= f->obytes;
        loop invariant \base_addr(f->buf) == \base_addr(f->data) == \base_addr(p);
        loop invariant f->buf <= p <= f->buf + f->bufsiz + 32;
        loop invariant \valid(p+(0..f->obytes-1));
        loop assigns f->obytes, p, f->pub._IO_eof, f->pub._IO_error, rv;
        loop variant f->obytes;
    @*/
    while (f->obytes) {
        rv = write(f->pub._IO_fileno, p, f->obytes);
        if (rv == -1){
            if (errno == EINTR || errno == EAGAIN) continue;
            f->pub._IO_error = true;
            return EOF;
        } else if (rv == 0){
            f->pub._IO_eof = true;
            return EOF;
        }

        p += rv;
        f->obytes -= rv;
    }

    return 0;
}
```

**Listing 11.** __fflush implementation and contract

loop invariant. From the point of view of verification this function is very problematic, because of its dependencies. If the input buffer contains some bytes the
function fseek is called, which in turn invokes either the system call lseek or
__fflush again. On the other hand, if the output buffer is not empty its contents
are written to disk with the write system call. Writing a deep contract for this
function is thus at this point not possible, because both cases will depend on the
outcome of system calls. Nevertheless we were able to specify some functional
and memory safety properties. Using Z3 we were able to discharge most (but
not all) of the VCs. This partial verification is due to reasons explained above
and not to the choice of prover.

## 5    Evaluation of Results and Difficulties

As a general remark, we note that a standard C library contains inherently low-
level code, which makes it hard to verify formally, due to the presence of system

calls. Verification tools of the class employed here are only capable of verifying source-level code, and of course the implementation of the system calls is in machine language – there is no way to prove their correctness. It is possible to write a basic contract for a system call, but the verification of the calling functions will always be dependent on its assumed conformance to this contract.

The Fluorine release of the WP plug-in represents a major step as the verification of properties of low-level code is concerned. In fact, in the previous Oxygen release of WP only a few type casts were supported, such as unsigned char* to char*. In order to avoid the problems raised by this limitation we were forced to modify the code being verified, which is hardly a recommendable approach. Also, in our attempt to approach the verification of the file API with the Oxygen release we were forced to use the complex Runtime memory model, and we were unable to verify even the simplest properties of functions from <stdio.h>. These difficulties were eliminated in the Fluorine release, which made possible the work reported in Section 4.

A recurring problem detected in various functions from <string.h> is an *underflow* error present in the while loops (this is detected by all the WP releases used in our experiments). Basically, the problem is that an unsigned variable is decremented when its value is zero. Because of this, the RTE assertions cannot be proved. We have produced modified versions of these functions to make sure that no decrement is performed when the variable reaches zero.

In the verification of mutually recursive functions that share pointers between them we noticed that it is necessary to include in both functions' contracts the assigns clauses corresponding to the side effects produced by the code of both functions. This actually makes sense, but perhaps it would be more productive if functions could inherit assigns clauses from called functions whenever a pointer is shared (in the same way that some 'continuous' loop invariants are automatically present, such as assertions regarding variables not assigned in the loop body).

A present limitation of the WP plug-in is the lack of support for dynamic memory allocation. Even though ACSL defines clauses to deal with dynamic allocation (such as **fresh**, **allocable**, or **freeable**) these are not yet supported in the Fluorine release. According to the developers, support will be included in the next major release of the tool.

We also noted that using some provers required a heavy consumption of resources. For instance with CVC3 many threads are created but not killed in the end. We do not know if this problem is created by the prover itself, by Frama-C, or by the Why platform. Since CVC3 requires a large amount of memory very rapidly, this bug often results in forced reboots.

## 6   Concluding Remarks

The main goal of our experiments was to see how far one could go with verifying a low level library with Frama-C and WP. Due to the limitations described previously we ended up with partial verifications for some of the functions. Nevertheless, we were able to completely verify 14 functions out of 34 from <string.h>, and 13 out of 23 from the `<stdio.h>` file API. A full list of the approached functions and the present verification status (including, in the unsuccessful cases, the number of VCs left undischarged with each prover) can be found in Appendix A. The corresponding library with all the annotations is publicly available.[2]

Regarding the performance of the different automated provers employed, Alt-Ergo and CVC3 seemed to be better at handling string-related functions and behaviors, while Z3 was much more powerful dealing with the unsupported casts required to verify the file API. Within the string-related functions, Alt-Ergo was able to discharge less VCs when compared to CVC3; however, for those that were successfully discharged the computational cost was lower, and the huge amount of memory consumed by CVC3 was avoided. Since Alt-Ergo is natively supported by Frama-C, WP is able to take advantage of its built-in theories, making it a competitive option as an SMT solver.

Regardless of the partial verification results obtained for some functions, we believe we have shown without doubt that it is now viable to verify low level C code. Whatever the gravity of the problems identified in practice may be, their detection reinforces the interest of formally verifying code even when it has been widely validated by large numbers of users, as is the case of library code.

During the experiments we have identified limitations and bugs in Frama-C/WP that were properly reported to the developers. The Frama-C team is well aware of its users' needs, as evidenced by the release of the new memory model and the optional feature to support unsafe casts. The forthcoming release including support for dynamic memory allocation will very likely be another landmark in the practical applicability of deductive program verification tools.

**Acknowledgment.** This work is funded by ERDF - European Regional Development Fund through the COMPETE Programme (operational programme for competitiveness) and by National Funds through the FCT - Fundação para a Ciência e a Tecnologia (Portuguese Foundation for Science and Technology) within project **FCOMP-01-0124-FEDER-020486**.

# References

1. Meyer, B.: Applying "Design by Contract". IEEE Computer 25(10) (1992)
2. Burghardt, J., Carben, A., Gerlach, J., Hartig, K., Pohl, H., Völlinger, K.: ACSL By Example – Towards a Verified C Standard Library. DEVICE-SOFT project publication. Fraunhofer FIRST Institute (2011)
3. Baudin, P., Cuoq, P., Filliâtre, J.-C., Marché, C., Monate, B., Moy, Y., Prevosto, V.: ACSL: ANSI/ISO C Specification Language (June 2013)
4. Hatcliff, J., Leavens, G.T., Leino, K.R.M., Müller, P., Parkinson, M.: Behavioral interface specification languages. ACM Comput. Surv. 44(3), 16:1–16:58 (2012)
5. Leavens, G., Cheon, Y.: Design by Contract with JML (2003)
6. Correnson, L., Cuoq, P., Kirchner, F., Prevosto, V., Puccetti, A., Signoles, J., Yakobowski, B.: Frama-C User Manual (June 2013)

---

[2] https://github.com/Beatgodes/klibc_framac_wp

7. Marché, C.: Jessie: An Intermediate Language for Java and C Verification. In: Stump, A., Xi, H. (eds.) Proceedings of PLPV 2007. ACM (2007)
8. Baudin, P., Correnson, L., Dargaye, Z.: WP Plug-in Manual (June 2013)
9. Baudin, P., Correnson, L., Hermann, P.: WP Tutorial (September 2012)
10. Hermann, P., Signoles, J.: Frama-C's annotation generator plug-in (June 2013)

# A List of Functions

## A.1  <string.h> Functions

| Function | Alt-Ergo | CVC3 | Z3 | Combined provers | Unsafe casts | Depen-dencies | Obs |
|---|---|---|---|---|---|---|---|
| bzero | ✓ | ✓ | ✓ | | ✗ | memset | |
| memccpy | ✗(15/21) | ✗(18/21) | ✗(13/21) | ✗(18/21) | ✗ | | Problems with PosOfChar axiom |
| memchr | ✗(16/18) | ✗(16/18) | ✗(14/18) | ✗(16/18) | ✗ | | Behavior not proved, see strchr |
| memcmp | ✓ | ✓ | ✗(15/19) | | ✓ | | |
| memcpy | ✗(13/14) | ✓ | ✓ | | ✗ | | |
| memmem | ✗(37/42) | ✗(37/42) | ✗(36/42) | ✗(37/42) | ✓ | memcmp | Behavior not proved |
| memmove | ✓ | ✓ | ✓ | | ✗ | | |
| memrchr | ✗(12/14) | ✗(12/14) | ✗(12/14) | ✓ | ✗ | | |
| memset | ✗(13/14) | ✓ | ✓ | | ✗ | | |
| memswap | ✗(17/19) | ✓ | ✓ | | ✗ | | |
| strcasecmp | Does not schedule all VCs due to Frama-C bugs | | | | | | |
| strcat | Dependency strchr and strcpy not verified | | | | | | |
| strchr | ✗(14/17) | ✗(14/17) | ✗(13/17) | ✗(15/17) | ✗ | | Behavior not proved, see memchr |
| strcmp | ✓ | ✓ | ✗(14/22) | | ✗ | | |
| strcpy | ✗(16/23) | ✗(16/23) | ✗(15/23) | ✗(16/23) | ✗ | | |
| strcspn | ✓ | ✓ | ✗(4/5) | | ✗ | strxspn | |
| strdup | Suffers from dynamic allocation problem | | | | | | |
| strlcat | ✗(15/27) | ✗(15/27) | ✗(13/27) | ✗(15/27) | ✗ | | Has no post-conditions |
| strlcpy | Does not schedule all VCs due to Frama-C bugs | | | | | | |
| strlen | ✓ | ✓ | ✗(7/9) | | ✗ | | |
| strncasecmp | ✗(17/23) | ✗(17/23) | ✗(17/23) | ✗(17/23) | ✓ | toUpper | |
| strncat | ✗(12/23) | ✗(12/23) | ✗(9/23) | ✗(12/23) | ✗ | strchr | |
| strncmp | ✗(31/35) | ✗(31/35) | ✗(19/35) | ✗(31/35) | ✗ | | Behaviors not proved |
| strncpy | ✗(12/16) | ✗(13/16) | ✗(13/16) | ✗(13/16) | ✗ | | Has no post-conditions |
| strndup | Suffers from dynamic allocation problem | | | | | | |
| strnlen | ✓ | ✓ | ✗(13/15) | | ✗ | | |
| strpbrk | ✓ | ✓ | ✗(7/14) | | ✗ | strxspn | |
| strrchr | ✗(17/22) | ✗(17/22) | ✗(14/22) | ✗(17/22) | ✗ | | Behaviors not proved |
| strsep | ✓ | ✓ | ✗(19/20) | | ✗ | strpbrk | |
| strspn | ✓ | ✓ | ✗(4/5) | | ✗ | strxspn | |
| strstr | Dependency memmem not proved | | | | | | |
| strtok | Dependency strxspn not proved | | | | | | |
| strtok_r | Dependency strxspn not proved | | | | | | |
| strxspn | ✗(32/40) | ✗(33/40) | ✗(31/40) | ✗(34/40) | ✗ | memset | Proved under assumption |

## A.2    &lt;stdio.h&gt; Functions

| Function | Z3 | Unsafe casts | Dependencies |
|---|---|---|---|
| clearerr | ✓ | ✗ | |
| fclose | ✓ | ✓ | fflush |
| fdopen | ✗(19/25) | ✓ | |
| __init_stdio | ✗(5/10) | ✓ | fdopen |
| feof | ✓ | ✗ | |
| ferror | ✓ | ✗ | |
| __fflush | ✗(20/23) | ✓ | fseek |
| fflush | ✓ | ✓ | __fflush |
| fgetc | ✓ | ✓ | |
| fgets | n/a | ✗ | fgetc |
| fileno | ✓ | ✗ | |
| __parse_open_mode | ✓ | ✗ | |
| fopen | ✓ | | __parse_open_mode, fdopen |
| fputc | Dependency _fwrite not proved | | |
| fputs | Dependency _fwrite not proved | | |
| _fread | ✗(18/37) | ✓ | __fflush |
| fseek | ✓ | ✓ | __fflush, lseek |
| ftell | ✗(10/11) | ✓ | lseek |
| fwrite_noflush | ✗(26/39) | ✓ | __fflush |
| _fwrite | ✗(29/34) | ✓ | |
| lseek | ✓ | ✗ | __llseek |
| rewind | ✓ | ✓ | fseek |
| ungetc | ✓ | ✓ | |

# Author Index

Antonino, Pedro R.G. 31
Arlt, Stephan 313

Baier, Christel 285
Bardsley, Ethel 230
Bartels, Björn 98
Bernardeschi, Cinzia 209
Bridge, James 188
Bryans, Jeremy W. 31

Carvalho, Nuno 343
Cofer, Darren 1
Correnson, Loïc 215
Curzon, Paul 209

Danish, Matthew 158
da Silva Sousa, Cristiano 343
Daum, Marcus 285
Denman, William 203
Donaldson, Alastair F. 230
Dubslaff, Clemens 285
D'Urso, Enrico 209

El Ghazi, Aboubakr Achraf 173
Engelen, Luc 258

Fedyukovich, Grigory 300
Ferrari, Alessio 264

Garoche, Pierre-Loïc 246
Gascón, Adrià 270
Gladisch, Christoph 173
Gurfinkel, Arie 300

Hierons, Robert M. 62
Hoffman, Dustin 92
Horsmanheimo, Seppo 77
Howar, Falk 246

Immler, Fabian 113

Jackson, Paul 188
Jähnig, Nils 98
Jensen, Peter Gjøl 307
Jones, Paul 209

Kahsai, Temesghen 246
Kamali, Maryam 77
Klein, Joachim 285
Klüppelholz, Sascha 285
Kolehmainen, Mikko 77
Kristensen, Klaus E. 31

Larsen, Kim Guldstrand 307

Masci, Paolo 209
Mazzanti, Franco 264
Mehlhorn, Kurt 46
Merz, Stephan 143
Mihaila, Bogdan 328
Miller, Steven 1

Neovius, Mats 77
Noschinski, Lars 46

Oladimeji, Patrick 209
Oliveira, Marcel Medeiros 31

Paulson, Lawrence 188
Pedro, André de Matos 16
Pereira, David 16
Petre, Luigia 77
Pinho, Luís Miguel 16
Pinto, Jorge Sousa 16, 343

Rizkallah, Christine 46
Rönkkö, Mauno 77
Rubio-González, Cindy 313
Rümmer, Philipp 313

Sampaio, Augusto C.A. 31
Sandvik, Petter 77
Schäf, Martin 313
Schneider, Stefan-Alexander 252
Schumann, Johann 252
Shankar, Natarajan 313
Sharygina, Natasha 300
Simon, Axel 328
Sørensen, Mathias Grund 307
Sogokon, Andrew 188
Spagnolo, Giorgio Oronzo 264
Srba, Jiří 307

Taankvist, Jakob Haar    307
Taghdiri, Mana    173
Tagore, Aditi    92
Tahar, Sofiène    128
Thimbleby, Harold    209
Thirioux, Xavier    246
Tiwari, Ashish    270
Tomb, Aaron    343
Türker, Uraz Cengiz    62
Tyszberowicz, Shmuel    173

Ulbrich, Mattias    173

Vanzetto, Hernán    143

Weide, Bruce W.    92
Wijs, Anton    258

Xi, Hongwei    158

Yousri Mahmoud, Mohamed    128

Zaccai, Diego    92
Zhang, Yi    209